MANAGEMENT: Theory and Practice

McGRAW-HILL SERIES IN MANAGEMENT

KEITH DAVIS, Consulting Editor

MANAGEMENT:
Theory and Practice
second edition

Ernest Dale, Ph.D.
Wharton School of Finance and Commerce
University of Pennsylvania
and Ernest Dale Associates

McGRAW-HILL BOOK COMPANY
New York St. Louis San Francisco London
Sydney Toronto Mexico Panama

Acknowledgments

Material from the *Journal of Abnormal and Social Psychology* reprinted by permission of the publisher, The American Psychological Association.

Chart and material from Seymour Melman, *Dynamic Factors in Industrial Productivity*, reprinted by permission of Basil Blackwell, publisher.

Selection from Stephen Vincent Benét's *John Brown's Body*, from *Selected Works of Stephen Vincent Benét*, published by Holt, Rinehart & Winston, copyright 1927, 1928 by Stephen Vincent Benét, copyright renewed (c), 1955 by Rosemary Carr Benét, reprinted by permission of Brandt & Brandt, New York.

Chart from Victor Lazzaro (ed.) *Systems and Procedures: A Handbook for Business and Industry*, copyright 1959 by Prentice-Hall, Inc., Englewood Cliffs, N.J., reprinted by permission of Prentice-Hall.

Quotations from the following reprinted by permission of the Harvard University Press:

Francis X. Sutton, Seymour E. Harris, Carl Kaysen, and James Tobin, *The American Business Creed*, copyright 1956 by the President and Fellows of Harvard College.

Chester I. Barnard, *The Functions of the Executive*, copyright 1956 by the President and Fellows of Harvard College.

F. J. Roethlisberger and W. J. Dickson, *Management and the Worker*, copyright 1939 by the President and Fellows of Harvard College.

Sidney Schoeffler, *The Failures of Economics*, copyright 1955 by the President and Fellows of Harvard College.

C. R. Walker and E. Guest, *Man on the Assembly Line*, copyright 1952 by the President and Fellows of Harvard College.

Management: Theory and Practice

Library of Congress Catalog Card Number 69-17145

15163

1 2 3 4 5 6 7 8 9 0   HDBP   7 6 5 4 3 2 1 0 6 9

This Book Is Dedicated to My Parents

Preface

In the four years since the first edition of *Management: Theory and Practice* was published, there have been a number of developments in the management field:

1. Greater use of computers and management science (operations research), including application to new types of problems
2. A growing trend toward multinational companies that allocate their resources on a worldwide basis—so much so that proposals are now being made that such corporations be chartered on an international basis
3. Further developments in behavioral science and growing interest in it
4. Growing interest on the part of management in its social responsibilities
5. A decline in the demand for "organization men" and greater emphasis on creativity, especially, of course, in research, but also in management itself

This edition incorporates the new knowledge in these and other areas. The chapters on organization and direction include more material drawn from behavioral science sources; the international section has been updated and an appendix on Japan has been added to it; and the chapter on innovation has been greatly revised. In addition, a great deal of new material has been added to the section on computers and operations research. There are now two chapters on computers—one designed to make clear what a computer can and cannot do at present, and what it is likely to do in the future, and the other dealing with the effect of computerization on organization, management jobs, and employment in general. The chapter on operations research has been revised, and a fuller explanation of the techniques has been included; also, an appendix made up of mathematical problems (with solutions) has been added for those who wish a broader background in the subject. In addition, there have been other revisions in accordance with suggestions from teachers and readers.

Despite the new material that has been added, there are now only thirty chapters instead of thirty-five as in the first edition. Among the changes that have made this possible are some shortening of the material on the concepts of the scientific management movement and compression of it into one chapter; presentation of the two chapters "Who Are the Managers?" and "The Road to the Top" as an appendix to the first section of the book; and elimination of some of the older material formerly included in these two chapters. The chapter on management ideology has been combined with the chapter on representation, for it is becoming increasingly evident that *what* management represents is as important as—if not more important than—the public relations techniques that constitute the method of representation.

The fundamental aim of the book, however, remains the same: to equip the reader with a solid background of management knowledge that will make it possible for him to evaluate realistically both current theories and practices and those that may be introduced in the future.

The book is designed as an introductory textbook, but at the same time it contains material of sufficient sophistication to make it suitable for more advanced students and for experienced managers who may wish to gain an overall view of the field. The approach has been to assume no previous knowledge on the part of the reader but to lead gradually from the simpler concepts to the more difficult ideas and techniques and to illustrate abstractions by practical examples, many of them drawn from the author's experience in working with companies here and abroad.

The author wishes to express his appreciation to Edward E. Barr, senior vice-president, Sun Chemical Corporation, who made valuable suggestions on Chapter 5; to Professor Gordon C. Shaw, York University, Toronto, for his help with the chapters on decision making and management science and for preparation of the appendix to the management science chapter; and to Russell L. Ackoff, professor of Statistics and Operations Research, and William F. Hamilton, lecturer in industry and senior research staff, Management Science Center, Wharton School of Finance and Commerce, University of Pennsylvania, for many helpful discussions and comments on the management science chapter.

Others to whom the author is grateful for comments and suggestions include Professor F. D. Barrett, York University, Downsview, Ontario, Canada; Professor William Wolf, University of Southern California, Los Angeles; Professor Joseph A. Litterer, University of Illinois, Urbana, Illinois; Professor Robert T. Sullens, John Carroll University, Cleveland, and treasurer of the Cyril Bath Company; Professor Vernon Titus, head, Department of Management, Rochester Institute of Technology, Rochester, New York; Professor Richard Brandenburg, Carnegie-Mellon University, Pittsburgh; Leonard Marks, Jr., Assistant Secretary of the Air Force, U.S. Department of Defense; Townsend Hoopes, Principal Deputy for the Assistant Secretary of Defense, Internal Security Affairs, and T. T. Paterson, professor of management, Strathclyde University, Glasgow, Scotland.

The author is grateful to the many members of the Academy of Management who made suggestions for improving the content of this book when he met them in his capacity of president of the Academy of Management.

The author wishes to acknowledge his deep indebtedness for his intellectual training to the late Sir Dennis Robertson, the great monetary economist of Cambridge University, who wrote an outstanding work on management (*The Control of Industry*, Cambridge University Press, London, 1960); to Lord Keynes, who was both a great thinker and practitioner of management; and to Francis Leavitt Impey, who was the author's first boss and for whom he served as assistant in manufacturing, marketing, and accounting at the Kalamazoo Loose Leaf Equipment Company in England and South America.

The author also gratefully acknowledges the help and inspiration of two academic officials with whom he worked at Cornell University—the late Edward H. Litchfield, formerly chancellor of Pittsburgh University, and C. Stewart Sheppard, former dean of the Cornell Graduate School of Business and Public Administration and now with the Graduate School of Business, University of Virginia. The author is also indebted to members of the University of California Graduate School of Business at both Berkeley and Los Angeles.

The author's greatest debt is to Dean Willis Winn, Edward B. Shils, Acting Chairman, Department of Industry, and Herbert R. Northup, chairman, Department of Industry, Wharton School of Finance and Commerce, University of Pennsylvania, for their encouragement, for making facilities available, for the opportunity of heading the teaching of the introductory management course, and for their financial support of the computer research.

The author is also extremely obligated to Alice Smith, who did a great deal of the research and revision of a number of chapters and who was particularly helpful to the author in making complex ideas intelligible and the teaching of management issues enjoyable; to Charles Meloy, who did the bibliographical research, the index, and the revision of the chapter on compensation; and to Della Jaffee, who typed many drafts of the revision.

The author would appreciate receiving comments for further improvement from readers of the book, in the spirit of Mary Parker Follett, who wrote that "the improvement of this world will come through a multitude of specific relationships."

Ernest Dale

Contents

1

Management and Its Environment

Before one can understand the various theories of management and their application to situations in the real world, it is necessary to determine what managers actually do. In the first chapter of this book, therefore, the management functions are listed and defined. These are the functions that all true managers perform, to a greater or a lesser extent, whether they are business managers or managers of other types of organizations.

But definitions so generally applicable are necessarily rather abstract and divorced from actual situations. A manager is always managing *something;* he cannot operate in a vacuum. Chapter 2, therefore, pictures the work of five actual managers of business organizations, or departments of business organizations, so that the abstractions may be related to definite tasks. It will be noted that although these men were engaged in different types of work, each one performed several of the management functions in the course of a single day.

What a manager does is also determined by the environment within which he operates, the framework—or rather, frameworks—that circumscribe his actions. The internal environment, the ''climate'' within the company, depends on a great many variables, but the corporate structure provides an overall framework within which the variables act and react. The theory of the corporation and some of the ways in which the corporate system works in practice are explained in Chapter 3. Chapter 4 deals with the extent to which the corporate framework circumscribes the actions of the top manager and the extent to which he makes his own role.

In addition, there is the external environment in which the company itself operates, which places constraints on the top manager and all the managers under him. This is discussed in Chapter 5.

1
WHAT
IS
MANAGEMENT?

Under any social order from now to Utopia a management is indispensable and all-enduring. . . . The question is not: "Will there be a management elite?" but "What sort of elite will it be?" Sidney Webb

1 The idea that management is a distinct type of work, different from all other work, comes naturally to most people. Practically everyone has observed cases in which men of outstanding technical competence have proved themselves unable to manage enterprises or sections of enterprises. Thus a fine doctor may be a poor hospital administrator, an outstanding engineer may fail as head of an engineering company, and a highly skilled craftsman may not be a good foreman.

When a man becomes a manager, he may or may not continue to do part of the actual work, but he also takes on new duties that are entirely managerial in character. He must plan work for others, decide what each of his subordinates should do, motivate those under him to do their best, and check on their progress.

Knowledge of the work itself may be indispensable, but managing requires something more. Even when he knows exactly how he would go about a job if he were to do it all himself, he may be unable to explain to others how it should be done or to decide on the best sequence when several people are to handle parts of it. Or he may find that people resent his orders or are apathetic toward their work no matter how hard he tries to arouse them to enthusiasm. Or, if he is not in a position to oversee each detail personally, many of the things he has decided should be done may not be done or may be done badly, and he may not discover this until it is too late to correct the resulting difficulties.

But if a manager needs more than knowledge of the work itself, what exactly does he need to know? Or is management an art that can be practiced effectively only by those with special natural endowments?

There is general agreement that management is, at least at the present time, partly an art; there are no foolproof rules that do away with the need for judgment and common sense. But there is a growing body of knowledge about the field that anyone who aspires to management can learn, given intelligence and application. And regardless of his natural talent or lack of it, he will be a better manager because he has acquired this knowledge than he otherwise would be.

In order to determine what a manager should know, it has been necessary, of course, to define management itself. One frequently quoted definition is "Management is getting things done through other people." And it is, in part, of course, especially if it is management of a large organization.

But, as James L. Hayes, dean of the School of Business Administration of Duquesne University, once observed:

> The man who is new in management hears it [the definition] this way: "Management is getting things done *through other people.*" Now, at last I have a kingdom and someone to work for me. . . . Then he can sweep down to his subordinate all the nasty jobs he never has wanted to do. . . . However, he later reaches the point of maturity when he hears the definition with a little different emphasis: "Management is *getting things*

done through other people." It is when he gets the sense of responsibility for accomplishment that he is a manager.[1]

Thus the manager must not only understand how to get people to do what he wants them to do; he must also know what they should be doing—what results should be achieved, what each person and group should contribute to the common effort, and how the results can best be achieved without duplication of work or lost motion.

Again, it is sometimes said that "management is decision making," and it is quite true that many of the most important actions managers take are simply decisions—to expand a business in a certain way; to hire this man or dismiss that one; to adopt a new marketing strategy or a new personnel policy.

But the definition of management given earlier also implies decision making. If management is getting things done through other people, the manager must decide first of all what he wants the people to do; then he must decide who can best do each part of the job and how he can ensure that each person does a *good* job. If the study of management is to foster better decision making, the management job must be broken down into the areas in which decisions are made. Only then will it be possible to ascertain what knowledge the modern manager needs.

THE MANAGEMENT FUNCTIONS

One useful breakdown is that suggested by Luther Gulick,[2] who coined the word POSDCORB from the initial letters of management functions: planning, organizing, staffing, directing, coordinating, reporting, and budgeting. With some modifications and additions, this will be the breakdown used in this book. The management functions will be presented here as:

Planning   The manager must first decide what he wants done. He must set short- and long-run objectives for the organization and decide on the means that will be used to meet them. In order to do this, he must forecast, as well as he is able, the economic, social, and political environment in which his organization will be operating and the resources it will have available to make the plans work out. As one example, plans that are entirely feasible in a time of prosperity may be utterly impractical in a period of depression. Planning may be said to encompass Gulick's *budgeting,* since a budget is a plan to spend a certain amount of money to accomplish certain objectives.

Organizing   The objectives and the work that will be necessary to attain them dictate the skills that will be needed. In organizing, the manager decides on the positions to be filled and on the duties and responsibilities attaching to

---

[1] At a management seminar conducted on October 17, 1960, at the Rochester Institute of Technology.
[2] "Notes on the Theory of Organization," in Luther Gulick and Lyndall Urwick (eds.), *Papers on the Science of Administration,* Institute of Public Administration, New York, 1937, p. 13.

each one. But the work done by the members of the organization will necessarily be interrelated; hence some means of coordinating their efforts must be provided. Coordination is, in fact, an essential part of organization rather than, as Gulick suggested, a function in itself.

Staffing   In organizing, the manager establishes positions and decides which duties and responsibilities properly belong to each one. In staffing, he attempts to find the right person for each job.

An established company, of course, already has both an organization and people to fill the positions that have been set up. Nevertheless, both organization and staffing are likely to be continuing jobs since changes in plans and objectives will often require changes in the organization and occasionally necessitate a complete reorganization. And staffing obviously cannot be done once and for all, since people are continually leaving, getting fired, retiring, and dying. Often, too, the changes in the organization create new positions, and these must be filled.

Direction   Since no one can predict just what problems and opportunities will arise in the day-to-day work, lists of duties must naturally be couched in rather general terms. The manager must, therefore, provide day-to-day direction for his subordinates. He must make sure that they know the results he expects in each situation, help them to improve their skills, and in some cases tell them exactly how and when to perform certain tasks. If he is a good manager, he makes his subordinates feel that they want to do the best possible job, not merely work well enough to get by.

Control   In directing, the manager explains to his people what they are to do and helps them do it to the best of their ability. In control, he determines how well the jobs have been done and what progress is being made toward the goals. He must know what is happening so that he can step in and make changes if the organization is deviating from the path he has set for it. Gulick's *reporting* is a means of control rather than a separate function. Reports are made so that the manager, his superiors, or his subordinates may see what is happening and change course if necessary. And a budget is not only a plan; it is also a means of control. If there is a budget overrun, the organization is spending more for something than it had planned to, which means that some adjustment must be made somewhere to compensate for this.

Innovation   But many people would consider even this list incomplete. If, they would say, the manager attempts merely to continue doing what he has been doing in the past, making the best possible showing in view of external circumstances and the resources available to him, his organization will be a static one at best. Further, it is more likely to decline than to stay in the same place, particularly if it is in a competitive field.

"Managing a business," Peter Drucker writes, "cannot be a bureaucratic, an administrative, or even a policy-making job. . . . [It] must be a creative rather than an adaptive task."[3] In other words, the real manager is always an innovator.

Thus we may number innovation among the true functions of the manager, and the manager may innovate in any one of several ways. He may develop new ideas himself, combine old ideas into new ones, pick up ideas from other fields and adapt them to his own use, or merely act as a catalyst and stimulate others to develop and carry out innovations.

It could be argued that the planning function encompasses innovation, since the manager should plan not only how to adjust his organization to future conditions but how to change those conditions in order to improve the possibilities open to him. This is logical enough, but it may lead to a lack of emphasis on the need for innovation in all phases of a business, including innovations in the handling of the other management functions. For this reason, innovation will be discussed separately in this book.

Representation   Finally, the manager's job includes representing his organization in dealings with outside groups: government officials, unions, civic groups of one kind or another, financial institutions, other companies in the industry, suppliers, customers, and the public generally. Sometimes this function of representation consists merely of making himself accessible and pleasant; at other times it is a matter of delicate negotiations. But there are few managers who do not have to spend part of their time on it—from the foreman who must represent the company in a discussion with the union steward to the chief executive of an influential corporation who goes to Washington to discuss a price rise with the President of the United States or to present the views of his industry to a Congressional committee.

There are a number of other functions that might be mentioned, but they are actually subfunctions. For example, it is sometimes said that communication is a major part of a manager's job, and so it is. Unless the manager is able to make his subordinates understand what he wants them to do, he cannot get them to do it. And if he cannot get them to talk freely to him, he may be kept in ignorance of some of the things he should know about—to say nothing of the possibility that he may miss hearing some good ideas. But achieving good communications is clearly part of the directing function, in which the manager attempts to ensure that each of his subordinates contributes as much as he is able to the success of the whole operation.

RELATIVE IMPORTANCE OF THE FUNCTIONS

The various functions of management enumerated above—planning, organization, staffing, direction, control, innovation, and representation—are all part of the manager's job, but the importance attached to each one may vary at different times and in different places.

[3] *The Practice of Management,* Harper & Row, Publishers, Incorporated, New York, 1954, p. 47.

Immediately after World War II, for example, the rapid growth of many companies made organization (or rather, the lack of it) a matter of very serious concern to many managers. They spent a good deal of their time realigning responsibilities and creating new coordinating positions because their companies had outgrown some of the more informal methods of coordination that had served well enough up to that point. In the 1960s, however, many managements felt that the most important problems in the organization area had been dealt with. Moreover, economic conditions appeared more uncertain once the pent-up demands generated by wartime shortages of goods had been largely satisfied. Then planning and control seemed more important. And representation vis-à-vis the government was of little concern to American management in its early days since government itself was little concerned with business. Today Federal and state laws and municipal ordinances limit the manager's freedom in many ways.

Interest in innovation has also grown rapidly in recent years. Generally this has taken the form of greater interest in research and development, but many managements have become more receptive to innovations in all phases of company activity than they were ten, or even five, years ago.

Again, in many underdeveloped countries, planning does not present many difficulties. There is so much that obviously needs to be done, and that can be done if the available resources are allocated properly, that the main difficulty is execution or direction—actually getting things done. Many excellent plans for starting new industries, improving agriculture, and so on have not produced results because those responsible for the direction phase have been unable to get the enterprises off the ground.

WHY STUDY MANAGEMENT?

What does the breakdown into the seven functions tell us about what a manager needs to know? Analysis shows that management, insofar as it can be scientific, must use what is termed an interdisciplinary approach—that is, the theories and techniques of many sciences must be used in the management job.

For example, planning cannot be done without forecasting, and this requires some knowledge of economics. The manager need not be an economist himself—if he is the chief executive of a large corporation he will probably have an economist on his staff—but he needs to know something about how forecasts are made in order to judge how much faith he can place in them. It is he, not the economist, who must decide whether to plan for an expanding market or a contracting one.

In the area of organization, there have been many studies of difficulties traceable to poor organization and of organizational practices in successful corporations. While there are differences of opinion among the writers and researchers in this field, much is available that will help the manager make decisions in this important area by alerting him to the various possibilities. How does he decide, for example, whether a certain duty should be performed by one department or another? How many levels of subordinate managers should there be? What means of coordination can be used? Since the experts disagree, the manager is not relieved of the need to use judgment; but if he is familiar with the ideas that have been suggested and with the ways in which they have worked out, he will be saved initial confusion and much of the trial and error that would be necessary if he attempted to learn merely by experience.

The fact that an important part of the manager's job is selecting people to fill the positions under him immediately suggests that he should be aware of any help psychology can provide. Psychology may help him also in the directing phase of his work; that is, in getting things done through people. And since his relationships will be with groups as well as with individuals, some of the findings of sociology will be of value to him as well. Moreover, the organization itself is made up of people; hence the insights developed by both psychologists and sociologists may be needed in actually structuring the jobs.

Fairly exact techniques are available in the field of control, particularly in the area of financial control. Developing the financial controls may be the job of the company controller, but the manager needs to know what is possible in this area and how to interpret the figures that the controller sends him. And he should be aware, also, of the other types of control needed and available: the control of product quality, for example.

Recently, managers have begun to use another type of mathematics in both planning and control. With the advent of the computer, forms of analysis not heretofore possible have become fairly common in large organizations, and a whole new technology—known as "management science" or "operations research"—is now available to help managers with their decision making. The manager of today needs to understand what the computer and the operations research techniques can and cannot do for him, and what their future possibilities are.

Under the heading of innovation, the potential manager can learn how innovations come about, something of the type of company climate that fosters them, and what steps must be taken to bring a good idea to fruition. Invention, whether of a new product or a new method of marketing, is only partly a matter of inspiration; a good part of it arises from recognition of needs and careful study of what has been done before, which may suggest some new possibilities.

Finally, the man who aspires to management must learn something about his role as a representative of his organization and about the groups to whom he will represent it.

These seven functions—planning, organizing, staffing, direction, control, innovation, and representation—are common to all business management and management in other fields as well, although the ways they are carried out will differ in different fields. Emphasis in this book will, however, be on business management, and the ways in which it can utilize the theories and techniques available.

And if the potential manager aspires to business management he will need to understand how a corporation is organized and to know something of the general framework within which business operates. He should learn how managers are judged and why one manager is better than another, what ideologies managers commonly hold and why, and how the various concepts and theories of management were developed.

Management is thus a very complex subject in which material drawn from many fields is integrated with material found in no other science or art into a body of knowledge directly applicable to the management job. And that job is a very important one, for resources cannot be used for the good of mankind if capable management does not exist.

The manager must learn from actual experience on the job before he will be capable of high-level management work. But he will start with an advantage if he already knows the theories and techniques that have been developed by thinkers and practitioners in the field. He will also be better able to interpret his own experience and to formulate theories that will guide him in the future.

JUDGING THE THEORIES

Many people discount the importance of theory in practical business situations. But decisions, if they are at all rational, are always based on some theory, whether the man who makes them realizes it or not. For example, if a supervisor decides that his subordinates "need a good bawling out," he is acting on the theory that the best way to get people to do good work is to make things unpleasant for them if they don't. Conversely, if he decides to sit down with each of them and explain the goals they should strive for and how they should attempt to reach them, he is acting on a quite different theory about human nature.

In this book a number of theories regarding the various management functions are presented. While some complement each other, others are to some extent contradictory. Hence it is important that the student consider how he can distinguish good theory from bad. Following are some tests that can be applied:

1. Was the theory developed in as scientific a way as possible? If it was based on observations or studies in depth, one must consider to what extent the researcher has reported all the pertinent facts. Has he selected merely those that tend to prove a point of which he was already convinced, or has he started without preconceived notions and reported only what the facts justify? If the researcher states that certain things happened *because* certain things were done, is it possible that other causes, which he overlooked or chose to ignore, were operating at the same time? Is the

theory based on enough instances to permit generalizations, or were the facts gathered in only a few situations that may have been special cases?

2. Is the theory a plausible one in the light of the reader's own experience, or does it throw new light on experience that he has been unable to explain satisfactorily before?

3. Finally and most important, does the theory make it possible to predict that if certain things are done, certain results will always, or almost always, follow?

One cannot expect that a theory about management will make possible predictions as exact as those that can be made in the physical sciences, or that the research can be conducted in such a way as to eliminate all possibilities of misinterpretation of facts. To measure one variable in a situation with complete accuracy, it is necessary to hold all the others constant during the experiment. This is seldom if ever possible in a management situation, in which there are likely to be innumerable factors at work, all of them variable.

However, since one must necessarily act on theory, it is important to have a means of judging the *relative* value of the theories offered, and the three tests listed above will provide guidance in this.

SUMMARY

The job of management may be broken down into seven functions: planning, organizing, staffing, direction, control, innovation, and representation.

Although judgment, common sense, and knowledge of the field in which he is operating are necessary to the manager, many academic disciplines provide both theory and techniques that will help him. He may draw on economics, sociology, and psychology, and also on a body of knowledge derived from study and experimentation in the management field itself.

In the course of his study he will encounter some contradictory viewpoints, and it is up to him to decide which is the most valid. To determine the value of a theory, three tests may be applied: (1) Was it developed in as scientific a way as possible? (2) Is it plausible? (3) Does it permit reasonably accurate predictions?

Review Questions

1. What are the seven functions of management listed in the text? Define them in your own words. Do you believe this list is complete, or would you add other functions? Or do you believe that some of these functions are not properly considered managerial functions?

2. How does organization differ from staffing?

3. Distinguish between direction and control.

4. Why may the definition, "Management is getting things done through people," be inadequate?

5. How would *you* define "management"?

██

Case Study / The Suburban Bank and Trust Company*

██

During the 1920s, Henry Davidson, chief loan officer of the Suburban Bank and Trust Company, maintained a strict loan policy despite pressure from other bank officers and influential depositors. Some businessmen withdrew their deposits because he refused to grant them loans.

Suburban was, however, the only one of seven banks in the area that reopened after the bank moratorium in the 1930s, and depositors who had transferred their funds from Suburban suffered severe losses. Thus Suburban established a reputation for soundness that led to steady growth.

In 1949, Davidson was made president. He works hard at his job, coming to the office at 7 A.M. to open all the mail and seldom leaving before 5 P.M. He supervises every department personally, and very few decisions, even routine decisions, are made before he has approved them. In some cases he has over-ruled decisions made by department heads, and some of the latter complain that their employees have fallen into the habit of going directly to Davidson whenever they have a question.

In dealing with customers Davidson is abrupt, and many of them prefer to talk to the executive vice-president.

Davidson formulates investment policies which are very conservative, but he has displayed unusual skill in selecting investments that provide relatively high yields, and his record compares very favorably with records achieved by professional staffs of larger banks.

In the matter of loans, Davidson still insists that the bank should not lend money unless it is sure beyond a reasonable doubt that both principal and interest will be paid on schedule. Loans amount to only 25 per cent of deposits, whereas the average bank in Suburban's class usually has a maximum loan limit of 35 to 40 per cent.

Deposit growth has been steady but at a lower rate than that of other banks in the nation.

Davidson has said, "If a customer walks through the door, we're glad to serve him, but we're definitely not going outside to try to get him in here." Thus the bank does not have a new-business department, although most of its competitors do. Some of these competitors have been successful in increasing deposits by calling on businessmen and explaining the various services they offer; one competitor obtained $1 million in new accounts last year. Competition for the depositor's dollar is increasing, especially since savings and loan

---

* This is a very much shortened version of a case appearing in *Policy Making and Executive Action*, 2d ed., by Thomas J. McNichols, McGraw-Hill Book Company, New York, 1963. (Copyright, 1959, by Northwestern University. All names and organizational designations have been disguised. Northwestern University cases are reports of concrete events and behavior, prepared for class discussion. They are not intended as examples of "good" or "bad" administration.) Rev. ed., p. 77.

associations and savings banks can offer higher rates of interest than commercial banks like Suburban.

Suburban's earnings have also increased, and while cash dividends have not risen for the last five years, the bank declared a 50 per cent stock dividend at the end of last year. Earnings per share are sufficient to permit the bank to pay the same dividend on the new shares that it has been paying on the old. Thus the stockholders will now receive a 50 per cent increase.

Davidson has an announced policy of promotion from within, but during the last two years two key positions have been filled from outside because no one within the organization was considered qualified for them. Suburban has no training program, and younger men claim that they have no chance to learn anything but their own jobs because the bank operates with a minimum number of personnel and they are kept too busy. Salaries are generally higher than in comparable banks, and for this reason turnover has been low among male employees. Just recently, however, two young men with recognized potential left for other jobs that pay less but give them more chance to learn and advance.

1.   Would you say Davidson is a good manager?
2.   Which of the management functions, if any, is he handling badly? Which, if any, is he handling well?
3.   Is he performing any functions that cannot be classed as management?
4.   If you were a stockholder in the bank, would you want the bank to get a new president? Why or why not?

Selected Readings

The Theory of Economic Development, Joseph A. Schumpeter, Harvard University Press, Cambridge, Mass., 1949, pp. 74–94. A great economist presents the history of the concept of management and a definition of the manager as innovator.

Dynamic Administration, Mary Parker Follett in Henry C. Metcalf and L. Urwick (eds.), Harper & Row, Publishers, Incorporated, New York, 1941. The concept of the manager as a leader in a creative society; presented from the viewpoint that management is developing into a profession.

The Functions of the Executive, Chester I. Barnard, Harvard University Press, Cambridge, Mass., 1938. An analysis of executive responsibility and authority by a former president of the New Jersey Bell Telephone Company and the Rockefeller Foundation.

Business Enterprise in Its Social Setting, Arthur H. Cole, Harvard University Press, Cambridge, Mass., 1959. A summary of studies of the concepts of management in different environments.

The Reality of Management, Rosemary Stewart, William Heinemann, Ltd., London, 1963. Part Two of this book deals with the manager's job and is based in part on interviews with 1,500 managers, conducted by the author over a period of twelve years.

2

HOW MANAGERS CARRY OUT THEIR FUNCTIONS

Management, like war, is made up of long periods of routine divided by short bursts of intense activity and peril. John Tyzack

2 The last chapter listed the management functions in the abstract as planning, organizing, staffing, direction, control, innovation, and representation. How do managers actually carry out these functions in their day-to-day work?

There has been little literature on the daily tasks of management. Most books and articles tend to describe somewhat broadly and theoretically what an executive ought to do rather than how he deals, or fails to deal, with the problems that confront him at his desk each morning.

Managers are not, of course, a homogeneous group. Some head great businesses with worldwide ramifications. Others manage small enterprises or single departments of larger businesses. Some devote all their time to management functions; others perform some tasks that are distinctly not managerial at all. For example, one of the nineteenth-century heads of the Du Pont Company, General Henry du Pont, refused to have a stenographer, wrote all his letters with a quill pen, and opened the mail himself.

Also, managers have different ways of operating. Some like to run a one-man show and insist on making even minor decisions themselves. Others divorce themselves from detail to such an extent that they really have no idea of what is going on even two or three levels below them. Many others, of course, steer a course somewhere between these two extremes. Again, some managers operate bureaucratically and are greatly concerned about procedures; others prefer as little red tape as possible.

In part, the way a manager operates is determined by the circumstances in which he finds himself: by conditions in his industry and his company. To a large extent, however, it depends on his own nature, for he will tend to gravitate toward the type of organization in which his natural way of working brings success. If he doesn't, he may not remain a manager for very long.

The sketches of managerial activity in this chapter are not invented. The author gathered some of the material by sitting in the offices of executives for days on end. In other cases, the managers themselves noted down exactly what they did. One of them actually kept an hour-by-hour diary for a period of several weeks.

These managers include men at various levels of company organization and in companies of various sizes. Among them are the following:

A tycoon The tycoon is the big businessman of legend, who also exists in fact, the man who builds an industrial empire with worldwide ramifications. The tycoons of several decades ago are perhaps best known to the general public; the names of John D. Rockefeller, Andrew Carnegie, and Henry Ford immediately come to mind. In today's economy, tycoonship is more difficult to attain than it used to be, if only because big business is bigger than it was and the tycoon must spread his empire very far indeed, farther almost than is possible in the span of one lifetime, to qualify for the title. High taxes are another stumbling block. Perhaps the only genuine new tycoons are oilmen (like Paul Getty, who is said to be the world's only billionaire), who enjoy certain tax advantages because of depletion allowances.

A medium-sized-company president   The job of the president of a medium-sized or small company tends to differ greatly from that of the big-company president. He is closer to the scene of action and more likely to be interested in details because he has less margin for error. One bad season, one important miscalculation on an important contract, can make a major dent in his company's prosperity and may even be disastrous. In contrast, the Ford Motor Company was able to spend around $300 million on the ill-fated Edsel and then abandon the venture without losing stride. It generally takes several bad mistakes, or mismanagement over a long period, to shake a giant corporation seriously.

An executive vice-president and plant manager   At one time the title vice-president connoted only one thing: the man who was second in command to the president. Today it is not uncommon for a company to have eight or ten vice-presidents, each in charge of a different function and all on the same level. Hence it has been necessary to find a new title for the true vice-president. Generally he is known as the executive vice-president,[1] though sometimes the title senior vice-president is used. The executive vice-president whose day is described in this chapter is also the manager of his company's one plant.

A sales manager   Sales manager, like vice-president, is a somewhat ambiguous title. There are sales managers who are part of the top management group. Others are actually only salesmen. The man whose day is described in this chapter is somewhere between the extremes.

A personnel manager   The personnel manager is another executive whose title gives little clue to his status. In one white-collar organization employing perhaps 2,000 people, he does little more than interview applicants for clerical positions. In another company, he may be a member of the top policy-making group and have the title of vice-president.

The man whose day is sketched later in this chapter is among those enjoying higher status. Though he does not, at least as yet, have a vice-presidential title, he heads the personnel function for an entire company and three other personnel managers (one at each of the company's three plants) work under him. Since he handles union as well as employee relations, which some personnel managers do not, he is in charge of the entire range of the personnel function.

THE TYCOON

Mr. B, as he was known to his associates, built up three fortunes in the years between 1910 and 1960. A European tycoon whose home base was the

---

[1] Some large companies now have more than one executive vice-president, but in general, the executive v.p. is second in command to the president.

Netherlands, he was in many ways typical of tycoons everywhere, particularly in his single-minded devotion to business.

When he passed his sixtieth birthday, Mr. B announced his retirement from the company he had founded and pushed to worldwide proportions, but this made little difference in his activities. The only change was that he gave up his office and began operating from his hotel suite and transacting more business by telephone. Not long before his death, he asked a consultant to help him set up an organization that would enable him "to control the company from beyond the grave."

Mr. B began his career with a steel warehousing company in the Netherlands. Such an organization acts purely as a middleman or distributor, buying steel from producers and selling it to industrial users. Steel, of course, comes in many different types and shapes for different purposes. The successful distributor must know where each type can be obtained and where it can be sold to best advantage. He must also be a good negotiator since his profit depends on getting more for the product than he buys it for. It soon appeared that Mr. B was something of a genius at locating sources of steel, finding buyers for it, and negotiating low purchase prices and high selling prices. By the time he was thirty, he was making $100,000 a year.

His first success went down the drain when the post-World War I depression struck. His company folded, and with it went both his job and his savings. Instead of seeking a new job from one of his many contacts, B decided to start a business of his own on borrowed money. In picking a product to make and sell, he was guided by three criteria:

1.   It would have to be a steel product, because he knew more about steel than anything else. He had devoted some fifteen years of his life to learning about it.
2.   It would have to be a product sold to industry rather than to consumers, again because of his past experience.
3.   It should be an item that accounted for a very small part of the total cost of the customer companies. This would give him leeway to charge high prices if he could produce a superior product. The customers' decision to buy would be based on quality rather than cost since the price they paid for a minor item would have little or no effect on their own costs and prices.

B hit on the idea of producing steel drums for the shipment of oil and other liquids. This was a wide-open field at the time; wooden drums were the rule, but steel drums had many advantages over them. Further, the oil industry, the largest potential customer, was expanding rapidly, and the expansion seemed likely to continue indefinitely.

The business was an unqualified success. Soon B had branches all over Europe and was beginning to formulate plans for a worldwide organization. He was also able to branch out into other fields.

One of the ingredients of his success was his immense capacity for assimilating detail without losing sight of overall considerations. Calouste Gulben-kian, the "mystery" oil millionaire, used to say, "Check, check, check," and "Nothing escapes my attention; nothing." B might have said the same thing. After his retirement, he spent his time reading reports of the far-flung operations of his empire and could spot a single figure out of line in any of them.

Mr. B lost his second fortune when the Nazis overran Holland. His business was taken from him, and he himself was forced to flee for his life. He was able to save only one asset—a group of horses from a circus he owned (ostensibly to publicize his product, but probably because he had a weakness for circuses). During the war, he brought the horses to the United States, and made a living by exhibiting them. Circus riding was one of the skills he had managed to acquire while building up his business.

At the end of the war, his properties were restored to him, and he set about building up the business again and making it even larger than before. His reputation for excellent service stood him in good stead, and he regained lost customers. Soon he had plants and sales offices all over the world.

For decades, Mr. B followed a grinding daily schedule. He rose at 5 A.M., had a cup of coffee, and began going over memoranda and reports received the previous day. From 6:30 to 7, he did calisthenics and had a massage and a hot and cold shower. Then his secretary came in to take dictation. (Mr. B believed in giving customers unusually good service and charging premium prices for it, and he paid his subordinates premium salaries but demanded long hours in return.)

B was a meticulous correspondent, and the dictation took two hours. Then from 9 to 10, he saw his general manager, a man who like himself had grown up in the steel warehousing business and was almost as shrewd a negotiator as his boss. Together they went over the principal problems of the business. Mr. B asked searching questions, made decisions or postponed them pending further information, or perhaps delayed them because he felt the time was not ripe. (He placed great emphasis on proper timing.)

From 10 to 1, each of the heads of the great departments appeared to report on his stewardship and to discuss problems and new possibilities. Between their visits, Mr. B read detailed reports—daily, weekly, monthly, and long-range breakdowns of sales and expenses—giving special attention to wage rates and fringe benefits.

At 1, with an eight-hour day behind him, Mr. B took a recess. He had a leisurely lunch to the accompaniment of nineteenth-century music, which he preferred to anything later, then slept for an hour.

The afternoon was devoted to special projects. At 7, he had a good dinner, usually in splendid isolation. Then would come two hours of telephoning to his managers around the world. From 10 to 11, he read the day's papers. A half-hour's walk before bed completed his day.

The special projects might include anything—planning a new plant, hiring a new act for the circus (or firing some of the current performers), or dealing with labor difficulties.

For the last, Mr. B, an unreconstructed capitalist of the old school, in later life developed a special cure. He was likely to apply it to any strike, but particularly to one occurring in France since he disliked the French and labor unions equally. His first move was to fly to the site of the stoppage and walk down the picket lines handing out 100 francs to each of the pickets. If this turning of the other cheek proved ineffective (and it generally did), his next step was drastic. During the night a special fleet of trucks arrived at the plant. Equipment, furniture, and fixtures were loaded at top speed and quickly driven away to another of the company's factories. When the pickets arrived the next morning, there was nothing to picket—only the empty and deserted building.

Behind these ruthless tactics was less a desire for money than an extreme devotion to the business itself, a belief in it as a monument that should be perpetuated. Hence any attack on the business was to be resisted by any means at its owner's command.

B could be generous with money; in fact, he gave largely to causes of all kinds and left the business itself to a charitable foundation. (His children were already generously provided for.)

Such a course of action is characteristic of the tycoon. His early and middle life are devoted to building up a business and acquiring money, and he seldom questions the value of this activity. To him, a successful business is the most worthwhile activity that any human being can engage in, and he enjoys every minute of it. In later life, one nineteenth-century tycoon was inspired to write a poem, which went in part:

> I early learned to work as well as play
> My life has been one long, happy holiday.

To such a man, the money is the badge of success rather than an end in itself, and the business that he builds is a life work that he cannot bear to see destroyed or curtailed in the slightest degree. What the tycoon wrote about himself may not even be good doggerel, but it contains a great truth as a tycoon sees it—work, especially work at making money, is the best holiday any man could desire.

THE PRESIDENT OF A MEDIUM-SIZED COMPANY

Daniel Brewster is president of a company in a small Southern town with a population of 10,000. Now in his forties, he has grown up in the company, which is family-owned, and has been president since his father resigned some years ago to become chairman of the board. He lives in the town where the plant is located, in a house that is, in his phrase, "a fast five minutes or a slow eight minutes" away from his place of business. He has an office or study at home as well as one at the plant and often works at home for a couple of hours before leaving in the morning.

His company is small by comparison with such giants as General Motors and U.S. Steel, but it is fairly important in its own field. Its principal product is medium-priced underwear for men and boys, but it also manufactures other types of clothing, including hosiery and sport shirts. It employs 500 people. For the most part, the products are sold by the company's own sales force. In a few cases, however, the plant produces goods for other companies to sell under their own brand names. Also, the hosiery it manufactures is distributed through a converter who performs the finishing operations.

In addition to running his business, Brewster spends a day or two each week at a university some distance from the town. A few years ago he obtained his master's degree in one of the physical sciences by such part-time study, and he is now adviser to the business school at a nearby university. He also takes a prominent and often time-consuming part in community activities and church affairs—he even preaches a Sunday sermon on occasion. In addition, he is active in his industry trade association, which means that he must take an occasional trip North to attend the meetings. He utilizes whatever time is left over on these trips by getting together with company sales representatives in the area or with major customers. Since the company has its own trademarks and it is important to protect them, he also goes to Washington at times to confer with lawyers there on steps to be taken in cases of infringement. Whenever he is out of town, work continues to pile up on his desk back at the plant.

Brewster is very conscious of the importance of time and devotes a good deal of thought to methods of conserving it. Once he made the following calculation: "If you are forty years old, you will probably retire in twenty-five years. Whatever you accomplish in business during the rest of your life will be done in that length of time. Taking out sleeping time, you have only 146,000 hours left in which you must do everything you hope to do." His car is fitted out with special lights, a working table, and a dictaphone so that he can continue working during his frequent trips between the university and his office.

Brewster is not an autocrat who believes he must pass on every detail. He leaves many decisions to his chief subordinates. But inevitably there are questions that he alone can decide since they involve matters that cut across departmental lines and affect the profitability of the company in an important way.

There are always new products to be considered that will involve changes in manufacturing methods and possibly investment in new equipment. For example, should the company start making a men's girdle? A New York designer has sent in a model that looks very promising. (After conferring with the heads of the finance, manufacturing, and marketing departments on various aspects of the question, Brewster made a final test. He encased his own form in the girdle for a week or two to see how it felt.)

A sales department head reports that one major customer wants a higher-quality shirt that will be somewhat more expensive to produce. Should the company agree to make it, and if so, for this customer alone? Or should it substitute the model for one it is presently producing for other customers and thus obtain the advantage of purchasing the cloth in larger quantities?

Brewster has recently initiated several major changes in various aspects of the business that he believes are desirable for future progress: He has renovated the equipment in the knitting mill and established a new cost accounting system and a market research program. It is necessary for him to keep in touch, through conferences with various executives, on the way things are working out.

Day-to-day more or less one-of-a-kind problems also arise. Should the underwear mill operate on Saturdays—at extra labor cost, of course—in order to ship out a large customer's order a little faster? There has been delay in getting out certain orders, and one of the company's big sales points is its ability to deliver quickly. Is the delay in manufacturing or in the shipping department?

Finally, there are the unexpected visits from customers or from representatives of other companies with whom the plant does business. They will be better satisfied if they can talk to the head man for at least a short while before being turned over to the departments with which they are really concerned.

Brewster's chief subordinates are his vice-president, who is in charge of finance and manufacturing; a manager of research and development; and the heads of the five principal sales divisions: retail sales, discount sales, military sales, sales to supermarkets and drug stores, and civilian exports and foreign licenses. Working directly under him also are a sales assistant, who coordinates (but does not supervise) the work of the sales division heads and handles a few accounts under Brewster's personal supervision; a research assistant, who is making studies of such matters as possible mergers and the European Common Market; and a private secretary.

While there is no "typical" day, it is perhaps possible to abstract such a day from the time sheets of a couple of weeks:

5:10 to 7:10 A.M. Worked in study at home on a science article to be presented later for publication.

7:10 to 8 A.M. Exercise and breakfast.

8:05 A.M. Arrival at office.

8:05 to 8:30 A.M. With private secretary going over plan of day, disposing of mail, working on assignments and follow-ups for various subordinates.

8:30 to 8:45 A.M. Report by sales assistant on major market developments, follow-up on major customer who has become a credit risk, with a view to stopping production and delivery to him.

8:45 to 9:45 A.M. Meeting with research assistant for a report on Common Market possibilities for the company. (After studying the data, Brewster later turned the report over to the manager of research and development and the controller for development of the comparative cost picture vis-à-vis European competitors.)

9:45 to 11:45 A.M. Executive committee meeting with his father (chairman of the board) and the heads of departments. Items discussed included:

1. The operations forecast, which is made up each week. The committee goes over all the figures in the previous week's forecast and compares them with actual orders. The actual sales are also compared with sales for the corresponding period the previous year, with the production forecast, with actual production, with the inventory of each item, and with the projected inventory of each. Then the next week's production is planned.
2. The advisability of employing an outside consultant to develop procedures for control of inventory, shipping and order processing, production planning, raw material procurement.
3. Employment of a purchasing agent (purchasing is now split among several different executives).
4. Policies relative to price increases.
5. The stocking of a new item.
6. Costs. These are reviewed at the end of each accounting period, with detailed consideration of the reasons for variances from budget.

11:45 to 12:15 P.M. Discussion with the advertising manager regarding the copy for some planned advertisements. Also a discussion with him and the sales assistant regarding the possibility of new outlets for substandard goods.

12:15 to 12:45 P.M. Meeting on the site of a new building the company is planning to erect with the architect, the vice-president of manufacturing, the vice-president and treasurer, and a representative of a brick company. This was to decide the type of brick to be used.

12:45 to 1:30 P.M. Lunch, interviewing a candidate for school principal.

1:30 to 2:30 P.M. Discussion with the manager of research and development, the vice-president of manufacturing, and the retail sales manager about the possibilities of a new product that the R & D department has devised. Consideration was given to desirable modifications of the product, from both a sales and a manufacturing viewpoint, and a thorough analysis was made of the costs. A deadline was set for final decision on these matters—after that, the R & D department was to give the sales department a limited number of samples so that it might check the market.

2:30 to 3:15 P.M. Meeting with the president of a customer company at which an important contract was signed. Brewster had sown the seeds of this deal some time earlier at a meeting in New York on one of his trips.

3:15 to 3:30 P.M. Meeting with a city councilman who called to leave reports and an engineering drawing relating to a special parking problem in space near the plant.

3:30 to 3:45 P.M. Discussion with a local man who has been doing some research on a new device for production machinery. The idea for it originated with Brewster, but development was turned over to a physics professor at a nearby college.

3:45 to 4:15 P.M. Telephone discussion with the New York office: report on a contact with a very large account and on the possibility of a license agreement with a firm in Hong Kong (the Hong Kong salesman was in New York).

4:15 to 5:15 P.M. Meeting with the buyer for a chain of stores and his two assistants. Buyer called primarily to introduce a new assistant, but discussion also covered prices and deliveries.

5:15 to 5:45 P.M. Meeting with the vice-president and treasurer and an out-of-town banker on short- and long-term financing. The banker was impressed with the company's prospects and seemed inclined to grant loans on favorable terms.

5:45 to 6:15 P.M. Conference with the sales managers on the matter of concessions to certain customers. Reports indicated that a re-evaluation of policy might be necessary.

Even after such a day as this, Brewster seldom goes home empty-handed. There is usually a batch of notes, memoranda, and sometimes reports for him to read and ponder in his study at home, and he may get up as early as 5 in the morning in order to study them.

THE EXECUTIVE VICE-PRESIDENT AND PLANT MANAGER

Ferdinand A. Fischer is an old-timer in the chemical industry, a man whose experience spans some forty years. He is not, however, so old as the length of his working life would indicate. In his early teens illness compelled him to leave high school, and he never went back. Instead, he began working in a laboratory and rose to become head of the largest plant of one of the largest chemical companies in the country. Along the way he acquired the equivalent of a college education with a major in chemistry by taking courses at night. Though he has no degree, he has immense knowledge of the technology of his particular field, the production of dyestuffs.

Fischer's job with the big company lasted until he reached his mid-forties. Then, unaccountably, he was fired, a casualty of one of the sudden shake-ups that sometimes take place in big companies in the course of a power struggle at the top.

Many executives who find the ground cut from under them in this way lose their confidence and are never able to reach comparable levels again. Fischer was made of tougher fiber. He found a job in a smaller company as executive vice-president and manager of its one plant. The president, a young man of thirty-one who had inherited his job, was glad to lean on his experience and know-how.

One of the advantages of the smaller-company post is that he can do more to affect the profit and loss statement. In the larger organization, his efforts were sometimes almost entirely nullified by others over whom he had no control. Thus when the profits amounted to 35 per cent on factory costs, the commercial overhead charges added to take care of the top-heavy organization at headquarters pared this down to 3 per cent. Nor did he find that the experts employed by the central organization provided any really vital help. One of the most difficult technical problems he encountered in his career was solved in his plant long before the central laboratories produced an answer. And in some cases—notably in collective bargaining—the specialists from the home office were more a hindrance than a help.

"If a man from headquarters is there," he says, "the plant manager knows he will relay a report to top management. Inevitably, then, you find yourself talking to impress the headquarters man rather than to persuade the union men across the table."

Fischer was a manager in the days when there were no unions and workmen were accustomed to autocratic supervision. It might be expected, therefore, that he would find it difficult to adjust to the present-day "human relations" approach. But he has been far ahead of the human relations experts all along. He is not soft; he can and does fire a man who can't handle a job, and he will not put up with sloppy work. But his attitude is that most men want to do a good job and that it's not necessary to drive them. As for rules and regulations, he feels that the principal one, applicable to management and labor alike, is "Act like a gentleman." That's what he expects; and that, for the most part, is what he gets from his work force.

His present plant has some 70 employees, and he knows them all personally. (He also found it possible to know most of the 900 people in the larger plant.) It's not unusual for a man to stop him as he walks through the yard and offer a suggestion or a criticism of present practices.

The plant is unionized, but there has never been a strike, though the union is one that is considered "difficult" by many employers.

Fischer's day generally begins with reading: going through his mail and the notes and memoranda left on his desk. He also keeps in daily touch with the various sales offices in order to be sure that the plant is turning out products of the kind and in the quantity that can be sold. Not long ago, for example, the sales manager presented him with an opportunity and a problem: If the plant could triple its output of one of its products, the company could obtain a large and lucrative contract, one that could continue indefinitely.

Fischer called a meeting of the foremen to investigate the possibilities. If the plant were to put on a second shift, supervision would be required. Could they recommend any members of the rank and file who could be promoted to night foremen? What extra equipment was available, if any? What equipment modifications would be necessary?

Two of the foremen were able to recommend two or three experienced workmen who could supervise a night shift. Another remembered that there were some small tanks not being used that could be brought into service, and so on. Fischer was able to telephone the sales manager to take the contract, and the trebled production was achieved easily.

This day was an exception; contracts of this size are not usual for a small plant. A more typical day would be the one that began with the need to trace down the causes of off-standard product in company with the technical director. After that, Fischer lunched with two union representatives to discuss general problems of operation under the contract and in the afternoon planned for the plant vacation closing.

In many companies, the informal meeting with the union representatives at lunch would be an impossibility. The union men would not dare to get together with management informally without a large group present for fear their constituents would charge them with "selling out." Similarly, some management men would hesitate to let down their guard lest the union officials win some extra concessions not in the contract. In Fischer's plant, these difficulties do not seem to arise.

The vacation closing was a departure from past practice, which had been to keep the plant operating and stagger the vacations. As more and more employees acquired the length of service necessary to qualify for two weeks with pay, this became increasingly inconvenient. Most departments were short-handed from June through September.

Making the decision to close down was not a simple matter of saying "Yes, we'll do it." It was necessary to decide how much extra inventory should be built up to take care of orders that would come in immediately after the reopening. The extra production had to be scheduled and purchases rescheduled. Suppliers and customers had to be informed.

The inventory needed was set on the basis of sales in the previous year at the same time with additions to take care of expansion since then. The shutdown itself was timed to coincide with the shutdowns of the major customers, which Fischer had had the salesmen ascertain some time before. And instead of sending out a formal notice, Fischer delegated the job of informing the customers to the salesmen—it would give them a good reason to make extra calls and perhaps extra sales.

Though he grew up in the production end of the business, Fischer believes that the sales department is the most important in the company. Unlike many production men, he is aware that the most efficient production in the world is valueless if the output cannot be sold, and that production must always adapt itself to the needs of the market. Perhaps this is one reason why he is executive vice-president of the company instead of merely the plant manager.

THE SALES MANAGER

Joe Polansky, sales manager for the Evans Stationery Company, began his day with a telephone call to a customer. His phenomenal memory makes it possible for him to quote any one of his firm's hundreds of items by stock number, size, quantity, and price, and to talk about the special advantages of each. In this case he persuaded the customer, a stationery dealer, to double his order for New Year's diaries. Then he checked the customer's inventory over the telephone and managed to sell him another dozen items and interest him in a new type of paper.

His next move was to look over the morning mail and give the orders it contained to his assistant, who put them on order cards. Then he visited the stockroom to make sure that all the orders would be shipped out during the day. He always tries to have every order filled and shipped the day it is received. If the stockroom cannot fill the order, he often calls the factory for quick service.

After the orders, Joe turned his attention to the salesmen. He has a private office, but it is enclosed in glass so that he can see everyone and everyone can see him. The salesmen's desks are lined up in a row outside, in what Joe calls the "compound" or the "service station." Instead of calling the salesmen to him, he visited each one in turn.

There are four experienced salesmen, and with these he merely chatted casually, asking about their prospects and giving them advice only when they asked for it. With one of them, Gus Weber, a high-strung man who produces $1 million in orders every year, he was very careful. Joe talks rather slowly, which makes Gus nervous, and Gus also finds one of Joe's favorite phrases, "Repose yourself," particularly irritating. So Joe tries to interfere with him as little as possible.

The rest of the salesmen, a half dozen in all, are the younger men whom Joe is training, a group known as "Joe's stable." On these Joe lavishes most of his time and attention. Every day he goes over the results of the day before with each one, praising, counseling, correcting, listening to their ideas, and sometimes letting them make mistakes and learn from them if the consequences will not be too serious.

During all this time, Joe was being interrupted by calls from dealers who were asking questions, looking for advice, or merely complaining—often about personal problems since Joe tries to anticipate complaints about the Evans Company. No matter how often Joe has heard similar stories, he always acts as though each problem were unique. "Ye gods and little fishes!" he will exclaim in astonishment as the dealer recounts his troubles.

Lunch was, as always, with a customer, at a good but not ostentatious restaurant. Joe makes it a point to lunch at least once every two months with each of his principal customers, and if the business can be increased or if there is trouble, he lunches with a customer more often. It gives him a chance to talk and listen without the interruptions that occur when meetings are held at the customers' stores or in his own office. Joe believes profoundly that he can learn something from everyone. Naturally, the customer—the stationery store owner—likes to "tell the company." But subtly and indirectly, Joe Polansky educates the dealer in turn, and he can do so because he knows dealers' problems intimately.

In the afternoon, Joe visited a dealer's store, accompanied by one of his young protégés. He began by discussing the trend of business—what was selling, what was slow. Then he answered questions from the dealer, providing counsel drawn from his long experience and his knowledge of what other dealers were doing. And in the process, he sold the dealer more of a number of items and gave him tips on how to move them. Finally, he left his young man behind to help the dealer take inventory (and so learn the product line better).

Back at the office, Joe took care of more dealers' calls and inquiries, in the meantime answering and signing the mail. Finally, he checked on the day's sales, compared them to quota, and made a plan for the next day (and thereafter) to bring about improvements.

THE PERSONNEL MANAGER

At the Avalon Corporation, a medium-sized electronics company with 4,000 employees in three plants, office workers start their day at 9 A.M. and leave at 5:30 P.M.; plant employees work from 8 to 4:45.

Joel Black, director of personnel and industrial relations, is generally in his office in the main plant at 7:30 or 7:45. He stays "until I'm through," which is usually around 6 at night. Sometimes he is there until 10 P.M.

Black is in charge of employee and union relations for the three plants. His immediate subordinates are three personnel managers, one for each plant; the manager of the cafeteria in the main plant; and the head of the medical department there. His boss is the company president.

Black has a good-sized glassed-in office on the ground floor of the plant, which is located in a suburban area and surrounded by treeless lawns. Directly across a narrow aisle and enclosed only by a shoulder-high partition is the main assembly floor of the plant, a vast expanse in which several hundred men and women are engaged in precision work. There is no noise from this area since the assembly is delicate work, done mostly by hand.

Black chose this location for his office because he believes he should be accessible. On the same principle, he had the frosted glass removed from his office walls and plain glass substituted. Sometimes he passes up the executives' dining room for a meal in the company cafeteria, a move designed both to add to the impression of accessibility and to enable him to check up on the food there.

One of Black's shorter working days occurred last winter. He arrived at the office a few minutes after 8, which he considers "being late," and left a little before 5. He had returned home from a business trip at 1 A.M. the night before.

At 8:10 he began dictating a report on his visit to one of the company's major competitors the day before in order to get everything down while it was fresh in his mind. Avalon was negotiating a new union contract and wanted to know what other companies in the same industry were paying for various jobs: not merely the straight hourly rates, but the incentive payments, if any, and how much others were putting into such fringe benefits as insurance, pensions, pay for holidays, and so on. The wage and salary administrator, who is a member of Black's department, had conducted a mail survey on this, but it took a personal visit to elicit all the details from the major competitor.

After dictating the report, Black directed that copies be made for the wage and salary administrator, the benefits manager, and a young management trainee currently working in his office. (Part of Black's job is to plan the programs for the management trainees, no matter what department they are eventually slated for. Most of this training is conducted by rotating assignments, to give the trainees a chance at a number of different types of work.)

Then he dictated a thank-you note to the industrial relations manager who had supplied the information for the report. It was now 9 o'clock, and the rest of the office had come to work.

Black's next job was to review the file folder of an executive who was being gently booted out after six months on the job—that is, he was being allowed to "resign" rather than have a discharge appear on his record. Most discharges are said to be due to personality clashes, but this was a clear-cut case of poor performance or nonperformance in an important job.

"I'd interviewed the man before he was hired," Black said, "and I wanted to find out where we'd gone wrong. I discovered that I had had some serious doubts about him in the beginning. But since we needed a man in a hurry, we'd moved faster than we should have."

Next Black talked to the man himself. This was partly to find out whether the poor performer had understood what was expected of him, and if not, why not. Could the department head have been somewhat at fault in the way he oriented him to the job? Was the man possibly salvageable for another job in a different department?

During the interview it developed that the man did, indeed, feel the department head was to blame. He had never, he said, been told how he was expected to proceed.

Black recognized that this was quite possibly only a normal defense mechanism. "Nobody," he says, "ever really accepts the fact that he has fallen down on the job. I know I wouldn't. If my boss were to fire me, I'd be convinced that he hadn't been close enough to the work to understand what I was doing or that he had been listening to malicious gossip—that it was anybody's fault but my own. And I'd think so no matter what I'd done or left undone."

Nevertheless he decided to explore the matter further to be sure that no injustice was being done. On several occasions the department head had complained of the man's work, and each time Black had asked, "Have you talked with Conifer himself about this?" The answer had always been yes. Was it possible that the department head had not actually done so? Or had not made himself clear? Black's next move was to ask the department head to join the meeting.

The department head stated, in Conifer's presence, that he had told Conifer of his shortcomings. He admitted that he had not supervised him very closely, but he pointed out that the man had been hired precisely because he was supposed to be a seasoned executive able to take hold and do the work immediately. And his salary had been set accordingly.

Black could not but agree. He had gone along with the selection of Conifer in the first place despite misgivings because the man had a background that indicated he knew what the job involved and how he should go about it. The company would not have set the salary at $20,000 a year if the job had called for a trainee or a man who would need six months or a year to orient himself.

Since Conifer had to go, Black applied himself to the second purpose of the interview: to ease the man out as humanely as possible, help him to salvage his pride and avoid discouragement. The real trouble, he told Conifer, was quite possibly that Conifer was not suited to Avalon's way of working; perhaps in a larger company or a smaller one, or one that operated in a different way, the same difficulties would not arise.

When Conifer, reconciled if not cheered, left the office, it was 10:30, and Black was called to a meeting in the controller's office. Here he found an outside consultant, the controller, a cost accountant, and an operating vice-president gathered to discuss another possible dismissal, this time of the head of the purchasing group.

Black knows more about the operations of the various company departments than most men in the industrial relations field because he serves as chairman of a general management committee made up of vice-presidents. He was convinced that the inefficiency in purchasing was due less to any one person than to general company procedures that the purchasing man had inherited. At his suggestion, the group agreed to defer any action until the consultant had drawn up a plan for revision of procedures and a possible realignment of job responsibilities. A date a few days later was set for another meeting.

On the way back to his own office, Black was cornered by the public relations manager, who wanted to know why he had not attended any of the sales meetings then in progress. These meetings are an annual event at the home office, and Black and other corporate executives are usually present for at least part of the time.

On this occasion Black had not been there simply because he could not be in two places at the same time; he had had to choose between conflicting duties. He made his excuses as best he could and escaped back to his own office.

Once there, he spent forty-five or fifty minutes with one of the management trainees, explaining what the next assignment would be and why he thought it would afford valuable experience. The trainee had had some doubts about it.

Now it was 11:55, and Black took five or ten minutes off to call his broker and authorize some stock purchases—the only noncompany business he transacted during the day. Then he went to the executives' dining room for lunch.

After lunch, he had a meeting with the personnel manager of the main plant and the wage and salary administrator to discuss the findings of the wage and salary survey and the information he had obtained from the company's chief competitor. The management trainee was present also and was encouraged to ask questions and contribute what he could.

A little later, one of the general administrative executives joined the group to discuss a change proposed by the union in a contract clause. This was merely a revision in one of the many nonfinancial clauses that appear in any union contract—clauses covering distribution of overtime, conditions under which leave of absence will be granted, and similar matters.

Black, who has had long experience in bargaining, knew that a demand for a change of this nature generally comes up because of some incident that occurred in the past. In this instance he remembered a case some three years earlier in which the union had felt that a strict interpretation of the contract worked hardship for one of its members.

Evidently the union was attempting to plug up what it considered a loophole. But the wording the union had suggested was unclear; in fact, none of the management representatives was quite sure exactly what it did mean.

Black decided that an attempt to clarify matters and to work out a less ambiguous wording should be the subject of the next bargaining session, scheduled for 3 P.M. the same day. He found this convenient because he did not want to plunge right into the monetary demands, which the union had presented only the day before. These were excessive—and purposely so, he knew, because a union always asks for more than it has any hope of getting in order to allow leeway for compromise later. Yet he was sure that if he returned a flat "no" only a day later, it would appear that the company was turning down the demands without giving them due consideration, and the sessions would get off to a bad start. He preferred to begin by discussing a relatively noncontroversial matter and to explore it with the union representatives from the viewpoint that it might be possible to arrive at a solution that would be good for both sides.

As soon as the conference was over, Black reviewed the notes the trainee had prepared on the bargaining session the day before. Ordinarily, Black does not plan "make-work" assignments for trainees; he places them where there is real work to be done and holds them accountable for performance. But he believes that sitting in on the negotiations is the only way to get the "feel" of union relations and that no academic instruction can take its place. Since the young man could scarcely be expected to speak up at the meeting—and, of course, it would be unwise to allow him to do so—Black had had him take notes to keep busy.

Discussion of the progress of the bargaining session out of the way, Black had time to dictate two letters. One was to a college student, holder of a company scholarship, and the other to a second union in the plant, advising its president that he was terminating the contract as of February 18th—the regular expiration date—but was ready to start negotiating whenever the union wanted him to. He also had a telephone discussion with an executive in another company about a new committee being formed to encourage industry to locate in the area.

At 3 o'clock Black, the plant personnel manager, and the vice-president for manufacturing met the representatives of the first union for a session on the new contract. Black served as spokesman, as he always does during negotiations. The meeting broke up shortly before 5 o'clock.

How typical was this day? Of course, the company does not fire a $20,000-a-year executive every day; and since he works on the corporate level, Black would not, except in special circumstances, concern himself with discharges of those in lower echelons. But he might well have spent an equal amount of time interviewing candidates for a similar job, discussing a transfer on the same level, or reviewing a change in organization structure, which might mean meeting with several department heads.

Similarly, the company is not always in process of negotiating a new union contract. One of Black's achievements, in fact, has been persuading the union to agree to contracts that run for two years instead of one. But there are always problems that come up during the contract term: there may be disagreement over the meaning of the clauses, for example, or the union may claim that some supervisor has disregarded the terms. Moreover, there are two unions in the plant, and negotiations with each may be spread over several weeks.

Also, preparation for collective bargaining is time-consuming. Black must study all the data bearing on the demands and know what effect granting all or some of them will have on profits and on daily operation. And if he has to say no, he must give logical reasons for his answer. Otherwise he would be destroying the good union relations he has been working to build up.

Working with the management trainees is also a continuing part of his job. He must plan their assignments—and this entails conferences with various department heads—and he must counsel them on their progress.

WHAT THESE MANAGERS WERE DOING

All the managers whose activities have just been described are spending most of their time on management as a distinct and separate activity, although it may not be easy to discover which of the managerial functions—planning, organization, staffing, direction, control, innovation, or representation—they are carrying out at any particular moment. It may even seem as though the activities of any two of them have little in common, except that they all spend a large part of their time in discussions with other people.

Yet it is possible to fit practically all the many activities that make up their days into one or more of these categories. The managers' constant conferences are devoted to *planning* steps the company is to take (or to keeping themselves informed of new developments so that they can plan wisely), to *direction* of their subordinates (which includes teaching, explaining, and suggesting as well as giving orders), or to *controlling*—that is, to checking on how well previous plans have been carried out. For example, in reading the very detailed reports of sales and expenses, Mr. B was keeping close control of his widespread enterprises.

Organization matters also cropped up in some of the managers' days—for example, when Brewster considered placing purchasing under a single head. Joel Black, the personnel manager, naturally devoted a greater part of his day to *staffing* than the other managers did (firing is as much a part of staffing as hiring), but Fischer was also engaged in staffing when he discussed the selection of new foremen for the night shift.

SUMMARY

The subject matter with which managers deal differs widely. The problems and possibilities they will be found working on will vary according to their positions, their companies, and the circumstances of the moment. But to the extent that they are managing—as opposed to performing some of the actual work—they are engaged in one or more of the seven management functions.

It is often difficult to classify what a manager is doing at any given moment into one of these seven divisions, because he may be performing more than one of the seven functions at the same time. For example, he may, in an interview with a subordinate, be both planning and controlling—and directing as well. And during the discussion, he may develop the germ of a new idea (innovation) or stimulate his subordinate to suggest an important innovation.

In the course of these activities, managers naturally must make decisions, but "a decision is only a moment in a process."[2]

Review Questions

1. Did any of the managers whose days are described in this chapter perform any duties that were not strictly managerial in character? Specify.
2. List the activities performed by the managers that might be classified as planning.
3. Give three instances besides the one mentioned above (Mr. B's report reading) in which managers were performing the control function.
4. List three instances in which the managers were performing the representation function.
5. Were there any instances in which they were innovating?

Case Study / Daniel Brewster

In the case of Daniel Brewster, classify each of the tasks he performed under one of the seven management functions, or else specify that it was nonmanagerial in character.

[2] Mary Parker Follett, in Henry C. Metcalf and L. Urwick (eds.), *Dynamic Administration,* Harper & Row, Publishers, Incorporated, New York, 1940, p. 146.

Selected Readings

Executive Behaviour: A Study of the Work Load and the Working Methods of Managing Directors, Sune Carlson, C. A. Strömberg, Aktiebolag, Stockholm, Sweden, 1951. A description of the methods used and the results found in a lengthy study of the working days of twelve European managing directors (the equivalents of chief executives). The book presents data on the time spent on major management functions, the principal types of decisions, and the persons with whom time was spent.

What's Past Is Prologue, Mary B. Gilson, Harper & Row, Publishers, Incorporated, New York, 1940. An account of the work day and the problems of a personnel director.

Executive Suite, Cameron Hawley, Houghton Mifflin Company, Boston, with Ballantine Books, Inc., New York, 1952. A novel covering the dramatic few days in which a new chief executive is selected in a company in which there is considerable rivalry for the top job.

Managers and Their Jobs: A Study of the Similarities and Differences in the Ways Managers Spend Their Time, Rosemary Stewart, Macmillan & Co., Ltd., London, 1967. A realistic account of how managers spend their time. One hundred and sixty managers took part in the research on which the book is based by keeping diaries over a period of four weeks.

APPENDIX

THE ROAD TO THE TOP

Management is generally classified in three groups: lower, middle, and top. The lower (or first-level) management group is made up of foremen and white-collar supervisors, men and women who are only one short step above the rank and file. Then comes middle management, a vast and diverse group that includes sales managers, plant managers, personnel managers, controllers, and many other department managers as well as some people in less important positions. Finally, there is top management—the board chairmen, the company presidents, the executive vice-presidents—the men who direct and coordinate all the specialties and make policy for the company as a whole.

This classification is, however, a very loose one. Even in medium-sized corporations there are usually more levels than three—some companies have a dozen or more. Those toward the bottom of the scale (including some who can, if they wish, classify themselves as middle managers) may be so circumscribed by rules and set procedures that they do little actual managing. At the other end of the hierarchy, some of the heads of specialized functions may have reached the policy-making level.

Many researchers have attempted to determine how men reach the top executive positions, and of course, this subject may be explored in several different ways. Thus one may attempt to determine:

1. The extent to which family background plays a part in success. That is, to what extent is there equality of opportunity in the United States? And is U.S. society hardening into a class structure or becoming more open?
2. How do the men who reach the top differ from those who do not? Are they more intelligent, more persuasive than those who remain on the lower levels or superior to them in some other way?
3. What departments or specialties contribute the largest number of top men? Has an accountant a better chance than a production man, for example, or does sales offer the best chance of eventually rising to the top?

Most of the research that has dealt with family background has tended to prove, as one might expect, that it does have an important effect, but not a conclusive one, except in family-owned businesses. And in general, the research has shown that despite the rags-to-riches tradition of the United States, this has always been true. Moreover, some studies[1] have found that the opportunities are broadening because higher education is more possible for people from poorer families than it was earlier. One of the most recent

[1] See, for example, W. Lloyd Warner and James C. Abegglen, *Big Business Leaders in America*, Harper & Row, Publishers, Incorporated, New York, 1955.

projects,[2] on the other hand, has found that the amount of social mobility is just about what it always was but that the American occupational structure has always been more open than radicals have claimed, although, of course, true equal opportunity does not and never has existed.

Studies of success characteristics have been inconclusive. Although successful business executives tend to be more intelligent than the average man, the most intelligent executive is not necessarily the one who reaches the top. Thus attempts have been made to identify a "personality configuration" that makes for success, but the findings may apply only to the particular samples that were studied. Also, it seems that the man who starts his own business and runs it successfully is likely to differ widely from the man who is successful in a large corporation.

Studies of the specialties that are most likely to lead to the top have also reached different conclusions, but this is not surprising since industry has different needs at different times and companies differ from each other in this respect. Thus in some companies at some times the man who starts out in sales is most likely to reach the top; in others, the field has been production, finance, or something else. For example, in 1967, the management consulting firm of Heidrick and Struggles, Inc., conducted a survey of presidents in the largest industrial firms and found that an administrative post, rather than a position in manufacturing or sales, was the best springboard.[3]

On the other hand, there is evidence that the increasing technological complexity of modern industry is making it more and more necessary for the top executive to have a scientific background. Drawing on evidence produced by various surveys (his own and those of others), Jay M. Gould, reports:

> The percentage of corporate heads with technical degrees was below 7 in 1900, reached 20 by 1950, and shot up to 33 in the past decade. An additional 5% of the 1964 crop of corporate heads . . . had no formal college degree in science or engineering but had sufficient on-the-job training to be regarded as having come up through "technical" ranks.[4]

Dr. Gould also found that opportunities for those from poorer families are increasing if they acquire the necessary technical background.

On the other hand, there will probably always be some industries and some companies in which a technical background will not be the most important factor. Also, it appears that the choice of a chief executive often depends on the problems a company is facing at the time the choice is made. For example, Alfred P. Sloan, Jr., was selected president of General Motors in the 1920s because, in the words of an unnamed spokesman quoted in the *Wall Street Journal:*

[2] Peter Blau and Otis Dudley Duncan, *The American Occupational Structure,* John Wiley & Sons, Inc., New York, 1968.
[3] *Business Week,* Oct. 14, 1967, p. 130.
[4] *The Technical Elite,* Augustus M. Kelley, Publisher, New York, 1966, pp. 82–83.

The company needed an organizer and financial expert. . . . By the time William S. Knudsen came along, we needed a production genius, and we got the man who later ran the war output program. In Mr. Wilson's day, among other things, we faced labor troubles. That was a field Mr. Wilson knew and was interested in. It made a big difference in our labor relations.

Mr. Curtice, in my opinion, is still the greatest instinctive stylist and salesman this industry has ever seen—and that's exactly what was required to spark the terrific postwar auto boom that gave G.M. the billion-dollar profit. All those men were different, and all of them were great presidents, but they were chosen to do a specific job that needed doing right at that time.[5]

When Harlow C. Curtice retired in 1958, Frederic G. Donner was chosen chief executive (with the title of chairman of the board). According to the same spokesman, what the company needed most at that time was financial guidance to enable it to continue its record as a top money-maker, and Donner was a financial man. Since he had spent his entire life in finance, the no. 2 man elected to the presidency at the same time was a production executive who had been in charge of the body and assembly divisions, John F. Gordon.

Planning a career to the top is an extraordinarily difficult task, as anyone knows who has attempted it. Requirements for top posts vary not only among different industries and among companies in the same industry, but even, as the General Motors story shows, at different times within the same company.

The very qualities that will take a man to the top in one company or at one time may actually hamper his progress in another company, or even in the same company at a different time. There is no certainty, no matter how well thought out the plan or how competent the planner. The most that can be done is to ensure the *possibility* of a rise, and here there are three critical stages to consider:

1. The break-in, or entry, stage; that is, getting a first job, or a first full-time job.
2. The breakthrough into a position in middle management.
3. The breakthrough into a position at or near the top where it is possible to influence broad policy.

Entering a company

Many college graduates receive several offers of employment. They may be tempted to take the one that pays the best or to accept a position with the company whose recruiter makes the most glowing promises of opportunity for advancement. Instead, they should make searching analyses of their own. While a mistake at this point is not fatal, it can slow up a career and entail a painful readjustment later.

Most young men understand that a "growth" company offers more oppor-

[5] August 26, 1958.

tunities for advancement than one that has reached its peak or is even in process of slow decline. But how does one identify a growth company?

Choosing an industry   First of all, it is necessary to consider the industry. If the industry is declining, only a few companies can hope to swim against the tide, and the chances are that the company which is offering the job will not be among them.

In making a decision on this point, one must do more than follow a general impression, such as "Electronics is the coming thing." The general impression may very well be correct, but there are many different types of electronic products, and not all have equal prospects. Also, a company may be "in electronics" but only to a minor extent. The bulk of its business may be in some other field. Again, its electronics business may be entirely dependent on government contracts subject to cancellation at short notice.

It may be well, therefore, for the graduate to do a little library research on the industry in general and the particular segment of the industry in which the company is engaged. Government figures and other published material often provide very interesting sidelights on industry prospects.

Some industries often seem to pay far higher salaries than others for comparable jobs, and there are many different theories as to why this is so. But the salary differentials among companies of various sizes are more evident at the top than down the line; therefore this matter may be unimportant in the beginning.

Another point to consider is how transferable the skills learned in the industry will be. There are certain companies and certain industries in which the knowledge an executive acquires is so specialized that it will be difficult for him to convince another company that his experience will be valuable in another field, even a closely related one. He is then at a major disadvantage if it becomes necessary or advisable for him to change companies.

On the other hand, many of the companies in these industries offer great security to the man who is willing to stay with one organization all his life. He can be as sure of continued employment and some advancement as anyone ever is in this life, and of an excellent pension when his working days come to a close. Some utilities fall into this classification.

Which company?   Once the industry has been considered, it is, of course, even more necessary to consider the company itself. Automobiles were undoubtedly a major "growth industry" in the early twentieth century, yet many of the companies then starting off with high hopes fell by the wayside or were absorbed into others.

Company material is usually available in profusion. The brochures offered to prospective employees will be of some help, but naturally they are designed to create as favorable an impression as possible. On entirely factual matters, one may take everything they say as accurate. Where the statements are a matter of opinion, it is best to discount them. Take the paragraphs on "chances of advancement." Every company that is not on the verge of bankruptcy is likely to offer some chances of advancement for some people; therefore every company can be expected to list this among the pluses.

Moreover, the brochures seldom give factual information on sales and profit trends, which are the real clue to growth. Data on these points can be obtained from company annual reports for several years in the past, or sometimes a single annual report will recapitulate a ten-year record of sales and profits. Even more informative will be a perusal of 10K reports made to the Securities and Exchange Commission by all companies with more than $2 million in stock outstanding. These may be examined in the offices of the SEC or in Stock Exchange libraries. Or, if the student does not have access to these collections, he may obtain copies from the SEC in Washington if he pays a small charge for the reproduction.

Also informative are the prospectuses issued when new securities are offered. Announcements of these issues appear in metropolitan papers, and copies of the booklets may be obtained from the underwriters, whose names will be mentioned in the news stories and advertisements. If the company is not issuing any new stock currently, copies of past prospectuses may be obtained from the SEC, again by paying for the reproduction.

Still other sources of information are the many directories available in most large libraries. For example, a directory put out by the National Academy of Sciences—National Research Council gives material on the types of research being done and the size of the research staffs for an enormous number of industrial laboratories, both independent and company-sponsored. The *Advertising Register* (National Register Company) lists the advertising budgets of a large number of companies—a point of interest to anyone who is planning a career in this phase of the business. In another volume, it lists the accounts of practically all advertising agencies in the country. Moody's Investors Service gives the financial history of each company listed in its directories—the trends in sales and profits, the amount of stock outstanding, the mergers that have taken place, and so on.

Using the last source alone, it was possible to predict that one company which enjoyed a splendid reputation for growth was actually riding for a hard fall. It was issuing enormous quantities of new stock and using this to purchase other companies in fields far removed from its original activities. Its growth was, therefore, only paper growth; it was becoming larger, but earnings per share of stock had been steadily falling. About a year after this analysis, the management was ousted and a period of strict retrenchment began.

Small versus large companies   Many young graduates prefer large companies to small ones on the theory that the large organizations are bound to have many more higher job openings. This is true, but it is also true that they will have many more people competing for the openings that do occur, and the policy-making jobs will be at a greater distance from the beginning jobs.

Of course companies in the same size group differ widely from one another.

Nevertheless, a few generalizations about the differences between large and small companies are possible:

1. In a small company, the new employee has a greater chance of direct contact with top management. Hence he has more opportunity to show the people who control his business destiny what he can do. On the other hand, many small companies are family-held, and no one has much chance at the really top posts unless he is a member of the family or marries into it.

2. The large company usually provides more formal training, the small company more opportunity for on-the-job training in diversified activities, with actual responsibility for results at an early date.

3. It is probably easier to get fired from a small company than from a large one since many big organizations suffer from a kind of inertia that permits people who are not very competent to continue in their jobs for years unless they make conspicuous and costly mistakes. This may not be an argument for the large-company job, however. If a young man cannot do well in a given field or company, it may be better for him to be fired fairly quickly. Otherwise, he may find himself unemployed at a time when he has greater family responsibilities and has reached an age when it will be more difficult for him to get a new job. Offsetting this is the fact that if a man cannot do well in one job, the large company may have others to which it can transfer him, whereas the small company may have no other openings.

4. Large companies usually provide more generous benefits in the form of pensions, insurance, and so on. On the other hand, the various benefits are tending to spread throughout industry, and this factor is likely to make less difference in the future. Moreover, small companies can be more flexible in this respect than large ones and will often do more for a well-liked employee who meets with extended sickness or other hardship. The large organization must always take into account the fact that it may be setting a precedent that will prove awkward later. In the large company the man who makes the decision on a matter like this probably will not know the employee personally; hence he will be more likely to think in terms of general policy.

5. In the matter of long-term security, the advantage probably lies with the larger company, but not overwhelmingly so. A small company is more likely to go out of business entirely than a diversified giant is. It is also more likely to be bought up by another company, and it is very difficult for anyone in a key position to hold his place when such a major change occurs since the buyer will probably have men ready and willing to step into the management of the various functions. But the giant companies can and do cut off entire departments and activities, sometimes rather suddenly, and neglect to find comparable positions or any positions at all for those who are left without work. If the worst comes to the worst.

however, and a man finds himself out of a job, the fact that he has had good experience in a well-known company may make his résumé more attractive to prospective employers.

6. As to general treatment on the job, it may be said that when the small company is good in this respect, it is very good indeed, and when it is bad it is likely to be impossible. This is because, much more than the large company, the small company is the "lengthened shadow of one man." If the top boss is intelligent, fair, and kindly, a small-company job is likely to offer greater intrinsic job satisfaction. Each man's efforts affect final results more directly, and there is no feeling of being only a small cog in an enormous machine. In the large company, the personality of the man at the top does make itself felt, but not to the same extent. It is more likely that the department head sets the tone, and if the jobholder does not like the climate that surrounds him, he can sometimes arrange for a lateral transfer to some other department.

How specialties rank   Another factor, more important than the size of the company, is the status of the candidate's specialty within the company. A man who wants a career in research should seek out a company in which research is important and likely to continue so. This will rule out many, though not all, small companies since few of them have the resources to finance large laboratories, particularly laboratories for research that will not pay off for a long time.

The status of a personnel department, an advertising department, a financial department, or even production or sales will vary widely in different companies and in different industries. "In the large oil companies," says an executive in one of them, "I notice a strong tendency for top management to be drawn exclusively from the ranks of men with considerable background of line operating experience. This is in partial contrast to industries that manufacture a wide variety of products and those in which sales promotion and sales effectiveness constitute such a large part of the profit-making ability."

Such industries as soaps and cosmetics and packaged foodstuffs are those in which sales promotion and sales effectiveness make the largest contribution. Thus Neil H. McElroy joined Procter & Gamble as a clerk in the advertising department after his graduation from Harvard in 1925 and rose to become manager of advertising and promotion. From that post he was promoted to vice-president, then to vice-president and general manager, and three years after that, to president of the company.

If the specialty in which a man is working is considered, rightly or wrongly, comparatively unimportant to total results, it may be very difficult for him to advance into a policy-making position or even to obtain the money to make the improvements that will call attention to his capabilities. "When you go up there [to top management to ask for an appropriation]," one maintenance manager observed, "you're just expense. But production is a golden god."

Without actual experience in a company, it is very difficult to tell how the various departments rate in the company hierarchy. One indication that will help to differentiate between the ''just expense'' departments and the golden gods is the department head's place in the organization chart. In general, though this is not an infallible clue, the higher his status the more important the department. Another indication is the size of the department in relation to total employment in the company. A third is the scope of the department head's job: the number of functions that come under his jurisdiction.

Self-analysis   Just as important as analysis of the industry and company is a searching self-analysis. The candidate must decide what he really wants out of life and what his qualifications—technical and personal—really fit him for. To some extent, he may have already made the choice by his selection of a college course, but there are many different ways of using the same background. An engineer, for example, may have a choice among a number of types of engineering (e.g., process, development, technical sales, research, sales service, and so on).

First of all, the candidate should ask himself whether he has the foundation knowledge and enough interest to acquire all the technical knowledge necessary to advance in the field he is preparing to enter. A man may know enough accounting to obtain a position as a junior accountant, but if he is not really interested in the whole subject of finance and not able and willing to learn, say, the possibilities of computers and other forms of highly mechanized accounting, the operations of the money market (of which the stock market is only a part), the complications of the tax laws and Securities and Exchange Commission regulations, he is not likely to reach a high post through the financial management route.

Second, he must regard the function as important. If he considers certain types of staff activities a form of boondoggle, he will be neither happy nor successful in working at them. If he thinks of salesmanship as a mere exploitation of one's personality and not work really worthy of an intelligent man, he will not be able to put his heart into selling and will most likely fail at it.

Would he rather work in a small town or a large city? What part of the country does he prefer? Most locations have some advantages, and the choice must be an individual one. There are many people who would rather make less and live in the type of community they prefer, and the candidate should consider this point carefully since it may influence his decision on size of company. A large company with many locations may transfer executives often. A small one generally has only one location, and a man who takes a job with it can be reasonably sure where he will be living five years later.

Important, too, is the extent to which the candidate's personality ''fits in'' with the organization. If most of the people in the top and near-top posts come from rich families and are graduates of top prep schools, the graduate with the more rough-and-ready background may not find it easy to advance very far. (Manners and attitudes can be learned, but the learning makes for extra strain and requires an ability to notice nuances that many people do not possess.) Similarly, in a company in which most of higher management is the rough-

and-ready type, the too smooth employee may be regarded as weak. Often there is a "company type," which will be recognizable after the candidate has met several executives (as he usually will before a serious job offer is made), and only those who fit the specifications advance very far in the organization.

Allied with this consideration is the question of how much conformity a man would like or can take. In recent years, "conformity" has become an ugly word in business, and everyone feels called upon to deny that he likes it for himself or demands it of others. Yet many people do like an organization in which conformity is general, and many organizations do demand a great deal of it.

Of course no one would say, "I want to be made to conform." The man suited to a conformist organization would say, rather, that he likes to know "where he's at"—meaning that he would like to know exactly what he is supposed to do in every situation, be rewarded for acting in the prescribed manner, and perhaps see others duly punished for not acting in the same way. He feels hesitant in situations where he is supposed to work out his own methods and find new ways of handling new problems.

Conformity is generally more prevalent in large organizations than in small ones, but it is not possible to judge its extent by company size alone. The handbooks distributed to new or prospective employees offer one clue: On how many questions has the company found it necessary to set hard and fast rules? The degree to which interviewers, other than the original recruiter, talk frankly and informally is another indication. If they appear to be giving canned speeches, if they show irritation at an unexpected question—these are hints that they are operating within set grooves and do not dare depart from them without higher sanction. If he gets a chance, the candidate may also judge from the exchanges between subordinates and superiors and between executives on the same level. Are contacts frank and informal, or does each man seem to be watching his step?

One cannot ask an interviewer about conformity, nor would the query elicit an honest answer. The only thing the candidate can do is weigh the indications and decide whether there seems to be too much or too little conformity for his taste.

In passing, it might be noted that no one except a hermit can be completely nonconformist. Working with other people always makes the observance of some rules necessary. If being five minutes late in the morning after an hour's overtime work the night before is considered a major crime, one may logically conclude that the company is very interested in conformity. But no one should expect to work only when the fancy takes him. If all executives appear to go to the same tailor for exactly the same kind of suits and all smoke the same brand of cigarettes (the kind the top man smokes), that is conformity. But no one should expect that sloppy dressing, hair that needs cutting, or dirty fingernails will not hold him back.

The man who is just entering industry cannot hope that his first job will satisfy all his criteria perfectly. Undoubtedly, he will have to compromise on some points. But he should weigh the relative importance of the various factors mentioned and make the best possible compromise in the light of his own real desires and qualifications.

The first breakthrough

For the college graduate, the breakthrough into the lower ranks of middle management may be possible merely by virtue of seniority and performance that is at least up to the average. The man who counts on that method of promotion, however, is not likely to go very far; certainly he has few prospects of reaching the top.

Doing more than is expected   Consistently outstanding performance is a less uncertain method. Contributions above and beyond the call of duty are also likely to accelerate the promotion process. Thus the salesman who consistently outsells the others, who builds up a lagging territory to a volume beyond expectations, who proves adept at opening new accounts, puts himself in line for a job in sales management. If he devises new promotions or new applications of the company's products, or opens up new markets of one kind or another, he has a better chance, particularly if his methods are applicable to territories other than his own and produce an overall gain for the company. The process engineer who devises improvements that produce major savings is also likely to attract attention and move up the ladder. The research man who makes a real discovery will probably be appointed leader of the group that works on its development.

Innovation for success   A new idea, well worked out and presented through the proper channels, will often work wonders. For example, Gerard Swope, president of General Electric from 1922 to 1939, started with Western Electric Shops in 1895 at $7 a week after his graduation from MIT as an electrical engineer and, as he afterwards recalled, "was assigned to the dirtiest work in the shop . . . tearing down old machines that had been returned for repairs."[6] Here he did such a good job of inventorying the machines that the general foreman had him draw up an inventory for the whole department. This was recognition of a sort, but Swope was afraid that it might lead only to other jobs of a clerical nature.

He was already supplementing his income by publishing articles in engineering journals; now he decided to broaden his field. He drafted a plan for a new district sales organization in St. Louis, and it was accepted by the vice-president in charge of sales. Though an older man was put in charge of carrying it out, Swope went along as his assistant. Later he was promoted to sales manager for St. Louis, and when he landed a big contract against heavy competition, he was made president of a subsidiary organized to handle Western Electric business throughout the territory.

---

[6] David Loth, *Swope of G.E.,* Simon and Schuster, Inc., New York, 1958, p. 25.

This was a long time ago, but the method still works. Quite recently a purchasing agent found himself stymied. He was doing good work in his own field, but no one seemed to notice it, and promotions were not forthcoming. So he asked himself: What improvements are needed around here?

In thinking over the possibilities, he decided that the company could save a good deal of money if it had a "materials manager" who would be in charge of purchasing materials, receiving, storage, and related functions. These operations were currently spread among different departments—a situation that was causing duplication of work and many failures to get the materials to production on time. He worked out the plan in detail—the functions, the costs involved, the savings in time and money—and presented it to his immediate superior. The superior liked the idea and passed it upward. Eventually, top management accepted it and the purchasing agent was given the new job at an increase in salary. Better yet, he had made top management aware of his existence and had put himself in line for consideration for further promotions.

The technique of the new idea is one of the best, but there are precautions to be observed in using it. First, a vague general idea will arouse no interest. "We ought to get our products into the supermarkets" means nothing. The idea must be embodied in a plan of action that explains in detail how it can be carried out, what the extra costs will be, and what returns may be expected. This often means unpaid overtime work at home since no one looks with favor on the man who neglects the job at hand to work out some grandiose scheme for his own advancement.

Second, it is well to take the plan up with one's immediate supervisor first. There have been cases in which men have scored by going to higher management at once, but there are probably more instances in which those who tried it have found themselves out of a job in very short order. Will the superior steal the idea and pass it off as his own? That is a chance the man must take, and very often faith in the superior's honesty will be justified. Even if the superior does take the major share of the credit, he will be likely to let a little percolate down to the man who originated the idea. In any case, the wisest plan is not to go over his head unless one has accepted the alternatives of "up or out." Further, the superior, with his greater experience, may be able to suggest some improvements that will make the plan more acceptable to the top.

Asking for promotion   Finally, there is nothing wrong with asking for a promotion when a new job on a higher level opens up. But if the request is to be granted, the applicant must have spent some time preparing himself for the opportunity by taking courses, on-the-job learning, or both. Only in the most routine jobs is there little opportunity to learn some of the functions of the higher positions, and in many companies positive help in doing so is provided.

The road may be long   Reaching a middle management position does not mean that a man is now ready to try for the top; often he must advance slowly through various middle management jobs, sometimes making lateral transfers to broaden his background. Here are the positions held by two fairly high-level officials of a nationally known oil company over the years:

S.M., Administrative vice-president of the production department
1927 Hired as assistant production engineer (already had a few years' experience as a geologist with another oil company)
1929 Production foreman
1933 District superintendent, production department
1935 Production engineer
1936 Assistant general superintendent, production department
1946 General production superintendent
1947 Assistant manager, production department
1949 Manager, production department
1951 Vice-president and manager, production department
1955 Administrative vice-president, production department

A.C., Administrative vice-president and general manager of marketing
1928 Hired as order clerk
1929 Salesman
1931 District superintendent of marketing
1934 City manager of marketing
1939 Assistant division manager, marketing
1947 Division manager, marketing
1951 Regional general manager, Eastern region
1953 General manager, marketing
1958 Administrative vice-president and general manager, marketing

These two men started their business careers in the 1920s, which means that they encountered the major depression of the thirties before they were very far along. For this reason their progress was undoubtedly slower than it would otherwise have been. S.M.'s transfer from district superintendent to production engineer may well have been a demotion, occasioned not by any lack of ability on his part but by the general contraction that practically every company experienced during the slump. But the outline of their careers does indicate the number of steps that may exist between the lower levels and a vice-presidency.

To the top levels

When Gerard Swope was appointed president of the St. Louis subsidiary in 1901, he was actually nowhere near the top despite his title. The subsidiary was a sales subsidiary, and his post was that of a glorified territorial sales manager. Superlative performance, however, led to an enlargement of his territory and then to a headquarters position as assistant supervisor of all branch houses and national sales manager of the company's machinery business. Here he paved the way for further advancement by more good performance and several new ideas of a general management nature: detailed expense analysis and a plan for coordinated control of autonomous departments, among others. Very shortly after, he was put in charge of all the company's electrical machinery business—engineering and manufacturing as well as sales. Among his achievements in this position was development of a plan that settled a serious strike.

In 1908, only nine years after he had initiated the plan that led to his breakthrough into middle management, Swope was appointed general sales manager in charge of the marketing of all products, and his contributions in that position (which included negotiation of the purchase of patents essential to the automatic telephone) led to promotion to vice-president and member of the board of directors. Then the General Electric Company sought him out for the presidency of its international organization. He became GE president a few years later.

The rapidity of Swope's rise was due in part to outstanding performance in each position, but perhaps more to the initiation of many new and successful ideas. It will be noted, also, that he was careful to broaden his background. Starting as an engineer, he switched to sales, and in the course of his career he learned all he could about finance—a subject in which many sales executives and engineers find it difficult to take an interest.

A man in whose success an original idea played a decisive role was Donaldson Brown, at one time treasurer of the Du Pont Company and later a General Motors vice-president and a member of that company's board of directors. "An event occurred in 1914 which proved to be the turning point of my business career," he wrote in his autobiography.[7] "The circumstances which led up to it were accidental, and I have often wondered what might have been my fate and fortune in industrial management if I had not, that summer, hit upon the mathematical equation."

Brown, originally a salesman for Du Pont, had been transferred to the headquarters staff "to take care of analytical matters." (At that time the company was a good deal smaller than it is now.) Then, in the important summer of which he speaks, the president of the company, Coleman du Pont, called for a study and report on the performance of the operating departments, and Brown undertook the job of providing a method of measurement. The result of his work was the mathematical formula

$$R = P \times T$$

R in this case stood for the rate of return on invested capital, which Brown characterized as the final and fundamental measure of industrial efficiency. T stood for the ratio of sales to investment, and P for the percentage of profit on sales. Thus if the total investment figure were $100,000 and net sales were

[7] *Some Reminiscences of an Industrialist,* Ernest Dale (ed.), Alfred A. Knopf, Inc., New York, 1969.

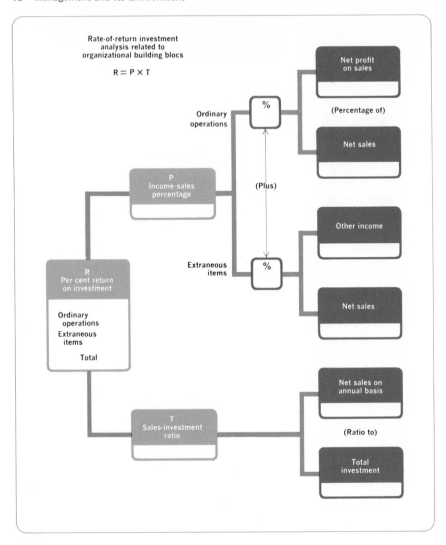

FIGURE 1 This chart was part of Donaldson Brown's explanation of his formula $R = P \times T$.

$200,000, the ratio of the sales to the investment would be 2 to 1. If total cost of sales were $180,000, the profit on the net sales figure would be $20,000, or 20 per cent on an investment of $100,000.

This was an ingenious and accurate way of measuring performance in various divisions of the company. Dollar profit figures would not be significant since more would be invested in some activities than in others.

It should not be supposed that Brown presented his idea in the summary form outlined above. He worked it out very carefully in a paper showing all the components of cost of sales and investment in such a way that a poor return on investment in any segment of the business could be traced back to its cause or causes.

The immediate effect of this plan on Brown's career was a promotion to the post of assistant treasurer of the Du Pont Company. Four years later the treasurer was made a vice-president and Brown became treasurer and, shortly afterward, a member of the board of directors. His transfer to General Motors occurred in 1921, when Du Pont, which owned a large block of GM stock, was forced to take a hand in the management because the automobile company had run into difficulties. Brown went to GM as vice-president in charge of finance.

Changing jobs   In Swope's and Brown's cases, the climb up the ladder was largely with one company. The same results may often be achieved by a series of judicious job changes. A man who learns all he can and extends the boundaries of his job as far as company policy will allow may gain experience that will enable him to apply for a higher job in another organization if he wins no recognition in his own. In the matter of job changes, however, there are several precautions to be observed.

First, if he can possibly arrange it, a man should never quit one job until he has another. Confronted with an unemployed applicant, the man who does the hiring may think, "If he's so good, why is he out of work?" Even more important, the employed applicant is in a better bargaining position, both financially and psychologically. Few people can afford to remain off a payroll long, and financial pressure may drive the man who has quit to improve his status to take a job that is less desirable than the one he left. And unemployment tends to rob people of confidence, which means that they are not at their best in applying for a new position.

Second, job changes should not be too frequent. When a man reaches the age of, say, forty, too many shifts constitute something of a blot on his record. If he has held a great many jobs that lasted only two or three years, a prospective employer is likely to conclude that the man is either an incompetent who has been frequently fired or a prima donna who quits every time something does not go exactly to his liking.

Third, it is important to be sure that the new job represents an actual step up. More money is, of course, one way of judging this factor, but unless it is much more, it may not be the most important one. A chance at more responsible work and an opportunity to learn may be just as valuable, particularly if they are accompanied by a title that implies a higher status.

Fourth, the company should be investigated, perhaps even more thoroughly than the company with which the man took his first job. At this point, he will be better equipped for the investigation because he will know more about the business world and what he really wants from it.

Promoting the department   Still another method of rising to the top, and one which almost every department head attempts to pursue, is to raise the status of the department within the organization to the point where top management will begin including its chief in the policy-making group. This may be done by enlarging the department's functions at every opportunity and/or making unexpected contributions to overall company success. A part of the technique may be a judicious public relations program within the company—calling attention to the department's achievements by means of periodic reports and similar measures.

To employ this means of self-advancement it is necessary, of course, that a man have reached the position of department head, and it works best when his efforts are bolstered by trends within the industry or within the company itself. The rise of unionization in the 1930s gave industrial relations an unparalleled opportunity to improve its status; so did the shortage of labor during World War II. Many heads of industrial relations emerged from these periods as vice-presidents. Automation may offer a similar opportunity to maintenance departments since keeping the expensive machinery running will become more and more important to profitability.

Entrepreneurship

Finally, of course, one may start a business of one's own and rise with it. This may produce the greatest rewards both in money and in job satisfaction, but it also entails the greatest risks. Though many people have made fortunes in this way, many more have lost their savings. Statistics indicate that it is only the exceptional business that is still going five years after it is started, and some of these survivors fail before another five years have passed.

The first requisite for a new business is a good product, which may be either a tangible product or a service. Preferably it should fill a need so far unsatisfied, or it should be substantially better than other products on the market. Or the new business should have what the economists call "time and place utility"—that is, it should be able to provide quicker service or service in an area where it has so far been unavailable.

A better product   William C. Durant, the founder of General Motors, who was a carriage maker before he was an automobile manufacturer, achieved his first success by using the technique of a better product. A friend took him for a ride in a two-wheeled horse-drawn cart that was substantially superior to anything of its kind he had seen before. It had a new type of suspension that gave a smoother ride on the rough roads of the day, and it was unusually attractive-looking as well.

That same night Durant took the train to the town where the plant was located. The next morning he was talking to the owner, offering to buy a part interest in the firm, which was a very small one. Though he had no money of his own, he was confident he could borrow enough to finance the purchase.

The manufacturer refused to sell a part interest but was willing to sell out completely for the modest sum of $1,500. Durant left with the contract and returned to his home town of Flint, Michigan, to raise the money. He had some fairly rich relatives, but he did not go to them for the loan. As he explained in his unfinished and unpublished autobiography, written in part in the third person:

> The next morning, the eventful 18th of September, 1886, we find our friend on the corner of Saginaw and Kearsley Streets thinking hard. Across the street was the Genesee County Savings Bank. Ira Wilder, the cashier . . . was approachable and it would seem that that was the logical place to apply for a loan. But there was one thing against the proposition. The young man's uncle was president of the bank and he had a relative or two on the board of directors. . . . Figuring quickly, he arrived at the decision, "If I make a failure of the venture, I will never hear the last of it. *Nothing doing.*"

Instead, he sought out another bank and obtained $2,000 without much difficulty. Then he told a friend, J. Dallas Dort, who clerked in a hardware store, about the proposition and sold him a half interest for $1,000. In the course of a single day, he obtained the $1,500 purchase price and another $1,500 for working capital.

Even a superior product does not sell itself, as the original manufacturer of the road cart (as the product was called) had evidently found out, since he was so willing to sell at a small price. The entrepreneur must know the markets and he must be able to sell, or he must have an associate who possesses these qualifications.

Durant himself was a superlative salesman and probably knew a good deal about the carriage-making business since Flint was a small center of the industry. Though he was less than twenty-five years old at the time, he already had eight years' business experience—in his grandfather's lumberyard, as manager of the Flint waterworks, and as a salesman of real estate, bicycles, and insurance.

Having acquired the company, he knew exactly what to do to promote sales. Most of the state fairs were over, but there was one in Wisconsin to be held shortly. He took a sample cart, which had come with his purchase, to the fair, and won a blue ribbon with it. On the same trip, he persuaded two or three established businessmen to act as sales agents. Before returning to Flint, he had contracts for more than 600 carts. On the same trip he arranged a production contract with a carriage maker who agreed to turn out 1,300 carts at $12.50 each.

From then on, the company grew steadily, and Durant and Dort both made modest fortunes out of it during the next three decades. After that Durant switched to the automobile business. He had even greater success until 1920, when he overextended himself and was forced out of the company (General Motors) which he had organized.

Personal service in filling needs   An example of a company built on filling needs that had been going unsatisfied and providing time and place utility is National Steel, fifth largest steel company in the United States. Its founder, Ernest Tener Weir, grew up in the steel business, learning both the production and the sales functions. Like Durant, he had a natural talent for raising money. When he and a partner purchased a small run-down tinplate mill, they did not try to buck U.S. Steel directly. Instead, they sought out smaller customers and provided a type of personal service these organizations felt they were not getting from Weir's giant competitor.

Later he went into the production of steel itself and merged his company with Great Lakes Steel, which was located in a suburb of Detroit near the growing automobile industry—one of steel's largest markets. (At that time, the big steel companies were all located in Pittsburgh.)

The salable product and the ability to sell it are two of the main ingredients of success in a new venture. Durant's road cart was distinctly superior to anything else of its type on the market. Weir entered the production of tinplate at a time when more and more food was being packed in cans and the market for his product was growing. Moreover, he provided a new type of personal service for his small customers, and with the Great Lakes Steel plants he put himself in a favorable position to supply the big automobile market quickly.

Pitfalls of entrepreneurship   In considering demand for a given product, however, it is important to distinguish between a trend and a fad. Some fads produce an enormous market almost overnight (hula hoops, for example, and earlier, miniature golf courses); then they collapse almost as quickly. In general, a very quick rise in demand for a product may indicate that it is one the public will soon tire of. The first entrepreneurs in the field often make a great deal of money, but those who come later usually lose a great deal. Slow, steady growth is a surer sign of a long-term trend.

Another point to consider is how easy it will be for some larger company to become a major competitor. A case in point is that of the manufacturer of a foreign car who projected continually rising sales after an initial success. But it was in the cards that the U.S. Big Three would begin manufacture of smaller cars if the foreign cars started to take an appreciable part of the market, and so it happened.

Even when a product may count on a good market for a long time to come, there are other pitfalls. One is financing—many small businesses have failed because they lacked the capital to tide them over the starting period and make needed improvements, and have been forced to close even though success was only a short while away. There are also entrepreneurs whose reasoning is simply, "If I make it for $7 and sell it for $10, my profit will be $3." They take insufficient account of overhead (sometimes they do not consider it at all), possible credit problems, and other important costs.

Production often offers another pitfall. A working model that appears perfect may develop unexpected bugs in mass production. In the case of Durant and Dort, this was not a major problem because the production was farmed out.

In any case, production problems were simple. Moreover, since Durant himself had worked in a lumberyard while his partner knew hardware, they were familiar with the materials necessary to produce the cart.

There are also the unforeseen problems. In the case of a retail establishment—and many of the thousands of new ventures started every year are retail stores—a big competitor may suddenly open up down the street, the state road may bypass the store and leave it high and dry, or the character of the district may change. A manufacturer who is making a product for industry may find that his customers are changing their production processes and his product is no longer in demand.

Another hazard is too rapid expansion. Too much money is tied up in inventory and receivables. Or perhaps debts are incurred to finance larger quarters, and the interest charges eat too far into profits.

Insufficient energy on the part of the venturer is also a hazard. The man who starts a new business must be prepared to say good-bye to regular nine-to-five hours for a long time to come. If the plant or store is open eight hours a day, he will often have to spend that time supervising the operations, and handle his planning, analysis of results, and so on, at night.

Dun and Bradstreet lists poor management as a major cause of the failure of new enterprises. Poor management has many facets: It may grow out of insufficient knowledge of some phase of the business; it may consist of lack of understanding of the basic principles of accounting or a tendency to make too optimistic forecasts that lead to unwarranted expansion; or it may be the result of simple laziness.

Taking a job overseas

Since many observers are predicting that business will become more and more international in the future—and there are, in fact, many more companies that both produce and sell abroad than there were even ten years ago—a background of experience in foreign operations may provide an extra advantage for the young man who hopes to rise to the top.

Moreover, to many young men a job in a foreign country seems to offer an exciting and romantic prospect, and some even prepare themselves for work abroad in college. The decision to seek a career in the management of foreign operations is, however, one that should not be made lightly. The advantages are often more evident at first glance than the disadvantages.

Life abroad On the plus side there is the attraction of seeing new places, meeting new people, learning more about the world. Often, too, a man will be paid more in consideration of the fact that he must leave his own country; the salary and the generous allowances may add up to much more than he could earn at home. In addition, he may, because of differences in wage levels, be able to maintain a sizable establishment with more than one servant, which may sound to him like the height of luxury.

The difficulties he may encounter may not be so visible, though some companies try to provide advance warning for both overseas personnel and their wives.

In the first place, the cost of living in some foreign countries is just as high as or higher than it is at home and the attractive salary may not go so far as the young man thought it would. Second, unless he genuinely likes the nationals of the other country and can enjoy life among them, he may find that his social life is as circumscribed as it would be in a very small town at home. In Germany, where many Americans have chosen to live in sections by themselves, the Germans sometimes refer to the American residential districts as "golden ghettos," and a ghetto is always a little confining even if it is golden to the point of luxury. And in some countries there may be only one American company in a given town or city; thus the American expatriate who confines his social life to contacts with other Americans sees the same faces day after day both at work and after hours.

Finally, the difficulties of everyday living may be much greater than they are at home. Even in European countries, many of the conveniences to which an American is accustomed may not be readily available to him. In underdeveloped countries, the food may be unpalatable. For example, in some places, butchers may not supply a steak or chops or a standing roast on demand. Meat is meat, and the customer takes the part of the animal that the butcher feels should be cut off next. And the overseas employee may find that the servants are more a hindrance than a help; because their work is so highly specialized, some things never get done at all, and he and his wife will lose face if they do them themselves.

On the other hand, life in foreign countries is pleasanter to some people than life at home. They find the pace more leisurely, and they like it that way. And in England, Western Europe, and the capitals of Latin America, daily living is not likely to present any insuperable difficulties, nor will customary amusements be lacking. In England and on the Continent, too, it is easy to take vacation trips to new countries. Some people even like the life in one of the underdeveloped countries and readily fall in with local customs.

Career prospects   A job abroad should, however, be considered not only from the viewpoint of whether or not the man and his family will like the life, but from the viewpoint of career security. While no job is entirely or even largely secure, there are peculiar hazards attached to foreign operations that do not exist in domestic employment.

During his stay abroad, the manager may achieve an excellent record, but it will be difficult to sell himself into a domestic job on the basis of his experience if he wants, or is forced, to return home. The fact that he knows all there is to know about markets in, say, Burma or Venezuela may not do him much good if he is applying for a job as Midwest sales manager in the United States. If he has worked in an undeveloped country, he may have performed miracles of improvisation in the face of enormous difficulties, but companies operating domestically may feel that the experience is inapplicable. There is also, in many countries, the possibility that political upheavals may make doing business there impossible, and he may have to close out the operations and return home. If his entire experience has been in a single country, his own company may not find a spot for him, and other companies may be reluctant even to send him to a different foreign country, again feeling that his experience will be inapplicable. And since he has been out of the country for several years, he may lack contacts in the business world at home.

On the other hand, it is undeniable that foreign operations will be expanding over the long run, especially since the advent of the European Common Market and the possibility of similar arrangements elsewhere in the world. This should make more opportunities for those with training and experience in foreign operations. This will be particularly so in the international companies whose influence is growing.

SUMMARY

Company requirements, which vary among companies and even in the same company at different times, have an important bearing on the choice of a chief executive. It is, therefore, not easy to map a road to the top or the near-top with any degree of certainty. The best that an ambitious man can do is:

1. Select a company that has possibilities for growth.
2. Choose the field in which he can make the greatest contribution.

Other things being equal, excellent performance plus contributions above those normally expected seems to offer the best chance of advancement. Many men who have risen have done so by introducing and effectuating entirely new ideas.

If a man starts a business of his own, his rewards may be greater than any salary he would be likely to get. But the risks are also much greater. A new business has the best chance of succeeding if it offers (1) a product or a service that is needed but is not being supplied at all to the market that the entrepreneur is planning to reach or (2) one that is in some way better than competing products or services.

Case Study One* / Butler's Skating Rink

Locational factors   Butler's Skating Rink was a large roller-skating recreation hall located on a major highway going out of Providence. Although the area

---

* This case study and the one following it are drawn from *The First Two Years: Problems of Small Firm Growth and Survival* by Kurt B. Mayer and Sidney Goldstein of the Department of Sociology and Anthropology, Brown University, published by the Small Business Administration (Government Printing Office), Washington, D.C., 1961.

contained several small businesses such as a grocery store, a coffee and doughnut shop, and a gas station, the immediate area in which the rink was located was primarily a middle-income residential area. For the most part, the housing units and business establishments in the area were well constructed and fairly attractive in appearance.

The roller-skating rink was located on the first floor of a large building, which it shared with an adjoining small grocery store and a residential apartment above, in which the proprietors of the rink lived. The building was approximately thirty years old and, at the outset of the study, was badly in need of painting and repairs—both internally and externally. At that time, the physical nature of the premises was described by adjectives such as dank, dreary, decrepit, and disorderly. At the same time, however, evidence indicated that steps were being taken to remedy this situation, and by the time a year had passed, its physical appearance had undergone a radical transformation: both the interior and exterior had been completely remodeled, giving the business a modern and very attractive appearance.

Personal characteristics   Butler's Skating Rink was operated by Phillip Butler and his wife Jane, a childless Yankee couple aged fifty and forty-six, respectively. The division of labor was such that, although both regarded themselves as jacks-of-all-trades as far as their contribution was concerned, most of the business decisions and plans were made by Phil, who had had considerable experience in this line of business. Jane, who had worked for a catering firm from 1940 to 1950 and as a chef from 1950 to 1951, acted primarily in the capacity of bookkeeper. Neither one had had any formal training for a career in business; Phil had graduated from high school and had had some postgraduate technical training, whereas Jane had left high school during the Depression after having completed only two years. Both, however, gave the impression of possessing good common sense, as well as sound business judgment.

Although both were intensely interested in the business, and although both exhibited the capacity for business judgment, Phillip Butler appeared to be the driving force behind the operation of the business—because of his very strong love for this particular line and because of his extensive prior experience, which had acquainted him with the special problems involved in operating a skating rink.

After finishing high school, Phil went to work as an apprentice machinist for a tool company in Providence, a job he held from 1925 to 1928. From there, he went to a large machine tool factory in Providence where he worked as a foreman until the Depression threw him into the ranks of the unemployed in 1931. He then worked at a variety of odd jobs—including a five-year stint as a department foreman at another large factory in Cranston, after which he entered the civil service. From 1939 to 1945, he held a civil service appointment as an instructor at the United States Naval Base in Newport; he was laid off in 1945 in the wake of the postwar reduction in manpower. From there, he went to work in a supervisory capacity for a factory in Massachusetts until 1950, when he decided to go into business for himself.

During the early years of his occupational career, Phillip Butler was a devoted roller-skating enthusiast. In the late 1940s, he began to tire of changing from one job to another and of "taking guff from above." He began to think about going into business for himself. Specifically, he began to think about "combining business with pleasure" and opening a roller-skating rink. He broached his thoughts to a few of his friends, who tried to discourage him, but this only added to his desire to become an entrepreneur. This is brought out quite clearly in his response to the question pertaining to when he first decided to open his own business:

> Well, it was around 1950, I'd say. I happened to mention the idea and my friends said I couldn't make a go of it. This really did it, for here was a challenge I couldn't refuse.

Aside from this "challenge," however, Phil went into this line of business for two very practical reasons: he liked it, and he strongly believed that there was a lot of money to be made in it. Again, this is best illustrated by his own answer to the question asking why he went into the roller-skating business:

> Roller skating was a hobby of mine. I really enjoyed it. I felt that it was an economical and healthful pastime and so would have a strong appeal. I felt, too, that its appeal was growing and hadn't anywhere near reached its peak. So there you have it: I enjoy it, and I felt there was a good deal of money to be made in it.

And so Phillip Butler went into business for himself. His first roller-skating rink in Massachusetts lasted from 1951 to 1954, at which time it was destroyed by Hurricane Carol. He then opened another rink in a Rhode Island community. He operated this successfully until 1957, when he received notice that his place of business was condemned for highway construction. At this point, with the help of *Roller Skating Rinks of America*, he began to look around for a new location. He finally decided on the present one. In making this decision, money was the decisive factor. In looking for other possible locations—even as far away as Canada and California—he was unable to find anything within his price range:

> Everyone wanted replacement value, and I didn't get a bite under $60,000. This place was my last resort, and in this, the price ($30,000) was the deciding factor. . . . I knew of the place, and I knew that the guy who was running it wanted to get out. He hadn't been very successful, but that was his own fault. He lacked vitality and imagination. Also, I heard he was running it for a relative and that his heart wasn't in it. So, I offered him a price and he bit.

The price offered by Phil was $30,000. He made a down payment of $18,000 and obtained a mortgage of $12,000 from a friend at 5 per cent interest with up to ten years to pay. He paid most of this off at a later date when he received a settlement from the state for his earlier business. On March 3, 1958, Butler's Skating Rink was opened for business.

Business growth   Butler's Skating Rink was primarily a roller-skating rink. However, it also sold various items connected with skating, such as roller skates and skating skirts. In addition, it contained a small soda fountain which was operated as an "accommodation" for the customers—selling soft drinks, candy bars, ice cream sodas.

From the very beginning, it was apparent that the Butlers were determined to make a success of their business venture. By the end of the first months in business, they had already invested some $6,000 of their savings for repairs and remodeling, and they were anticipating making even more improvements pending the settlement from the state for their prior business. Plans were also under way to advertise the business quite heavily by means of vigorous campaigns to acquaint the people with the advantages of roller skating as a pastime in general and with Butler's Skating Rink ("under new management") in particular. Accomplishing this task was regarded by Phillip Butler as the biggest problem the business faced:

> My big problem is in getting the public to realize the basic decency, the good supervision, and the all-around healthful atmosphere that a properly run rink provides for their children and themselves. . . . We must make the public aware of our new operation. We plan to do this through various promotional activities. By promotional activities, we mean establishing ourselves with the churches and schools, by having skating parties and showing them the good points of our operation. This is the backbone of our business. Out of this, we hope a word-of-mouth spread will lead to increased good will, increased business, and increased profits.

At the time of the first interview, the interviewer gained the impression that the Butlers, under Phil's driving force, would succeed in their endeavor, although it was apparent that the business still had a long way to go—both physically and in volume of customers. Although his formal education was limited, Butler was obviously an extremely intelligent and capable person who had ambitious dreams for the future. He was by no means a "dreamer," however, as his successful operation of two similar businesses, both of which he lost due to circumstances beyond his control, amply testifies. In short, he was a vigorous, personable man, with high ambitions and the necessary drive to work for their achievement. Although much still remained to be done to convert the forbidding structure into a successful skating rink, the prospects for the future looked good.

As the business progressed, this initial impression turned out to be well founded. When the business was next contacted in August, 1958, it was grossing enough to cover operating expenses. This was all that the proprietors had expected it to do until repairs were finished. Also, having received his settlement from the state, Phil was all squared away financially. The promotional campaigns to stimulate business had not yet been started, since the premises were still in the process of being rejuvenated (the Butlers had invested an additional $2,000 in the business since the initial interview), but plans were being made to send out letters and flyers to various churches, schools, and other organizations in the fall. No particular problems had arisen, and the Butlers were patiently waiting until the remodeling was completed and were still anticipating a bright future.

When the third interview was conducted in October, 1958, Butler's Skating Rink had undergone a radical transformation. In addition to basic construction changes that gave the building a modern design, it had been painted and shingled, and it looked very attractive. The inside also underwent major renovation; a large part had been done over in knotty pine, and the remainder was rapidly nearing the completion stage. In short, the physical appearance of the establishment had changed from one that was dismal and dilapidated to one that was modern and attractive, and one that would certainly act as an inducement in increasing attendance.

More important, the gross sales seemed to be reflecting the improvements in the physical appearance of the business. Phillip Butler reported at this time that his gross for the previous month of September was $2,000. This was his peak gross to date, but the respondent stated that it had been gradually building up to that figure each month since he had opened. In spite of the gradual increase in gross income, the Butlers had not as yet withdrawn any money for their own expenses; all profits had been reinvested in repairs of the building. In addition, they had hired a professional skating instructor who was drawing a salary of $100 a week.

The advertising, which Phillip Butler referred to as "promotional work," was just getting under way; ads were being run in the local newspaper, and flyers were being sent out to various organizations in the area. With the winter coming up (roller skating is an indoor sport that is most actively participated in during bad weather), the Butlers were anticipating a substantial increase in business. However, when the business was next contacted in January, 1959, the expected increase had not materialized. Nevertheless, there had been some improvement in gross income, and with the completion of the major remodeling activities, their expenses had been reduced. The Butlers were now able to make withdrawals regularly for their living expenses. There had been an intensification in their advertising or promotional activities: more flyers and leaflets were being sent out, and they were running special events—such as roller hockey—every now and then. The future still looked bright, and the proprietors were, if anything, becoming more and more sure of their chances of eventually having a "really successful" business.

The business continued to maintain its slow but steady growth during the following months, and after its first full year in business, Butler's Skating Rink was clearly on its way to being a successful business. The gross for the first year had been $20,000, of which $7,000 was net income. Out of this net income they had taken between $4,000 and $5,000 for themselves and had reinvested the remainder in their business in their "continuing policy of remodeling." Although Phil did not expect the business to remain at the level it had then attained, he was satisfied with the progress it had made so far. In his own words:

> We went into business expecting to exercise our patience to the fullest. This we have had to do, but we are now seeing our operation begin to grow. This, of course, is the most satisfying part, watching it grow.

In short, Mr. and Mrs. Butler were well satisfied with the business, so far as it had progressed, but were still expecting it to grow. This it did. Throughout the second year, business became progressively better, which may reflect the fact that advertising continued to play an integral part in the business. In addition to using flyers, newspaper ads, and radio ads, Phil had personally contacted various organizations and had managed to sign up whole groups, such as the Girl Scouts, for skating instruction classes. As the months passed, the business continued its gradual growth, and when the final interview was conducted on March 7, 1960, it was clear that the Butlers had built their rink into a successful business. They had grossed $29,000 during the second year (nearly $10,000 more than the first), which yielded a net income of approximately $10,500 after deducting for purchases, overhead (about $5,000 of which went for advertising), and employee wages. Of this net income, the Butlers took $5,400 for their personal expenses and again reinvested the bulk of their income in the continuously improving business.

Although very much satisfied with the progress made by the business, the Butlers were quick to point out that they did not expect it to stay at its present level. Rather, they steadfastly expressed the view that it would continue to get better. In this respect, they were planning to exert even more effort than previously in their promotional activities. As Phil stated when asked about his plans for the future:

> The only plans for the immediate future are to continue with the work on the rink, to make it even better than it is. We are going to try and plan more skating parties, even hire busses for outside groups. We are also going to try and sign up more groups like the Girl Scouts for skating lessons. This is the sort of thing we will be hitting hard all the time to build up the business. Once we have established "going skating as the thing to do" among the young people, the business will take care of itself. In order to do this, we are going to hit advertising harder this coming year than ever before—several thousand dollars worth. The momentum of the business is a thing that must be kept going.

In short, although Phil and Jane Butler had worked hard and spent a lot of money to build up a successful business, their plans for the future called for working even harder and spending even more money in order to build up an even more successful business.

Case Study Two / Werner's Market

Locational factors   Werner's Market was located on a fairly heavily traveled major traffic artery which runs into the fringe area of the downtown central business district of Woonsocket. At its beginning, the street was primarily commercial, with occasional low-income-type residences located above the retail and service establishments. As it continued away from the city, however, the number of commercial enterprises decreased while the number and quality of residences increased. By the end of the street, the area was predominantly residential, consisting largely of two-family homes inhabited by middle-income blue-collar and white-collar persons. Werner's Market was located about midway between these two extremes, in a neighborhood that can be described as an area of working-class apartments with scattered retail and service units. Within a 100-foot radius of the store were located two other grocery stores, a bicycle repair shop, a linoleum store, and a beauty parlor. The residential units in the neighborhood were largely semidilapidated apartment buildings housing from 100 to 300 people, most of whom were of French extraction and of low socioeconomic status.

The particular business was located on the first floor of one of the apartment buildings. Its physical character could be described as typical of the hundreds of retail units that may be found in such transitional zones—small in size, unattractive on the outside, and unattractive, crowded, and run-down on the inside. This particular store occupied no more than 600 square feet of ground space, and although it was generally more attractive than the building as a whole, the run-down appearance of the store front was in keeping with the seeming lack of prosperity in the neighborhood. Similarly, although the stock was neatly arranged, the interior of the store was physically unattractive: the shelves and floor were old and worn, as were the counters, and the ceiling was cracked in several places and yellowed with age. Even though it was fairly clean, it was badly in need of painting and repairs.

The business had been in its present location for some thirty-six years under the previous proprietorship, but had obviously been neglected in recent years as the prior occupant got along in years and began to look forward to selling the store and retiring. Into this environment came Richard Werner, a likable young man, aggressive and with a strong ambition to get ahead in the world. He took over the business on March 13, 1958, changed the name to Werner's Market, seemed to prosper momentarily, but eventually reached the point where it was costing him money to remain open. At this point, the business was closed—after exactly six months' operation.

Personal characteristics   Dick Werner was a good-looking young man of twenty-three. He was rather short, standing about 5 feet 5 inches, with curly black hair and a fair complexion. He was of French-English extraction, married, and had two children—both under two years of age at the time of the initial interview. Although his wife was unemployed when he first took over the business, she eventually went to work in one of the local mills in order to facilitate Dick's struggle to keep the business alive after it started on its downhill run.

Upon graduation from high school in 1951, Dick went to a Massachusetts college and took a business course, but financial problems necessitated his stopping after a year and a half. He then "played around" from one unskilled job to another until he was drafted into the Army in 1953. Upon being discharged from military service, he went to Connecticut, where he held a job as an "internal expediter." He worked at his job until September, 1958, at which time he left to go into business for himself in his home tow : of Woonsocket.

Dick decided during the fall of 1957 that he would like to be a businessman. His reaching the decision at this time was closely related to the work slowdown at his place of employment and the increased number of layoffs from that firm. Dick feared that he too would be laid off. Being a family man with responsibilities, and being afraid that the "tight" economic conditions prevailing at that time would hinder his chances of getting another job, he began thinking about going into business for himself.

When asked directly why he went into business, Dick stressed the desire for independence:

> Independence, more than anything else, is the reason I want to be a businessman. I have no particular desire to get rich. I just want to make enough to live on comfortably—$80 to $100 a week—just so I can afford the necessities of life with one or two luxuries. The main thing is I don't want to spend the rest of my life working for someone else.

Although he stressed the idea of independence, his major reason for going into business seemed to have been a desire to escape from the fear of unemployment. As he himself said:

> Things were slowing down and it looked like I would soon be laid off, so I thought I'd look around for a business near home.

At the time he was last contacted (October 11, 1958), Richard Werner was unemployed, although his wife was still working. He said that the only jobs that were available were "minimum wage jobs" at which he could make only $40 a week, in contrast to the $48 he could collect as unemployment compensation. Moreover, by staying at home while his wife worked he was able to save $12 a week on babysitter fees—which meant that by not working he was making the equivalent of $60 a week.

When Dick closed the business early in September, the only thing he was able to sell was the refrigerator; he stored the meat case, counters, shelves, and groceries in his parents' home. If he should eventually be able to sell these fixtures and the remaining stock and get the price he thought he should, he estimated that he would have lost about $1,000 in his business venture.

At the time, however, his financial loss was between $3,000 and $4,000. When he was last interviewed, Dick was planning to collect his unemployment benefits at least until January of 1959. Later, it was learned that he had taken a position as a mechanic.

Choice of business   Having once reached the decision to go into business, Dick began reading the Woonsocket newspaper ads to see what he could find. His reasons for trying to find a business for sale instead of starting one of his own related to the type of business he wanted to have. He was primarily interested in opening a package liquor store; however, due to a city ordinance which limited the number of package store licenses, his only hope of getting such a business was to buy one already in existence. No opportunities of this nature came along.

As his imminent layoff in Connecticut approached, he began looking into other business opportunities. It was at this time that he came across a grocery store that was for sale. He came to Woonsocket, talked to the proprietor, and then went back to Connecticut to talk it over with his wife. On the basis of Dick's unemployment situation and the fact that he had had experience working in his uncle's grocery store during high school vacations, they decided to buy the business. The decision to buy the grocery store was therefore a function of the fact that it became available at a time when Dick's uncertain employment status led him to the decision to go into business on his own in an attempt to create job security for himself.

Although he talked with his uncle, who ran a similar type of establishment, Dick did not really seek any advice before going into business for himself. He examined some of the earlier records of the previous occupant and noted that the business had grossed between $70,000 and $80,000 annually during the three years prior to World War II. No records were available for the war years, but those for more recent years indicated that the business had been falling off steadily since 1946 and yielded an average annual gross of only $50,000. Although Dick was well aware that the business had been getting progressively worse, he attributed this to the age and declining health of the prior occupant, and took the view that all that was needed to build the business up again was some young blood.

Moreover, in spite of the fact that there were no less than seven similar stores within a radius of one or two blocks, Dick did not seem to regard competition as a serious problem—his opinion being that a store that had been established for thirty-six years would be able to hold its own. Actually, a little more careful checking on Dick's part would have indicated the importance of the competition factor. According to a subsequent interview with one of the wholesalers who supplied many of the stores in the area, the [proprietor of the] store directly opposite Dick's, which he passed off as primarily dealing in meat, had the area "pretty well sewed up." Evidence for this lay in the fact that he had steadily been increasing his purchases over the years while those of all the other stores, including the one that Dick took over, had been progressively declining. In any case, Dick apparently thought—because he was young and willing to work hard—that he could make a success of the business.

Additional incentive for taking the business, even though he knew it had been falling off, concerned the price. Dick was able to purchase the whole business (lock, stock, and barrel) for $3,500:

> I got the store for a "steal," only $3,500; but that was the old man's price, not mine. The refrigerator case alone is worth about $2,000 and the whole business is worth at least $5,000. But $3,500 was the price he set, and I wasn't going to argue about it.

Although Dick initially thought he was getting a "good deal" when he got the business for only $3,500, he later changed his mind and came to think that he was the one who was "robbed." Moreover, this may actually have been the case, since he was later able to get only $50 for the refrigerator which he had apparently been led to believe was valued at $2,000.

The $3,500 with which he bought the business came from his own savings. Other opening expenses were $12 for miscellaneous licenses, $75 in legal fees for clearing and transferring the title of ownership, and $129 for additional stock during the first week he was open. This represented a total investment of $3,716—all of which came from Dick's personal savings and which, as he noted, nearly exhausted his bank account.

The fact that he "blew his wad" in buying the business was subsequently cited by one of his suppliers as one of the reasons for his eventual failure:

> He had to sink quite a bit into the store as an initial investment, which meant that he was in no position to carry himself over the rough spots; and when things got rough this summer, he either had to quit or lose money that he didn't have.

Business decline   When Dick took over his business, he seemed to be in pretty good shape. At the time of the initial interview in June, 1958, the business was all paid for and he was grossing about $400 a week. This was more than enough to keep the business going. Each week, he was able to take $78 for expenses (which actually amounted to his approximate gross profit)—$40 went for living expenses for himself and his family, and $38 was set aside for overhead expenses which consisted each month of $50 for rent, $8 to $9 for the telephone, and about $20 for electricity. Anything that was left over he set aside for later use in expanding the business. However, he soon had to use the small surplus he had built up in order to keep the business running. Moreover, his wife had to go back to work during the summer because Dick could no longer afford to take out $40 a week for the family.

At the time of the second interview in July, business had started to fall off somewhat, and his average weekly gross was running just over $300. This point marks the beginning of a decline which reached a low of $189 for the week prior to his closing the business. According to Dick, the presence of supermarkets and the failure of his friends to support the business were the factors behind his failure to make a success out of the business:

> You can't expect a small store like this to be able to compete with the supermarkets. . . . When I first started, I used to get a lot of business from my friends, but that started falling off after the first couple of months. Their wives want to get the Green Stamps, and "shop around" the supermarkets for sales. . . . It's the women who rule in this world. I counted on getting a lot of business from my friends but they let me down.

From the beginning, the business was a sole proprietorship having no employees other than the proprietor, although Dick's mother and wife helped out occasionally so he could take a "breather." Although he did have a meat case and did some business in meats, he dealt primarily in groceries. Originally, he had planned to put in a freezer and add a line of frozen food; but his plans here never materialized because of the financial situation that developed.

The only advertising he did was to give $2 a week to the church to get his name in the weekly newsletter. He did not even advertise his opening; apparently, he agreed with the opinion of the previous occupant that it would be better if he worked in gradually and quietly took over the business. To this end, Dick worked in the store for two weeks prior to taking it over—so that customers would "get used to seeing me around" and thus make the transition of ownership a smooth one.

At first, Dick did all his buying by the case, both because most wholesalers did not like to break up a case and because, if they did, they charged more. As time passed, however, and as business began to fall off, he began buying in smaller quantities. This meant that he was paying more for his stock than formerly, but was getting the same sale price. As a result, his margin of profit was reduced at a time when he could least afford it. Later, he made an arrangement with a friend of his who worked in a large supermarket to purchase stock in small quantities at what it cost the friend, but this apparently came too late to help the business get back on its feet.

Other than the change of suppliers and the steady decline in gross sales beginning in July, no significant changes occurred in the business during the six months in which it was in operation. His earlier plans for remodeling and expanding were thwarted by the progressively worsening state of the business, which Dick attributed to his inability to compete with the supermarkets and the failure of his friends to patronize the store. Dick's ultimate reaction to this state of affairs was to close the store.

1. Contrast the objectives set by Butler with those set by Werner. Which did more effective planning? Why?
2. What innovations did Butler introduce that contributed to his success?
3. Can you think of anything Werner might have done to increase his chances of success?

3

THE

CORPORATE

FRAMEWORK

*Institutional doctrine is never a frank description
of the practice . . . of the institution.*
Thurman Arnold: *The Folklore of Capitalism*

3 Many businesses begin as owner-managed firms. The owner-manager provides the capital (cash and merchandise or machinery) needed to get started and becomes an entrepreneur. He literally undertakes the risks of investment.

In these cases, the investor generally becomes the chief executive, and legally he has the right to make all the decisions so long as he does not transgress the laws that apply to business in general or to his industry. The golden rule of capitalism has been stated as: "Where the risk lies, there the control lies also," and this still holds, in both theory and fact, when there is a sole owner. According to the British economists Sir Dennis Robertson and Stanley Dennison, the rule rests on two premises: "that the power of making decisions will be most wisely exercised if it rests in the hands of those who stand to lose most heavily" and "that the risks of industry will be most bravely shouldered if those who shoulder them are not obliged to hand over to others the power of making decisions about the use of the resources which they put to the hazard."[1]

Individual proprietorships are still the most numerous of all forms of enterprise in the United States; there are several million of them in existence today. But for the most part they are small enterprises in such fields as retailing, construction, and the services.

A change in the type of ownership occurs when the capital of the individual owner is no longer sufficient to finance the needs of a growing business. Then the owner may acquire partners: either silent or "sleeping" partners, who merely provide capital and share in the profits but take no part in the management, or active partners who help with the management. But to obtain very large amounts of money it is generally necessary to form a corporation and issue shares. In that way even a person with a very small amount of capital can buy into the ownership by purchasing only one or a few shares, and the number of possible "partners" is greatly increased.

Shares may be of two types: preferred stock or common stock. Owners of preferred stock, although they are among the owners of the corporation, assume less of the risk than the common stockholders because their dividends have first claim on the corporation's profits: they must be paid before the common stockholders get anything. And since their risk is smaller, they have less chance of making a great deal of money if the corporation prospers because they are usually limited to a set percentage return on their investment. The common stockholders, on the other hand, can get any amount the corporation decides to pay.

Thus the status of the preferred stockholders is somewhat like that of bondholders, who are simply people who have lent the corporation money and receive interest on it until the principal is paid off, usually on a date some years later. Interest on bonds, however, takes precedence over dividends to the preferred stockholders because the bondholders are creditors and the stockholders are owners.

[1] *The Control of Industry*, James Nisbet & Co., Ltd., Welwyn, England, and the Cambridge University Press, London, in association with The University of Chicago Press, Chicago, 1960, p. 75.

THE THEORY OF THE CORPORATION

The concept of the corporation originally implied a "franchise" or "grant" given by the state (the national government) to a number of investors in a specific enterprise. Often it provided a monopoly, such as the exclusive right to trade with some colony in a product. In return for the grant, the state or the monarch might participate in the profits. Some of the great trading corporations of the sixteenth and seventeenth centuries, such as the East India Company and the Hudson's Bay Company, were established in this way. And if the company was successful, it tended to become a more or less permanent institution. Gradually, through statutory and common law, as well as by custom and practice, the present concept of the corporation developed. Among the principal characteristics of a corporation are the following:

Separate "personality" or identity   The corporation is an entity distinct and separate from its owners, and they are not personally liable for its debts. It has a right to hold property and do business in its own name. It can sue and be sued as a person, and the suits in no way involve the owners personally, although, of course, results may affect the capital they have invested and the profits they get.

Perpetuity   A corporation continues its existence as an entity even though the individuals who own it are constantly changing. (In contrast, a partnership may be automatically dissolved on the death of one of the owners unless special arrangements to take care of such a contingency have been incorporated in the partnership agreement.)

The specific grant of identity separate from that of the owners is found in the "certificate of incorporation," usually known as the corporate charter, which in the United States is issued by a state. This might be termed the company's constitution; it outlines the arrangements the owners are making with each other and covers such matters as the following:

1. Name, location, scope, and objective of the corporation. Unlike the rulers of the sixteenth and seventeenth centuries, the states grant no monopoly powers so far as doing business is concerned, but the corporation does get a monopoly on the use of the name it has chosen. For this reason, it cannot adopt a name identical with that of any other corporation within the state.
2. The total number of shares to be issued. The incorporation papers will also state the par value of the shares—which is usually the price at which they will be issued—or if they are not assigned a par value, the papers will specify that they have no par value.
3. Provisions regarding the conduct of the business, the distribution of the profits, and the disposal of assets.
4. The names of the incorporators.

5. The method of selecting directors.
6. A clause affirming the fact that the owners will not be personally liable for the debts of the corporation.
7. A clause stating that the corporation is to be perpetual.

Charters were once issued by state legislatures; now a state official is responsible. Laws regarding incorporation vary from state to state, and in some states (notably Delaware, New Jersey, and Florida) are more liberal than in others, "liberality" in this case meaning that the corporation is allowed greater flexibility. For example, a Delaware corporation may pay dividends out of surplus as well as out of earnings, and directors need not be shareholders.

The corporate charter is usually supplemented by bylaws, which are a set of standard rules making more detailed provision for the regulation of the corporation's affairs. The bylaws set forth such matters as the time and place of stockholder meetings and specify the officers (by title rather than by name) of the corporation. Bylaws sometimes contain summaries of the officers' responsibilities and authority.

The common stockholders are the true owners of the corporation and in theory have the power to control it, just as an individual owner has a right to control his own business or the parties to a partnership control theirs. Directors are elected at the annual meeting of shareholders, and they in turn select the president and other officers of the corporation who will make up its top management. The shareholders may have to approve all changes in the corporate charter and bylaws, such as a change in the number of shares or a plan to permit officers to purchase stock on favorable terms. They may also have the right to approve (or disapprove) changes in the compensation of the officers and in their benefits.

At the annual meeting, also, the directors and officers present a report on their stewardship in the form of financial statements for the previous year, together with a summary of the year's activities and a review of prospects for the future. Shareholders present can address questions to the board and the officers of the company. As an ultimate resort, a dissatisfied shareholder or group of shareholders can sue the directors for mishandling the property.

The government of a large corporation whose shares are widely held may be pictured as somewhat like an hourglass (Figure 1). At the top are the thousands of stockholders. Then the government narrows down to a dozen or so directors, then still further to the board's executive committee. The waist represents the chief executive, often the president of the corporation. Under him is a comparatively small group of top managers, then a larger group of middle managers, a still larger group of first-line supervisors, and finally the employees. In quite a number of large organizations, the stockholders are as numerous as or more numerous than the employees.

The board of directors constitutes the bridge between the shareholders and the managers. It is often characterized as exercising broad supervision rather

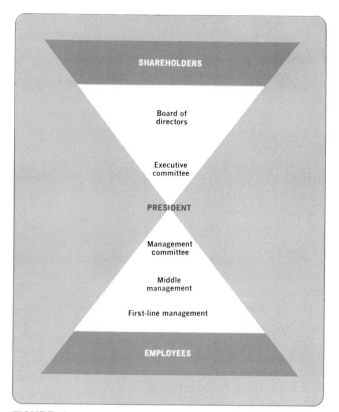

FIGURE 1

than executing details; setting objectives rather than planning how they should be achieved; establishing policy rather than administering; appraising rather than controlling.

The laws of the states under which corporations operate are, however, broader than this. They specify that the boards of directors "manage the affairs of the company" and are responsible for its welfare. Elected as representatives of the shareholders, the directors must (1) pay a decent amount of attention to the business, (2) show fidelity to the interests of the corporation, and (3) exercise a reasonable prudence in the management of the corporation's affairs;[2] i.e., in the words of a famous court definition of "a prudent man" in 1830, the director "is to observe how men of prudence, discretion, and intelligence manage their own affairs not in regard to speculation but considering the probable income as well as the probable safety of the capital to be invested."[3]

[2] Adolf A. Berle, Jr., and Gardiner C. Means, *The Modern Corporation and Private Property*, The Macmillan Company, New York, 1933, p. 221.
[3] *John McLean v. Francis Amory, Trustee*, Supreme Court of Massachusetts.

If a director neglects these duties, he may be sued by the stockholders and forced to make restitution for resulting losses out of his own pocket. In the past, however, his position was not so risky as it might have appeared to be. For example:

A director was unlikely to be held in any way liable because he made an honest mistake, because he did not foresee what eventually happened, or simply because his corporation failed to make money and went into bankruptcy. Rather, the liability would be likely to exist only if he accepted a proposition which on the face of it would be anathema to a prudent man. Thus in one case, a bank agreed to buy the securities of a corporation and sell them back at the same price six months later if the corporation wanted to buy them. Under such an arrangement, the judge pointed out, the corporation would be sure to buy back its securities if the market price rose and would certainly not buy them back if it fell. Thus the bank would risk a loss with no compensating possibility of gain. "Whichever way we look at this transaction, therefore," he stated, "it was so improvident, so dangerous, so unusual and so contrary to ordinary prudent banking practice as to subject the directors who approved it to liability in a derivative stockholders' action."

The fact that the directors held the bonds after the repurchase agreement had expired when they were entirely free to sell them was considered merely a mistake in business judgment for which they were not liable. The lack of prudence was in the agreement itself; therefore they were liable only for the loss that occurred during the time it was in force and they had to hold the securities for possible repurchase by the corporation.[4]

Recently, however, stockholder suits have been increasing in number, and the courts have become more sympathetic to them.

THE CORPORATION IN PRACTICE

So much for theory, the formal setup in the large majority of corporations. But how does it actually work out?

One way of finding out is to study the actual exercise of leadership in corporations to determine who makes the decisions that vitally affect the accomplishment of basic objectives, such as profit, and who exercises a check on how the objectives are accomplished.

The stockholders

In theory, of course, the shareholders do both. "You may own only a few shares, yet without you there is no home in the country, no company plane, no corporation-owned limousine at his [the president's] disposal. . . . You are a mighty important man and you are becoming more powerful every day."[5] This is the traditional view.

---

[4] Ralph J. Baker and William L. Cary, *Cases and Materials on Corporations*, 3d ed., The Foundation Press, Inc., Brooklyn, N.Y., 1958, pp. 404–412 (*Litwin v. Allen*, 25 N.Y.S. 2d 667.)
[5] David Karr, *The Fight for Control*, Ballantine Books, Inc., New York, 1956, pp. 1–2.

Since the stockholders are the legal owners of the corporation, it might seem that they would have the right, if all or even a majority of them were in agreement, to remove directors and managers at will, decide on the sale of assets, change the bylaws; in fact, conduct all the corporation's affairs as they saw fit. They have, however, lost many of the powers that would ordinarily accrue to a legal owner. For example:

1.   Courts have held that the stockholders have no power to remove a director during his term of office merely because they want to. They must show that he has failed in his duties in some obvious and important way.
2.   In some states, only the directors can amend the bylaws, and the stockholders have no power to do so unless that power is specifically reserved to them in the articles of incorporation.
3.   Under many state statutes, a very large number of shares—far more than will be issued and sold in the beginning—may be authorized. Then the directors may, in effect, issue new shares whenever they want to.

All this, and other enlargements of the directors' power, would not alter the fact of the stockholders' control if they actually had the power to select the directors. In a small, closely held corporation they do possess this power; in fact, the directors and the shareholders are likely to be the same people for the most part. But in a large corporation, few stockholders are able to attend the annual meeting, either because of the press of other business or because it is held at a distant spot. Instead, they are asked to appoint proxies to represent them, and the proxies are preselected for them by the board of directors. The names are printed on cards (often called "proxies") that are sent to stockholders in advance of the meeting so that they may vote by mail.

The proxy card that the shareholder returns may state one or two propositions (a proposal for an increase in stock might be treated in this way) and make provision for the stockholder to indicate whether he is in favor of them or against them. But in all other cases, the stockholder must simply put his trust in the judgment of the person he appoints as his proxy. Moreover, he is generally presented with a single slate of directors. Thus he has little choice but to vote for the men whose names are suggested to him or to refrain from sending in his proxy and lose his vote.

If the stockholder could get together with enough of his fellows to muster a majority of the shares, they would, of course, be able to nominate and elect a different slate of directors. But this is just what small stockholders are unable to do; it would take time and money that they do not possess. The "proxy fights" that are publicized in the newspapers are always sparked by a man or group of men who have bought up a great many shares and have the money to circularize the smaller shareholders.

Under the rules of the Securities and Exchange Commission, a stockholder may also initiate a proposition for a vote and have it included on the proxy statement. But he must put it in one hundred words, which leaves little space for argument. If he wants to corral support for it from other stockholders, he will have to spend his own money to do so.

"The proxy machinery has thus become one of the principal instruments not [as it was designed to be] by which a stockholder exercises power over the management of the enterprise, but by which his power is separated from him."[6]

In corporations in which the stockholders' control is atomized because each holds only a small percentage of the shares, it has been said that the stockholder "elects but does not select" the board of directors and may "propose but not oppose" the corporation's course of action—that is, he may oppose it but not successfully. He can write a letter to the board of directors or ask questions at a stockholders' meeting, but in either case he may be put off with a soft public relations answer.

This situation does not exist in all large companies, even in all the very largest. In about a quarter of the 200 largest manufacturing companies, there are individuals or families who control, not a majority of the shares, but a large enough proportion of them to exert a strong influence on management. This type of shareholder might be termed a "partial proprietor" since the degree of influence he can exercise is somewhere between the complete control enjoyed by the man who owns the majority of the stock and the complete absence of any say-so that is the lot of the alienated owner who has no effective voting power.

For example, the du Pont family still owns a large block of shares in the company bearing its name; and since the Du Pont Company owned 23 per cent of the shares of General Motors until forced to divest itself of the stock by the Supreme Court,[7] it might be said that the du Ponts were partial proprietors of GM as well. Another example is the Mellon family, which is a partial proprietor of both Gulf Oil and the Aluminum Company of America. Also, aside from the du Ponts, GM long had partial proprietors in the shape of retired company executives, each of whom held several hundred thousand shares.

But these large shareholders are rapidly becoming extinct. High income taxes make the accumulation of enough money to buy large numbers of shares harder than it was in the past. In addition, steep inheritance taxes make it difficult for a son to replace his father in the capacity of partial proprietor since he may have to sell a good part of the stock to pay them. Companies may in some cases serve as partial proprietors of other companies, but this can bring them into conflict with the antitrust laws. Since the Du Pont-GM decision, the danger seems greater, for in that instance the Supreme Court made it clear that it is not only what a company does with its power over another corporation that matters but what it might possibly do if it had a mind to.

---

6 Berle and Means, *op. cit.*, p. 139.
7 Since Du Pont supplied automobile finishes to GM, it was held that the situation presented a violation of the antitrust laws, the theory being that Du Pont was in a position to force GM to buy its products. Even if it had not actually done so, the Supreme Court said, the situation should be terminated because it might do so.

The only type of partial proprietor whose numbers seem to be increasing is the institutional investor. Investment trusts, banking trusts, pension funds, brokerage houses, and foundations hold very large amounts of stock in many large companies. Because of their holdings they are sometimes called "the new tycoons." But although they are comparatively new as partial proprietors, they do not often act like tycoons. When they are dissatisfied with corporate performance, they tend to sell their shares rather than attempt to improve matters; and in these cases they actually exert no more influence than the small stockholders. However, there seems to be some tendency for these collective shareholders and the increasingly sophisticated financial analysts to ask more discerning questions and occasionally offer advice.

Then there are still some large companies that are owner-managed in that one person or a small group, perhaps all members of one family, holds all the stock. In these cases, all or nearly all the stockholders serve as directors or have a personal representative on the board—a legal adviser, say, or a trustee for an estate, or a close relative. Also, one of them generally acts as chief executive.

The privately held company is one that has never found it necessary to raise money by selling shares to the general public, and most of the large ones that are still private have avoided doing so because, as one representative of such a company said, they "like privacy."[8] They need not make their reports public or explain their actions to financial analysts or large numbers of stockholders, nor do they have to conform to the regulations of any stock exchange. Since they do not need to raise money from the public, they do not have to care what "the market" thinks of them.

Another reason why some of the owner-managers prefer to keep the company private is that they believe they have greater flexibility than they would have if they had to account—even if only in general terms—to a large group of stockholders. Stockholders' or directors' meetings can be easily called at any time; thus important decisions can be made quickly.

The board of directors

In a publicly held company, the board of directors is generally a group of about a dozen men, though it may be either larger or smaller than that. Small companies tend to have smaller boards; some types of companies, such as banks and railroads, have larger ones.

Each board has a chairman and a secretary and conducts its affairs more or less by parliamentary procedure: Motions are made and seconded and passed or disapproved by majority vote at monthly or quarterly meetings. Members receive no salaries for their services; they are compensated by fees, which may range from $100 to $750 a meeting, and possibly by retainers ranging from $3,000 to $10,000 a year. Sometimes they are given options or rights to buy company stock.

[8] "Behind Closed Doors," *Forbes*, Feb. 1, 1965, p. 33.

Directors select (and possibly dismiss) the chief executive and other corporate officers, determine their compensation, and act as a court of last resort when managers disagree. They may, as has been seen, even amend the bylaws and in effect issue new stock by putting unsold but authorized shares on the market. Generally, they must authorize capital spending above a certain amount, and increasingly they concern themselves with corporate objectives and with strategy, such as the kinds of business the corporation should enter or leave. In all cases, they determine what part of the corporation's profits will be paid out in dividends and what part will be retained in the business. In addition, they nominate their own successors, and the nomination is usually tantamount to election. Usually, too, they can confidently expect that the stockholders will rubber-stamp such proposals as they care to make for the issuance of new stock, the purchase of other companies, and similar measures.

As in the case of the privately held companies, a director of a publicly held company may be simultaneously a large shareholder and a full-time member of management. In other cases, directors may be large shareholders who are not members of management or they may be representatives of large shareholders. Sometimes retired executives who have acquired a considerable number of shares may serve as directors after their retirement.

A third type of director represents a bank or other financial institution which has played a part in financing the enterprise. If a company borrows money for expansion, for example, the institution that lends it may insist on having its own representatives on the board to act as watchdogs.

In the earlier days of American business these men, especially the bankers, played an important role in financing new enterprises, in rescuing those that were declining, and in merging companies into industrial empires. The U.S. Steel corporation was put together largely by J. P. Morgan, head of the famous financial house bearing his name.

A fourth type of director is important not because of his shareholdings but because he can contribute to the profitability of the enterprise. That is why major customers sometimes sit on boards of railroads, why major suppliers who are vital to the survival of an enterprise may be appointed directors, why a company that depends largely on defense business may invite a retired general or admiral to sit on its board.

Men may be selected also because of what they can contribute in the way of knowledge. Sometimes the financial men are chosen because they can advise the company on its fund raising. Inventors like Kettering and Vannevar Bush often sat on boards because of their knowledge of technology and future possibilities.

A fifth type of director is a man of outstanding public stature who will inspire confidence among the investing public. He may be the chief executive of another corporation, the head of a foundation or a university, or a former prominent figure in government.

Finally, a director may be a member of management who has been appointed, even though he holds no stock, or very little, as a reward for good performance or because the other directors believe he can contribute to their deliberations. Company presidents are usually directors as well; often other corporate officers are also.

Directors who are not company officers, large shareholders, or the representatives of groups or individuals who have substantial holdings generally gain their places when a company "goes public"—that is, puts shares on the market for anyone to buy. A company that has passed through the stages of individual proprietorship, and perhaps partnership, and has become incorporated may for a long time continue to finance its growth out of retained earnings and borrowings. But eventually it is likely to reach the point where the few shareholders are unable to raise enough money for further expansion. Then the company must take in more owners through the sale of stock, and quite likely its management will be not too familiar with the process. The board of directors may find it well, therefore, to take in some representative of a financial interest, or a lawyer versed in the procedure, or perhaps executives of other corporations who have had experience in the field. Moreover, the addition to the board of people who are well known in the business or financial world, or perhaps of public figures, is likely to further the sale of the stock. Investors feel that the company is a going concern when such men are associated with it.

Committees of the board

Next to the board of directors in the hierarchy are the board committees. Because these groups are smaller than the full board, they are able to get together more easily and perhaps transact business more quickly.

The most important of these directorial groups is the executive committee,[9] whose function in most companies is to transact urgent business. As a rule it consists of a few directors who live near enough together to meet on short notice and who are both congenial and competent. Such a committee may be set up by virtue of the bylaws or by the board itself.

The executive committee meets during intervals between board meetings, and its function, in addition to approving matters requiring immediate decision, is to sift and funnel matters to the board. If a proposal passes the executive committee, it is likely to be accepted by the other directors.

The best-known executive committee is probably that at Du Pont, founded originally because of a problem of succession. Du Pont had been run very successfully during the last part of the nineteenth century by General Henry du Pont, and when he died there was no single person who could take his place. Hence the du Pont family decided that the power should pass to a group of men more or less equal in status who would "sing in the choir" rather than be outstanding soloists. The idea was to expand managerial competence by bringing more than one mind to bear on the problems.

Initially, this committee worked like most management committees: it

---

[9] The executive committee is not to be confused with the executive committees composed of department heads that exist in some companies. A board committee includes only members of the board.

agreed with the president. It took years to eliminate the notion that, though the committee members might be equal, the chief executive was "more equal" than anyone else. Now the Du Pont executive committee is perhaps one of the few examples of genuine group management in American industry.

Much less common, but possibly more important where it exists, is the finance committee, which passes on the major financial requests and may, therefore, have a decisive influence on corporate policy. It may decide or counsel on such matters as budgets, taxes, corporate investment portfolios, financing and issue of securities, dividend policy, debt structure, and acquisitions. Some finance committees actually make decisions on appropriations.

Among the most common of the other board committees are those on executive compensation and audit. The first is generally made up of directors who are not also executives of the company and will, therefore, not participate in any bonuses or stock option plans—thus any charge of conflict of interest is avoided. The audit committees select independent outside auditors and review audit results and procedures.

The board and management

The potential power of the board over the management of a corporation is absolute. No company officer can defy the board's edicts with impunity when it acts as a unit. Legally and actually the board is his "boss" who has placed him where he is and can cast him down again. And whereas the "atomized" stockholders have no way of getting together and agreeing on a new board of directors, the directors are not limited in this way. They meet regularly and they are a small enough group to come to agreement merely by talking things over.

Often, too, one or more directors may be "influential" enough to make it wise for management to obey their suggestions without specific direction from the board as a whole. The source of the influence may be public prestige, authority of knowledge in a particular field, large shareholdings, or just political skills. Influential directors can and do exercise "control," influence decisions, and sometimes even make them. Usually an "expression of concern" or questioning by one or more influential directors can at least arrest management action in a particular case.

The power of the chief executive is, however, often greater than might appear. He may have a strong influence over the board by reason of his persuasiveness, or simply because the directors are aware that he knows more about the workings of the company than they do. Directors who are not members of management are likely to have other jobs and other interests; they may not be able to spend time on the detailed study of the company that would be needed to refute claims and proposals of internal management.

Thus in one company that had been losing both money and share of the market for some time, the president convinced his board that things would shortly be very different by laying before it an elaborate plan of cost control developed for him by a respected firm of outside consultants. The plan, however, was never put into effect. Only when the losses had continued for two more years was the board finally moved to retire the president and put in a new man. The very next year the company started making money again.

Such showdowns rarely occur. Even an "influential" director can seldom carry the entire board with him unless there has been a long record of poor performance.

Occasionally, too, the chief executive becomes so influential that his nominations for the board are accepted by the directors. In that case he may come to control the board itself by ensuring that it is made up of his own subordinates or people who are dependent on his good will, either because he can throw business their way or because they regard board membership as an honor and are aware that they owe it to him.

A board made up entirely of members of management is known as an "inside" board, and there is considerable difference of opinion over whether it is a good thing or not. If the managers are also large shareholders, their interests may coincide almost completely with those of the small stockholders, and they may properly represent them. If their stockholdings are negligible and the greater part of their income comes from salaries and bonuses, they may be tempted to increase their own compensation unduly. This has happened, but it would be unfair to say that most, or even many, inside boards act in this way.

Inside boards do have certain advantages. Members can meet at any time; they are likely to have more or less the same basic outlook and talk the same language; and they can easily deal with confidential matters confidentially. It may be argued also that company officers have a greater knowledge of the company's needs than outsiders could have and that, since their entire careers are bound up with the corporation, they have a greater interest in its welfare.

On the other hand, some authorities believe that the majority of the board (some say 75 per cent of it) should be not only financially independent of the corporation but completely independent of inside management. Otherwise, they point out, there will be no one to meter management's performance, and its power may be abused. This is not to say that all managements necessarily need metering, but the absence of even potential rebuttal power may be dangerous.

The small owner-manager is effectively metered by the forces of the marketplace. If he does not do a good job, his firm will go under and he will lose both his ownership and his managership. Competition provides a check on large companies also, but it acts very slowly in many cases, and reserves accumulated by former managers may make it possible for an inefficient chief executive to continue his rule undisturbed until his retirement on a generous pension.

Aside from the negative contribution of preventing management inefficiency or greed, capable outside directors can also contribute in many positive ways.

Frequently they have technical knowledge—of products, markets, finance, economics, or research—that is specifically useful in solving specific problems; or perhaps even more valuable, they may have general business acumen acquired through experience in other corporations. Top executives of successful corporations are much in demand as outside directors; so are the "directors' directors" who sit on many boards and have gained experience in many industries.

Second, directors can be helpful in the training of top management. The counsel they give may provide the officers with a broader viewpoint. They may also be able to spot younger talent within the corporation, or because of their contacts they may help in the recruiting of capable outsiders.

Third, they may be able to suggest acquisitions, mergers, new products, cheaper sources of materials, new outlets, and new ideas that can considerably improve a company's financial position.

Finally, capable independent directors tend to preserve top management from the delusion of infallibility, which often attacks those whose power verges on the absolute. The freedom of discussion that is possible when ten or twelve equals sit around a table may carry over into the management of the company as a whole. It may ensure that a number of minds are brought to bear on every problem and that the top man is not told only what he wants to hear—a situation that may prevail where there is a single absolute ruler rather than a group of equals at the top.

Divorce of ownership and control

The divorce of ownership and control in large corporations has been discussed by many writers, notably James Burnham in *The Managerial Revolution*[10] and Adolf A. Berle, Jr., in *Power without Property*[11] and earlier books.

One method of giving at least a measure of greater power to the small stockholders is the practice of cumulative voting. Ordinarily a stockholder votes for a slate of directors, rather than for individuals, and has one vote for each share he owns. Under cumulative voting, his votes equal the number of his shares multiplied by the number of directors, and he may cast them all for a single director if he chooses. In this way, a comparatively small group of stockholders might find it possible to put at least one man of their own choosing on the board.

But the practice is not widespread since so many of the large corporations are incorporated in Delaware, where the law provides only that cumulative voting is permissible. Fairly frequently, some stockholder exercises his right to put a proposal of it on the proxies, but stockholders are likely to turn down the idea. Whether this is because too many are not sufficiently interested to vote for it or because the large holders, such as financial institutions, make a practice of voting "with management" it is impossible to say. Certainly managements generally recommend a "no" vote on this.

Another possibility is that the institutional stockholders, who hold large

---

[10] The John Day Company, Inc., New York, 1941.
[11] Harcourt, Brace & World, Inc., New York, 1959.

blocks of stocks in many corporations and probably could muster a controlling interest by pooling their votes, should take a more active part in the selection of the directors and managers. There is little likelihood that they will do so on any large scale in the near future, however, since most of them seem to prefer to sell their stock if matters are not going to their liking rather than make a fight for a new management.

Neither of these possibilities seems likely to materialize in most corporations, and there are some who feel that corporations do better under the control of "professional managers" than they do under the control of owners. Certainly many of the small stockholders have neither the ability nor the desire to exercise control. They feel little interest in the corporation, not even in the possibility of rising dividends over the long term. Rather, they buy stock as they might bet on a horse race, in the hope that it will rise rapidly and enable them to make some money quickly.

The trend toward the control of the corporation by those who do not own it—either independent directors or managers—probably cannot be arrested, though it will not become a universal phenomenon as long as there are many businesses in which entrepreneurs can get a start. Whether it eventually results in greater control by government will, as Berle points out, depend on how well the self-perpetuating directors and managers do their jobs, since their power ultimately rests on public acceptance of their role.[12]

SUMMARY

A corporation is an entity quite apart from its owners, and it retains its identity even if the owners are constantly changing. The owners are the shareholders, who elect a board of directors to represent them. The board of directors in turn selects the top management of the corporation.

In theory, therefore, the shareholders, or owners, control the board of directors, and the board controls the top management of the company. In practice, however, the top management may be more independent of both owners and directors than a simple statement of the mechanics would imply. Since the board of directors nominates its own successors and presents the stockholders with a single slate, they do not have much choice, especially since they may constitute such a large and scattered group that it is impossible for them to get together and agree on an alternate slate.

Further, the company president often controls the board of directors in fact if not in name, either because it is an inside board made up of his subordinates or because he is so persuasive that he is able to get it to go along with anything he recommends.

The effects of such a situation are not necessarily bad, since the chief executive is likely to know more about the company than the directors unless they are also members of management. But there are some potential dangers

[12] *Ibid.,* pp. 110–116.

if the president is not very competent or is tempted to put his own interests above those of the owners, for whom he is supposed to be acting.

In a small company, there is less likely to be a divorce of ownership and control since the shareholders may be few in number and themselves make up the board of directors. Moreover, one of them may serve as chief executive. In some large companies also, there are what may be called "partial proprietors"—individuals or companies who own large blocks of stock although they do not have a majority of the shares outstanding. Usually such an individual or a representative of such a company will be a director, often an influential one.

In most very large companies, however, this situation does not exist. The trend toward reduction of the power of the stockholders seems to be a continuing one.

Review Questions

1. A corporation is an entity, quite apart from its owners. What are some of its other characteristics?
2. How is a corporation chartered?
3. What is meant by the "divorce between ownership and control" in large corporations? Are there any advantages to this? What are the possible disadvantages?
4. May a company own stock in another company?
5. What is an "institutional investor"?
6. What are some of the functions a board of directors usually performs?
7. What is cumulative voting? Do you believe it would be a good or a bad thing for a company to have? Why?
8. When may a director be sued by an owner for losses sustained by a corporation?
9. Define "inside" and "outside" directors. What are the advantages and disadvantages of having an inside board rather than one that includes mainly outside directors?

Case Study One / Retirement of Directors

The board of directors of a company passed a resolution making the retirement of directors mandatory at age sixty-five. Shortly before this resolution was passed, the board had elected a new president who was in his mid-thirties. The majority of the board consisted of men at or near retirement age. This older group of directors had at one time rescued the company from near-bankruptcy by diversifying its activities so that it became less dependent on a declining market.

One of the directors to be retired felt that the new ruling was designed to prevent, or at least reduce, independent thinking on the part of the board. He believed that the new president—who had proposed the resolution—wanted to surround himself with his own men. The director, therefore, started a proxy fight to overturn the ruling.

Set forth the arguments for and against the mandatory retirement age:

1. As you see them
2. As the new president would present them
3. As the director over sixty-five would present them

Case Study Two / Subpoena of Directors

The board of directors of the subsidiary of a large foreign international corporation was asked to give evidence on the charges of a canceled dealer, who felt he had been treated unfairly. Members of the board had never had any discussion regarding dealer policies, much less any discussion of this particular dealer. The dealer's lawyers also tried to subpoena the top management of the foreign concern when any of its members came to the United States.

The only board member of the subsidiary who had had any business with the dealer was the general manager and vice-president of the U.S. subsidiary. He answered his own subpoena, but opposed any appearance by other directors or by members of the parent company's management.

1. Do you think the dealer was justified in subpoenaing the directors of the subsidiary? Of the parent company abroad? Why or why not?
2. What do you think would be the outcome of the case?

Case Study Three / The Dwyer Mobile Home Company

During World War II, there was an Army camp near Frank Dwyer's home in Arkansas, and the wives of many of the officers had trouble finding living quarters nearby. Frank conceived the idea of providing the needed housing by building automobile trailers that would be more suitable for housekeeping than those currently available. Since he was a carpenter and a general all-round mechanic, he was able to build such a "mobile home" himself, in back of his garage.

Frank's first mobile home was sold immediately to an Army wife, and several others agreed to purchase homes from him if he would build them. He set up operations in a large barn and hired some assistants. His wife, who had had some secretarial and bookkeeping experience, helped him in the accounting, purchasing, and customer promotion.

Word of the high quality of his homes spread around, and new demand arose from a nearby construction camp and an oil drilling camp. Frank had to set up a real factory and arrange financing so that his homes could be paid for over a period of time. He had accumulated some savings, but they were inadequate; so he got a bank loan and secured the services of a finance company. He also got loans from friends.

By the end of the war, Frank was selling about ten mobile homes a week, and he believed that the demand would increase since he foresaw that many young couples who could not afford regular houses would buy mobile homes. So he decided to increase his production, allow the customers more time to pay for their homes, and cut the interest rate. He got one of the finance companies to support his scheme.

Demand rose rapidly because of the quality of the homes and the easy payment terms. Frank expanded his manufacturing facilities, hired more labor, engaged a sales force, and acquired dealers. To do all this, however, he had to increase his borrowing, both from the banks and from friends. But since sales and profits were rising, he felt he could afford the greatly increased interest costs. And finance companies undertook to help him finance the loans to his customers.

Everything seemed to be going well until Frank set up branch plants in other parts of the country. All these required heavy investment, especially since Frank preferred large-scale production as mechanized as possible.

Unfortunately for Frank, competitors had the same idea and also set up branch plants to be closer to their customers. Frank had neither the time nor the staff to run his branches, and he had no dealer organizations in the areas where the branch plants were located.

Although his sales managers had given him glowing forecasts of sales in the areas near the branch plants, only the home plant seemed to make money. Its profits helped to meet the increasingly heavy interest charges and the losses elsewhere. But Frank was so short of cash that he lost the discounts for prompt payment of bills. He had to let his own collections be made by factors (who charged 15 per cent of the receipts for their services). Finally he mortgaged his land and incurred extremely heavy interest charges (30 per cent per annum) on a final loan, which he hoped would save him.

You are an outside independent director on Frank's board.

1. What would you advise Frank to do to get back to financial solvency and sanity?

2.   What opposition would you be likely to encounter?
3.   How could it be overcome?

Selected Readings

The Corporate Director: A Critical Evaluation, Stanley C. Vance, Dow Jones, Richard D. Irwin, Inc., Homewood, Ill., 1968. The thesis of this book is that in the modern large corporation, the board of directors must provide the dynamism formerly provided by the individual entrepreneur. With this in view, the author considers how boards are made up and how they operate.

Handbook for Corporate Directors, Mortimer Feuer, Prentice-Hall, Inc., Englewood Cliffs, N.J., 1965. A detailed practical study of the responsibilities and duties of directors and their relations to stockholders and management.

The Board of Directors and Effective Management, Harold Koontz, McGraw-Hill Book Company, New York, 1967. A study of board functions and operations and of the relationship between company directors and the chief executive. Includes a chapter on the liabilities of directors.

The Corporate Director, J. M. Juran and J. Keith Louden, American Management Association, New York, 1967. An in-depth study of the responsibilities and powers of the corporate director. Also discusses the working relationships between board members.

The Director Looks at His Job, C. C. Brown and E. E. Smith, Columbia University Press, New York, 1957. Report of a round-table discussion by students and practitioners.

The Modern Corporation and Private Property, A. A. Berle, Jr., and G. C. Means, The Macmillan Company, New York, 1933. A famous study, analytical and empirical, of the separation of ownership and control and its consequences.

4
IN
THE
HEARTLAND
OF
MANAGEMENT

THE ROLE OF THE CHIEF EXECUTIVE

The head of a large-scale business . . . remains a human being and his main lines of policy and organization will vary with his individual character, his antecedent environment, the conventions of his social class, and various psychological stimuli to which he is exposed.
P. Sargant Florence: The Logic of British and American Industry

4　The divorce of ownership and control, as outlined in the last chapter, has meant that the office of the chief executive (generally the president, but in quite a number of cases the chairman of the board) is often the real power center of the company, the fulcrum around which everything, or at least most things, in the corporation turn.

True, the chief executive's power is not really absolute. Although the board of directors may be willing to do what he wants in most cases, it may rebel if he chalks up a poor record over a number of years. The external environment of the company also imposes substantial restrictions on him. In addition, he must bear in mind that subordinates who do not agree with his policies have many ways of silently sabotaging them without appearing to do so. But by and large, the chief who controls the directors, either because they are beholden to him in some way or because he is very persuasive, has immense power, and both he and his subordinates are continuously conscious of that fact.

First of all, the chief can exercise great powers on legal grounds. The bylaws of most corporations provide for the appointment of a chief executive who has practically full powers except as they are limited by the board of directors.

Secondly, the chief executive can strengthen this power by judicious use of rewards and punishments. Complying subordinates can be given salary increases, bonuses, stock options, benefits of all kinds, and status symbols, such as large offices, free cars, and credit cards. Conversely, he can withhold these and other privileges from subordinates who oppose his views. And he need not resort to discharge to make his displeasure even more evident. He can send men to a "managerial Siberia"—some post where they have nothing of importance to do—or gradually withdraw responsibilities from them until they become disgusted enough to quit. It is not necessary for the chief executive to take drastic steps very often. If he has occasionally done so in the past, few will care to challenge his power.

Further, the status of the chief executive, the recognition he receives both inside and outside the company, may endow him with a standing such as to give his behavior toward a subordinate the most extraordinary significance. The frequency of access to the chief executive, the treatment received while talking to him (or rather being talked to), consultation on vital issues, participation in trips and meetings, his praise, blame, or neglect—all these can make or break a subordinate's status among his colleagues and his own feeling about his chances in the company.

THE ROLE OF THE CHIEF EXECUTIVE

Unlike others in the corporation, the chief executive knows that there is no insider who can really check him. His decisions are final, and this in itself imposes a burden. Before he assumed his present job, he had a boss with whom he could share a tough decision; now he has no one. He can, and generally will, get plenty of advice, some of it conflicting perhaps; but the actual decisions that affect the main course of the business are his alone.

For this reason, he is likely to be a lonely man in his business life, even though he is constantly surrounded by people. If he confides his doubts and hesitations to his subordinates, they may lose faith in his leadership. Outside directors may be too busy to help him or may be unfamiliar with the situations confronting him. And he himself is often not entirely familiar with all the areas in which he must make decisions, for he cannot be simultaneously an expert in production, marketing, finance, research, and industrial relations—at least not in a big company where each of these areas would require a lifetime of study.

It was an awareness of these things that led one chief executive to say, "I am a lonely wanderer on the wrong side of the fence, deciding on a program whose implications I don't understand and whose real results I do not know."

He must also bear in mind that he is a *symbol*, both inside and outside his corporation. He represents more than himself, for he is often considered the personification of the corporation itself. Rightly or wrongly, the way a president acts, even looks and dresses, affects the opinion both the general public and the employees have of the enterprise. The symbol or image is sometimes such as to create a belief in the omnipotence of the chief executive. It may appear to his subordinates, who are dependent economically and to some extent emotionally on his favor, that he can do anything he wishes to do. And so it may appear to the chief executive himself if he has an inactive board of directors that will rubber-stamp anything he proposes and if the company is strong enough to survive an occasional very bad mistake or a period without profits.

Although many company presidents have formal job descriptions, in actual practice their jobs tend to be what they want them to be. Some are intent on building themselves up in the view of the general public and may devote a major part of their time to making speeches to outside groups. They may even keep a publicity man or two busy issuing releases on their views. Others look upon the necessity for even an occasional public appearance—and most presidents must make some—as an interruption to their real work. Some regard their role as primarily that of idea men; others believe that it is the job of their staffs to develop new ideas and that the president should merely pass on proposals thoroughly worked out before they are even presented to him. Some concentrate on sales, some on production, some on finance (that is, on the function they know best); others try to apportion their time among all these functions.

Some common types of chief executives and the ways in which they look at their jobs may be listed:

The financier He is, of course, primarily interested in the monetary aspects of the business and attempts to increase his holdings, if necessary by large-scale reinvestment. He is more interested in sudden growth through acquisition and merger than in slow and solid advancement through research or gradual broadening of markets. Often he is smart at picking people who can handle other aspects of the business for him and ruthless in dismissing them if they do not show results fairly quickly. He tends, however, to be poor at internal administration and coordination. He may inflate his empire too far, with the result that a business depression puts it in real danger of dissolution. Then only heroic effort on the part of his successors, and their ability to reestablish the confidence of the financial community, can keep the company going.

The salesman   His most important quality is his persuasiveness. He can charm his board of directors, the members of the financial community, his associates, and his important customers.

If he is backed up by good production and financial men and is willing to listen to them, he may be very successful. But if he begins to believe that he is infallible in these areas, his company is in for trouble, for he does not really understand figures or place much importance on them, and his controller will have great difficulty in getting him to pay attention to hard facts. He tends to be overoptimistic about prospects.

His associates will probably like him, since he is quite willing to go out of his way to be pleasant to them; but he may also be a harassing factor in their lives. As he can sell easily, so he can himself be sold without too much difficulty; hence he may be continually steamed up about some new idea—in administration, in techniques, or something else—that he may have heard about at a management meeting or from some of his opposite numbers in other companies or industries.

The technician   The technician has the great advantage of knowing what he is administering. However, he may be weak in finance and in selecting and dealing with subordinates except when they need to have a technical background similar to his own. He may tend to become so interested in innovations in his own field that he neglects other functions.

The administrator   The manager who views himself primarily as an administrator and coordinator will attempt, at least partially, to substitute system for the intuition and genius which may have guided his predecessor if the latter was the founder of the business. He is likely to be in favor of reinvestment of surplus profits in order to ensure survival of the enterprise and its successful defense against competition. He is probably a good coordinator. On the other hand, he may tend to be too conventional, too cautious, and too slow in permitting the introduction of innovations. In selecting people, he may too often choose those who are much like himself.

Ideally, of course, the chief executive would possess the virtues of each of these types and none of their faults. While such paragons are seldom found, some chief executives do approach the ideal. Others are conscious of their own weaknesses and try to ensure that they have associates who can fill the gaps in their backgrounds.

There are really no rules about how a chief executive should conduct himself, what image he should present to the public and his subordinates, which phases of the business he should take into his own hands, and which he should delegate. Successful chief executives have played all possible roles, from the democratic hail-fellow-well-met to the aloof aristocrat, from the father of a family to the ruthless money seeker. They have been innovators, and they have been mere coordinators and umpires. They have made themselves into supersalesmen and spent a major portion of their time mingling with important customers, and they have stayed in their offices checking over figures.

REWARDS AND DANGERS

The biggest reward of most chief executives is in the actual handling of the job—the conception, the planning and organizing, and the accomplishment of results. The feeling of purposefulness and fulfillment is often their highest incentive. As the last founder—part-owner-manager in the steel industry (Ernest T. Weir, National Steel) used to say, quoting Einstein, "The only way to escape personal corruption from praise is to go on working. One is tempted to stop and listen to it. The only thing is to turn away and go on working. Work—there is nothing else."

Secondly, the chief executive may enjoy the power to do good by building something tangible that may be helpful to many people—providing jobs and products.

Thirdly, there is what the economist calls "psychic income," the satisfaction derived from position, status, perquisites, and the feeling of having gotten to the very top.

Finally—and not least by any means—there are the money income and other economic perquisites, such as company cars and planes, generous pensions, and large expense accounts.

The power the chief executive wields brings satisfactions, both tangible and intangible. But it also brings dangers, especially when he is accountable to no one because he himself controls the board of directors.

There is, first of all, the danger that his decisions may be wrong, and they may not be easy to correct if they involve large corporate aggregates. If successful accomplishment is his chief pleasure, his failures—and he is bound to have some—are proportionately painful. He may try to soften the blow by blaming subordinates, to himself and to others, but in his heart he must know that since he selected the subordinates—or at least did nothing to replace them—he himself is really responsible.

Second, there is the danger that he may lose the capacity for hearing unpleasant truths and so be unaware of pitfalls until they engulf him. If he is impatient with those who offer objections to his ideas and interprets disagreement as disloyalty, subordinates will readily fall into the habit of telling him only what they think he wants to hear. And it is very easy for the chief executive to create the impression that he does not want to be told unpleasant truths, even if this is not the case. No one who has, say, developed a new idea can manage to look pleased when associates greet his explanation of it with reasons why it won't work or even with "Yes, but . . . ." Though he may have no intention of holding the objections against them, his subordinates will judge merely from the fact that he seems momentarily annoyed and make up their minds not to question his ideas again.

Many chief executives, in fact, are surprised at the weight their subordinates place on their lightest words. "We seem to have too many rules," one of them remarked. "Every time I comment on something, I find someone has made a rule about it. If I say, for example, that an office could look neater, I later find out that someone has made a rule about what can be kept on desk tops—and that's much more than I ever intended."

Then, there are certain moral hazards. With no check on his behavior, the chief needs a very strong conscience to place the corporation's interests above his own or even on the same level with them. If the board of directors will grant him a salary increase or a large bonus every time he suggests it, where is he to stop? If there is no one to limit his expense account, what prevents him from indulging in as many whims as he or the company lawyer can explain satisfactorily to the Internal Revenue Service?

THE DUARCHY

Often, however, the power of the president is modified by a form of dual control: two executives, supposedly working in tandem, at the top instead of one. The two may be the president and the chairman of the board of directors or the president and the executive vice-president, senior vice-president, or first vice-president. One of these two tends to be more important than the other, but his power is less absolute than that of the single chief executive since he often has no real control over his partner. Their powers may be split in any one of the following ways:

	Chief decision maker	Second decision maker
1	Policy	Operations
2	Outside relations	Inside relations
3	Staff*	Line*
4	All decisions (line and staff) except..........	Finance, law, or public relations
5	Line	Staff

In addition, there are some cases in which no division of responsibilities is set up, and all top decisions are made—or are supposed to be made—jointly.

The principal reason for tandem top management is, of course, that a single chief executive tends to be overloaded with work. Or it may be that the top man has come up through one department and his knowledge is somewhat specialized. Therefore another man who has been trained in a different field may be needed to supplement him. Thus a chief executive who has come up through finance may have a marketing man or a manufacturing executive as

---

* In general, staff departments perform advisory or auxiliary functions (e.g., personnel), while line departments are directly concerned with the main business of the company. Production and sales, for example, are line departments. The distinction is explained in more detail in Chapters 11 and 12.

the second decision maker. Or the second job may be created to train a successor to the top man; sometimes a president who is due for retirement is made chairman of the board and works closely with the new president.

The most frequent division of responsibilities is the one listed first in the table: the top man is designated as the policy maker while the second-in-command runs the operations. If, in such a case, the top man has no staff to prepare, implement, and coordinate his policies, he cannot have too much influence on the company's activities, and the real power passes to the second-in-command. Or even if the top man has a staff, the second-in-command may be able to isolate him so completely that his policies are not actually observed very closely.

Staff functions under one executive and line functions under another should work well since the plan will leave the line chief free to work on coordination and the staff chief free to develop and assess new ideas. However, the split between line and staff may be too wide, with the result that the staff is not available to assist the line or attempts to control the line rather than advise it.

Where outside relations are delegated to one of the two decision makers and inside relations to the other, the inside man is likely to be the real power. In the case where the chief decision maker is responsible for everything except finance, law, or public relations, he is again in practically sole command. An exception might be where the second-in-command is in charge of finance and can thus keep a check on activities by refusing to provide money for them, particularly if he has influence with the board of directors.

Finally, there is the undefined joint relationship between the chief and the second-in-command described as "the marriage." But compatibility is doubtful, and split-ups are not infrequent. Once there is a second man, he may try to make himself first, with the result that the two become rivals and enemies.

GROUP CONTROL

Because of the unsatisfactory nature of the "duarchy" or "tandem" approach, many companies that try it either retreat to the system of having a single decision-making executive or move forward toward group decision making. In group decision making, some top executives may be freed from work on day-to-day operations to devote themselves entirely to overall problems, or at least spend only a part of their time on their functional responsibilities. Such a body may confine itself to overall issues involved in planning, organization, and control, or it may also deal with specific functional issues.

The basic advantage of such a system is that it brings more than one mind to bear on the most important problems of the corporation. And, since the members of the group are on a more or less equal footing, there can be more freedom of discussion than is likely between a superior and his subordinates. Again, one person who has almost absolute power may go overboard for a new idea with insufficient consideration of its disadvantages, whereas someone among a group of men who are not afraid to speak their minds freely will be sure to point them out.

On the other hand, a group is likely to be more conservative since one or two of its members may object to almost any new idea on one ground or another. Thus the company may miss golden opportunities by moving too slowly. Group management also blurs accountability because there is no one person who can be held responsible for success or failure. The result may be confusion, a multiplication of red tape, and eventual stagnation.

The group approach works very well in some companies; in others it works poorly. The degree of success possible seems to depend largely on the personalities of those making up the group. Members of some groups work well together, supplementing each other's knowledge and stimulating each other's ideas; in other cases, the group method seems to dilute the sense of responsibility among the members and give rise to a tendency to postpone action.

OTHER FACTORS

Other factors in the internal environment that may act as checks on the chief executive's power may grow out of past decisions and company tradition. Some decisions—as one example, a decision on the location of a plant—in part determine what a company can and cannot do for a long time to come. Also, company tradition may be hard to change because those who have been accustomed to following it are simply unable to think in a different way or to work for new goals, and ordering them to do so will have no effect. Although the chief executive may have the legal power, say, to fire all his department heads, as a practical matter he cannot do so without disorganizing the company completely. Hence he may have to work more slowly than he would like to in setting his firm on a new course, gradually replacing the men he finds it impossible to change and educating the others in the value of the new approach.

An even more important internal check on the president's power is growing naturally out of technological advances and the increasing complexities of administration. No single person can possibly be at once familiar with all the physical sciences used in a large and diversified company, with consumer tastes and the possibilities of various marketing techniques, and with finance. Then there are the ins and outs of collective bargaining, which is no longer a simple matter of "How much will the union take not to strike, and can we afford it?" Rather, it involves a whole range of work rules and various other provisions that affect management decisions—day-by-day decisions in the case of the first-level foreman and occasionally top management decisions on such matters as plant location.

Hence top managers must surround themselves with experts who are able to delve deeply into such subjects and provide advice. But how does one judge an expert if one is not very familiar with his field? This is a problem that It is illegal for an employer to discriminate against an employee or threaten

> We sit at our desks all day, while around us whiz and gyrate a vast number of special activities, some of which we only dimly understand. And for each of these activities, there is a specialist. . . . All of them, no

doubt, are good to have. All seem to be necessary. All are useful on frequent occasions. But it has reached the point where the greatest task of the president is to understand enough of all these specialties so that when a problem comes up he can assign the right team of experts to work on it.[1]

SUMMARY

The chief executive, who may be either the chairman of the board or the president, is usually the chief power in the company, particularly if there is a large and scattered group of stockholders. In general, therefore, his job is what he wants to make it.

If he has a complaisant board of directors and so is accountable to no one but himself, he will be in danger of falling into the delusion that he is infallible. And even if he is not prone to think so, he may have difficulty finding out what is actually happening since subordinates may be reluctant to tell him things they think he doesn't want to hear.

Sometimes, however, the power of the chief executive is modified by a form of dual control; that is, there are two executives at the top instead of one: the president and the chairman of the board, or a president and an executive vice-president. In that case they may divide the work in any one of several ways, each of which has advantages and disadvantages.

Another way in which the power of the chief executive may be modified is by the appointment of experts in various fields. Since he cannot know everything about every area of the business if it is a large one, he may be increasingly forced to pass on suggestions without being able to judge their value with assurance.

Group management is used in some companies; that is, top management consists of a committee rather than an individual. This works very well in some instances, but in others it merely serves to blur responsibilities and slow things down.

Review Questions

1. What are some of the ways in which the powers may be divided between the president and the chairman of the board or the president and the executive vice-president?
2. Can you think of any ways in which the president can ensure that he is assigning the right team of experts to work on a problem?
3. What are some of the ways in which a chief executive may encounter moral hazards?
4. If you were a chief executive, what are some of the decisions you would want to make yourself?
5. Do you think a company president should view himself mainly as an administrator?

[1] John L. McCaffrey, "What Corporation Presidents Think about at Night," *Fortune*, September, 1953, p. 128.

Charles Hall, who owns 60 per cent of the outstanding stock of the Management Dynamics Corporation, has been serving as president, handling all the top management functions and some of the middle management functions as well: appointment of personnel, decisions on compensation, production scheduling, purchasing procedures, inventory determination, union negotiations.

Hall is in his fifties and is being worn out by the steadily increasing volume of responsibilities and the pettiness of some of the problems he feels he must solve but hates to handle. He would also like to give his younger managers (in their forties) greater opportunity.

Therefore he appoints Frank Hennessy, who has been his senior vice-president, to the presidency and John Towne, formerly vice-president of operations, as executive vice-president. He himself becomes chairman of the board.

In making these changes, Hall is deeply concerned with maintaining (1) the power to protect his ownership interests and (2) his status as top man in the eyes of the outside world. On the other hand, the new president and executive vice-president want to have real power to run the business and also to represent it to the outside world.

You are asked to be a "managerial Solomon" and distribute the powers among the three men so that they will all be satisfied they have adequate powers of decision making and adequate status. How would you distribute the responsibilities and authority?

Albert Berenschott Van de Water started with nothing and achieved high success in one of the most competitive industries in the country, one in which survival depended on imagination, quick decision making, and trading instinct.

In his thirties he was a multimillionaire and began to feel he had had enough of the hurly-burly. So he bought into a company in a more stable, established industry and became its president. He appointed some outstanding men from the business world to his board of directors to confer prestige on it and hired a number of staff men who had made fine records in other industries. He also brought with him some friends from his old business and got rid of some of the old-timers in the new company.

Next he set up a new organization structure, dividing the company into a number of semi-autonomous profit divisions, each producing and selling a different product and each with its own general manager and staff. Experts in manufacturing, sales, finance, personnel, and public relations were added to headquarters, and most of the existing operations were expanded because Albert ("call me A. B.") felt that growth was imperative.

A. B. loved new ventures. In rapid succession, he acquired one company after another, mostly in fields unrelated to the original business. As a result, he was asked to make many public speeches telling others how he managed to be so "dynamic."

But after five years in the presidency, A. B. found that the return on investment in the company was far less than his predecessors had been making, although he had always been scornful of them for being "timid" and "ultra-conservative."

There is still nothing wrong with the traditional product lines in A. B.'s company except that they may be managed by too many people, some of whom do not know what they are managing. But the new and exotic lines have only added deficits. The directors are getting restive. Stockholders are complaining about lower earnings and dividends. Wall Street brokers are advising against the purchase of the company's shares. Worst of all, A. B.'s confidence in himself, once so supreme, has been shaken.

You are a management consultant and A. B. has faith in you and likes you. He asks you to advise him how he can make money again. What is your advice? You know that his personality is not going to change very much and that as soon as he gets over his present discomfiture he is likely to want to start on new plans for expansion by acquisition.

Selected Readings

The Great Organizers, Ernest Dale, McGraw-Hill Book Company, New York, 1960. Studies of the behavior and techniques of top managements of major corporations, plus a discussion of possibilities for improving management accountability in the absence of ownership control.

The Boss, Roy Lewis and Rosemary Stewart, Phoenix House, London, 1958. The lives and careers of businessmen, mostly English and American.

My Years with General Motors, Alfred P. Sloan, Jr., Doubleday & Company, Inc., Garden City, N.Y., 1964. Mr. Sloan, for many years chief executive of the General Motors Corporation, details the management methods he and his associates used.

Business Leadership in the Large Corporation, Robert Aaron Gordon, The Brookings Institution, Washington, D.C., 1945; 2d ed. with new preface, University of California Press, Berkeley, Calif., 1961. Contains a competent study of the chief executive, his functions, and his relationships, drawn from published sources.

5

THE

EXTERNAL

FRAMEWORK

*Every American enterprise today takes a
position in a highly organized world which it
did not create, and—necessarily—
takes it as it finds it. Adolf A. Berle, Jr.:
The American Economic Republic*

5 As the last two chapters have explained, the broad framework provided by the corporate structure often places few limitations on the chief executive. Moreover, other internal constraints—the effects of tradition and past decisions and the possible opposition of important subordinates—can be overcome in time if the top man is really determined to have his own way. He can even reduce his dependence on the experts by learning enough about their fields to evaluate their advice himself. Thus, to the manager further down the line who is limited by company policy, by the nature of his job, by his budget, and perhaps by the personalities of his superiors, it may seem that practically unlimited freedom exists at the top.

It is true that the framework within which the top manager exercises his talents is far broader than that which circumscribes a subordinate manager. But it is no less rigid; it can, in fact, be even more rigid. The manager down the line is limited mainly by the decisions of his superiors, who, like all human beings, may sometimes be persuaded to change their minds. The top manager, on the other hand, is limited largely by impersonal forces, for the corporation itself is a framework within a framework, and the larger framework is its external environment. The dimensions of the larger framework are determined by a variety of factors, chief among which are the state of the economy; the policies of competitors, financial institutions, and labor unions; government regulations; and the current state of technology in the industry or industries of which the corporation is a part.

The man in the heartland of management may have many immediate subordinates and thousands of employees, great decisions to make, and the symbols and perquisites of high office. These may make him feel omnipotent, or very nearly so. Yet when anyone in such a position of great power examines his situation closely, he is bound to find that there are distinct limits to what he can do, even if his own organization is completely responsive to his will.

The principal constraints imposed on top management by the external environment may be grouped under four headings: (1) financial limitations; (2) legal limitations; (3) limitations imposed by unions; and (4) technological limitations.

FINANCIAL LIMITATIONS

In every case, the financial limitations are to some extent a product of the external environment. Even in privately held companies that can get along without either borrowing from financial institutions or offering stock to the general public, the price level and the interest level will affect top management decisions on major matters. Construction costs, which the company cannot very well regulate, will influence decisions on building new facilities, and the current interest rate may dictate a decision on whether or not the company should take money out of the bank and invest it in some other way.

Also, every company's financial condition is affected by such factors in the external environment as the size of the market for its products, the number and strength of its competitors, and the prices it can obtain for its products.[1]

The primary fact of business life is that every company is limited by its financial resources, which in all cases are affected by the state of the economy and in many cases depend on how much money the company can raise from outside, by borrowing or by selling stock. Income must surpass outgo, at least in the long run, or the business will not survive.

This hard fact is made harder still by another truism: Every step the top manager takes to increase income is likely to increase outgo. Will a new plant enable the company to produce more efficiently and make a larger profit? It will take money to build, lease, or buy one. Are greater sales and advertising efforts needed? Money is again essential. Is the company's product becoming obsolete because of new inventions or a change in public taste? A switch to a new one will be expensive. As the popular saying goes, "You have to spend money to make money." Moreover, the spending has to come first.

"If I could just buy that new press," says the production manager, "I could produce the same amount of product with 10 per cent fewer people. The equipment would pay for itself in two years. Why can't top management see it?"

"With a few more salesmen," the regional sales manager mourns, "we could beat competition to a frazzle in the Cleveland area. Why can't top management see it?"

Even in the largest companies, there is never enough money to do all the things that might be profitable. Hence one of the major jobs of top management is allocating this scarce resource in the wisest way: putting it where it will produce the greatest return. Each of two divisions wants a new plant, but there is only enough money to build one of them. The fact that one of the proposed plants will earn 20 per cent on the investment may be irrelevant if the other one can earn 30 per cent.

The amount of money the corporation has in its reserves depends only partly on what top management has done in the past; in large part it depends on the prosperity or lack of it in the country as a whole and in the industry. And if the company must raise money from outside, it comes squarely up against limitations imposed by its environment, including those imposed by financial institutions.

Equity financing

When a company issues new stock, it is taking in more owners, which means that the profits will be divided among a larger number of shares and people and that each of the original owners has a smaller percentage of the total stock outstanding (dilution of equity). If the returns are much larger because

[1] Although some very large companies may appear to dominate their markets to such an extent that they can raise prices at will and be confident that their smaller competitors will follow suit, there is always the possibility that charging too high a price will produce a smaller market, for there are few products for which no substitutes are available. Also, a price rise may make foreign competition more likely.

the new money produces larger profits, well and good. But if not, earnings per share will be less. Moreover, although the original stockholders will have shares in a larger company, their stock may actually go down in value and produce a capital loss as well as an income loss.

Further, issuing stock may be an expensive proposition in itself. The executives can't stand on the street corner, or even on the floor of the stock exchange, and peddle it. Usually they must engage underwriters who make a specialty of stock issues and pay them for doing the job. The underwriters may buy the issue at a discount and then proceed to sell it for what it will bring, or they may charge a fee for their services or get paid in other ways— by stock options, for example. Sometimes the price will include the addition of a representative of the underwriting firm to the board of directors. And the small or financially weak company may find that the best underwriters are unwilling to handle its issues; in other words, it may come face to face with limitations imposed by other institutions.

Debt financing

Debt financing by selling bonds or debentures or borrowing from banks and other financial institutions imposes the burdens of interest and sometimes requires the services of an underwriter also. Convertible debentures, which are debt certificates convertible into stock at a later date, may carry a lower rate of interest because the lenders expect to make a capital gain by the conversion. But this form of financing requires interest payments now, and it may dilute the owners' equity later if the lenders decide to make the conversion.

The advantage of equity (or stock) financing is that it carries no interest burden; if the company does not make money on its new investments, it does not have to pay the stockholders, whereas bondholders or other creditors can put a company that does not pay its debts into receivership. On the other hand, if the company does make money, the interest on the debt will be deductible from its income tax, whereas payments to stockholders are not. Also, some companies have a historical dividend policy under which the rate of payment on equity money may be higher than the interest on debt.

Further, in times of rising prices, a debt that loomed large when it was first incurred may appear smaller later on because it represents less purchasing power. The opposite effect will be felt if prices fall very far. The reason for the recurrence of mortgage foreclosure in late-nineteenth-century popular drama, one economist held, lay in the experience of the farm population during the long price decline of the 1870s. A farmer who took out a mortgage amounting to, say, the price of 1,000 bushels of wheat would find that he had to raise 2,000 bushels to pay it off if the price of the grain fell by 50 per cent.

Leasing

The third principal method of financing is some form of leasing arrangement. Leasing involves neither equity nor debt financing, and it offers tax advantages as well. It is being used increasingly widely, especially in plant, warehousing, and computer financing.

For example, a company might sell a new plant and lease it back from the new owner under a long-term lease, with an option to purchase at book value or less. The entire rent is, of course, tax-deductible as a business expense, whereas the cost of a company-owned plant may be deducted only over a period of years as depreciation. In addition, the company does not have its capital "tied up in bricks and mortar," as businessmen are fond of saying, but can use it for other new projects. Also, while a long-term lease may affect a company's debt capacity (the total amount it will be able to raise by borrowing), the effect is not so great as that of a long-term debt.

But there are drawbacks to leasing as well as to the other methods of financing. Perhaps the principal one is that the lessor naturally expects to make money on the transaction. Hence the rent of a leased plant will amount to more than the interest the company would have to pay if it borrowed the money to build and retained ownership.

Uncertainties

Thus there is no way of raising new money for expansion without paying a price for it. If the return on the new money is greater than the cost of acquiring it, the move will be well worth while. It would be, for example, very sound business to borrow money at 6 per cent and invest it in a plant that would make 20 or 30 per cent on the investment.

Further, when a company borrows only part of the money it needs for expansion and uses retained earnings for the remainder, a factor called "leverage" comes into the picture, which means that its return on its own investment may be huge. Suppose it borrows $9 million and invests $1 million of its own, then makes 20 per cent annually on the investment, or $2 million. Subtracting interest payments at 6 per cent, it earns well over $1 million, or more than a 100 per cent return on its own investment each year.

But even though everything looks promising, the plant may not make the 20 per cent or anything like it. Economic conditions can never be predicted with entire accuracy. Sales may be lower than expected, or costs may be higher—both the initial costs and the continuing costs of running the new plant. Hence in adversity, the result may be merely an additional interest charge of over $500,000.

Another point management must bear in mind is what has come to be known as the "time value" of money. The $100 a company or an individual has today is worth more than the $100 due to come in a year from now, regardless of price changes—for the simple reason that the $100 in hand today can be earning a return during the year, whereas the $100 that comes in next year is earning nothing in the meantime. Thus in figuring the return on an investment, a company may discount both costs and revenues expected in the future. (Tables are available for this.)

Also, it is not always possible for a company to get its first choice among the methods of financing. As one financial officer of a medium-sized company that had recently built a new plant phrased it, "When you are ready to choose your financing method, you will find the financial market loaded with all kinds of transactions, arrangements, lures, nostrums, and cure-alls, but your choice is limited. . . . Unless you are top-flight, blue-chip, and loaded, you are going to be limited to a single choice." In other words, limitations imposed by other institutions—banks, underwriters, and so on—will tend to narrow down the possibilities.

Even companies that *are* "top-flight, blue-chip, and loaded" do not have absolutely unlimited freedom in this matter. For example, if a number of new stock issues have just been placed on the market, there may not be enough money floating around to pick up a large new one, and it may be necessary to wait in order to sell it at a good price. It may also be necessary to wait if stock prices have suffered a severe drop.

LEGAL LIMITATIONS

Among the most important of the institutional limitations are the legal limitations: Federal, state, and local.

Over the years, the Federal government has imposed increasing restraints. Laws passed by Congress affect almost every area of business decision, from purchase of other companies to treatment of employees. Some of these apply to business in general; others affect only specific industries—such as foods, drugs, railroads and airlines—or apply only to work on government contracts.

Then there are numerous state laws. Some reinforce Federal laws by setting the same standards for intrastate commerce that the Federal legislation sets for interstate commerce. Others impose new restrictions.

Regulations developed by the various Federal and state agencies charged with administering the laws passed by Congress and the state legislatures sometimes broaden the interpretation of the statutes. These regulations are known as "administrative law" and represent an impressive body of restrictions.

For example, the Texas Railroad Commission is empowered to determine how much crude oil may be produced in Texas, officially to conserve crude, but actually to prevent supply from outrunning demand and keep prices stable. The commission's power to achieve the objective is reinforced by Federal laws against the sale or movement of oil produced in excess of assigned production limits and by Federal import quotas for oil.

But in the case of administrative law there is always the final safeguard of appeal to the courts, and ultimately to the Supreme Court of the United States, and the courts may apply the rule of reason rather than absolute standards that are unfair in specific cases.

Finally, there are local ordinances regarding safety, fire hazards, zoning, and similar matters. These dictate the kind of buildings that may be constructed and often restrict location.

It is obviously impossible to discuss the large and growing file of government restraints on business enterprise. However, it may not be inappropriate to review four major areas of limitation by government. The first of these is the limitation on certain types of growth by means of antitrust laws; the second, the corporate income tax law, which has a major effect on business decisions in many areas; the third, antipollution legislation (Federal and state); and the fourth, legislation dealing with labor.

Antitrust laws

The maintenance of free competition is one of the cornerstones of the American system. Legislation designed to ensure it is intended to preserve free entry into the various industries by new entrepreneurs and to enable them to compete on equal terms.

These goals are usually not achieved when one producer has a monopoly or when there are only a few firms in the industry (oligopoly) which combine to prevent the entry of others who might "spoil the market" for them (e.g., by reducing prices or introducing product improvements that those already in the field do not find it feasible to copy).

Now there are many cases where only one producer is needed to supply all of a given commodity or service required by the public and to have more than one producer would mean needless duplication of facilities and an economic waste. Examples are public utilities, such as telephone companies and electric power companies. In cases like these, the government usually sets up a public commission to pass on rates and regulate the conduct of the business. Among these commissions are the Federal Power Commission, the Interstate Commerce Commission (the oldest public utility commission, which determines railroad passenger and freight rates), and the Civil Aeronautics Board.

Sherman Antitrust Act   But for the most part, the threat to competition appears to be greatest in industries in which corporations might get together in order to reduce or eliminate competition by fixing prices, allocating contracts, restricting output, and other devices.

In the late nineteenth century, sellers in many industries banded together to acquire enough financial power to drive out the little men. This happened in railroads, sugar, nails, copper, steel, oil, tinplate, and many other fields. Prices could be reduced to the point where new or smaller firms could not make a profit; then they might be raised when competition had been driven out. Or special concessions could be forced from railroads and unfair competitive advantage gained. In agriculture, middlemen might combine to drive down prices to the farmer while ensuring that the consumers continued to pay high prices. And in both cases the monopolizers were aided by financial interests, such as banks and insurance companies.

It was against the destruction of the small producer and monopolization of the market to the detriment of the consumer that the populist drive rose at the end of the nineteenth century and the later trust-busting campaign of President Theodore Roosevelt was directed. There arose a widespread feeling that "there must be a law to make it right." Clearly to most people the common law was inadequate because it was not able to take action against conspiracies to fix prices and restrict output, and the advantages of conspiring to do just that had become great enough to tempt many businessmen.

The result was the Sherman Antitrust Act, which was passed in 1890. Chief Justice Hughes called it a "charter of freedom" for American business, which it was. But if it gave freedom to some businesses, it also placed restrictions on other businesses, restrictions that have grown tighter—through further legislation and through interpretation—in later years.

The act made illegal all contracts, combinations, and conspiracies for the restraint of trade or monopolization of trade among the several states or with foreign nations. Violation of it might result in seizure of property in the course of transit and the award of triple damages to the injured parties.

With the advent of the Theodore Roosevelt administration, prosecutions were undertaken against some of the great trusts or combines. While some of these were unsuccessful, the vast Standard Oil Company, among others, was compelled to dissolve itself into several different companies. But in the case of Standard Oil in particular, "The holding company was not required to sell its stockholdings to outsiders, merely to distribute them to its own stockholders—and continuity of management prolonged practices of cooperation . . . among these companies."[2]

The Clayton Act and the Federal Trade Commission   The trust-busting efforts of the first decade of the twentieth century appeared to be largely unsuccessful because the law dealt with monopoly only when it was a *fait accompli*. Therefore new legislation was passed by Congress to halt monopoly in its "incipiency." The most important additional restraints were imposed under the administration of President Woodrow Wilson: the Clayton Act and the act that created the Federal Trade Commission, both passed in 1914.

Perhaps the most important single clause of the Clayton Act was section 7, which forbade corporations to acquire stock in other corporations if the effect of the acquisition would be to lessen competition between the acquirer and the acquired. Other important provisions specified that:

1. There could be no price discrimination between competing customers, except in such cases as quantity discounts or discrimination "made in good faith to meet competition."
2. Companies in competition with each other could not have directors in common ("interlocking directorates"). Recently the rulings on this point have become much stricter.
3. Companies could not make it a condition of sale that the purchaser would refuse to handle the merchandise of their competitors ("exclusive dealing").

[2] Melvin G. de Chazeau and Alfred E. Kahn, *Integration and Competition in the Petroleum Industry,* Yale University Press, New Haven, Conn., 1959, p. 88.

In addition, the powers of inquiry into the conduct of business were greatly strengthened by creation of the Federal Trade Commission. Not only could it collect information and subpoena witnesses; it could investigate the practice of any organization, require annual reports, protect consumers, investigate violations of the antitrust acts, see how the court decrees were being carried out, make recommendations, and even investigate conditions abroad. The Commission can decide what are and what are not "unfair and deceptive" acts of competition, and after trial require companies it considers offenders to "cease and desist."

These 1914 acts, although they were passed more than fifty years ago, put some real teeth into the Sherman Antitrust Act. Rather than attempting to dissolve the large corporation—which is generally considered to be imprac- tical—government control has taken the form of outlawing "unfair" and "unreasonable" methods of competition. While growth was to be encouraged in the main, growth by acquisition of other companies was to be discouraged where it tended to produce monopoly. Interpretation of the acts has tended to place more emphasis on protection of competition than on direct protection of consumers, in the hope that competition will accomplish the same result.

In the next few years, clarifying amendments to this legislation were passed, but not much new was added. In fact, it was weakened in one important respect: Under the Webb-Pomerene Act of 1918, associations concerned exclu- sively with export trade were permitted, under certain circumstances, to join international associations in order to compete with foreign cartels.

In the 1930s, however, there was some tightening of the legislation. The Robinson-Patman Act of 1936, an amendment to the Clayton Act, was passed mainly to protect small retailers. It reiterated the provisions of the Clayton Act regarding price discrimination, with the additional proviso that the Federal Trade Commission might, after hearings, "establish quantity limits on particu- lar commodities or classes of commodities where it finds that available pur- chasers in greater quantities are so few as to render differentials on account thereof unjustly discriminatory or promotive of monopoly." And in 1938 the Wheeler-Lea Act, an amendment to the Federal Trade Commission Act, out- lawed false advertising of "food, drugs, devices or cosmetics."

Generally speaking, American business had enjoyed a moratorium from restraints in the monopoly field between the end of World War I and the advent of the Franklin D. Roosevelt administration. Under the latter, the public esti- mate of the threat of monopoly changed, partly perhaps as the result of detailed investigations of the concentration of economic power by the Tem- porary National Economic Committee.

Limitations on outcompeting rivals   Then, following World War II, the climate of restraint became increasingly tighter. The number of cases initiated annually by the Antitrust Division of the Department of Justice doubled and those initiated under the Federal Trade Commission Act and the Robinson-Patman Act rose to several hundred annually—mostly because of an increase in the number of complaints and an increase in the government staffs charged with processing them.

Also, section 7 of the Clayton Act was strengthened by the O'Mahoney-Celler-Kefauver Act of 1950, which prohibits acquisition of either the stock or the assets of any other corporation where the effect of the acquisition may be to lessen competition substantially or to create a monopoly.

There has also been a change in interpretation, which imposes still further restraints.[3] Now it is considered that not only mergers that lessen competition in general but those that are likely to injure smaller competitors should be banned. Horizontal mergers—of companies selling to the same market—were always likely to be restrained if the merged organization would take a substantial share of the market. Now it appears that vertical mergers—mergers of producers and their suppliers or their marketing outlets—are also likely to be disallowed. So are conglomerate mergers—mergers of two companies in somewhat different fields—if they might tend to injure smaller competitors.

One of the most important cases won by the government was that of the Brown Shoe Company, an instance of vertical merger. Brown, a shoe manufacturer, accounted for only 4 per cent of total shoe manufacture; and the company it proposed to acquire, a chain of shoe stores, sold only 1.6 per cent of all shoes retailed. The merger was not permitted on the ground that further combination of production and retailing would reduce the outlets available to small shoe manufacturers who had no outlets of their own. Brown's own outlets sold Brown's shoes, and it was expected that the new outlets would be compelled to handle them. It was also argued that the vertical integration would reduce costs and make possible price reductions that smaller competitors could not meet.

Thus there is a definite tendency for government to prevent larger companies from outcompeting small ones. This seems to have been confirmed by a number of other important cases, most notably that of the Humble Oil Company, which had planned to acquire the marketing outlets of the Tidewater Oil Company on the West Coast. Humble stopped the process when the Federal Trade Commission announced that it would oppose the merger on grounds not substantially different from those outlined above.

Also, Procter & Gamble's acquisition of Clorox was challenged not because this would give P & G too large a share of the market, but because its large resources and lower advertising costs *might* enable Clorox to increase its share of the liquid-bleach market at the expense of smaller competitors. In this case, the Supreme Court held in 1967 that "all mergers are within the reach of Section 7 [of the Clayton Act], and all must be tested by the same standard, whether they are classified as horizontal, vertical, or conglomerate."

Again, the General Dynamics Corporation was forced to divest itself of CO_2 operations even though it had not violated any antitrust law, merely because it was a large customer of potential CO_2 users and the latter *might* be subject to indirect or inferred pressure. And the Supreme Court decision that required

[3] The following is largely drawn from Jesse W. Markham, "Antitrust Trends and New Constraints," *Harvard Business Review*, May–June, 1963.

Du Pont to divest itself of its holdings in General Motors forty years after they were acquired rested on the mere possibility that Du Pont might use its part ownership to force the automobile company to purchase some of its products.

Thus it is no longer necessary for a company actually to violate the law. If even a reasonable probability of restraint of trade exists at the time of the suit, a company may be required to divest itself of its holdings in another company. And the reasoning applied in the Clorox case could be applied to any type of conglomerate merger if one of the parties were a large company.

These rulings may even affect decisions on new products. A company that already holds substantial stock in another concern that would be a potentially large customer for a new product may have to decide whether it is better to sell the stock or forego the new product.

Then there are other uncertainties that existed even before the Du Pont decision. For a company to obtain by acquisition of other companies so large a share of the market that it shuts out competition is, of course, illegal, but what is the market? In another case against Du Pont (this one decided in favor of the company), the ruling was that although the company produced almost 75 per cent of the cellophane sold in the country, cellophane accounted for only 20 per cent of flexible packaging material sold. In other words, the market was not the market for cellophane but the market for all flexible packaging materials. However, this was a narrow decision that might well have gone the other way. And in some cases, the market is defined as a marketing section of the country rather than as the whole of the United States. In that event a single company's share may amount to a large percentage even though it is not a very important factor in the U.S. market as a whole.

Thus it is not surprising that the antitrust laws have made some companies wary of competing too strenuously. If they were to push their sales efforts as hard as they could, they might—in view of the quality of their products, their ability to make them cheaply, and their resources—end by driving their main competitors out of business or achieving so large a share of the market that they would be liable to prosecution. And it is not any given percentage of the market that is likely to cause trouble since the matter is decided on a case-by-case basis.

The penalties for violating antitrust laws may be heavy. It is true that criminal action and prison sentences are not likely except when deliberate violation (such as conspiracy to fix prices) is believed to have taken place. But even civil actions, which are much more frequent than criminal actions, may bring difficult consequences. A company may have to go to considerable trouble and expense to divest itself of an acquisition that has been found illegal, or it may have to discard plans in which it had placed great hopes because the Department of Justice will not permit a proposed merger.

Tax laws

Many companies, of course, are in little danger of trouble from the antitrust laws; they are operating in crowded fields in which competition does not let up for an instant. However, taxes affect management decisions in practically every case, not only Federal but state and municipal taxes as well.

The principal tax, and the one that most widely affects business decisions, is the Federal corporate income tax, which is levied on company profits. The rate for a number of years has been around 50 per cent on profits above $25,000. This, of course, cuts the profits available for distribution by the same amount. Further, it limits the amounts that can be plowed back into the business.

The effect of the corporate income tax on methods of raising new money has already been noted, but there are a number of other ways in which the tax rates influence business decisions. One of these has been to make some companies more liberal with their spending. Profits are what remains after all costs have been paid; hence a company is actually cutting its profits by only about half a dollar for every dollar it spends.

It cannot, however, consider that a new plant will cost only around 50 cents on the dollar, because money spent for expansion is what is known as "capital money." A simple illustration will show how this differs from "expense money," which is tax-deductible: If a company has $1 million in the bank and builds a new plant at a cost of $1 million, it now has a plant worth $1 million instead of the cash. In other words, it has merely changed the *form* of its assets; it has not spent them. Money spent for necessary repairs to a plant, on the other hand, would most likely be considered expense and would be tax-deductible as part of the cost of doing business. Thus it may be the part of wisdom, other things being equal, to do things in such a way that as many expenditures as possible are expensed rather than capitalized.

Another feature of the corporate income tax law is one of the most important determinants of business policy: the provision for tax-loss carry-forwards. If a company sustains a loss of earnings in any one year, that loss can offset an equivalent amount of earnings in any of the following five years. Thus a company that lost $1 million in each of two years might pay no taxes on earnings of $1 million in each of the next two. This provision tends to encourage mergers with companies that have sustained losses in past years but have good prospects of earning money in the future, although there must be some economic or technological justification for such tax-loss mergers if the benefits are to be realized.

Even the form in which the accounting records are kept may affect taxes. For example, a company has an inventory of steel ingots, bought at different times for prices ranging from, say, $100 to $200 a ton. These ingots are identical and are used to make the same product. Should the cost of the material be considered $100 or $200? In times of rising prices, companies have found it advantageous to use what is known as the last-in–first-out method (LIFO) of inventory accounting, under which the latest price is considered the cost, and profits for tax purposes are reduced. If prices are falling, however, the material first purchased will have cost more, and the opposite method—first-in–first-out (FIFO)—will enable the company to keep a larger percentage of its income.

Either of these methods is permissible under the income tax laws, but there is a catch. A company cannot elect one method one year and another the next. It must keep its records on a consistent basis, no matter where the chips may fall. Thus when a company elects a given method, it must bet that its view of current price trends is the correct one.

Finally, recent studies seem to indicate that many corporations are tending to treat profits substantially as an after-tax phenomenon. Thus the corporate income tax is considered a cost of doing business rather than a result of profit maximization. In this case, the corporate tax is one of the main variables taken into account in all planning.

Antipollution laws

Of growing importance in recent years, also, are the laws against the pollution of air and water. These are mainly state laws, but the Federal government is empowered to act in certain cases, as when pollution originating in one state affects the air or the water in another state.

Many industrial processes produce dusts or fumes that can be harmful or annoying to human beings or damaging to materials or vegetation. This has always been true, but when plants were smaller and fewer, the concentrations were not so great and in any case were likely to affect only small areas. Now there is so much industrial activity that the clean-air problem has become very serious, and legislation has been enacted as a result. There is a rising social cost which is not being paid for from private gains.

Similarly, a very small operation is unlikely to pollute river water to any great extent; but if it becomes large—or if several plants are discharging effluent from, say, plating baths to a river—the water may become so polluted that all marine life dies, swimming and boating are impossible, and other plants that need the river water for their processes find that they cannot use it.

New processes and changes in processes may also contribute to the pollution—as one example, there may be danger that radioactive materials will be discharged to a river and affect the water even a hundred miles downstream.

When a company is ordered to cease discharging pollutants into the atmosphere or the public waterways, it may have to comply within a given length of time or shut down its operations. Thus it may have to spend large amounts of money for expensive treatment facilities or change its processes in some way to ensure that they produce fewer pollutants.

This, of course, is only just. No one can seriously argue that any individual or organization has a right to pollute the air and water that are the common property of all. But it does limit top management's freedom to act, since in reckoning the cost of an expansion or a change in processes, it must take into account not only the cost of purchasing the new equipment necessary for production and installing it but also the cost of any new equipment it must install to control possible pollutants. Occasionally, the control of pollutants makes it possible for the company to recover reusable material and even produces a net gain. But, more often, the control simply increases costs.

Labor laws

Labor laws narrow the framework of management in two ways. In some cases, they impose direct restraints; in others, they make it easier for employees to form unions and impose still further restraints.

The first type of legislation is exemplified by the Fair Labor Standards Act of 1938, which sets a minimum hourly wage (raised from time to time) for workers in interstate commerce or engaged in production of goods for interstate commerce. It also provides for the payment of time and a half for hours over forty a week. There are many state laws of this nature, too, and some that deal with the hours and working conditions of women and minors.

The other type of legislation, that governing relations between management and unions, has perhaps had more far-reaching effects.

In the early part of the nineteenth century, labor unions were often held to be "criminal conspiracies," and those who organized them could be punished by the courts. This later gave way to the idea that unions were entirely legal, but could expect no help from the law. Thus a businessman was free to require his employees to agree not to join a union as a condition of employment. He could also get the courts to enjoin most of the actions that would make a strike effective. "There is and can be no such thing as peaceful picketing, any more than there can be chaste vulgarity," a Federal court held in 1905.[4]

The Clayton Act exempted unions from the Sherman Antitrust Act and also made peaceful picketing legal. But state laws designed to make the latter provision effective were held unconstitutional.

Some strong unions did exist under these circumstances, but the great mass of industrial employees was largely unorganized and had to bargain individually with employers on wages and hours. In times of labor scarcity, the employer might find it necessary to offer concessions in order to get people to work for him; but for the most part he could set wages and hours unilaterally.

The first break in this situation came in 1932,[5] when the Norris-La Guardia Act forbade the use of the injunction in labor disputes and outlawed the "yellow dog" contracts (as union men called them) under which the employee signed an agreement not to join a union. The employer was still free, however, to fire him if he did join.

With the passage of the National Labor Relations Act of 1935 (the Wagner Act), however, union organization received a tremendous impetus. Under this

4 Benjamin Aaron, "Changing Legal Concepts and Industrial Conflict," in Arthur Kornhauser, Robert Dubin, and Arthur M. Ross (eds.), *Industrial Conflict*, McGraw-Hill Book Company, New York, 1954, p. 420.
5 The first break, that is, so far as labor in general was concerned. As early as 1892, hours of labor on government contracts (with several exceptions) were limited to eight unless the employer paid time and a half for the overtime (the Eight Hour Law); and the Davis-Bacon Act of 1931 made it necessary for government construction contractors to pay "prevailing wages" in the area in which the work was done. In 1926 the Railway Labor Act compelled employers to bargain with the unions.

law, employers were forbidden to fire employees for union activity; moreover, they were compelled to bargain in good faith with a union if a majority of the employees in a given group or "bargaining unit" voted to be represented by it.

The National Labor Relations Board was created to administer the act— to decide on cases of "unfair labor practices," including discharge of workers because of union activity, and to conduct elections to determine whether or not employees wished to be represented by a union and if so, by which one. It also had the power to define the bargaining unit—that is, those who were entitled to vote in a representation election. This last power is an extremely important one because the inclusion of groups of workers among the voters can drastically affect the results of the election. For example, white-collar employees, who are generally much less inclined to unionization than factory workers, have not been allowed to influence union acceptance by production and maintenance employees.

The Wagner Act was entirely devoted to setting forth the rights of employees and unions. It was based on the premise that the employers had all the rights to begin with and that the balance could be redressed only by restricting their actions. For example, the only unfair labor practices listed were those that could be committed by employers.

In 1947, however, a new labor relations act was passed: the Labor Management Relations Act of 1947 (the Taft-Hartley Act). This listed possible unfair labor practices by unions as well as employers, made it possible for employers to sue unions for violation of contract, and outlawed closed shop contract provisions, under which employers may hire only union members.

The basic provisions of the Wagner Act, however, remain largely unchanged. It is illegal for an employer to discriminate against an employee or threaten him because of union membership, or to refuse to bargain collectively with a union that has proved, by an NLRB election, that it represents the majority of the employees in a given bargaining unit.

In addition, of course, there are many state laws governing relations between employees and employers, conditions of work, and the rules under which collective bargaining is conducted.

LIMITATIONS IMPOSED BY UNIONS

There are two types of unions: craft unions and industrial unions. The former include only members of a given trade or craft (carpenters, say, or electricians); the latter attempt to take in all the rank-and-file employees in a plant.

Craft unionism is somewhat the older form. Although there had been attempts at industrial unionism earlier, it never gained much of a foothold until the 1930s, when the American Federation of Labor, whose membership included most of the craft unions, appointed a Committee on Industrial Organization under the leadership of John L. Lewis, president of the United Mine Workers. Many of the industrial unions, which were organized rapidly shortly after this, later split off from the AFL and formed their own federation, the Congress of Industrial Organizations, or CIO.

Some of the industrial unions remained in the AFL, but its membership was in general made up of the older craft unions, which tended to practice what is known as "business unionism"—that is, their main aim in collective bargaining was to obtain higher wages and/or shorter hours for their members. The CIO unions, on the other hand, leaned toward "welfare unionism"—the pioneering of new demands for various types of fringe benefits, such as company-paid pensions, life insurance, hospitalization, paid holidays, and so on—and toward political action.

With the passage of the years, however, the two federations came closer together. Many AFL unions became quite as interested in welfare as any CIO union, and obtained many of the same benefits. By the early 1950s, there was no longer much real distinction between the two, and in 1955 both recognized this fact and united under the name of the AFL-CIO.

Not all unions belong to the Federation, however. Some have been expelled for bad behavior (because they were thought to be dishonestly run or because their leadership seemed to be tainted with communism). Others have never cared to join, and still others have "disaffiliated" because they disagreed with Federation policies (e.g., the United Mine Workers). A third type of unaffiliated union is the "independent," whose membership is usually confined to employees of one company.

Unions making up the Federation are known as national or international[6] unions. Membership in these bodies is organized into locals, which generally include employees of a single company or a single plant. Thus when a man joins a union, he becomes a member of the local, which automatically makes him a member of the national or international union, and his dues are divided between the local and the parent body.

In negotiations to arrive at a union contract, management may bargain either with the local representatives or, if it is a very large company, with the representatives of the parent body. In the former case, however, representatives of the national or international are likely to be on hand to assist the local officers, and the parent union may refuse to okay a union contract unless certain minimum concessions are obtained. And sometimes a contract negotiated with the national or international union is supplemented by extra clauses negotiated by the local.

Thus it is first the national or international, and second the local, that impose restrictions on management through the process of collective bargaining. The extent of those restrictions depends on the strength of the union vis-à-vis management, locally and in the country at large, and on what management, both in the company and in the industry, has agreed to in the past. The restrictions, therefore, differ among industries and among companies. However, certain clauses are common to practically all contracts.

---

[6] Some unions have members in Canada, Puerto Rico, and other areas outside continental United States, but none is international in the sense that it has, or claims, worldwide jurisdiction. For a more detailed description of the organization of unions see Neil W. Chamberlain, *Sourcebook on Labor*, McGraw-Hill Book Company, New York, 1958, pp. 53–177.

Effect on costs

In the first place, the union contract is likely to increase costs, since most unions are able to negotiate higher wage rates than are called for in the Fair Labor Standards Act or than the company would otherwise have to pay in order to obtain workers in the current labor market. Second, whereas the Fair Labor Standards Act provides merely for time and a half for overtime, a union contract may call for double time, or even triple time, for overtime over a certain amount. Again, under the Fair Labor Standards Act, the normal working week is considered to be eight hours a day and forty hours a week. But some unions have succeeded in shortening the "normal" time so that overtime payments begin sooner. Premium pay for second- and third-shift work is also common.

These provisions reduce not only management's control over its costs but its flexibility in making changes in work schedules. For example, it might wish to increase production by adding an extra shift or an extra day to the workweek but find the cost prohibitive because of the premium pay.

But the money clauses are only part of the story. There are two other usual clauses that provide further restrictions.

Grievances and seniority

One of these is the clause providing for a *grievance procedure*. Under this provision an employee who feels that he has not been accorded his rights under the union contract may bring a formal grievance and take it up through several steps, the last of which is likely to be a hearing before an arbitrator who is hired, and paid, by both the union and the company. The arbitrator's decision is binding on both parties.

> A *Three-step Grievance Procedure*
> Step 1   The aggrieved employee, in company with the union steward (a fellow employee elected to union office by the men in the shop), discusses the grievance with his foreman. If he is not satisfied, the grievance is put in writing and taken up by—
> Step 2   The plant manager and the head of industrial relations on the company's part, and the international representative and the union steward on the employee's part. If an agreement that satisfies the employee and the union cannot be reached—
> Step 3   The grievance is taken to arbitration.

Theoretically, an employee may bring a grievance only when the company or one of its representatives has violated a provision of the union contract. In practice, grievances are apt to cover a much wider area since the union contract will not deal with all possible cases and in some cases its language will be ambiguous.

One of the commonest types of grievance is the protest against disciplinary action: An employee who is fired or laid off without pay for what management considers good cause will take the case up through the procedure to arbitration. The arbitrator may summarily rescind the penalty and order reinstate-ment (with back pay) or reduce the punishment; dismissal may be changed to a few days' layoff, for example.

Grievances may arise also over such matters as the operation of an incentive system, the transfer of an employee to lower-paid work, coffee breaks, over-time, and any number of other things. The attitude the union is likely to take, therefore, is a factor in management decisions in these areas.

The second practically universal clause in union contracts is the *seniority clause,* under which length of service brings certain rights. If a company finds it necessary to lay off a part of its work force, it must generally let men go in reverse seniority order: those who were hired last must be dismissed first. Then, when it calls back employees who have been laid off, it must call back those with the most seniority first. Seniority may also affect promotions.

Most managers have no quarrel with seniority as a general principle. In fact, other things being equal, it would probably be their policy to give prefer-ence to senior men in promotions, layoffs, and recalls. But seniority as a hard and fast rule involves complications. If a senior man's job is abolished, he may have the privilege of "bumping" another man with less seniority and taking his job. Then the second man may bump someone else with still less seniority, and the game of musical chairs will go on until the most recently hired man turns out to have no job at all. If all employees had the same skill and were doing the same kind of work, the system might not present too great a problem for management. But this is hardly ever true, and management may lose some of its most valuable men in the process while retaining others who are not of great use.

Again, seniority is likely to affect management's freedom of choice in mak-ing a promotion to, say, first-line foreman. Commonly the union contract will specify that where ability is equal, seniority will prevail. But it is very difficult to "prove" that one man has greater ability than another. Further, unions usually try to have such a clause interpreted to mean that the man with the most seniority should get the job if he *can* do the work, even though someone with less seniority might be able to do it better.

Other union restraints

The matter of overtime is another moot point. Since overtime pays time and a half, workers generally like it; and unions try to give all their members a chance at it. Hence they will generally seek a clause providing for "equalization of overtime" within departments or subgroups. But this may be difficult to arrange. Take a repair that must be made during the off-shift hours when the machines are not operating. There may be several men who qualify as machine repairmen but only two or three who have experience on the particular machine. Thus it will be hard to equalize overtime if that particular piece of equipment is a frequent cause of trouble.

Then there are the jurisdictional matters that arise when management deals with more than one union, as it quite often does. Each union will want to keep its members employed so far as possible; therefore each will insist that certain types of work are within its jurisdiction, and management will be caught in the middle. Conversely, some unions may have rules regarding work that their members cannot do because they consider it unworthy of skilled men. Thus a company may have to have an electrician disconnect a machine and a mill-wright carry it down to the shop for electricians and machinists to work on. Even where all are members of an industrial union, which is one that includes all crafts, distinctions of this nature may exist, and they make for an inflexible work force.

And in even more important matters, unions may impinge heavily on what management considers its right to manage. Contract clauses may restrict its right to move work from one plant to another, to purchase parts from outside, to hire construction contractors. Management may even find that it is not free to close one plant and open another without difficulties with the union.

TECHNOLOGICAL LIMITATIONS

A company is, of course, free to develop new technology if it has the ability to do so, but only in exceptional cases can it free itself from the technological limitations imposed by the equipment currently on the market. And other technological limitations are the result of external conditions entirely beyond its control—for example, the location of the sources of its raw material.

The technology may dictate the comparative importance of the various departments within the company. In companies that depend on a flow of new products, for example, the scientist is of increasing importance. And the growing complexity of the technology in many industries has dictated the hiring of more engineers, which may mean that top managers will come from the engineering ranks in the future.

As one gets to know more managers, it seems increasingly possible to identify them as "automotive men" or "oil men," just as one may recognize the geographical origin of a man from the South or the Midwest. Although management makes many decisions about the product, the product tends to shape the manager to some extent. The raw material specifications, the nature of the production process, the kind of machinery, the requirements of quality control—all these tend to influence and to limit the style of management.

Among the principal ways in which technology imposes limitations are the following.

Location

Management's actions always have been, and still are, limited by the need to observe certain principles in the location of its operations. In the days before efficient transportation, distribution of the product was confined to an area within a short radius of the place of production, the more so the bulkier the product. Thus the increased efficiency that might have been obtained through operations on a larger scale would often have been offset by the cost of the extra transportation necessary to tap a wider market.

In spite of greatly improved transportation, this factor is still a major limitation on management today. For example, in one of the newer industries, the production of mobile homes, it is crucial. Since it costs $1 a mile to transport a single home, a plant that produces a home at a cost $500 below that of a competitor 500 miles away will be barely able to meet the latter's prices in his home city. Thus the size of a plant may depend on the radius of the circle within which its goods can be profitably distributed and on the density of the population within that circle.

In determining the place of production, management is likely to be limited by the following considerations: If the raw material is heavier and more expensive to carry than the end product, then production must take place near the place where the material is available. If, on the other hand, the final product is more costly to carry than the raw material because it is heavier, bulkier, or more fragile, then production must be carried on at or near the place of final consumption. (A conventional house, for example, would be much more expensive to transport in its completed form than the raw materials; hence it is built on the site where it will be used.) If several materials that are expensive to transport will be used, management must weigh a number of factors in relation to each other.

Another technological limitation on location is the availability of water and power, and the former is likely to become increasingly important because the demand for water has been growing much faster than the population. Many industries require enormous quantities of water; therefore they must locate either near a river or in an area where water is close enough to the surface of the ground to make well digging practical. Again, it may be worthwhile for a large operation to construct its own power plant, but a smaller one will find it more economical to locate its factory where power is readily available from a public utility.

If a plant is located in or near a large city, many advantages (called "external economies") are available to it, advantages that it cannot get if it "goes out into the cornfield," as building far out in the country is often called. There will be, for instance, suppliers who can rush parts to it when machines break down, whereas the plant in a remote location may have to maintain a large inventory of spares (often an expensive proposition) or wait days or weeks for replacement. In addition, there will probably be skilled labor available in a densely populated area; in the cornfield, the company may have to spend extra money and time on training.

But city land is more expensive, and a location in a densely populated area often limits expansion drastically. It may be simply impossible to obtain more space, even at a premium price, because the plant is bounded by public streets or by buildings whose owners have no desire to sell them.

Size

To produce a single copy of a metropolitan daily newspaper, complete with news, features, pictures, and advertisements, would cost almost as much as it does to produce the hundreds of thousands of copies ordinarily printed. The editorial and advertising departments could be no smaller; the same amount of type would have to be set. The only savings would be in newsprint, ink, the pressroom, and the circulation department.

This illustrates the big advantage of mass production. Once production is set up and ready to go, costs do not increase in direct proportion to increases in output. But this factor itself imposes limitations on top management.

In the dress industry, which is still largely unmechanized, a small plant can be profitable. In the automobile industry, on the other hand, costs of tooling up to produce a single model and setting up the production are so heavy that only a large plant is possible.

Thus the economic size of a plant depends on the technology of the products, and management must figure as nearly as possible what that size is. If the plant is too small, the overhead component of unit cost will be so large that management can never make a profit even if the plant produces at capacity. If the plant is too large, it may reach the point where communication and coordination become so difficult that waste and confusion develop.

There is no general agreement on what the optimum economic size of plant is in any given industry. It is possible to calculate how small a plant may be and still make a profit (provided one is sure that prices will not drop too far); but the point where diminishing returns set in from increasing size is more difficult to determine. Some companies discover it only by trial and error.

However, most companies do have a general idea of economic size and try not to have any single plant exceed it. This means that after a certain point, expansion must take the form of opening new plants rather than of increasing the size of the original operations.

Often plants big enough to be of economic size, and especially multiplant operations, impose additional limitations on top management. In a small operation, the manager is in personal contact with and in direct command of all his subordinates; hence he requires little in the way of formal management techniques. In a somewhat larger operation, he may still know all his subordinates but be unable to oversee their work. He must, therefore, work through subordinate managers. The final and most difficult stage is reached when the manager has to get results through a great many people, most of whom he may never even meet. At this point he has to introduce many formal methods of management to overcome the difficulties of communication: policy guides, job descriptions, organization charts, committees.

Mechanization and automation

Advances in technology have come rapidly in recent years. While the mechanization of work, that is, the substitution of machinery for hand labor, took a long time, there has been a speedup with the advent of automation processes in which products or parts are passed automatically from one automatic operation to another, emerging in a finished state without the need for human hands.

For example, there is a machine that can turn out hundreds of glass incandescent lamp bulbs a minute, performing a series of operations that were once performed separately. Only one operator is needed, as compared to the large number required for separate processes. And in addition to producing lamp bulbs, it can turn out other related products.[7]

Feedback, or self-monitoring, is another feature of automation. Many machines can sense when they have made a mistake and either correct the error or flash a signal that attention is needed. For example, a grinding machine can automatically correct itself if it has ground a piece with a diameter either too small or too large and make the next piece either smaller or larger as necessary.[8]

Numerically controlled machines and systems are run by punched tape, which provides all the directions they need to continue performing an operation. Thus:

> A reading device transmits to the machine the proper feeds and speeds, moves the work table into the proper position. . . . It does the work of the human operator in preparing the machine for the next operation to be performed, "remembering" a long series of required operations and repeating them without error and without hesitation.[9]

Like other advances in mechanization, automation has freed management from some technical limitations, especially limitations on the amount of output possible with a given number of workers. But it has not by any means removed all technological limitations imposed by production processes.

In the first place, not all industries are automated, nor can they be at the present stage of technology. In some, many hand operations are still needed, and in others only partial automation is feasible. Even in the automobile industry, which is considered quite highly automated, it is not possible to throw in material at one end of a transfer machine system and have a finished car emerge at the other end. Only parts and sections of the car can be produced automatically. Completely automatic production is generally possible only in the production of bulk products, such as chemicals, steel, or oil.

In the second place, many of the old technological limitations on management still exist, despite greatly improved equipment. And in the third place, automation itself has introduced some new limitations.

[7] Robert A. Brady, *Organization, Automation, and Society,* University of California Press, Berkeley, Calif., 1963, pp. 236–237.
[8] M. A. Hollengreen, "Automation in the Metal Working Industries," in Howard Boone Jacobson and Joseph S. Roucek (eds.), *Automation and Society,* Philosophical Library, Inc., New York, 1959, p. 59.
[9] *Ibid.,* p. 60.

Since automation increases the costs that go on whether a plant is producing or not, management may not have the same flexibility in responding to
market demand that it had formerly. Plant and equipment must be fully utilized
because of the higher overhead costs. Therefore management cannot expand
or contract its operations as easily as it could when it could do so merely by
hiring or laying off people.

Flexibility is also reduced because changeover from one type of product to
another, or even to a greatly changed model, may be more difficult.

Then closer tolerances may be required if the transfer machines are to
handle the parts efficiently and turn and position them between one operation
and the next. Further, the more complicated the transfer mechanism, the more
likely it is to cause difficulty. For this reason, it is sometimes easier and
cheaper to interpose manual operations at some stages in the system.

A further difficulty is that a failure in one part of the system may be more
serious than a failure that occurs where separate machines are being used.
Parts may be piling up at the point where the breakdown occurs while the
system beyond it may be "starved" for something to work on.

Sometimes the automated system is so large that different manufacturers
must be engaged to build parts of it. Then the various parts may not work
together when they are finally assembled. In any case, some debugging is
likely to be required after the system is installed in the purchaser's plant. This
may range all the way from simple adjustments to redesign of many components.

SUMMARY

The external environment of the corporation limits the possibilities open to top
management in many ways. First of all, there is the state of the economy,
which has a major influence on the amount of money a company can hope to
take in, and hence on its plans for the future. And if a company wants to
borrow money or raise new capital by selling stock, it is limited by the practices of financial institutions and by the amount the general public is willing
to pay for its securities.

Top management is also circumscribed by laws, Federal and state, and by
municipal ordinances. The chief Federal laws that affect the conduct of business in general are the antitrust laws, the Federal tax laws, and the various
laws governing management's conduct toward its employees and their unions.

A third type of limitation is imposed by unions, which may succeed in
obtaining contracts that both affect major management decisions and impose
restraints on managers all down the line in the day-to-day management of the
work. Actually, at some times and in some places, unions have participated in
decisions on plant location, on price and dividend policy, and even on products. And, in addition to influencing wage rates and other labor costs (e.g.,

the cost of fringe benefits), a union often limits management's ability to hire and fire, to make promotions and transfers, to impose discipline, and to make job assignments and employ contractors.

Technological limitations are imposed by the product and the production process. They may dictate decisions on plant location, the size of the plant, and the amount of capital that is necessary. Mechanization, and later automation, have freed management from some limitations that existed in the past, but they have also imposed new ones. The technology of the industry may also influence the importance of the various departments within the plant and the type of manager required.

Review Questions

1. What is equity financing? What is debt financing?
2. If you were head of a company that wished to raise new money, which type of financing would you prefer today? Why?
3. What are the advantages of leasing?
4. What is the "time value of money"?
5. What is the difference between "vertical" and "horizontal" mergers?
6. What are the main provisions of the Sherman Act and the Clayton Act?
7. How did the Labor Management Relations Act of 1947 (Taft-Hartley) modify the provisions of the National Labor Relations Act (Wagner Act) of 1935?
8. What are some of the ways in which unions may restrict management's freedom to manage?
9. What is the difference between a craft union and an industrial union?
10. What is a jurisdictional dispute?
11. How does the nature of the product sometimes dictate company location?
12. What limitations may technology impose on size?
13. What are some of the limitations imposed by automation?

Case Study One / Audubon's New Plant*

The Audubon Plumbing Company, maker of plumber's tools and equipment, operates in an old plant in downtown Newark, New Jersey. The plant—dark, multistory and hemmed in by slums—was built around the turn of the cen-

* Reprinted by permission of Peter F. Drucker.

tury and is not at all adapted to modern production methods. The fact that modern flow of materials and parts is hardly feasible because of the plant's multistory character means, for instance, an addition to manufacturing costs conservatively estimated at 10 per cent, or $300,000 a year. And it is likely that there are other costs that would not occur in a modern single-story plant with enough elbowroom.

In addition, expansion is impossible in Newark. The plant is surrounded by residential buildings, and even if they could be bought up for a reasonable amount, a city ordinance forbids additional manufacturing in the area. Nor is there any way out through multishift operations. In fact, the plant is only allowed to operate one shift, again because of a city ordinance, and would not be able to get away with any violation of this order since its air blower can be heard twenty blocks away.

For these reasons the company has long thought about building elsewhere and has actually bought a suitable piece of land some 25 miles outside Newark. For management and for most of the workers, the new location would actually be more convenient because it is closer to some of the newer suburbs than the downtown district.

To build the new plant—one-story with some room for expansion—would cost about $3 million. In addition, the company would have to rent small sales offices and a small warehouse in downtown Newark to cater to local trade, which is about one-third of its total business. The rental cost is estimated at $45,000 a year minimum.

There is one more piece of relevant information: About one-third of the company's present machinery is getting obsolete and will have to be replaced soon at a minimum cost of $450,000 if the company remains at its present location. However, in a new plant this machinery would not be needed and could simply be scrapped without replacement. Two-shift operations would be possible there, and the company has enough first-rate modern machinery to turn out its entire volume on it, given two shifts rather than one.

The company has enough money to buy the new machinery it needs. But it does not have the capital for a $3 million building; it would have to obtain the capital from the outside—something it has never done before. The company is family-owned; and, except for an occasional credit on receivables or raw material inventories, it has never gone to the banks. Net profit, before taxes but after generous salaries to the members of the family in the management, has been running at 8 per cent of sales, i.e., at $300,000 a year.

1. Should the company build the new plant? (Disregard all questions of timing.)
2. If so, what are the factors the Audubons should consider in regard to the financing? What would be the ideal financing for them?
3. Do you know enough about the capital market today to say what kind of financing they are most likely to get, and what it would cost them?

Case Study Two / Union Opposition to Computerization

A large company wanted to install a computer to speed up the reporting of vital statistical information. Its clerical workers were unionized, and the union representative strenuously objected to (1) shifting workers to other jobs, to which they would not be accustomed and which they might not like and (2) the possibility that some workers might be laid off because of the greater mechanization of the clerical work. The union therefore requested that some of the new employees—programmers, coders, systems builders, and administrators—join the union if the computer were installed. Management flatly rejected the union's request.

1.   What were management's reasons?
2.   What action do you think the union took?
3.   What do you think the final outcome of the dispute was?

Note: In this case, the company is in an industry whose labor relations are regulated by the Railway Labor Act. This differs from the National Labor Relations Act in that subordinate officials may be included in the bargaining unit, although there is no definition of "subordinate officials" as distinct from true managers. A body known as the National Mediation Board has the power to determine the bargaining unit, and it might quite possibly determine that the new employees were members of the unit. If so, in any representation election they would be easily outvoted by the more numerous clerical employees.

4.   Can you write a definition that will distinguish management from those who properly belong to the bargaining unit?

Case Study Three / Sleeping Employees

An employee was discovered by his foreman asleep on the job. Up to this point the foreman had considered him an excellent employee—skilled, intelligent, and willing. In fact, he was studying engineering at night, with company encouragement, and it was probably because of his heavy schedule that he fell asleep during working hours.

The foreman who discovered him asleep merely woke him up, accepted his apology, and told him to "watch it" in the future.

Later on, he discovered another man sleeping on the job, reported the matter to his superiors, and gained their consent to discharge the offender. The second man brought a grievance, claiming that he was being discriminated against because he was active in the union and had brought up several grievances against the foreman in the past. The union supported him, and the case went to arbitration.

The foreman and the company contended that the nap was only the last straw. The man was an inept workman, truculent and disagreeable at all times; in fact, there had been some talk of discharging him during his probationary period, but the foreman had decided to give him the benefit of the doubt. To which the union replied, "You're claiming all these things now, but there's no proof that they are true. If the man didn't make the grade, you could have discharged him while he was on probation. When you took him on permanently, you tacitly admitted that he was qualified—you say you had doubts, but if so you never said anything to him about them. It's a clear case of a man's being fired because he has insisted on his rights under the union contract. Another man who fell asleep wasn't fired."

1. If you were the arbitrator, what would you decide? Why?
2. Assuming the foreman was telling the truth, what could he have done earlier to make a stronger case for the company's position at this point?

Selected Readings

Financial limitations

The Financial Manager: Basic Aspects of Financial Administration, Jerome B. Cohen and Sidney M. Robbins, Harper & Row, Publishers, New York, 1966. Discussion based on actual practice and the latest developments in financial theory.

Basic Business Finance, Pearson Hunt, Charles M. Williams, and Gordon Donaldson, Richard D. Irwin, Inc., Homewood, Ill., 1958. A book dealing with many phases of business finance, including control of investment in inventory, receivables, plant investment, sources and uses of funds, capital budgeting, government regulations (Federal regulation of new issues, limitations imposed by the Securities & Exchange Commission), dividend policy, recapitalization, mergers and failures, financing new enterprises.

Enterprise and Environment: The Firm in Time and Place, Neil W. Chamberlain, McGraw-Hill Book Company, New York, 1968. The author finds that although the constraints imposed by the environment are continually closing off opportunities for business firms, at the same time the changes in the environment are opening up new opportunities for them.

The Financial Policy of Corporations, 5th ed., Arthur Stone Dewing, The Ronald Press Company, New York, 1953, 2 vols. A clear explanation of the nature of the corporation and of many aspects of business finance, including valuation of a corporation, administration of income, methods of financing expansion, and financial reorganization.

Security Analysis, 4th ed., B. Graham, D. L. Dodd, and S. Cottle, McGraw-Hill Book Company, New York, 1962. An analysis of the major types of securities financing from the viewpoint of the stockholder.

Legal limitations

Legal Foundations of Capitalism, John R. Commons, The Macmillan Company, New York, 1924. An important book in which one of the great realistic economists considers the discontinuity of the economic process and the difficulty of making predictions, which he believes arise from institutional limitations on business and from the fact that social objectives can be set only by collective reasoning.

The Legal Environment of Business, James L. Houghteling and George G. Pierce, Harcourt, Brace & World, Inc., New York, 1964. The processes by which the law is created and molded to meet changing needs, and its application to specific cases.

Competition as a Dynamic Process, John Maurice Clark, The Brookings Institution, Washington, D.C., 1961. An analysis of modern analytical thinking on competition and its objectives.

Social Control of Business, 2d ed., John Maurice Clark, McGraw-Hill Book Company, New York, 1939. The development and purpose of government controls, their principal instruments, control of utilities and trusts.

Competition, Cartels and Their Regulation, John Perry Miller (ed.), North Holland Publishing Company, Amsterdam, 1962. Nine essays by well-known American and European authors. They discuss the evolution, content, and experience of a public policy for competition in the United States, England, and various European countries.

Cases in Antitrust Policy, Paul W. Cook, Jr., Holt, Rinehart and Winston, Inc., New York, 1964. A short volume of case material that emphasizes policy rather than legal or historical issues.

Effect of Federal Taxes on Growing Enterprises, J. Keith Butters and John Lintner, Division of Research, Graduate School of Business Administration, Harvard University, Boston, Mass., 1945. Restraints imposed by Federal taxes and opportunities for saving.

Limitations imposed by unions

The Union Challenge to Management Control, Neil W. Chamberlain, Harper & Row, Publishers, Incorporated, New York, 1948. A theoretical and field study of the extent of union participation in management decisions.

Collective Bargaining, 2d ed., Neil W. Chamberlain and James W. Kuhn, McGraw-Hill Book Company, New York, 1965. An up-to-date account of the limitations imposed by unions, especially at top union and management levels as well as with public authorities.

Technological limitations

Organization, Automation and Society, Robert A. Brady, University of California Press, Berkeley, Calif., 1963. One of the most comprehensive studies of the impact of technology in a number of selected industries by a noted student of big business in large industrial countries.

2

The Beginnings of Modern Management

Men have, of course, written on the management of political states for centuries, but they were seldom concerned with business management as such or with the applicability of their theories to business. In contrast, today's management studies are almost entirely concerned with business management or with the type of government management that is very closely related to business management—for example, the administration of government departments in a businesslike manner.

Although there are many men who might be described as pioneer management thinkers, those whose work is discussed in this section typify the three mainstreams of management thought today.

First, there is the view that management is or can be, at least in part, an exact science, based largely on mathematical calculations. Although some men had approached the subject in this way earlier, it was the work of Frederick Taylor and his associates in the scientific management movement that brought about widespread acceptance of the concept. Now the mathematical approach has been given tremendous impetus by the introduction of computers, and today "management science," in which mathematics play a major part, is a recognized part of management studies. (This is discussed in Chapter 29.)

The second major approach to management today is the behavioral approach, based on the theory that management is largely a matter of developing good interpersonal relationships. Members of the scientific management movement were not unaware of the importance of good human relations, but they (Taylor especially) tended to believe that pay rates were the most important factor in developing them. Elton Mayo and his associates, on the other hand, aroused management's interest in nonfinancial incentives of various kinds and in the ways they could be used to improve morale and productivity. A very large part of the experimentation and theorizing on management today is concerned with these factors and has covered not only the direction of small groups (which was Mayo's principal interest) but all other phases of management.

Henri Fayol's ideas on administration have wide influence also. In fact, up until recently, much of the work on organization theory was largely an elaboration and expansion of the fundamental concepts he expounded.

No student of management can afford to be unfamiliar with the ideas of these pioneer thinkers on management. Not only are the theories and practices they developed constantly referred to in the literature, but their concepts include much that is of practical value and use today.

However, each of the three approaches has some shortcomings; thus the good manager must use them in an eclectic way. To do so he needs to know something about the men themselves, for their predilections and experiences naturally influenced their ideas. He should also know something about the situations that gave rise to their theories. Part Two provides this background information.

6

THE

SCIENTIFIC

MANAGEMENT

MOVEMENT

Exact scientific knowledge and methods are everywhere, sooner or later, sure to replace rule-of-thumb. Frederick W. Taylor: Testimony before the Special House Committee

6　It is often said that automation and computerization are producing a "second industrial revolution" with consequences as far-reaching as those of the original Industrial Revolution. There was, however, an earlier development that was hailed as a "second industrial revolution"—the scientific management movement that hit its stride early in the twentieth century.

The founder of the movement, Frederick Winslow Taylor, began his career in the 1870s as an apprentice in a small machinery-making shop in Philadelphia. (His father was well-to-do, and he had originally intended to go to Harvard; but he had strained his eyes studying by the light of a kerosene lamp, and his doctor advised him to avoid close work.) Later he became a machinist foreman and in that capacity began the work that made him famous as "the father of scientific management."

As a foreman, the young and ambitious Taylor was naturally anxious to see his men turn out as much production as possible, but he knew it would be difficult to arouse any enthusiasm among them. They had nothing to gain if they did work harder, and it was common practice for them to do as little as they could and still get by. Taylor even sympathized with their attitude; he himself had followed the same system when he was a day laborer. Later he wrote:

> When a naturally energetic man works for a few days besides a lazy one, the logic of the situation is unanswerable: "Why should I work hard when that lazy fellow gets the same pay that I do and does only half as much work?"[1]

Some jobs lent themselves to piecework—that is, the men were paid so much per piece produced—but employers were very likely to cut the piece rate as soon as production rose. In consequence, there was more holding back on piecework than there was when the men worked for a daily wage.

Since he had been a machinist himself, Taylor was familiar with the tricks used by the men and knew very well that output was about a third of what it might have been. He asked the machinists to produce more, and nothing happened. He operated a lathe himself and showed them that it could be done. Again nothing happened. Finally he decided to take "the next step," which, he had warned them, would be "a durned mean one."[2]

The durned mean step was to bring in some of the more intelligent laborers and teach them how to run lathes. In return for the opportunity to learn a good trade, they promised to do a fair day's work. But the pressures from their associates were too strong. The laborers who had been trained as machinists kept production down just as much as the original machinists did. So Taylor cut their pay rates in half. Later he testified:

> These men, of course, went to the management and protested I was a

---

[1] "Shop Management," in *Scientific Management*, Harper & Row, Publishers, Incorporated, New York, 1947, p. 31.
[2] "Testimony before the Special House Committee," in *ibid.*, p. 81.

tyrant . . . and for a long time they stood right by the rest of the men in the shop and refused to increase their output a particle. Finally, they all of a sudden gave right in and did a fair day's work. . . . [Then] they played what is usually the winning card. . . . Every time I broke a rate or forced one of the new men to work . . . at a reasonable and proper speed, some one of the machinists would deliberately break some part of his machine as an object lesson to demonstrate to the management that a fool foreman was driving the men to overload their machines until they broke.''[3]

Taylor had known this was coming and had told his superiors what would happen. And he had obtained their promise to back him up when he attempted countermeasures. What he did was to fine every man whose machine broke down and to accept no excuses whatsoever—he knew that a "good excuse," impossible to disprove, would always be forthcoming. So he told them, "I don't care if the roof falls in and breaks your machine, you will pay all the same.''[4]

After three years of battling, Taylor had his way, but he found the hostility he encountered in the shop during the transition period unbearable, particularly since he had been on very friendly terms with the men originally. If there were no better way of bringing about increased productivity, he felt he would rather get out of the business entirely and find some other kind of work.

THE TAYLOR SYSTEM

The real trouble, Taylor decided on reflection, was that no one knew how much work it was reasonable to expect a man to do. Either employers gauged a "fair day's work" by a general impression—gained from observation or, as in his case, by actually working on some of the jobs themselves—or they had a record of the shortest time in which certain jobs had ever been performed. And there was plenty of room for argument about either standard. Therefore he asked the president of Midvale Steel for permission to make a series of studies of the motions used in performing the various operations and the time it took to perform each one.

To this end, Taylor employed a young man to time each motion with a stopwatch. These small segments of the job (e.g., picking up a bolt and a clamp, inserting a bolthead in a machine) he called "elements," and he arrived at the total time necessary to complete a job by totaling the element times and adding allowances for brief rests and unavoidable delays. Thus it would be possible, Taylor believed, to say how much a man could produce if he did "a fair day's work," and no one could argue about the figure because it had been scientifically determined. In addition, Taylor studied both the motions themselves and

[3] *Ibid.*, pp. 83–84.
[4] *Ibid.*, p. 84.

the tools employed, with a view to learning how fewer or shorter motions could be used to accomplish the same result.

This was one beginning of time and motion study. Although there were earlier and parallel developments elsewhere, it was mainly Taylor's work that started systematic use of the plan in industry.

Another phase of the Taylor system was a new payment plan that Taylor called "differential piecework," a plan designed to enlist the cooperation of the workers. Under this system, a man received one piece rate if he produced the standard number of pieces and another rate if he met or surpassed the standard, and in the latter case, the higher rate would be applied to all the pieces he produced, not merely to those over the standard. For example, if the regular rate were 50 cents per piece and the differential rate were 60 cents per piece, the man who produced only three pieces a day would get $1.50, whereas the man who produced four would get $2.40, or 60 per cent more. Management, Taylor said, could well afford to pay the higher rates because of the economies achieved through better methods and the elimination of slowdowns.

These industrial engineering systems were not the only radical changes Taylor proposed, however. He also called for a drastic reorganization of supervision. His system embodied two new concepts: (1) separation of planning and doing and (2) functional foremanship.

When Taylor first entered industry, it was customary for each man to plan his own work, generally following a pattern he had learned by watching others when he was an apprentice. The order in which the operations were performed, for example, was entirely up to the man insofar as it was not dictated by the nature of the job; so was the selection of tools. The foreman or gang boss simply told the worker what jobs to perform, not how to do them—except, possibly, in the case of entirely new work.

Taylor's plan retained the gang boss but supplemented him with a number of functional foremen, each of whom was a specialist in one type of work— for example, in the use of a lathe or a grinder. The specialists occupied a "planning room," and each gave orders to the workmen on his specialty. Thus, if the gang boss assigned a worker to a job that called for several different operations, the man would be told how to proceed by seven or eight other bosses.

But the essence of scientific management, Taylor believed, lay in none of these techniques; rather it was in the mental revolution he was sure they would produce in both management and labor. If workmen were paid handsome amounts for producing more and were shown how to do so, they would cease their slowdowns. Since management would be enjoying the fruits of increased productivity, it would be happy to pay the larger wages. Interests of management and labor would be identical, and there would be no reason for strife between them. Neither side would be interested in getting a larger percentage of the pie because both would profit so much more by working together to increase its size. This would automatically mean bigger slices for both, and relative shares would be unimportant.

Under the differential piecework plan, workers who were capable of high production could, and often did, earn very high daily wages by the standards of the period. (One man, for example, increased his pay from $1.65 a day to $2.85.) But those who could not—or at any rate did not—meet the standards fared badly since the piece rates for below-standard production were depressed to offset the high rates paid for the extra production. This often created inequitable situations. In addition, machine breakdowns, defects in material, and bottlenecks in production might bring down the earnings of even a first-class workman to a very low point indeed.

These difficulties with the Taylor plan were corrected to some extent by one of his disciples, Henry Laurence Gantt, who devised what was known as the "task and bonus plan." This is the foundation of many incentive plans in industry today.

The bases of the plan were the daily task—for example, production of a certain number of pieces per day—and the payment of a daily wage whether or not the worker succeeded in completing that task. But if a man completed three hours' work in three hours or less, he was given four hours' pay (at the day rate). And those who could not complete the task still got the regular daily wage.

Similarly, many incentive plans today use standard hours, which are measurements not of time but of work, a standard hour being the amount of work a man may normally be expected to do in an hour. (The man who completes ten standard hours in eight hours gets ten hours' pay.) A daily wage plus premium pay for production above standard is, in fact, a feature of most modern incentive plans, though straight piecework is still common in some industries. In some cases, too, premiums are paid for all production above, say, 80 per cent of standard, an arrangement which, in effect, provides a bonus simply for meeting the standard.

Though Taylor and his disciples are best remembered for their introduction of the stopwatch and time study, they made a number of other contributions to industry. Taylor pioneered in the use of tungsten steel for cutting tools and invented a process for hardening it through heat treatment at temperatures close to the melting point.

One of Gantt's contributions was the invention of the Gantt chart, on which progress can be plotted continuously against time. Figure 1 shows a modern adaptation.

GILBRETH'S WORK

Frank Gilbreth and his wife Lillian, who became widely known to the general public through the book *Cheaper by the Dozen*[5] and the motion picture made

[5] Frank B. Gilbreth and Ernestine Gilbreth Carey, Thomas Y. Crowell Company, New York, 1948.

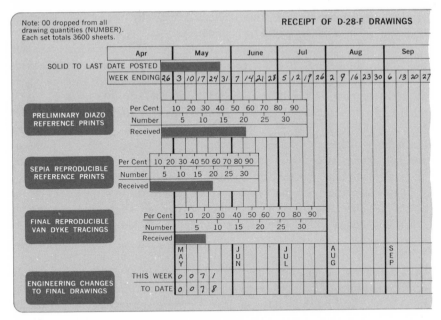

FIGURE 1 A modern Gantt chart. [From Victor Lazzaro (ed.), *Systems and Procedures: A Handbook for Business and Industry,* Prentice-Hall, Inc., Englewood Cliffs, N.J., 1959, p. 91.]

from it, were contemporaries of Taylor and Gantt but pioneers on their own account in the use of time and motion study.

Frank Gilbreth's family had wanted him to go to MIT, but he decided he would make money faster if he went to work immediately after completing high school. So he became a bricklayer's apprentice.

Like Taylor, he wanted to get ahead as fast as possible, and his boss, who was also a friend, had promised him rapid advancement as soon as he learned his trade. He began by asking his fellow workmen how to lay bricks, but each one gave a different answer. What was more confusing, none of the bricklayers followed his own recommendations on the job.

Gilbreth's curiosity about the best way to do a given job was soon translated into a system of shortcut motions for bricklaying. He was not so much interested in how long it took to do a piece of work as he was in the best way to do it. Gilbreth's "one best way" was the way that required the fewest motions performed in an accessible area and in the most comfortable position. He designed more efficient scaffolding, rigging, and hods for carrying bricks. Materials and working areas were kept at levels that eliminated excessive stooping, bending over, walking back and forth, and time-out waiting for materials.

After rising to construction foreman and then to superintendent, Gilbreth felt he could go no further working for someone else. Ten years after his start as an apprentice bricklayer, he went into business for himself and continued to devise improvements in methods and equipment. Later he became a consultant.

Gilbreth's system became known as "speed work," but it was not what unions refer to as speedup. The speed came not from hurrying but from a reduction in the amount of work through the elimination of unnecessary motions. Wage rates on Gilbreth's jobs were generally higher than was customary; he could afford this because more was accomplished in a shorter time.

Although Taylor did a good deal of work on improved methods, including some study of individual motions, Gilbreth's attempts to find the one best way of doing each job were much more far-reaching and constituted the basis of modern motion-study techniques. He identified seventeen basic elements in on-the-job motions, which he christened "therbligs." (Therblig is Gilbreth spelled backwards with a transposition of one letter.) These were (1) search, (2) find, (3) select, (4) grasp, (5) position, (6) assemble, (7) use, (8) disassemble, (9) inspect, (10) transport loaded, moving hand or body with a load, (11) pre-position, (12) release load, (13) transport empty, (14) wait—unavoidable, (15) wait—avoidable, (16) rest—necessary for overcoming fatigue, and (17) plan.[6]

Of course, not all these therbligs are actually motions in the exact sense of the term. But they do constitute the fine divisions of physical work, though each activity will not necessarily include all of them in the order given.

Gilbreth also created the flow process chart (Figure 2), which facilitates study not of a single task but of an operation. It calls for breaking the operation down into steps, which may be performed by several different employees. With a written record of exactly what is done in producing a product or a component, it is possible to discover whether some of the steps can be eliminated or shortened, or whether a change in the sequence of steps will eliminate backtracking.

Lillian Gilbreth worked with her husband from the time of their marriage in 1904, at first helping him with his writing and later becoming a partner in his consulting business. The Gilbreths had twelve children, but she was able to find time for a career through application of scientific management to the home. After her husband's death, she carried on his business, specializing in human relations work.

C. BERTRAND THOMPSON

Other important contributions to the scientific management movement were made by C. Bertrand Thompson, who in 1910 became one of the first lecturers on management at the Harvard Graduate School of Business Administration.

[6] William R. Spriegel and Clark E. Myers (eds.), *The Writings of the Gilbreths*, Richard D. Irwin, Inc., Homewood, Ill., 1953, p. 284.

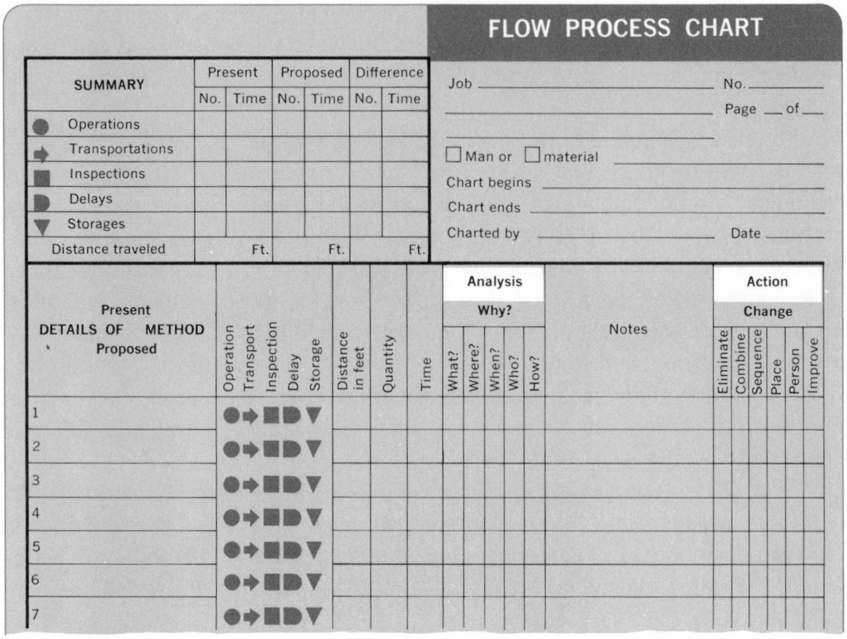

FLOW PROCESS CHART

SUMMARY	Present		Proposed		Difference	
	No.	Time	No.	Time	No.	Time
● Operations						
➡ Transportations						
■ Inspections						
▶ Delays						
▼ Storages						
Distance traveled		Ft.		Ft.		Ft.

Job _____ No. _____
_____ Page __ of __
☐ Man or ☐ material _____
Chart begins _____
Chart ends _____
Charted by _____ Date _____

Present DETAILS OF METHOD Proposed	Operation / Transport / Inspection / Delay / Storage	Distance in feet	Quantity	Time	Analysis — Why? (What? Where? When? Who? How?)	Notes	Action — Change (Eliminate / Combine / Sequence / Place / Person / Improve)
1	●➡■▶▼						
2	●➡■▶▼						
3	●➡■▶▼						
4	●➡■▶▼						
5	●➡■▶▼						
6	●➡■▶▼						
7	●➡■▶▼						

FIGURE 2   Flow process chart.

Not only did he write widely on the subject[7] and introduce the Taylor system in a number of plants in the United States and other countries, but he was one of those who helped to improve the techniques.

For example, Thompson suggested to Gilbreth that he use a large clock with the dial divided into hundredths of a minute as a background and take motion pictures of various operations. In this way, it would be possible to study motions—and the time it took to perform them—more easily and get more accurate results. Gilbreth adopted the practice and made many of the pictures, which he called "chronocyclegraphs," in his studies of motion.

Thompson also worked with Taylor and other associates in the development of a system of classification of accounts, which—except that it used letters rather than numbers—was very similar to systems used today for keeping costs by computer.

However, Thompson felt that the single most important contribution made by the scientific management movement was Taylor's "exception principle"— the theory that in order to avoid getting enmeshed in too many details, the manager should concentrate on cases in which results are especially good or especially bad, since study of these cases will suggest possibilities for improvement. (This principle is perhaps more widely used today than ever before because the computer has made it easier to identify the exceptional cases.)

[7] For example, he wrote *The Theory and Practice of Scientific Management*, Houghton Mifflin Company, Boston, 1917.

Finally, unlike many of his colleagues, Thompson was successful in enlisting the support of labor unions when he introduced scientific management, and his method of doing so was in line with that advocated by many modern sociologists and psychologists: he invited the participation of the unions from the beginning. For example, when he installed the Taylor system in the French General Electric Company, where a radical union had organized the workers, he had a union representative work with him at every stage of the installation and report to the union what was being done. As a result, the union raised no objections when the system was put into effect.

Younger than most of his colleagues in the movement, Thompson is one of the very few of the early proponents of scientific management who are still working. At the age of 85, he is now engaged in cancer research in Uruguay.

HARRINGTON EMERSON

A big impetus to the spread of the scientific management movement arose out of a hearing conducted by the Interstate Commerce Commission in 1911. The railroads of the northeastern section of the United States filed for an increase in freight rates, pleading increased costs, which they laid to an increase in wages. Shippers banded together to oppose the rise, and Louis D. Brandeis, later a justice of the Supreme Court, acted as unpaid counsel for them, undertaking to prove that the trouble lay with inefficiency in management. To this end, he called a number of engineers and plant managers to testify to the possibilities of scientific management.

One of these was the engineer Harrington Emerson, whose startling testimony that the railroads "could save a million dollars a day" by the introduction of more scientific management methods caught the imagination of both businessmen and the public and did a great deal to popularize not only the term "scientific management" but the new occupation of efficiency expert, of which he was a member.

Emerson's scientific management was somewhat different from Taylor's in that it did not concentrate so heavily on work measurement and financial incentives, though these were part of it. Also, it was less concerned with management in the shop than with the whole conduct of the business. Specifically, in a book published in 1912,[8] he listed twelve principles of efficiency, including:

Ideals   By this term, Emerson meant clearly defined goals, in general all stemming from the objective: the best product in the shortest time at the least expense—and the dissemination of this objective down through the organization.

It might be supposed that in businesses organized for profit making, this objective would be so obvious that it would need no statement. Emerson was,

[8] *Twelve Principles of Efficiency*, The Engineering Magazine, New York, 1912.

however, able to cite a number of examples in which it had been totally disregarded.

Common sense   In his explanation of this principle, Emerson called for less attention to bigness for its own sake. The railroads, he said, had a "tonnage mania":

> A railroad superintendent had occasion to send one of the locomotives to the central shop several hundred miles away for repairs. The locomotive was quite capable of hauling a two-thirds load, but this was not permitted. . . . [It] was not even permitted to go under its own steam. It was put in a freight train and bumped over the road to its own detriment and that of the train and track. The superintendent was adding to his tonnage record.[9]

Under this principle, he also pointed to the necessity for careful evaluation of new machines and changes in layout to ensure that they would pay for themselves and benefit the company:

> On one of the great transcontinental lines a gravity grade was eliminated at a cost of $5,000,000, entailing a fixed charge forever of $1,000 a day. The operating cost of the helper locomotives able to handle all the traffic up the grade did not exceed $100 a day.[10]

Reliable, immediate, adequate, and permanent records   These records should cover costs and efficiencies of machines and manpower utilization:

> We ask the price of coal per ton, but rarely know whether it contains 10,000 or 15,000 heat units per pound. . . .
> The ordinary industrial-plant furnace, boiler and engine use five to seven pounds of coal per horse-power hour. By buying better coal, better furnace, better boiler, better engine, and better service, coal consumpiton can be reduced to two pounds, in some instances to one. . . .[11]

> Labor, like material, consists of both quantity and quality. . . . When [labor cost] seems too high, there is generally an insane desire on the part of those in control to reduce wages . . . [but] I have known industrial plants to engage 600 men when 300 would have been sufficient. . . . I have known men that ought to have been earning $6 a day, in reality earning only $3 because they were in the wrong place, paid $3 for work that a $1 a day boy could have performed better.[12]

Workers using improper methods or doing nothing because of hiatuses in the supply of work, expensive machines used for only a few hours a day—

---

[9] *Ibid.,* p. 108.
[10] *Ibid.,* p. 109.
[11] *Ibid.,* pp. 210, 216–217.
[12] *Ibid.,* pp. 219–220.

these were some of the inefficiencies that Emerson saw around him and that proper records would have gone far to alleviate.

Too often, also, he found that railroads not only lacked the records they really needed for cost control but had large clerical forces accumulating records they did not need:

> It has not been unusual in a great corporation's records to find a great variety of monthly tabulations, and when inquiry is made it is finally unravelled that twenty years before some president wanted a certain set of records, that his successor wanted a different set, which were started in parallel, that a third and fourth incumbent added their requests, but the old tabulations continue to be made and painstaking clerks work their monotonous lives away in neat compilation that no one has looked at, much less used, for a decade.[13]

Dispatching   Emerson used the term "dispatching" for what is now called production scheduling and control, because the word was in common use on the railroads. The dispatching of trains was, in general, very efficient—it had to be if timetables were to be met and wrecks avoided. Why, he asked, should not work in the railroad repair shops be dispatched with equal efficiency?

When a locomotive was out of service, Emerson pointed out, the cost to the railroad was $35 a day (a much more impressive sum in 1911 than it is now), and the more quickly repairs could be made, the more money the road would save. He therefore suggested not only that locomotives be scheduled for return to service in a definite number of days, the length of time depending on the seriousness of the repair needed, but that each separate step in repair be scheduled in the proper sequence so that the work could be completed in the shortest possible time.

It is interesting to note that only in comparatively recent years has there been great interest in the "dispatching" of repairs in many industries, although production in the same industries may be scheduled as a matter of course. Since union rules—and sometimes custom, where there is no union—prevent one craft from giving another a hand, lack of scheduling can mean that men being paid $3 or $4 an hour must stand around doing nothing until preliminary work is completed.

Standards   Emerson listed a number of principles that may be summed up under this heading: "standards and schedules," "standardized conditions," "standardized operations," and "standard practice instructions." He felt that there should be rational work standards, based not only on time and motion study but on proper placement of each worker, and that conditions and operations should be standardized so that work measurement would be meaningful.

---

[13] *Ibid.*, p. 209.

He also advocated standardization of parts and designs and standard procedures:

> I have before me one volume of the standard-practice instructions
> covering the manufacturing of the gasoline automobile truck car. It
> contains 278 isometric designs or illustrations, 314 pages of printed
> matter, and spaces for the times and rates of 1,231 distinct operations.
> Each one of these operations was preceded by many designs until one
> was accepted as approximately good. The design was split up into its
> component parts, investigation made as to material of each piece, how
> strong it should be, what heat treatment should be given, on what
> machines it should be shaped, in what sequence by which worker. As to
> each piece and operation many time studies are made, and finally from
> the mass of accurately ascertained or available information, a carefully
> pre-studied work-instruction card is made out. . . . A modern activity,
> whether the operation of an industrial shop or a railroad, or of the
> turrets and guns of a battleship, is part of a gigantic, automatic machine;
> and it pays to plan in advance, not to trust to the haphazard. . . .
>
> The difficulties are very real and there is a middle ground between
> the optimism that underrates them and the despair that refuses to mas-
> ter them. There are between 8,000 and 16,000 separate pieces in a loco-
> motive, and each railroad in the country wants a different design. One
> great railroad used 256 different styles of locomotives; so that there is
> an appalling lack of standards, but the more reason for beginning at
> once.[14]

EFFECTS OF THE MOVEMENT

The time and motion study inaugurated by Taylor and Gilbreth did indeed
produce large improvements in productivity in many cases. After Taylor had
installed an incentive payment plan for shovelers at Bethlehem Steel and
showed the men how to shovel correctly, it was found that 150 men could do
work formerly performed by 450. Using Gilbreth's motions, a bricklayer could
lay 2,800 bricks in the time it had previously taken him to lay 900.

But the "mental revolution" on the part of both management and labor,
which Taylor considered the heart of his scientific management, never materialized, except perhaps in isolated instances and for short periods of time. Some
thirty years after he had first introduced his plan at Midvale, Taylor stated that
there was not a single company in the country that was actually practicing
scientific management in its entirety, though many were using time and motion
study.

Why did scientific management fail to produce the result Taylor had envisioned? There were a number of reasons.

14 *Ibid.*, pp. 304–306.

Some unregenerate employers went back to their old practices of cutting piece rates when productivity went up. Unions and employees foresaw large blocks of unemployment if the same amount of work could be done by a half or a third of the number of men then required, and many mistakenly regarded the plan as simply a new form of speedup designed to make men exhaust themselves in the interest of higher production. Taylor's system was even investigated by a congressional committee, and laws were passed against the use of the stopwatch on government operations.

Time and motion studies have played an important part in increases in productivity, but few companies believe that unlimited cooperation can be obtained from employees merely through financial incentives based on "scientifically determined standards." In many cases the standards are used only in scheduling the work.

Other features of the Taylor plan, such as functional foremanship, never really caught on. Companies found that having a man take orders from seven or eight different bosses resulted in confusion, to say nothing of the increase in overhead implicit in such an increase in supervision. In many cases they have divorced planning and doing by allocating the planning function to various other groups, such as methods departments; but the plans are transmitted to the foreman, and he alone bosses the men.

Taylor was said, and is still believed by many, to have lacked all sympathy with the workingman, and the failure of his mental revolution has been attributed to this fact. Some of his descriptions of workers lend force to this criticism—for example:

> Now one of the very first requirements for a man who is fit to handle pig iron [as a shoveler] as a regular occupation is that he shall be so stupid and so phlegmatic that he resembles . . . the ox.[15]

But the criticism is not really justified. If he recognized the obvious truth that some of the workmen had little more intelligence and sensitivity than an ox, he was equally ready to admit that others whom he met in the shops were more intelligent though less well educated than he was. These men, he felt, could and should be promoted to planning jobs as the increased productivity made expansion possible. Even with the oxlike, he approached matters on a perfectly logical basis that indicated respect for them as human beings. In effect, he said to them, "Do you want to earn more money? Do what I tell you and you will." And he kept his promise. When he fined the men for breaking their machines in protest against his methods, he was firm in his insistence that the money should not revert to management. Instead, he organized a mutual benefit association for the workmen and used the fines to help support it.

---

[15] "The Principles of Scientific Management," in *Scientific Management, op. cit.,* p. 59.

Taylor felt so strongly about the benefits of his system that eventually he began devoting his entire time to promotion of it, working without pay. He wrote:

> It ought to be perfectly evident to any man that no other human being would devote the whole of his life and spend every cent of his surplus income for the purpose of producing higher dividends for a lot of manufacturing companies in which he has not the slightest interest. . . . On the contrary I have devoted nearly all of my time and money to furthering the cause of Scientific Management . . . entirely with the idea of getting better wages for the workmen . . . so as to make them all higher-class men—to better educate them—to help them to live better lives, and, above all, to be more happy and contented. This is a worthy object for a man to devote his life to.[16]

The real reasons for the failure of the Taylor system to produce the mental revolution that might seem implicit in it at first glance are complex and difficult to determine, but several possibilities might be discussed.

One of the most frequently mentioned is that no man is entirely an "economic man"—that is, he does not always act as his financial interests dictate. He has other needs that move him far more potently than his desire for money, at least after he has risen above the starvation level. Thus public opinion within a group may tend to keep the work pace down to that of the slowest—or at least the average—employee, and few will care to buck it.

Moreover, the separation of planning and doing, and the greater specialization inherent in the system, tended to reduce the need for skill and produce greater monotony of work. Gilbreth's systems were designed to benefit the worker by reducing fatigue as well as by making it possible for him to earn more money. A man, he said, actually made fewer motions laying 2,800 bricks under his system than had been necessary to lay the customary 900. But many people were instinctively repelled by the idea of prescribed motions and felt that the system represented an infringement of personal liberty.

Most important of all, Taylor was never able to provide a satisfactory answer to the argument that men would be displaced by his system and some unemployment result. Advances in methods and better tools and machines do tend to eliminate some workers, and except in times of unusually high employment, many of them do find it difficult to get other jobs. True, in the long run the advances mean larger employment than ever, but as a union official once observed, "Try to tell that to the worker. He doesn't live in the long run. He lives in the short run and has to pay his bills in the short run."

Management, too, sometimes lives in the short run. A profit made now by cutting rates may seem more attractive than a possibly greater profit later on, which may not even materialize because there may be no demand for the increased output. It is mainly because of a long history of rate cutting that the force of public opinion in the plant often tends toward restriction of output. (A

---

[16] Frank B. Copley, *Frederick W. Taylor: Father of Scientific Management*, Harper & Row, Publishers, Incorporated, New York, 1923, vol. II, pp. 237–238.

man who exceeds the norm is known as a "rate-buster.") True, many of the companies that use financial incentives today have strict rules against rate cutting, but suspicions aroused over a long period die hard, and there are many subsidiary problems that a simple statement of the Taylor system does not encompass. Sometimes, for example, a rate is miscalculated, so that the men on the job are making far more than others doing work of comparable difficulty. Or the worker himself may discover new and better methods and be able to produce far more and earn far more than was originally contemplated.

Again, not everyone admits that time study and motion study are entirely "scientific." Two time-study men may time the same job and come up with entirely different answers. And there are many who deny that there is such a thing as "one best way" so far as the component motions are concerned.

Taylor and Gilbreth and other members of the scientific management movement did, however, point the way to great increases in efficiency:

1. They focused attention on the need for systematic study to discover better methods of performing work. If there is not necessarily one best way of doing a job, study is likely to produce a way that is better and quicker than the haphazard methods likely to prevail when each man works as his fancy dictates.

2. They were instrumental in introducing time study, which makes more accurate scheduling possible. If each job is timed, it is possible to predict when it will be completed and the next operation can be started; thus there will be fewer delays between operations because each shop will be ready to start its part of the work at the scheduled time. (Of course unexpected delays do occur, even so, but the schedules can be more closely adhered to if the times have been calculated in advance.) Also, when management knows how long each job is likely to take, it finds it easier to calculate costs in advance.

In some cases, too, financial incentives have increased productivity substantially, even if not so much as Taylor expected they would.

In introducing these improvements, Taylor was not actually developing a science *of* management. Rather he developed a new science *for* management, a series of techniques to be applied to a single company function: production. He contributed nothing that would help in the handling of other company functions—or in the coordination of them, which is one of the fundamental management jobs.

Taylor might, in fact, be called the father of industrial engineering rather than the father of scientific management. But by his promotion of the term and the controversies he aroused, he did publicize the idea that management could be at least partially a science, and thereby encouraged the search for new principles and techniques. To some extent, acceptance of the idea that management could be scientific was in itself a mental revolution, although not of the kind Taylor expected. When managers began to think of management as a science, they began to view all problems as susceptible to rational solution if enough time and attention were devoted to them.

SUMMARY

Frederick Taylor's system embodied several features: (1) the separation of planning and doing, (2) functional foremanship, (3) time study of the elements of jobs through the use of a stopwatch, (4) the study of motions with a view to the development of improved methods of performing work, and (5) a differential piecework method to encourage men to put forth their best efforts.

Taylor believed that it would be possible to determine the exact amount of work a man could do in a given time without in any way straining himself and that time-study findings would be so "scientific" that there could be no argument about them. Then, since employees would be able to earn a great deal more by meeting the standards, they would no longer have any reason to slow down; and since management would profit from the greater productivity, it would be willing and able to pay the higher wages. Then, Taylor said, both management and labor would undergo a "mental revolution" and begin to work together wholeheartedly.

Frank Gilbreth's work paralleled that of Taylor but was independent of it, and he placed more emphasis on motion study and the development of improved methods than on time study. But in general, the work of the two men was complementary. Out of their systems came present-day industrial engineering, which encompasses not only time and motion study but improvements in machinery, in scheduling, and in other phases of production.

There were many other men who contributed to the scientific management movement, too many to mention here, and the work of only a few of them has been touched on in this chapter. Harrington Emerson is noteworthy in that, unlike Taylor, he concentrated not on techniques to be applied at the first-line level of management but on techniques to be used by higher management: more accurate cost accounting, standardization of parts and machines, and so on. Gantt and Thompson, perhaps, showed greater understanding of human relations than Taylor did, and both contributed to the development of the scientific management techniques.

Case Study One / Applying the Taylor System*

H. K. Hathaway worked in the machine shop of the Midvale Steel Company (where Taylor had introduced his system) and rose from apprentice to foreman or overseer. Then he accepted a position as superintendent with a smaller

---

* The above case was related by H. K. Hathaway himself at a meeting of the American Society of Mechanical Engineers. It is told here in third person, but the wording is largely Hathaway's own.

company, where the employees, under the sole direction of one overworked foreman, ground their tools to suit themselves, repaired and cared for the belts on their machines, and followed their own judgment or inclinations on the feeds, speeds, cuts, and kind of tools to be used.

He was amazed at the light cuts and slow speeds he found and at the many peculiar shapes of tools in use. When a belt slipped, it was the custom to reduce the speed or feed to a point where it would pull—the workmen thought that was less trouble than tightening the belt. Another drawback was that the tools were of every conceivable kind of steel, a bar or two having apparently been bought from every tool-steel salesman who came along. Because the workman had no means of distinguishing the tools made of good high-speed steel from those made of old carbon or early self-hardening steels, he ran the machine at the speed suited to the latter, to be sure that his tool would not give out during a cut.

In many cases a workman who was told to use a certain feed, speed, or depth of cut answered in a convincing manner that "the machine wouldn't stand it" or that the job he was working on was of such a peculiar nature that a heavy cut would spoil it. If the foreman insisted, the workman might proceed, more in sorrow than in anger, to prove the truth of his statements.

Hathaway managed to get the belts, tools, and driving mechanisms on a few of the machines in such a condition that something like the proper speeds and feeds could be used. But he found that it was utterly impossible with one over-worked foreman ("who did not take very kindly to my notion of speeding up anyway") to ensure that these conditions were maintained. He might get a workman to run the proper speed on a job on a certain day, but the next time the same job came up, the man would be running at the old speed and giving the old reasons for doing so.

Then Hathaway attempted to install a Taylor incentive plan and to get the speed up to what he knew was possible. After three months, he had a strike on his hands that very nearly put the company out of business.

What should Hathaway have done? Should he have allowed things to go on as they were? Or was there some other course he could have adopted?

Case Study Two / The Ambidextrous Employee

On one operation the company's incentive system, based on time and motion study, enabled the average man to earn 20 per cent more than his daily wage if he worked steadily using the motions that the industrial engineers had determined made up the one best way. Over a period of years several men held the job, earning from 110 per cent to 130 per cent of the base pay, with the average around 115 to 120 per cent.

Then a new man came on the job and after a short while began producing so many pieces that he earned two or three times his day rate. Yet he did not seem to be exhausting himself. Investigation showed that the man had been a juggler for several years. He was completely ambidextrous and was able to move his hands much faster and with greater economy of effort than most people.

The production manager thought the time standard was now too loose. He wanted the job restudied so that it would not be possible for the man to earn more than 20 to 30 per cent above his base pay, particularly since the man's total wages were far above those being paid to other people on the same level.

Do you think a new time study of the job was in order? Give reasons for your answer, considering both the company's viewpoint and the viewpoints of the man and his fellow workers.

Case Study Three / £14 a Week versus £20*

In a large modern factory in Glasgow, Scotland, certain semiskilled workers were averaging £14 a week under an incentive system. The manager of the department pointed out to them that workers in the United States who were using the same machines were constantly producing at a rate that would make possible earnings of £20 a week under the incentive plan in force in the Glasgow plant. The workers appeared uninterested in this possibility. Instead they demanded a reduction in work load with no loss of pay. Why, asked the manager, did they not take this chance to make as much money as would provide them with far better living conditions?

What might be some of the reasons for the workers' attitude?

Case Study Four / Application of the Twelve Principles

F. L. Impey, Sr., was the owner of a firm that manufactured loose-leaf binders and accounting record sheets. His sales were around $1 million, mostly to business firms in different parts of England.

* Drawn from T. T. Paterson, *Glasgow Limited: A Case-study in Industrial War and Peace,* Cambridge University Press, London, 1960.

He was particularly careful about quality. He made binders that would last a lifetime or two, and this made for high production costs and high prices. In addition, he was willing to make the products to customers' specifications, which also resulted in high costs since ink and paper had to be changed for each new order and new type had to be set up almost every time. And there was no systematic scheduling because each foreman made his own decisions, often without consulting the others. There was little mechanization, and the printing equipment was never repaired until it broke down.

Impey, Sr., employed few specialists; he felt he could be his own expert on production, sales, research, and control. But since he was an admirer of Ruskin, most of his time went into the improvement of workmanship and little into coordination of his enterprise, which had some hundred-odd employees performing different tasks. And even though he manufactured record books, he had no records himself—he "never got around to" installing a record-keeping system.

While he was kind to his employees, he treated them, not according to their contributions, but as the fancy struck him. Some of his favorites got thumping Christmas bonuses, but others who were contributing quite as much got much less. He had no standards for measuring work; his judgment of employees was based on his general impressions.

Impey, Sr., wanted to make a lot of money, but he also wanted to produce binders and print sheets that were enduring works of art. And since anyone with a knowledge of printing and a little capital could enter the business and many buyers were satisfied with no more than adequate serviceability, he began losing customers to firms that offered lower prices. In addition, his policy of making almost as many different types of product as he had customers necessitated a very large and diversified stock of binders and literally tens of thousands of different types of accounting sheets.

Eventually he went bankrupt, but his son, F. L. Impey, Jr., managed to raise enough capital to take over the business. Impey, Jr., was a devotee of Emerson's *Twelve Principles of Efficiency*, and he made the business successful by applying them.

How would you apply the twelve principles to the Impey company?

Review Questions

1. How did Taylor determine a fair day's work?
2. What did he mean by an "element" in a job?
3. What is functional foremanship?
4. What is a Gantt chart? A company has an order for 1,000 widgets, which must be delivered within two months. Each widget includes five components that are produced separately and then assembled. At the end of a month the company has on hand: component 1, 1,000 units; component 2, 500 units; components 3 and 4, 700 units each; component 5,

250 units. Draw up a Gantt chart showing the status of the order. What does the chart suggest might be done to speed up delivery?

5.   What is a flow chart? What are the advantages of using such a chart in studying operations?

6.   What "mental revolution" did Taylor expect his system would produce? What are some of the reasons why this mental revolution did not occur?

7.   What is motion study? How does it differ from time study?

8.   Which do you think would be more helpful to *top* management: Emerson's principles or the systems developed by Taylor and Gilbreth?

9.   What did Emerson mean by "ideals"? By "dispatching"?

10.   How did Emerson believe proposed capital expenditures should be judged?

11.   Why did the scientific management movement arouse opposition? Do you think the opposition was justified? Why or why not?

12.   What were the major contributions of the scientific management movement?

Selected Readings

"The Principles of Scientific Management," *Scientific Management*, Frederick Winslow Taylor, Harper & Row, Publishers, Incorporated, New York, 1947. Taylor's own description of his principles and ideas, written originally in 1909 for the American Society of Mechanical Engineers and published by Taylor at his own expense in 1911.

The Pattern of Management, Lyndall F. Urwick, University of Minnesota Press, Minneapolis, 1956, chap. 3. This chapter contains a sympathetic account of F. W. Taylor's theories. A somewhat longer account is given in Colonel Urwick's centenary address to the International Management Congress in Paris, 1957, published as *The Life and Work of Frederick Winslow Taylor*, Urwick, Orr and Partners Ltd., London, 1957.

The Writings of the Gilbreths, William R. Spriegel and Clark E. Myers (eds.), Richard D. Irwin, Inc., Homewood, Ill., 1953. A full selection of the writings of the Gilbreths.

"Motion and Time Study," Marvin E. Mundel, and "Trade Unions and Industrial Engineering," William Gomberg, in William Grant Ireson and Eugene L. Grant (eds.), *Handbook of Industrial Engineering and Management*, Prentice-Hall, Inc., Englewood Cliffs, N.J., 1955. The first of these articles is a description of modern methods of time study. The second discusses the attitude of the early proponents of scientific management toward trade unions and explains why unions often object to time study and other branches of industrial engineering as they may be presently practiced.

Scientific Management and the Unions 1900–1932: A Historical Analysis, Milton J. Nadworny, Harvard University Press, Cambridge, Mass., 1955. An account of the relations between advocates of scientific management and trade union leaders, relations which have varied from hostility to active cooperation. Over the years, the author shows, the union attitudes have modified the application of scientific management, and scientific management has exerted a direct influence on the evolution of trade union policy.

Efficiency as a Basis for Operation and Wages, 4th ed., Harrington Emerson,

The Engineering Magazine, 1919. Emerson's first book, which appeared originally in 1909. Chapter 8, "The Location and Elimination of Wastes," and Chapter 9, "The Efficiency System in Operation," give a good idea of Emerson's method of utilizing his principles when he acted as a consultant.

"The First Principle: Clearly Defined Ideals," Harrington Emerson, in Harwood F. Merrill (ed.), *Classics in Management,* American Management Association, New York, 1960. Emerson's explanation of the need for objectives in business, taken from his book, *The Twelve Principles of Efficiency.*

Taylorism at the Watertown Arsenal: Scientific Management in Action, Hugh G. J. Aitken, Harvard University Press, Cambridge, Mass., 1960. A detailed account of the introduction of scientific management in a government plant, the results it made possible, and the conflicts that developed. It was the situation at Watertown that gave rise to the political pressures which led eventually to a ban on the use of the stopwatch on government operations.

Efficiency and Uplift, Samuel Haber, The University of Chicago Press, Chicago, 1964. This is a critical examination of the "progressive era" (1890–1920), during which "efficient" and "good" seemed to mean the same thing.

7
ELTON
MAYO
AND
THE
HUMAN
RELATIONS
SCHOOL

If our social skills had advanced step by step with our technical skills, there would not have been another European war.
Elton Mayo: *The Social Problems of an Industrial Civilization*

7 "It has been proved in most work," the Gilbreths wrote, "that more output can be achieved by applying oneself steadily for short periods, and then resting, than by applying oneself less steadily and having no rest periods."[1] It was through a study designed originally to confirm this view that some entirely new theories developed which were greatly at variance with those of the scientific management movement.

In the 1920s, Elton Mayo, an associate professor at the Graduate School of Business Administration at Harvard, joined a group who had undertaken a long-term investigation into the effect of worker fatigue on productivity and the possibility that rest periods would result in a rise in output. In this they were given a free hand by executives of the Hawthorne plant of the Western Electric Company in Chicago, where the experiments were conducted.[2]

THE RESEARCH

The most famous of these Hawthorne experiments was the one concerned with the assembly of telephone relays, a repetitive operation performed by women. Each unit consisted of a coil, an armature, contact springs, and insulators, all of which were placed in a fixture and secured there by means of four screws. Since the job was in no way machine-paced, output depended largely on the speed with which the operators worked and the extent to which they kept steadily at the job. An experienced operator could assemble a unit in about a minute.

A financial incentive plan was already in effect for the work. Operators were divided into groups of about one hundred, and the extra pay of the individual worker depended on the output of her group.

Five experienced workers from the regular assembly floor were selected to take part in the experiment, with their own full knowledge and consent. Without their knowledge, however, a record was kept of each girl's production for weeks before any changes were made. This was to provide a basis for estimating changes in output as various changes in schedule were introduced; hence it was necessary that the girls work along as usual. If they had known a record was being kept, they might—consciously or unconsciously—have speeded up or slowed down and invalidated future comparisons to some extent.

At the end of this time, the five girls (and a sixth to bring them parts) were moved to a room by themselves, where a standard assembly bench seating five workers had been installed. In order to minimize any effects that might be due to this change alone, all conditions were kept otherwise unchanged during a period of five weeks thereafter.

Then a change in the incentive plan was introduced. Instead of being based on the output of a large group, the extra payments were made dependent on

[1] "Fatigue Study," in William R. Spriegel and Clark E. Myers (eds.), The Writings of the Gilbreths, Richard D. Irwin, Inc., Homewood, Ill., 1953, p. 309.
[2] For the complete account of the Hawthorne experiments, see F. J. Roethlisberger and William J. Dickson, Management and the Worker, Harvard University Press, Cambridge, Mass., 1939.

the production of the five. Since this gave each girl a more direct opportunity to influence her own rate of pay, they were allowed several weeks to get used to the new plan. At this point, the investigators believed, they might safely assume that any changes in output thereafter would be due to the changes in schedule they were about to introduce. The experiment then began in earnest, each change in schedule being discussed in advance with the operators. The changes were, successively:

1. The girls were given two rest periods, each five minutes long, one at 10 in the morning and another at 2 in the afternoon. This continued for five weeks.
2. The rest periods were increased to ten minutes each for a period of four weeks.
3. Again for four weeks, the number of rest periods was increased to six and the time of each one shortened to five minutes.
4. The rest periods were reduced to two of ten minutes each, and the girls were served soup or coffee and a sandwich during the morning rest and something light in the afternoon. (Since they often came to work without breakfast, it was felt that this might possibly stimulate their productivity.) And, finally, in order to give them more time to eat, the morning rest was lengthened to fifteen minutes.

Schedule 4 was then continued for a period of months, and various other changes in the working day were introduced. At one time, the experimenters cropped an hour off the end of it, allowing the girls to leave at 4 instead of 5. At another point, for a period of twelve weeks they eliminated the Saturday work that was standard at the time.

During all this time, output of the group kept rising. There were some minor fluctuations, it is true. For example, it declined slightly when the girls were given six rest periods a day, and the workers themselves felt that such a schedule created too many interruptions. When Saturday work was eliminated, weekly production was somewhat lower, though daily production was higher. In general, however, the trend was steadily up.

It might have been concluded that rest periods in some form, particularly when accompanied by refreshments, were highly conducive to productivity, and that possibly a shorter working day would be advisable in the interest of raising output. But the next change brought some surprising results.

For a period of twelve weeks, beginning in September, 1928, rest periods, refreshments, and shortened working days were all eliminated, and the schedule in force before the start of the experiment went back into effect. And at that point output rose to a new high and stayed there during the entire period.

Then rest periods and refreshments were again introduced, and output rose still higher. During the no-rest-period time, each operator had produced about 2,900 relays per week, as against 2,400 before the experiment proper began. When rest periods were reintroduced, the number rose to 3,000.

In short, during the course of the experiment, which continued over several years, there was an upward trend in output independent of the changes in rest periods. Further, regardless of the changes in schedule, the girls in the test room were out sick only about a third as much as the operators in the regular assembly room. They seemed "eager to come to work in the morning," and it was observed that practically no supervision was required. The girls in the test room could be depended upon to do their best.

It was evident that something in the nature of the "mental revolution" that Frederick Taylor had believed financial incentives would spark had occurred. Moreover, it had occurred spontaneously without the provision of extra pay.

The girls themselves had no clear explanation of why they worked so much faster than they had at first; they were not conscious of any speedup. On the contrary, they said, they "felt under less pressure" than before and attributed much of their increase in output to the fact there was "no boss or slave-driving."

The test room, it must be remembered, was mainly under the supervision of the experimenters. They were trying to isolate the effects of rest periods from other factors and therefore hoped to keep all other influences constant. To this end, they took special pains to enlist the wholehearted cooperation of the girls, explaining moves in advance, soliciting suggestions, sometimes allowing the operators to make decisions on the course of the experiment, and taking a personal interest in each one. Moreover, a girl could vary from a fixed pace without drawing a reprimand.

NONDIRECTIVE INTERVIEWING

One conclusion possible from all this was that certain supervisory practices on the regular assembly floor were actually holding down output, and a series of interviews throughout the organization began in consequence. At first the interviewers asked a series of set questions, but finding that the workers tended to be uncommunicative, they abandoned this technique in favor of what is known as "nondirective interviewing," in which the person is merely encouraged to talk freely. Finally, they observed conditions within the factory and compared their findings with the complaints voiced by the workers. Here again, though they did uncover some specific conditions that needed correction —poor ventilation in certain areas, for example—they learned very little about supervisory practices that tended to inhibit productivity. Mayo wrote:

> Complaints about persons, or for that matter about supervision, in the great majority of instances had to be disregarded. Such complaints served indeed to draw attention to something of interest in the personal history and present attitude of the person being interviewed; but the validity of the external reference was minimal. . . . At the outset, then, the inquiry was baffled, and in two ways. First, one range of facts of which . . . management wished to know more were the facts of interpersonal relation incident to organization and supervision. And these facts when first discovered seemed, alas, to be not facts but prejudiced

judgments. The second source of puzzlement was consequent on the first. The interviewing group could not willingly believe that the larger group of persons . . . consisted of individuals who were generally unbalanced in their personal judgments. Such a belief was repugnant to common sense.[3]

MAYO'S THEORY

Mayo's eventual conclusion, covering employee relations and administration in general, was that what he called the "rabble hypothesis" must be disregarded. This hypothesis is that workers in a plant—or in any other organization—are a disorganized rabble of individuals, each of whom is acting in his own self-interest as logically as he is able. Good administration therefore is achieved by showing each individual that his self-interest is best served when he behaves as management wishes him to. In essence, this was the theory on which Frederick Taylor based his studies.

Rather, said Mayo, work is a group activity, and in an "atomistic society" such as we have at present, in which traditional groupings and ties have weakened, the work group is especially important. Yet technological advances and changing conditions tend continually to disrupt the formal and informal working groups that form within industry and hence to disturb the worker's sense of belonging and to deprive him of the recognition he has gained within a cohesive group. It is this disturbance that often manifests itself in complaints about supervision or working conditions:

> Generally speaking . . . the responses of any adult individual to his surrounding are of three types:
> (a) *Logical.* . . .
> (b) *Nonlogical.* . . . The individual's actions may be adequate to the situation, but any intelligence they exhibit is socially and not personally derived. This form of response is the effect of training in a social code of behavior.
> (c) *Irrational.* Nonlogical response is typical of social adjustment. Irrational response . . . is symptomatic of social maladjustment and shows all the signs of obsession.
> The nonlogical response, that, namely, which is in strict conformity with a social code, makes for social order and discipline, for *effective collaboration in a restricted range* of activity, and for happiness and a sense of security in the individual.
> The industrial worker, whether capable of it or not, does not want to develop a blackboard logic which shall guide his method of life and work. What he wants is more nearly described as, first, a method of living in social relationship with other people and, second, as part of this an economic function for and of value to the group. . . . Socialism, Communism, Marxism would seem to be irrelevant to industrial events of the

[3] *The Human Problems of an Industrial Civilization*, The Viking Press, Inc., New York, 1960, pp. 92–93.

20th century. These doctrines probably express the workers' desire to recapture something of the lost human solidarity. . . . As we lose the nonlogic of a social code, we must substitute a logic of understanding. If at all critical posts in communal activity we had intelligent persons capable of analyzing an individual or a group attitude in terms of, first, the degree of logical understanding manifest; second, the nonlogic of social codes in action; and, third, the irrational exasperation symptomatic of conflict and baffled effort; if we had an *élite* capable of such analysis, very many of our difficulties would dwindle to vanishing point. . . . Our leaders tend to state these problems in terms of systematic economics, and since the gravamen of the issue is human and social and not primarily economic their statements are not relevant.[4]

What is Mayo really saying here? Does he mean that workers must be brought to understand the logic of management? Or is he arguing that the manager must understand the limitations of logic as a method of persuading his subordinates to a course of action and turn to formation of cohesive work groups such as existed in the Hawthorne test room? His words do not make this point clear, but the whole tone of his writing, particularly his use of the term "elite," makes it appear that the latter is the case. Mayo has, in fact, been criticized for implying that management is always completely logical, whereas the workers are largely driven by their emotions and the need to feel a "sense of belonging."

The small group in the relay test room was able to develop this sense of belonging. The girls formed a homogeneous and stable group and often saw each other outside working hours. The type of supervision provided, which was interested and sympathetic rather than authoritarian, contributed greatly also.

SUMMARY

Mayo's name has been very largely associated with the Hawthorne experiments, although he was not the originator of them or even one of the chief researchers.

The conclusion he drew from these experiments was that employees would be happy and productive only if they could belong to a cohesive and stable work group, that the "sense of belonging" was more important to them than anything else.

The Hawthorne experiments also focused management attention on the importance of first-line supervision in the creation and preservation of morale.

Review Questions

1. What did the Hawthorne researchers originally plan to test?
2. What unexpected results occurred?
3. What did Mayo mean by the rabble hypothesis?

[4] *Ibid.*, pp. 157–158.

4. What did Mayo believe was most important in developing good morale and higher output?
5. Do you believe that it would be a good idea for all companies to have employee counselors?
6. What is nondirective interviewing?
7. Do you believe that the type of supervision provided and the relationships on the job are more important to most people than the amount of money they earn?

Case Study / Mayo's Prescription for Reducing Labor Turnover*

During World War II, Elton Mayo and several associates from the Harvard Graduate School of Business Administration examined the causes of high labor turnover in the West Coast aircraft industry.

In one large plant with total employment of 40,000 people, for example, they found that there were more than 30,000 severances in a twelve-month period, 65,000 transfers within the plant, and approximately 150,000 "loans," or temporary transfers for a day or less than a day, from one plant department to another. Thus the labor turnover was 75 per cent, transfers 157 per cent, and "loans" 360 per cent—or a total of nearly 600 per cent.

You are the manager of the plant. If you planned to correct this situation by utilizing Elton Mayo's theories, what would you do?

Selected Readings

Hawthorne Revisited, Henry A. Landsberger, New York State School of Industrial and Labor Relations, Cornell University, Ithaca, N.Y., 1958. A summary of the work of Mayo and his associates and an appraisal of its significance.

The Social Problems of an Industrial Civilization, Elton Mayo, Division of Research, Graduate School of Business Administration, Harvard University, Boston, 1945. An exposition of Mayo's basic ideas.

The Human Group, George C. Homans, Harcourt, Brace & World, Inc., New York, 1950. A good account of the theory of groups by one of Mayo's students, later a professor at Harvard.

"Contributions of the Behavioral Sciences to a General Theory of Management," Fritz J. Roethlisberger, in Harold Koontz (ed.), *Toward a Unified Theory of Management,* McGraw-Hill Book Company, New York, 1964.

Counseling in an Organization: A Sequel to the Hawthorne Researches, William J. Dickson and F. J. Roethlisberger, Division of Research, Graduate School of Business Administration, Harvard University, Boston, 1966.

---

* From Elton Mayo and George F. F. Lombard, *Teamwork and Labor Turnover in the Aircraft Industry of Southern California,* Graduate School of Business Administration, Harvard University, Boston, 1944.

8

TAYLOR AND MAYO— WHO WAS RIGHT?

All philosophers find
Some favorite system to their mind.
In every point to make it fit
Will force all nature to submit.
T. L. Peacock: *Headlong Hall*

8 Frederick Taylor and Elton Mayo represent opposite points of view. To Taylor, as to Karl Marx, man at work was entirely an economic man; therefore, he would work harder only if he could improve his economic position by doing so. To Mayo, even intelligent workers were people motivated largely by a need for "togetherness" and for individual recognition within a small group whose standards they accepted.

Each man, strangely enough, was able to prove his point. Under the Taylor system productivity rose sharply in many instances, and Mayo's theories were borne out not only by the records of the Hawthorne test room but by other studies.

Mayo's findings have received substantial acceptance in industry generally, just as Taylor's time study has; but the mental revolution among industrial workers has yet to occur. Productivity in this country rises year by year, but mainly because of new machines and better methods; not, it would appear, because employees are putting forth greater effort. Industrial relations problems, group and individual, continue to be among the most harassing management faces.

It would be an oversimplification to conclude that the truth lies somewhere between the two extremes, or even that both methods—financial incentives and the development of cohesive work groups—will motivate people to work harder. Combining the two systems, provided each is handled skillfully, can probably help to raise productivity higher than it would otherwise go, but neither separately nor together do they elicit the full cooperation of the worker, except in isolated instances.

The most probable answer seems to be that there are human motives and elements in the work situation that eluded both investigators because, as all human beings must, they viewed objective happenings through the lenses of their own preoccupations.

TAYLOR'S BACKGROUND

Thus Taylor was representative of the socially approved ambitious young man of his time, willing to start at the bottom but expecting to move upward in the managerial hierarchy by hard work and display of intelligence. When he found himself one of a group of young college graduates employed by an engineering company, he voluntarily offered to come in and work at night or on Sunday if he was needed, and in this way he made himself known to all the superintendents. Later he attributed his rapid promotion to this move.

When he looked at the men in the shop, he understood their reluctance to produce to capacity. He himself was willing to do so because he was a man of education from a good middle-class family who might logically expect promotion. The men with whom he worked had no such advantages; they could expect only ten, twenty, or thirty years more of the same type of work and at substantially the same low rates. Extra pay for extra effort, plus the chance for advancement to planning positions for the more intelligent, would, he concluded, transform their lack of interest into something like his own dynamism.

MAYO'S EXPERIENCE

Elton Mayo, on the other hand, was a psychologist by profession, and many who have studied his writings believe that he was a man to whom all conflict was distasteful, even if it took the form of peaceful disagreement.

Born in Australia in 1880, Mayo was originally destined by his family for the medical profession but gave up his studies before completing them. In 1905, his father purchased a partnership in a printing firm for him, and shortly afterward he began combining his work with studies for a B.A., specializing in psychology. Later he became a lecturer at the University of Queensland and did some clinical work on the treatment of the shell-shocked soldiers of World War I. He came to the United States in 1922 with the aid of a Rockefeller grant.

The psychologist often finds the causes of psychological difficulties within the individual in opposing tendencies that do not cancel each other out but produce tension, or "conflict." When Mayo branched out into sociology, he apparently applied this concept to groups and concluded that groups as well as individuals were not healthy if they were not "integrated" in the psychological sense.

It is possible also to speculate whether Mayo's own experiences did not tend to make him exalt togetherness and social skills. In *The Social Problems of an Industrial Civilization* he wrote:

> It was indeed the appearance in universities of students brilliantly able but unhappy and ineffective that first called attention to the more general problem. . . . Such students . . . are always almost devoid of social skill. . . . . The personal histories are monotonously iterative of circumstance that prevented active experience in early life of diverse social groups and different social situations.[1]

Was Mayo himself originally such a student, and did he, upon solving his difficulties, ever afterwards place more importance on belonging to the group than he would have if he had never felt himself an outsider? The bare facts of his life indicate that this is at least a possibility. At the age of fourteen, he was a brilliant student who had won a classical scholarship, but from then until he took up the study of psychology, he appears to have lost interest in academic work. Eventually he abandoned his studies and drifted from job to job over a period of years—journalism in London, lecturing at a workingman's college, a laboring job in West Africa.

Whatever the cause, Mayo, as everyone must, viewed the industrial scene through glasses tinted by his own preoccupations, and the tint seems to have

[1] Division of Research, Graduate School of Business Administration, Harvard University, Boston, 1945, p. 23.

been especially heavy in his case. "Democracy," he wrote in 1919, "has done nothing to help society to unanimity."[2]

Complete unanimity is probably impossible among any group of human beings except for short periods. Outward dissent from the prevailing view may be largely, though not entirely, smothered by force, but Mayo wanted spontaneous cooperation. It is extremely questionable also whether unanimity, either spontaneous or enforced, is at all desirable. If no differences of opinion existed, there could scarcely be any progress.

Mayo was not against progress. He recognized that the modern company must continually change its methods and technology and that there could be no return to the stability that prevailed in the Middle Ages, a period for which he seems to have felt some nostalgia. His aim was rather to provide "a sense of belonging" in the work group that would enable it to adapt itself to the changes as they occurred. But if unanimity prevailed throughout an organization and not just at the lower levels, the workers might not have many changes to adapt to.

WAS MAYO'S ANSWER THE RIGHT ONE?

Given his background and his predilections, it was natural that Mayo would disregard some of the clues the Hawthorne research provided. The girls in the test room at Hawthorne told the investigators that they could produce more because they "felt under less pressure" and had no "slave-driving bosses." Granted that the regular supervisors were not slave drivers and that it is necessary to look behind these ostensible reasons for the true cause of the change, are Mayo's conclusions the only possible ones? For example, two of Mayo's critics (Bendix and Fisher) point out:

> It is conceivable that the "sense of social function" depended as much in the end upon separation from the common run of the factory as upon the non-invidious attachment of the group members to each other. To sever the ties which relate the work group to the process of production may make observation of the group manageable. It will obscure the fact, however, that the worker is subject to the authority of the employer. If the factory were not in some measure an authoritarian institution, production would break down.[3]

The Hawthorne experiments did, however, produce some valuable findings regarding morale and productivity, and the principal account of those studies[4] contains much that can be of value to management. And although Mayo was only one of many who contributed to the studies, his own writings did much to publicize them and to stimulate management to take account of the importance of nonfinancial incentives.

---

[2] In "Democracy and Freedom," quoted in Reinhard Bendix and Lloyd H. Fisher, "The Perspectives of Elton Mayo," *The Review of Economics and Statistics*, November, 1949, p. 313.
[3] *Ibid.*, pp. 315–316.
[4] F. J. Roethlisberger and William J. Dickson, *Management and the Worker*, Harvard University Press, Cambridge, Mass., 1939.

Mayo's theories and those of Taylor are not untrue, but either singly or together they are somewhat incomplete. Later researchers whose work is discussed in Chapter 19 on direction have been attempting to fill in the gaps.

Review Questions

1. Why do Taylor and Mayo represent opposite points of view?
2. Can you think of any elements in a work situation that might be as important to morale as those identified by Taylor and Mayo?
3. Can you think of any situation in which you derived intense satisfaction from work? Can you suggest any reason why this experience was particularly satisfactory?

Case Study / The Inefficient Cleaners

In the Biltmore factory, each department has one or two clean-up men who clean around the machines and also take care of the washrooms, hallways, and other areas. The cleaning job has the lowest status of any in the plant, although the pay is fairly good because the plant has found it difficult to get enough cleaners.

There are twenty cleaners in all. They report to the foremen of the departments in which they work, but the foremen are very dissatisfied with them. A common complaint is that as soon as a man knows what is expected of him and learns to do it right, he quits. Moreover, the cleaners are frequently absent and often come late.

Mayo and Taylor are engaged as consultants to work on this problem. Each works independently and each makes a separate set of recommendations.

1. What do you think their recommendations would be?
2. Can you think of any new problems that acceptance of either solution, or of both solutions, might cause?
3. What would you yourself do?

Selected Readings

Work and Its Discontents: The Cult of Efficiency in America, Daniel Bell, Beacon Press, Boston, 1956. Trenchant criticism of both Mayo and Taylor with emphasis on the factors both ignore.

Motivation and Productivity, Saul W. Gellerman, American Management Association, New York, 1963, chap. 1. A brief account of Hawthorne and some of Mayo's other studies, together with analysis and criticism of his theories.

9

FAYOL

THE

UNIVERSALIST

At what moment in my life I became convinced
that social phenomena are, like physical phenomena, subject to natural laws independent
of our will, I cannot say. It seems to me that
I have never doubted it.
Henri Fayol: *L'Eveil de L'Esprit public*

9 Taylor and Gilbreth were concerned mainly with *techniques* that management might use and on the rank-and-file level at that. So, too, was Elton Mayo, although his approach to the problem was different. Harrington Emerson considered the subject from the viewpoint of higher management and the direction of the business as a whole, but he was also concerned mainly with techniques: dispatching, cost accounting, standardization, and so on. None of them attempted to deal with management as a function entirely separate from the various specialties. That task has been undertaken by others.

One of the most famous of the analyses of management itself is that made by Henri Fayol, a French engineer born in 1841. Fayol was chief executive (Directeur général) of a large coal and steel combine from 1888 to 1918, and during that time brought it from the verge of bankruptcy to high success. As a mining engineer, he had become accustomed to working with principles and techniques that embodied scientific truth. When he became a manager, he sought to develop something similar for management, and he eventually came to the conclusion that there was a single "administrative science" whose principles could be used in all management situations no matter what type of organization was being managed.

Fayol emphasized, however, that he used the word "principle" only for convenience. His principles, he said, were not immutable laws but rules of thumb to be used as the occasion demanded.

Thus he was a universalist only in that he thought the principles would be useful to all types of managers; he did not consider that a manager needs nothing more than a knowledge of management principles in order to manage successfully. At higher and higher levels, he said, a manager depends less and less on technical knowledge of what he is managing and more and more on knowledge of administration, but even at the very top he needs some technical knowledge and familiarity with the field.

In 1916, Fayol published a paper embodying his conclusions in the bulletin of a French trade association, under the title "Administration industrielle et générale" (General and Industrial Management). This was later published in book form, and is now considered one of the classics of management literature. It has had considerable influence not only on the theories of management current today, but on the actions and aims of many managers in important positions. Many who have never read Fayol's book have learned his principles at second- or third-hand and applied them to their own organizations.

Fayol defined the functions of administration as:

1. To plan
2. To organize (both men and materials)
3. To command—that is, to tell subordinates what to do
4. To coordinate
5. To control

FOUR IMPORTANT PRINCIPLES

He laid down a number of principles for the administrator, the most famous of which are the following:

1. *Authority is not to be conceived of apart from responsibility.* In explaining this maxim, Fayol stressed that those who have authority to issue orders should be willing to accept responsibility for the consequences. "Generally speaking," he wrote, "responsibility is feared as much as authority is sought after."[1] Today the converse of this proposition is often stressed: *Authority should be equal to responsibility.* That is, if a man is responsible for the results of a given operation, he should be given enough authority to take the actions necessary to ensure success.

2. There should be *unity of command.* That is, for any action whatsoever, an employee should receive orders from one superior only. This principle, of course, runs directly contrary to Taylor's recommendation that workers be directed by several functional foremen, each of whom would be a specialist in one particular phase of the operation. "I do not think," Fayol wrote, "that a shop can be well run in flagrant violation of this [the unity of command]. Nevertheless, Taylor successfully managed large-scale concerns. . . . I imagine that in practice Taylor was able to reconcile functionalism with the principle of unity of command, but that is a supposition whose accuracy I am not in a position to verify."[2]

3. There should be *unity of direction.* There should be "one head and one plan" for a group of activities having the same objective. How this differs from the preceding principle can be shown by a simple illustration: A company could conceivably split up a sales force of twenty men, all selling the same product in the same territories, and have two sales managers, each in charge of ten men. Each of the salesmen would take orders from only one man, but there would be no unity of direction unless all sales plans were coordinated at a higher level.

4. *Gangplanks should be used* to prevent the *scalar chain* from bogging action down. What Fayol meant by this is illustrated by the following diagram taken from his book:

A on the diagram represents the top man in the organization, who is directly over B and L. B, in turn, is over C, and L is the immediate superior of M, and so on down the line. In a strict observance of "channels," any communication from F to P would go all the way up one side of the triangle to A and down the other side, a time-consuming process.

Fayol suggested that a "gangplank" (the dotted line) could be thrown across without weakening the chain of command. It would only be necessary for the

[1] *General and Industrial Management,* trans. Constance Storrs, Sir Isaac Pitman & Sons, Ltd., London, 1949, p. 22.
[2] *Ibid.,* p. 69.

superiors of *F* and *P* to authorize them to treat directly with each other, provided each informed his superior of any action taken. Fayol wrote:

> It allows the two employees *F* and *P* to deal . . . in a few hours, with some question or other which via the scalar chain would pass through twenty transmissions, inconvenience many people, involve masses of paper, lose weeks or months to get to a conclusion less satisfactory generally than the one which could have been obtained via direct contact. . . .
>
> Is it possible that such practices, as ridiculous as they are devastating, could be in current use? Unfortunately there can be little doubt of it in government department affairs. It is usually acknowledged that the chief cause is fear of responsibility. I am rather of the opinion that it is insufficient executive capacity on the part of those in charge. If supreme authority *A* insisted that his assistants *B* and *L* made use of the "gang plank" themselves and made its use incumbent upon their subordinates . . . the habit . . . of taking responsibility would be established.[3]

OTHER PRINCIPLES

In addition to these, Fayol listed the following ten principles:

1. *Division of work,* or specialization. He wrote:

> Specialization belongs to the natural order. . . . The worker always on the same part, the manager concerned always with the same matters, acquire an ability, sureness, and accuracy which increase their output. Each change of work brings in its train an adaptation which reduces output . . . yet division of work has its limits which experience and a sense of proportion teach us may not be exceeded.[4]

2. *Discipline:*

> General opinion is deeply convinced that discipline [obedience, application, energy, and outward marks of respect] is absolutely essential for the smooth running of business. . . . I would approve unreservedly of this . . . were it followed by this other, "Discipline is what leaders make it." . . . Experience and tact on the part of a manager are put to the proof in the choice and degree of sanctions to be used, such as remonstrances, warnings, fines, suspensions, demotion, dismissal. Individual people and attendant circumstances must be taken into account.[5]

The best means of maintaining discipline, he said, are to have (*a*) good superiors at all levels; (*b*) agreements (made either with the individual employees or with a union, as the case might be) that are as clear and fair as possible; (*c*) penalties judiciously applied.

3. *Subordination of individual interest to general interest.* "The interest of one employee or group of employees should not prevail over that of the concern."[6] To ensure this, he added, there must be firmness and good

---

3 *Ibid.,* pp. 35–36.
4 *Ibid.,* p. 20.
5 *Ibid.,* pp. 22–23.
6 *Ibid.,* p. 26.

example on the part of superiors, agreements that are as fair as possible, and constant supervision.

4. *Remuneration.* Wages and salaries, Fayol stated, should be fair. They should depend both on circumstances (the cost of living, general economic conditions, the demand for labor, the economic state of the business) and on the value of the employee. The plan should reward well-directed effort, but should not lead to overpayment "going beyond reasonable limits."[7] The method of payment—by the day, by the job, by the piece, or by the day plus bonuses—would depend on the circumstances; each method had advantages and disadvantages. As to profit-sharing plans, which were to some extent in use in his day, he was extremely dubious, though he thought such a plan might be useful in some instances, particularly for managers. Profits, he pointed out, often depended on many factors other than individual capability even on the part of the highest managers. He was generally in favor of non-financial incentives (good working conditions, housing, etc.), though he believed they were possible only for large-scale concerns.

5. *Centralization.* Like division of work, Fayol felt, centralization belonged to the natural order. "In every organism . . . sensations converge towards the brain or directive part, and from the brain or directive part orders are sent out which set all parts of the organism in movement."[8] The question of centralization or decentralization, he said, is a simple question of proportion. In small firms, where the managers give orders directly to subordinates, there is absolute centralization; in large concerns, where a long scalar chain is interposed between managers and the lower grades, orders and counterinformation too have to go through a series of intermediaries.

> What appropriate share of initiative may be left to intermediaries depends on the personal character of the manager, on his moral worth, on the reliability of his subordinates, and also on the condition of the business. . . . Seeing that both absolute and relative value of manager and employees are constantly changing, it is understandable that the degree of centralization or decentralization may itself vary constantly.[9]

6. *Order.* By order Fayol meant a place for everything and everything in its place, a place for everyone and everyone in his place—and the right man in the right place. Moreover, he believed that this kind of order "demands precise knowledge of the human requirements and resources of the concern and a constant balance between these requirements and resources. Now this balance is . . . the more difficult the bigger the business."[10]

7. *Equity.* This Fayol defined as justice tempered with kindness.

8. *Stability of tenure of personnel.* Both managers and employees, and especially managers, he pointed out, need time to learn their jobs; if they leave or are removed within a short time, the learning time has been wasted. Generally, he said, the managerial personnel of prosperous concerns is stable; that of unsuccessful ones is unstable. But since—aside from the changes

[7] *Ibid.,* p. 27.
[8] *Ibid.,* p. 33.
[9] *Ibid.,* p. 33.
[10] *Ibid.,* p. 37.

inevitable because of death or retirement—the incompetent must be removed and some of those who do well must be promoted, stability of tenure is also a matter of proportion.

9.   *Initiative.* The manager must sacrifice his own vanity to encourage and inspire those under him to show initiative, within the limits of respect for authority and for discipline. The plans and proposals made will contribute to the success of the business and to morale.

10.   *Esprit de corps.* The manager must encourage cohesiveness and *esprit de corps* among his subordinates. Here Fayol cautioned particularly against two temptations the manager may be subject to: (1) divide and rule, and (2) abuse of written communications. Dividing up enemy forces may be clever, he said, but to apply the same tactics to one's own team is not. And a manager should give his subordinates oral rather than written directions and explanations whenever possible, because face-to-face contacts make for speed, clarity, and harmony.

SUMMARY

Fayol believed that there is an "administrative science" applicable to all kinds of administration in any type of industry or in government.

He defined the functions of administration as planning, organizing, commanding, coordinating, and controlling. Among the more important principles or guides he developed for the administrator were unity of command, unity of direction, responsibility equal to authority, and the use of "gangplanks" in cases where going through the channels of the scalar chain would take too much time.

Review Questions

1.   In what way are Fayol's functions of administration similar to the functions of management outlined in Chapter 1? How does his analysis differ from that in Chapter 1?
2.   What was Fayol's view of authority and responsibility?
3.   What did he mean by unity of command? How does this differ from unity of direction?
4.   What is the scalar chain? How did Fayol suggest it could be made less rigid?
5.   Which of Fayol's principles do you think would be of most help to a manager?
6.   Why may Fayol be considered a universalist?

Case Study / The French Postal, Telephone, and Telegraph (the P.T.T.)*

After Henri Fayol retired from business in 1918, he devoted his time to writing and speaking on the science of administration. He was particularly concerned

* From *L'incapacité industrielle de l'état: Les P.T.T.*, Dunod, Paris, 1921.

with what he considered the absence of good management in the public service. Hence he devoted some study to the French Postal, Telephone, and Telegraph Services, which were run by the government. He summarized their shortcomings as follows:

1. The services were headed by an undersecretary of state, a political appointee chosen by the Cabinet subject to parliamentary confirmation. Since the undersecretary was a political appointee, his tenure was uncertain: he would be out of a job whenever the Cabinet fell, which happened quite often under the Third Republic. His superior was the Minister of Public Works.
2. There was no long-range plan.
3. There was no budget.
4. There was excessive and abusive intervention by members of Parliament.
5. There was no incentive for effort and insufficient compensation for services rendered.
6. Since the undersecretary usually did not remain in office very long, he could not be held accountable for the shortcomings of the services.

The functions of the undersecretary were the preparation of laws and decrees, the signing of numerous orders and instructions, collection and expenditure of funds, approval of legislative bills and budgets, and the appointment of members of P.T.T. committees. He was assisted by a chief executive officer, a chief of service, and a central service, and worked with many committees: a management committee, a technical committee, an improvement committee, an organization committee, a marketing committee, a building committee, an examination committee, a promotion committee, and a disciplinary committee.

The following services reported to the chief executive officer: the central service, personnel and accounting, postal service, telegraph service, telephone service, postal checks and postal savings, and the inspection service.

1. In the light of Fayol's theories, what would he consider the principal shortcomings in the setup?
2. What would his principal recommendations for improvement probably be?

Selected Readings

Foreword by L. Urwick to *General and Industrial Management*, Henri Fayol (trans. Constance Storrs), Sir Isaac Pitman & Sons, Ltd., London, 1949. An account of the life, work, and significance of Henri Fayol.

The Philosophy of Management, Oliver Sheldon, Sir Isaac Pitman & Sons, Ltd., London, 1923. Another view of administration as a science in itself, applicable to all types of organizations.

3

The Management Functions

In the first chapter of this book, the management job was subdivided into seven basic functions: planning, organization, staffing, direction, control, innovation, and representation. This part explains some of the theories on which a manager may act in carrying out these functions and some of the techniques that have been developed to facilitate managerial action.

In some cases, the student will notice that there is more than one school of thought among the theorists, and that one school may tend to be somewhat critical of the other. This is true, for example, in the case of theories of organization; on one hand there are what are known as the "classical theories," on the other, a whole new set of theories developed by behavioral scientists, some of whom would discard the classical theories altogether. The author does not believe, however, that the two sets of theories are so incompatible that it is necessary to use one to the absolute exclusion of the other. In the last part of Chapter 11 on organization theory, therefore, he has endeavored to show how the manager who is aware of both can use both to advantage.

Again, in the matter of direction (Chapter 19) a number of different theories regarding leadership, motivation, and morale (management as the "direction of people") are considered, all of which the manager may need to take into account in formulating his own "leadership style," even though he may accept none of them without some reservations.

Chapter 23, the final chapter in Part Three, covers the theory and practice of decision making. While, as Chapter 1 points out, decision making is not a function in itself, it is a very important part of each of the seven main managerial functions.

10

WHAT

IS

ORGANIZATION?

*The agents of production are commonly classed
as Land, Labour and Capital . . . it seems
best sometimes to reckon Organization apart
as a distinct agent of production.*
Alfred Marshall: *Principles of Economics*

10 We sometimes speak of organization in connection with the work of one person, as when we say that a man is inefficient because he does not organize his work properly. In management literature, on the other hand, the term is commonly used only in cases where two or more people are working together for a common end. In that same literature, however, we find "organization" used in two somewhat different senses: to designate a process and to describe the results of that process.

ORGANIZATION AS A PROCESS

When two or more people are working toward the same objective, each one must know what part of the job he is supposed to do. Otherwise there will be confusion and duplication of effort. And no matter how precisely the work is divided, the efforts will not dovetail exactly unless some means of coordination is provided.

Considered as a process, then, organization includes (1) breaking down the work necessary to achieve the objective into individual jobs and (2) providing means of coordinating the efforts of the jobholders. In a small group, of course, both phases can be handled informally and orally and changes in assignments can be made easily if it turns out that one part of the work is proceeding too slowly to mesh with the other parts. But when achievement of the objective requires the work of a large number of people and the performance of many different tasks, some sort of permanent or semipermanent division of the work is usual; so is a formal system of coordination.

Perhaps the first social scientist to discuss the process of organization was Max Weber. According to Weber, the process includes:

1. Distributing the regular activities in a fixed way as official duties
2. Arranging a hierarchy of jobs, with each jobholder's authority to give commands strictly prescribed, including his authority to apply various means of coercion
3. Preparing written documents ("the files") to govern the general conduct of the institution[1]

THE RESULT OF THE PROCESS

The result of the process of organizing is "the organization"—the people employed and the network of relationships among them. When the organization was structured in the way he described, Weber said, the result would be a bureaucracy, which he thought would be the most efficient form of organization possible. He wrote:

[1] See Weber's essay "Bureaucracy," in H. H. Gerth and C. Wright Mills (eds.), *From Max Weber: Essays in Sociology*, Oxford University Press, Fair Lawn, N.J., 1958, pp. 196–239, translated by the editors from chap. 6, *Wirtschaft und Gesellschaft*, J. C. B. Mohr, Tübingen, Germany, 1925.

The fully developed bureaucratic mechanism compares with other organizations exactly as does the machine with non-mechanical modes of production.

Precision, speed, unambiguity, knowledge of the files, continuity, discretion, unity, strict subordination, reduction of friction and of material and personal costs—these are raised to the optimum point in the strictly bureaucratic administration.[2]

Since everyone would know what was expected of him and would have both the skills to do it and impersonal rules to guide him, Weber believed, the system would enable the organization to act as a unit, particularly when it was "monocratic"—that is, when there was one-man rule at the top. Coordination would be provided through the hierarchy of officials: If A were over B, C, and D, he would coordinate their efforts, and his own efforts would be coordinated with those of others on his level by a common superior, and so on, up to the top. Moreover, Weber specified that decisions made at one level could be appealed to the next higher level, thus ensuring further coordination when necessary. Still further coordination would be provided through the documents in the files since the jobholders could have recourse to them when there was a dispute over the way activities were being carried on.

Weber did recognize that the organization so structured would not function automatically in all cases. He acknowledged that there would be special cases in which the decisions could not be based on the documents in the files or on directions from the top, but he believed that even if the bureaucracy would not be perfectly efficient, it would be more efficient than any other type of organization.

To modern ears, the claim that a bureaucracy moves with greater speed and precision than any other type of organization may seem strange. We are accustomed to think of bureaucracies as slow and inefficient, bound down by red tape. However, Weber's point was that bureaucracy substituted a rule of rational law for rule by the whims of those who happened to be in charge and also made it more probable that the various jobs would be distributed to those competent to handle them. "The more complicated and specialized modern culture becomes," he said, "the more its external supporting apparatus demands the personally detached and strictly 'objective' *expert* in lieu of the master of older social structures, who was moved by personal sympathy and favor, by grace and gratitude."[3]

Weber's ideal bureaucracy, in which the man or men at the top can make a decision and be confident that the organization will move with speed and precision to carry it out, is still the goal of many practical administrators. Many of them accept his view that an organization must be built on (1) specialization, (2) a hierarchy of officials, each of whom possesses a planned amount of authority, (3) impersonal rules, and (4) managers trained for their jobs. Moreover, such an organization is not necessarily "bureaucratic" in the unpleasant

[2] *Ibid.*, p. 214.
[3] *Ibid.*, p. 216.

sense, for the impersonal rules may be few and not very constricting and people at all levels may have a considerable amount of freedom to use judgment.

Actually, an organization, even one in which there are many rules and a strictly organized hierarchy, cannot function like a machine. Although, by and large, the men at the top can rely on the people down the line to carry out orders in most cases, the action that follows a top management decision is not always undertaken as speedily or as precisely in accordance with top management plans as Weber thought it would be. People are not like parts of a machine designed for a specific purpose and that purpose only, and they are seldom so completely submissive that they will obey orders blindly. How they respond is affected by the extent to which they accept the goals of the organization, the way in which they interpret the instructions, and their relations with others in the organization. "Personal sympathy and favor" are always present no matter how rigid the bureaucratic structure.

For this reason, many writers on organization prefer to describe an organization as a social system in which each person is a variable who reacts to his associates and is himself the cause of the reactions of others. These interactions are, of course, influenced both by the way in which the duties are divided and the authority structure and by the personalities and attitudes of the members of the organization.

Like any society, also, the business organization has a culture (in the sense that anthropologists use the term), and this culture influences the members of the organization and is, in turn, influenced by their concepts, habits, and predilections. Each organization has a culture of its own, "its customary and traditional way of thinking and of doing things, which is shared to a greater or lesser degree by all its members, and which new members must learn, and at least partially accept, in order to be accepted into service in the firm."[4]

Because of this, what is known as the "informal organization," in which both the division of duties and the authority structure are somewhat different from those formally prescribed, may grow up side by side with the formal structure. In the process of developing a formal structure, therefore, the aim is to produce a system that will function as planned and to ensure that any informal organizations that develop within it will not function in such a way as to make attainment of the formal objectives less likely.

DESCRIBING AN ORGANIZATION

One of the simplest ways of presenting a picture of an organization—although it does not give a complete or wholly accurate picture—is to draw up an organization chart, which is simply a diagram of the formal authority structure. This shows by job title who reports to whom, that is, the subordinate-boss relationships. (In business, a subordinate is said to be "reporting" to his

[4] Elliott Jaques, *The Changing Culture of a Factory,* Tavistock Publications, Ltd., in collaboration with Routledge & Kegan Paul, Ltd., London, 1951, p. 251.

superior. This term has found favor, perhaps, because it sounds more democratic to say that Jones reports to Smith than to say that Smith is Jones's
boss. Also, it carries the important connotation that Smith can hold Jones
responsible for doing certain work.)

A chart of a small branch sales office might look like the chart in Figure 1.
If the office were larger, it might be necessary to insert another layer of supervision between the sales manager and the rank and file, as shown in Figure 2.
Here only the assistant sales manager and the office manager report to the
sales manager directly, and each of the rank-and-file employees reports to
one or the other of the two second-level managers.

The chart of a really large company would, of course, include more levels
of supervision between the rank and file and the top man and would be too
long to be shown on one page. Hence it is customary to use several charts: one

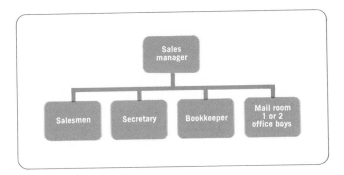

FIGURE 1

FIGURE 2

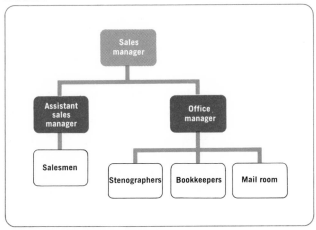

for the top management organization (the chief executive and his immediate subordinates) and one for each of the main departments. Sometimes the subgroups within the departments are also charted.

The chart shows each person in the group who his boss is and each boss who comes under his jurisdiction. But it leaves many questions unanswered. Is the office manager in Figure 2 empowered to give a stenographer a raise, or must he get permission from the sales manager first? Suppose he wants to fire one of the bookkeepers. May he do so without checking with the sales manager? May the assistant sales manager realign the territories of his salesmen without permission from the sales manager? May he, or the sales manager, permit a salesman to cut prices without permission from even higher authority? Does the sales manager's job include advertising and promotion, or are these functions handled by a department or departments in the home office?

The chart, then, shows who has authority over whom, but it does not show the extent of that authority or the duties each person in the organization is expected to perform, except insofar as duties are implied by job titles.

For this reason, larger companies often prepare organization manuals that include job descriptions in addition to the charts. Commonly, job descriptions state the objectives of each position,[5] that is, the results the jobholder should be trying to bring about, list the duties each one should perform, and endeavor to make clear the relationships between the positions. Figure 3 is an example of a job description.

Together, the charts and descriptions make up a plan of organizational behavior. They show who is supposed to follow whose directions, what part of the necessary work each person is supposed to do, who coordinates which segments of the organization, and what relationships should be maintained. They designate the official channels of communication from the top down and from the bottom up, and they enable superiors to determine whom to question if some part of the work is not completed on time or in the right way.

It is not, of course, always necessary to reduce these things to writing. In a small company, the division of duties and the authority structure may be so well understood that no written documents are necessary. Even some large companies do not attempt to picture their organization structures in diagrams and job descriptions, finding that oral instructions and explanations are sufficient. However, as firms become larger and more complex, they generally feel it is necessary to have charts at least, for the structure becomes too complicated for people to keep a clear picture of it in their heads.

To the extent that an organization structure has been well planned and the inducements in the form of money or other rewards are sufficient to bring about cooperation, the resulting organization will function more or less as the planners expected—although not, of course, with the precision of a machine. Stress has been laid here on the "bureaucratic model of organization," as it

[5] That is, for each position above a certain level. Descriptions may exist even for rank-and-file jobs, but they are seldom included in the manual.

SUPERVISOR, ACCOUNTING SECTION, MANUFACTURING DIVISION

I. FUNCTION

Furnishes functional guidance to the plant superintendents on, and provides services in connection with, accounting, auditing, budget, inventory and stock control, payroll, and tax activities.

II. RESPONSIBILITIES AND AUTHORITY

The responsibilities and authority stated below are subject to established policies.

1. Administers approved policies and procedures pertaining to accounting, auditing, budget, payroll, and tax activities, making such recommendations as he deems necessary to the comptroller through channels.

2. Administers approved policies and procedures pertaining to inventory and stock control activities, making such recommendations as he deems necessary to the manager of the Supply and Transportation Department through channels.

3. Consolidates the financial, accounting, budget, inventory and stock control, payroll, and tax reports and statements of the plants, and prepares such reports and statements for the division.

4. Establishes and maintains necessary accounting records for the division.

5. Establishes and maintains necessary cost control records for the division.

6. Maintains necessary inventory and stock control records for the division.

7. Maintains necessary production records for the division.

8. Maintains necessary records of receipts and disbursements and has custody of funds on hand for the division office.

9. Maintains necessary payroll records and accounts; prepares and pays division office payrolls and confidential payrolls of the division.

10. Conducts all tax activities for the division.

III. RELATIONSHIPS

A. General Manager, Manufacturing Division

Reports to the general manager.

B. Plant Superintendents and Section Supervisors

As directed, or as requested by the plant superintendents and section supervisors, advises and assists them in the accomplishment of their respective functions in all matters within his province.

C. Outside Auditors

Cooperates with independent auditors.

D. Others

Conducts such other relationships as are necessary to the accomplishment of his function.

FIGURE 3   Job description. (From *The Management Guide,* prepared by George Lawrence Hall with the assistance of other members of the department on organization of the Standard Oil Company of California; 2d ed., edited by Franklin E. Drew and George Lawrence Hall, Standard Oil Company of California, March, 1956, p. 63. Now out of print.)

is called, because most business organizations and, in fact, most large organizations in the modern world are bureaucracies in the sense that they embody a hierarchy, prescribed duties, some objectively determined rules, and managers trained for their jobs (if not through formal courses, then by precept, example, and experience).

Some students of organization, however, are beginning to believe that the bureaucratic pattern is not the only one that will enable people to work together for a common end but that there are other types of organization that would work better. These will be discussed in the next chapter, which deals with theories of organization.

SUMMARY

Organizations are formed to enable people to work together for a common objective. In the process of organizing, the work necessary to achieve that objective is divided into segments that make up jobs for individuals. The result is "the organization," a system in which people interact with each other in various ways—for example, following directions or not following them, stimulating each other to further efforts or hampering each other's efforts.

The formal organization, which may be described in organization charts and manuals and which generally is so described in the case of a large company, sets forth a pattern of behavior for the institution as a whole and for the various parts of it. Certain informal organizations may exist side by side with the formal organization because of the impact of the various personalities on each other, but by and large, the formal organization structure is likely to determine much of the behavior of the organization members unless it is so poorly conceived that it is impossible for it to function as the planners thought it would.

In the modern world, most organizations of any size are bureaucracies. That is, they have hierarchies of officials, each chosen for his supposed expertise in some phase of the work, and a man or a group of men at the top charged with coordination of the entire effort, plus a more or less strict division of duties for those below the top, plus some impersonal rules. They are not necessarily bureaucratic, however, in the sense that they are bogged down in red tape.

Some of those who have studied the actual behavior of organizations, however, believe that this form of organization may defeat its own ends by making it less likely that the members of the organization will work together cooperatively.

Review Questions

1. Assuming that an organization is fairly large—that it includes, say, more than 1,000 people—do you think it is necessary to have a hierarchical structure? If not, can you think of any other way in which it might be organized?

2. Weber thought that in a bureaucracy officials might qualify for their posts by passing examinations. This is often the case in the civil service—in fact, Weber appeared to be thinking largely of civil services in describing his ideal bureaucracy. Do you think that managers in business should have to pass examinations to qualify? What sort of examination would you prescribe?
3. What are the main characteristics of a bureaucracy?
4. What two steps are necessary in organizing?
5. Why is "an organization" sometimes described as "a social system"?
6. Would you prefer to work under impersonal rules or under a system in which restrictions were applied and rewards granted on the basis of "personal sympathy and favor"? Why?
7. What means of coordination did Weber postulate for his bureaucratic form of organization?
8. Can you think of an example of the way in which an informal organization might develop side by side with the formal structure?

Case Study / The Perfect Organization

John E. Walsh, a recent graduate of a school of business that places heavy emphasis on the formal aspects of organization, has joined a small company run by a father and son. The father is chairman of the board and in charge of finance; the son is the president and in charge of manufacturing and sales. The company's success has been largely due to innovations in the electronics field, most of which were developed by the technical director, and to the sales manager's contacts in Washington.

There is a great deal of conflict between the father and the son (because the former tends to make all important decisions) and between the technical director, who wants to emphasize quality, and the sales manager, who is mainly interested in low costs and fast delivery. On the basis of his college studies, Walsh believes that these problems can be solved if the company has an organization chart that shows relationships clearly and job descriptions that set forth functions and authority in a way that leaves no room for misunderstanding.

Is Walsh's plan likely to succeed if he can get the chairman and the president to agree to it? Give reasons for your answer.

Selected Readings

"Organization as Affected by Purpose and Conditions," Russell Robb, in Harwood F. Merrill (ed.), *Classics in Management,* American Management Association, New York, 1960. A lucid explanation of why organization is necessary and why it takes different forms under different circumstances.

Modern Organization, Victor A. Thompson, Alfred A. Knopf, Inc., New York, 1961. See especially Chapter 2, which deals with Max Weber's theory of bureaucracy and the characteristics of modern bureaucracy.

The Bureaucratic Phenomenon, Michel Crozier, Phoenix Books, The University of Chicago Press, Chicago, 1967. An analysis of the effects of truly bureaucratic (in the sense of inflexible) organization, based on a study of bureaucratic organizations in France.

11
THEORIES
OF
ORGANIZATION

A hypothesis is important if it "explains"
much by little. Milton Friedman:
Essays in Positive Economics

11 In planning an organization structure, an organizer needs some definite guidelines to follow if he is to answer such practical questions as: How should the work be divided by departments and by individuals? How much authority to make decisions should be given to each jobholder? What means of coordination should be provided? Since the organizations shown in the charts in the preceding chapter are small and simple, these problems may not seem very difficult; but in many organizations there are hundreds, even thousands, of different activities to be performed, and the way in which each one of them is handled will affect the way in which others are, or can be, performed. Dividing the work and ensuring that the various segments are properly coordinated then become very complex tasks.

For quite a long time, both managers and writers on management have been in search of principles that will provide some guidance for the organizer, and a good many books advocating principles of various kinds have been published. Unfortunately, there is currently no general agreement on the validity of the principles proposed.

THE CLASSICAL THEORIES

What have come to be known as the classical theories of organization—"classical" largely because they are of comparatively long standing—are in part derived from Fayol's analysis of management and are sometimes cited as principles of management since organization is such a large part of management.

The most commonly mentioned are five whose initial letters form the name OSCAR: objectives, specialization, coordination, authority, and responsibility. Stated in the form of guides for the organizer, they take the following form:

O   The organization should have a clearly defined objective (or objectives). Also, each position should have an objective logically related to the overall objective in such a way that if each jobholder meets his goal, the goals of the entire organization will be met. If we accept the definition of organization as a means of enabling people to work together for a common end, this principle scarcely needs stating. And, in fact, the founders of an organization always do have objectives in mind, whether the organization is a government, a business, a philanthropic organization, or an organization of any other type.

S   So far as possible, the work of each person should be confined to a single function, and related functions should be grouped together. This principle of specialization, it may be noted, was used in structuring the branch sales office whose charts were shown in the last chapter.

C   Means of coordinating all efforts toward the common goal must be provided.

A   The organization must have a supreme authority, and a clear line of authority should run from that person (or group) down through the hierarchy— e.g., from the chief executive through the vice-president in charge of manufacturing, through the plant manager, through the production manager, through the foremen to the rank-and-file production employees, and from the chief executive through the marketing manager, through the general sales manager, through the regional sales manager, through the district sales manager to the salesmen. This is often referred to as the "scalar principle," and the resulting hierarchy is known as the "chain of command."

R   Authority should be commensurate with responsibility; that is, when anyone is made responsible for achieving a given objective, he should be given enough authority to reach it. This principle might be illustrated by a reference to budgets. If an executive is given a budget and held responsible for keeping within it, it is often found necessary to exclude certain expenses that will be charged against his department in the accounting records simply because he has no part in the decision to incur them. The expenses that he is made responsible for are those he has been given authority to approve or disapprove.

Other classical principles cited by writers on management include the following:

Efficiency   The organization should be so planned that the objective can be attained with the lowest possible cost, which may mean either money costs or human costs or both.

Delegation   Decisions should be made at the lowest competent level; that is, responsibility and commensurate authority should be delegated as far down in the organization as possible. It is sometimes said that responsibility cannot be delegated; in fact, some writers state as a principle that the responsibility of a superior for the acts of his subordinate is absolute. It may seem that there are two contradictory principles here, but it is not illogical to accept both. Let us say that A is B's immediate superior and that B, in turn, has a subordinate C. B is free to delegate decisions to C, but he is still accountable to A for the results of the decisions. It is part of B's responsibility not to delegate decisions to the incompetent, and if his judgment of C's competence was in error, he cannot expect A to excuse him simply because he personally did not make a given mistake.

Unity of command.   Each person should be accountable to only one superior. In the example above, C is accountable to B, while B is accountable to A. In the strict observance of this principle, A will never tell C what to do or correct him if he doesn't do what he is supposed to do. If C makes a bad mistake, A will talk not to C but to B about it, and B may pass along as much or as little of the complaint as he deems wise. Similarly, C should not be permitted to go to A with a request for help on a problem; he must go to B, even though B may have to consult A before taking action.

The span of control   No superior should have more than six immediate subordinates whose work is interrelated. (Some authorities use a different figure—say, four or eight.) As nearly as can be ascertained, this principle was first asserted by Gen. Sir Ian Hamilton, who commanded the British forces in the Battle of Gallipoli in World War I. "The average human brain," he wrote, "finds its effective scope in handling three to six other brains."[1]

Hamilton's principle was later publicized by a management consultant, V. A. Graicunas, and has been strongly supported by Lt. Col. Lyndall F. Urwick, a British authority on management and organization.

The Graicunas-Urwick principle stresses that the limitation applies only when the functions are interrelated and is based on the idea that every interrelationship is a point at which coordination is called for. Graicunas wrote:

> If Tom supervises two persons, Dick and Harry, he can speak to each of them individually or he can speak to them as a pair. The behavior of Dick in the presence of Harry or of Harry in the presence of Dick will vary from their behavior when with Tom alone. Further, what Dick thinks of Harry and what Harry thinks of Dick constitute two cross relationships which Tom must keep in mind in arranging any work over which they must collaborate in his absence.[2]

Graicunas believed that a superior with only two subordinates whose work is interrelated may have no less than six relationships to coordinate: two direct single relationships, two direct group relationships, and two cross-relationships (Harry with Dick and Dick with Harry). Using this as a basis, he calculated that supervising a group of twelve would involve the coordination of some 2,000 relationships, an impossible burden for the superior.

A short chain of command   There should be as few levels of supervision between the supreme authority in the organization and the rank and file as possible. Obviously, if directions flow down from the top through the chain of command and reports on what is actually happening follow the same channel, the longer the chain, the greater the chance that the directions or the reports will be distorted on the way.

Balance   The organization must be continually surveyed to ensure that there is reasonable balance in the size of the various departments, between standardization of procedures and flexibility, and between centralization and decentralization of decision making.

Imbalance between departments occurs because the amount of work to be

[1] *The Soul and Body of an Army,* Edward Arnold (Publishers) Ltd., London, 1921, p. 299.
[2] "Relationship in Organization," in Luther Gulick and Lyndall Urwick (eds.), *Papers on the Science of Administration,* Institute of Public Administration, New York, 1937, p. 184.

done by various groups changes as a company develops new products, new methods of production, new marketing plans, and so on. If the company decides to rely on advertising rather than on direct sales in marketing its products, it will probably need a larger advertising department and find it possible to reduce the size of its sales department. Greater mechanization or automation will reduce the need for production workers but increase the need for maintenance men since keeping the machines running will be a complicated task.

Again, standardized procedures are necessary in any large organization, but there is always the danger that they will spread over too much of the work and be enforced too rigidly. Then the organization will find it difficult to act as quickly as it should in many situations. To cite one possible case: It may be good policy for a company to require competitive bidding on large construction jobs, but to extend this policy to small alterations might mean holding up work to the point where new products would not come on the market until after competitive products had become well established. Thus in adopting a policy, management must balance the need to get the work done quickly with the need to have it done at the lowest possible cost.

Balance is necessary also between the principle of the span of control and the principle of the short chain of command, for shortening the span of control generally means lengthening the chain of command. If a company president has twelve executives reporting to him, about the only way he can reduce his span is to insert another layer of management, as in Figure 1. Then A, B, C, D, E, F, G, H, I, J, K, and L, who originally reported to the president, report to executive vice-presidents, each of whom has a span of six, while the president's span has been reduced to two. But the chain of command has been lengthened by an extra level of management.

FIGURE 1

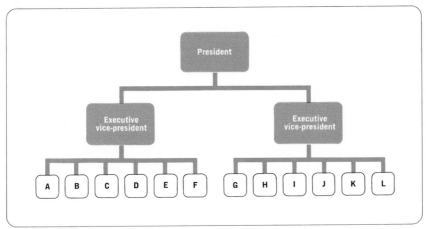

Further guides

But how does the organizer determine where one job begins and another leaves off? And how does he decide which jobs are sufficiently related to be grouped together in a single department or section? Here, too, classical theory offers some guidance.

For example, Luther Gulick, an authority on the subject who served as a member of the President's Committee on Administrative Management in the Roosevelt administration, suggested that each person in an organization might be classified in four ways:

1. By the major purpose he is serving, such as (in a municipal government) furnishing water, controlling crime, or conducting education.
2. By the process he is using, such as engineering or accounting.
3. By the persons or things he deals with or serves, such as (again in a municipal government) immigrants, veterans, or automobiles.
4. By the place where his work is done.[3]

Figure 2 shows division by purpose and process. The organizer may then decide whether he should put each of the horizontal divisions together and have them provide centralized services to the vertical departments or allow each of the vertical departments to have its own clerical force, its own engineering section, and its own financial section.

The decision will depend on the situation. It may be less expensive to centralize the engineering services if a great many different types of engineers are required, since none of the departments may be able to utilize the full time of, say, an electrical engineer, a hydraulic engineer, or a construction engineer. Clerical services of some kind will undoubtedly have to be provided for each of the vertical departments, but it might be possible to have a central department for large-scale clerical jobs or one that all departments could call upon for help with peak loads.

Division by persons or things dealt with may be a subdivision within a department, and this may also be true of division by place. A sales department, for example, is a purpose division; its objective is to bring in revenue by selling the company's products. It is also a process division, for sales are made by face-to-face explanation and persuasion. The department may also be subdivided by things dealt with (e.g., by different types of products), by persons dealt with (different types of customers), and by place (geographical division of the sales force).

When a company grows very large, however, these secondary criteria may become the first to be considered. This is known as "*divisionalization.*" One man is put in charge of all functions necessary to make and market a single product or a group of products, or he is given responsibility for all business (both marketing and manufacturing) in a given area. The first type of divi-

---

[3] "Notes on the Theory of Organization," in *ibid.,* p. 15.

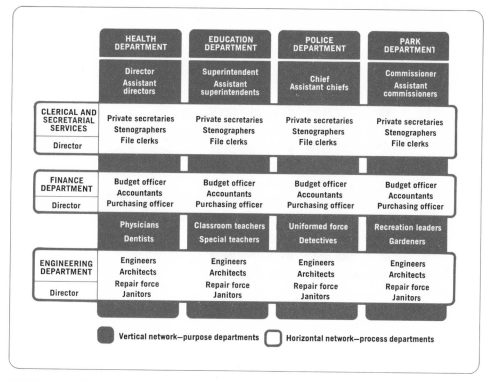

	HEALTH DEPARTMENT	EDUCATION DEPARTMENT	POLICE DEPARTMENT	PARK DEPARTMENT
	Director Assistant directors	Superintendent Assistant superintendents	Chief Assistant chiefs	Commissioner Assistant commissioners
CLERICAL AND SECRETARIAL SERVICES Director	Private secretaries Stenographers File clerks	Private secretaries Stenographers File clerks	Private secretaries Stenographers File clerks	Private secretaries Stenographers File clerks
FINANCE DEPARTMENT Director	Budget officer Accountants Purchasing officer	Budget officer Accountants Purchasing officer	Budget officer Accountants Purchasing officer	Budget officer Accountants Purchasing officer
	Physicians Dentists	Classroom teachers Special teachers	Uniformed force Detectives	Recreation leaders Gardeners
ENGINEERING DEPARTMENT Director	Engineers Architects Repair force Janitors	Engineers Architects Repair force Janitors	Engineers Architects Repair force Janitors	Engineers Architects Repair force Janitors

■ Vertical network—purpose departments   ☐ Horizontal network—process departments

FIGURE 2   Purpose and process subdivision in organization. Vertical network: Purpose departments. Horizontal network: Process departments. [Adapted from Luther Gulick, "Notes on the Theory of Organization," in Luther Gulick and L. Urwick (eds.), *Papers on the Science of Administration,* Institute of Public Administration, New York, 1937, p. 17.]

sionalization is known as product divisionalization, and the second type as geographical divisionalization. Geographical divisionalization is less common than product divisionalization, but it does exist—in oil companies and utilities, for example. In addition, many companies that are divisionalized by products lump all their overseas business into one international division.

Methods of dividing work have also been classified as "unitary" and "serial," as shown in Figures 3 to 5.

The division by persons or case numbers is the simplest method and requires a mere counting off (100 men to a century, six centuries to a cohort, ten cohorts to a legion).

The other types of unitary division require more examination of the actual content of the work. The geographical division of the sales force, for example, cannot be accomplished merely by dividing the total area of the country by

THE UNITARY METHOD FIXES LIMITS TO THE KIND OF WORK INVOLVED IN A POSITION:

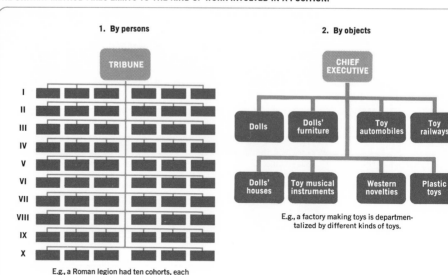

FIGURE 3   Differing methods of dividing work (1). (Adapted from Lyndall Urwick, *The Theory of Organization,* American Management Association, New York, 1952, p. 26a.)

the number of salesmen available, since the size of the market in each territory will vary, not by the number of square miles it includes, but by the number of potential customers there. Similarly, the division by objects (i.e., by products) necessitates examination of the production processes (the machines and methods used), and in the division by time, types, and incidence, it is necessary to examine the different types of cases that arise and the regulations that apply in each case. The advantage of this last type is that each group in the organization need become familiar with only one set of regulations. This method is, of course, a form of organization by process, just as the other unitary methods include division by place, people, or things dealt with.

Functional organization, another common method, demands still closer examination of the actual work to be done since it is often difficult to determine the limits of a function. Research engineering and industrial engineering are both engineering, but the work of the two types of engineers is so different that they would probably be in separate departments.

All the methods of division described in this section may be—in fact, often are—used in combination. Thus production is a function that may be subdivided by processes or groups of machines; and where all the people in one of the subgroups are doing the same type of work, there may be a further subdivision by persons (ten or fifteen men under each first-line supervisor), by

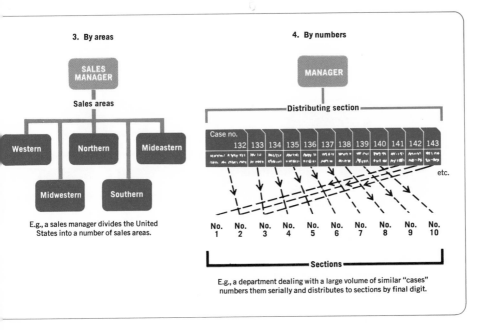

3. By areas

SALES MANAGER

Sales areas

Western   Northern   Mideastern

Midwestern   Southern

E.g., a sales manager divides the United
States into a number of sales areas.

4. By numbers

MANAGER

Distributing section

Case no. 132 133 134 135 136 137 138 139 140 141 142 143

etc.

No. 1   No. 2   No. 3   No. 4   No. 5   No. 6   No. 7   No. 8   No. 9   No. 10

Sections

E.g., a department dealing with a large volume of similar "cases"
numbers them serially and distributes to sections by final digit.

objects (ferrous castings and nonferrous castings in the foundry), or by areas
if the space covered by one department is too large for one first-line supervisor to manage effectively.

The classical organization

Observance of the classical principles produces an organization that is essentially a bureaucracy, although not necessarily one that is characterized by the
inflexibility and red tape often thought to be inherent features of bureaucracy.
Use of these principles also produces what is known as a line-staff organization
unless the enterprise is a very small one.

The distinction between line and staff in business is similar to the distinction between line and staff in armies. In either an army or a business, the line
organization is made up of those whose work contributes directly to achievement of the fundamental goal, the staff of those who assist the line in some
way, either by providing services or by developing plans, giving advice, questioning plans, or auditing performance.

The goal of an army is to win battles and wars; hence the line officers are
those who command the fighting groups, while staff officers are those who
provide supplies, transportation, and other auxiliary services and those who

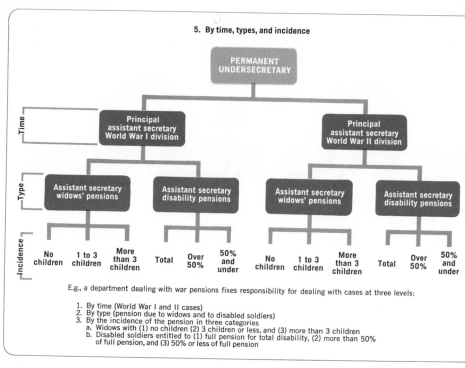

5. By time, types, and incidence

E.g., a department dealing with war pensions fixes responsibility for dealing with cases at three levels:

1. By time (World War I and II cases)
2. By type (pension due to widows and to disabled soldiers)
3. By the incidence of the pension in three categories
   a. Widows with (1) no children (2) 3 children or less, and (3) more than 3 children
   b. Disabled soldiers entitled to (1) full pension for total disability, (2) more than 50% of full pension, and (3) 50% or less of full pension

FIGURE 4 Differing methods of dividing work (2). (From Lyndall Urwick, *The Theory of Organization*, American Management Association, New York, 1952, p. 26b.)

work on strategic plans. Similarly, the main objective of a business is to make a profit by producing and selling goods or services, and only those who perform or supervise these services are members of the line organization. However, if the company is a financial institution that draws a large part of its revenue from investments, the financial executive may be considered a line man since his function itself produces a profit.

The line-staff organization is dictated by the scalar principle and the principle of unity of command; otherwise, it would be difficult to observe both in a company that had many specialists of different types. Under Frederick Taylor's functional-foremanship plan, each of the functional foremen was a specialist in some phase of the work and each gave orders directly to the workmen. This meant that there could be no unity of command and no single line of authority running from the top to each person in the organization; hence, the danger of conflicting orders existed.

Division of the jobs into line and staff activities gets around this difficulty. Thus an accounting department does not, at least in theory, issue orders to a department head or a foreman regarding his budget. Rather, the head of the accounting department reports further up the line to, say, the chief executive

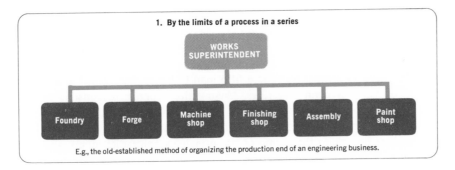

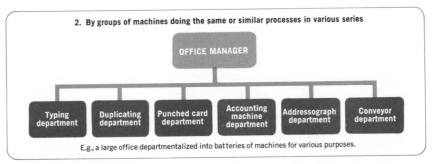

FIGURE 5   The serial method. (From Lyndall Urwick, *The Theory of Organization*, American Management Association, New York, 1952, p. 27a.)

of the plant or the company; then, if the chief approves the budget recommendations, he issues the orders down through the chain of command. Similarly, a methods department, which is responsible for developing improved methods of production, may report to the production manager, and he, rather than the methods man, will issue the necessary orders to the line foremen, who in turn will issue them to the rank-and-file employees.

Criticism of classical theory

The classical principles have met with widespread acceptance among writers on management and among managers themselves. But in recent years they have been encountering growing criticism.

A major criticism is that they are too broad to provide much help in the actual work of organizing. The principle of specialization, for example, does not tell the organizer how finely the tasks should be divided, and to say that an organization needs coordination is merely to state the obvious.

One of the more specific principles of classical theory is the span of control, and this, though it has ardent defenders, is often attacked as demonstrably untrue since a number of surveys have shown that spans in many successful companies are considerably wider than classical theory would permit. From the Graicunas formula, it appears that an executive with four subordinates will increase the number of relationships for which he is responsible by 127 per cent (from 44 to 100) if he adds a fifth man to his group. "This," one writer has said, "is just plain silly. . . . Making the superior responsible in any direct sense for all the relationships between and among his subordinates seems to extend unduly the functions of the executive."[4]

Again, critics claim that some of the principles contradict others and that therefore it is impossible to observe them all. The impossibility, in many cases, of providing both a short chain of command and a short span of control has already been noted. This difficulty can be resolved by a good compromise, but some critics find more serious contradictions. Thus, Herbert A. Simon, of Carnegie-Mellon University, has written that unity of command is incompatible with the principle of specialization:

> One of the most important uses to which authority is put in an organization is to bring about specialization in the work of making decisions, so that each decision is made at the point in the organization where it can be made most expertly. . . . If an accountant in a school department is subordinate to an educator . . . then the finance department cannot issue direct orders to him regarding the technical, accounting aspects of his work. Similarly, the director of motor vehicles in the public works department will be unable to issue direct orders on care of motor equipment to the fire-truck driver. . . .
>
> The principle of unity of command is perhaps more defensible if narrowed down to the following: In case two authoritative commands conflict, there should be a single determinate person whom the subordinate is expected to obey; and the sanctions of authority should be applied against the subordinate only to enforce his obedience to that one person. . . . Even this narrower concept of unity of command conflicts with the principle of specialization, for whenever disagreement does occur and the organization members revert to formal lines of authority, then only those types of specialization which are represented in the hierarchy of authority can impress themselves on decision.[5]

Simon's conclusion about some of the other classical principles was that they were "no more than proverbs"[6] and that administrative theory must be concerned with the weight that should be given to each of the various principles in any concrete situation. (This, of course, is in line with the classical principle of balance.)

Simon also found Gulick's suggestions for departmentalization more ambig-

---

[4] Mason Haire, "Biological Models and Empirical Histories of the Growth of Organizations," in Mason Haire (ed.), *Modern Organization Theory: A Symposium of the Foundation for Research on Human Behavior*, John Wiley & Sons, Inc., New York, 1959, p. 295.
[5] Simon, *Administrative Behavior*, 2d ed., The Macmillan Company, New York, 1957, pp. 23–26.
[6] *Ibid.*, p. 44.

uous than they seem at first glance. He pointed out that an education department may be viewed as a purpose organization (to educate) or a clientele organization (children) and that the forest service organization could be considered to be based on purpose (forest conservation), clientele (lumbermen and cattlemen utilizing public forests), or area.

In a later book, written in collaboration with James G. March and Harold Guetzkow, Simon characterized classical organization as representing "only a quite small part of the total theory relevant to organization behavior."[7]

But the most insistent criticism leveled against classical theory comes from exponents of the behavioral sciences, the sciences that deal with human behavior, such as psychology, sociology, and social anthropology. Writers identified with these fields claim that classical theory is too mechanistic and so ignores major facets of human nature. Some even say that the theory is incompatible with human nature. If this is true, it is a very serious deficiency, for formal organization structures are designed solely for the purpose of enabling *people* to work effectively together for a common end.

Those who base their criticism on this point feel that the classicists assume that top management need only (1) know what it wants done, (2) arrange a structure in which the various tasks are exactly dovetailed, (3) provide for coordination through common superiors or some other formal arrangement, (4) issue the necessary orders down through the chain of command, and (5) see that each person is held accountable for his part of the work. Then, the classicists are said to believe, the organization will function harmoniously and effectively, each person in it being spurred on by the hope of reward in the form of pay raises or promotions and by the fear of penalties in the form of denial of advancement or dismissal.

It is true that the classicists lay stress on the importance of leadership, or the ability to inspire *esprit de corps* at every level of management. But essentially they consider this the oil in the machine; the proper arrangement of parts, they believe, is the most essential factor.

THE NEWER THEORISTS

The newer theorists have developed a number of different approaches to the study of organization, and a number of different schools of thought have grown up. A very broad classification of the different approaches would be (1) the behavioral approach, (2) the decision-making approach, and (3) the biological or mathematical approach. However, there is considerable overlap among the three schools—for example, Herbert A. Simon, who is the principal exponent of the decision-making approach, built his new theory partly on the work of Chester I. Barnard, who was one of the first to take the behavioral approach. And those who have promulgated the mathematical theories—the newest approach—tend to be those trained in one of the behavioral sciences.

[7] March, Simon, and Guetzkow, *Organizations*, John Wiley & Sons, Inc., New York, 1958, p. 33.

Behavioral theories

Of late years, some behaviorists have been offering alternatives to the bureaucratic structure, but for the most part they have been less concerned with specific directions for organizing a company or a department than with pointing out the factors that classical theory does not cover and examining the ways in which organizations and their subdivisions actually behave, which may be very different from the way the formal structure would appear to dictate.

The behavioral writers are conscious that in an organization made up of human beings there are a great number of variables and that an attempt to alter any one of them is likely to start a sort of chain reaction. They point out that orders and policies, no matter how plainly stated, will be subject to reinterpretation according to the psychological "set" of those who transmit them or carry them out, the environment in which those down the line find themselves, and the conflicting pressures to which they are subject. These writers are aware that the people who make up an organization are motivated by many forces besides those taken into account by the classicists and may be seeking goals quite different from those assigned to them by the organization manuals.

For example, a man may want to head a large department, not because doing so will enable him to make more money or do a better job for his company, but because he obtains ego satisfaction from knowing that he is the boss of a large group. Again, a man may be incapable of acting in accordance with the spirit of a policy or an order and so be forced to find ways of appearing to follow it. This was probably the case with the manager who made a practice of giving each new employee a very poor score on his semiannual merit rating and then raising the mark gradually with each new review. He knew that his superiors considered developing those under him an important part of his job, but he was incapable of doing so or did not wish to bother. Hence he used the only means open to him of *seeing* to do so, indicating through better and better scores that he was fostering improvement. This had, of course, consequences that top management never intended when it wrote "developing subordinates" into his job description. All his employees knew what was happening (the older ones told the new ones), and they realized that their performance had little or no effect on the way they were rated—a discouraging situation, to say the least.

Chester I. Barnard　One of the first writers on organization to take a behavioral view of the subject was Chester I. Barnard, who at one time served as president of the New Jersey Bell Telephone Company. He was impelled toward this, he said, because:

> Nothing of which I knew treated of organization in a way which seemed to me to correspond either to my experience or to the understanding implicit in the conduct of those recognized to be adept in executive practice or in the leadership of organizations. Some excellent

work has been done in describing and analyzing the superficial characteristics of organizations. It is important, but like descriptive geography with physics, chemistry, geology, and biology missing.[8]

Barnard defined organization as a "system of cooperation," which is a definition any classicist could easily accept, for cooperation implies working together for a common purpose. However, Barnard gave far more weight to the psychological and sociological factors that affect the degree of cooperation than most classicists do.

Whereas classical theory implies that authority is delegated from the top down, Barnard thought of it as delegated upward:

> A person can and will accept a communication as authoritative only when four conditions simultaneously obtain: (a) he can and does understand the communication; (b) *at the time of his decision* he believes that it is not inconsistent with the purpose of the organization; (c) *at the time of his decision,* he believes it to be compatible with his personal interest as a whole; and (d) he is able mentally and physically to comply with it.[9]

To cite a hypothetical case that has many parallels in reality, let us say that foreman A is given a course in human relations in which he is told that he is expected to treat his employees with consideration and to explain the reasons for his orders whenever possible. If subordinates make mistakes or disobey orders, he is told, he should not bawl them out; rather he should attempt to show them why they were wrong and try to persuade them to do better in the future. His past practice (the practice foremen used when he was an apprentice) has been to bawl out those who made mistakes or broke rules, and if they persisted in error, to punish them with a day's layoff or even dismissal if he could get the latter approved by the higher-ups.

The new ideas are couched in plain language in the course, but foreman A does not really understand them. His translation would be: "Management is getting soft," or "Management is so afraid of the union it wants to coddle the employees." He believes that putting the instructions into effect would be contrary to the interests of the organization ("You can't get out production that way") and contrary to his own interests since he will be judged by the amount of production he gets out. Thus, although higher management has issued an order that it supposedly has the authority to issue, it *cannot* get that order obeyed unless it changes the foreman's attitude or replaces him with someone else.

Barnard felt, also, that most earlier discussions of organization had put too much emphasis on economic motives: ". . . it seems to me to be a matter of common experience," he wrote, "that material rewards are ineffective beyond the subsistence level excepting to a very limited proportion of men; that most men neither work harder for more material things, nor can be induced thereby to devote more than a fraction of their possible contribution to organized

[8] Barnard, *The Functions of the Executive,* Harvard University Press, Cambridge, Mass., 1938, p. viii.
[9] *Ibid.,* p. 165.

effort." [10] Far more important, he said, were such inducements as the opportunity for distinction and power, desirable conditions of work, a chance to experience pride of workmanship, the feeling of working toward altruistic ideals, pleasant associations with others, the opportunity for participation in the course of events, and what he termed "the condition of communion," by which he meant membership in a group that provides not only an opportunity for companionship but mutual support in personal attitudes—the "feeling of belonging" that Elton Mayo felt was all-important.

Barnard was not naive enough to think that all men are moved by all these incentives all the time or that any organization could provide all of them for everyone: ". . . different men are moved by different incentives or combinations of incentives, and by different incentives or combinations at different times. . . . A second fact is that organizations are probably never able to offer *all* the incentives that move men to cooperative effort, and are usually unable to offer adequate incentives." [11]

For this reason, Barnard believed, the organization must use "persuasion" as a means of motivation, and although he recognized that coercion can be considered a form of persuasion, he thought other types more important and more effective.

Barnard's analyses take in more territory than those of the classical theorists, but his writings have been more useful in alerting managers to factors undreamed of in the philosophy of the classicists than as practical guides. In the end, he fell back on leadership and the proper selection of leaders as the really important factor in organization, which is only another way of saying that it takes good management to develop a good organization.

Role conception   Many of the sociologists who have been studying the effects of various types of organization have laid great stress on role conception and role interpretation as points to be studied in considering the motivations that prompt action by people within the organization.

As Herbert Simon explains this idea, ". . . the captain goes down with his ship because he has accepted the role of captain, and that is what captains do in our culture." [12] Foreman A, whose human relations training passed through his head without affecting his attitude at all, had a conception of his role as boss—as a man who tells people what to do and bawls them out if they don't do it. Similarly, people have conceptions about other people's roles. A man whose idea of a boss is like that of foreman A might feel that a superior who practiced the procedures taught in the human relations class was weak and indecisive.

Bakke and the fusion process   E. Wight Bakke of the Yale Labor and Management Center has approached the subject of organization from the viewpoint

---

[10] *Ibid.*, p. 144.
[11] *Ibid.*, pp. 148–149.
[12] Simon, *op. cit.*, p. xxx.

that it embodies a fusion process. The individual, he points out, hopes to use the organization to further his own goals, while the organization attempts to use the individual to further its goals. In the fusion process, ". . . the organization to some degree remakes the individual and the individual to some degree remakes the organization."[13]

Bakke lists the individual's goals as security, progress, and justice with respect to (1) possession of means; (2) optimum performance; (3) health or internal harmony; (4) understanding; (5) autonomy, or freedom of movement and decision; (6) integration, or significant and effective relatedness; (7) respect.

The attempt to make the formal organization a means of accomplishing these goals Bakke terms the "personalizing process." The "fusion process" is the fusion of the personalizing process and the "socializing process," which is accomplished through the "bonds of organization," such as the formal organization, the informal organization, the work flow and the work assigned, and the system of rewards and penalties.

Bakke's model of the fusion process is shown in Figure 6. "Standing" in this case is the standing the man desires to occupy (e.g., leader, follower, critic, honest man, loyal man). It is the fusion of these personal goals and his actual position and function in the organization that determines his role in the organization.

Bakke's theory is designed to describe what actually happens within an organization rather than to lay down rules about organizing, though some guides to both executive conduct and organization structure may be implicit in his theory. For example, he notes the reciprocal character of each person's role:

> For one man to play the role of "benevolent supervisor," another has to play the role of "grateful subordinate." For one man to play the role of

[13] *The Fusion Process*, Labor and Management Center, Yale University, New Haven, Conn., 1953, pp. 12–13.

FIGURE 6   (From E. Wight Bakke, *The Fusion Process*, Labor and Management Center, Yale University, New Haven, Conn., 1953, p. 20.)

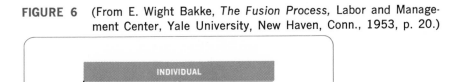

"presidential leader," another has to play the role of "citizen follower." . . .

One is led to wonder whether this situation doesn't throw some light
on why industrial paternalism fails to produce desirable results in many
cases. No man can play the role of "paternalistic employer" successfully
unless others will play the reciprocal roles of "child-like employees."[14]

Again, he says:

The question about the writing of individual and team job specifications
becomes not merely, "How can these specifications be written to assure
that all the activity required by a successful organization shall be performed?" but also, "How can the organizationally necessary tasks
incorporated in the activity required of participants be made more compatible with the activity the participant needs for personality realization?"

The question about loyalty to the organization is not merely "What can
the organization do for or to its participants in order to win their loyalty?" but also, "How can *what the participant does*, i.e., his organizational function, be so arranged that loyalty is generated as a by-product
of his organizationally and personally effective participation in organizational activities?"[15]

Bakke's associate, Chris Argyris, has stated that a basic conflict will exist
between the personalizing and the socializing process if the socializing process
requires people to work at jobs which:

1. Would tend to permit them little control over their workaday world
2. Would tend to place them in a situation where their passivity rather than
    initiative would frequently be expected
3. Would tend to force them to occupy a subordinate position
4. Would tend to permit them a minimum degree of flexibility and fluidity and
    tend to emphasize the expression of one or a few of the agent's relatively
    minor abilities
5. Would tend to make them feel dependent upon other agents (e.g., the
    boss).[16]

These conditions, he believes, are most likely to obtain where there is great
task specialization and strict observation of the unity-of-command and span-
of-control principles. In fact, he concludes that there is a basic incongruency
between the needs of a mature personality and the requirements of formal
organization developed in line with the classical principles. Such an organization, he says, requires employees to be passive, dependent, and subordinate,
to have a short time perspective, to use a few skin-surface abilities, and to
produce under conditions leading to psychological failure. Moreover, if
employees are mature, this inevitable incongruency increases (1) as the formal
structure based on the classical principles is made more clear-cut and logically

---

[14] *Ibid.*, p. 21.
[15] *Ibid.*, p. 45.
[16] E. Wight Bakke and Chris Argyris, *Organizational Structure and Dynamics*, Labor and
Management Center, Yale University, New Haven, Conn., 1954, pp. 21–22.

tight, (2) as one goes down the line of command, (3) as jobs take on more and more assembly line characteristics.[17]

Actions and reactions   In another phase of their work, some of the newer organization specialists have been calling attention to important side effects of the prescriptions offered by the classical theorists.

R. K. Merton has pointed out that the demand for control on the part of top management makes itself felt as a demand for reliability, that is, a demand that people down the line behave as expected. This produces:

1. A reduction in personalized relations. Each official reacts to other members of the organization not as unique individuals but as representatives of positions that have specified rights and duties.
2. Internalization of the rules of the organization. Rules become ends in themselves.
3. Increased categorization of decision making. Each decision is pigeonholed and handled according to definite procedures and criteria. This tends to make deciding more mechanical, and the criteria used in selecting alternatives may not include all the factors that bear on the situation.[18]

The rigidity that develops makes it easier for management to predict what people down the line will do, but it tends to foreclose the possibility of major contributions that require a breaking away from accepted procedures. This is the trend to conformity that has been pilloried in such books as W. H. Whyte, Jr.'s, *The Organization Man*[19] and Allan Harrington's *Life in the Crystal Palace.*[20]

Another writer, P. Selznick,[21] has pointed out that delegation of authority tends to increase administrative costs through such factors as the following: (1) increased training costs; (2) more conflict, which may develop with greater subdivision and more semiautonomous units; and (3) divergency of the subunits' goals from those of top management.

One type of chain reaction might be:

1. Management institutes a formal organization in which tasks are very finely subdivided and supervision is close.
2. Because they are left so little scope, employees tend to become apathetic about their jobs.
3. Since they find so little satisfaction in the actual work, employees seek it through such means as socializing during working hours and taking longer coffee breaks.
4. Management sees this as a failure on the part of the supervisors and therefore prescribes their role more carefully.
5. Supervisors themselves become apathetic.

[17] *Personality and Organization*, Harper & Row, Publishers, Incorporated, New York, 1957, p. 66.
[18] March, Simon, and Guetzkow, *op. cit.*, pp. 38–39.
[19] Simon and Schuster, Inc., New York, 1956.
[20] Jonathan Cape, Ltd., London, 1960.
[21] March, Simon, and Guetzkow, *op. cit.*, pp. 40ff.

6. Failure of the supervisors to do more than blindly enforce rules leads management to insert another layer of supervision between the first-line supervisors and the level above them.

(The foregoing is intended only as an illustration of what could happen. It is not contended that the chain of reactions actually would take this course. There are many other ways in which it could proceed.)

Motivational approach   In a sense, all the behaviorist organization specialists take a motivational approach to the company structure. They are concerned with the ways in which the goals of individuals and those of the organization can be made to fuse, or at least coincide to some extent. There is, however, a special approach which has been christened "the motivational approach" by its author, Rensis Likert.

Likert's approach is based on a number of empirical studies conducted by the Institute of Human Relations at Ann Arbor, Michigan, on the differences between good supervisors and bad ones—good supervisors being those whose groups achieved high productivity, and bad ones those in charge of low-productivity groups.

Likert follows Elton Mayo in stressing the importance of the work group. He says:

> It can be concluded, therefore, *that management will make full use of the potential capacities of its human resources only when each person in an organization is a member of one or more well-knit, effectively functioning work groups that have high skills of interaction and high performance goals.*[22]

Therefore, he believes, management should establish groups that meet these criteria rather than adhere to the traditional man-to-man pattern. These groups in turn should be linked by means of overlapping groups of supervisors, as shown in Figure 7. And in order to ensure that the "linking pins" perform their functions adequately, "It will usually be desirable for superiors not only to hold group meetings with their own subordinates, but also to have occasional meetings over two hierarchical levels."[23]

One foundation for this theory is a research finding that good supervisors tend to have more influence on their own superiors than poor supervisors. When supervisors who had above-average influence with their own bosses followed procedures that are generally considered to be good supervisory behavior, their subordinates tended to react favorably. But when supervisors who were below average in the amount of influence they had with their superiors practiced the same desirable supervisory procedures, they usually failed to obtain a favorable reaction from their subordinates and not infrequently got an adverse reaction. Strengthening the bonds of organization by the linking-pin method is believed to ensure three-way communication (up, down,

---

[22] "A Motivational Approach to a Modified Theory of Organization and Management," in Haire (ed.), *op. cit.,* p. 192. (Likert's italics.)
[23] *Ibid.,* p. 203.

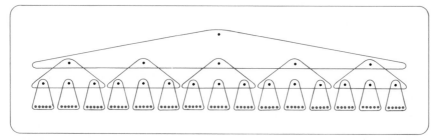

FIGURE 7   [From Rensis Likert, "A Motivational Approach to a Modified Theory of Organization and Management," in Mason Haire (ed.), *Modern Organization Theory: A Symposium of the Foundation for Research on Human Behavior*, John Wiley & Sons, Inc., New York, 1959, p. 193.]

and sideways between people on the same level) and to permit each supervisor some opportunity to influence his boss. In this way, it is thought, the goals of the persons in the organization and those of the organization itself will become compatible if not exactly identical.

Ideas for the organizer

If the organizer follows the classical theories, the resulting structure will necessarily be characterized by a hierarchy, a division between line and staff, and a series of rather precisely defined jobs and relationships. Those who have been examining organizations in the light of behaviorist findings, on the other hand, do not necessarily prescribe any one type of organization.

Some of them appear to accept the hierarchical form but believe it can be much improved by less narrow specialization, by permitting more participation in decision making on the part of the lower ranks, and by a more democratic attitude on the part of managers at all levels. None of these features is impossible to achieve where classical principles are observed, unless they are used too rigidly, but many behavioral scientists believe that they usually are used too rigidly and that managers need to focus more attention than they customarily do on their human resources.

Rensis Likert's "linking-pin" plan would, of course, require some sort of change in the formal structure, but not a very drastic one. However, a few others have recommended more far-reaching changes.

One suggested organization structure based on behavioral theories is what is known as the "organic organization"—a structure in which there is a minimum of formal division of duties. Theoretically, then, everyone pitches in and contributes to the best of his ability to the solution of any problems that arise, and so far as the regular work is concerned there is more or less general agreement about who should do what since each person is known to possess certain skills and to lack others.

Some very small enterprises are, in fact, largely organic in structure. People may have job titles which indicate that they are expected to do certain types of work, but the boundaries of their jobs are not set formally or precisely, and they often do work that is ordinarily not expected of one with a similar title—work demanding either a higher or a lower skill than they ordinarily exercise. Probably also, some small groups within larger organizations are essentially organic in nature.

Moreover, at least one company in the United States, Non-Linear Systems, Inc., a California manufacturer of electronic instruments, once introduced organic organization throughout. It achieved extraordinary results on the lower levels by breaking up a production line into small "organic" groups, but it later reverted to a more classical form of organization at higher levels.[24]

Another behavioral idea regarding the actual division of the work is the view that organizations will be made up of temporary task forces or matrices in which membership will shift as needs and problems change. Warren G. Bennis, of MIT, argues that bureaucracy—that is, the classical structure—is too rigid to be serviceable in a time of rapid technological change and that it will, therefore, eventually disappear, to be replaced by the task-force type. Of the organization of the future, he says:

> First of all, the key word will be temporary. Organizations will become adaptive, rapidly changing *temporary systems*. Second, they will be organized around *problems-to-be-solved*. Third, these problems will be solved by relative groups of *strangers* who represent a diverse set of professional skills. Fourth, given the requirements of coordinating the various projects, *articulating points* or "linking pin" personnel will be necessary who can speak the diverse languages of research and who can relay and mediate between the various project groups. Fifth, the groups will be conducted on *organic* rather than on mechanical lines; they will emerge and adapt to the problems, and leadership and influence will fall to those who seem most able to solve the problems rather than to programmed role expectations. People will be differentiated, not according to rank or roles, but according to skills and training. . . . Though no catchy phrase comes to mind, it might be called an *organic-adaptive* structure.[25]

The decision-making approach

Barnard's theories were further developed by Herbert A. Simon in his book *Administrative Behavior*. Like Barnard, Simon emphasized that the equilibrium or survival possibilities of an organization depend on its ability to induce cooperation. And in discussing decisions, Barnard wrote:

> The general executive states that "this is the purpose . . . the direction in which we wish to move, before next year." His department heads . . . say to their departments . . . "This means for us these things now, then others next month, then others later, to be better defined after experi-

24 See Arthur Kuriloff, *Organization on Behaviorist Lines*, in Ernest Dale (ed.), *Readings in Management: Landmarks and New Frontiers*, McGraw-Hill Book Company, New York, 1965, pp. 228–229, for an account of Non-Linear Systems' experience.
25 "Organizational Developments and the Fate of Bureaucracy," *Industrial Management Review*, MIT, Spring, 1966, p. 52.

ence." Their subdepartment . . . heads say: "This means for us such and such operations now at these places, such others at those places, something today here, others tomorrow there." Then district or bureau chiefs in turn become more and more specific, their sub-chiefs still more so. . . . But meanwhile, back and forth, up and down, the communications pass, reporting obstacles, difficulties, impossibilities, accomplishments; redefining, modifying purposes level after level.[26]

Simon expanded the idea of this hierarchy of decision making into a method of actually structuring an organization. He suggested that the structure be designed through an examination of the points at which decisions must be made and the persons from whom information must be required if decisions are to be satisfactory.

Another writer has suggested what he calls the "functional teamwork" approach to organization as a means of ensuring that decisions regarding various areas are made by those most expert in the areas. He suggests that the distinction between line and staff be done away with and that all functions be given authority and decision-making power in their own functional areas, as shown in Figures 8a and 8b. He writes:

There is a logical sequence of decisions. . . . Thus, the first decision relates to the product and service mix; and once that is made, then manpower planning makes decisions about manpower, size of the staff, composition; finance makes decisions about financial requirements; manufacturing makes decisions as to production schedules; marketing makes decisions as to its sales effort to achieve the called-for sales results; and so on.

. . . There is teamwork, *but only to the extent that decisions of one function impinge on the operating efficiency of another.*[27]

Biological-mathematical theories

An organization has many properties in common with a living organism. To mention just a few: It comes into existence, then grows, reaches a peak, then often (or even usually) declines, and finally dies, and it reacts to its environment. Also, like a biological organism it is made up of many parts that interact with each other in varying and complex ways.

This has led some writers to conclude that an organization, like an organism, cannot grow and still function unless the balance between its various parts is maintained in some fairly exact ratio, or even some exact ratio, like the ratios in geometry. (For example, the relation between the radius of a circle and its circumference remains the same no matter how large or how small the circle is.)

In support of this idea, Mason Haire has developed what he calls the "square-cube" theory. As the mass of an object is cubed, its surface is only squared, and Haire believes that something similar occurs in organizations.

26 Barnard, *op. cit.*, p. 232.
27 Gerald G. Fisch, "Line-Staff Is Obsolete," *Harvard Business Review*, September–October, 1961, p. 77.

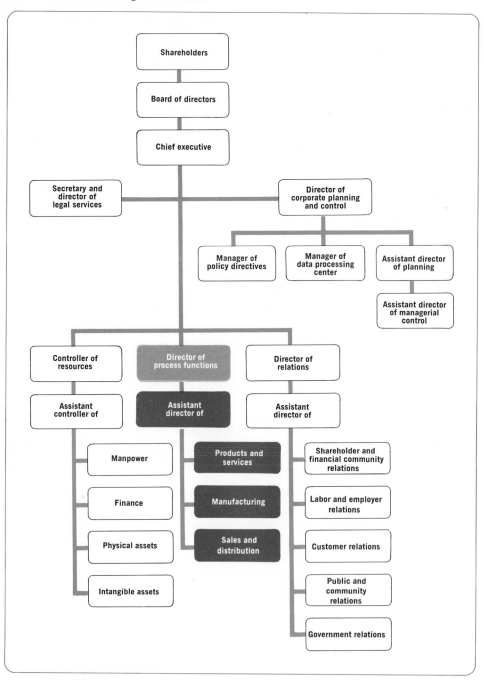

FIGURE 8a How a company might be organized under the functional team-work concept. (From Gerald G. Fisch, "Line-Staff Is Obsolete," *Harvard Business Review*, September–October, 1961, p. 76.)

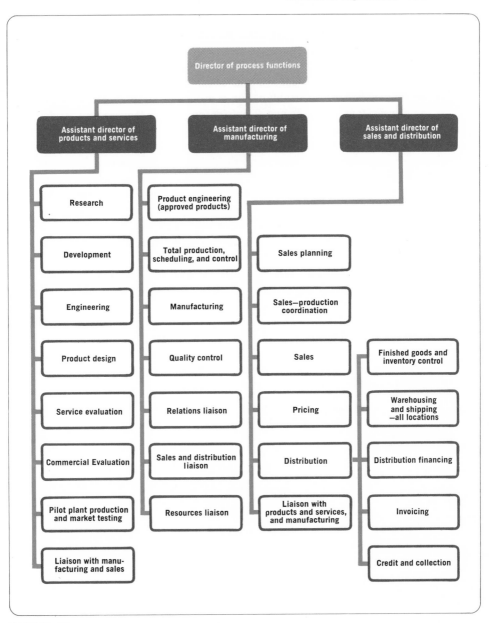

FIGURE 8b

By examining what happened in a number of growing companies, Haire discovered that a constant relationship continued to exist between "surface" employees (that is, those maintaining relationships with customers and others outside) and "inside" employees. If, for example, the cube root of the number of inside employees doubled, the square root of the number of outside employees would also double. Thus if an organization started with 27 inside employees (cube root 3) and 9 outside employees (square root 3) and grew to the point where it had 216 inside employees (a doubling of the cube root to 6), the square root of the number of outside employees would double and the organization would have 36 people in this category.[28]

While some other studies have shown a similar relationship, it is quite possible that the ratio is not an inevitable one like the relationship between the circumference of a circle and its radius. W. H. McWhinney has suggested that the original relationship may have occurred because economy of scale dictated the size of each group, and the ratio may have remained constant because of tradition.[29]

Another line of exploration has been the possibility of predicting the results of various organization changes through the use of computers, since this makes it possible to take a very large number of variables into account. However, the variables that affect the functioning of an organization are not only numerous but difficult, if not impossible, to express in numbers, and the use of a computer requires quantification. Probability theory has been used to determine how large certain groups should be,[30] but this is a different matter from using it to structure an entire organization.

EVALUATING THE THEORIES

It would be impossible to recapitulate all the organization theories that have been developed in the last few years since almost every writer on the subject has a new theory or at least a new approach to the study of organization and some new observations of the way in which organizations actually behave under given circumstances.

Where does all this leave the practical man who must figure out a good way to divide the work in a steel mill, an automobile plant, a department store, or an advertising agency? On the one hand, he has the classical rules and on the other, a vast number of warnings that adherence to them will probably entail consequences that he does not expect and will not like.

It must be remembered, also, that practically none of the theorists—classical or nonclassical—derived his ideas a priori in an ivory tower. Many of the men who developed classical theory had a good deal of practical experience in managing organizations and were highly successful in doing so. And if many of the later theorists are academicians, most of them, perhaps all,

---

[28] "Biological Models and Empirical Histories of the Growth of Organizations," in Haire (ed.), op. cit., pp. 272–306.
[29] "On the Geometry of Organizations," *Administrative Science Quarterly*, December, 1965, pp. 356–357.
[30] This technique is discussed in Chapter 29, "Operations Research—Management Science."

have conducted experiments in real companies, experiments that they have attempted to make as nearly scientific as possible. They have gone into plants and offices and talked with people at all levels, observed the working out of different forms of organization, and derived their generalizations from what they have observed.

The principal quarrel is between the behaviorists and the classicists; the decision school does not reject the hierarchical form of organization but only suggests new criteria for dividing the work, and the mathematical theories are as yet little more than tentative ideas that might be used in conjunction with either the classical theories or the behaviorist suggestions.

One explanation of the classical-behavioral dispute is that the theorists in each group may be influenced by their own predilections and by their times. A man of authoritarian turn of mind finds something aesthetically satisfying in the idea of the chain of command and a high degree of specialization. A man who is primarily concerned with the happiness and satisfaction of human beings, on the other hand, may tend to look upon a mechanistic approach with something approaching horror. Again, classical theory was formulated at a time when an authoritarian approach was regarded as quite normal in business, while the newer thinkers are influenced by the great emphasis on "human relations" in recent years. This emphasis, in turn, has grown out of developments that have tended to rob the rewards and penalties management can dispense of some of their force. Unions have curbed management's power to hire and fire at will, and comparatively full employment, unemployment compensation, and the existence of new opportunities have mitigated the impact of the extreme penalty of dismissal.

Fortunately, the practical man need not be concerned with developing a plan that will be applicable to all organizations. He need only do the best he can by his own organization in the light of its objectives, the resources available to it, and the type of people he is dealing with.

Moreover, there is some evidence that technology may have an important effect on the extent to which any given principle should be observed. A group of British researchers came to this conclusion after studying a number of companies of different types:[31]

1. Companies engaged in job-shop production: those producing units or small batches to customers' requirements, those making prototypes, and those fabricating large equipment in stages
2. Companies engaged in large-batch and mass production
3. Process production companies engaged either in intermittent production of chemicals in a multipurpose plant or in continuous-flow production of some type

The structures of the firms in the first and third groups had a great deal in common. In both, the distinction between the line and staff was blurred and the structures were beginning to verge on the organic. In the job-shop type of

31 See Joan Woodward, *Industrial Organization: Theory and Practice*, Oxford University Press, Fair Lawn, N.J., 1965.

production, the first-line supervisors tended to possess enough technical knowledge to dispense with staff assistance, and in the process production companies, the staff frequently had line authority. And in some of the latter that did observe the line-staff distinction, the line executives and the staff executives were interchangeable, and a man might shift from line to staff and back again quite easily.

Of the large-batch and mass-production companies, on the other hand, the more successful tended to observe the classical principles: a clear definition of duties, unity of command, separation of line and staff functions, and a short span of control for the chief executive. In her report on this research, Joan Woodward observes:

> The tendency to regard large batch production as the typical system of modern industry may be the explanation of this link between success and conformity with [classical] management theory. The people responsible for developing management theory no doubt had large batch production in mind as they speculated about management.[32]

Using the classical principles

The classical principles are still widely used in organizing and reorganizing companies today. In a survey of large and medium-sized companies conducted for the American Management Association,[33] companies were asked what principles they had found useful and to what extent they were using behavioral ideas. The vast majority mentioned one or more of the classical principles, and some who said they were using behavioral ideas actually cited classical principles as examples.

However, the classical principles are undoubtedly more useful when they are used—as Fayol said his principles should be—as general guides and not as immutable principles.

For example, most business organizations would find it hard to function effectively without a supreme authority and a chain of command. The supreme authority, however, need not necessarily be a single person—it may be a committee made up of the heads of various functions.

Not all organizations have a single supreme authority, however. For example, the U.S. government operates under a system of checks and balances. Thus the President cannot overrule Congress, though he can influence—and in some cases almost dictate—its actions. The Supreme Court can overrule Congress by declaring the laws passed unconstitutional, but Congress can, in turn, modify the rulings of the Supreme Court by amending the Constitution, although an amendment is difficult to achieve since it requires a two-thirds vote. Thus it cannot be said that the President is answerable to Congress or to the Supreme Court or that the Supreme Court is under Congress or over it.

It could, of course, be contended that the supreme authority rests in the voters, who elect both the President and Congress. But the voters have no real

[32] *Ibid.,* pp. 71–72.
[33] Ernest Dale, *Organization,* American Management Association, New York, 1967.

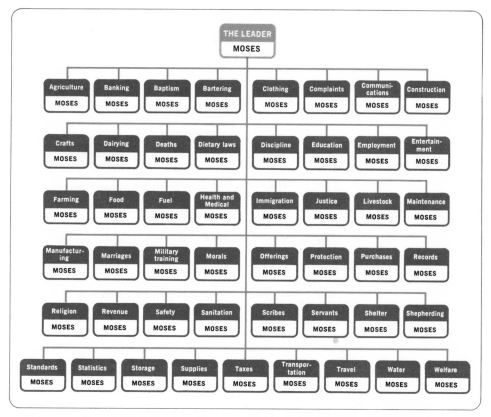

FIGURE 9 Disorganization. Perhaps the earliest recognition of the fact that the span of control can be too large is found in the Bible. The Book of Exodus, Chapter 18, tells how "Moses sat to judge the people: and the people stood by Moses from the morning unto the evening." Moses' father-in-law, Jethro, saw this and told him, "The thing thou doest is not good. Thou wilt surely wear away, both thou, and this people that is with thee: for the thing is too heavy for thee; thou art not able to perform it thyself alone." Figure 10 shows the organization Jethro proposed.

control over the Supreme Court, whose members are appointed for life and cannot be removed from office except by impeachment.

Even in business there are instances in which more than one authority exists. Two equal partners, for example, must iron out their disagreements as best they can without appeal to higher authority. The company from which the vast Shell Oil Company grew was at one time managed by two brothers, Marcus and Samuel Samuel, neither of whom could act independently under the terms of their partnership:

> They had to reach agreement, but never did so, on any single subject, without a violent quarrel. Members of the staff remember the sounds of

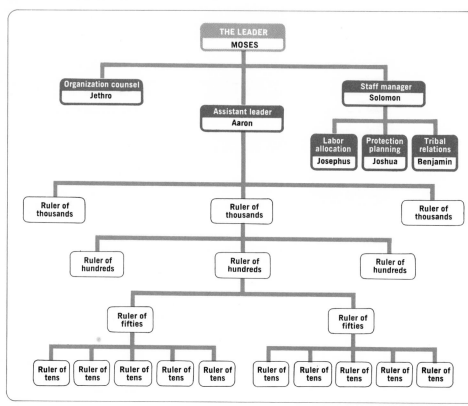

FIGURE 10   Organization. The subordinate rulers, Jethro suggested, could judge "every small matter" and bring the great matters to Moses. Up to this point, the Israelites had spent thirty-nine years on a journey that had taken them only about halfway to the Promised Land. After the reorganization took place, the remaining half of the journey was completed in less than a year.

terrible combat, anger, and recrimination . . . that could be heard through the door of the office that they shared. Sometimes a clerk would be summoned to bring information, and while he waited "the two brothers would always go to the window, their backs to the room, huddled together close, their arms round each other's shoulders, heads bent, talking in low voices, until suddenly they would burst apart in yet another dispute, Mr. Sam with loud and furious cries, Mr. Marcus speaking softly, but both calling each other fool, idiot, imbecile, until suddenly, for no apparent reason, they were in agreement again. . . . Then Mr. Marcus would say: 'Sam, speak to him on the telephone,' and would stand at his brother's shoulder while the telephoning took place."[34]

[34] Robert Henriques, *Marcus Samuel: First Viscount Bearsted and Founder of the "Shell" Transport and Trading Company, 1853–1927*, Barrie and Rockliff, London, 1960, p. 53. Material in quotes embodies the words of a Mr. X, a pensioned employee of the firm, who preferred to remain anonymous.

Again, it is probably impossible to make authority and responsibility exactly equal down through the organization because the work of each person is affected by the work of so many others over whom he cannot be given authority if any degree of specialization is to be preserved. Nevertheless, the organizer must bear in mind the need to make authority and responsibility as nearly equal as possible. To hold a man accountable for getting certain things done but allow him so little authority that his hands are tied is to place him in an impossible position.

Similarly, the man who has two bosses who disagree may also be placed in an impossible position. But unity of command need not be made a fetish. It is often entirely feasible to make a man accountable to one superior for one phase of his work and to another for another phase.

Then, while it may not be either feasible or desirable to limit the span of control to a definite number, there is a limit to the number of subordinates one man can supervise, even though that limit may differ with individuals and with the nature of the work. In diagnosing the ills of an organization, it is often helpful to examine the spans of the president and the other top officers to see whether they have not extended themselves to the point where they no longer have time to learn what is actually being done, to provide the necessary direction, or to evaluate what is really happening.

In addition, while some of the classical ideas of departmentalization may be less exact than their proponents have believed, they do at least offer a point of departure for a rough plan of dividing the work. This can then be modified in the light of, say, the points at which decisions are to be made. Without some approaches such as the classicists suggest, it might be difficult for the organizer even to know where to begin.

Insights of the newer theorists

The organizer who hopes to develop a successful organization structure, however, must be cognizant of the findings of the sociologists and psychologists who have been studying the field.

It is often possible to utilize their findings within a largely classical structure. For example, it may be impossible for some companies that have organized the work on an assembly line basis to dispense with conveyor-paced operations in order to allow each man a broader scope. To do so might be prohibitively expensive—might, in fact, raise costs to the point where it would no longer be possible to make even a small profit. But in many other companies it would be feasible to decrease specialization and so increase interest in the job on the part of both employees and subordinate managers. What is known as "job enlargement"—including more varied tasks within the scope of a single job—has been known to raise output rather than decrease it. Not as much has been done in this area, probably, as would be possible if organizers were more flexible in their use of the classical principles.

The chain-reaction theory is of particular importance. In making changes within an organization, the organizer should constantly bear in mind that the changes he contemplates are practically bound to produce other changes, and he should endeavor to predict what those changes will be. Then he can consider whether further adjustments should be made.

Thus the great value of the newer theories is that they alert the organizer to the many possibilities, quite a few of which he might overlook if he went entirely by the classical rules.

The comparative approach

Perhaps the trouble with organization theory is that most of the theorists have been trying to take in too much territory. (The research reported by Joan Woodward supports this idea.) Both classicists and behaviorists have been attempting to evolve theories that will apply to all organizations of human beings.

Lt. Col. Lyndall Urwick, a militant supporter of classicist views, writes: "There are principles . . . which should govern arrangements for human associations of any kind. These principles can be studied as a technical question irrespective of the purpose of the enterprise, the personnel composing it, or any constitutional, political or social theory underlying its creation."[35]

And the newer theorists do not quarrel with this viewpoint, however much they tend to minimize the value of the classical principles. "We suggest that the concepts are adequate for describing the nature of *all* types of social organization," E. Wight Bakke and Chris Argyris state in *Organizational Structure and Dynamics.*[36]

It is undeniable that all human organizations do have at least one thing in common: they all require division of the work and coordination of it. But they have widely differing objectives and different sets of exterior circumstances to contend with, and the work to be done differs widely. Moreover, human beings enter different kinds of organizations for different reasons. Most people join a business organization primarily to make a living. A man may have other goals as well: he may want prestige or interesting associations with others congenial to him. And in some cases one of these goals may take precedence over the financial incentive, but nearly always the need to make a living is the primary cement that holds the members of a business organization together. In an organization of a different type, this bond is likely to be entirely lacking, although some people do join social or philanthropic organizations for business reasons.

For these reasons, better results might be obtained if what can be called the "comparative approach" to organization theory were adopted, that is, if theorists of all schools were to examine several truly comparable organizations (of the same size, in the same industry, with similar facilities) and endeavor to find out which type of structure was producing the best results and why, as the Woodward group did. The generalizations arrived at by this method would be

---

[35] "Organization as a Technical Problem," in Gulick and Urwick (eds.), *op. cit.*, p. 49.
[36] *Op. cit.*, p. 6.

more limited than those so far developed, but they might provide more definite guidance.

It might be possible to state, for example, that in a company of a given size in a given industry, organization structure is most efficient when certain departments are grouped together; or it might be found that more authority and responsibility should be delegated down the line in some departments than in others. It might also be found feasible to set upper and lower limits for the span of control, not for all organizations, but for certain similar organizations.

Such studies require both immense work and immense insight on the part of the researchers, for it is necessary not only to examine the similarities and differences in the organization structures of the less successful and more successful companies but to judge the extent to which organization structure itself was responsible for success.

Lacking such studies, the practical organizer can regard the theories only as suggestions that may or may not apply in the particular cases he deals with. He must be aware also that every step he takes is likely to entail losses as well as gains and that the best he can do is try to ensure that the gains outweigh the losses.

In the following chapters, which deal with the actual structuring of organizations, the discussion will be confined to business organizations. Even this category is a very broad one, but some attempt will be made to illustrate methods of structuring in different industries.

First, there will be a discussion of the line-staff question, then of the mechanics of organization: breaking down the work, fitting the various functions into a coordinated whole, and creating a hierarchy of jobs, not of people. The assumption here is that when a task or a group of tasks constitutes the logical duties of a single job, someone can be found who will fit that job exactly.

This, of course, is never more than approximately true. Especially in the case of higher jobs, it is to some extent necessary to mold the job duties to the individual. The third part of the discussion will, therefore, consider the modifications that may be necessary because of the human material the organizer is actually working with. This phase of the work has been termed the "dynamics of organization."

SUMMARY

Organization theorists, in general, take one of two main approaches to the subject: the classical approach or the behavioral science approach. The first school of thought has developed a number of guides, some of which are fairly definite, while the ideas of the second are more diffuse and cover more ground, in that they take into consideration many aspects of human behavior that classical theory often seems to ignore.

The main difference between the two, however, is in the stress placed on different aspects of organization.

In the view of the classicists, organization itself is a science with its own rules. Thus Lyndall Urwick writes:

> It may be objected that . . . the organiser . . . can't sit down in a cold-blooded, detached spirit and draw an ideal structure, an optimum distribution of duties and responsibilities and relationships, and then expect the infinite variety of human nature to fit into it.
> To which the reply is that *he can and he should.*[37]

Behaviorists, on the other hand, tend to view sociology and psychology, rather than organization itself, as the underlying sciences. Since organization is a system of cooperation among human beings, they believe that it is more fruitful to consider how work can be organized to maximize the cooperation.

Yet classicists do not deny—certainly Urwick does not—that modifications will have to be made in the "ideal structure" because of the human beings who make up the organization. Nor would the classicists ignore the findings of sociology and psychology. But they do believe that the goal toward which the organizer should be striving is the mechanically perfect organization that will function more or less as Weber thought a "perfect bureaucracy" would.

Nor do the behaviorists contend that people are to be taken as given and the organization structure adjusted completely to their needs, regardless of the rationale of the work itself. But they do believe that more emphasis should be placed on the effect of human beings on organization and of organization on human beings than is commonly the case in industry today.

Thus the difference between the two may be more one of emphasis than of complete disagreement, although some of the behaviorists would throw out the classical principles completely and others consider them only a small part of the total organization theory needed.

On the whole, research on organization has tended to move away from the mechanistic point of view. Overemphasis on the goals of the enterprise without sufficient attention to those of its individual members is believed to lead to a loss of morale and of motivation to produce that will, in the end, hamper efforts to reach the goals of the organization itself. Hence there is increasing emphasis on the organization as a social system rather than as the machine that Weber visualized.

Review Questions

1. What are the classical principles of organization?
2. How does Barnard's idea of the source of authority differ from the classical view of delegation of authority?
3. If you were organizing a company, do you think that the classical principles of organization would be of more help to you than the findings of the behavioral scientists, or vice versa? Why?

[37] *The Elements of Administration,* 2d ed., Sir Isaac Pitman & Sons, Ltd., London, 1947, p. 36. (Italics added.)

4. What is an "organic organization"?
5. Why does Chris Argyris believe that close adherence to the classical principles of organization is unwise? Do you agree with him?
6. What did Bakke mean by the fusion process?
7. What form of organization does Rensis Likert suggest?
8. What unfortunate effects does R. K. Merton believe may follow from the demand for reliability down the line? What is meant by "reliability" in this context?
9. Would you rather work with a group in which the structure was organic or with a group in which there were definite, more or less permanent assignments and coordination was achieved through a superior? Why? How do you think most people would feel about this?
10. What is the decision-making approach to organization?
11. What guides to the actual division of the work do the classicists offer? Do you believe these would be helpful, or would you rather approach the matter in some other way?

Case Study / The Overworked Research Director

Harold Jones is director of research for a large chemical company. The research laboratory consists of about 500 professional chemists, chemical engineers, physicists, and other scientists, assisted by 300 lab assistants and clerical personnel. The research, which covers a wide range of products, varies from "basic" in an industrial sense to commercial.

Dr. Jones is an extremely domineering individual. He is mortally afraid of making a mistake. His own experience in research as well as the nature of his company has encouraged a strong one-man policy. The company is quite enamored of the flat organizational structure.

Jones reports to Adolph Muhler, vice-president in charge of research. Muhler is a member of the management committee, where he represents the interests of the research department. An outstanding academically trained man, he was educated at Heidelberg, has a low opinion of everyone else, and has adopted the typical German professional attitude. He uses his assistants as one might use repairmen or technicians and believes that he is the only one who generates original ideas.

Muhler makes all presentations, financial requests, and progress reports to the management committee personally. He insists on being briefed in all these matters by his research director. For this reason Jones feels that he must know the status of all major projects as well as of many minor ones in considerable detail.

Before he became an administrator, Jones did excellent research for years, loved his work, and made some important contributions in his field. Today he is much respected for his research competence and still has great interest in specific technical problems.

The organization structure of the research department is shown in the chart below.

It can be seen that Jones has twenty-two men reporting to him. The work of these people is specialized and quite varied. The nine heads of regular research sections each have from twenty-five to sixty research scientists under them. Three major special projects are going on, and there are "research teams" made up of different scientists who change their assignments frequently. A number of outstanding senior scientists reports to Jones; one is a scientific consultant, a position that is a kind of resting place for a distinguished man who no longer works on research. Finally, there is a large group of administrative staff men in accounting, office services, personnel, purchasing, building, security, and safety.

There are many additional contacts that Jones has to handle. He maintains personal liaison with the ten division managers and their research labs, with the legal and patent departments, with the commercial development group, with the finance department, and with the advertising and sales heads. He also does a good deal of liaison work with outside consultants, research directors of other companies, and industry, academic, and governmental contacts. Moreover, he represents the company in local community work and public relations. He does church work and voluntary agency work. He serves on several governmental advisory bodies and has to go to Washington several times a month. Finally, he is much in demand as a speaker in scientific organizations and universities.

Besides his close interest in the technical aspects of the research, Jones does a great deal of administrative work. Since he is unfamiliar with it and since research administration is not well developed or systematized, and especially since he believes he is accountable for all administrative work under him,

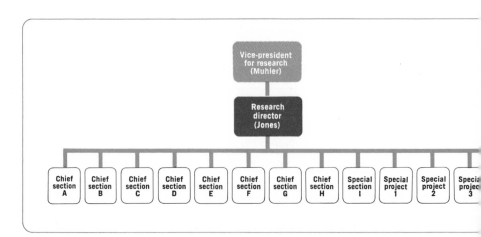

he tends to handle much of it himself. He opens all the mail personally and answers all letters; he draws up all the budgets and checks expenditures; he passes on all personnel changes, including salary changes and the hiring of secretaries. His average day is ten to twelve hours. He usually works a seven-day week. He has short vacations and rarely takes a day off. He has acquired hypertension and two ulcers; he is overweight; and he gets a skin rash each time he has to talk to Muhler.

Jones has no time for long-range planning. Even immediate problems get delayed and inadequate attention. He is a hard man to see; his office is like Grand Central Station. He insists on personally resolving all differences of opinion. He is unable to meet all the demands from various parts of the company.

1. If you were chief of section A and were offered the job of assistant to Dr. Jones, would you accept?
2. In case you were to step into this job, how would you conduct yourself?
3. Construct an organization chart that will ease Jones's burden and give him more opportunity for planning.
4. How should such a change in structure be sold up the line?

Selected Readings

"Bureaucracy," *From Max Weber,* H. H. Gerth and C. Wright Mills, Oxford University Press, Fair Lawn, N.J., 1958. Discussion of organization theory by a great sociologist.

The Elements of Administration, L. Urwick, Harper & Row, Publishers, Incorporated, New York, 1943. A short, concise statement of the principles of organization as seen by a classicist.

Organization, Ernest Dale, American Management Association, New York, 1967, Chapter 1. Contains a summary and appraisal of the major theories of organization.

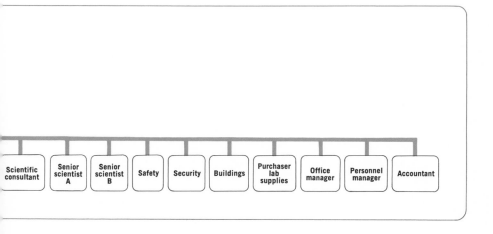

Some Theories of Organization, Albert H. Rubenstein and Chadwick J. Haberstroh (eds.), The Dorsey Press, Inc., and Richard D. Irwin, Inc., Homewood, Ill., 1960. A collection of articles dealing with studies on organization from a number of different disciplines.

Organizations, James G. March and Herbert Simon, with Harold Guetzkow, John Wiley & Sons, Inc., New York, 1958. A survey and analysis of major theories of organization. Also includes a number of new propositions on organization theory.

Modern Organization Theory, Mason Haire (ed.), John Wiley & Sons, Inc., New York, 1959. A collection of excerpts and articles on organization theory, drawn mainly from the writings of psychologists and sociologists.

The Functions of the Executive, Chester I. Barnard, Harvard University Press, Cambridge, Mass., 1938. A pioneering work that analyzes the forces that make for equilibrium in the organization. Discusses the roles of the principal members of the organization (owners, employees, and customers) in cooperating with one another, the informal organization as distinct from the formal organization, and the concepts of efficiency and effectiveness as used in appraising the organization.

Personality and Organization, Chris Argyris, Harper & Row, Publishers, Incorporated, New York, 1957. Deals with the incompatibility of the individual and the formal organization structure of the corporation.

Organizational Behavior and Administration, Paul R. Lawrence, Joseph C. Bailey, Robert L. Katz, John A. Seiler, Charles D. Orth, James V. Clark, Louis B. Barnes, and Arthur N. Turner; Richard D. Irwin, Inc., Homewood, Ill., 1961. Case descriptions, plus statements of concepts and theory useful in analyses of the cases.

Management Theory, T. T. Paterson, Business Publications Limited, London, 1966. A discussion of organization, decision making, and administration from the viewpoint that a firm is a social organism that "shows those characteristics, which, according to biologists, distinguish living from nonliving."

12

THE

DEVELOPMENT

OF

STAFF

But I remember, when the fight was done,
When I was dry with rage and extreme toil,
Breathless and faint, leaning upon my sword,
Came there a certain lord, neat, and trimly dress'd,
Fresh as a bridegroom . . .
He question'd me . . .
. . . he made me mad
To see him shine so brisk, and smell so sweet,
And talk so like a waiting-gentlewoman
Of guns and drums and wounds,—God save the mark!—
Shakespeare: *King Henry IV, Part One*

12 The distinction between line people (those who contribute directly to the goals of the enterprise) and staff people (those who assist the line in some way) was explained briefly in the last chapter. How this works out in practice may be illustrated by reference to an actual company.

In Figure 1, the only line executives shown are the board chairman, the company president, the vice-president of marketing, the vice-president of manufacturing, and the plant managers. All the others are staff men.

The executive committee, although it is made up of both line and staff executives, is a staff group. According to the company's organization manual, its function is to advise the president; thus it issues no orders to the line as a result of its deliberations. Similarly, the work of the new-product development committee, although both the sales and the manufacturing vice-presidents are members, is "to investigate and advise the president of the possibilities for the development of new products and the expansion of product lines." In theory at least, the president makes the decisions on new products and issues the orders concerning them to the line organization, even if in practice he customarily accepts the committee's recommendations.

FIGURE 1

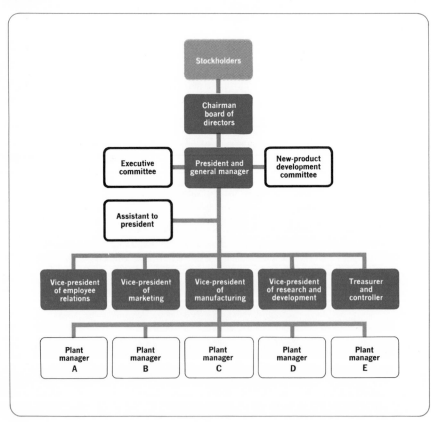

In addition, the heads of both line departments, i.e., marketing and manu-facturing, have staff departments of their own, as their organization charts (Figures 2 and 3) show.

The line of authority runs directly from the vice-president of manufacturing to the plant managers, then through their supervisors and foremen down to the workers at the bench. Manufacturing control and manufacturing engineer-ing are staff departments providing specialized services for the vice-president.

The marketing chart (Figure 3) shows three line executives and four staff executives reporting to the vice-president in charge of marketing. Line execu-tives are the sales manager (domestic), the manager of government contracts,

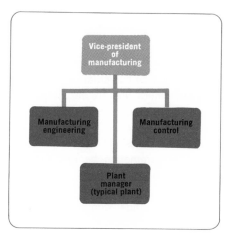

FIGURE 2

FIGURE 3

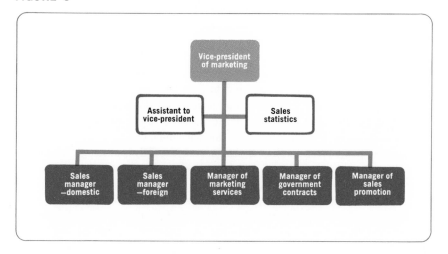

and the manager of foreign sales. Each of these men exercises direct line control over a field sales force: the first over those selling to domestic commercial customers, the second over those selling to the government, and the third over those selling to customers in foreign countries. The marketing services manager is responsible for market research, forecasting sales requirements, and the management of warehouses and inventory. In other words, he serves the regular sales forces by determining what can be sold and by ensuring that it is on hand when it is needed. Sales promotion, which in this case includes advertising, helps the line to sell by providing the materials it needs—special displays, literature for the salesmen to distribute, and so on—and insofar as possible presells the market through the written word.

The fourth staff department in the marketing organization, sales statistics, assists the vice-president with the management function of control by providing him with the data he needs to determine whether his plans are working out as expected, and thus enables him to take action before any real downtrend occurs. This group will, for example, provide him with figures on the sales of each product by geographical area, by type of customer, and perhaps even by individual customer in the case of customers who are very important to the company. If sales in any area or to any industry are falling off, the marketing vice-president can then investigate the causes: Is the decrease the fault of sales managers or salesmen? Is delivery too slow? Do the products need improvement? Should the advertising and promotion be revised? Has heavier competition developed, and should the company therefore spend more on its sales effort? Note that it is the marketing vice-president—not the staff statisticians, who are outside the line chain of command—who must make the decision and issue the orders for correction of any difficulty. As a staff department, sales statistics has no authority over the sales managers and their field forces even though it appears to be higher on the organization chart.

This is an example of a line-staff setup at the top level of the company. Similar forms of organization may exist—in fact, probably do exist—further down in the organization if the company is at all large. Thus the plant manager may supervise three department heads, each of whom supervises four or five foremen, who in turn supervise the production workers. This is his line organization. But he may also have a personnel department to recruit and train workers, keep their records, and manage such employee services as the cafeteria; a production control department to plan production; a methods department to improve efficiency; and other specialized departments. And a field sales manager is likely to have at least a clerical staff whose members will work directly under him but not "over" the salesmen.

A further point to remember is that a staff executive, although he has no authority over the regular line, will have line authority *over his own subordinates*. The methods manager, for example, is likely to have line authority over a group of time-study men; the personnel manager over a group of interviewers, over the clerical staff in his own department, and perhaps over the cafeteria manager, the supervisor of employee benefits, and others who handle various personnel functions. The head of a staff function at any level has line authority of this kind unless he is a one-man department.

The last chapter pointed out that the distinction between line and staff was necessary to reconcile the classical principles of specialization and unity of command. However, the distinction antedates classical organization theory, particularly in military organizations.

WHY STAFF DEPARTMENTS DEVELOPED

The need for staff services in both armies and businesses has grown out of three developments: (1) large-scale organizations, (2) technical developments, and (3) more recently, changes in the climate of opinion prevailing generally and in the laws that reflect those changes. Since armies have included thousands of men for centuries and most business organizations were fairly small until the last half of the nineteenth century, the concept of staff developed first in the military and business borrowed it.

In a small primitive army composed of, say, a couple of hundred men, a general could shout his orders and be heard by everyone. There would be no need for a supply service since such an army probably would not attempt to carry on a sustained campaign. Each man would carry his own provisions or perhaps get them from the countryside by looting the stores of the unfortunate inhabitants. If intelligence services were needed, one or two scouts from the regular line organization might be sent ahead.

This situation could not endure when armies became larger. Since battlefields were spread over larger areas, at the very least the commander required messengers (or aides-de-camp) to transmit his orders to subordinate commanders in the field. When sustained campaigns rather than sudden forays were contemplated, he would have to have some sort of organized supply service if his men were not to starve.

It is known that rudimentary staff services, organized as groups apart from the line, existed as early as 1600 B.C., although detailed descriptions of the way they functioned have not come down to us.[1]

Development was not continuous even in the ancient world, however; and in the Dark Ages, warfare reverted to small-scale operations again. But by the seventeenth and eighteenth centuries, most European armies had staffs of some sort. In 1645, Oliver Cromwell's New Model Army included a chief of staff and such specialized officers as a "commissary general of victuals," a "commissionary general of horse provisions," an intelligence chief ("scoutmaster general"), treasurers, a judge advocate general, physicians, a clerical staff, and aides-de-camp.[2]

This is, however, a rather simple organization compared with the modern military staff. Technological developments have made necessary highly com-

---

[1] J. D. Hittle, *The Military Staff: Its History and Development,* The Stackpole Company, Harrisburg, Pa., 1961, p. 14.
[2] *Ibid.,* p. 118.

plex engineering and research work. In the United States, there is a large organization within the Department of Defense headed by a Director of Defense Research and Engineering, under whom are directorates responsible for such functions as electronics and information systems, research and technology, strategic and space systems, and tactical warfare programs. Matters concerning nuclear technology have become so voluminous as to require an Assistant to the Secretary of Defense for Atomic Energy. And problems associated with public affairs, international security affairs, and systems analysis have become so great as to require sizable departments under Assistant Secretaries of Defense to cope with them.

And, of course, the enormous size of the modern military establishment and the widespread areas in which it must operate have made necessary greater complexity within the staff organizations. Whereas Oliver Cromwell had a supply service consisting of two groups—one to provide victuals for the men and the other to supply victuals for the horses—the U.S. Defense Department has an enormously complicated logistics department, whose organization chart (as of 1967) is shown in Figure 4. In addition, a new Defense Department organization, the Defense Supply Agency, now performs many of the functions that Cromwell's supply service once took care of, i.e., the feeding and clothing of the soldiers.

FIGURE 4   (As of 1967.)

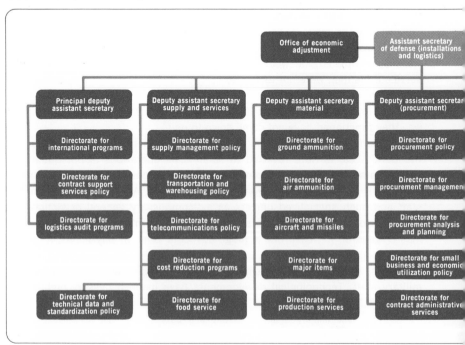

The fact that the Joint Chiefs of Staff have line authority may seem confusing in view of the stress laid earlier on the purely advisory and service capacity of the staff. The discrepancy is due to the fact that the Constitution requires civilian control of the armed forces, with the President as Commander-in-Chief, coupled with the fact that highly specialized knowledge is now required for direction of the forces. On matters of policy, the Chiefs' function *is* advisory; but under the direct authority of the Secretary of Defense, they administer the operations of certain joint or unified commands (e.g., the Pacific Command and the European Command). In addition, they administer individually, under their respective Secretaries—Army, Navy, and Air Force—the operations of the Armed Forces.

In business, the first staff people were probably the clerks who kept accounts and wrote or copied letters and the couriers who, like the aides-de-camp in an army, carried the messages. Both became necessary as soon as business began extending its sphere of activity over a wide area, as some enterprises did even in the Middle Ages.

Nevertheless, the division of work tended to be largely informal up to the time of the Industrial Revolution—in many cases, even up until the twentieth century. For example, one partner might engage in research on new products because he had the knowledge and the inclination to do so; another would

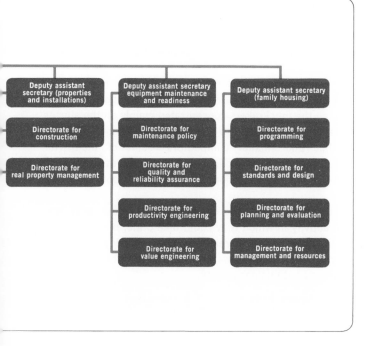

concentrate on finance for the same reason. And there were many organizations in which one chief executive handled all management functions himself. The staff of the head of the Whitin-Machine Works, a New England manufacturing company, consisted of half a dozen clerks until a great expansion of business in 1899 and thereafter forced him to delegate purchasing to the man who had been his secretary.[3]

The development was, of course, uneven, and it varied from industry to industry. For example, one of the first research departments in the oil industry, if not the first, came into being when Standard Oil bought out a small refinery whose owner had invented a new process, then set that owner to work in a laboratory. This was in 1888, and in 1889 the company hired a young Ph.D. to assist him.[4] Yet in many industries, research departments became common only after World War II, and many companies today do not have them, and some do not really need them.

Perhaps the best illustration of how increasing size, technological developments, and general social climate have fostered the growth of specialized staff can be found in the development of the personnel or industrial relations department, which was affected by all three factors.

This staff department actually began as two separate functions: welfare work and employment management. The two functions were later amalgamated into a single division or department.

Welfare work had, of course, existed in isolated instances for a long time, the work of Robert Owen in the early part of the nineteenth century being a case in point. But early in the twentieth century it took on the proportions of a general movement. The influence of Frederick Taylor and his followers was in some part responsible for this, since the scientific management movement stressed that better working conditions would produce greater efficiency. Contributing, too, were a certain amount of social unrest and some rather large strikes.

The early twentieth century was also a period of rather widely read attacks on business by a group of journalists called "muckrakers" by those who disagreed with them. Although the muckrakers concentrated mainly on the abuses of power by the "trusts" or large business combinations—abuses affecting mainly the general public and smaller competitors—some of them (for example, Upton Sinclair in *The Jungle*) denounced the treatment of employees. Under such heavy attack, industry was anxious to put its best foot forward in every respect.

Thus a good many businessmen became convinced that welfare work was not only a philanthropic activity in which they could take pride, but good business from the standpoint of both public relations and efficiency. No doubt some who were of a kindly cast of mind were glad to justify following their natural inclination as hardheaded business sense.

---

[3] Thomas R. Navin, *The Whitin-Machine Works since 1831: A Textile Machinery Company in an Industrial Village*, Harvard University Press, Cambridge, Mass., 1950, p. 285.
[4] Paul H. Giddens, *Standard Oil Company (Indiana): Oil Pioneer of the Middle West*, Appleton-Century-Crofts, Inc., New York, 1955, pp. 6–7.

By 1916 Ida Tarbell, one of the foremost of the muckrakers, whose exposé had touched off investigations that resulted in the breaking up of the Standard Oil trust, was writing lyrically about "our new workshops" and the excellent treatment of employees in them.[5]

Welfare work included such things as encouragement of employee clubs and sports, health services, suggestion systems, better lighting, and sometimes pension and insurance plans. Often the people put in charge of it were drawn from social work rather than from business.

Employment management, on the other hand, grew out of the increase in company size, the development of psychology and its application to vocational guidance in the schools, and perhaps out of the very high turnover that developed in some plants as industry grew and more jobs opened up.

In a small organization, the chief executive may handle all hiring and firing. In a larger one he can delegate it to the foremen, but they cannot be expected to draw very heavily on the science of psychology. And if turnover is high, the selection will take too much of their time.

Both company growth and the development of such aids to selection and placement of employees as psychological tests occurred in the years just before World War I, and it was in these years that the job of employment manager originated. In 1912 there was already a Boston Employment Managers Association. In 1916, a survey of thirty concerns with a total of more than 50,000 employees showed that eighteen of them had established separate employment departments, but in only a few cases had the departments been in existence more than five or six years (i.e., before 1910–11).[6]

Frederick W. Taylor had suggested that the personnel function be placed under the supervision of one man, to be known as the "disciplinarian." The scientific managers did not visualize him as the stern dispenser of punishments that this title connotes; in fact, Lillian Gilbreth suggested that in practice he would be "rather the friend of the worker than of the employer if the two interests can possibly be separated."[7] But in view of the fact that the title alone would be enough to make him suspect among employees, it is not surprising that companies preferred the less emotionally charged name "employment manager."

Combining the employment department and the welfare department was a natural step since both were concerned with employees. But as late as 1918, a book published in that year[8] was in the main a plea for this amalgamation. The author's suggestion was that such a department be called an "employee service department," though the terms "personnel department" and "industrial relations department" were already in use.

Actually, welfare had acquired a bad name despite the good intentions of its proponents. As one early industrial relations manager, who came into

[5] New Ideals in Business, The Macmillan Company, New York, 1916, chap. 1.
[6] Roy Willmarth Kelly, "The New Profession," Hiring the Worker, The Engineering Magazine, New York, 1918.
[7] The Psychology of Management, Sturgis & Walton Company, New York, 1918, p. 73.
[8] Kelly, op. cit.

industry from the Railroad YMCA, wrote: "Most employees resented such dispensations as paternalistic. . . . Much welfare work, although benevolent and well intentioned, was construed by many employees as largely intended to tie the employee to the company even though he was dissatisfied with wages or working conditions."[9]

In the 1920s personnel and industrial relations departments became quite common. The growth of unions in the 1930s gave still greater impetus to the movement as companies felt themselves competing with the labor organizations for the loyalty of their workers, and sometimes hoped through various welfare measures to forestall unionization altogether. A speaker at a management meeting once quoted a company president as saying, "Well, we've got the union; so I guess I'll fire the personnel department." In addition, new laws, such as the National Labor Relations Act and the Wage and Hour Act, made it necessary to have specialists to keep abreast of legal developments and their application to company operations.

World War II gave further impetus to the movement. Labor, especially skilled labor, became scarce as the draft took men from industry, and production increases raised the demand for workers. There were new employment regulations to cope with, too. For example, wage stabilization, at a time when employers were quite willing to raise wages as much as necessary to get the workers they needed, imposed rules that made it more difficult to pay higher rates, and interpreting the rules was often felt to require a specialist. So did presentation of cases to the regulatory bodies when the employer wanted permission to go beyond the letter of the law. And at the end of the war, labor unions sought to make up for lost time by demanding large wage increases, which meant more work for the industrial relations department in the form of actual collective bargaining sessions and digging up facts and figures to back up company cases.

At present it would be hard to find a company of any size that lacks a personnel or industrial relations department. In general, persons engaged in this function in a given company are likely to number around 1 per cent of the total work force (that is, 1 personnel specialist to each 100 employees), though the number fluctuates to some extent. Often, the head of the function is a vice-president of the corporation.

THREE MAIN TYPES OF STAFF

The staff organizations mentioned above all have in common the fact that they are auxiliary to the main functions of the business. There are, however, different types of staff, and there is often some confusion about this, particularly in a business organization where the same person may handle more than one type of staff work. The three main divisions may be listed as:

---

[9] Clarence J. Hicks, *My Life in Industrial Relations: Fifty Years in the Growth of a Profession,* Harper & Row, Publishers, Incorporated, New York, 1941, p. 43.

1.   Personal staff
2.   Specialized staff
3.   General staff

Personal staff   In an army, the personal staff man is typified by the aide-de-camp, whose function is to care for the well-being of the chief as an individual. The aide-de-camp may accompany the chief on his rounds, keep his notes for him, look after his maps and personal papers, conduct his private correspondence, arrange interviews, run his headquarters mess, and act as a social secretary—in short, do anything and everything the general may ask him to do. An eighteenth-century writer, Francis Grose, advised the aide-de-camp: "If your general keeps a girl, it is your duty to squire her to all public places and to make a humble third of a party at whist or quadrille; but be sure never to win."[10]

In business, the personal staff is typified by the private secretary, who may keep the executive's personal checkbook, buy his Christmas presents, and arrange his appointments. Generals or business executives are given personal staff assistants on the same theory: their time is too valuable to be spent in handling the details of daily living.

Specialized staff   The specialized staffs are those which handle specialized functions—e.g., accounting, personnel, engineering, and research. It is now impossible for one man to familiarize himself with all the various specialties needed in the modern large business or the modern army. Hence the general or the company president, and perhaps the department head, is provided with experts in each field to counsel him on the various specialties and to handle supporting activities. (Some authorities believe that functions of this type are more properly called auxiliary or service departments rather than staff, since they actually carry on a good deal of work necessary to the business, even though they do not produce or sell goods or services. Generally, however, they also counsel the chief on policy.)

But although the specialized staff men relieve the chief of the need to become an expert in a number of different specialized fields, they also increase his burdens since he must coordinate their work as well as that of the line men.

Staff departments are often a fecund source of new ideas: for improving employee relations (personnel), for new products (research and development), for new financial controls (accounting and finance), for public relations activities, and for other new programs and policies. But it is the chief executive who must gauge the overall result of these proposed policies and projects because many of them will have far-reaching effects throughout the business and may impose burdens on the line departments that will offset the benefits seen by the promoters.

Not surprisingly, the programs and policies submitted by any staff depart-

[10] *Advise to Officers of the British and Irish Armies, 1782,* republished with drawings by Frank Wilson, Jonathan Cape, Ltd., London, 1946, p. 23.

ment are practically always calculated to enhance the status of that department and perhaps increase its size. The more a department head can build up his department, the more important he becomes; and it is asking too much of human nature to expect him to propose that expenses in his department be cut or that the number of people under him be reduced. Moreover, he is usually honestly convinced that his department *is* about the most important in the company. He would not have entered the personnel field, for example, if he had not been convinced that personnel work was of supreme importance. The same can be said of a research director or a public relations man.

No one can attend a meeting of specialists all in the same field but drawn from different companies without becoming conscious of this. In discussion from the floor, perhaps the most frequent comment is, "We all know such and such a program is a good thing to have, but how do we get top management to see it?" Usually the speaker is perfectly sincere, yet the dispassionate observer can often think of many reasons why the program will not be of any special value—or perhaps will be actually detrimental—in some company situations.

The company president must evaluate these proposals, and he cannot do so by off-the-cuff decisions. He must read the written reports submitted by the proposers and bear in mind that they are, in effect, intended as sales literature and that he can expect to find in them only the pros and none of the cons. If he wants to uncover the disadvantages, he will have to spend time discussing the idea not only with its originator but with heads of other departments. And time is a commodity with which company presidents are not very well supplied.

It is here that the general staff man comes in.

General staff   Any decision that cuts across departmental lines must be made by the chief executive. It cannot be delegated to the head of a specialized staff group or to a line department head since other department heads will naturally resent interference in their departments by someone who is in no way their superior. A typical case would be a change in the organization structure of the company as a whole: the combination of two departments under a single head, for example, or the organization of a new top-level department.

It is with these functions that cannot be delegated that the general staff men can provide assistance and save the time of the top man. True, the chief cannot delegate any one of these functions to a general staff man, but he can often delegate parts of each of them.

The title of the general staff man is most often "assistant-to" the company president, or other executive, though it may also be executive assistant, administrative assistant, or even vice-president. The "to" in the title is significant. An assistant president (if such a title existed in industry) or an assistant production manager (a title that frequently exists) is second in command to his chief and replaces him in his absence. An assistant-to, on the other hand, is not second in command and has no authority over his chief's immediate subordinates, even in the absence of his chief. The assistant-to the company president is no more the boss of the vice-presidents than the president's private secretary is.

What, then, is his job? In his capacity as a general staff man, he handles parts of some or all of his chief's principal functions (organizing, coordination, and so on), but no one function in its entirety.

Suppose, for example, the personnel department presents a proposal for the introduction of a management development course, together with a detailed outline of proposed subject matter, schedules of sessions—a complete package. The company president is then confronted with a twofold decision:

1.   Should the company have a management development program? What will be the benefits, if any, and will they outweigh the cost of the program— that is, offset not only the actual out-of-pocket expenses for materials, speakers, and so on, but the intangible costs incurred when men are detached from their jobs for study?

2.   Granted that the answer to the first question is yes, is the program proposed the very best one for the company? What other possibilities are there?

If the costs incurred by such a program were a simple matter of so much money for books, so much for classroom space, and so much per hour for the time to be spent, the accounting department could run up the answers. But, as mentioned, there are intangible costs. If an executive is detached from his job for days, or even hours, the cost may be greater than the money that is paid him for time not actually spent working, for his absence may disrupt the work of others. And the value of the training will be largely intangible.

Here is where the assistant-to can save his chief valuable time. He can talk to department heads and get their views on whether any formal training is needed for their subordinates and, if so, what type. He can also examine what other companies are doing and what types of development programs are available.

This digging for information takes time, time that the chief does not have to spare. A succinct report from an assistant can enable him to ask the right questions when he talks to the man who proposed the project. One assistant's method of working may be instructive:

> When a problem was assigned to him, he would first develop a plan of action, drawing on his own knowledge, reading about the problem as widely as possible, thinking out its implications, and preparing the relevant questions. Then he would discuss his proposed investigation with his chief and have him approve the plan.
>
> Next Thornton [the assistant-to] interviewed the executives concerned with the problem, taking . . . careful notes on each interview and working out the practical implications of the suggestions. Results of all these different contacts were put together in a memorandum which analyzed the problem and recommended action. This memorandum was reviewed by his chief, subjected to many questions, comments and criticisms, and then done over as many times as the chief required.

When the chief was finally satisfied, the memorandum was submitted to the top management committee for comment and again redone as many times as necessary. When the basic policy changes were finally approved by every principal concerned, they were drafted for adoption.[11]

General staff may also exist in the form of a committee or a department. For example, when General Motors was reorganized in 1921, the new plan provided for a general advisory staff whose purpose was:

> . . . to advise the chief executive . . . concerning problems of technical and commercial nature which are themselves so broad and require so much study as to be outside the scope of a single operation and which will be, when developed, of importance in the guidance of all operations. . . . The Control of the General Advisory Staff is under a chief executive who is a Vice President of the Corporation. He is supported by such assistants as he may designate who, together with the Staff Secretary, constitute the executive side of the General Advisory Staff.[12]

Similarly, when General Brehan Somervell became chief executive of the Koppers Company some years ago, he introduced a general staff in the form of a control section, which was planned as an "extension of the eyes and ears of the chief executive." In the group was an organization administrator whose duties included:

1. Keeping abreast of new and existing organization concepts and analyzing them with the needs of the company in mind.
2. Reporting and recommending for further study any deficiencies in procedure, planning, scheduling, or coordination that might be observed in connection with organizational studies and audits.
3. Studying and reporting to appropriate management the need to provide for succession to key positions.

A second member of the control section was a planning administrator. One of his primary duties was described as "obtaining, analyzing, evaluating, and consolidating forecast results and cooperating with the finance department in translating the data into finished programs." Other duties were:

1. Development of ways by which the company's progress might be appraised through comparison with its own past record and with the performance of competitors.
2. Study of the distribution of capital investment in the various businesses in which the company was engaged.
3. Collection and analysis of data of interest to the company in planning its operation and recommendation of new objectives for future operations.

A third part of the control section was a group whose primary job was to

11 Ernest Dale and Lyndall F. Urwick, *Staff in Organization,* McGraw-Hill Book Company, New York, 1960, pp. 202–203.
12 *Ibid.,* pp. 187–188. Quotation is from a memorandum by Alfred P. Sloan, Jr., embodying a plan for reorganization of General Motors (1920).

study inter-unit relationships and recommend standard procedures for ensuring smooth dovetailing of the work.

Note that all the duties described cut across departmental lines. Hence they are the province of the chief executive and cannot be delegated to a department concerned with only one phase of the business as all line and specialized staff departments are. Note also that in no case does the general staff man actually make the decision; he merely assists the chief by uncovering pros and cons, keeping abreast of all the possibilities, and transmitting the views of those down the line to the president and vice versa. But he does not handle the whole of any of the three management functions: planning, organizing, coordination.

It is sometimes difficult to understand the nature of the general staff function in an actual business situation because the same man may be at once a general staff man, a specialized staff man, and a personal staff man. An assistant-to the company president may be, for example, the chief publicity man of the organization or the chief economist and may function as head of his specialty (perhaps with some assistants of his own over whom he has line authority). Similarly, a president may delegate certain personal staff functions to an assistant whose job is primarily of a general staff nature. Thus the assistant may help his chief with planning, organization, and evaluation of new ideas (the president's own or those of other departments) and may also arrange travel schedules for him, keep his appointment book, purchase theater tickets, and perform other duties of a similar nature.

No particular difficulty may be experienced when two or perhaps even three types of staff jobs are combined in this way, provided the assistant himself and those with whom he comes in contact understand the scope of his authority and responsibility. If he is to handle some personal staff functions, the division of labor between the assistant-to and the private secretary should be made clear so that she will not feel he is infringing on her territory. Similarly, if he handles a specialized staff function, such as public relations, his relationship to those in related staff functions, such as advertising and promotion, should be spelled out.

A comparatively new development in industry is the use of chiefs of staff, general staff men who supervise all or several of the specialized staff groups, approve or disapprove their recommendations, and advise the company president on a number of subjects. This, of course, makes it possible to reduce the chief's span of control, which may have become wider and wider as more and more specialized staff groups were found necessary.

DIFFICULTIES WITH STAFF-LINE RELATIONSHIPS

The theory of line-staff organization is quite clear and seemingly simple to understand. Operating in accordance with it, however, is not easy. For example, some organization authorities and some staff men advocate what has come to be called completed staff work. This has been described as follows:

Completed staff work is the study of a problem and presentation of a solution by a staff officer, in such form that all that remains to be done on the part of the head of the staff division, or the commander, is to indicate his approval or disapproval of the completed action. . . .

It is your job to advise your chief what he ought to do, not to ask him what you ought to do. He needs answers, not questions: Your job is to study, write, restudy, and rewrite, until you have evolved a single proposed action—the best one of all you have considered. Your chief merely approves or disapproves.

Do not worry your chief with long explanations and memoranda. Writing a memorandum to your chief does not constitute completed staff work, but writing a memorandum for your chief to send to someone else does. Your views should be placed before him in finished form so that he can make them his views simply by signing his name. In most instances completed staff work results in a single document prepared for the signature of the chief without accompanying comment. If the proper result is reached, the chief will usually recognize it at once. If he wants comment or explanation, he will ask for it.

When you have finished your completed staff work, the final test is this:

1. If you were the chief would you be willing to sign the paper you have prepared and stake your professional reputation on its being right?
2. If the answer is in the negative, take it back and work it over because it is not yet completed staff work.[13]

But if the staff produces a finished product as described, is it not actually taking away a good part of the line's decision-making power? Note that the staff man is told to "select a single proposed action—the best one of all" he has considered. Thus the chief is given no knowledge of possible alternatives, and he must have a great deal of blind faith in his staff man if he is willing to stake his reputation on the latter's choice without inquiring about the discarded possibilities. And if he does inquire about them, can he expect an impartial answer from a man who has already made up his mind that only one answer will do?

If the line chief is the staff man's boss, of course, he is in no danger of finding his decision-making powers weakened by the work of the staff unless he wants it that way. But line executives further down tend to feel that they are to some extent actually under the control of the staff men who assist their superiors. Harrington Emerson, a strong advocate of a well-developed staff system, wrote more than half a century ago: "Each separate staff man is regarded as an invading enemy by each and every line head, and all the lines will combine against all the staff. Even if many of the men are amiable, sensible, patient, the conditions leading to discord and trouble are constant."[14]

The time that has elapsed since Emerson wrote those words has seen some

---

[13] Adapted from an official paper by Maj. Gen. Archer L. Learch, former Provost Marshal General.
[14] *The Twelve Principles of Efficiency*, The Engineering Magazine, New York, 1912, pp. 410–411.

diminution of this hostility, but the difficulty remains. Some thirty years later, when William Knudsen, top production man at General Motors, went to Washington to organize production for World War II and was asked about the difference between line and staff, he is reported to have said, "Well, you know, at General Motors we say that line people are the fellows who bring in material, put it together, and ship it out. And the staff people are the fellows who are trying to prevent the line from doing the job."

Certainly staff activities, even in the absence of completed staff work, do diminish the authority of every line boss except the superior to whom the staff men report. This is true even though the staff observes protocol and issues no direct orders to the line. If a staff develops a program, gains the approval of the line boss to whom it is subordinate, and has him issue the necessary orders, the line is not fooled. It knows where the program originated. Subordinate managers may expect their bosses to tell them *what* to do—to specify sales or production quotas, for example—but they do not like to be told in detail *how* to do it. And often it is the how that the staff departments specify.

For example, in a plant that had expanded rapidly foremen had been accustomed to planning the sequence of work and the methods of doing it. When a methods department was organized, they spoke of its instructions as something "dreamed up" and continued to do their own planning.

The personnel department in the same plant also aroused resentment. One department hired a man of sixty-odd and thought itself lucky to get him. He had owned his own business, sold it and retired, then gone back to work to keep himself busy. Because he had very broad production experience, he was able to help the department head reorganize the operation and bring order where a considerable amount of chaos had existed before. Soon other departments were asking, "Where can we get a man like that?" But when the personnel department processed his records, it telephoned the department head, "You can't keep that man. He's over the age limit, and he'll have to go."

These two cases, it must be noted, occurred during World War II, when the plant was in process of changing over from very specialized experimental work to mass production of items desperately needed by the military. Where methods and personnel departments are well established, the conflicts are seldom so overt. But they do exist. Specifically, the line has the following complaints against the staff:

First, it usurps authority that properly belongs to the line. The very fact that staff people sit in the head office near the company president, the plant manager, or the department head, as the case may be, arouses suspicion that they are likely to be "dreaming up" programs that will make extra trouble for the line. Also, some line people feel that staff men tend to be more articulate than line men and better able to sell the boss their ideas.

Second, line men sometimes feel that staff men are not really familiar with what is going on where actual work is done, and that therefore they tend to promote unrealistic projects.

Third, the line believes that the staff causes an excessive amount of paper work. Some line people say that they have to spend two or three hours a day preparing reports for staff use and defending the data they have sent in.

Nor is the discontent entirely one-sided. Staff men have grievances against the line, of which four stand out prominently:

First, many staff men think that the line does not utilize their services enough. They feel that they could help the line materially in many areas that the line prefers to keep entirely in its own bailiwick.

Second, staff people feel that line men tend to push responsibilities they dislike onto staff people and then, when something goes wrong, say: "Well, yes, but we did exactly what you told us to do."

A third complaint is that when the line does ask for advice, it often does not make the problem clear or neglects to allow sufficient time for the staff to provide an answer.

Fourth, some staff people feel that if they report to operating men they cannot exercise their skills as they should. A typical example might be a quality control manager who reports to the plant manager. He may feel somewhat timid about criticizing the quality of the product because such criticism could be construed as criticism of his boss. He might, therefore, prefer to report directly to the chief of quality control on the central staff, to whom he would feel free to express his real opinions.

How prevalent are difficulties occasioned by line-staff conflicts? Although in many cases the line and most parts of the staff probably rub along without much difficulty most of the time, in a survey the author of this book conducted for the American Management Association, 41 of 100 large companies that answered a question on this point reported that significant conflicts had occurred or were occurring and another 4 companies said they had experienced minor conflicts.[15] And it is, of course, possible that some of the men who answered the questionnaire were not aware of the conflicts that occurred in their companies or did not wish to admit that their organizations were not completely harmonious.

The most usual way of attempting to cope with the line-staff difficulty is to foster rapprochement between the people who happen to be occupying the various jobs. Both sides are advised to adopt a conciliatory attitude and to learn to understand each other's problems. Sometimes formal meetings are held for exchange of ideas. This helps, but it is not a complete answer, for although some disagreements may occur because of personalities, fundamentally the trouble arises because of the formally prescribed roles.

In the case of some staff activities, some companies have attempted to put the relationship on an entirely different basis. In these instances, the services of the staff department are neither there for the asking nor forced on the line—each line department pays for them out of its budget, and if it can get the same service from an outside supplier at a lower cost, it is free to buy outside. But this arrangement, although it may be used for such activities as

---

[15] Ernest Dale, *Organization*, American Management Association, New York, 1967, p. 67.

construction and maintenance, and sometimes for training, is not suitable for all staff activities.

Another possibility, of course, is to dispense with the distinction entirely, under the plan described in Gerald Fisch's article "Line-Staff Is Obsolete," which was cited in the last chapter.[16] But while the distinction may become blurred in some companies, it is doubtful whether any large company has actually tried so drastic a change in the usual structure. It is also possible that disagreements would still exist under such a system, for the manager of operations might well claim, for example, that the manpower manager had underestimated the personnel requirements and that, therefore, operations could not produce according to plan.

However, the power, or at least the influence, of the staff departments seems to be increasing. In the survey conducted by the author for the American Management Association, 62 of the 100 large companies covered reported that the influence—in some cases, the formal authority—of the staff groups appeared to be increasing in industry, and only 4 reported that staffs had become more subordinate to the line. Of 66 medium-sized companies included in the survey, 41 believed staffs were gaining in influence or power and, again, only 4 stated that staff groups were becoming more subordinate to the line. (The rest of the respondents either could discern no marked change or said that the trends were mixed, that is, that some staffs were gaining influence and others were losing it.)[17]

SUMMARY

By definition, line people are those who carry out the functions that contribute directly to the achievement of the organization goal, and staff people are those who contribute indirectly by helping the line to do its job or by auditing its performance.

There are three types of staff: (1) personal staff, (2) specialized staff, and (3) general staff; and each performs a different type of function. Executives are provided with personal staff merely in order to relieve them of the details of daily living—answering telephone calls, scheduling appointments, typing letters. The specialized staff performs work requiring expertise in a specialized field, such as accounting. The general staff helps the manager to whom it reports with functions that he cannot delegate in their entirety by gathering and assessing information on which he can base a decision.

In classical organization theory, staff men have no authority over line men. If they devise programs that the line must install, the line superior approves them and issues the necessary orders to the line. But often the new programs suggested by the staff men deal with areas that the line executives consider extraneous to the real job, and it seems to the line that the staff spends its time thinking up ways to make the line's own work harder or more compli-

16 *Harvard Business Review*, September—October, 1961.
17 Dale, *op. cit.*, p. 76.

cated. In addition, the line often feels that the staff does not understand conditions in the shop or in the sales territories and that the programs are, therefore, unrealistic, and sometimes the line is right in thinking so.

On the other hand, the staff feels that since it possesses far greater expertise in certain areas than the line, its recommendations should be followed wholeheartedly, and sometimes it is right in thinking so. In fact, some observers have begun to feel that the line-staff distinction is obsolete and that the members of specialized staffs should be given authority to make decisions in their own areas.

Review Questions

1. List some of the jobs in a college and in a city government that might be considered line jobs.
2. Is the Postmaster General of the United States a line man or a staff man?
3. What is personal staff? General staff? Specialized staff?
4. What are some of the complaints of the line about the staff? Of the staff about the line?
5. Over whom may a staff executive have line authority?
6. What are some of the advantages a chief executive might derive from having a chief of staff? Can you think of any disadvantages the plan might entail?

Case Study / The Frustrated Vice-president*

A few years ago an old and prosperous company in an old industry hired a very young personnel vice-president from the outside. The company had never had such an officer; in fact, it had never had any personnel function as such. And the young man had never worked in the industry; he had made a rapid and brilliant career for himself in an entirely different type of business.

The young man was hired because the management of the company felt that its personnel relations, its union relations, and its management organization were in very poor shape—a belief that was borne out by the facts—and that something had to be done. However, no one in the company had any very clear idea of what that something might be. That was why the company went outside, a step it had never taken before, and brought in an "expert."

Most of the new vice-president's colleagues had more years of service than he had of age. But despite this, and despite a strong tradition of promotion from within, the young man was cordially received. In a short while he gained

* By Peter F. Drucker.

both the confidence and the friendship of most of the men in the management group.

Three years later the young vice-president received a tempting offer from one of the country's large companies—an offer of a position with a higher salary, more authority, and better prospects. Nevertheless his instinctive reaction was to turn down the offer without even considering it. When he analyzed this feeling, which surprised him by its intensity, he found that it was caused by the fact that in his three years with the company he had actually accomplished nothing.

He had brought all his knowledge of good personnel management to bear on the company's problems. For example, he had worked out new ways of handling union relations; and with 60 per cent of the company's expenses going into direct labor costs, good union relations were obviously essential and bad relations a source of real danger. He had worked out a new wage and salary plan to bring order out of total chaos, a chaos admitted and deplored by everyone in management. He had developed a new organization structure to end the deeply frustrating conflicts over authority and responsibility. He had worked out a systematic policy of recruiting, training, and testing management successors to overcome the twin evils of an overaged management and promotion largely by seniority—evils which everyone he met, from first-line supervisors on up, had been drawing his attention to.

Every one of his proposals had been accepted immediately—after all, wasn't he the expert?—but although they were accepted, announced in letters, speeches, and orders by the chairman of the board and the president, and put formally into effect, none had actually been carried out.

There had been no resistance. In fact, his associates were not even conscious of their behavior. They thought they were doing everything he wanted them to do and considered him a great success. But actually there had been no change in attitudes, policies, and practices whatsoever. The organization worked exactly as it had been working when he first started out.

The young man made two decisions—whether they were the right ones is not our concern here since he was obviously emotionally unable and unwilling even to discuss them: (1) He wasn't going to quit. (2) He wasn't going to "surrender" either and relax into comfortable and well-paid inertia.

But his ideas about what he was going to do to change the situation were entirely indefinite. What could he hope to achieve? And how? He went to an old friend for advice.

The friend realized immediately that he must not do what the young man had asked him to do; that is, make a decision for him. But he might help him come to a decision by outlining the possible alternatives of action and behavior, together with the major arguments for and against each course. He could not make up the young man's mind for him, but he could help to clarify his ideas.

You are that friend. Just what would you put on your agenda for a long, leisurely discussion with the frustrated vice-president?

Selected Readings

Staff in Organization, Ernest Dale and Lyndall F. Urwick, McGraw-Hill Book Company, New York, 1960. This book examines the various types of staff found in business today, analyzes the theory and use of staff in military organizations and in government, and discusses the theory and practice of improved staff-line relations at length.

The Military Staff: Its History and Development, J. D. Hittle, The Stackpole Company, Harrisburg, Pa., 1961. This detailed history of the development of staff from the earliest times to the present day presents rich source material.

"The Network of Authority," O. Glenn Stahl, *The Public Administration Review,* vol. 18, no. 1, Winter, 1958. [Reprinted in Paul Pigors, Charles A. Myers, and F. T. Malm (eds.), *Management of Human Resources,* McGraw-Hill Book Company, New York, 1964, pp. 35–37.] This is an article critical of what it calls the "conventional approach" to line-staff relationships. It suggests that the chief executive should settle the conflicts by holding all lines of "the business checkerboard."

"Changing Staff-Line Relationships," Melville Dalton, *Personnel Administration,* March–April, 1966, pp. 3–5, 40–48. This article examines a case in which staff actually had authority over the line and discusses the results.

"Innovation in Business Organizations: Some Factors Associated with Success or Failure of Staff Proposals," William M. Evan and Guy Black, *Journal of Business,* University of Chicago, October, 1967, pp. 519–530.

13

THE

MECHANICS

OF

ORGANIZATION

It is important . . . to ask at the outset whether there are any features of form or structure which most organizations have in common. We shall find that there are such features; that, in fact, it is possible to construct a general model of an organization which embodies in somewhat abstract form the essential features of all organizations.
Kenneth Boulding: *The Organizational Revolution*

13 The point of departure in dealing with the mechanics of organization is the company objective: What is the organization trying to do? This immediately suggests two other questions: (1) What work must be performed if this objective is to be reached? and (2) Which of these jobs can best be coordinated by the same person, or in other words, which functions can be grouped together under a single boss?

A categorical answer to the first question can be given in very general terms. Every business is attempting to make a profit by doing one (or more than one) of three things:

1. *Producing products and selling them at a price higher than the cost of producing and distributing them.* This is the case with mining and manufacturing companies.

2. *Providing a service and selling it at a price higher than the cost entailed in supplying it and marketing it.* In this category are enterprises ranging from advertising agencies to laundries.

3. *Buying goods and reselling them at a price that will more than cover the purchase price and other expenses.* All companies that are merely distributors—retailers and wholesalers—fall into this group. In a sense these companies are providing a service—making it easier for customers to buy. But both retailers and wholesalers sell *goods;* they do not sell a service as a trucker sells transportation or an advertising agency sells the writing and placing of advertisements.

A fourth method of making a profit might perhaps be added: *investing funds,* which is a very important source of profit in some companies, notably banks and insurance companies. In order to obtain the funds to invest, however, these companies have to create and sell services. A bank must provide services for its depositors (e.g., protection of their money, checking facilities) as well as pay them interest for the use of their funds. An insurance company provides a service in the form of protection against the hazards of life.

DIVIDING THE WORK

Every company, therefore, needs to do some form of selling, through advertising, personal sales, or both. The marketing function is a primary one. Similarly, every company must keep financial records, for without them it would not even know whether it was making money or losing it. Finance and accounting and marketing are consequently two functions no company can dispense with. The rest of the answer to question 2 at the beginning of the chapter will depend in large part on the type of company under consideration.

The manufacturing company

The objective of the manufacturing company is to produce goods and sell them at a profit. Hence it requires production management as well as marketing and financial management. The main divisions of a manufacturing company must include marketing, finance, and production. So now we can draw a chart of the basic organization as in Figure 1.

In a small company, of course, the president may be the sole owner, and in that case we could dispense with the two top boxes on the chart. But in most companies of any size the owners tend to be stockholders who are investors only, with neither the ability to manage the company nor any interest in doing so.

If all jobs could be grouped under the three main functions considered so far, the mechanics of organizing a company would be simple. The three do not conflict in any way, and each requires a different type of ability and knowledge. It would be a fairly easy task to specify the responsibility of each, and the president's span of control would be well within the limit set by the classical theorists since he would supervise only three men directly.

But it is not always, or even usually, possible to fit all the positions under these three headings, especially when the company is a large one. There are too many functions that impinge on all three of the main departments.

Take the personnel function: Employees must be recruited, selected, and trained for all departments. Should not the personnel manager, therefore, report to the company president?

Or consider a research department charged with developing new products. All three of the main functions (production, marketing, and finance) must be concerned with the results of its work. Marketing must have products it can sell. New products generally require some change in production arrangements; some of them may even make it necessary to build new plants. Finally, new products require new investment, often of substantial size—a matter that certainly concerns the financial department. It is not, therefore, feasible to place a research department under any one of the three since its operations

FIGURE 1

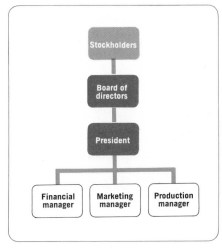

will have a company-wide effect. The same could be said of a number of other functions: public relations, the legal department, and purchasing, for example.

In a great many companies, also, the accounting or record-keeping function is separated from the management of the company's capital. In these cases there will be a controller in charge of all accounting functions and a treasurer whose job is to manage the company's capital: handle banking matters, stock issues, and so on. Moreover, it is only recently that management has begun to think of advertising and selling as part of the same function, and it is very common to have separate advertising and sales departments, with the heads of both reporting to the company president. A chart like the simple one in Figure 1 is, in fact, very rare. A more usual one would look like Figure 2.

It can be seen that it is far from easy to keep the president's span of control very short. Without even adding the purchasing director, who, since he may purchase for all departments, may properly belong in the top group, or the director of public relations, whose job also cuts across departmental lines, the president is already responsible for the direct supervision of seven men. Some companies even have organization departments which, since they assist the president with the organization of the company as a whole, must report directly to him. *The Management Guide,* a booklet prepared by the Standard Oil Company of California and widely used by other companies, suggests that the major divisions be as shown in Figure 3. Here there are eight executives reporting to the company president, or two more than the top number sometimes cited as the feasible span of control, and this seems to be a more typical arrangement than one that follows classical theory exactly.

In a survey conducted by the author[1] fewer than one-fourth of 100 large

[1] See Ernest Dale, *Organization,* American Management Association, New York, 1967, pp. 95–96.

FIGURE 2

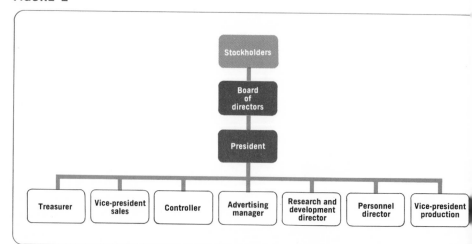

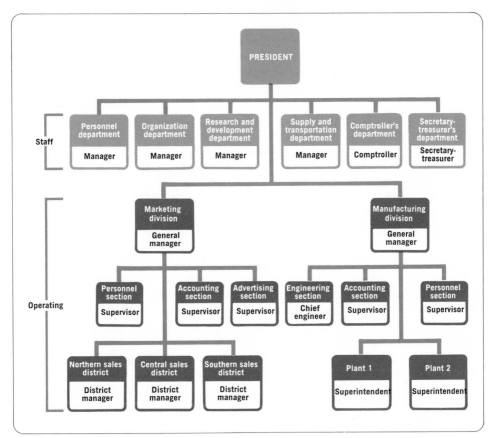

FIGURE 3   (From *The Management Guide,* prepared by George Lawrence
Hall with the assistance of other members of the department on
organization, Standard Oil Company of California; 2d ed. edited
by Franklin E. Drew and George Lawrence Hall, Standard Oil Company of California, March, 1956, p. 35. Now out of print.)

companies reported that the chief executive's span of control was six or less.
For others, the figures were as shown on page 252.

The 7 other companies making up the sample of 100 appeared to have a
form of group management at the top. Each chart showed a number of executives in the top box along with the chief, and the line of authority led from the
group to the executives on the next highest level.

Also, spans of control seemed to have changed but little from the early
1950s, when the author conducted a similar survey,[2] and surveys by others
show similar results. In the interval between the author's two surveys, some

[2] See Ernest Dale, *Planning and Developing the Company Organization Structure,* American
Management Association, New York, 1952, pp. 57–59.

Span of control	Number of companies
7	13
8	8
9	10
10	7
11	8
12	5
13	4
14	3
15	1
16	1
17	1
18	2
19	1
20	1
21	2
23	1
24	1

functions had been consolidated under one head (an executive vice-president or an administrative vice-president) in some cases, but in others new functions reporting directly to the top had been added. Thus the general picture remained about the same.

Aside from the heads of production, marketing, and finance and the executive vice-presidents and administrative vice-presidents, the executives who may be found working directly under the president often include the legal counsel and the heads of such departments as industrial relations or personnel, purchasing, research and development or new products, public relations, advertising, traffic, organization, economic research, quality control, and patents.

Production   Down the line, too, there are difficulties growing out of the twin needs for specialization and coordination. Consider, for example, the functions of a production department.

If all the production workers were doing the same type of work, a simple division by numbers (such as prevailed in the Roman legion) would be sufficient, as shown in Figure 4.

Or if the foremen became too numerous for one production manager to supervise directly, another level of supervision could be inserted as in Figure 5.

And even if producing the product required several different operations, the division could be made by one of the methods shown in the charts in Chapter 11 on theory. Finally, if the company has several plants or several different products, still a third layer (of plant managers) may be inserted.

So far as direct production labor is concerned, supervision is often subdivided in this way in a large company, although the titles are by no means constant. The production manager who supervises several plants is likely to

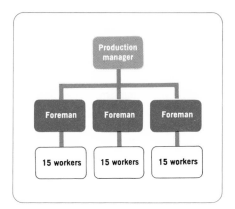

FIGURE 4

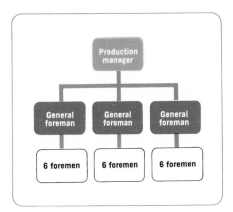

FIGURE 5

be a vice-president in charge of production, a vice-president of operations, or a vice-president in charge of manufacturing. The men who are known as general foremen in some companies may be called supervisors in another; or the first-line foremen (those in direct charge of the rank and file) may be known as supervisors and their superiors as foremen.

This division of labor is fairly clear-cut. Men performing the same operation can be grouped together under a single foreman, or closely related operations can be grouped together. But a plant requires many auxiliary services:

1. Someone must ensure that raw materials are available when they are needed. The purchasing department will buy them, but it must get requisitions from production first because only the production department is in a position to know what will be needed and at what times.
2. Materials must be received and put into a storeroom. Inventory records must be maintained.

3. Materials must be brought to production operations in the right quantities and at the right times. If they are not there when needed, the men who operate the machines will have to waste time waiting for them. But too large a quantity cannot be brought to the production floor at one time; there simply will not be room.
4. Parts on which several operations must be performed must be routed to the right machines in the right sequence.
5. Parts must be fed to subassembly lines and subassemblies to the final assembly when they are needed. If one component is missing, the entire product may be held up.
6. Finished products must be packed and shipped.
7. Quality must be controlled. Defects in parts must be caught before the parts are incorporated in subassemblies or assemblies, and final assemblies must be inspected before they are shipped.

It is evident that steps 1, 3, 4, and 5 are part of a process: getting materials to production on time through advance planning of the flow of production from raw material to finished product. They also involve a closely related set of decisions:

a. Given the fact that the plant is to produce 300 units of product X, what materials will be needed in what quantities?
b. If product X is produced by several operations, in what sequence should they be performed? And if the plant is also producing product Y, which requires several of the same operations, how can the production be dovetailed so that one product does not hold up the other?
c. How much time should be allowed for each operation to ensure that there is no delay?

Data on which the production planning is based, however, will most likely have been worked out by another group. A methods department will have determined the operations necessary to produce the product, and the unit times for various operations will have been calculated by a time study group using the stopwatch techniques first introduced by Frederick Taylor. These two functions may be combined in an industrial engineering department.

Generally, also, there will be another separate group charged with inspection of parts and finished products. The foremen who direct the production workers cannot very well handle this function since their main objective must be to see that their departments produce as much as possible in the shortest possible time, and the duties of quality control, which include rejection of some pieces, would involve them in a conflict of interest. In addition, quality control is now often achieved by a sampling method that requires statistical knowledge not possessed by the average foreman. Therefore the inspectors are likely to be under a quality control manager.

Another combination of duties might be shipping, receiving, and storage, and still another utilities and maintenance, since many of the same skills are needed in both (e.g., both need electricians and pipefitters). For the same

reason, maintenance will usually handle any new construction or rearrange-
ment of departments. The man at the head of the maintenance and construction functions is generally known as the plant engineer.

In a single-plant company, then, we might have an organization chart like
that in Figure 6. The functions under the chief production executive, the plant
manager, are shown in detail.

There is, however, no standard form for the organization of a manufacturing
plant. To cite just a few examples of the variations in use: Since inventory
represents money temporarily tied up, it may be under finance; in other cases
it may be the responsibility of purchasing. Or there may be a separate utilities
department, particularly if the plant supplies its own power. The organization
is likely to be somewhat different also in a chemical plant or other operation
in which production is continuous.

Marketing   The primary marketing function is, of course, direct face-to-face
selling. In some companies a simple geographical division of the sales force

FIGURE 6

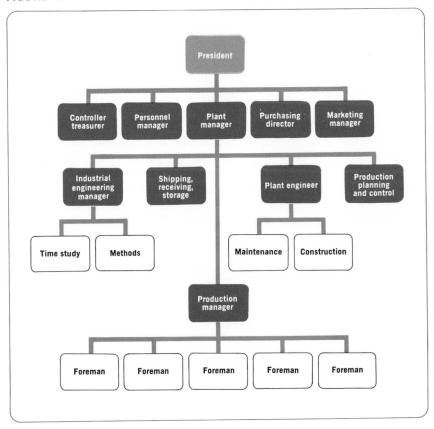

will suffice. The country, or the section of it in which the company sells its products, may be divided into districts and regions and a sales manager placed over each.

For a company selling diverse types of products, a division according to products or customers may be necessary because the selling processes may be different. In companies that make both products sold to consumers through retailers and wholesalers and products for industry, those who sell to industry must often be engineers who can plan industrial applications and discuss them intelligently with the engineers of customer companies. Again, some companies in which sales to the government are important have special sales departments to handle the contacts with government agencies.

The strict division between sales and advertising that exists in some companies has been due to a division by process. The actual work of an advertising department (writing advertisements and placing them or working with an agency on these tasks) was so different from the face-to-face selling process that it seemed logical to separate the two. The growing recognition that both are designed to serve the same *purpose* has sparked the trend toward combining them into the single function of marketing. It might also be argued that the division makes little sense if organization is thought of as based on decision making. To have the advertising department stress one line of products while sales is concentrating its efforts on another would be wasteful.

Another division of the marketing process is marketing research, which is both a purpose and a process group. Its purpose is not to sell directly, either in person or through the written word, but to find out how much of a given product can be sold, who are the most likely prospects for sales, where they are located, and what changes in products will make them more salable. The processes it uses are largely the study of figures from various sources and the construction of questionnaires to ascertain what customers want and why they buy. Marketing research may also set up "test marketing"—arrange to have a product introduced in a single area first, to ascertain consumer reaction before proceeding with full-scale distribution. But in this case it will merely establish the procedures; the actual selling effort will be carried out by the sales and advertising departments. In general, it may be said that the marketing research people provide data on which sales and advertising can base decisions.

Still another division of marketing may be sales promotion, which is a function whose place in the structure differs in different companies. Its work includes preparation of kits for salesmen and other material that will help them in sales, development of special promotions to be conducted at the retail level, and sometimes direct mail advertising. In some companies it is considered part of the advertising department; in others, part of the sales department; in still others it is a separate department reporting to the company president.

Finance If the need to combine, or at least closely coordinate, sales and advertising is fairly obvious, it is not necessarily true that there will be any advantage in combining treasury functions and controllership functions. Strictly speaking, they differ in both purpose and process.

The treasurer handles stock issues, borrowings, relations with stockholders, company investments. Since many of these matters have legal aspects, he may be a lawyer rather than an accountant. He will need a fairly good knowledge of accounting, however, since he cannot make decisions in any of these areas unless he is able to understand accounting records.

The controller, on the other hand, keeps the accounting records. He is much more than a glorified bookkeeper, however, since, as his title implies, it is his job to develop financial data that will make possible control of financial expenditures before they have been incurred: budgets, unit costs of various products, most economical inventory levels, and so on.

Multiplant companies   In a company like the one in Figure 6, writing job descriptions that specify authority and responsibility will not be too difficult. Possibilities of conflict exist, as they do in any situation involving human beings, but policies can be developed that will indicate who will make the final decision when a disagreement occurs. If plant engineering insists that a machine must be taken down for repairs and production is equally insistent that it needs the machine to produce an order, the plant manager, who is responsible both for the facilities and the output, can be given authority to decide. If sales wants to fill an order for a customer who is not a good credit risk, the financial department may be given the power of veto, or the two departments may take the case to the president.

In the case of a multiplant company, however, a different situation prevails. Then the plant manager may need an accounting organization of his own since it might take too long to issue the payroll checks and obtain cost data if the raw data had to be transmitted to a central organization some distance away for calculations. He will need a personnel department as well, for hiring workers locally and handling other personnel problems on the spot. Similarly he may need a purchasing department.

Yet all these functions will probably have to be duplicated at headquarters. Figures from the various plants must be coordinated if the company president is to know what the company as a whole is doing; central purchasing of some items may make for economy; if there is no central methods group, there can be no organized way of passing on improvements made in one plant to the others. Nor can the company president allow each plant manager to set his own wage rates and personnel policies. If there is a union, this is quite likely to be impossible; even if there is not, the manifest inequalities that would soon appear would be likely to cause trouble.

At once the possibility of conflicting authority arises. Should the plant accounting department report to the headquarters controller or to the plant manager? Should the straight line of authority run from the company president through the plant manager to the plant personnel manager or from the company president through the vice-president in charge of personnel and industrial relations to the personnel manager in the plant?

This problem is not peculiar to manufacturing companies; all companies that have more than one location are afflicted with it to some degree.

The consensus among companies seems to be that the plant controller, the plant personnel manager, the plant purchasing agent, and the rest should report to the plant manager, but that headquarters staff men should exercise "functional" control over them. Functional control is generally indicated by a dotted line on the organization chart (Figure 7).

To determine where the division can be made between functional and direct control, Herbert Simon's decision-making approach described in Chapter 11 may be helpful. Which decisions must be made at headquarters and which may be left to the discretion of the local executives?

In the case of the controller, for example, it is evident that all figures sent

FIGURE 7 Relationship of staff functional authority to direct line authority.

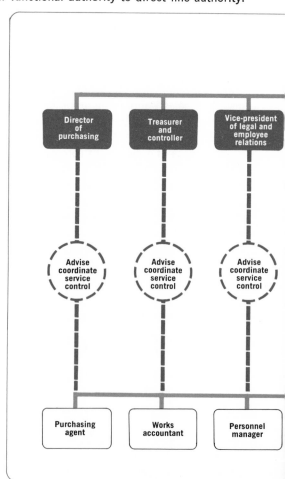

to headquarters should be calculated on the same basis; otherwise the company will have no basis for comparing the costs and profitability of its different plants. Therefore decisions on accounting systems would naturally be reserved for headquarters. Again, wage rates, vacation policies, the number of paid holidays, and similar matters are likely to be uniform throughout all plants, either because all are covered by the same union contract negotiated by the headquarters group or because top management believes that fairness and logic demand uniformity in these matters. Then, as long as he does not order the controller or the personnel manager to violate any of the general company policies, the plant manager may be given control of his staff men.

The system of making the staff men completely independent of the local plant manager and responsible only to their headquarters counterparts may

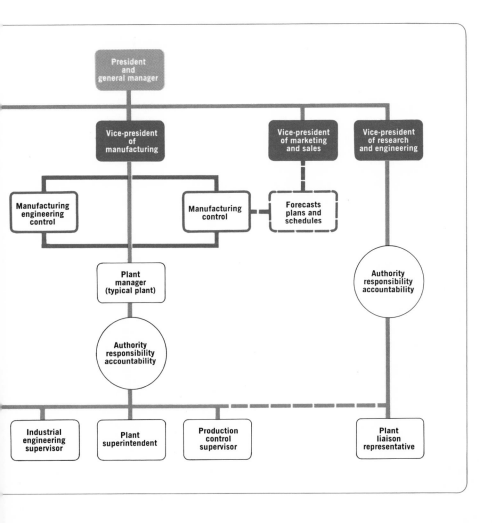

be in effect in some companies even today, but it is fraught with even greater difficulties than the division between functional and direct authority.

Up until the late 1930s, when a major reorganization took place, Westinghouse Electric Corporation was organized along completely functional lines: the works [plant] manager at the gearing division plant reported to the general works manager, but his engineering department reported directly to the engineering department at East Pittsburgh, and a similar situation prevailed in regard to his other staff departments. "There were more executives in my plant not working for me than there were working for me," the works manager, H. C. Philips (later vice-president in charge of manufacturing), once observed, and, he added, he had to ask a jury of about a dozen men before making any decision of consequence. Even unimportant matters went all the way up one chain of command and down another before anything could happen.

The service company

Companies that create services and sell them are of so many different types that few generalizations are possible about them. Like manufacturing companies, however, all require the financial and sales functions and, since they are creating a service, something roughly analogous to the production function. Figure 8, for example, is the organization chart of an advertising agency.

The sales department here is the one called the "account service department" since the account executives are those who contact the clients, present and prospective. (Some agencies also have a special new-business man or department.)

The job of creating the service, or the function that could be called "production" if the company were a manufacturing organization, is entrusted to three departments in this case: public relations, the creative department, and the media and merchandising department. Some explanation of the terminology used is necessary to make this clear since the functions are different from those performed by manufacturing company departments with the same names.

The job of the public relations department in a manufacturing company is to make the company and its products well and favorably known. The advertising public relations department, though it may help to publicize the agency itself, is there primarily to provide public relations services that the agency sells to the clients. In the case of this particular agency, the public relations department evidently has its own sales forces—"public relations contact"—as well as a group that provides the service. The functions of the production and traffic departments also differ from the functions of departments with the same names in a manufacturing company. In the advertising agency, production handles only a part of the actual production of the service; the creative department writes the advertisements, and the production department mainly provides liaison between the creative people and the printers and publications. Whereas traffic in a manufacturing company is concerned with shipping routes

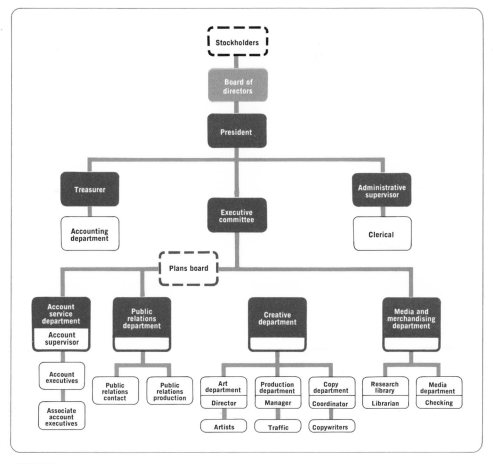

FIGURE 8

and schedules, traffic in an agency is charged simply with getting copy and art to publications and scripts and recordings to broadcasting stations on time.

The agency, then, is actually producing three services: public relations, advertising copy and art, and placement in the various media. The public relations department produces the public relations services; the copy and art departments produce the advertisements; and the media department handles selection of media, which is one of the agency's services.

The executive committee and the plans board shown on the chart are coordinating groups composed of the heads of important departments.

In insurance, the main sales job is done by a corps of independent agents in the case of a stock company, or a regular sales force in the case of mutual companies. But the stock company as well as the mutual must have its own sales department of special agents to oversee the work of the agents. Here again terminology may cause confusion. Insurance executives commonly refer to sales as "production." "Production costs" in an insurance company are actually marketing costs.

The financial function is likely to be of particular importance in an insurance company. Not only does the company need a host of records; it derives a good part of its income from its investments.

What the company sells is the protection afforded by the policies. The work that corresponds most nearly to the production work in a manufacturing company or the creative work of an advertising agency is the work of the actuarial department, which develops the statistics on which coverage is based, and that of the underwriting department and the clerical workers who prepare the policies. Another important function is the investigation and settlement of claims, which has no exact parallel in any other business.

Retailers and wholesalers

Distribution companies differ from manufacturing companies in that they do not actually produce anything. What they sell they purchase from outside. The main functions, in addition to finance, are purchasing and selling.

Purchasing of articles for resale is an entirely different matter from purchasing for the company's own use. The purchasing agent in a manufacturing company need not worry about the sales of the final product; his only job is to buy, on the best terms possible, the materials and parts that other groups have determined will go into it. Purchasing for resale, on the other hand, requires primarily a knowledge of what will sell. For this reason purchasing and selling are usually combined under a single head. In a department store, a "buyer" is the head of a department sales force.

COORDINATING THE WORK

As human knowledge broadens, it becomes more and more difficult for any one person to know "all about" a given field. This leads to narrower and narrower specialization.

Small companies are not too greatly affected by this trend. Take a small chemical company that produces only a single line of products. It is quite possible for a single chemical engineer to acquire, say, all the knowledge needed about the way in which these products induce corrosion in the process equipment and the structural members of the building, and to discover the materials most resistant to their effects. But in a larger company producing hundreds of products, the problem will take the full time of a group of men. Thus there will be a group of corrosion engineers who constitute a division of chemical engineering, which is itself a specialty. Or take accounting. In the small company, one general accountant may be able to ascertain unit costs for each of the few products; the larger company will require a cost accounting division of the accounting specialty.

Narrow specialization in middle-level professional jobs may not have the deadening effect it does at lower levels, where a man may have to specialize in inserting four screws. But it does lead to disunification of manifold activities that should be aimed toward a common goal. The centrifugal forces in a large organization may be very strong. Without constant efforts toward coordination, there is likely to be duplication of work and work at cross-purposes.

First of all, those who spend their time on specialties come to regard their activities as ends in themselves rather than as means to another and bigger end. Often there is danger that one department or section will attempt to improve its showing at the expense of other departments, or even at the expense of the company as a whole.

Sales and manufacturing may be at odds. Sales wants products that will sell; it would like to satisfy every whim of every customer. Manufacturing wants high volume at low cost—that is what it will be judged on. Slight changes in design may mean extra processing; quicker delivery dates may mean that manufacturing will have to keep its force working overtime at time and a half. The question here is: What is the optimum? What course of action will enable the company to make the highest profit? It may be that the extra sales are worth the higher manufacturing cost, or conversely, that sales should be curtailed if that is the only way manufacturing costs can be kept down. Or it may be that some compromise between the two viewpoints is necessary. But neither sales nor manufacturing is capable of finding the optimum point independently.

Moreover, most executives feel pushed for time. Caught in a network of problems of their own, they overlook the need to talk over proposed actions with other departments that may be affected by them. And because they have concentrated so wholeheartedly on their specialties, they often have little appreciation of the fact that something they propose will affect other departments.

Again, departments and functions are often widely separated geographically. Quick communication is difficult. The head of one department who attempts to throw one of Fayol's gangplanks across to the head of another may find himself stymied. If he calls on the telephone, the man he is trying to reach may be out of the office. If he writes a memo, it may lie around unread because the other man is being deluged with reports of all kinds from his superiors and his subordinates.

For this reason, formal methods of coordination are increasingly employed as companies get larger. In part, of course, this coordination is achieved through common superiors. But every superior, like every subordinate, is hampered by lack of time. He cannot police every small decision made by his subordinates; he has decisions of his own to make that require study.

In part, too, clearly written objectives and job descriptions will foster coordination; but again there is a catch. Circumstances may arise in which the welfare of the company as a whole demands that the objective of one department be partially sacrificed for a time. But the department head who has been told by his superiors in writing what his objective is, and who knows he will be judged by how well he meets it, is not likely to accept this idea if it is presented to him by someone on his own level.

Coordination by committees

A working definition of a committee is that it is a group of people (usually no more than can sit around a table) which makes decisions or presents viewpoints and whose conduct is governed by a set of rules.

A committee may have a purely advisory function in some cases. Thus a committee composed of the heads of the chief functions may meet regularly or irregularly to counsel the company president on his decisions. In this way he is assured of taking all points of view into account. He can decide whether a course of action that may be advantageous for some phases of the business will be disadvantageous for other phases and determine whether the advantages offset the disadvantages. Or he may seek the committee's advice on some problem to which he himself has as yet no solution.

On the other hand, a committee may be a decision-making body that can itself choose a course of action or approve or disapprove a proposed course. In that case, it may decide by majority vote, or it may determine to act favorably on an idea only when it has reached unanimous agreement. In the latter instance, of course, the proposal may have to be modified considerably before a consensus can be obtained.

Use of committees both at the top and down the line has grown enormously during the post-World War II period, mainly because companies have grown larger. As *Fortune* once stated:

> As soon as a manager is forced by the growth of his company, the variety or complexity of its products . . . to establish broad policies . . . chart high strategy . . . the manager finds himself in conference with his peers. Whatever he chooses to do he confronts committees, *ad hoc* if nothing else. If the organization of his corporation is too monolithic and he decides on decentralization, he usually winds up with a series of committees. If, on the other hand, organization is loose, the usual consequence of unification is again a series of committees.[3]

And the trend toward use of committees is not confined to the United States. A large Dutch company found that roughly 1,000 meetings of its interdepartmental standing committees were being held each year, with from three to twenty or twenty-five people taking part in each one. "This means," it reported, "that, at a rough estimate, about 30,000 manhours are absorbed in meetings of this kind."[4]

The committee form of coordination has both defenders and attackers. There are those who hold that a decision made by a group is likely to be

[3] "Management by Committee," April, 1953, p. 146.
[4] *Economy of Time and Money at Meetings*, a brochure issued to its executives by A.K.U. (Algemene Kunstzijde Unie, or United Rayon Manufacturing), whose headquarters are in Arnhem, the Netherlands.

better than one made by an individual, even if that individual knows more about the subject than all the others put together. Members of this school of thought appear to have an almost mystical belief that when a group meeting takes place, the whole is somehow greater than the sum of its parts. On the other hand, there are those who are severely critical of committees on several grounds. Some believe that committees tend to become mere sounding boards for a dominating personality (generally the chief executive) and so defeat the very purpose for which they are organized: interchange of viewpoints and information. It is also charged that when all members concur in a decision it is likely to be based on the lowest common denominator. That is, the course of action adopted is merely the one that arouses the least opposition and may not be the best course by any means. The commonest complaint, however, is that committee meetings take too much time, time that executives could better spend getting on with their own jobs.

To some extent, company experience with committees depends on the circumstances and the personalities involved. Thus when U.S. Rubber adopted a system of committee management that had worked well at Du Pont for decades, the plan seemed to be more a hindrance than a help. When it was abolished, the company found the results good:

> In an important test of quick action on a larger scale, the new management decided at the beginning of the 1957–58 recession to close down the company's old Fort Wayne plant. Within a few weeks, the plans were approved and the machinery started for abandoning this uneconomic facility. Veterans of the old executive committee say such a step could have taken a year under the old system. Some feel that at least one member of the old committee would have had a soft spot in his heart for the old plant and its demise could only have come about through rather long wrangling and perhaps needless compromise.[5]

It should be noted, however, that U.S. Rubber did not abolish *all* committees; it merely assigned decision-making responsibilities that had formerly devolved on the top executive committee to individuals and organized a new operating policy committee to advise the president and the chairman of the board on production and research and development.

In fact, it is doubtful whether it is possible for a modern large company to operate without some committee meetings. The problem is to keep the number of committees and the number and length of the meetings within bounds.

Certainly some committees accomplish a great deal by saying comparatively little. For example, the executive committee of the Standard Oil Company of New Jersey meets frequently—several times a week. But since its members have known each other for years, relatively little argument may be needed to come to a conclusion.

Probably the first characteristic of a good committee is that its members have open minds and be willing to be convinced by facts. Homogeneity of

[5] *Business Week,* Oct. 22, 1960, p. 104.

general outlook is also important; that is, the members should be generally committed to the same overall objective. If each member sees the company goals differently, no agreement can be reached. Again, a committee can have no real homogeneity if it is dominated by one man (usually the chief executive) who feels that "although we each have one vote, mine is more than equal to all the others." Equally unsatisfactory is a committee torn by two rivals, who may deliberately range themselves on opposite sides of any question.

Finally, although the committee members should have more or less the same outlook, each should be skilled in a different phase of the business. Thus their contributions can supplement each other.

Some other tentative generalizations about committees may be summarized as follows:[6]

1. High performance depends on the contributions of many; on much rather than little interaction.
2. Small committees (groups) tend to be superior to large ones when the material lends itself to immediate formation of opinions; larger ones tend to be better when it is desirable to reject incorrect proposals quickly.
3. The tendency toward agreement tends to diminish with an increase in size (and so does the influence of the chairman).
4. The freer the discussion, the better the results. Each member's remarks should be judged on their own merits, and each should feel as free to utter aloud in the presence of the group what he would think to himself privately.
5. Agreement as a desirable end of committee discussion tends to be less fruitful than exploration of differences.
6. "The effort to understand is the beginning of reconciliation."

As to the conduct of committee meetings, some very practical pointers are offered by A.K.U., the Dutch company mentioned above, in its brochure for executives:

Members
1. Periodical meetings are apt to attract many members. *Have the right members been invited and is their attendance really necessary? Do not duplicate unnecessarily.*
2. Could the meeting be reduced to a *standing* core and other members invited only as and when required?
3. Is it absolutely necessary for all members *to be present during the whole of the proceedings?* If not, has the agenda been drawn up with due regard to that fact?

Notice
1. Is the meeting really necessary, or could it be combined with one at a later date?

[6] From John Cohen, *Humanistic Psychology,* George Allen & Unwin, Ltd., London, 1958, pp. 141–154.

2. Does this meeting have to be convened periodically and at these intervals of time?
3. Should documents be sent together with this notice which would arrive too late if enclosed with the agenda?

Agenda

1. Are there *enough important points*, or is this meeting being convened to discuss a "ragged" agenda? Ring up members and ask them if they have any points to go on the agenda. It is better to postpone the meeting than to hold one facing an unimportant agenda.
2. Are the points of the agenda *mature for discussion,* or do they require further preparation? A complicated subject should sometimes be discussed within a small circle, or else preliminary advice or an informatory note should be submitted.
3. Sometimes the same points reappear on the agenda regularly under the same titles, despite the fact that various aspects of them have been disposed of. Has it become a routine? Subdivide general subjects so that members may realize that progress is being made.
4. Arrange the points that take up most time in order of importance. Let the meeting begin with a few points in which only statements are made. Keep for the end such points as you wish to have discussed more thoroughly at subsequent meetings.
5. *Do not introduce each point yourself,* but let the most expert or qualified do it. Have his name put down on the agenda and let him know in advance that you expect a short introduction from him. If many figures or facts are to be put before the meeting, ask the introducer to present an *informatory note* or write these data on the blackboard in advance.
6. Are the *points of the agenda* well described? Is each point adequately *explained?* Do not place any points on the agenda which could be decided outside the meeting equally well or to better advantage.
7. Is the *question to be put* to the meeting important enough to recur regularly on the agenda? If it is important but, for lack of sufficient time, cannot receive the attention it deserves, why not let it lead off the agenda at stated intervals?

Preliminaries

1. Even if the minutes are not read to the meeting, make yourself acquainted with the *decisions taken last time* and, after the meeting has been opened, ask whether the necessary has been done to give effect to those decisions. This does not apply to the points recurring on the agenda.
2. Try to make up your own mind as to roughly how much *time* is to be *allotted* to the most important points on the agenda.
3. Allow for enough *breaks.* Do not continue the discussions during lunch if a meeting runs on for an exceptionally long time.
4. Make a note beside each point on the agenda of the name of the person most *qualified* to speak on the subject and make up your mind *to call on him first.*

5.   Do not deal *with any point on the agenda* which could equally well be dealt with outside the meeting.
6.   *Have the telephone disconnected* and let your secretary or the Exchange know who will act for you while you are at the meeting.
7.   When the question is put to the meeting, ask members to suggest *points to be put on the agenda for the following meeting.*

Conducting the Meeting

1.   Ask whether the minutes of the previous meeting call for any comment, but try to avoid duplicating it.
2.   Consider the expediency of dealing first of all with points on the agenda for which certain members have been specially convened, so that they need attend for only a short time.
3.   If possible, let other members take the chair from time to time.
4.   Analyze the problems together with the members, sum up the essential points and take stock of the opinions held by the group.
5.   Encourage members to take part in the discussion.
6.   Link the views expressed and see that members discuss their experience.
7.   Keep the discussion well in hand; prevent it from becoming too emotional; do not let anyone (including yourself) monopolize.
8.   Lay down the points of agreement.
9.   Sum up from time to time.
10.   Direct the discussion toward a conclusion.
11.   At the end, recapitulate clearly and briefly any conclusions and arrangements come to.

Questions

Proceedings can also be guided by asking questions, e.g.,

1.   *In order to draw attention to a point which has not yet been discussed:*
   Might I have your opinion on an aspect which no one has brought forward so far? I mean. . . .
2.   *To test an argument:*
   Mr. A has just advanced a new argument. Could you tell me how much that weighs with you?
3.   *To test the value of the source of information submitted:*
   Now, where did that information come from?
   Who is this Mr. X to whom you referred just now?
   Where does Mr. X find his facts? Is he a qualified man?
4.   *To arrest digressions:*
   What point are we really discussing?
5.   *If the discussion was disappointing, or the problem has not yet come to maturity:*
   What would you say to our thinking over the whole question quietly by ourselves and having it put on the agenda again in a month's time?
6.   *If the group is prejudiced:*
   I wonder whether our own interest in this matter is making us take too one-sided a view of it?

Obstacles to the discussion

Language:

1. *Using vague terms.* It is useful, but not enough, to ask your opponent to give a definition. If you do not understand a term, or cannot see clearly what it is intended to imply, ask for concrete examples by way of illustration.

2. *Exploiting the emotional value of words* for the conscious or unconscious purpose of disguising a weak argument by the frequent use of emotionally charged words. Remedy: Substitute "neutral" words for these, thus facilitating an objective appraisal of the reasoning and making its true value plainer.

Judgment:

1. *Generalizing* by basing a categorical judgment upon insufficient evidence. Remedy: Ask the speaker to state the grounds upon which his opinion is founded. "Are you sure you have examined enough cases to warrant such a sweeping statement? Have you made due allowance for those cases which do not fit into the picture?" Advise speaker to keep his mind flexible, i.e., to be prepared to change his mind if new facts should call for it.

2. *Oversimplification,* i.e., "settling" a complicated matter in a few words. Remedy: Point out calmly that matters are not quite as simple as your opponent makes them out to be.

3. *Loose thinking,* exemplified by stating that something "is" this or that because it "ought to" or "must be." Remedy: Point out that conclusions with regard to the facts can only be based on other facts, hence not on the speaker's conviction that something "should by rights be so-and-so" or "surely must be so."

Argument:

1. *The "ding-dong" argument,* i.e., doggedly repeating one's own opinion without touching on opponent's arguments. Remedy: Point this out to your opponent and then advance the for-and-against arguments for discussion. If this also fails, break off the discussion.

2. *Measuring by two standards,* i.e., accepting an argument in one case and abruptly refusing to accept it in another. Remedy: Ask him if he wishes to adhere to the argument as it is. Then apply this argument in both cases.

3. *Facing somebody with a dilemma.* Remedy: Refuse to recognize the alternative and put it to the person in question that he is flatly ignoring all the possible compromises.

4. *Sidetracking.* One way is to tempt a speaker to digress from his initial theme by unobtrusively shifting the discussion to another sphere. Remedy: Bring the discussion back to its starting point.

5. *Driving someone into a corner,* e.g., by insidiously imputing a statement to him which he has not made at all, or has not made in that way. Remedy: Do not allow yourself to be put out and stick quietly to your initial position.

Minutes

1. Do the minutes of this meeting serve any useful purpose?

2. Do the names of those who have received copies appear invariably on all the minutes? After each meeting discuss with the secretary who else should receive a copy to enable him (them) to put the decisions into effect.
3. Make a note in the margin of the minutes of the name of the person who has undertaken a task, or underline beside every decision the words: "Mr. X has undertaken to. . ."
4. Discuss with the secretary whether the minutes are to be a true record of all opinions expressed, or a businesslike résumé of the decisions come to and the instructions issued as a result of the discussions.
5. Quote the numbers and descriptions of the points on the agenda in the report.

Follow-up

1. The chairman and/or secretary should make it a practice to ascertain whether the decisions made at the meeting have been or are being carried out and, if not, take the necessary steps to see that they are.
2. Consider giving the meeting time periodically to criticize the proceedings and the chairman's leadership. Encourage them to offer suggestions for improvement.

The general staff

Use of the general staff man or group constitutes another device for ensuring coordination.

Figure 9 illustrates the pattern of communication in a company where twelve executives, all on the same level, are charged with self-coordination. Each of them must decide which of the others should be informed of any proposed action. If he makes a practice of informing all of them in every instance, an enormous number of useless reports and memoranda will be circulated, for not all will be interested in every proposal. Moreover, if executives are continually getting reports that are of no possible interest to them, they will fall into the habit of putting memoranda from their colleagues aside and may miss something important. If, on the other hand, a colleague attempts to send his memos only to those who will be interested in them, he may make some bad mistakes, for the more tasks become specialized, the harder it is for the specialists to appreciate the effects of their projects on other functions.

The general staff group can mitigate this situation by acting as a clearing house, as shown in Figure 10. The twelve executives need only inform the general staff of their plans, and that group then becomes responsible for seeing that those who will be interested are informed promptly. Because of its central position, it will be able to gauge which of the departments will be affected by any given course of action. It can also maintain standard lists showing who should get what data.

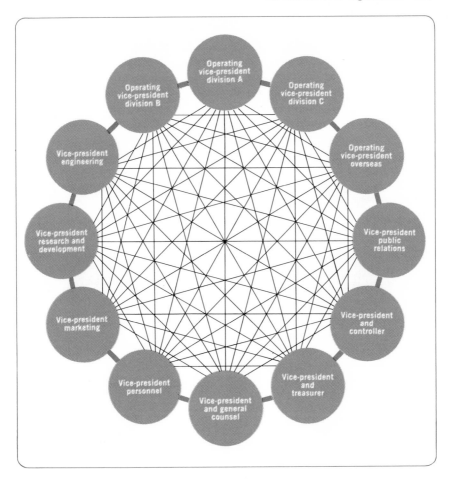

FIGURE 9 Communications pattern resulting from self-coordination.

Special coordinators

Still a third device is the appointment of individuals to serve as special coordinators of various phases of the business.

One coordinating position, which has become increasingly common in recent
years, is the contract administrator. When the company gets a large contract,
from the government or from a commercial customer, the work might be
expected to flow smoothly from sales to engineering to production. In practice,
this is seldom the case. The customer changes his mind about certain details
of design and wants to know how much the changes will cost him. Or he
wants additional work done, or a quicker delivery date. Up to the time he
signed the contract, his contact has been the salesman or sales engineer, but
the latter cannot spare the time from his marketing work to shepherd the
changes through and coordinate the engineering, estimating, and production

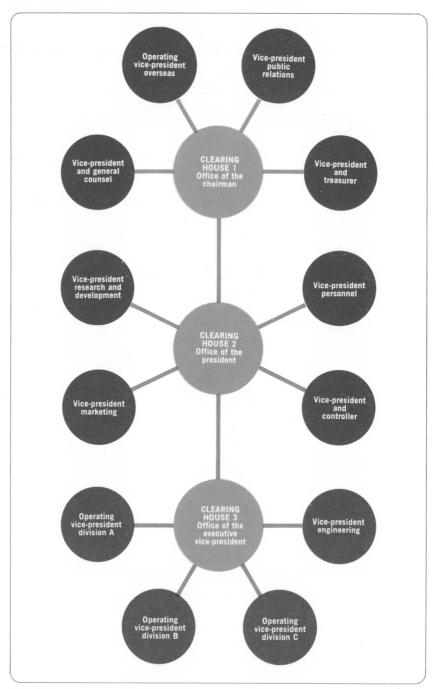

FIGURE 10   General staff groups as coordinators.

work on them. The contract administrator fills the gap, providing liaison and coordination between the customer, his own engineering department, and the production force.

Again, some companies that make a variety of products (soap and cosmetic companies in particular) have product managers who are responsible for coordinating all the work necessary to make a single product or a family of products salable: the marketing research, the packaging, the advertising, the sales promotion, and the pricing. A product manager does not, however, usually have control over all these functions, just as the contract manager is not charged with supervision of production and engineering. Each man must work by suggestion and persuasion.

On the other hand, the job of the project manager, who is another type of individual coordinator, usually does carry some line authority over those whose work he coordinates. For many years project managers, who are usually men transferred from other jobs temporarily, have been used to coordinate new construction work; now they are used for many special projects that require the task force or matrix form of organization.

Another example on a somewhat lower level is the maintenance coordinator sometimes employed in paper mills. Many paper mills run continuously 24 hours a day, seven days a week, which means that it is difficult for the maintenance department to make needed repairs to machines. If the machines are stopped for replacement of parts that are wearing out, or if they are allowed to run to breakdown, production time will be lost. But production itself stops the papermaking machines at times to change the wires (screens on which water is shaken from the pulp mixture) and the felts on which the sheet is dried, and these changes take at least an hour, and probably longer. It is obviously important, therefore, to utilize this time for lubrication and repairs, but the production foremen, busy as they are with their own jobs, do not always remember to inform the maintenance department when they are expecting to make the changes. Here is where the coordinator comes in: He maintains liaison between the two departments, keeps a list of repair jobs that need doing, and has men on the spot ready to work when the machine goes down for a felt or wire change.

SUMMARY

A company's organization structure is generally determined by its objectives and the work entailed in reaching them; hence the organization structure may differ according to the industry.

Functions common to all business organizations are marketing and finance. The production function is common to all manufacturing companies and to all companies that produce a service, although in the latter case it is not always labeled as such. These three major functions—which have different purposes and use different processes—are easy to separate organizationally.

In large companies, and even in some fairly small companies, however, there are many other functions that must be departmentalized, and often these affect the functioning of the three main departments and of one another. For this reason, it is difficult to keep the president's span of control as short as classical organization theory demands.

In companies that have more than one location, still another important problem exists: Should staff groups report to their counterparts at headquarters or to the line manager at their location? Probably the commonest way of handling this difficulty is to state in the organization manual that the local groups report to the local manager in a line relationship but functionally to the groups at headquarters.

Division of the work is one important phase of setting up an organization, but it is equally important to make provision for coordination. Primarily, coordination is achieved through common superiors. In a small company, this—plus informal consultation—is probably all that is necessary. In a large company, on the other hand, further formal means of coordination are necessary. These means are almost sure to include committees of one kind or another. General staff men may also be valuable for this purpose. In addition, companies often employ special coordinators of one kind or another to coordinate special phases of the work.

Review Questions

1. Why is a production planning and control group necessary in a large manufacturing plant? Is it a line or a staff group?
2. Why do companies often place advertising and sales under the same superior?
3. What do dotted lines on an organization chart represent?
4. What are some of the disadvantages of having staff groups at the plants report directly to their counterparts at headquarters?
5. What are the "products" of the advertising agency whose chart is shown in Figure 8?
6. How do the functions of the purchasing agent in a manufacturing company differ from those of a buyer in a department store?
7. Is the purchasing agent line or staff? Is the buyer in a department store line or staff? Give reasons.
8. What are some of the means used to ensure coordination?
9. What are the advantages and disadvantages of committee management?

Case Study One / Peter Williston and Sons Company*

Peter Williston, aged sixty-two, the son of the founder of the Peter Williston and Sons Company, retired from active management of the concern in 1967. Peter Williston's sons—James, aged forty-two, and John, aged forty—suc-

* This case is adapted from *Problems in Industrial Management*, by Erwin H. Schell and Harold H. Thurlby, A. W. Shaw Company, Chicago, 1924, pp. 171–179.

ceeded their father in the active management of the business. James had been with the company for twenty-three years and had been in complete charge of manufacturing for twelve years. He was quiet, reserved, and a hard worker, and he had the respect of his foremen. John Williston was of the hale-fellow-well-met type. He was in charge of the selling activities and was highly respected not only by his customers but also in civic and social circles.

Peter Williston and Sons Company is engaged in the manufacture of wooden hay and garden rakes, wheelbarrows, snow shovels, handles for axes and for metal garden tools, clothes racks, trellises, and a fair variety of wooden toys. About 180 men are employed during the busy season. The products are sold to a small number of hardware jobbers, who give a fairly wide distribution to the firm's products and also to metal garden tools and other hardware.

Associated with the Williston brothers at their own plant are a general foreman, three foremen, an auditor, and a stockkeeper. The general foreman assists James Williston in shop matters and has charge of the implement department. The stockkeeper is in charge of the storerooms, purchasing, and shipping. The auditor keeps the general ledger accounts, maintains relations with the bank, and with the assistance of a bookkeeper, supervises both the financial and the cost accounting. One foreman has charge of the small sawmill which is operated by the company; the other two foremen are in charge of the trellis and toy departments, respectively. Departments have been organized on the basis of products, although similar operations are performed on many of the products and some duplication of machines is required.

Production is largely for stock. Orders to manufacture are issued by James Williston to the general foreman as brief memoranda.

Sales are almost entirely to hardware jobbers, and John Williston, with two traveling salesmen, handles the distribution. Over a third of the business is done on direct orders received by mail from the customers. The company has no advertising other than the printed catalogues which are furnished to jobbers. The possibility of increasing the sales of clothes racks and of trellises by the use of circular advertising and canvassers has been considered for some time, but no effort has been made along this line.

The total sales of the company were approximately $1,250,000 in 1967. An examination of the balance sheets of the company shows a fairly steady growth during the last twenty years, although the total increase of sales has not been over 20 per cent. Costs of manufacturing, however, have been comparable when corrected for cyclical variations over the entire period.

Less than a mile from the plant of Peter Williston and Sons is located the plant of the Williston Company, which makes shovels, spades, crowbars, steel wheelbarrows, and contractors' hand tools; and metal rakes, hoes, and other garden tools, including such edge tools as pruning shears, scythes, and sickles. Recently a small line of lawn mowers and several sizes of wheel hoes have been added to the line, the castings being purchased. These products are sold to jobbers and by them to contractors, construction companies, and retailers. About 500 men are employed fairly steadily. The company is for the most part made up of younger men, and the management is aggressive in its policy. The balance sheets for the last decade have shown a rapidly increasing surplus, which has been secured by lower manufacturing costs and a considerable increase in sales. Sales have been tripled during the decade and in 1967 approximated $2,400,000.

President Daniel Williston, recently deceased, had been a strong man. Both aggressive and attractive in personality, he had inspired his associates and had kept them producing to the limit of their abilities. Anxious to keep abreast of the times, he had installed the latest methods and equipment for the manufacture of all his products in increasing quantities.

Now, in 1968, the executives in this organization are the general superintendent, chief accountant, plant engineer, planning manager, personnel manager, sales manager, purchasing agent, and storekeeper, together with the heads of several departments, such as the master mechanic, the boss blacksmith, and the foremen.

Mr. Meyers, the general superintendent, is a man of sixty years who was with Daniel Williston when he first started the manufacture of iron tools. At that time Meyers was a young foreman with little education but with the knowledge of a good machinist. He became master mechanic and held that position for a number of years, and has been superintendent for the last eight years. His greatest value to the organization lies in his control over the men in the shops. The men address him as Tom, and his loyalty to Daniel Williston is exceeded only by his men's loyalty to him. Without him the Williston Company would not have attained its success since Mr. Williston's own points of contact with the men were mostly points of irritation.

To assist the general superintendent, a planning department was inaugurated in 1961. This department was under the charge of an industrial engineer during its development, but during the last two years it has been placed under Daniel Williston, Jr., who has been with the company three years. He is twenty-five years old and entered the company immediately after graduation from college. Young Williston has the aggressiveness of his father, and it has shown to good advantage in his work in the planning department. Meyers and Williston, Jr., are an excellent team, and relations between the two are extremely close.

As sales manager, Daniel Williston had selected one of his star salesmen, from whom he had expected great things in the future. The former salesman is only thirty-four years of age, however, and has not been able to control all the four older salesmen very successfully. The chief accountant, purchasing agent, and personnel manager are young men of average ability. The plant engineer and storekeeper are men of middle age and well qualified to carry on the functions assigned to them.

Proposed merger

When Daniel Williston, Sr., a brother of the elder Peter Williston and president of the Williston Company, recently died, it was found that the Williston Company had become very largely a one-man concern and that Daniel Williston had no understudy. There appeared to be no one in the organization to whom the responsibilities of management could be entrusted.

At a meeting of the directors called for the purpose of deciding what to do about this "riderless horse" situation, it was suggested by the president of the Manufacturers National Bank (Mr. Foster), who was a director in both companies, that the Williston Company approach Peter Williston and Sons Company with a proposal to buy the latter business for the purpose of consolidating the two companies. In this way the Williston Company could secure the managerial services of the "Williston boys" and the advice of their father. At a previous meeting, Mr. Foster had proposed that an outside man be secured for the presidency, but he had been unable in the interim to find a man who had the necessary experience.

It was found that the brothers and their father were willing to enter into such an arrangement. A plan of consolidation and financial reorganization, drawn up by Mr. Foster and the attorneys for the concerns, was accepted by the owners. The companies were combined under the name of the Williston Implement Company, with Peter Williston, his two sons James and John, Mrs. Daniel Williston, Mr. Foster, and Mr. Fisher (a former director in the Williston Company) as the directorate. The former stockholders in the Williston Company received stock in the Williston Implement Company in exchange

Organization chart submitted by *John Williston* for the Williston Implement Company.

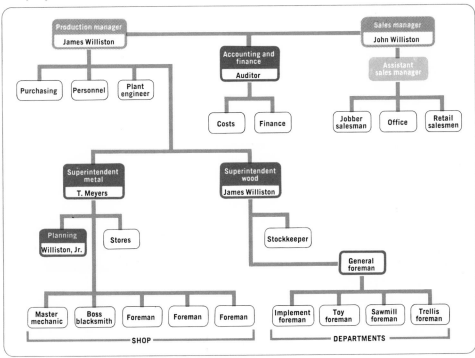

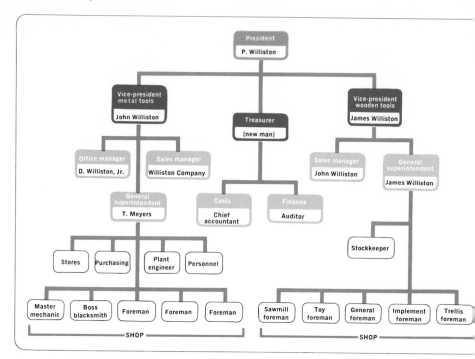

Organization chart submitted by *A. E. Foster* for the Williston Implement Company.

for their small holdings, but were not elected directors. Mrs. Daniel Williston and Peter Williston were the largest stockholders in the new enterprise, but neither held a controlling interest. The financial arrangements having been completed, the development of a general and manufacturing organization for the Williston Implement Company became necessary.

1. Be prepared to criticize or commend the attached organization charts. Make a list of the good and bad things about each.
2. Draw an organization chart that you recommend for the new Williston Implement Company. Be prepared to defend what you have done.

Case Study Two / Divisional Authority*

As explained in Chapter 11, large companies often utilize a divisional form of organization. That is, instead of having all marketing operations report to one executive and all production operations to another, the organization is split up

---

* This case was developed by the Westinghouse Electric Corporation and is reproduced here with the permission of that company.

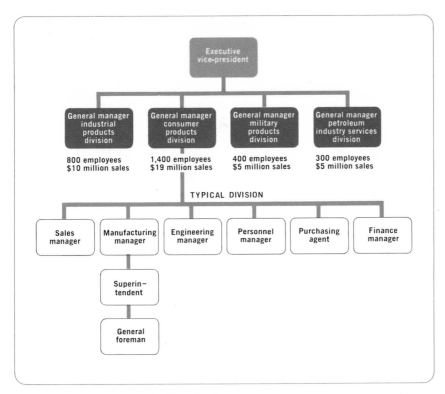

Colossal Behemoth organization chart.

into several semiautonomous divisions, each of which produces and sells a single product or a single family of products or handles all production and marketing in a given area.

The Colossal Behemoth Company is divisionalized on a product basis, as shown on the chart. All the division managers have been on the job for at least three years, and each is responsible for the profits of his division. Although the division organizations are not identical, each division has key executives who are responsible for sales, manufacturing, engineering, personnel, purchasing, and finance.

A full set of financial statements is prepared for each division annually, showing assets and profits. Detailed profit objectives are established each year, and division performance is measured by success in meeting them.

Business conditions have been fair, and all the divisions have been profitable, although not as profitable as the board of directors would like. In addition, each division has at least one major product line that has shown losses, and there is real pressure from the board to get these profit drains stopped.

You are the executive vice-president of the Colossal Behemoth Company, and all the division heads report to you. On the attached questionnaire, indicate the degree of authority you would grant to the division heads on each of the matters listed.

	Complete delegation		Veto option		Abdication	
	1	**2**	**3**	**4**	**5**	**6**
	Take action without any contact with you.	Take action; mention the action taken later if he happens to see you.	Advise you in advance of the action he intends to take; act unless you tell him not to.	Advise you in advance of the action he would like to take; delay action until you give him approval.	Give you an analysis of the alternative actions possible, with their merits and disadvantages, supporting his choice of the one he recommends for your approval.	Give you as many facts about the case as possible so you can identify alternatives and select the action
1. Hire a replacement for the Division Manager's secretary who is leaving.						
2. Authorize a temporary $50,000 increase in division raw material inventory in anticipation of a possible steel strike.						
3. Establish next month's manufacturing schedule for the division, at an increased level which will require the hiring of two additional people in the factory.						
4. Establish next month's manufacturing schedule, at a substantially higher level which will require the addition of 50 people in the factory.						
5. Pass final approval on the design of a new product, and authorize work to start on production tooling.						
6. Postpone the scheduled introduction of a new model by 45 days, and authorize a crash program estimated to cost $100,000 which will modify the design and permit incorporation of a recently developed design feature.						
7. Establish the list price of a major product line, which in the aggregate amounts to 30% of division volume.						
8. Increase the price of an existing product line by 4%, to attempt to recover cost increases that have taken place in material and labor; this will place the price above the competitive level.						
9. One product line has an extremely seasonal pattern, with all sales occurring in the summer. Authorize the production schedule for the year, which will create a $6 million shipping stock of this product at the time of its peak selling season.						
10. Make a change in the division inventory standards, which will reduce field shipping stocks but increase factory work-in-process inventory, maintaining the same total investment.						
11. Increase the investment in inventory on a different product by approximately $1 million, because the sales department feels that they can get more sales if they have greater product availability.						
12. Initiate a computer activity, estimated to cost $1 million for feasibility study and programming, and which will require a commitment for a computer that will ultimately cost $200,000 per year.						

	Complete delegation		Veto option		Abdication	
	1	2	3	4	5	6
	Take action without any contact with you.	Take action; mention the action taken later if he happens to see you.	Advise you in advance of the action he intends to take; act unless you tell him not to.	Advise you in advance of the action he would like to take; delay action until you give him approval.	Give you an analysis of the alternative actions possible, with their merits and disadvantages, supporting his choice of the one he recommends for your approval.	Give you as many facts about the case as possible so you can identify alternatives and select the action you want to be taken.
13. Introduce a new system into the factory, that is recognized to have a 20% chance of precipitating strong opposition possibly leading to a strike on the part of the union.						
14. Change advertising program for the division, reducing magazine advertising, increasing direct mail and trade show promotional activities.						
15. Authorize the manager of manufacturing to increase the methods and industrial engineering activity and reduce the size of the quality control department, maintaining the same total manufacturing expense.						
16. Authorize the marketing manager to increase the number of salesmen in the field, reduce the number of manufacturing engineers by a corresponding amount to maintain the same total cost.						
17. Select the replacement for the manufacturing superintendent who will retire soon.						
18. Take the superintendent off the job for poor performance; replace him with another man now serving as a general foreman.						
19. Select the replacement for the general foreman position now open.						
20. Increase the number of general foremen positions in the division from four to six. Select the individuals to fill the new positions.						
21. Authorize an 8% salary increase for the manufacturing superintendent, allowed for in the budget and within the rate range for the job.						
22. Authorize an 8% salary increase for the division sales manager, allowed for in the budget and within the rate range.						
23. Authorize the factory to work overtime two Saturdays next month to reduce the backlog of overdue orders.						
24. Increase the job classification and rate range for the engineering manager, to reflect the growth of his department and the increased responsibility of his position.						
25. Authorize a change in job classification for the six general foremen in positions, as a result of changes in their responsibility.						
26. Cancel two engineering development projects included in this year's program, and concentrate the $250,000 effort on a new development believed to have real commercial potential, identified as a result of research performed in the corporate research center.						

Selected Readings

Top Management Organization and Control, Paul E. Holden, Lounsbury S. Fish, and Hubert L. Smith, McGraw-Hill Book Company, New York, 1951. A detailed survey of the practices and procedures of outstanding large companies that is still useful and interesting.

Organization: The Framework of Management, E. F. L. Brech, Longmans, Green & Co., Ltd., London, 1965. This is a thorough treatment of the principles and practice of organization, with many illustrations and job descriptions drawn from British and European industry. An appendix outlines the history of thought on organization.

Organization, Ernest Dale, American Management Association, New York, 1967. Covers the theory and practice of organization, including the results of a survey of 100 large companies and 66 medium-sized companies. Contains sections on conducting a reorganization and on the organization of international operations.

14

THE

DYNAMICS

OF

ORGANIZATION

If you take a flat map
And move wooden blocks upon it strategically,
The thing looks well, the blocks behave as they should.
The science of war is moving live men like blocks. . . .
But it takes time to mold your men into blocks
And flat maps turn into country where creeks and gullies
Hamper your wooden squares.
Stephen Vincent Benét: John Brown's Body

14 In the mechanical phase of organization, the organizer considers only the work to be done; he takes no account of the possible peculiarities of the persons who are to do it. As Alvin Brown, a leading exponent of the classical theory and a man with very broad management experience, put it, "In principle, organization should come before the selection of personnel; organization, that is, should determine the need for personnel rather than personnel determine the manner of organization."[1]

This is incontrovertible. The best organizer in the world would be hard put to it if he started by hiring a group of people and then attempted to slot each one in the job he was best fitted for. The company might find itself with ten excellent financial men, ten industrial engineers, and six personnel managers, but no salesmen or sales manager.

Brown further observes, "In organizing, the principle of specialization is applied in two different ways. In the first place, it says that jobs should not overlap. . . . In the second place, it says that the various duties of a job should be as similar as possible, so as not to make exorbitant demand for talent in the man who will perform it."[2]

This, too, makes sense. To have two people duplicating each other's work is obviously wasteful. And while one might, perhaps, find a financial executive who was also a good sales manager or a personnel man with a talent for industrial engineering, this would be a purely fortuitous case. It is much easier to find a good sales manager, a good industrial engineer, or a good personnel man.

Like the classical theories, the mechanics of organization are purely rational. And although, as the later theorists have pointed out, an organization that is based on pure rationality ignores many facets of human nature, one must at least start by attempting to be as rational as possible. Otherwise, there will be complete confusion. Modifications and concessions can be made later to take account of the varied talents and proclivities of the human beings who fill the jobs. This is, in fact, what most companies do, are forced to do by the dynamics of organization, or the way in which the members of the organization influence the structure as they themselves are influenced by it—the fusion process described by Bakke.

The results of considering organization as a process of locating the points at which decisions are made, as proposed by Simon, would probably not be too different in general outline from those achieved by the more classical methods. As a practical matter, Simon's method is probably more useful in structuring individual departments and in planning line and staff relationships than it is in drawing the broad outlines.

Bakke's suggestion that "the basic ingredient in the concept of 'organization' is the arrangement of successive steps in the flow of productive work" would probably produce very little change in the overall company structure, and making decisions on the mechanics on that basis might be more difficult

---

[1] "Some Reflections on Organization: Truths, Half-truths and Delusions," *Personnel*, American Management Association, July, 1954, p. 33.
[2] *Ibid.*, p. 34.

than considering purpose and process or skills used. Bakke's method can be very useful, however, in considering the structure of the various departments and the amount of authority to be allocated to each position.

But even on paper it is impossible to produce a completely rational organization in which lines of authority are wholly clear. The dotted lines of functional authority that appear on organization charts are testimony to this. Moreover, the various functions are never so compartmentalized as they appear to be on the chart, and it is impossible to make them so. Because of the way one department impinges on another, we find such statements as the following in organization manuals:

> The activities of the Director of Contract Administration are subject to policy direction from the Vice-president of Finance [not his boss] with reference to the financial aspects of contract negotiations.
>
> The Director of Contract Administration maintains surveillance over plant facilities activities [not actually within his jurisdiction] relating to contracts.
>
> The Director will coordinate general customer specifications and statements of work and the terms of contracts with all members of management whose responsibilities may be affected.

THE INFORMAL ORGANIZATION

If it is difficult to divide work and responsibility and prevent overlapping on paper, it is twice as difficult to do so in fact because human beings never fit into neat little boxes. One production head, for example, may be a genius at developing new methods, and because of his obvious superiority in this activity, he may gain *de facto* jurisdiction over the methods department even though methods comes under engineering on the organization chart. Another production head may concentrate on face-to-face direction of his men and succeed in setting personnel policies for his department and in taking the leading role in union contract negotiation, which the organization manual assigns to the industrial relations department. A line boss may, because of pressure of work or simple laziness, shift much of his authority to a staff assistant or a staff department.

These deviations from the division of authority and responsibility shown on the formal chart produce the "informal organization." A chart of such an organization is shown in Figure 1.

To the man in the small box marked "organization planning," the situation depicted may seem to be entirely bad, but it is not *necessarily* so. It depends on what the company's problems are. The overlapping responsibilities might be unavoidable, and if they do not mean that different parts of the organization are working at cross-purposes, they could be unimportant. Even conflicts may serve a purpose by bringing issues out into the open and making more informed decisions possible.

Assuming that this is so—though it probably is not—should the company then attempt to bring the formal organization into line with the informal groupings? By no means.

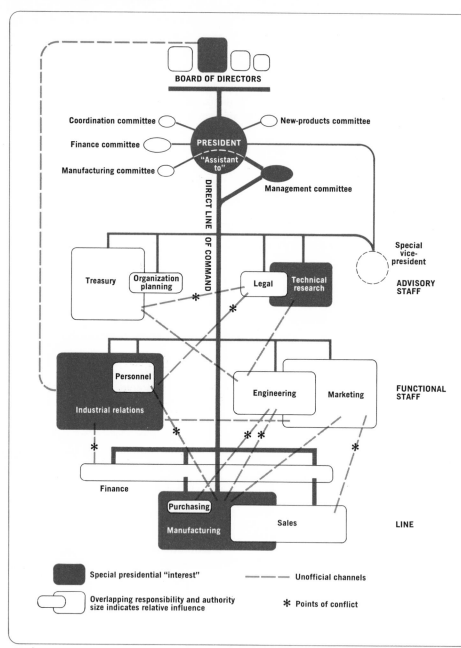

FIGURE 1 An informal organization. (From Perrin Stryker, *A Guide to Modern Management Methods*, McGraw-Hill Book Company, New York, 1954, p. 112.)

For example, let us assume that industrial relations has gained its present position because it has alleviated a bad labor situation that manufacturing had allowed to develop and that this is why the weight it carries in management councils (shown by the size of its box) is greater than that carried by manufacturing. To formalize this situation would be to make manufacturing subordinate to industrial relations. Then industrial relations would have authority as well as influence, and there is a great difference between the two. The manufacturing manager might find that he had to judge every action by its effect on industrial relations rather than by its effect on output, and the company might no longer produce enough to remain solvent. As it is, manufacturing can fight back if it feels that new industrial relations policies will hamper operations too much. If it loses some of its battles, it undoubtedly wins others because it, too, has direct access to the company president.

Moreover, the informal organization has no stability. Alliances are formed and broken; new conflicts arise within it; a change in the incumbent of a single executive job can change its character entirely. No company could hope to develop and reach clear-cut goals if it built its organization structure on the shifting sands of the informal organization.

If the chief executive should not revise the formal chart to make it conform to the informal one, should he then try to eliminate the informal structure entirely? It will be impossible for him to do so as long as human beings are human beings. He can, however, make gradual changes that will help to minimize its destructive aspects and maximize those that are constructive. If overlapping responsibilities are causing two departments partially to nullify each other's efforts, he can clarify responsibilities and authority by making a few changes in the job descriptions of the department heads. Or perhaps he can transfer some of the debated activities to a third department. Transfers of individuals from one job to another will sometimes alleviate a bad situation.

Actually, the formal organization of the company in Figure 1 is not too rational. Sales and marketing, really parts of the same function, are separate departments in conflict with each other. A more logical plan would be to place sales under marketing in the direct line of authority since both have a common objective. Also, the committees as presently constituted do not appear to be serving any useful purpose. The manufacturing committee has not been able to prevent conflicts between engineering and manufacturing; it might well be abolished and its functions transferred to the management committee. Another candidate for abolition is the coordination committee, which seems to have been singularly unsuccessful in producing coordination. Treasury and legal functions, now in conflict, could be combined under one head, who might be given the title of company secretary.

MAKING CHANGES

If a new president should be appointed for the company in Figure 1, he might be inclined to make drastic changes—to draw up an entirely new organization chart and new job descriptions that embodied a complete shake-up of job responsibilities and authority and present it to his executives with the fiat, "From now on, this is it."

Many presidents have used this earthquake approach. Some of them have been new presidents who have inherited cumbersome organizations that were obviously in need of major repairs; others have found that organizational defects with which they have jogged along for years have worsened and suddenly become intolerable. Still others have become entranced by organization theory, as expounded by some expert at a management meeting, and returned home to put their new ideas into effect as soon as possible.

Too sudden changes should be avoided if at all possible. Sweeping organization changes introduced overnight are likely to destroy organization efficiency. Old relationships are broken up, informal channels of communication become blocked, and executives become fearful and unable to concentrate on the work at hand because they are worrying about possible loss of status.

Thurman Arnold in his well-known book, *The Folklore of Capitalism*, has cited an excellent example of a case in which badly needed changes, made too suddenly, produced completely negative effects:

> Paramount Publix [a motion picture company] grew to be a colossus in the amusement industry by virtue of the most wasteful and extravagant habits imaginable. It was a combination of the personalities of Lorenzo the Magnificent and Jean Jacques Casanova in the motley crowd of business enterprises, many of which affected the dour attitudes of our Puritan fathers. Came the reorganization. A distinguished business man named Hertz was given power over the budget to effect economies. From a puritanical standpoint, this was an easy task. Waste was everywhere. Hertz cut down expenditures about twenty-five million dollars in one year. He was promptly forced to resign. Every economy that he instituted was entirely defensible. Yet the institution, instead of improving, appeared to be going to pieces under the strain. The persons whom he discharged were, no doubt, parasites. Yet fear and anxiety spread to the most useful members of the organization. Mr. Swaine, the hard-boiled and able attorney for the bankers, had difficulty in explaining before the Securities and Exchange Commission why the activities of Hertz were stopped. . . . Yet what he said seemed inescapably true. It was as if a father was trying to reform a drunken and profligate son by putting him in a straitjacket. Dogs cannot be trained that way, neither can persons, neither can organizations. Changes in institutional habits are made only by gradual substitution of new habits. Failure to realize this factor of institutional personality brings the efforts of most reformers to futility.[3]

This was a practical demonstration of one of the major points stressed by the newer organization theorists: The organizer who starts adjusting the structure in one respect is likely to find that his changes bring others in their train, and sometimes these secondary changes may work against the very effect he is trying to bring about.

---

[3] Yale University Press, New Haven, Conn., paperbound ed., 1959, pp. 351–352.

Few, if any, companies can go along indefinitely without any changes in structure. Often quite far-reaching alterations are necessary because of company growth; because of changes in products, markets, or the economy; or because of the death or retirement of key people. The problem is to minimize the disturbing effects of the necessary changes.

More productive than the earthquake approach is the long-run plan in which needed changes are put into effect over a period of years. In this approach, the first step is to study the existing organization and determine its shortcomings. Here it should be borne in mind that transgression of one of the classical rules is not necessarily a shortcoming. Symptoms of poor organization are of a strictly practical nature: delay in decision making or frequent and serious errors in decisions, bottlenecks, inadequate communication, lack of clear-cut objectives, frequent and serious clashes between departments. The situation that prompted a far-reaching reorganization at Westinghouse in the 1930s is a good illustration. As *Fortune* described it:

> It was a stubborn company that Mr. [A. W.] Robertson [chairman of the board] had on his hands at the beginning of the depression. Bulky as a hippopotamus, with its directing brain handling everything from East Pittsburgh, the company could not always tell its manufacturing extremities in Mansfield, Ohio, and Chicopee Falls, Massachusetts, the correct thing to do. Nor could it be counted on properly to interpret the stimuli it received from these extremities. Westinghouse engineers would perfect something—say, the grid glow tube, which stimulated the development of photoelectric cells and electric eyes—and the Westinghouse sales promoters would often miss the train to market with the product. The company was slow in styling; its goods were trustworthy but incorrigibly humdrum in appearance.
>
> These were symptoms, big and little, of a central administrative heaviness.[4]

Once having determined the ways in which the organization structure itself is hampering effectiveness, the organizer can proceed to structure the company as he would if he were able to start from scratch without any consideration of personalities. The resulting organization will be the "ideal"—not necessarily the perfect organization, but the best possible for his company in its current circumstances. Then he should avoid the earthquake approach by working toward the ideal gradually.

Each time an executive dies, retires, or resigns, the company can move a step nearer the ideal organization. To illustrate: If the sales manager of the company whose informal organization is shown in Figure 1 leaves the company, it will be very easy to combine sales and marketing. A new man will accept the situation as a matter of course since he will be told when he takes the job that sales is part of the general marketing responsibility.

No company can ever reach the ideal, of course. In fact, the ideal itself will

---

4 February, 1938, pp. 55, 59.

not remain static; it must constantly be revised to take care of new circumstances. But if this type of continuing attention is devoted to organization
problems, the necessary changes can be made so gradually that they cause a
minimum of disruption.

Sometimes, of course, it is not possible to postpone fairly sweeping changes
for a period of years; it may become clear that the company cannot survive
unless it takes action sooner. Even in that case, it is better not to announce
the changes suddenly as a *fait accompli*, but rather to hold meetings at which
executives can express their opinions and perhaps contribute to the new plan.
It must be remembered that the view from the top or that of the organization
specialist, who is to a certain extent outside looking in, may not encompass
all the pertinent facts. Seldom, if ever, is it necessary to make drastic changes
overnight; a few weeks' or months' delay is not likely to be fatal.

SOME UNRESOLVED PROBLEMS

As was noted in Chapter 13, not all the problems of the mechanics of organization have been solved. The staff-line structure is fraught with potential (and
often actual) difficulty; jobs do not always fit into neat little boxes with clear-
cut responsibility and authority; and it is difficult to provide for coordination
without entailing a diffusion of responsibility and accountability.

These problems are minor, however, compared to the unresolved problems
growing out of the dynamics of organization. If jobs cannot be compartmentalized, people are even less amenable. Seldom does a man exactly fit into his
organization box. If it is too small for him, he is actually prevented from contributing to the full extent of his powers and will tend to lose interest even in
the contribution he is permitted to make. On the other hand, if he is rattling
around in a box too large for him, he will tend to devote most of his time to
covering up his inadequacies and neglect the parts of his job he really might
handle capably. Even more common may be the man who is at once too small
and too large for his box. He is capable of doing more than he is permitted
to do in some areas, but not quite as much as he is expected to do in others.
His is perhaps the most frustrating position of all.

The whole problem of making company goals and individual goals coincide
is also largely unresolved—although identity is achieved by some persons,
and even by practically all persons in some companies. But no one knows of
any precise formula for ensuring this, or for solving a related and perhaps
identical problem: How can people be inspired to put forth the very best efforts
of which they are capable?

The latter problem is complicated by the fact that the space at the top of
an organization is narrow. Structures tend to take the form of a pyramid, or
at least a pyramid with the top sliced off. This means that many people who
make steady progress during their early careers eventually reach a point where
they can expect no further advancement. For some, realization that they have

gone as far as they will ever go comes slowly; for others, it comes in the form of a sudden shock when they are passed over for a promotion they expected to get and realize that another opportunity is not likely to arise.

Placed in such a position, a man may shift his entire objective. Instead of trying to do the best possible job, he may hope only to do well enough to avoid unfavorable attention so that he can continue to collect his salary and later his pension. How can a company motivate this man to continue his interest? No satisfactory answer has yet been found, though various attempts have been made, such as the creation of high-sounding titles that mean nothing.

And how, in a situation where people necessarily compete for advancement, can they be motivated to pull together wholeheartedly and submerge individual interest in the common interest? Again there is no formula. It is true that companies often consider a man's record for teamwork in weighing his "promotability," but there are many ways of appearing to be a team worker while actually pursuing individual goals.

Finally, there is the question of how companies can use the nonconformist. If businesses never changed, business could well get along without him. But they do change, which means that innovators are needed; and innovators are likely, almost by definition, to be nonconformists, for the man who does not question accepted ways of doing things will not try to discover better ways.

Yet organization is itself a device for enforcing a certain amount of conformity through predetermined objectives, a high degree of specialization, and prescribed areas of action. Top management *must* seek reliability in those down the line; that is, it must be sure when it determines the overall objectives and the steps to be taken in reaching them that the planned course of action will be followed. Without a degree of such assurance, the organization could not function at all.

No form of organization that will resolve this conflict between the twin needs for innovation and reliability has yet been devised.

However, close coordination of research with other functions is necessary only after its results have been achieved, when the new products or processes are ready for production and marketing. Thus it is not too difficult to allow researchers a great amount of freedom in conducting the research itself.

Where exact coordination is required, much less room for nonconformity seems to exist in a large organization. A partial answer to the problem may be achieved by decentralization, but decentralizing is still far from a complete solution.

SUMMARY

In the mechanical phase of organization, the company structure is set up without reference to the individuals within the organization; only the work itself is considered. But in the course of the fusion process described by

Bakke, the people who occupy the boxes in the organization chart tend to modify the nature of their jobs. These changes in the structure that occur without formal action constitute the dynamics of organization.

Through the dynamics, some people relinquish some of the authority to which their positions entitle them or have it wrested from them. Others gain in stature and influence.

The dynamics of organization operate to create an "informal organization," which may be either advantageous or disadvantageous to the company. Where the informal organization works to slow progress toward company goals, it is often a symptom of faults in the formal structure, and in that case the latter should be modified.

Review Questions

1. What are some of the ways in which the dynamics of organization produce deviations from the formal structure in actual day-to-day operation of the company?
2. Can you suggest a few cases in which the informal organization might produce beneficial results?
3. Can you suggest some reasons why there are conflicts between manufacturing and engineering in the company whose informal organization chart is shown in Figure 1?
4. Why is a sudden reorganization likely to be disruptive to a company?

Case Study / Ajax Insurance Company—Dallas Office Case

The Ajax Insurance Company is a medium-sized firm writing three lines: ordinary life, accident and health, and group. John Ralston, president of the company, tries to keep close tabs on as much of the company's activity as he can from the home office in Richmond, Virginia. However, the company has grown rapidly during the six years of his presidency, and Ralston has somewhat reluctantly allowed the three operating vice-presidents (one for each line) to take on larger burdens of responsibility, reporting to him only on matters of defined import.

Meanwhile Ralston, while not neglecting the accident and health and group lines, continues to devote a major portion of his energies to the ordinary life field, which was his first love. He started with the Ajax as a life agent in 1932 and moved steadily up from there. He was made vice-president in charge of life in 1958 and became president in 1964.

The Ajax Company has branch offices in fifteen major cities, including Dallas, Texas. Generally, the offices are jointly managed by three branch man-

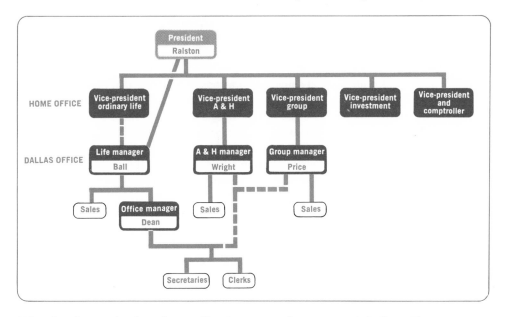

Abbreviated organization chart—Ajax Insurance Company and Dallas office.

agers (one for each line); each has his own staff of salaried field representatives and clerical employees. The field representatives recruit and train
agents and maintain relations with brokers. The branch managers, in turn,
report directly to their respective vice-presidents in Richmond. In the Dallas
office, however, a slightly different organization exists. Although he has known
of this divergence for years, Ralston has only recently become aware of the
problems it presents. (A chart of the Dallas organization is presented here,
but Ajax itself has never drawn one.)

The Dallas office was established in 1951 largely through the efforts of
Ralston and Edward Ball, a long-time personal acquaintance of Ralston and
formerly a very successful agent in Dallas for another company. As one of the
most active and widely respected agents in the Southwest, Ball was able to
bring a number of big cases to Ajax after it opened the Dallas territory. Reflecting on this, Ralston sometimes feels that it is Ball's aggressive personal
dynamism and his contacts, rather than the Ajax Company itself, that have
kept the sales volume increasing in Dallas.

It is primarily because of Ball's abilities that the Dallas office has its unique
organizational setup. In effect, Ball is director; under him he has a staff of
sales supervisors and an office manager, Tom Dean (who is in immediate
charge of accounting, field underwriting, expense control and personnel). The
other two managers, Leonard Wright (accident and health) and Cecil Price
(group), have their own clerical people among Ball's staff, and in addition both
have their own salaried sales supervisors and field representatives.

Ball tends to supervise the office staff personally and generally handles the hiring and firing through Dean. In some instances, Ball will consult Wright and Price, but these two managers both feel that they have less to say about the operation of the office than they would like. They feel that secretaries and sometimes other clerical employees are chosen for them; that they do not know or have anything to say about what these subordinates are paid; and that there are occasionally visible signs of split allegiance among these people.

Wright and Price have discussed the problem openly with each other and in a general way with their home office vice-presidents, but nothing has been done. They know vaguely of Ralston's leaning toward the ordinary life side of the Ajax Company, but their own pursuits have been heretofore unaffected by this. They are also aware of the close friendship between Ralston and Ball and Ball's importance in giving the Dallas branch its initial impetus.

The organizational situation came to a head recently when Wright returned to Dallas after a four-day trip to see agents and brokers out in the territory. He found that Dean had released one of his clerks as part of a program insti- tuted by Ball to cut down the branch office overhead. Dean explained to him that the dismissal was a "financial necessity" and that Ball had felt that this particular clerical job (consisting largely of keeping accident and health pro- duction records) was unnecessary to the operation of the office. When Wright confronted Ball, these reasons were reiterated.

Wright by now was openly irritated and insisted that the clerk was highly competent and vital in the accident and health operations in Dallas. He told Ball that the Ajax Company was, after all, writing three lines and that he saw no reason for his line to be slighted because of Ball's prominence in the South- west, Ralston's personal interests, or the relatively small percentage of acci- dent and health business in the Ajax Company's total operation. Lastly, Wright emphasized that his accident and health sales had been the fastest-growing line in the Dallas office for each of the past two years.

When Ball remained adamant on the issue of "financial necessity" and the "definitely expendable" clerk, Wright contacted the vice-president in charge of accident and health in Richmond. He, in turn, passed the issue along to Ralston.

1. What should Ralston do about this situation in Dallas? List a step-by-step procedure, with reasons.
2. What attention, if any, should be given to the company-wide organizational situation, apart from the immediate problem in Dallas?

Selected Readings

Organizational Behavior and Administration: Cases, Concepts and Research Findings, Paul R. Lawrence et al., Irwin-Dorsey, Homewood, Ill., 1961. Reports of research findings on work groups, supervisory behavior, and intergroup behavior; discussion of remedial action and organization change.
The Organization from Within, Cyril Sofer, Tavistock Publications, London,

1961. A study of organizational change and the human problems of a business enterprise, a hospital, and a technical college as observed by a consultant from a psychological point of view.

Exploration in Management, Wilfred Brown, John Wiley & Sons, Inc., New York, 1960. An analysis of the ideas and practices that turned a company into a cohesive enterprise, written by the chairman of the company.

Organizations in Action: Social Science Bases of Administrative Theory, James D. Thompson, McGraw-Hill Book Company, New York, 1967. Especially Chapter 9, which deals with the exercise of discretion on the part of individuals within the organization.

15

HOW

AN

ORGANIZATION

GROWS

*"I wish you wouldn't squeeze so," said the
Dormouse, who was sitting next to her.
"I can hardly breathe."*

*"I can't help it," said Alice very meekly:
"I'm growing."*
Lewis Carroll: Alice's Adventures in Wonderland

15 Seldom does a company start out on a large scale, plan its organization in the light of its goals, and then proceed to hire people to fit the boxes on a predetermined organization chart. Rather it rises from small beginnings, tacking on specialists here and there as they are needed and modifying the structure, in part or in whole, every once in a while to bring the functions into more logical alignment.

Perhaps the simplest type of business organization is what is known to sales departments as the "Momma and Poppa" store, the small retail outlet in which the owner and his wife spell each other behind the counter and the children provide extra help before and after school. The objectives of such an enterprise are merely to buy merchandise from manufacturers, wholesalers, or jobbers and sell it at a profit, and to build up a group of satisfied customers so that the profit making can continue.

Assuming that the store is already in business, what functions must be performed on a continuing basis? Primarily there are only two: buying and selling. But there is need also for a number of auxiliary functions: Bills must be sent to customers, and the store's own bills must be paid. Records must be kept, taxes calculated and paid. The store and merchandise must be kept clean, purchases unpacked. Advertisements must be prepared and placed in the local newspaper or sent through the mail. Orders must be packed and delivered to the customers, inventory checked. And someone must decide how much inventory will be carried, what new items will be stocked, what old slow-selling lines will be discontinued. Decisions must be made on prices also, and it will probably be necessary to obtain bank loans for expansion, when this is warranted, or for tiding the business over slack seasons.

Now let us say the store is a paint store in which some of the merchandise is processed on the premises. Then another important function is added.

In the terms used to describe the functions in a larger business, these various jobs stack up like this:

General management

Determining the lines to stock and the amount of merchandise to be kept on hand (inventory minima and maxima), deciding what part of the merchandise will be made on the premises and what part purchased from outside, setting prices.

Specialized functions

Marketing. Selling, advertising, window and other special displays, arrangements of merchandise within the store.

Finance and accounting. Arranging for banking facilities, keeping records, paying bills and taxes, billing customers, taking inventory.

Production. Preparing the paint and putting it in cans.

Maintenance. Keeping the store clean and in order, making minor repairs or arranging to have them made.

Purchasing. Seeing salesmen, obtaining comparative prices, ordering merchandise.

Receiving and shipping. Unpacking shipments of merchandise, packing up customers' orders and delivering them.

The specialized functions are so called because they require specialized knowledge only. General management decisions, on the other hand, must be made on the basis of overall knowledge of all the functions, acquired either by first-hand study or experience or through the counsel of the specialists. This will be clear if we suppose that each of these functions is handled by a different person. In that case:

The purchasing agent decides mainly *where* to buy. *What* to buy is a general management decision since it involves the whole conception of the store's function. Does it plan to cater to do-it-yourself painters only, or does it hope to sell professional painting contractors as well? Will it feature low prices or high quality? How large a line of accessories (brushes, rollers, spray guns) does it plan to sell? Thus the purchasing agent may need largely a knowledge of sources. The question he must decide is: What manufacturer or wholesaler can supply the merchandise that general management tells him is needed at the lowest price and in the shortest time?

The marketing man need know only how to induce customers to buy. He may, however, advise general management what the customers are most likely to buy and at what price.

The production man is not required to know what will sell or in what quantities, merely how to produce paint consistently of the quality needed and in the quantity required.

The financial man specializes in bookkeeping (or accounting), and since setting a value on the inventory is primarily an accounting problem, it will probably be part of his job to keep records on it and to devise the record-keeping systems.

The maintenance man will need to be something of a mechanic, even in a small store. If production utilizes machinery, he will take care of that also.

· Receiving and shipping in the Momma and Poppa store require mainly physical effort. But if the organization is a little larger and begins shipping outside the neighborhood, it will require the traffic function: decisions on shipping methods (train or truck) and shipping schedules.

The decisions the general manager must make are of an entirely different character, and if each of them is examined in turn, we can easily see how broad a knowledge they require. To determine what lines to stock he needs to know what can be made economically, what is available from manufacturers and wholesalers and at what prices, and what can be shipped economically; and he must balance these considerations against customers' needs and desires. To set his prices intelligently, he must take into account the effect of prices on sales. Higher prices may mean fewer customers, but they will produce a larger unit profit. Determining where the optimum point lies is a general management decision since it will be based on data from two different functions: marketing and accounting.

Determining how much inventory to stock is also a decision that cuts across departmental lines. A large inventory may enable the store to supply all the customers' needs and so increase sales. But will the increase in volume be large enough to pay the cost of carrying the extra stock and produce extra profit as well? Since purchased goods or materials must often be paid for before they can be sold, the larger the inventory, the more of the owner's money is tied up in it. He may even find that he has to borrow money and pay interest on it in order to pay the suppliers. Or the owner may have to take the money out of the bank where it could be earning interest. And even if the money is ready to hand in a checking account that is earning no interest, the general manager must consider whether it could be more profitably spent in other ways. Would devoting the same amount of money to advertising, for example, produce more sales than carrying a larger inventory?

In the Momma and Poppa store the question of who can best do each job will be answered on the basis of sheer necessity and individual talents and preferences. A strict division of functions would, for example, give the general management functions, production, finance, and purchasing to the husband; marketing to the wife; maintenance and shipping and receiving to their high-school-age children.

In practice, it may be advisable for the husband to handle the advertising and the wife to take care of window displays, perhaps with the help of the children; for the husband to purchase some of the items of merchandise and the wife others; and for the whole family to pitch in and help with the selling when the store is crowded. It would be foolish for the husband to stand idle while customers waited for service if he had already prepared enough paint to last for a few days, or for either the husband or the wife to allow dirt to accumulate merely because the maintenance force (the children) was at home studying for school examinations. And both husband and wife may take a hand in general management.

STAGES OF GROWTH

If the business grows, however, more help will be needed, and the greater the growth, the more tendency to specialization there will be.

Suppose the store gains a reputation for providing special types of paints that are prepared on the premises, and these products sell to the extent that the preparation becomes a full-time job for two or three people. In that case, those hired will be chosen on the basis of their ability to prepare paints and will have nothing to do with the other functions.

Then a full-time bookkeeper may be added, and perhaps a typist to help take care of the billing, and the organization will have the nucleus of an office force. The children may be relieved of their duties because they are attending college, and a full-time delivery man and a handyman may be hired. With the growth, some extra sales people may be needed.

At this point, too, the husband and wife may find it necessary to divide supervision of the specialized functions between them since the volume of work in each will have grown beyond the point where it can be handled on a catch-as-catch-can basis. Now a plan of organization that can be charted can be discerned, even though the owners probably will not attempt to put it down on paper at this stage of the growth. The chart would look something like that in Figure 1.

Then let us say new stores are opened, and the production operation grows to the point where it necessitates acquisition of a small factory, which supplies not only the stores owned by the proprietor but other outlets as well. Now income is sufficient to support other specialists and to enable the wife to stop working and the husband to devote all his time to general management duties, including planning for further expansion. He will acquire an accountant to take charge of finances, a sales manager to supervise sales to outlets he does not own, a manager for each of his own stores, and a general store manager to supervise them. He will acquire an advertising agency and perhaps an advertising manager to work with it on his advertising needs. Then the plan of organization will look something like the chart shown in Figure 2.

What becomes of purchasing, receiving and shipping, and maintenance? Purchasing may be split up between the factory manager, who will purchase the materials needed for production, and the manager of store operations, who will purchase merchandise from outside suppliers. Or the purchasing of both may be done by a specialist who reports to the proprietor himself.

Receiving and shipping will be one of the departments in the factory. Individual store managers will have their own receiving and shipping forces, though the manager of store operations may arrange a unified system of trucking to make deliveries for all the stores.

Maintenance of the factory building and equipment will come under the plant manager, who perhaps will have a maintenance manager to supervise a force of skilled mechanics. Store maintenance will be under the direction of the individual store managers.

Long before this point, the business will have found it advantageous to

FIGURE 1

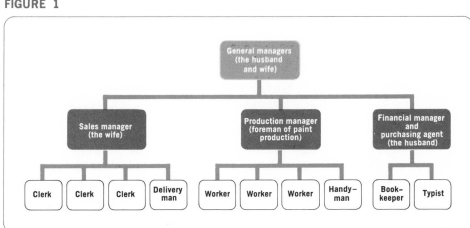

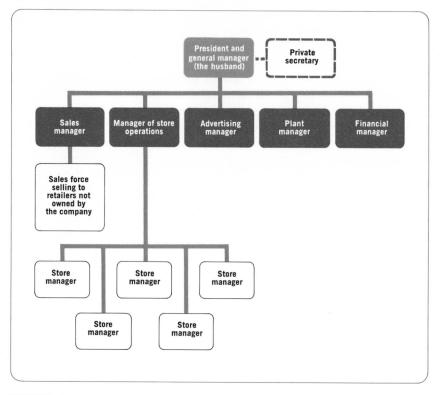

FIGURE 2

incorporate, and it may even have undertaken the sale of stock to finance expansion. In any case, handling banking relations and planning for new financing may have made it necessary to have a full-time treasurer. If the original accountant is thoroughly conversant with the treasury functions and the money market, he may assume the title and continue to supervise accounting as well, though he will delegate more of the actual duties. It is more likely that a treasurer will be hired and will report directly to the president on the same level as the chief accountant, who will probably be given the title of controller.

This is, of course, a hypothetical case. It may now be pertinent to examine some of the charts of actual paint companies at various stages of growth.

ACTUAL CASES

Figure 3 shows the top organization of a comparatively small company whose business is quite similar to the hypothetical operation described above, in that it has a group of stores of its own and a factory which sells both to these stores and to other outlets. Duties of the top-echelon executives whose positions are shown on the chart are as follows:

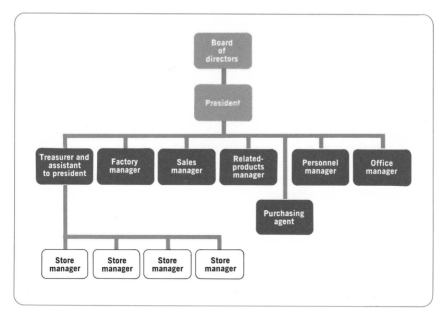

FIGURE 3

The *treasurer* handles the usual treasury functions (relationships with banks, stock issues, and so on) and, in his capacity as assistant to the president, helps with the overall management of the company. He is also in charge of the company-owned stores and of credit for state customers.

The *factory manager* is in charge of the plant that produces the paint.

The *sales manager* is in charge of paint sales only; sales of related items (brushes, rollers, and so on) are under the direction of the *manager of related products,* who is also in charge of factory shipping schedules.

The *office manager* is also the controller and is in charge of credit to accounts within the city.

The *purchasing agent* handles buying of raw materials, equipment for the factory, and the related items that the company sells but does not manufacture.

The *personnel manager* is in charge of preliminary screening of both office and factory personnel and advises the president on personnel policies.

Factory sales are $3 million annually, and total sales are around $4.5 million since the company manufactures only the paints and purchases the accessories it sells from outside. The company's own stores are set up as separate corporations in which the parent company owns all the stock. The wholly owned store corporations take 50 per cent of the factory's output. Products the company manufactures account for 68 per cent of total sales; the items it buys and wholesales for 32 per cent.

The chart and the division of duties here are not calculated to delight the heart of a doctrinaire organization theorist of the classical school. He would probably consider it poor practice to have credit management divided between the office manager and the treasurer, and to have the latter handle store operations—which are primarily selling—and to keep them separate from the other sales. He might also want to put the factory shipping schedules under the factory manager.

However, in view of the company's modest size and the nature of its operations, the structure may be the most economical and effective one possible.

First, there are only eight top executives, including the president, which means that they can easily coordinate their efforts by informal consultation. It would not make any sense to hire, say, a high-priced marketing manager to coordinate the different types of sales effort if equal coordination can be achieved by daily conversation.

Second, the company-owned retail stores are separate corporations; hence the performance of the individual store managers can easily be judged by their profit records. Thus it is quite logical to place them under the treasurer.

The division of the credit function is logical also. A large proportion of the

FIGURE 4

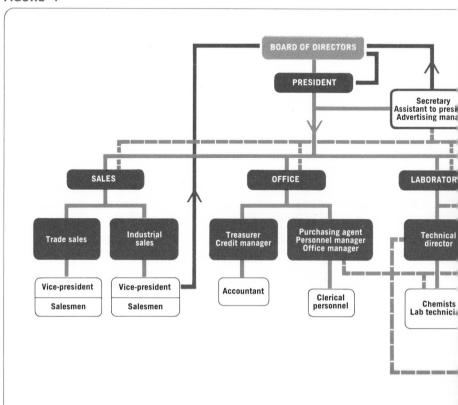

customers, and all the smaller ones, are within the city. Checking on their credit is a routine duty that the office manager can easily handle, either personally or through one of his subordinates. The treasurer and assistant to the president, on the other hand, could not spare time for these routine checks. In contrast, the state customers are the larger ones, and a credit loss in their case could well be a large one and properly the concern of the treasurer.

Similarly, since the manager of related items needs complete familiarity with shipping requirements to handle his regular job, it is economical to have him in charge of shipments from the factory as well and avoid the expense of a special factory traffic manager.

A somewhat larger paint company, which has no retail outlets of its own, divides the main functions as in Figure 4. The responsibilities of the executives are as follows:

Board of directors. Seven members, including three active employees, three outside stockholders, and one retired officer. All but one of the active employees are stockholders.

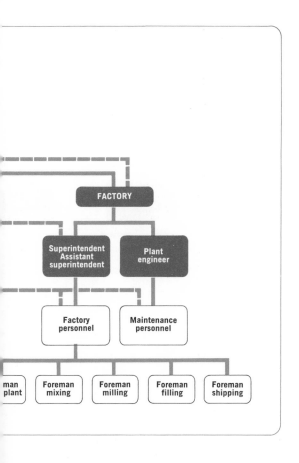

President. Actively and directly supervises all phases of company activity.

Secretary, assistant to president and advertising manager. Assists president in all duties. Actively supervises all phases of company activity, acting for president. Supervises and directs merchandising, advertising, and sales promotion. Secretary of corporation and director.

Vice-president, trade sales. Directly supervises all dealer sales and relations. Hires, trains, supervises, and assists trade salesmen. Spends at least 50 per cent of his time in the field working with salesmen.

Vice-president, industrial sales. A director of the company. Works actively as industrial salesman, but does not supervise other industrial salesmen.

Treasurer. Direct responsibility for all company finances, credits, and collections. Supervises accountant in keeping of company books.

Purchasing agent, personnel manager and office manager. Title self-explanatory. Directly supervises all office clerical personnel. Responsible for hiring all factory and clerical personnel.

Technical director. Directly supervises laboratory functions and personnel.

FIGURE 5

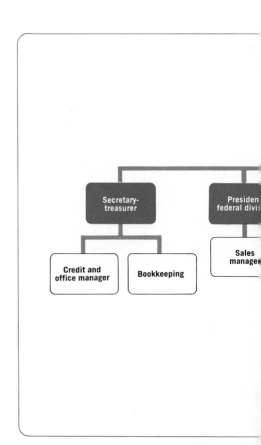

Responsible for quality control in plant. Directly supervises resin plant functions.

Superintendent. Directly supervises all plant productive functions. Handles plant personnel in conjunction with personnel manager. Responsible for production planning, as well as all manufacturing and shipping functions.

Plant engineer. Directly supervises all new construction, maintenance, and repair. Handles maintenance personnel in conjunction with personnel manager.

A chart for a still larger company (sales $9 to $12 million) is shown in Figure 5.

Not all paint manufacturing companies by any means start as Momma and Poppa stores, and certainly all manufacturing companies do not. Yet there are some that do. A large candy manufacturer (since merged with others) began as a small retailer selling products cooked up by Momma in a kitchen at the rear. And Smith, Kline & French, now a large pharmaceuticals manufacturer, started as a one-man corner drugstore.

Some manufacturing companies are established by inventors, like the

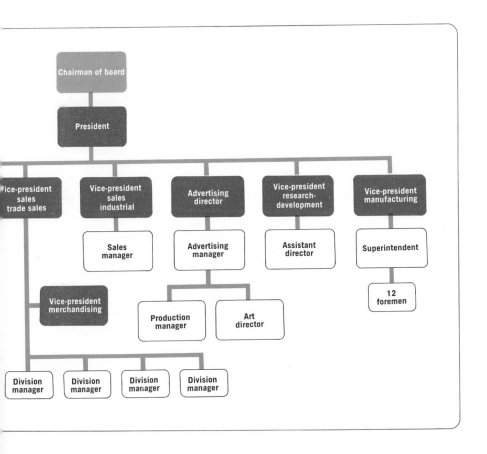

Edison Electric Company, which grew out of Thomas A. Edison's laboratories after he developed the electric light. After merger with other companies, this company became General Electric. In other cases, a man who has learned the various phases of a business by working for someone else may decide that there is room for one more company in the field and go ahead on his own.

In still other cases, an engineer, who may or may not be the inventor of a new product, and a salesman team up to start a new company. This was the way the Yarnall-Waring Company of Philadelphia, which now has a sales volume of around $12 million, began more than fifty years ago.

Two friends—one an engineering assistant who was helping Henry Laurence Gantt install the Taylor system in a machinery manufacturing plant and the other a salesman for a pen manufacturer—agreed to start their own business as soon as they could and to hold onto their jobs in order to finance it. They had no particular products in mind, although, of course, they intended to enter some field where their experience would be of value.

Their first step was to advertise in trade papers for "articles of merit" whose inventors were looking for backers. A large number of offers came in— a great many, probably, at no value at all—but one was from a young draftsman who had invented a line of pipe-joint clamps and who had some other related specialties in mind.

At first, the partners had the product produced by other companies and sold it through direct-mail advertising and advertising in trade papers. Their office was in the engineer's home, and they handled the distribution and bookkeeping at night. Eventually, they quit their jobs to devote full time to the business and rented space in an office building. Later the company acquired shop facilities and added many new products. Today its products are sold in practically every country in the world.

In some cases, too, companies are organized on a moderately large scale at the start, either because the organizers are able to raise enough capital to build a plant and hire a full-scale marketing force or because the type of industry requires it. Chrysler Corporation started as a large organization in the 1920s.

FURTHER STAGES OF GROWTH

The hypothetical paint company has already achieved a measure of vertical integration since it has its own retail outlets. Later it may decide to seek "backward integration" (to suppliers) by starting plants to manufacture painting accessories as well as paints. Perhaps it may even begin producing its own raw materials.

The motive for and the method of vertical integration have been well described by the president of a large steel company:

> We are producers of coals; we have got modern collieries, thoroughly equipped. . . . Mr. Whitwell is in charge of the next stage in the ladder,

namely pig-iron . . . leading on to steel works which we hope to acquire and for which we are at present in very close negotiation. Then we pass on to our shipbuilding yard, where the steel will be readily absorbed, and . . . at the present moment we are suffering in our output chiefly on account of the lack of raw material. It is very essential therefore that we should secure our own steel works with the least possible delay. . . . From the shipbuilding yard we pass on to ship-owning, and in carrying on and supporting our ship-owning we are building up a very large coal-exporting business and a timber-importing business. Mr. Whitwell, at his iron works, requires our ships to bring back the iron-ore to keep his blast-furnaces going. We pass on to marine insurance, and in this connection we are closely connected with Lloyd's. There is not a string that we are neglecting in this great aspiration of ours that we should be self-contained, and be able to carry on the business in such a way that in cycles of depression and prosperity it will give a constant regular dividend to the shareholders and secure their principal.[1]

Other companies seek a similar safety, not by integrating all operations from the raw material production to the sales to the ultimate consumer, but by diversification through the production of entirely different products. William C. Durant, for example, bought Frigidaire for GM because he thought it would provide something for the car dealers to sell if the demand for automobiles should drop.

The diversification into many new lines increases the difficulty of coordination. And if the original Poppa who started the business and grew up with it dies or retires, the difficulty is increased since his successors are likely to lack his encyclopedic knowledge of it. At this point, the company may decide to decentralize.

Decentralization

Essentially, one or more of the following characteristics mark a program of decentralization in a large corporation:

1. *The administrative unit that usually covers the company as a whole as well as all its plants is broken down into smaller administrative units, often on either a geographical or a product basis.* Each is headed by a manager who may be compared to the head of a smaller enterprise. Usually he has fairly complete control over basic line functions; if he also has staff services, such as accounting, engineering, research, and personnel, the unit may be largely self-contained.
2. *Provision is made for utilization of a centralized staff of specialists to aid the decentralized operations.*
3. *A series of general staffs may be provided for the chief executive.*
4. *Centralized controls are designed to ensure that the chief executive can*

[1] Sir Dennis Robertson and S. R. Dennison, *The Control of Industry,* Cambridge University Press, London, 1960, pp. 27–28.

find out how well the delegated authority and responsibility are being exercised.

A common form of decentralization is through divisionalization on a product basis; that is, more or less autonomous divisions are set up to manufacture and sell single products or single lines of products. A division manager is very similar to the president of a smaller company, except that he is not responsible for obtaining the capital he uses; this is allotted to him by the parent company. Then he is judged on his profit and loss statement.

In one large company, for example, there is a paint division with sales of $76 million, headed by an operating vice-president. (This company did not start out as a paint company but diversified by adding paint to its other product lines, which are somewhat related to paint.) In this case, the decentralization has continued in the divisions themselves on a geographical basis. The line organization is broken up into regions, each headed by a regional director who supervises trade sales, industrial sales, and the manufacturing and technical departments.

When companies become divisionalized, it is often necessary to have large central staff groups to assist the divisions with their planning and to coordinate their activities. Another method of coordination where there is a large number of divisions is to appoint group vice-presidents, each in charge of a group of divisions. The group vice-presidents rather than the heads of the operating divisions report directly to the president, and in that way the president's span of control is kept down.

No final form

Neither diversification nor divisionalization is necessarily permanent, however. Companies that went in heavily for diversification in the late 1940s and early 1950s often added unrelated products and operations and found that they could not make them profitable. When that happens, a company is likely to sell off some of its product divisions.

Again, many companies that decentralize with great fanfare quietly recentralize again after a few years because of difficulty in controlling the decentralized operations and because, in many cases, decentralization increases administrative expenses—more staff people must be added to provide services for the divisions.

SUMMARY

All the *functions* that exist in a large company are likely to exist in a small one whose field of operation is the same. The difference is that there is less specialization in the small company, and one person will handle several functions.

As the company grows, it begins to hire specialized executives and to departmentalize. In a very small company, the owner may be the general manager and the sales manager and, in fact, may do all the selling himself. When it is necessary to hire several additional salesmen, he will probably find that he can no longer devote enough time to supervising them, and he may have to hire a sales manager. As the company becomes larger, he will have to departmentalize other activities as well.

At later stages, he may have to divisionalize his organization in order to devote more time to overall planning, coordination, and control. Decentralization through divisionalization is not, however, necessarily permanent. Some companies have recentralized after trying the divisional form of organization.

Review Questions

1. What is the difference between departmentalization and divisionalization?
2. Would you change the organization of any of the companies whose charts are given in the text if you were the president? How? Why?
3. Why does specialization become more and more necessary as a company grows?
4. What is diversification?
5. Why do companies seek integration?

Case Study/The Growth Problem of the Du Pont Company

Shortly after the end of World War I, the Du Pont Company was confronted with a major organization problem arising from:

1. *Growth in size.* The number of men working for Du Pont rose from 5,300 in the fall of 1914 to more than 85,000 in the fall of 1918. The management group (at that time all who were getting $4,200 a year or more) rose from 94 to 259. Over the same period, gross capital increased from $83.5 million to more than $300 million.

2. *Diversification.* During the war the company had concentrated largely on munitions, for which demand naturally dropped at the end of hostilities. This drop had been foreseen, and the company's development department began planning for diversification while the war was still going on. (The company was debarred from further expansion in the peacetime powder and explosives field, its original area of activity, by a Supreme Court decision based on the Sherman Antitrust Act.) The postwar expansion, therefore, occurred in (a) industries into which the company had already entered, such as artificial leather (Fabricoid) and celluloid-type products (Pyroxlin); (b) industries whose products had been in short supply, such as dyes; (c) products that could utilize raw materials from existing plants (i.e., paints and var-

nishes), although this meant difficulties in that the products would have to be marketed to consumers, whereas Du Pont was more accustomed to industrial marketing.

3. *Need to provide opportunity for younger men.* The company felt keenly its need to provide expanding opportunities for its younger executives, including the 165 who had joined the company during the war.

4. *Increase in centralization.* The exigencies of war, the shortages of materials and men, and the close accounting needed on governmental work had led to an increase in centralization. More decisions were made at Wilmington headquarters. The organization itself was also quite centralized, with all production (see chart) under a single executive and all sales efforts under another.

Thus the top functional heads determined policies and plans for a number of different products. For example, the top marketing executive had to manage both sales of products like paint that required merchandising to the consumer and sales of products sold in bulk to industries.

Integrated forecasting, control, and appraisal became increasingly difficult. Communication up the line was slow, and a number of the new ventures

Du Pont production department, 1919–1921. (Adapted from Alfred D. Chandler, *Strategy and Structure,* M.I.T. Press, Cambridge, Mass., 1962, chap. 2.)

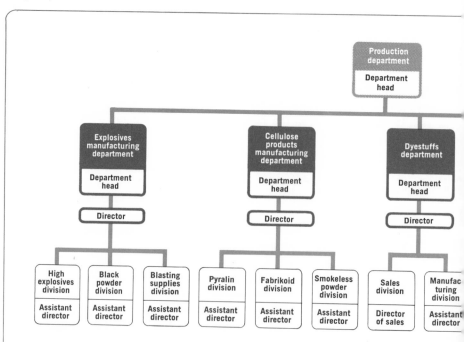

showed losses in 1919. For example, there was a loss of $489,000 on $4 million in paint sales.

At this point, the company president appointed a committee on organization structure.

1. If you were a member of that committee, what changes in organization would you recommend?
2. Draw a chart and analyze the advantages and possible disadvantages of the new structure as compared with the old one.

Selected Readings

Business Enterprise: Its Growth and Organisation, R. S. Edwards and H. Townsend, Macmillan & Co. Ltd., London, and St. Martin's Press, New York, 1958. A comprehensive study of the growth of companies, the factors conducive to it, and the impact on organization. The analysis is based on studies of many corporations, principally in England.

The Theory of the Growth of the Firm, Edith Tilton Penrose, Basil Blackwell, Oxford, 1960. A stimulating theoretical study of the various aspects of growth of an enterprise, with special reference to international changes, diversification, acquisition, and merger.

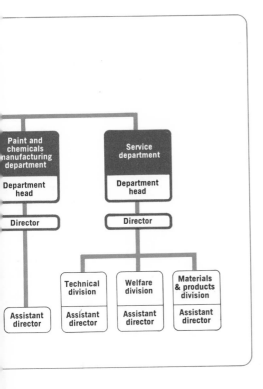

16
PLANNING
AND
FORECASTING

*The fact that a problem will certainly take a
long time to solve . . . is no justification for
postponing the study. . . . Our difficulties of
the moment must always be dealt with somehow, but our permanent difficulties are
difficulties of every moment.*
T. S. Eliot: *The Idea of a Christian Society*

*But since the affairs of men rest still incertain,
Let's reason with the worst that may befall.*
Shakespeare: *Julius Caesar*

16 A plan may be described as a statement of objectives to be attained in the future and an outline of the steps necessary to reach them. And since future possibilities depend on future circumstances, planning is inextricably bound up with forecasting.

Some planning goes on in every company, even though the plans may consist of little more than a few ideas in the chief executive's head based on an informal forecast derived from past experience, known facts, common sense, and a few hunches. Planning of that type needs no explanation; everyone does it in his daily life. This chapter will deal, rather, with formal planning in which definite techniques and procedures are used and written plans are produced.

One may distinguish two broad categories of formal planning: strategic or corporate planning and functional planning. In strategic planning, the managers determine the general objectives of the business and how they can best be reached in the light of the resources currently available and likely to be available in the future. Functional planning, on the other hand, is planning for greater efficiency, generally in some functional area. Strategic plans must be made by top management or at least approved by the top man or men. Functional plans, on the other hand, are usually made by department heads.

REASONS FOR CORPORATE PLANNING

Impetus to overall strategic planning was provided by World War II, when companies engaged in war work realized that the end of hostilities would mean that they would no longer be able to sell so large a proportion of their output to the government and would have to find new customers, perhaps new products as well, if they hoped to stay in business. This meant that they had to find the answers to such questions as: What will we sell after the war? Whom can we sell it to? What facilities will we need that we do not now have? How will we finance the new activities? How will we organize for them? In other words, complete plans covering all phases of the businesses were needed since it seemed very likely that their entire course would have to be shifted. Then the idea of "postwar planning," as it was called, spread to companies producing entirely for civilian markets because it was evident that peace and the end of wartime shortages would change their environment drastically.

But even without this push, it is likely that formal corporate planning would have developed fairly rapidly because of industry growth and technological and social trends.

In a large and diversified company—and many companies have become both larger and more diversified in the past two decades—there are many more factors to be taken into account in judging prospects and setting goals. A comparatively small company with a single product line has few problems in connection with the allocation of whatever funds it may have set aside for reinvestment in the business. Where product lines and activities are many, arriving at the proper emphasis on each means taking into consideration many different markets, profit margins, and other factors and determining the optimum among the vast number of possibilities.

Again, the increasing technical complexity of many products, on the one hand, the faster obsolescence on the other have given rise to the need for more careful planning. Before a company goes ahead with a product requiring expensive research and development, it must attempt to be sure that sales will be large enough and continue over a long enough period of time to make the investment worthwhile.

This can be illustrated by Figure 1, which shows in simplified form the life-span of various military systems and the time or cost[1] of development. For instance, at the time of Trafalgar, Lord Nelson's flagship was 40 years old and still an excellent ship. It cost very much less to build than Admiral Halsey's World War II flagship, which became obsolete within a few years. The B-36 airplane was ten years in the development stage and in use for only three. The *Navajo* missile cost a half billion dollars and was obsolete before it became operational.

Automation has also increased the need for advance planning. Since the equipment is usually very expensive, a company must be sure it can sell enough of the greatly increased output to justify the investment. Fixed costs

[1] Time and cost may be equated because elapsed time may be shortened by putting more people on the job.

FIGURE 1 (From Melvin E. Salveson, "Planning Business Progress," *Management Science*, April, 1959, p. 226.)

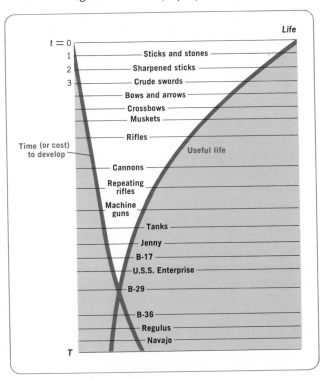

that continue whether production is in progress or not will be higher. In a labor-intensive plant (one which employs a great many people in relation to investment in equipment), the cost of depreciation is less important than the costs of labor and material, which may cease or drop sharply in a shutdown. The automated plant is a capital-intensive plant and has more continuing expenses.

But even wage costs, which are generally regarded as variable—that is, bound to drop when production does—are taking on something of the nature of fixed costs. Automated equipment requires many fewer production workers but many more maintenance workers, and some of the latter must be retained even if production is zero to keep the plant from deterioration. (The same would be true, of course, in a plant that was largely unmechanized, but not to anything like the same extent.) Moreover, in many industries it is no longer possible to cut the wage costs of direct production workers in proportion to the cut in production. Increasingly union contracts contain provisions for supplementary unemployment compensation, which compel companies to pay a percentage of wages for six months or more after a layoff.

SETTING OBJECTIVES

Finally, there is the matter of objectives. Plans must ensure that everything that is done contributes to progress toward them. In a small company, the objectives can be transmitted orally and progress toward them determined by simple reports, some oral and some in the form of figures. In any case, the objectives are likely to be quite generally understood. In a larger organization, there are so many different activities, a number of which contribute only indirectly to primary company objectives, that no control is possible unless the goals of each department and division are spelled out in detail and dovetailed.

Every organization is, of course, born with an objective since organization is a means to an end, not an end in itself. In a business organization this objective is to make the highest profit possible.

"The highest profit possible" is, however, a phrase susceptible to many definitions. It may mean the largest dollar amount, the highest profit on sales, or the greatest return on investment. The last is probably the most logical figure, though not all companies emphasize it.

How much a company may reasonably expect to earn on its capital will depend on the industry it happens to be in, on past performance, and on whether it considers profits before or after taxes. Somewhere between 15 and 20 per cent may be a reasonable pretax figure, since it allows a good return for the risks of entrepreneurship after payment of the corporate income tax. Some companies make more, in good years quite a bit more; other companies make less.

In any given year, or even for a longer period, short-run profit may be sacrificed for higher returns expected later. Many new companies, especially, must reconcile themselves to this prospect because they must make invest-ments before they even start operations, build up their sales volume slowly, and overcome many obstacles. This does not, however, alter the primary objective; they are still planning for the highest return on investment in the long run.

Planning for profit making may require planning for subsidiary goals as well, which may include such things as company growth, diversification into entirely new types of business, development of new products, penetration of new markets, getting a larger share of the market that already exists for the prod-ucts, or integration, that is, self-sufficiency. (A fully integrated steel company, for example, owns the mines that produce its raw materials as well as the steel-making capacity.)

Companies may also have social objectives: to pay good wages, to make their plants and offices good places to work in, to provide useful products, and to ensure that their operations do not detract from the appearance of the communities in which they are located or from the comfort of those who live nearby.

Social objectives may be forced on a company by the threat of legislation, the possibility of unionization or a strike, or because sales will be lost if the company acts in a way offensive to public opinion. Thus a company that erects unsightly buildings may find itself zoned out of many communities; one that discharges poisonous wastes into a stream may provoke legislation that will require stricter control of processes than would have been necessary had it acted voluntarily in the first place; and a widespread reputation as a bad employer or a bad neighbor may react on sales.

It should not be cynically concluded that all companies have social objec-tives merely because neglect of them may interfere with the money-making process. Companies are run by people, and many people have ethical stan-dards that they will not violate to make a few extra dollars; also, most people want the respect of their neighbors for its own sake.

In the long run, pursuit of the social objectives may contribute to profit-making capacity. But in specific instances, profit and social objectives may dictate opposite courses of action, and the decision to compromise on one or the other, or a little on each, is one of the planning tasks. So is the decision to adopt subsidiary objectives, such as diversification, in order to further the primary goal of profit making.

GOALS AND RESOURCES

Once objectives have been set, the planners must decide how far they can proceed toward them in view of the resources available, which include the money on hand, the money that sales will bring in, and the funds that may be obtained by borrowing or selling equities. The decision to borrow or sell new stock will, of course, be part of the planning process and will depend on the return expected on the investment.

Finally, the planners must decide on the allocation of the funds to the various company activities and the way in which these funds will be used to generate greater income in the form of sales revenue. The volume of sales is, in fact, the key factor in all corporate planning. One of the simplest ways of showing this is by a breakeven chart, as illustrated in Figure 2.

Certain expenses are fixed: They will go on whether the company sells a hundred units or a thousand, and they will not rise with increased sales. Others, such as the labor and material used in actually producing the product, rise in direct relation to sales. The cost line CD therefore starts at a point well above zero (A) and rises with sales. The point where line AB, representing unit sales, crosses the cost line is known as the breakeven point—the sales volume at which the company exactly meets its costs but makes no profit. It will be noted that thereafter the profit tends to grow faster with further increases in unit volume because the fixed expenses (or overhead) are spread over a larger number of units and account for a smaller and smaller percentage of unit costs.

The breakeven point in the chart in Figure 2 comes, let us say, when the company sells 10,000 units at $5 apiece. Obviously, if it were to raise the price to $10 it would need to sell only 5,000 units to break even. But a price rise is apt to reduce sales volume, and the company might never reach the breakeven point. That is, while line AB would rise more steeply, it might not rise so far, and the total profit might be less than at a lower price. Finding the optimum point is, of course, a part of planning.

FORECASTING

But how can a company forecast sales at any given price level when volume depends on the actions of consumers over whom it has no control? The answer is that it cannot, with certainty, but that it can often come close by judicious use of available forecasting techniques, which might be listed as

FIGURE 2   Breakeven chart.

(1) extrapolation, (2) economic forecasting, and (3) marketing research, though the three are not mutually exclusive.

Certainly it is necessary for some companies to plan on given sales volumes very far ahead because they depend on a constant inflow of new products which require time for research and development or because they cannot meet increased demand for their services without extensive construction. An electric utility company, for example, must plan on new power plants and new cables before the demand makes itself felt.

Firm plans are seldom made for more than a year in the future, and even then there is generally provision for review and adjustment every quarter, or more often. (A production man for a manufacturer of rubber footwear complains that the sales forecast is changed every time it rains.) Quite a few companies have five-year plans, but these are likely to be firmed up only year by year. Ten- and twenty-year plans, though they do exist, will be more tentative still.

Extrapolation

Extrapolation is the simplest form of forecasting since it is merely the projection of the trends of the past. Thus if a company sold x dollars' worth of product last year and sales have been rising around 10 per cent per year for the last few years (sometimes just in the last year alone), it forecasts sales of x plus 10 per cent dollars for the coming year.

Extrapolation has its place, especially in long-term forecasting, where changes are slow (e.g., population growth, life expectancy), although it should be used in conjunction with other techniques if possible. Thus the electric utility mentioned above may decide tentatively how much capacity it will need ten years from now by extrapolating population trends in its area and trends in the use of power per capita, which is rising steadily. It will not need to commit itself for any but fairly near-term construction and in the meantime it can be considering where it can best get the money for the long-term expansion.

But extrapolation takes no account of the business cycle, which may make a tremendous difference in short-term demand, changes in consumer tastes, or the actions of competitors.[2] Extrapolation or trend forecasting based on 1929, 1933, or 1937 would have been disastrous. Economic forecasting and marketing research are, therefore, necessary to supplement it in order to foresee more accurately the turning points, which are crucial.

Economic forecasting

It is not, of course, possible to predict business cycles with complete accuracy. But signs of coming change in the level of economic activity do appear, and it is often possible to make an informed estimate. Even the 1929 stock market crash and the long depression that followed it were foreshadowed in available

---

[2] The electric utility will be affected by a recession if plants that draw on it for power are shut down, but as a utility it has no competition except from other sources of power, and trends to an entirely new source are likely to be visible well in advance.

statistics months in advance. It was the unwillingness of most of the business community and the public at large to accept the idea that the economy could not keep on rising indefinitely that made the disaster appear so sudden and so unpredictable.

The single most important indicator of the current state of an economy is the gross national product (GNP). This is the money value of the output of goods and services produced in a year. In the United States it amounted to about $785 billion in 1967,[3] or almost triple what it was in 1941.

To estimate the future of GNP or general business conditions, three principal methods are being used:[4]

1. The lead and lag method
2. The overshoot method
3. Weighing opposing factors

Lead and lag   In the lead and lag method, the past behavior of various types of statistics is examined to ascertain whether they have consistently moved in advance of general business trends, have moved simultaneously with the trends, or have lagged behind them.

The most sophisticated analysis of lead and lag is the voluminous work by the National Bureau of Economic Research,[5] based on examination of the behavior of more than 400 statistical indicators over a long period of time. The Bureau found that the turns, up or down, in each of eight series of statistics tend to precede business cycle changes, turns in another eight to coincide with business cycle changes, and turns in five to lag behind the changes. The three sets of indicators, the length of time the leaders lead by, and the sources of the statistics are shown below.

[3] A description and analysis of the method used by the government in measuring gross national product is found in the *National Income Supplement* to the *Survey of Current Business*, Office of Business Economics, U.S. Department of Commerce, Washington, D.C., 1954, pp. 27–158.
[4] From the classification of A. H. Hansen, *Business Cycles and National Income*. W. W. Norton & Company, New York, 1951, pp. 579–583.
[5] G. H. Moore, *Statistical Indicators of Cyclical Revivals and Recessions*, Occasional Paper No. 31, 1950, pp. 2–3. Published monthly since October, 1961, by the Bureau of the Census, U.S. Department of Commerce, as *Business Cycle Developments*.

LEADERS

Series	Source	Average lead
Business failures, liabilities	Dun & Bradstreet	9 months
Industrial common stock prices	Dow-Jones & Co.	6 months
New orders for durable goods	U.S. Department of Commerce	6 months
Residential building contracts	F. W. Dodge Corporation	5 months
Commercial and industrial building contracts	F. W. Dodge Corporation	3½ months
Average hours worked per week	U.S. Bureau of Labor Statistics	3½ months
New incorporations	Dun & Bradstreet	3 months
Wholesale price index (28 basic commodities)	Bureau of Labor Statistics	3 months

COINCIDENT GROUP

Series	Source
Employment in nonagricultural establishments	Bureau of Labor Statistics
Unemployment	Department of Commerce
Business profits (quarterly)	Department of Commerce
Bank debits outside New York City	Federal Reserve Board
Freight car loadings	Association of American Railroads
Industrial production index	Federal Reserve Board
Gross national product (quarterly)	Department of Commerce
Wholesale price index, excluding farm products and foods	Bureau of Labor Statistics

LAGGING GROUP

Series	Source
Personal income	Department of Commerce
Sales by retail stores	Department of Commerce
Bank rates on business loans	Federal Reserve Board
Consumer installment debt	Federal Reserve Board
Manufacturers' inventories	Department of Commerce

The most important of these series from the viewpoint of the forecaster are, of course, those that lead, though even they are not absolutely to be counted on, and certainly the length of the leads cannot be taken as more than approximate. There are even economists who claim that the fact that these series have led the business cycle turns in the past does not mean much, if anything. Since we do not know "upon what other variables the relationships depend, and how they depend upon them, we have no criterion whatever by which to gauge their applicability to various other time periods."[6]

Yet some of these indices have been right 80 per cent of the time, and it is fairly easy to see why in some cases. For example, building contracts precede the actual level of activity in the construction field, and new orders precede actual production. A lower GNP, lower employment and higher unemployment,[7] and lower corporate profits are the characteristics of a business recession; if these signs are not in evidence, there is no recession. To speak of them as "coincident" with the turn is almost analogous to saying, as Calvin Coolidge is reported to have done, "When people are out of work, unemployment results." Finally, people do not curtail their purchases in retail stores until

---

[6] Sidney Schoeffler, *The Failures of Economics: A Diagnostic Study*, Harvard University Press, Cambridge, Mass., 1955, p. 62.
[7] Employment and unemployment may rise or fall together, since numbers in the labor force change. If people are no longer looking for work, they are not counted as unemployed. Withdrawals from the labor force include students who return to school and housewives who decide to stay at home.

after a recession has set in, and manufacturers' inventories do not start to pile up until consumers have curtailed their buying.

At any rate, the leading series offer the best clues we have to what is likely to happen, and if they all show the same trend, they provide a fairly firm basis for expecting an upturn or a downturn. Usually, however, the trends are mixed.

An extension of the lead and lag method is the use of differences in the fluctuations of some of the indexes.[8] For instance, purchasing agents use a ratio of raw materials inventories to new orders as a means of forecasting raw materials prices since low inventories mean that companies will soon be in the market bidding for the available supplies. Again, the ratio of durable goods production to nondurable goods production is likely to increase in boom periods; hence an increased demand for durable goods is considered an indicator of rising economic trends. Still another such indicator, useful for long-term forecasts in the construction and the furniture industries, among others, is the ratio of family formation and the supply of housing, present and planned.

Use of the lead and lag method, with or without examination of the various ratios, cannot be a matter of mathematical formulas. A qualitative analysis must be made of each series to determine how important it is likely to be in the future, and a good deal of judgment must be used in striking a balance.

For example, increased consumer demand (especially for durable goods), a rise in construction contracts, rising consumer incomes, and government budgets that incorporate increased defense spending are all factors that herald a rise in the general level of the economy. But against these one might have to set such things as overcapacity in many industries, which will probably mean a drop in company expenditures for new plant and equipment, a trend toward maintenance of lower inventories in relation to sales, and an unfavorable balance of payments in international trade.

Overshoot and opposite factors   The overshoot method is less accurate than the lead and lag method. It is based on the rather general and well-known proposition that whenever business activity rises above "normal" a reaction is bound to set in—and the greater the rise, the greater the reaction that follows. The problem is, of course, to determine what is normal (the trend line) and predict accurately the length and extent of the deviation.

The third method (weighing opposite factors) consists merely of listing factors for and against expansion or contraction and striking a balance.

Econometrics   Increasingly, however, forecasting is based on econometrics, the science of measurement. The principal variables are combined in a series of equations that represent an abstraction simple enough to permit the calculation, but complex enough to bear some correspondence to reality. In forecasting GNP the economic variables used may include the past series of

---

[8] See Milton H. Spencer and Louis Siegelman, *Managerial Economics*, Richard D. Irwin, Inc., Homewood, Ill., 1959, pp. 34–35.

disposable income, government income and expenditures, the balance of foreign payments, inventories, the stock of money, and others. These will be assembled into a series of equations or a mathematical model of the shape of things to come.

The most important consideration in forecasting is, of course, accuracy. To forecast general trends is not very difficult, but the more accurately turning points and the size of a rise or a drop in general economic levels can be predicted, the greater the possibility of increasing profits. Very large losses can be incurred if the forecasts of turning points or of the amount of the rise or drop are wide of the mark.

Secondly, a forecast must be timely. Unless the data are produced well in advance of the need and yet are as up to date as possible, they cannot be a reliable basis for planning.

Thirdly, the data must be applicable to the solution of specific problems. Thus financial forecasts should be in dollars, production forecasts in terms of factory units.

Fourthly, the data should be inexpensive to collect and to analyze in terms of the results.

Finally and very important, the forecast should be intelligible to top management, whose members are likely to be neither economists nor mathematicians. This is perhaps the reason why many companies use oversimplified forecasts and eschew the sophisticated mathematical methods that may often be required to achieve any degree of accuracy.

With a general idea of prospects for the economy as a whole, it is possible to gauge prospects for the industry in which the company is engaged. Again, there is no absolute certainty, but different industries account for different proportions of the national product, and if one can figure approximately what the GNP will be next year or five years from now, it is possible to predict approximately what industry sales will be. Some account must be taken, of course, of possible changes in the industry's position, and here the extrapolation technique may be of use.

Knowing industry sales and the company's share of the industry market, the forecaster can arrive at an approximate figure for company sales—at least in certain industries. If the company plans to *increase* its share of the market, it must also plan for better products, intensified selling effort, more advertising, or other moves to make the increase a reality.

Figures 3 and 4 show these interrelationships. Thus if the company's share of the market is M (Figure 4) and total industry sales are B, then company sales will be C. If total industry sales rise from B to B', the company sales will be C'. But if the company market share rises to M', then, even though industry sales remain the same, the company's sales would rise from C to C."

Figure 5 shows the relationship of company sales to profits before taxes. Thus if company sales are at a level C, net profits before taxes would be D. If a cost reduction is achieved, profits would rise from D to D'.

Figure 6 shows company profits before and after taxes as a function of

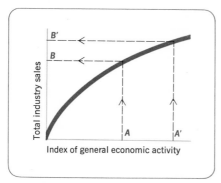

FIGURE 3   The company's economic environment (the total-industry-sales—
general-economic-activity relation). (From Robert S. Weinberg,
"What Does the Future Hold for Advertising and Marketing
Measurements?" *Proceedings of the Fifth Annual Conference of
the Advertising Research Foundation*, Sept. 25, 1959.) This and
Figures 4 to 7 copyright by the Advertising Research Foundation.

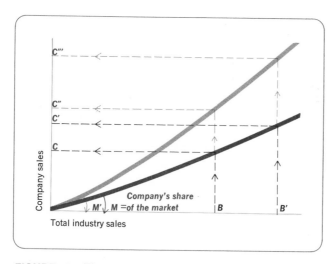

FIGURE 4   The company's competitive environment (the company sales-
total—industry-sales relation). (From Robert S. Weinberg, "What
Does the Future Hold for Advertising and Marketing Measurements?" *Proceedings of the Fifth Annual Conference of the
Advertising Research Foundation*, Sept. 25, 1959.)

the structure of tax rates (and perhaps the bargaining ability of the tax counsel). Thus when company net profits before taxes are *D*, net profits after taxes
will be *E*. An increase in profits before taxes to *D'* would lead to an increase in
profits after taxes to *E'*.

   These four interrelationships can all be put together in one chart (Figure 7).

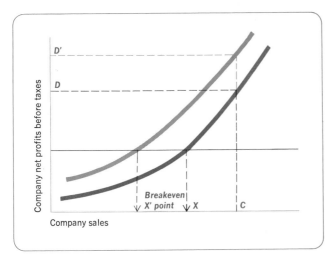

FIGURE 5 The company's internal environment (the company net-profits-before-taxes–company sales relation). (From Robert S. Weinberg, "What Does the Future Hold for Advertising and Marketing Measurements?" *Proceedings of the Fifth Annual Conference of the Advertising Research Foundation*, Sept. 25, 1959.)

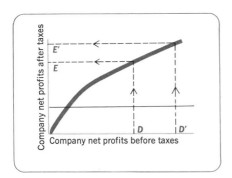

FIGURE 6 The company's institutional environment (the company net-profits-after-taxes–company net-profits-before-taxes relation). (From Robert S. Weinberg, "What Does the Future Hold for Advertising and Marketing Measurements?" *Proceedings of the Fifth Annual Conference of the Advertising Research Foundation*, Sept. 25, 1959.)

Thus if general economic activity is A, then total industry sales will be at level B. If the company's share of the market is M, company sales will be C, net profits before taxes D, and net profits after taxes E. And if the company's share of the market rises from M to M', sales and profits will rise to C', D', and E'.

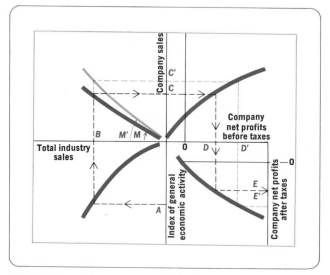

FIGURE 7   The company's general-economic-activity–net-profits complex. (From Robert S. Weinberg, "What Does the Future Hold for Advertising and Marketing Measurements?" *Proceedings of the Fifth Annual Conference of the Advertising Research Foundation,* Sept. 25, 1959.)

But even if the level of the economy and the level of the industry are as predicted, the company has no guarantee that it will be able to achieve the results it has planned for. Competitors plan too, and some of them may be planning to increase their market share.

Another way of considering some of the same factors is the building-block analysis[9] shown in Figure 8. Here the following factors are considered:

1.   The total market potential—how much the industry could sell if every possible prospect for the products were to purchase all he could possibly use.
2.   The market development rate—the extent to which the industry's products or the company's products are meeting all the needs of the market. For example, if there are four industries that could use products of the same general type and the company is producing items suitable for only two of them, its market development rate is only 50 per cent.
3.   The market realization rate—a measure of the extent to which the market is mature, that is, the extent to which the possible users of the products are actually buying them and are buying all they can use.

[9] The following is drawn from a paper by R. S. Weinberg, vice-president in charge of planning, Anheuser-Busch, St. Louis, given before the American Management Association in February, 1966.

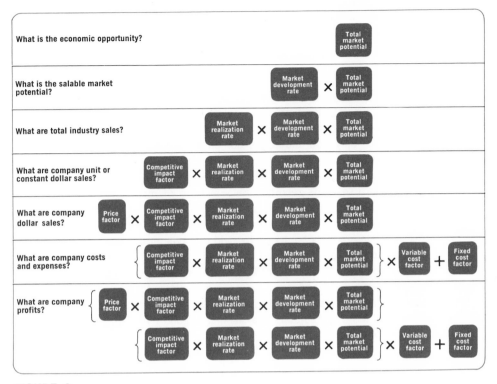

FIGURE 8

4. Total industry sales—these will equal the total market potential multiplied by the market realization rate and the market development rate. If the first two factors are 100 per cent, total industry sales will be equal to the total market potential, but, of course, they practically never are.
5. The competitive impact factor—the company's share of the market.

The other factors are self-explanatory. For example, dollar revenues depend on prices as well as on volume; and profits, of course, equal revenue minus costs.

To develop a strategy for corporate (or divisional) business growth, the company should have the answers to the seven basic questions shown on the chart, which indicate the opportunities for growth in the company's current market. The total market potential sets the outer limit of what is possible; then this figure is modified by the other factors in order to consider the matter more realistically. However, the ultimate success of any strategic planning program based on building-block analysis will depend on the ability of the market research and market planning personnel to develop the market structure data necessary to relate the company's prospects to those of the industry, and those of the industry to the economy. The computer with its capacity to analyze great masses of data very quickly is of inestimable value in this task.

Market research

Marketing, or market, research is defined as "gathering, recording, and analyzing all facts about problems relating to the transfer and sale of goods and services from producer to consumer."[10] Essentially, it is designed to discover not only how much the company can hope to sell, but where, to whom, and how.

Some part of the research can be done right in the company's own office through the use of its recorded data, a form of market research known as "sales analysis." This should provide information on which products are selling best, in what markets, and to what type of customer. It is very important that sales records be set up to yield this type of data in usable form.

Other sources of information on markets are the published statistics that give an indication of the size of the potential market in various localities. The Federal government and to a lesser extent state governments are valuable sources of this type of information. As a government statistician once observed: "Many consultants are making a good living merely because they know where to find the data provided by the government, and their clients are ignorant of the wealth of information that is readily available."

The main government sources are the publications of the U.S. Bureau of the Census and the Department of Commerce. Private sources of valuable market statistics include trade associations, trade papers (e.g., *Sales Management*), and many special publications—for example, a railroad or a utility anxious to bring new business to its territory will often publish a volume of statistics on the markets there.

From such sources as these, it is possible to obtain:

1. Figures on population, number of families, numbers in various age groups, population growth rates in various geographical areas. Many products are more likely to be purchased by families than by single persons (e.g., freezers), and age also affects purchases.
2. Figures on family and individual income and the proportion of that income spent for various categories of products, such as food, clothing, house furnishings.
3. Figures on manufacturing establishments in various industries and their size.
4. Figures on retail establishments and their size.

All these figures may be obtained broken down geographically: by states, counties, and cities, and sometimes even by smaller divisions. There are also data available that are directly related to the sale of specific products. For

---

[10] "1948 Report of the Definitions Committee of the American Marketing Association," R. S. Alexander, Chairman, *The Journal of Marketing* (American Marketing Association), October, 1948.

example, the number of automobile registrations shows the potential for an accessory purchased by car owners, the number of homes wired for electricity, the potential for various electrical appliances.

Note that these figures do not tell the company how much it actually *can* sell in a given territory. The mere fact that a man has a car does not mean he will buy all possible accessories for it even if he has a high income and can well afford them. Nor does a family necessarily purchase all possible electrical appliances simply because it has a wired home and the money to buy them. Moreover, in a competitive system, no company can hope to sell all the prospects in a given territory. Nevertheless, these data are extremely valuable in comparing territories and in judging potential for new products.

Statistics like these often set the top limit of the market potential. One cannot, for example, hope to sell more car radios than there are cars, more Rolls-Royces than there are families or individuals with very high incomes, more electronic control instruments than the sum total of those that are used, or could be used, by plants in industries to which they are adapted.

There are, however, many other factors to consider. Chief among them is the extent to which the company's product can win acceptance among those who may logically be expected to buy it. Mailed questionnaires are one possibility and often provide valuable data. They may be sent, for example, to present owners asking what they like and what they dislike about the product, what improvements they would like to see introduced, and what colors they prefer.

Polling   In the case of consumer products, however, it is more customary to use interviewers, who talk to a selected sample of consumers. The technique here is somewhat like that used in political poll taking. In fact, the political pollsters obtain much of their revenue from this use of their interviewing organizations; the political poll taking is sometimes merely by way of advertisement.

Selection of the sample to be polled is of the utmost importance; it must be truly representative of the people who may logically be expected to need and want the product and who are able to pay for it. And it must be large enough to give reliable results.

Sampling is a complicated technique in itself, but an example will illustrate the difficulties. In 1936, a now defunct magazine, *The Literary Digest*, predicted the election of Alfred Landon as the result of a very large mail straw vote it had conducted in all sections of the country. But his opponent, Franklin D. Roosevelt, was swept into office by a landslide. How was such a mistake possible? The *Digest's* big sample was taken from telephone books and automobile registrations; hence it contained an undue proportion of upper- and middle-income families (in Depression days, even a telephone was a mark of comparative affluence). The magazine's technique had worked in the past because *regional* differences played the major part in political results, and its sample was weighted only by the population in each section of the country.

Later political pollsters refined the techniques. Thus if 10 per cent of the population has incomes above $10,000 a year, 10 per cent of the sample will be in that income bracket. Such factors as religion, occupation, and union membership may also be taken into account if it is believed they will affect choices.

Still, some prominent political pollsters went wrong again in the 1948 election, when Harry S. Truman defeated Thomas E. Dewey. Also, they have often predicted results correctly but been fairly far off in percentages; in fact, they do not even claim to predict percentages exactly.

The use of interviewers does not preclude the necessity of drawing up a questionnaire just as carefully as if the research were to be conducted by mail, and the interviewers—who are generally part-time workers, perhaps housewives—must ask only the questions on the prepared questionnaire and in the exact words specified. This is important, because it is very difficult to draw up a question in a form that does not bias the answer or permit misinterpretation.

How wording of the question may affect the answer has been demonstrated by a number of experiments. For example, at the start of World War II, before the United States had entered the conflict, one pollster asked a question in two forms:

1. Should the United States convoy supplies to England?
2. Should we risk the lives of American seamen to get supplies to Great Britain?

Needless to say, the first question received many more yeses than the second, even though the people questioned probably knew that convoying involved a certain amount of risk to American seamen.

Even with a good sample and a well-constructed questionnaire, it is possible to get false answers, for the simple reason that people have many reasons for not telling the exact truth. For example, the person who is asked whether or not he expects to buy a new car next year may wish to impress the interviewer with his income status and answer yes when he knows very well he cannot afford to do so. It is possible, however, to include other questions that will provide some sort of check on the accuracy of the replies.

Motivation research   Finally, there is the difficulty that people themselves do not always know why they buy a certain product or a certain brand of merchandise. They buy a given make of car, for example, not because it is better mechanically, "rides easier," or is more attractive looking, but because they feel that ownership of that make gives them extra status in the eyes of their neighbors. Or a man may want a convertible because it makes him feel young and dashing.

Because of these factors, a whole new technique of market research, known as "motivation research," has been developed. This technique calls for more skilled interviewers and more searching interviews designed to uncover the hidden motives for buying that are based on deep human desires: status, security, even sex. Motivation researchers say, for example, that those who eat a great deal of candy are basically insecure people. Hence they have recommended that candy advertisements show closely knit family circles and similar scenes.

Undoubtedly, motivation research has discovered a portion of the truth about consumer buying habits, but too great a reliance on the hidden motives may be unwise. After all, people do buy a great many products for logical reasons: a washing machine because it saves work, foods simply because they like them, and so on.

For example, one writer—and skilled practitioner—of advertising has cited two advertisements for a curling lotion:

1.   "Girls—want quick curls?"
2.   "Does he still say 'I love you'?"

The first, it will be noted, is a straight logical appeal: The lotion provides curls, and it provides them quickly. The latter is based on an appeal to deeper emotions—a woman's desire to be loved. The first of these drew by far the greater response, if only because it was more believable.[11]

Market testing   Once as much information as possible has been gathered through market research, a technique that is often used in the case of new products is *market testing*. A product is put on sale to dealers or final consumers in a single city or in one or two areas to see what the response will be at a given price. Or it may be sold at different prices in different localities. Changes in packages can also be tested in this way.

This technique is not, of course, practicable for such products as automobiles, on which tooling up for a given model is expensive and cannot be done merely for test purposes. But it is very useful for soaps, detergents, and similar low-priced products.

THE CORPORATE PLANNING PROCESS

The sales forecast is the basis on which all the plans depend. It shows, for example, how much production will be needed, and this in turn makes it possible for the company to determine whether or not it will need new facilities and a larger work force. The market research phase indicates the prospects for new products, any changes needed in the design of the products, and even the themes that should be stressed in the advertising.

Content of a plan

One feature of a corporate plan is likely to be a series of budgets that translate company intentions into a series of assignments and provide the money to

---

[11] John Caples, *Making Ads Pay*, Harper & Row, Publishers, Incorporated, New York, 1957, pp. 105–106.

carry them out. Since a budget extends over a period of time, it represents a flow of assignments rather than a stationary approach, and changes can be made rather quickly, particularly if the budgets are reviewed monthly or quarterly.

Budgets are of two main types: capital and expense. Capital spending is investment, merely a change in the form in which assets are held. The money a company spends to carry on day-to-day business, on the other hand, represents actual out-of-pocket costs that must be recovered through sales during the year if the company is to show a profit.

The capital budget   The capital budget may provide the single most important way for a company to increase both sales and share of the market. Capital investment can make it possible for the company to produce a new product or a better product, to serve customers more quickly, or to reduce prices. A new modern efficient plant located nearer the major customers may well give the company a margin over its competitors.

No company has unlimited funds, of course, nor can it call on unlimited credit or always sell new equities at the price it would like to get. Therefore some scheme of priorities for projects must be adopted. The relationship of the supply and demand for capital projects is shown in Figure 9. There is a cutoff point at the volume of funds at which availability gives out.

FIGURE 9   Supply and demand for capital in a specific company. (Designed by Robert S. Weinberg.)

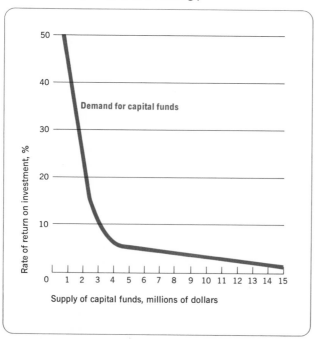

Now there are some projects that simply have to be undertaken regardless of the economic calculations since they must be budgeted for if the company wants to stay in business:

1. Projects required to meet the provisions of the law. There are numerous regulations (by municipalities, states, and the Federal government) relating to safety, avoidance of nuisance, employee welfare, and so on that may make new investment necessary. If pressure is brought on a company to stop polluting a stream with poisons from its processes, or if it is found in violation of legally required safety practices, it may have to spend a great deal of money for corrections, even though the projects bring in no return in the conventional sense.

2. Projects required by competitive exigencies. If a competitor is providing better and faster service, or a better or a cheaper product, the company may have to follow suit or lose its share of the market.

3. Repair and replacement. If fire destroys a plant, the company may have to appropriate capital funds over and above what it recovers from fire insurance because ordinarily the insurance will not cover the complete cost of replacement. Generally, too, when a company is compelled to rebuild, it will want to incorporate improvements.

4. Projects required to meet labor union demands. Labor unions may enforce (by threat of strikes) the provision of certain working conditions that require capital investment; e.g., better lighting or air conditioning. (In this way investments in Puerto Rican plants have gradually had to match those in mainland plants in the United States.)

Subtracting the unavoidable investments from the funds available leaves the amount that can be spent for desirable but not entirely necessary projects. And the criterion for judging among the latter is the rate of return on investment over the long term.

Since most managements must in fact combine a number of goals in making capital investments, there are different ways of accomplishing these, and the choice of the best combination tends to become important. The list on page 336 of goals and different plans to achieve them is adapted from the unpublished Ph.D. thesis of Professor Dale E. Zand, *An Analysis of Managerial Expenditure Decision Making* (New York University, 1954).

Expense budgets   Expense budgets allot the money to be expended for various activities. Some of these amounts will be fixed—interest on any debts outstanding, much of the overhead expense, and others. Other expenses will depend on the level of operations planned for—the amount of production, the sales effort to be expended, the amount of advertising to be done.

Generally budgets must include some cushion to provide for changes in expenditures beyond the company's control. The company knows, of course, what its wage cost is now at various levels of operation and how much it must spend for material to make a given volume of product. But it does not necessarily know what rises in material prices and labor costs will take place during

	Goal	Plans
1	Profits	Payout
		Necessity
		Rate of return on investment
		Highest comparable rate
		Discounted flow of cash
2	Survival	Minimum possibility of loss
3	Liquidity	Cash payback time
4	Consumer satisfaction	Cost per unit
		Comparative qualitative performance in terms of length of life
		Quality and speed of operation
5	Corporate leadership	Total sales compared with those of competitors
		Share of market
6	Employee satisfaction	Wage effect of the project
		Employment effect of the proposal
		Changes in workload
7	Stockholder satisfaction	Earnings and dividends per share
8	Community impact	In terms of employment, price-wage relationships

the year, or what other money it may have to spend because of unexpected occurrences.

Other budgets　In addition to the overall corporate and expense budgets, there will probably be a budget for each department (in fact, the corporate budget may be made up largely of the sum of the departmental budgets), and many departments will have capital as well as expense budgets. There may also be a manpower budget, showing the amount of manpower that will be needed in each department and when it will be taken on.

A very important type of budget to which companies are giving increased attention these days is the cash flow budget. A company may estimate that it will take in x dollars over the period of a year, and find itself in difficulty even if the estimate is accurate. Money seldom flows in evenly. In almost any type of business, there are periods of peak sales and periods of slack, and the cash flow is likely to lag behind sales in any case because of credit arrangements. In the meantime, the company needs money to finance its current operations.

Figure 10 shows what can happen to a business that pays no attention to cash flow. Mr. Jones of the ABC Company kept making a larger profit and putting more money into production for inventory to support his larger sales. On January 1, he had $2,750 and on June 1, nearly twice as much, $5,250. But he was actually worse off since all his money was tied up in inventory and receivables. In the meantime, he had to borrow money to continue in business because, even if he stopped producing, many of his expenses would continue without interruption. And, of course, the interest on the borrowed money cut into his profits.

As the year started, Mr. Jones of the ABC Company was in fine shape. His company made widgets—just what the consumer wanted. He made them for 75¢ each, sold them for $1. He kept a 30-day supply in inventory, paid his bills promptly, and billed his customers 30-days net. Sales were right on target, with the sales manager predicting a steady increase. It felt like his lucky year, and it began this way:

Jan. 1   Cash $1,000 Inventory $750 Receivables $1,000

In January, he sold 1,000 widgets; shipped them at a cost of $750; collected his receivables—winding up with a tidy $250 profit and books like this:

Feb. 1   Cash $1,250 Inventory $750 Receivables $1,000

This month sales jumped, as predicted, to 1,500. With a corresponding step-up in production to maintain his 30-day inventory, he made 2,000 units at a cost of $1,500. All receivables from January sales were collected. Now his books looked like this:

Mar. 1   Cash $750 Inventory $1,125 Receivables $1,500

March sales were even better: 2,000 units. Collections: On time. Production, to adhere to his inventory policy: 2,500 units. Operating result for the month: $500 profit. Profit to date: $1,125. His books:

Apr. 1   Cash $375 Inventory $1,500 Receivables $2,000

In April, sales jumped another 500 units to 2,500—and Jones patted his sales manager on the back. His customers were paying right on time. Production was pushed to 3,000 units, the month's business netted him $625 for a profit to date of $1,750. He took off for Florida before he saw the accountant's report:

May 1   Cash $125 Inventory $1,875 Receivables $2,500

May saw Jones' company really hitting a stride—sales of 3,000 widgets, production of 3,500, and a 5-month profit of $2,500. But, suddenly, he got a phone call from his treasurer: "Come home! We need money!" His books had caught up with him:

June 1   Cash $000 Inventory $2,250 Receivables $3,000

He came home—and hollered for his banker.

FIGURE 10   How to go broke while making a profit. (From *Business Week*, Apr. 28, 1956, pp. 46–47.)

Schedules   In addition to the budgets, the plan is likely to include a series of schedules specifying the production of each product each month; the dates when any new facilities will be started and completed; the dates when new products will be market-tested, put into commercial production, and on the market; the sales of each product each month; and similar figures.

A type of scheduling that is becoming increasingly popular is known as "critical path scheduling" or "arrow diagramming." It may be applied to almost any project, from getting a new product on the market to the planning and construction of a new building. It may be explained in this way:

In scheduling any step in an overall program or job there are three considerations:

1.   What must be done before each particular phase can be started?

2. What can be done concurrently?
3. What follows in sequence; or now that we have reached this phase, what can we do to further the project?

For example, in the first arrow diagram in Figure 11, jobs A and B must be completed before job C can be started. If A would take a week and B three days, the shortest elapsed time to reach node 2 and the point where job C can start would be a week. There would be no point in spending money to expedite job B, but there might be good reason for expediting A. The critical path is the longest path to completion of the project; in other words, the jobs along this path are those that must be speeded up if the elapsed time is to be shortened.

This is, of course, a very simple illustration, and it would be the work of a minute to figure out the best path to completion of the project. In large projects, however, the right path is less easily discernible.

Figure 12 shows the critical path diagram of a job somewhat more complicated than the simple one shown in Figure 11, but, of course, a far, far simpler project than, say, producing a missile. Once the crew is assembled, it can proceed to deactivate the pipe, erect the scaffold, and remove the old pipe,

FIGURE 11 Arrow diagramming. (From Thomas C. Hunter, Facilities Planning, International Business Machines.)

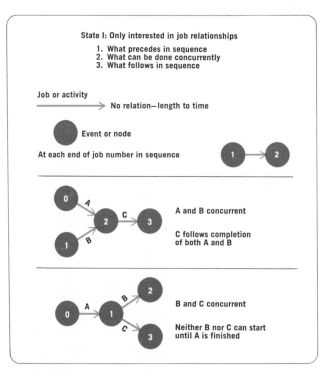

State I: Only interested in job relationships
1. What precedes in sequence
2. What can be done concurrently
3. What follows in sequence

Job or activity
⎯⎯⎯⎯⎯⟶ No relation—length to time

● Event or node

At each end of job number in sequence

A and B concurrent

C follows completion of both A and B

B and C concurrent

Neither B nor C can start until A is finished

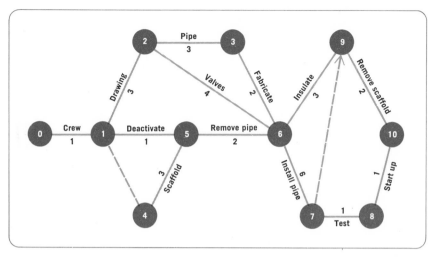

FIGURE 12 Arrow diagram of a simple job. (From Thomas C. Hunter, Facilities Planning, International Business Machines.)

which will take five days in all if the scaffold is erected while the deactivation is in progress.

But making the drawings will also take three days, the new pipe and valves cannot be ordered until the drawings are completed, and obtaining pipe and valves and doing the fabrication necessary will take five more days, or eight days altogether. So there would be no point in expediting the removal of the old pipe since there is a few days' "float" (extra time) for this part of the job. But a day could be sliced off the elapsed time by putting more men on the fabrication because the valves will be ready to install four days after the drawings are complete. Also, since the new pipe will not be ready to install for eight days, there is no reason to take the old one out of service on the first day; deactivation need not begin until the third day.

A further factor in critical path scheduling is the cost of expediting various parts of a job. In Figure 13, the critical job is 0-1, which will cost $30 per day to expedite. Job 0-2 could be expedited for $20 a day, but there would be no point in speeding it up because it can be completed in 10 days, whereas the other two jobs that must also be done before node 2 is reached will take 15 days. If job 0-1 could be expedited by five days, this would reduce the total time required to reach node 2 to ten days. Then further expediting would require speeding up both job 0-2 and job 1-2, but this would cost $60 per day.

On a large project involving hundreds of different jobs, a computer is used to make similar projections by finding the critical jobs that are least expensive to expedite. Then when the secondary paths (those with float) become critical, the planner moves on to find the next least expensive critical step, and so on.

A variation of this system, known as PERT (Program Evaluation Review Technique), was used in the Navy's *Polaris* program, which involved some

250 prime contractors and 9,000 subcontractors. PERT begins with three steps:[12] (1) every significant event that must occur before a project is complete is listed in very specific terms, (2) the sequence of the events and their relationships are shown by means of the PERT network or diagram (see Figure 14), and (3) a specific time is set for the start and completion of each event.

In order to ensure that the times set will be as accurate as possible, three estimates are made: the most *pessimistic* (i.e., the longest time), the most *optimistic*, and the *most likely* time considering the conditions that are likely to be encountered. An average of these three times (weighted to place greatest emphasis on the most likely estimate) is then calculated.

Expected times along all possible paths in the network are totaled by computer, which also determines negative and positive "slack times." Positive slack time is what is referred to as float in the critical path technique; negative slack time means that the jobs must be expedited (by overtime, for example) if they are to be completed in time for the next scheduled step. The final step

[12] Drawn from Howard Simons, " 'PERT': How to Meet a Deadline," *Think*, May, 1962, p. 15.

FIGURE 13   Cost to expedite. (From Thomas C. Hunter, Facilities Planning, International Business Machines.)

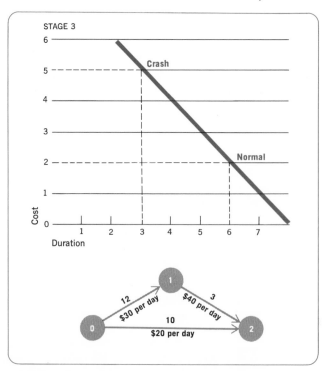

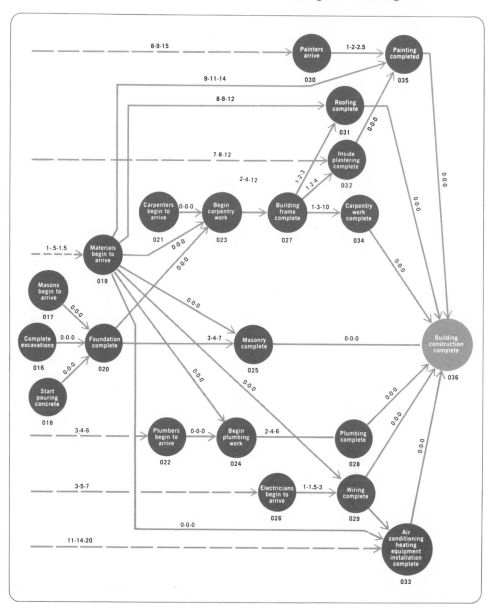

FIGURE 14 PERT diagram for building a house. (From *Think,* May, 1962, p. 15.)

in PERT is the production of printed material that focuses attention on the spots where management attention is most needed.

Another type of PERT is PERT/cost, in which dollar estimates for each job are made. This includes supplements that make it possible to determine the "best" plan, taking into account cost, time, and risk and weighting each in accordance with its importance. Another supplement may be used to determine the best allocation of resources—of skilled manpower, for example.

A complete plan   Figure 15 shows both the form a complete plan might take and the studies necessary to ensure that the most accurate decisions possible are made. This is a strategic plan for a major business research program,[13]

[13] This is not an actual plan, it should be noted; it might be called, rather, a "plan for a plan."

FIGURE 15   An illustrative "strategic" plan for a major business research program. (Developed by Robert S. Weinberg.)

Major research programs	Economic and industry relations (MRP I)			
Major research projects	Economic forecasting and analysis (MRP I, I)	Market research and analysis (MRP I, II)	New product development (MRP I, III)	New market and customer development (MRP I, IV)
Individual research projects	Long-term forecasting (PI, I, 1) Short-term forecasting (PI, I, 2) Forecasting the level of general economic activity (PI, I, 3) Forecasting specific industry trends (PI, I, 4) Forecasting technological change and displacement (PI, I, 5)	Consumer survey techniques (PI, II, 1) Industrial survey techniques (PI, II, 2) Motivation research (survey) (PI, II, 3) Consumer budget studies (PI, II, 4) Industrial purchasing policies (PI, II, 5) Community response patterns (PI, II, 6)	Capital requirements for new product developments (PI, III, 1) The development of joint and complementary products (PI, III, 2) Estimating the demand for, and distribution channels for new products (PI, III, 3) Development of new product "prototypes" of "functional least common denominators" (PI, III, 4) Acquiring new products or product lines through mergers (PI, III, 5)	The "economics" of geographic expansion (PI, IV, 1) Measuring new market potential (PI, IV, 2) The analysis of "latent" demand (PI, IV, 3) Acquiring new markets through mergers (PI, IV, 4) Input-output analyses for industrial market analysis (PI, IV, 5)
Technical research papers	Correlation techniques (TI, I, 1) Input-output analysis (TI, I, 2) Activity analysis (TI, I, 3) Dynamic economic models (TI, I, 4) Econometric model building (reduced form limited information) (TI, I, 5)	Sampling theory (TI, II, 1) Design of experiments (TI, II, 2) Consumer preference theory (TI, II, 3) Consumer family budget theory (TI, II, 4)	Engineering analysis and development of new products (TI, III, 1)	Consumer preference theory (TI, IV, 1)

but many of the same elements could be included in the corporate plan. The procedure calls for determining:

1. Long- and short-term prospects for the economy as a whole and for the industry
2. The products likely to be needed in the light of consumer demand (market research and analysis)
3. Methods and cost of acquiring new products through development or merger
4. Measurement of market potential

Competitive relations (MRP II)				Internal operating relations (MRP III)			
Advertising and sales promotion strategy (MRP II, I)	Pricing policies (MRP II, II)	The collection and evaluation of "economic intelligence" regarding competitor's operations (MRP II, III)	Planning long-term competitive strategy (MRP II, IV)	The production process (MRP III, I)	The distribution process (MRP III, II)	The financial process (MRP III, III)	The planning and control process (MRP III, IV)
The determination of "optimal" advertising and sales promotion expenditure levels (PII, I, 1) The allocation of advertising and sales promotion expenditure effort a) to media b) to market (PII, I, 2) Determining advertising and sales promotion effectiveness (PII, I, 3) "Optimal" distribution of sales (and salesman's) effort (PII, I, 4)	The impact of price upon demand (PII, II, 1) The impact of competitor's price competition on company sales (PII, II, 2) The interrelation between cost and price (profit) (PII, II, 3)	The evaluation of data and information sources a) government b) trade association c) customers and salesmen d) published reports (PII, III, 1) Mathematical models for "intelligence assessment" (PII, III, 2) The determination of the "behavior patterns" of the firm's competitors (PII, III, 3)	The derivation of long-term market penetration models (PII, IV, 1) The development of long-term competitive objectives (PII, IV, 2) The comparison of various alternative long-range competitive postures (PII, IV, 3)	Production control (PIII, I, 1) Production scheduling (PIII, I, 2) Inventory control (PIII, I, 3) "Make" or "buy" (integration) policy (PIII, I, 4) The analysis of the factors which influence and determine industrial productivity (PIII, I, 5)	"Optimal" warehousing policy (PIII, II, 1) "Optimal" transportation policy ("optimal" routing) & medium (PIII, II, 2) "Optimal" channels of distribution (PIII, II, 3) The control of administrative, general, and selling expenditures (PIII, II, 4) "Optimal" sales organizations (PIII, II, 5) "Optimal" plant location (PIII, II, 6)	The determination of working capital requirements (PIII, III, 1) Capital budgeting (PIII, III, 2) Activity accounting (PIII, III, 3) Mathematical models for budgeting (PIII, III, 4) Capital-output ratios (analysis) (PIII, III, 5) The financial aspects of merger policies (PIII, III, 6)	"Strategic" operations research models (PIII, IV, 1) The management decision process (PIII, IV, 2) Mathematical models of the firm (PIII, IV, 3) An analysis of communication flows within the firm (PIII, IV, 4)
Applications of game theory (TII, IV, 1) Long-term operational gaming models (TII, IV, 2)	Demand theory (elasticity of demand) (TII, I, 1) The derivation of statistical cost curves (functions) (TII, I, 2)	Statistical decision theory (TII, III, 4) Sequential sampling (TII, III, 2) Operational gaming (simulation) (TII, III, 3) Information theory (TII, III, 4) Symbolic logic (TII, III, 5)	Applications of game theory (TII, IV, 1) Long-term operational gaming models (TII, IV, 2)	Matrix algebra (TIII, 1, 1) Combinatorial algebra (TIII, I, 2) Linear programming (TIII, I, 3) Nonlinear programming (TIII, I, 4) Process analysis (TIII, I, 5) The derivation of statistical cost curves (functions) (TIII, I, 6)	Transportation models (linear programming) (TIII, II, 1) Distribution models (input-output models) (TIII, II, 2)	Allocation models a) Dynamic programming models b) Linear programming c) Calculus of variations (TIII, III, 1) The theory of investment of the firm (TIII, II, 2)	Activity analysis of the firm (TIII, IV, 1) Triangular models of the firm (TIII, III, 2) Communication (network) theory (TIII, IV, 3)

The plan will then include (see competitive relations) the amount of money to be appropriated for advertising and promotion, the pricing policies, the long-range competitive strategy. It will also cover production controls, production scheduling, inventory, which parts are to be made and which to be purchased outside, the warehousing and transportation policies, the sales organization needed, capital and expense requirements (under internal operating relations).

Few companies plan so carefully as this or make use of all the techniques shown, but it is likely that more will do so in the future as the investments needed, and hence the risks, grow larger.

WHO DOES THE PLANNING?

A corporate plan may, of course, be developed by the chief executive with the assistance of specialized planners. But it is better, and probably commoner, to have the planning start at the department or division level, both because those lower down are more familiar with the day-to-day problems and because they will be more interested in fulfilling the plans if they have a hand in constructing them. It is quite common to have each department make up its own budgets, with justifications[14] for any capital expenditures proposed.

A specialized planning group is often useful in this case also, to assist those down the line in drawing up plans for their segments of the organization, and later to help top management coordinate the various departmental and division plans into a unified whole.

At IBM   The planning system at IBM is shown in Figure 16. As can be seen, the top management of the corporation takes part in the planning process at several different times in the year. Early in the year it reviews the quantitative objectives that have been set for the corporation and revises them if revision is necessary because of changes in conditions or changes in assumptions about the future. Working independently, the corporate planning staff develops a set of revised planning targets as a basis for the proposed modifications, and if these are approved by top management, they are passed on to the divisions for use in developing one-year extensions of their strategic plans and possibly revisions of them. (As the chart shows, IBM plans cover seven years in the future; thus at the end of each year it is necessary to extend them by a year.)

Each division takes its financial targets—for example, the figures for expected net earnings and growth rates—and tries to build a plan that will enable it to meet or exceed them. This may necessitate reexamining the prospects for current product lines, adding new products, eliminating unprofitable products from the line, and/or modifying products or operations to increase profitability.

---

[14] Justification is provided by figures showing what the total investment will be and what return can be expected on it.

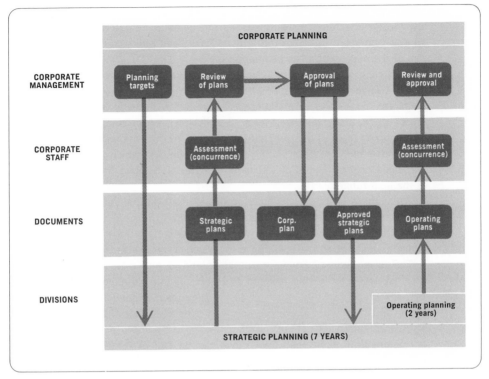

FIGURE 16   IBM Corporate Planning (time shown—one year)

Each department within a division develops its own plan, specifying the resources it will need (manpower, money, equipment, and so on) and setting forth a timetable showing when it expects to take each of the steps necessary to meet the objectives. In doing so, it works with the guidance of the divisional long-range planner, and it may also call on corporate specialists for help in the areas of their expertise. And, of course, it works within the corporate-wide policies originated by the corporate management.

Departmental plans are combined into the divisional plan, and this is checked against divisional objectives. In practice, of course, departmental plans must often be modified and adjusted before they can be combined. Sometimes they are reviewed several times because a change in one department's plan may necessitate changes in others.

When the divisional plans are submitted to corporate management, they are subjected to a staff review called the "assessment process." This process includes the negotiation necessary to resolve differences between the planning targets and the results likely to be achieved under the divisional plans. Some of the staffs may prepare written critiques of the plans; others may write letters of concurrence or nonconcurrence. In this way, items of disagreement or concern are brought to top management's attention.

After corporate top management has reviewed a divisional plan and settled any disagreements or discrepancies, it gives a tentative approval. Final approval comes only after all the plans have been reviewed and the total position of the corporation has been appraised.

Once their strategic plans have been approved, the divisions begin preparation of two-year operating plans based on the seven-year strategic plans. These plans are more detailed versions of the plans for the early years during which the strategic plans will be in force, and the divisional managers' commitment to live up to them is greater than in the case of the long-term strategic plans. Also, when the corporate staffs review the operating plans, they place greater emphasis on the means of implementing the plans than they do in the case of the long-range plans.

Thus, there is broad participation in planning throughout the organization. Top management sets the targets and conducts the final reviews; the staffs assist the divisions and assess the plans when they are submitted, but the divisions and departments within the divisions actually create them.

The advantages of having corporate planning and planning systems staffs are that attention will be focused more strongly on the planning process and that the staffs can take much of the burden of coordination off top management, and help those down the line with special studies that may be needed. The coordination, of course, is much more than a mere process of addition; it is more than likely that the various capital and expense outlays proposed will total more money than the company can safely make available. The specialists on the staff can examine the proposals and their implications in detail and present clear-cut alternatives for top management decision. They can also aid in "negotiating out" differences.

The value of such a staff depends, of course, largely on the skill of the specialists it includes, and above all on the ability of the man in charge of it, who needs a very broad background. He must be familiar with the environmental factors affecting the company and preferably should have had some general management experience, perhaps as assistant to the president or the executive vice-president, for he must be able to view the company as a whole. Ideally, he should have had experience in both the marketing and the production phases of the business, and certainly he should know something about its technology and about finance.

The danger in having such a staff group, many companies feel, is that it may attempt to do what it should not do: take over the planning process entirely. In this case it might be said to be superseding the line managers, even the chief executive himself.

This danger is an imaginary one, however, if the chief executive has clearly in mind the functions he wants the staff to perform and is careful to insist that line managers do the actual planning. In the case of the overall plan, the final decision must be made by the chief executive; those down the line must decide within the framework laid down by the overall plan what they propose to have their divisions or departments do. This is the theory on which IBM's plans and control staff works. Its functions are to (1) coordinate divisional planning for periodic consolidation into the overall plan, (2) provide advice and counsel for the divisional planners, (3) assist in the development of overall corporate and divisional objectives, (4) evaluate the results to be expected from the consolidated plan, and (5) gradually strengthen the planning process.

At Ford   At Ford Motor Company, there is no central planning group as such; the coordinating function is handled instead by the central finance staff. Various staff groups provide predictions of price levels, government fiscal policies, population trends, productivity rates, and other factors.

Two major objectives are set: (1) to increase substantially (by a specific amount which changes from time to time) the profits per share of stock and (2) to reach a specified rate of return on assets. The actual percentages are recommended by the finance staff and accepted or modified by top management.

Centrally, segments of the profits per share of stock are assigned to broad groups of activities: international operations, domestic passenger cars, and so on, but this goal does not concern the division managers, who are not responsible for the sources of the funds they use (e.g., equity or debt capital). Their goals are stated in terms of return on assets they are using since they control most of the factors that affect this figure.

Staffs set procedural rules so that all divisional plans will be developed on a uniform basis. For example, there is the "financial planning volume," which is an estimate of the annual sales of cars, trucks, and tractors. It is obtained by analyzing actual and projected industry volume and the company's share of it.

This figure is used for two reasons. First, a division may sell only to other company divisions, and it is impossible to judge the contribution to volume made by the component it manufactures. Second, basing plans on a constant volume helps to prevent development of new products in accordance with unrealistic assumptions of the extra volume they will produce. Constant selling prices are also assumed—divisions plan for increases only where the upgrading of the product is so significant that it can be expected to sell for a higher price even though competitors do not raise theirs.

Four types of plans are made: (1) divisional plans, (2) research plans, (3) supplementary plans, and (4) product plans.

A divisional plan incorporates the division's plans to reach the profit goal—the return on division assets—and is incorporated into the overall company plan after review and perhaps modification by the central finance staff and top management.

Research goals and plans, on the other hand, are not stated in profit and loss terms; rather they show who has been assigned to study what, when the reports will be issued, and what decisions must be made on the reports. They are designed to familiarize top management with the work research groups are doing so that it can determine which of the projects are most important and how they may be synthesized. (One very long-range research project is being conducted by a small central economics group that is trying to predict the future of transportation through the year 2000.)

Supplementary plans deal with such things as management development, product quality, dealer organization, and suppliers. These cover such points as recruitment and training of future managers, the location of dealers with respect to anticipated population movements, and the development of satisfactory suppliers.

The product planning process is particularly complex because it takes around three years to develop a completely new model. Thus Ford has a product planning office in each vehicle division and each of its principal foreign affiliates, plus a small central product planning group. A representative of the controller's office described the product planner's job as follows:

> The product planner must bridge the gaps between engineering, styling, sales, manufacturing and finance. . . . He tries to keep *out* any engineering developments that, in his opinion, don't add enough customer value to warrant the extra cost (no matter how delightful they may seem to the engineers who developed them). He tries to reconcile dramatic styling innovations that may be proposed by the artistically oriented designers with the nuts-and-bolts problems of building such designs with reasonable quality and cost. Throughout, he must be aware of the probable over-all financial result that is most likely to be achieved under a given product alternative.[15]

The first step in the planning process—three years before the new model is to be introduced—is the development by the styling, engineering, and product planning offices of possible product changes and improvements. The more promising of these are given detailed study to determine their market value and cost. Then the product planning groups develop tentative proposals, often more than one for each make of car.

During the next six months, a series of meetings is held, attended by representatives of product planning, engineering, styling, manufacturing, marketing, and finance, and discussions provide further guidance for the product planners, who are then ready to prepare a "paper program." This includes (1) estimates of required expenditures for plant, equipment, tooling, and launching of the new product; (2) comparisons of piece costs with those of earlier models and estimates of competitors' costs; (3) projected specifications (e.g., weight, dimensions) and performance (fuel consumption, acceleration, and so on).

The paper program goes to an operating policy committee made up of the company's top management. If it is approved, a clay model of the car will be made and measurements taken so that production problems can be anticipated. Drawings will be made and prototypes of the components built for test-

[15] "The Process of Long-range Planning at the Ford Motor Company," paper prepared by the Controller's Office, Ford Motor Company, for the Long-range Planning Research Seminar, UCLA, Sept. 13–14, 1962.

ing. (Throughout this stage the latest cost estimates and the effect of any changes are checked.)

Up to six or eight months before the new model is introduced, the program may still be modified without heavy losses. Thus a continuing check is kept on market conditions, probable actions of competitors, and cost trends. After that time, plans become final.

At a conglomerate   A conglomerate company is one that is engaged in several different industries, often industries that are in no way related to each other, and its divisions may have a large amount of autonomy. It is still necessary, however, for top management to coordinate the plans of all the divisions if it is to have any idea of where the company is heading and be able to allocate resources properly.

One company of this type used to pass out forms and carefully written instructions to the divisions and require them to make extensive forecasts. However, the results were not too useful; so top management installed a much simpler system.

Now there are no forms or written instructions at all. The division managers are simply told:

1. Stretch your imagination and think through as carefully as possible what you can foresee in the next five years: technological improvements, moves by competitors, changes among customers, and so on, and the challenges and opportunities that will result.
2. Against this backdrop, develop what you plan to do with your business: research and development programs, products, marketing efforts, facilities, people, and so on.
3. After you have done this, find out how you can do even better, and revise the plan.
4. Present the plan in the format that will best get the story across.

Each divisional manager reviews his plan with his superior, a group executive who is in charge of several divisions; then together they take the plan they have agreed on to the president's office for a conference on it. The only other person normally present is the vice-president for long-range planning, and he and the president rarely make suggestions. Instead, they confine themselves mainly to asking questions in order to be sure that each aspect of the plan has been thoroughly thought through and to enable the division head to spot any weaknesses himself. If enough weaknesses are discovered, the division head may rework his plan and return with a new version later.

Typically, the basic course of the business of each division during the next year is decided at such a meeting, and the review sessions are held throughout the year since each division has its own schedule. A session may take an entire day, and the president spends a major portion of his time on the planning process.

More specific financial forecasts are made after a review session and are then worked into the financial planning and control when the vice-president for long-range planning explains to the financial people the broad business directions agreed upon in the long-range planning sessions.

BRIDGING THE GAP

Suppose a company or division finds that, in view of the sales forecast, it is not likely to make the profit it believes it should make, even if no upsets occur in the form of economic recession or extraordinary moves on the part of competitors. The great problem in all planning, in fact, is to bridge the gap between what is desirable (stated objectives) and what is possible.

The first and most logical step toward preventing too wide a gap is to speed up development of products and services already planned. These are likely to be supplemental to the existing product line; probably they will fit into it from a technological point of view—that is, they will use the same production facilities. But partly because of this relationship, the prospect for the planned products may be declining too.

At that point, the company is confronted with the very basic question: What business should we be in? Obviously there must be an agonizing reappraisal of long-term prospects, and perhaps plans must be made to shift into another field.

Mergers as a means

One company that overcame a situation of this type, not once but twice, is the former Safety Car Heating & Lighting Company, now Safety Industries, Inc.[16] Founded in 1887, it has been compelled to change fields twice in the course of its existence—once because technological advance all but eliminated the need for its product, and a second time because the industry that provided its major market was contracting.

The company was founded to supply Pintsch gas for lighting and cooking on railroad cars and helped to make obsolete the kerosene lanterns and wood-burning stoves then in current use. The lamps and stoves were a major fire hazard when wrecks occurred; therefore the company's big selling point was safety, and it took its name from that.

Even now, Pintsch gas is used for lighting and cooking on some lines in Canada because it can be relied on when blizzards cut off electric power. But by 1910 the handwriting on the wall was clear: Electricity was bound to replace gas as gas had replaced kerosene and wood. The market would dwindle, and the company would dwindle with it unless it could diversify into other lines.

Since the company was accustomed to selling to the railroads, the obvious answer was for it to turn to electrical products for the same market. This it did, producing, first, electrical generating equipment and, later, voltage regu-

[16] The following is drawn from G. E. Byers, Jr., "Merging with Safety," *Dun's Review and Modern Industry*, May, 1957, pp. 41, 98–102.

lators, heating equipment, fans, and incandescent and fluorescent lights. Still later it began supplying air conditioning equipment for railroad cars. It also took a tentative step toward an advance into new markets by starting the production of grinding and mixing machines and dust collectors for other industries. But it continued to depend on the railroads for the major proportion of its revenue.

By 1952, however, it became apparent that the railroad industry could no longer support the company in the style to which it was accustomed. Between 1926 and that date, the number of passenger cars had dropped by 44 per cent, and further decline appeared likely.

Safety was not yet in anything that might be called financial difficulties in the ordinary sense. Balance sheet figures were extremely favorable. But profits were low and declining slowly but surely. If this trend were to continue, it was clear, the stockholders would be better off if the company were liquidated while its assets still outweighed its liabilities by a more than comfortable margin. They would be able to get a better return on their capital if they invested it somewhere else. With the competition from bus lines and airlines intensifying, it was unlikely that the decline in passenger cars would be stemmed.

The company had no intention of going out of business, however. Under the direction of a new president, Harold F. Kneen, it began to study the possibilities for new products. One way of finding new ones, of course, would be through research, and the research department was accordingly strengthened. But this was an answer only for the long run, and the need for a short-run answer was pressing. The company decided to diversify by buying corporations that were already established in markets other than the railroads.

But first of all, since the company executives had no experience with mergers or acquisitions, they embarked on a program of self-education in what to do and what not to do in an expansion program. A consultant was hired to assist in the training, and the executives also consulted officials of other companies who had had experience in the field. Then a complete survey of the company's resources—finances, manufacturing facilities, sales organization, and management know-how—was undertaken to determine the products the company would be capable of making and marketing. Eventually four criteria were drawn up. The company wanted:

1. High-quality products, complex in design and manufacture, in the electrical or mechanical field
2. Standardized products that could be improved by research
3. Complete products or assemblies
4. Products with partial patent protection

How did it set about finding companies that were producing such products? It advertised for them, not through publications, but through a brochure distributed to those in a position to know of companies that might be for sale—financial organizations, for example.

The first acquisition was Liquefied Gas Utilities, Ltd., of Canada. Unlike Pintsch gas, liquefied gas has many markets, but the know-how needed to produce the two products is somewhat similar. Moreover, Safety executives were accustomed to doing business in Canada.

The second acquisition was the Automatic Temperature Control Company, manufacturer of electrical controls, including some used in the promising field of automation. The third was the Howe Scale Company, whose products dovetailed neatly with those of ATC and Safety itself. ATC's controls were sold to process industries, a field in which market research showed there was considerable potential for industrial scales. Moreover, Safety already had a division, Entoleter, which was selling centrifugal and pneumatic conveying machinery to the same industries.

A fourth acquisition was the Star-Kimble division of Miehle-Goss Dexter, which was manufacturing electrical brakes, high-frequency generators, and specialized rotating electrical equipment, products akin to the electrical products Safety was manufacturing for the railroads. Thus it was possible to integrate the two manufacturing operations.

Results of this carefully planned program of diversification more than met expectations. The objective had been to double sales in five years; that increase was achieved in only two, and profits in 1956 were more than double those of 1955. Most important of all, perhaps, the company was no longer largely dependent on the railroads: 67 per cent of its sales were to other industries.

Companies do not, of course, face such drastic situations every year, or even every five years. Ordinarily the gap between objectives and possibilities can be closed or narrowed by less far-reaching moves.

Increasing return on assets

At one large company, for example, division managers develop their own plans to raise return on the assets they are using. The workbook supplied to them by the corporation points out that there are three possible ways of increasing that return: (1) increasing the sales volume, (2) increasing profits on sales, and (3) minimizing assets through better turnover of inventory.

Plans for increasing sales volume cover such things as product improvement, price modification, new products, improvements in delivery and service, improvements in distribution, sales training, improved advertising and sales promotion, and expansion of production capacity.

The effect on the ratio of income to assets is then calculated, taking into account any increase in assets necessitated by the programs to increase sales volume. Then the remaining gap between planned results and possibilities is considered.

The next attack is through programs designed to increase the profit margin on sales. A price increase might have a place here, but more commonly the effort will be to reduce costs. If a gap still remains, attention will be given to minimizing assets by pruning less profitable products from the line, reducing inventories, extending use of progress payments, and similar programs. Following are examples of how division managers might proceed.

Division A has a substandard return on assets. The manager sees that his asset turnover is good in comparison with that of other divisions, but his profit margin, only 6 per cent, is below the average. He is particularly impressed by the fact that division K, which has very similar characteristics, produces a return better than the company standard, despite a less favorable rate of asset turnover. He therefore decides to concentrate on improving his profit margin by attacking costs while endeavoring to maintain his asset turnover at its present favorable rate. His goal is to equal division K's profit margin on sales (12 per cent). This, in conjunction with his own rate of asset turnover, will produce a profit on investment higher than that of division K.

The manager of division J, which also has a substandard profit return, compares his division's performance with that of division L. He knows that it is essentially a similar type of operation and that the two divisions have almost identical profit margins. However, his overall result is depressed by a lower asset turnover (at the rate of 1.00 compared to 1.60 for division L). By further analysis, he finds that this deficiency stems almost entirely from the relative inventory turnovers of the two divisions. This leads him into a comprehensive study of inventory levels and controls. From this he concludes that his inventory excess is primarily the result of (1) a number of low-profit items, which in the aggregate constitute a considerable portion of his finished product inventory but a very small percentage of his sales; and (2) a number of profitable but relatively slow-moving items which are stocked in all his field locations.

As a result, he sets the long-range goals of an increase in asset turnover from 1.00 to 1.25 and a small increase in profit margin: from 16 to 17 per cent. If these are achieved, it will put his division well over the asset return standard and well over the current performance of division L. He plans to attain the improvement in asset turnover by increasing the inventory turnover, by weeding from his product lines the items that are spoiling his profit return, and by consolidating field stocks of slow-selling items.

These two examples illustrate some of the possibilities that exist for closing the gap, and there are many others. For example, sales efforts can be concentrated on the items that bring the widest profit margins. Inventories of raw material can be reduced by closer scheduling of production to ensure that material comes in the door only as it is needed and moves almost immediately to the production floor. Efforts can also be made to penetrate new markets.

Value analysis   One technique for increasing profit margins is value analysis, and many companies practice it regularly. Each material that goes into each component is scrutinized, each operation performed on it is considered—all with a view to determining what can be done to reduce the costs of making the product without lessening its salability. Perhaps the use of cheaper material for some of the components will in no way lessen performance, durability, or appearance. Perhaps a slight change in design that will not decrease the value in the eyes of the customer will make it possible to eliminate some of the operations.

New equipment may make it possible to get more production with less labor. While this will raise the investment factor, it may reduce expenses enough to increase the rate of return substantially, if not this year, at least in the years ahead.

Cutting out the fat   Finally, a company may tighten up all along the line by instituting a general cost reduction program to cut out the fat—the overgenerous expense accounts, the superfluous employees, and the general waste. It might be supposed that companies would be watching these things right along and would never allow waste to develop. Most companies try to, but when returns are good, many tend to become lax about cost saving. In fact, if a market is expanding and the economy is on the up and up, the manager may be better advised to spend his time and energy developing ways of taking advantage of the opportunities to increase revenue rather than concentrating on cost reduction.

At any rate, when harsh conditions drive them to it, most companies find that they can cut costs. Some do it rather blindly through, say, a 10 or 20 per cent cut in departmental budgets across the board—a system that is likely to do more harm than good. Not only may it produce a drop in revenue as well as in costs; it may encourage managers to pad their budgets and payrolls in good times in order that they may not find their operations completely hamstrung in poor ones. Selective cuts take longer but are likely to be more profitable. One of the advantages of planning is that it encourages the use of good judgment in cost cutting.

Despite the many possibilities for bringing performance closer to expectations, fulfillment of corporate plans is not always possible. If it were, everyone could get rich. A company can plan, for example, to increase its share of the market, take sound steps to achieve that goal and yet fall short. (There have been instances in which the market share plans of the various companies in an industry added up to more than 100 per cent.) Or it can plan for and achieve lower costs in some operations only to find that a rise in material or labor costs has more than offset the reduction. But the company that sets its goals in advance, plans definite steps for reaching them, and adapts itself to changing conditions has far more chance of progress than the one that operates haphazardly.

OTHER TYPES OF PLANNING

Perhaps the oldest type of formal planning is production planning, which became necessary as soon as there was any great amount of specialization. If one group of workers is making component A, another group is making component B, and a third is producing component C, it is obvious that some type of planning is required to get the components to the final assembly point at the same time so that the end product can be put together without delay.

In the case of modern products, the components may run into the hundreds, even into the thousands, and more than one operation may have to be performed on each of them. Further, there will probably be subassemblies as well as the final assembly. It is obvious that the plans cannot be carried in anyone's head and must be written out in advance. The complexity of modern production planning is illustrated by the following account of the way one producer of industrial trucks puts a new model into production.

When the new model is in the development stage, the estimating group reviews the prints of components and assemblies to determine costs. It checks with the purchasing department on the cost and availability of the material, builds up labor estimates based on similar jobs currently in the shop, and determines whether any new equipment will be needed. It may also recommend alternatives to development engineering so that excessive or nonprofitable capital investments will not become mandatory. The completed estimates of material, labor, and overhead permit the sales department to determine the market position of the new product and its value to the company.

Assuming the estimates are favorable, design engineering prints are released to the methods section, which reviews them to determine the compatibility of the new product with existing tools, tolerances, and methods, and may suggest that the design engineers make changes that will permit lower costs.

When the final design is decided upon, the methods section prepares the operation sheets, which indicate not only the sequence of operations by machine type, but also the travel sequence through one to four manufacturing departments. The section also requests the tools needed and issues assembly line change notices to define the line location of parts and assembly operations.

The tool design section produces drawings of the tools and gauges required, and in some instances it must also design test stands, welding fixtures, trunions, and machines. Then it issues orders to the toolroom showing the due dates.

Toolroom supervision logs the orders and requisitions the materials. When tooling is complete, the new tool number is added to the operation sheets.

Finally, the plant engineer's office asks production control to write the orders for a tool tryout run, and if this is satisfactory, the product is officially released to production and production control.[17]

Planning a new plant

Planning a new plant involves much more than merely deciding on a location and size and turning the job over to an architect with instructions about the general features to be included. Plants are built around processes, and the

[17] From O. B. Patton, "The Broad Responsibilities of Plant Engineering," *Techniques of Plant Maintenance and Engineering,* Clapp & Poliak, Inc., New York, 1958, pp. 126–127.

company itself must decide on the best possible process flow before it can give the architect the directions. This is often a long process, and sometimes three-dimensional models of equipment are used so that different types of flow can be tried out.

Coincidentally with the construction, the company must begin planning for start-up, which—especially in automated industries—involves much more than getting in the requisite number of employees and throwing a switch. In fact, where a large amount of equipment is interrelated, all components may be almost perfectly reliable and yet the complete system may have only a 45 per cent chance of operating as expected.

Figure 17 shows this in graph form. Components are 99.9 per cent reliable (upper line); yet if there are 300 in a single system, the system itself will have an availability of only around 75 per cent, and if it includes 1,000 components, its availability will be only 45 per cent. If the average component availability is only 99.5 per cent, a system with 1,000 components has practically no chance of operating. (This is why missiles, which are dependent on systems with a great many interrelated components, so often fail to rise as expected.)

Start-up planning at Du Pont, for example, begins many months before the expected completion of a plant. For example, some 231 man-months of preparation are required merely for one phase of the start-up: that handled by the works engineering department. Figure 18 shows the number of people who work on this phase and the times at which the various activities and plans must be started; Table 1, some of the tasks.

Marketing planning

One of the first decisions to be made in the development of a marketing plan for a new company or a new product, or when a complete overhaul of the

FIGURE 17   System start-up availability as a function of component reliability and number of components. (From J. C. Jessen, Du Pont Company.)

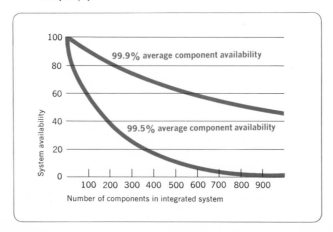

Pre-start-up function	1959 Nov.	Dec.	1960 Jan.	Feb.	Mar.	Apr.	May	Post-start-up function
Program coordinator	Program coordination (Nov–May)							Works Engineer
	Organization	Design liaison					Organization	
Training coordinator	Work plan—general mechanical training		Construction liaison					Maintenance supervisor
			General mechanical—selecting and upgrading procedures			Hiring—		
Spare-parts coordinator	Spare-parts plan	Preventive maint. plan	Spare parts analysis					Maintenance area supervisor —mechanical
		Shop and yard equipment rev.	Shop and yard equipment inspection					
Instructor		Port-able tools	G-2-b training preparation					Foreman—mechanical
			Overhaul procedures					
Instructor			Port-able tools	Training preparation				Foreman—mechanical
				Overhaul procedures				
Instructor			Training preparation	Port-able tools	Training preparation			Foreman—mechanical
					Overhaul procedures			
Engineer			Stores procedures	Administrative procedures				Planning and scheduling engineer
				Preventive maintenance schedules				
Engineer		Design liaison						Project engineer
		Project procedures and plant "how"			Construction liaison			
Engineer			Supervisory development	Instructor training	Spare-parts analysis			Engineer—design
Engineer								Engineer—design
Engineer					Overhaul procedures			Engineer—design

FIGURE 18   New plant—76 maintenance wage roll and 16 supervision— technical. Manpower schedule—works engineering. (From J. C. Jessen, Du Pont Company.)

existing marketing program is contemplated, is selection of the channels of distribution to be used. In part, the nature of the product will dictate the answer, but a good deal of leeway for choice remains.

A company may, for example, dispense with a sales force of its own and utilize what are known as manufacturer's agents. These are independent salesmen who maintain their own offices and sometimes sales forces of their own, and generally handle the products of more than one manufacturer, though not those of competing producers. Thus a manufacturer's agent who is selling pipe of various kinds to the chemical industry might take on a line of electronic instruments for the same industry, but he could not agree to sell other brands of pipe.

TABLE 1   PREMAINTENANCE PLANNING   (Based on a fairly complex plant of approximately $20 million investment)

Maintenance items	Approximate man-months required
1 Establish reference files	2
2 Select spare parts and extra machinery	12
3 Standardize packing and gaskets	1
4 Establish maintenance stores procedure	4
5 Establish maintenance organization requirements	1
6 Select supervisors	1
7 Supervisor orientation	1
8 Prepare job and position descriptions	2
9 Establish mechanics' selection and progression plan	1
10 General mechanic training	30
11 Control mechanic training	14
12 Special training programs	1
13 Welder qualification	1
14 Project procedures and plant "how" preparation	1
15 Set up maintenance systems	4
16 Prepare overhaul procedures	6
17 Establish preventive maintenance schedules	4
18 Specify lubrication equipment, frequencies, and routes	1
19 Check use of tabulating equipment	1
20 Special safety instructions	1
21 Program coordination	3
Power	
1 Power operating instructions	5
2 Power orientation program	3
3 Supervisory development	2
Total	102

Manufacturer's agents work on straight commissions, which must be high enough to enable them to pay their business expenses and still make a living. Since they are paid only for what they actually sell, they often afford an economical way of starting sales in a new section of the country or abroad. By assigning the selling to them, a company can get distribution in the new area without incurring the expense of setting up a sales force and opening branch offices before it knows what it can expect in the way of return. A common way of starting export sales, in fact, is to send someone abroad to appoint agents— already in business and selling to the market the company is seeking.

In most cases, however, companies prefer to have their own sales forces for domestic distribution since an agent, who is likely to be selling several lines, may not devote as much effort to pushing any one company's products as its own sales force will.

(The insurance industry is an exception here. All stock insurance companies sell through agents who work on the same basis as manufacturer's agents and sometimes even handle competing lines. Mutual insurance companies—that is, those that are owned by their policyholders as a mutual savings bank is owned by its depositors—often employ regular sales forces of their own.)

When a company has its own sales force, there are three main channels of distribution open to it. It may sell:

1. Directly to the users of the product.
2. To retailers, who will sell to the users.
3. To wholesalers, or jobbers, who will sell to retailers, who will sell directly to users. "Wholesaler" and "jobber" are now practically synonymous terms, although there was originally a distinction in that the jobber was one who dealt in odd lots.

Many companies will, of course, use more than one of these channels of distribution, even for the same product.

Selling directly to the user   While door-to-door selling of consumer products is not uncommon (one vacuum cleaner company uses this method exclusively), a manufacturer's sales force is more likely to sell directly to the user only if the products are industrial items, that is, products intended for use in industry rather than for use by individuals. The reason for this is simple: A company usually makes larger purchases than an individual does, which means that more money can be spent to get a single order. It is worth the company's while to have a salaried salesman spend hours, or even several days, getting a single order if the order and subsequent repeat orders will total hundreds or thousands of dollars. But if purchases by a single user are likely to be small, the manufacturer must channel the product to the retail level, where the customer comes to the seller rather than vice versa. In the retail store, the sale can be completed with relative speed, often in the space of a few minutes. The manufacturer's salesmen can then spend their time selling to wholesalers and retailers, who are buying for many individual consumers.

Wholesalers   Wholesalers are of many different types. Some of them merely take title to the merchandise and have it shipped directly from the manufacturer's plant; others buy it and keep it on their own premises. Some sell to retailers, others directly to large users of the product: companies, institutions, and so on. Some do both.

Wholesalers differ from manufacturer's agents in that they themselves actually buy the merchandise and are stuck with what they cannot sell. The manufacturer's agent, on the other hand, is at no point the owner of the wares he peddles, and need not take the risk of investing money in purchases.

Like the theater, wholesaling is often reported to be a dying industry, and again, like the theater, it manages to survive long after its imminent demise has been reported. Wholesaling has been criticized as an economic waste. The wholesaler adds nothing tangible to the value of the product and, unlike the retailer, does not provide obvious convenience for the ultimate consumer. Yet his costs and his profits go into the retail price, making it that much higher. He is one of the middlemen who are so often charged with responsibility for high prices.

It may be that in some industries and at some times the wholesaler has been guilty as charged. However, in most cases, little would be saved by eliminating him. Neither manufacturers nor retailers would deal with whole-salers unless they found an advantage in doing so.

For example, take the wholesaler who carries a stock on his premises. If he did not exist, the manufacturer would have to sell directly to the retailers—that is, to a larger group—and would need a larger sales force. If he did not expect the retailers to wait for their orders, he would have to open more warehouses around the country. Both of these courses of action would add to his cost. If he could not arrange for quick delivery, the retailer would have to carry a larger inventory because he often needs replacements in a hurry.

But what of the wholesaler who does not carry stock on his premises? He, too, may perform a valuable service that would have to be performed some-where in any case. Here, for example, is a lumber wholesaler who buys stock at mills in the West and South and maintains a sales force selling to manu-facturers of wood products in the East. If he did not exist, the lumber mills would have to maintain traveling sales forces of their own. As it is, the mills inform the wholesaler of the stocks they will have available, and he instructs his sales force, which knows immediately which customers will be interested. Then the lumber is shipped directly to the customer.

This wholesaler can get stuck, and stuck badly, if the lumber arrives in the East unsold because he will have to pay the railroads demurrage for using their freight cars as storage bins. Sometimes, in fact, lumber is already speeding across the continent before he has a buyer. But he depends on his proximity to the markets and his consequent knowledge of where to sell to prevent these incidents from occurring too often. Also, since he deals with a large number of mills and customers, he is able to effect certain economies in transportation by combining less-than-carload lots (lcl) into full carloads and so reducing the freight.

Retailers   Where a consumer product is concerned, the retail stores in which it is available are of the utmost importance. No consumer product can enjoy a large sale unless it gets into the stores that have a large number of customers for a product of its type. Sometimes the manufacturer finds it necessary to give the retailer an exclusive right to sell the product in a given territory in order to be sure he carries it. There have even been cases where retailers have found it possible to pressure manufacturers into providing them with expensive fixtures for their stores—agreeing, in return, only to carry the product.

The matter of a strong dealer organization is, in fact, of great concern to all marketing executives who do not sell directly to users, and what makes for strength in the dealer organization will differ with different products.

For example, a high-priced product is not likely to do well if it is sold through outlets that deal mainly in cheaper merchandise—the public may get the impression that it is merely low-quality merchandise at a high price. But a simple high-volume product like cigarettes needs all the retail outlets it can get.

There is, however, another consideration here. The more retail outlets the sales force must sell, the larger it must be, and this of course adds to the cost of selling. And since retailing outlets are constantly changing, the marketing manager must watch the trends closely so that he can deploy his forces to the best advantage.

Such questions as the following must be answered:

Are shopping centers likely to be more important than the traditional downtown retailing district?

What of supermarkets? There is no question that they afford a market worth cultivating for manufacturers of food items. But what of the other products they are adding? Such things as sheets and towels and drugs are now sold in many supermarkets.

Variety stores (originally typified by the five-and-ten-cent stores) have also greatly broadened their lines, and are selling not simply notions and other minor merchandise but furniture, hardware, and clothing.

Most observers believe this mixing of merchandise in the same outlet will continue and accelerate, but there is also a possibility that it will reverse itself in some lines. One example of this is the drug field: the drugstores were the original mix-masters in the retail field, and most continue to sell a wide variety of merchandise wholly unrelated to drugs. But at the same time, a number of drugstores have gone back to concentrating on drugs and medical supplies, even throwing out their soda fountains.

Marketing planning must also include dividing the country (or section of the country if the company does not sell nationwide) into territories that can be handled by a single salesman and setting quotas for each territory. (The decisions made here will depend on the market potential of the territories and the quotas may be changed almost every year.)

Some companies—a good many, in fact, the Sales Executives Club found in a survey—do no formal planning. The sales manager merely judges by past experience. But formal planning, based on market research, can take much of the guesswork out of the decisions. For example, if the company is selling equipment to the papermaking industry, it can ascertain the number of paper mills in the territory, their size, and the age of their equipment—all of which will indicate how much potential the territory possesses. Or suppose a firm is selling an expensive consumer product. If it knows the number of people in various income brackets in each territory and the number of retail outlets that carry merchandise of this type, it can pretty well gauge the potential.

Still another phase of marketing that must be carefully planned is the compensation of the salesmen, and the plan adopted must be tailored to the objectives set. Often, for example, the company wants certain products pushed more than others, and in that case it may want to pay a higher rate of commission on them. Or it may want the salesmen to do missionary work that will not result in immediate sales, and it cannot expect them to take much interest in doing so if it pays them on a straight commission basis. Sometimes, in the case of highly technical products, more than one salesman may have to work on a sale, and the division of the commission must be carefully planned.

Warehousing is another phase of marketing. In order to make quick delivery, the company must often store products in warehouses around the country, and the location of these will affect the speed with which it can serve its customers.

Other things covered by marketing planning include advertising campaigns (themes, media, tie-ins with local distributors), sales training, sales presentations, promotion, and many others. If a company has a formal plan, it can ensure that all phases of its campaign supplement and support each other.

WHY PLANNING MAY FAIL

Sometimes a company decides to engage in long-range planning but finds that no one bothers to do much of it, or if the plans are actually formulated, company activities bear little or no relationship to them. Perhaps the main reason why this happens is that the chief executive is not really interested in the planning process; he asks his subordinates to develop strategic plans but never checks to see that they have done so or does not appraise the plans carefully.

However, even when the chief is really interested, many staff planners fail to produce the results expected of them and eventually lose their positions. The reasons for this appear to be these:

1. *The planner lacks knowledge of the company.* This is particularly true of planners brought in from the outside. Even though the planner possesses considerable analytical skill and good judgment, he is handicapped by lack of familiarity with the company and with the man for whom the planning has to be done. It is often easier to have someone who knows the company acquire planning skills than to have an outsider acquire the necessary knowledge of the corporation.

2. *He takes an unrealistic approach.* Many planners ask operating men for information that is unavailable, time-consuming to get, or not worth having. They may demand projections so far into the future that any semblance to reality disappears. This situation may so discourage the line executives with the planning process that they will tend to pluck estimates out of the air. To avoid this, the planner should concentrate on the really vital data and permit the line to present them in simple and approximate form. From the most relevant facts, the planner can gradually work toward more comprehensive data.

3. *He has a tendency to follow rather than lead.* Many planners take a passive role. They lay out a scheme for obtaining the information needed and then sit back while the functional and divisional heads struggle to get it.

The planner should be an enthusiast, a teacher, a coordinator, and when differences arise, a mediator. Ultimately he will be judged by the results of his planning rather than by the logic of his presentation or the beauty of his charts. In keeping with their passive role, many planners neglect to follow up, to prod, to correct, and to improve execution, and many lack the subtlety to do so without assuming an authority they do not have. Getting results is difficult, for the planner cannot continually appeal to the chief executive for help in enforcing procedures. Although such appeals may be necessary at times, the planner's aim must be to inspire others to want to plan and to reach the goals set by the plans.

4. *He may have a tendency to produce alibis rather than to correct mistakes.* When plans are unfulfilled, the natural reaction of the planner may be to resort to self-justification and criticism of others rather than to offer constructive suggestions. A good planner is always able to pull additional rabbits out of his hat in a negative situation, but at the same time, he must never arouse hopes that cannot be fulfilled.

5. *He takes a short-run view.* Many planners try to achieve too much too soon. This leads to hasty collection and analysis of data, to undue pressure for quick results, and to expedient measures rather than correct ones.

OVERCOMING RESISTANCE TO PLANNING

Of course, some planners have difficulty because many of the division and department heads resist the whole idea. They do not like to commit themselves to reaching definite goals within a specified period of time. They prefer the calm, comfortable situation that may have existed in the absence of controls.

The planner cannot, by himself, overcome widespread resistance of this sort; he needs the help of top management. But he can reduce the resistance by showing that the goals are realistic and that managers will not be held accountable for meeting them if an unexpected situation makes attainment of them impossible.

Then there are executives who feel they are too busy handling day-to-day activities to take time out for consideration of fundamental problems. They must be convinced that solutions, or even partial solutions, to long-term problems will help to cut down their day-to-day problems and so save time.

Other objections come from executives who feel that it is impossible to forecast the future in their industry or in their particular field. The answer here is that informal forecasts based on the information available are better than nothing and can be modified and added to as more information becomes available. Although intuition may play a part in management success, it is far better to base decisions on such facts as may be available.

Some resistance to planning may arise because of too many changes in the objectives and the constituent parts of a plan. A temporary setback or sudden bad news may make for panic at the top; then projects that have already been approved may be suddenly dropped or curtailed. In that case, the confusion may be worse than it would be if there were no plan at all.

Although the worst of all plans is the completely inflexible one, a plan that is frequently changed in a drastic way is almost as bad. If planning is realistic in the first place, there should be no need, barring major catastrophes, for earthshaking changes.

Perhaps the most serious of all resistance may arise because of lack of understanding. This can be largely prevented by complete explanations and discussions before the planning is introduced. If there is a sudden announcement that executives are to begin at once to plan for five or ten years ahead, there is almost sure to be resistance. It should always be remembered that in planning it is the long-range results that count, and it is well worthwhile for both the chief executive and the staff planners to take the time necessary to explain the process thoroughly.

SUMMARY

Formal planning may be divided into two broad categories: strategic planning and functional planning. The first type covers the objectives the company expects to attain in the years ahead and the means it will use to meet them. Functional plans, on the other hand, are plans designed to increase efficiency, often only the efficiency of one particular function.

In strategic planning for the corporation as a whole, the first basic requisite is a reasonably accurate forecast of the state of the economy in the years covered by the plan. A number of techniques useful in forecasting the course of the economy have been developed, but a great deal of judgment is still needed to interpret the figures.

The key factor in all corporate planning is the sales forecast, for this determines the revenue that will be available. Data on the size of the total market are very important in this and are available from many sources.

Forecasts of the company's share of the total market may be based on its share in the past, on its advantages over competitors, and on any further advantages it can gain by increasing its sales force or its advertising or by improving its products.

Company overall plans are generally made with the help of groups skilled in economics, marketing research, and similar fields. Usually these are staff groups, which suggest, counsel, and work out possibilities, whereas the actual decisions are made by line executives. It is possible to have the planning groups work only with and for the chief executive, but many companies believe that it is better to allow the heads of departments and divisions to make their own plans, with only such modification at higher levels as is necessary to ensure that the plans are feasible and desirable from the viewpoint of the company as a whole.

Sometimes, of course, there is a gap between the revenue the company believes it should achieve and the revenue it is likely to attain in the light of the economic forecasts and the trends in its sales. In that case, it must find some means of bridging the gap between the two. The methods used may include anything from entering an entirely new field to simply making an effort to cut costs.

Plans may be expressed in many ways, but generally they will include budgets and schedules of many types.

Review Questions

1. Why is corporate planning more necessary now than in the past? How does functional planning differ from strategic planning?
2. What are some of the major advantages of formal planning?
3. If a company's fixed expenses are $10,000 and it spends $10 for labor and material for each unit it produces, how many units would it have to sell at $20 a piece to break even? Draw the chart.
4. Why is extrapolation often an inadequate means of forecasting?
5. What is the lead and lag method? What are some of the leading factors?
6. Of what value is the multiple (building-block) analysis? On what does the reliability of its forecasts depend?
7. What do statistics on population, income, and so on, tell about possible sales?
8. What is motivation research?
9. What is a capital budget? An expense budget? A cash budget? Why is cash flow important?
10. What is arrow diagramming?
11. What are some of the problems that lead to resistance and failure in planning? What steps can the planner take to help prevent them?

Case Study One / The Italian Plastics Plant

In view of a construction boom in Italy and the current popularity of plastics in the building materials field, your company has asked you to investigate the possibilities of putting up a plant there for the production of corrugated plastic sheets.

1. What facts would you endeavor to ascertain before making recommendations?
2. Suppose it is decided that the plant will make money. What steps would you take in setting up a plan for construction of it and for getting production and sales under way?

Case Study Two / The ABC Company's New Plant*

ABC Company was organized in 1952 to produce electronic equipment for missiles and space vehicles, and its present plant is located on the West Coast. Now it has developed an important new consumer product: a portable color television set that shows pictures in three dimensions.

Top management has decided: "The new plant should be separated geographically and administratively from West Coast headquarters at or near a prospective market center and close enough to a city, large or small, that will offer cultural and educational advantages for an eventual large staff of administrative and professional personnel. The plant will house 250 to 500 production people initially, but must lend itself to expansion to several times that size.

"At first, functions will be mainly research and development, assembly, test, and sales. Most of the parts, which will be of metal and plastics, will be purchased from outside in the beginning, but it must be possible to add integrated manufacturing operations later. Points to be taken into account include raw material supplies, transportation, and the need to dispose of effluents from both plating and chemical operations.

"About 50 staff men and supervisors will be transferred from headquarters, but the majority of the production people will be obtained through local recruiting. Additional professional people will be obtained through local and national recruiting.

"It is possible that an existing building will serve, but there must be no undue compromising. Perhaps an existing building can be used to train local production people while the plant is being built.

"While the company is financially able to provide all the facilities itself, it would welcome local assistance that would help it maintain a good cash position. But it is not looking for unhealthy short-range inducements. We would look favorably on the leasing of property, plants, and certain equipment in order to put more money into wages and salaries."

Your boss, who is in charge of picking a plant location, sends you to two or three towns in different states to get the facts on which to base a decision.

1.   What facts would you seek to ascertain?
2.   Where would you get them?
3.   Whom would you talk to?

Selected Readings

Corporate Strategy, H. Igor Ansoff, McGraw-Hill Book Company, New York, 1965. Presents an overall framework and a methodology for the formulation

* Adapted from *Industrial Building*, Clapp & Poliak, Inc., New York, 1961, vol. I, p. 59.

of product and market strategy and appraisal of the firm, plus an action program.

Sales Control by Quantitative Methods, R. Parker Eastwood, Columbia University Press, New York, 1940. A very systematic and practical analysis of forecasting techniques. A classic in its field.

Managerial Long-range Planning, George A. Steiner (ed.), McGraw-Hill Book Company, New York, 1963. A collection of case histories of corporate planning by large companies and some government agencies, with two analytical chapters by the editor.

Strategic Planning, Franklin H. Sweet, Bureau of Business Research, University of Texas, Austin, Texas, 1964. A theoretical assessment of the concept of strategic planning as a guide to a balanced combination of short-range and long-range planning efforts.

Long-range Planning, Warren E. Kirby, Prentice-Hall, Inc., Englewood Cliffs, N.J., 1966. Examines the entire process of long-range planning activity. Also considers the problems of matching short-term results with long-term plans.

"A Program of Research in Business Planning," H. Igor Ansoff and Richard C. Brandenburg, *Management Science,* February, 1967, pp. B219–239. A detailed and technical analysis of planning as a science.

Planning and Problem Solving in Marketing, Wroe Alderson and Paul E. Green, Richard D. Irwin, Inc., Homewood, Ill., 1964. A conceptual framework for planning, forecasting, and decision making in marketing.

Marketing Research: A Management Overview, Evelyn Konrad and Rod Erickson (eds.), American Management Association, New York, 1966. Seventeen articles on significant areas of marketing research by authorities in the field.

17

STAFFING

Personalities present unlimited manifoldness of talents and abilities . . . it necessarily follows that some are more, some less, fit for the particular economic task. In view of the far-reaching division of labor in our modern economic life, it is impossible to avoid the question how we can select fit personalities and reject the unfit ones.
Hugo Münsterberg: *Psychology and Industrial Efficiency*

17 It is important to have a good organization structure, but it is still more important to fill the jobs with the right people. A company may be successful with an organization structure that is very far from the best, but it will never be able to get off the ground if the people who run it and those who do the actual work are incapable.

Keeping the jobs filled with the right people is the staffing phase of the management job, and it includes several subfunctions:

1. Recruitment, or getting applicants for the jobs as they open up
2. Selection of the best qualified from those who seek the jobs
3. Transfers and promotions
4. Training those who need further instruction to perform their work effectively or to qualify for promotion

To these might be added administration of compensation plans since it is an important factor in both getting and holding qualified people. However, since it is a specialty in itself, it is discussed in a separate chapter (Chapter 18).

In his POSDCORB analysis described in Chapter 1, Luther Gulick includes "maintaining favorable conditions of work."[1] But favorable conditions of work depend so largely on the type of direction provided that this phase of the subject is discussed under that heading (Chapter 19).

Staffing is, as Gulick points out, part of the personnel function, but only certain phases of it commonly come under the personnel department. Every manager, up to the president of the company, must handle some phases of staffing, even though personnel may provide at least technical help in every case.

The extent to which personnel handles recruitment varies among companies, but in almost all large ones the department will recruit all candidates for rank-and-file jobs, plant or office, and for some of the lower and middle management jobs as well. As one goes up the line, the line managers are likely to take on more of the recruitment task.

Again, the personnel department seldom makes the final decision on selection, except in cases where large numbers of people must be hired at one time and the line managers would not have the time to interview them all. More commonly, even in the case of rank-and-file employees, it merely screens the applicants and picks out a few whom it considers the most promising. Then the immediate supervisors make a choice among these few.

Most personnel managers are quite content with this state of affairs. They view their departments as staff departments that exist to provide service to the line and not to assume any part of line management's responsibility. They realize that the line managers who are responsible for output must have some say in the choice of their own subordinates.

What is a sore point with many personnel managers, however, is that they

[1] "Notes on the Theory of Organization," in Luther Gulick and Lyndall Urwick (eds.), *Papers on the Science of Administration*, Institute of Public Administration, New York, 1937, p. 13.

are sometimes excluded both from recruitment and from selection when higher management jobs are involved. At the vice-presidential or department head level, the line boss may seek out the candidates and make his own selection without ever informing the personnel manager at all.

This situation is less common than it used to be, particularly in companies where the personnel manager has attained vice-presidential status, and even in companies where his judgment in the matter is given no weight, he may be asked to provide guides in the form of psychological test results.

Nevertheless, it may be said that the higher the position to be staffed, the less the part the personnel department is likely to take in staffing it. This is shown by the experience of a firm which conducts job campaigns for executives, sending out perhaps 150 letters for each of its clients. The letters are addressed to company presidents, and if the chief executive is interested in a man, he will frequently write or telephone himself. When the letter is passed down to the personnel department, it is generally only for the purpose of having someone write a polite rejection.

One reason for this may be the reluctance of men who have held or are holding high positions to go through the red tape that an application to the personnel department may entail. They may feel humiliated by being asked to fill out a lengthy application, submit to a preliminary screening interview by someone whose status may be little higher than that of a clerk, and perhaps wait some time even for that much. They may also feel that even the higher members of the personnel department know little about the actual content of higher line management jobs and that it will, therefore, be almost impossible for a candidate to make a real case for himself.

Another reason may be that to some extent personnel managers and top managers do not see eye to eye on the qualifications needed for management on the higher levels. In a survey conducted by *Fortune* magazine,[2] the majority of the company presidents questioned stressed the need for the old entrepreneurial qualities of initiative, aggressiveness, and so on. Personnel managers, on the other hand, tended to believe that the manager of today is primarily an administrator whose main job is to keep things running smoothly.

Or it could be that top management is inconsistent. "If our procedures are good for selecting members of the rank and file and lower management, why wouldn't they be equally successful in the selection of higher managers?" personnel managers ask. Perhaps this is a valid point, and the reason why many top managers continue to ignore it may be mainly habit. At any rate, the top managers are somewhat inconsistent in that they allow personnel departments a major say in selecting *potential* managers—the management trainees and others from whom they hope the company's future top men will come—but pay less attention to personnel procedures when they hire men from outside for high-echelon jobs.

In transfers and promotions, the role of the personnel department is some-

2 See William H. Whyte, Jr., *The Organization Man*, Simon and Schuster, Inc., New York, 1956, pp. 133–136.

what similar to that it plays in recruitment and selection. It has great influence in the transfer of rank-and-file employees and in their promotion to lower management levels, less when higher jobs are in question. But in nearly all cases it keeps records to help the line managers decide on these questions and advises them on the selection as well.

If a company has a training director, he will be a member of the personnel department, whether the training is designed for rank-and-file employees or for managers. While personnel department people seldom do the actual teaching, except in cases where their own specialty is involved (e.g., training in human or union relations), they organize and administer the programs. Sometimes this is because line management has asked them to provide training; sometimes it is because they see a need, develop a program, and persuade top management to accept it. This is true whether the training is for rank-and-file employees or for managers.

But every manager trains his subordinates himself, whether he is conscious of doing so or not. His example, the instructions he gives, the work he assigns to each man, the actions and attitudes he praises or blames—all help to train those under him. If he is a good manager, these will help to make his subordinates more proficient, and he will probably go further and attempt to enlarge their understanding by explanations and suggestions that go beyond the directions needed to complete the immediate tasks at hand.

RECRUITMENT

Recruiting may mean bringing in a few candidates for a single position or corralling hundreds or thousands for a major expansion. In any large company it is likely to be a continuing job since positions are constantly opening up as employees leave, retire, or die.

Where recruitment is for rank-and-file jobs or positions in the lower management ranks, the department that needs new workers will usually send the personnel department a job requisition stating the requirements of the job and covering such matters as the amount of education needed, the preferred age bracket, and the experience required.

Possible sources of candidates include applications already on file, newspaper advertisements, employment agencies, schools. If unemployment in the area is heavy, there may be a continual stream of applicants appearing every day; if the labor supply is tight, the company may have to go outside its own area to find enough people. In the late 1940s and early 1950s, for example, the automobile companies recruited widely among agricultural workers in the South. Sometimes employees already on the payroll are offered prizes or bonuses for bringing in friends who meet the company's requirements and stay with it for a given period.

College recruitment is now a recognized function of almost every large company's personnel department, and since World War II there has been heavy competition in the field, particularly for engineers. Some companies send recruiters to scores of universities and technical colleges armed with glowing brochures. Recruitment of technical personnel may also be carried on at engineering society meetings.

Recruiting of key executives, experienced men for important jobs, is a different proposition, and it is not always turned over to the personnel department, though generally the applicants will be tested and screened by that department at some stage in the hiring process.

Some companies say that all such positions are filled by promotion from within, but many of them find it necessary to go outside their own organizations at times, and there is no standard procedure in this case. Some will use such conventional means as newspaper advertisements and employment agencies. In others, top executives will merely inquire among their acquaintances or appoint someone whom they already know.

Management consultants may be asked for recommendations, and some of these (known as "executive recruiters") specialize in filling executive positions for a fee (a percentage of the first year's salary) charged to the company rather than to the successful candidate. These consulting companies institute what is known as an "executive search," which consists of combing applications they already have on file and attempting to pry qualified executives from other jobs. One technique is to write to a number of likely prospects asking whether they know of someone who would be qualified—in the hope that some of them will reply, "Why, I'd be interested in it myself."

SELECTION

Given two or more candidates for a job, there is no absolutely sure way of selecting the best one. Whether the position is that of sweeper or vice-president, the only tools available are examination of the candidate's past record, tests of actual performance in a trial situation (frequently not possible), psychological tests of various kinds, and the interview. These methods are not infallible, either separately or together.

Past records

Practically every company uses an application blank on which applicants are asked to list their education and past experience. Frequently also, the forms are designed to elicit information that will give clues to personality. For example, some psychologists have postulated that personality is, in part, dependent on the place in the family—the oldest of the children, the youngest, or in the middle—and a question on this may find a place in the blank. Other companies ask questions about hobbies, financial condition, occupations of parents and brothers and sisters, and how much other members of the family are earning. One form even inquired: "Have you any distinguished ancestors?"

Even so, for higher jobs, the application blank provides insufficient information on the past record. Commonly, therefore, if the candidate is seeking an executive or technical job, he will supplement this with a résumé of his education and experience that will devote more space to the things he has actually done in each job and the results. On a résumé, a salesman or sales manager can set down the increases in volume he has achieved and explain exactly what he did to bring about the improvement; a research man can note his discoveries and their effect on company prosperity; a production man can list the ways in which he reduced costs. Seldom does a printed application blank afford enough space for these things, and a job title does not necessarily indicate the extent of the responsibility.

On both the application blank and the résumé, the candidate will naturally try to put his best foot forward. And on the résumé especially he may claim credit for results that actually had little to do with his own performance. A sales manager may have achieved a remarkable record of volume increases because his company had a new product that practically sold itself, or because demand was rising so quickly that he could scarcely help getting a larger volume. A top manager's company may have prospered mightily during his tenure because of rising demand or the disappearance of a competitor, or because the company was just beginning to enjoy the fruits of hard spadework by his predecessor.

Checking with past employers is, of course, quite usual, but the man's former superior may not himself be aware of the part circumstances played in the subordinate's success. Further, most men are reluctant to spoil another man's chances and will give the applicant the benefit of the doubt if any exists. On the other hand, a man may be angry at his former subordinate for reasons that really have nothing to do with his performance or qualifications and so give him less credit than he deserves. A few superiors feel that anyone who leaves them is *ipso facto* disloyal; therefore they make a practice of criticizing former subordinates.

Finally, the qualities that make a man successful in one company may not make him equally successful in another. Whether or not a man does his best work depends on the circumstances, the way his supervisor acts, the company policies, and other factors. The environment in which one man thrives may stifle or baffle another.

Interviewing

The interview is the oldest form of selection procedure, and it usually carries the most weight. Many people believe that they can get a better idea of the applicant's total personality, including his intelligence and interest in the job, by face-to-face contact than in any other way.

Certainly there are some qualities that can be judged only in an interview—manners, neatness of appearance, ability to meet other people pleasantly and make a good impression at once—all very important in some jobs though not in all. To an alert interviewer, also, the interview will provide clues to intelligence, breadth of interests, general attitude toward work and life. Where the interviewer is the man who will be the successful applicant's boss, he can gain some idea of how well they could work together.

One trouble with the interview as a selection device is that many people tend to have preconceptions and prejudices: "Fat men are always lazy," or "People with low foreheads are stupid." Some interviewers, too, are not skilled in getting people to open up and talk naturally. If several interviewers are used, as they generally are when the position is of any importance, these difficulties will be minimized.

Nevertheless, the impression an applicant makes in an interview or even several interviews can be deceptive. A person who makes a good first impression may not wear well on further acquaintance. Some people talk intelligently, but do not act intelligently. Some can conceal unpleasant dispositions temporarily. Some who have a decisive manner are actually indecisive; others who look a little like Casper Milquetoast and seem very hesitant may act quickly, surely, and wisely in an actual on-the-job situation.

The psychologists who selected men for the Office of Strategic Services during World War II report:

> In a three-day program of assessment, a responsive, enthusiastic, genial, quick-witted, and perhaps humorous fellow is apt to make a favorable impression. His exuberance is inviting and contagious; he is facile in conversations and debate . . . both candidates and staff are likely to give him a high mark on Social Relations. . . . Some candidates of this type, however, have a number of annoying traits that they are able to hold in check for a short time, when their need to please is uppermost, but which emerge later when vigilance is relaxed. Also there are some ideas, attitudes, and mannerisms which on first appearance are entertaining but, on repetition, become exceedingly tedious and irritating. That it is difficult to pick out all the candidates who will not "wear well" on long acquaintance is evidenced by the fact that the OSS assessment staff recommended several men with exhibitionistic tendencies which appeared, when modulated at Station S or W, to be generally acceptable, if not appealing, but proved, when vented overseas, to be insufferable.
>
> Contrariwise, there is a tendency to underrate the shy, reserved and taciturn introvert because a person of this type is apt to take more than three days to warm up and display his full capacity for social relations and leadership. In a short time it is not possible to test the strength of such substantial qualities as integrity, loyalty, patience, and forbearance.[3]

Testing

When development of psychological tests began, it seemed to many that in time they might supply a complete solution to the selection problem. But after more than half a century of work on them, they are still merely aids to selec-

3 *Assessment of Men: Selection of Personnel for the Office of Strategic Services*, The OSS Assessment Staff, Holt, Rinehart and Winston, Inc., New York, 1948, pp. 458–459.

tion, not the complete answer. While a great many companies use them, most place more weight on other factors, or at least use the tests merely as a means of eliminating some of the candidates whose scores are below a previously set cutoff point.

A test is considered valuable to the extent that it possesses "validity" and "reliability." It is valid insofar as it measures what it is supposed to measure and reliable insofar as it gives consistent results. If a test were completely reliable, a person would make the same score on it now and three years from now, no matter who scored his performance. If it were completely valid, all those who lack the ability or characteristic it is supposed to measure would make poor scores; all those who have it would make good ones. No test or group of tests produces such perfect results.

Tests are generally validated by giving them to people whose abilities and characteristics are thought to be known, and then comparing the results with what is known about the people. In some cases, the publishers of the tests establish national norms by giving them to groups of people all over the country; in others, a company may devise its own test, give it to people already on the job, and compare their scores with their performance.

Intelligence tests Intelligence tests are among the oldest of the various types of tests, and have been given to millions of people. Every college student is familiar with these tests since they are widely used in schools and universities. They contain questions designed to measure vocabulary, ability to do mental arithmetic, ability to judge spatial relations, ability to produce logical conclusions from stated premises.

At one time, these tests were thought to be completely valid and reliable in measuring native intelligence or ability to learn, even though performance in school or in industry did not always correspond to test results. This was not, of course, an illogical view, since many other factors, emotional and situational, may affect performance over a period of time. More recently, however, psychologists have begun to believe that such factors as education affect the scores and that, in the case of children, family background is important. Thus a boy or girl who comes from a home in which the adults are educated and interested in learning is likely to make a higher score than one from a home in which there are no books, no stimulating discussion, and little interest in the child's development.

Since intelligence tests were first used on children, the score is generally expressed as the IQ, or intelligence quotient, which is the quotient obtained when the mental age is divided by chronological age. When such tests are given to adults, the chronological age is not used to produce the quotient because basic intelligence is not believed to increase much, if any, after the middle teens. Rather a given number of questions answered correctly is considered to indicate that the subject has a given IQ.

On these tests a score of 90–110 is considered "normal," and above that range such designations as "high average," "superior," and "very superior" may be used. Sometimes an IQ above 140 is called a "genius" rating. Scores below 90 may be listed in descending order as "dull normal," "moron," "imbecile," and "idiot." Where these tests are given to candidates for executive jobs, however, the standards may be higher. Thus "high average" may be high average compared to the scores obtained by executives and college graduates and would actually be "superior" if the comparison were with the population in general.

Some personnel managers believe that it is unwise to hire people with high IQs for routine jobs, holding that they will soon become bored and either quit or take to disruptive behavior. Indeed, some companies believe that people with subnormal intelligence may be better for work that is extremely dull. In general, though, a score at least within the normal range is considered a requisite for all jobs. And for such openings as apprenticeships in the skilled trades, higher office jobs, and executive positions, a good score on a test of this kind is considered a favorable indication.

Performance tests   For some jobs, it is possible to test an applicant's skill in the work by giving him an actual job to do. A typist may be asked to copy a page or two, or an advertising copywriter can be required to submit copy for some product.

Very few jobs fall into this category, however. One cannot, for example, ask prospective mechanics to dismantle a large machine and put it together again. That would mean taking a unit out of production for a long period. Neither is it feasible to have a candidate for an executive job take charge in a given situation and make decisions. Too much disruption of the work would be entailed, to say nothing of the danger that some of the applicants might make bad mistakes.

There have been some attempts to create tests that will simulate actual tasks. One was a piece of apparatus designed for repair mechanics in which knobs were turned or buttons pressed to indicate checks on various parts. A light flashed when the correct steps were performed in sequence, indicating that the machine, if it had been a real one, would be back in working order. The machine also recorded the number of false moves made before the solution was obtained.

Another, sometimes used for candidates for management trainee positions, is the "in-basket test," designed as a test of judgment. The candidate is given an in-basket of papers—letters, memoranda from various departments, reports, and so on—dealing with various situations that might arise on the job, and asked to state what he would do under the circumstances. Many of the facts presented in the material are interrelated, and it is not possible to satisfy all the demands of each situation. The candidate must, therefore, weigh the urgency of each problem and the effects of various courses of action on various departments.

Tests of this kind cannot, however, encompass all the tasks in a job that embodies several skills. Moreover, an actual situation is likely to include many more variables than can be simulated artificially.

Trade tests   Simpler to administer than the simulation test for mechanics described above are the paper-and-pencil or oral trade tests for skilled workers. On such a test an applicant may be asked questions regarding the particular language of the trade, how he would proceed on certain jobs, what tools he would use, and so on. A man who was entirely unfamiliar with the trade certainly could not answer these questions correctly.

A number of oral trade tests were developed by the United States Employment Service Occupational Analysis Section some time ago and proved to be exceedingly accurate in separating the experienced from the inexperienced. For example, on a test for machinists, the median score for those considered experts by their companies was 14, as against 4 for apprentices and helpers, and 0 for those without any experience in the trade at all (even though they had been working at related trades). The top score for those in the related group was 5, as against the 15 scored by the experts.[4]

On the other hand, proficiency in such trades as machinist, carpenter, and welder—the type of jobs for which these tests are used—involves more than simply *knowing how* to do the work. No matter what his knowledge of trade theory, a man who is all thumbs cannot be very good at them. Thus it might be said that while the tests will eliminate those who *cannot* do the work, they do not necessarily show the manager which of several experienced men will do it best.

Aptitude tests   Aptitude tests differ from trade tests in that they are designed to show capacity to learn a job rather than current skill in it. In this category are the tests of finger dexterity, in which the candidate has to perform delicate manual tasks, such as arranging very small pieces of material into some pattern. Aptitude tests may also be of the paper-and-pencil type. For example, one question on such a test (for mechanical aptitude) shows four irregularly shaped figures and three or four larger ones, each composed of the same number of pieces. The testee is asked which of the larger figures can be formed by putting the smaller ones together. Another question might ask which of two pictured tools would be better for a given job.

Personality tests   It is commonly said that more employees, including executives, fail on the job because of personality difficulties than because of lack of skill. A paper-and-pencil test that would reveal personality would, therefore, be of immense value in selection.

But there is also immense difficulty in devising a test of this kind in such a

4 C. L. Shartle, "New Selection Methods for Defense Jobs," *Personnel Series No. 50*, American Management Association, New York, 1941, pp. 30–40.

way that the applicant cannot guess the answers that the psychologist has decided are the right ones. If it asks, as some personality tests do, such questions as: "Do you frequently feel moody and depressed?" a reasonably intelligent applicant will answer no, regardless of the truth. He will realize that the cheerful, equable employee is likely to be preferred. Thus a test of this kind may work very well for a vocational counselor whose clients are really seeking to learn what they are best fitted for, but not at all in a situation where people are trying to get a job.

An applicant cannot fake the answers to intelligence, aptitude, or trade tests in this way. Either he knows them or he doesn't, and while he may make a few lucky guesses on multiple-choice questions, the probabilities are against his guessing right frequently enough to make much difference in his overall score. For this reason, there is more controversy over personality tests than over the other types.

There are some types of personality tests which proponents claim cannot be beaten by any applicant, no matter what his intelligence. These are the projective tests, "projective" because instead of being asked to choose a set answer by making a check mark, the applicant is required to make up an answer out of whole cloth and so project himself.

One of these, which is not often used in industry, is the inkblot or Rorschach test. Here the subject is shown a series of inkblots and asked to state what pictures the outlines seem to form.

Another type is the sentence completion test. This presents beginnings of several sentences which the applicant must complete. For example: "When he found that his subordinate had not completed the work at hand, he . . ." or "Right now, I wish I were. . . ."

A third is the Thematic Apperception Test (TAT), in which the applicant is asked to describe the situations portrayed in a series of pictures. One of these may show, for example, an aged woman looking over the shoulder of a young and good-looking girl; another, a man standing in a doorway looking out over a country landscape.

It may be that, as some aver, it is impossible for even the most intelligent applicant to outthink the psychologists who devised the projective tests and come up with answers that will show the characteristics presumed to be desirable. At any rate, a part of the validation procedure for the TAT was to have a group of psychologists take the tests twice: once under instructions to present the best possible personality configuration they could manage, and the second time, a month later, to present the worst possible picture of themselves. What happened has been described as follows:

> Let us say that Joe Doakes has agreed to take the tests. What we get in both cases is a picture of Joe Doakes plus a few responses that are real dillies. Or perhaps a picture of Joe Doakes plus a few nice, clinical, pathological responses. In other words the real personality of the man comes through in either case. And these are clinically trained people who

know a schizophrenic when they see one walking down the street, who have seen the responses of pathological groups and should know how to cheat if anyone does.[5]

Not everyone accepts this view of the projective tests, however. Whereas intelligence, aptitude, and trade tests can be scored mechanically by a clerk, the projective tests require a trained interpreter, and it is possible that the interpreter's own personality and predilections will get in the way of his objectivity. For example:

> David Riesman tells of a Thematic Apperception Test taken by a graduate student in history. . . . The . . . student, not too surprisingly, told a story about a famous historical figure who had had a difficult choice to make. Ah-ha! said the man who interpreted the tests, maladjustment. The student had talked about people who were *dead*. This was the first thought that a historical figure had called up in the mind of the tester.[6]

In another case, investigators gave the tests to a group of chief executives and found that the results indicated they had only two things in common: fear of illness and a tendency to depend on others when confronted with complex problems.[7]

The severest criticism of personality tests has been offered by Martin L. Gross in his book *The Brain Watchers*.[8] He cites such instances as:

> The woman psychologist who evaluated a finger painting by projective techniques and then found out it was done by a young chimpanzee.[9]

> The paper company that hired an inexperienced young man as a salesman because the tester found he was a "natural born salesman," and five years later was still waiting for him to produce.[10]

> A case in which the TAT was given to the same group twice, the second time after an interval of nine weeks, and the reliability score was .26, a ridiculously low correlation.[11]

No perfect system

Some managers say that it is more difficult to select effective salesmen than good candidates for other types of positions. "Yes," said a cynic, "because if a salesman is ineffective, it's immediately apparent in the sales figures in his territory. People in other jobs can do poorly for a long time before anyone gets around to realizing it."

At any rate, no amount of testing, interviewing, or examination of past records, as nearly as they can be ascertained, will enable a company to feel

---

[5] William E. Henry, "Executive Personality and Job Success," *Personnel Series No. 120*, American Management Association, New York, 1948, pp. 12–13.
[6] Whyte, *op. cit.*, p. 186.
[7] John B. Miner and John E. Culver, "Some Aspects of Executive Personality," *Journal of Applied Psychology*, October, 1955.
[8] Random House, Inc., New York, 1962.
[9] P. 82.
[10] Pp. 47–48.
[11] P. 249.

absolutely sure that it is really getting the best among the applicants who offer themselves. Certain errors may be avoided, but that is about all. Intelligence tests will eliminate people who are too stupid for a given job, trade tests those who are claiming more experience than they actually have. Projective tests may point out those too seriously disturbed to be worth the risk. Interviews will enable the company to spot those who are too gauche for certain positions. Past records will provide indications. Physical examinations, required by most large companies, will show who is physically incapable of handling the work. But among people who are, let us say, somewhat above the average in intelligence and as sane as most people, and who have reasonably good records, the choice will be difficult.

Further, selection procedures may work toward the elimination of some particularly good candidates. As one observer put it, the selection process is "often a series of hurdles, over which each applicant must pass. . . . You may even find that the course has been arranged in such a way that only one candidate survives."[12]

Those who fail to clear one of the many hurdles may in truth have some faults, but they may be so capable in some respects that their good qualities far outweigh their shortcomings. Thus the process may tend to produce mediocrities.

It may be questioned, too, whether the selection process has not been too greatly elaborated in the case of less important jobs. Some candidates become annoyed at the length of time required for the various steps and take other jobs in the meantime; others receive a poor impression of the company because of the delay in making a decision. One company, in fact, went so far as to publish a booklet for applicants explaining why the selection process took so long, and a single mention of this in a publication evoked a large number of inquiries from other companies which felt the need of something similar.

Also, these elaborate procedures cost money, and hence a type of circular reasoning may develop: "It costs us so much to put an employee on the payroll that we have to be extra careful not to make a mistake and have to go through the process all over again. Therefore we can spend more for further elaboration."

This is not to say that any part of the selection process should *necessarily* be omitted, only that there should be greater emphasis on the most important qualification for the job. And whether the post be that of machine operator or president, this is the ability to get results: quality and quantity of production in the case of the former, profits and company safety in the case of the latter. Either may have a less than perfect personality, provided it is not so bad as to be intolerable to associates and actually interfere with the results.

Further, there should be less a priori reasoning in developing selection procedures. It is not necessarily true that the man with the greatest empathy

---

[12] Glenn A. Bassett, "The Screening Process: Selection or Rejection," *Personnel* (American Management Association), July–August, 1962, p. 31.

for others will make the best supervisor—he may not set standards of work high enough. Again, quite a few companies interview wives of candidates for certain positions, on the theory that a man with a happy home life is likely to be better able to concentrate on the job. But sometimes the opposite is true. Because a man is unhappy at home, he may escape by putting more effort into his job. As one sales manager remarked: "Our best salesman has a witch of a wife. He doesn't like to go home; so he stays out on the road. And as long as he's on the road he sells."

If the obstacle course is so arranged that only one, or at best two or three, candidates survive it, the man who makes the final decision is deprived of the opportunity to handle the staffing part of his management function, which in the end is a matter of judgment that can be exercised only by the manager himself.

TRANSFERS AND PROMOTIONS

A "transfer" is generally a change in position without a change in status or pay. "Promotion," on the other hand, carries the implication that either or both (usually both) will be improved by the job change.

Sometimes a transfer is made to correct an original mistake in selection and placement. An employee or an executive is not doing well where he is, but his superior or the personnel department believes he has good possibilities and will do better at another type of work. Or the man himself may request a transfer because he does not like his immediate superior, because he believes that he will have greater chance for advancement in another type of job, or because he wants to gain wider experience.

Other transfers may be made because the company finds itself with a surplus of men in one group or department and a shortage in another. And, as noted in an earlier chapter, transfers may be forced by the union through the practices of "bumping" or "job bidding."

It might be supposed that picking candidates for promotion would be a great deal easier than choosing among new applicants. But in actuality it is almost as difficult to decide who among a given group should be promoted to the next higher job as it is to decide among a group of new applicants. And as one moves up the line, the task becomes even more difficult.

One reason for this is that a higher job is likely to require skills that are different not only in degree but in kind from the one immediately beneath it. The rank-and-file employee who is promoted to first-line supervisor must begin, even if only in a minor way, to plan not only his own work but that of others, to coordinate their efforts, and to see that they do what is expected of them. Getting results then involves more than simply *knowing how* the various tasks should be done.

Then, as a man goes up the ladder, he not only gets more deeply into the POSDCORB functions; he must plan, organize, direct, and so on, many more *different kinds* of tasks until, as president, he is directing such diverse functions as personnel and financial management, production and public relations.

Another difficulty is that the man who makes the final decision on promotion may not actually be familiar with what the various candidates have been doing and how well they have been doing it, since he may not be, probably is not, the immediate superior.

And even the immediate superior may base his recommendations on a general impression—perhaps indelibly imprinted on his mind by one or two incidents that occurred during the first few months of employment. Companies are much concerned these days about their "images"—the general impression the public has gained of them through its dealings with them or through what it has read in the papers. Thus they will try to hammer home, through publicity, advertising, and their general conduct, such images as "a progressive company" or "a company that treats its employees well" or to associate some other favorable quality with the company so closely that it immediately springs to mind whenever the company name is mentioned. People, too, have images in the minds of their associates, and once they are formed it is very difficult to change them. Thus a man may be seen as "brilliant but erratic," "dependable but slow-moving," or merely "a good man" or "not much good."

Yet a reputation for brilliance may be based on a single idea or the chance remark of an associate, and the same thing is true of the other qualities, good and bad. So eager are people to put their fellows into definite categories that they are quite likely to clutch at any indication and rarely reexamine it unless overwhelming evidence forces them to do so.

Still a third difficulty is that management may not know what talent it has available currently within the company. One executive recruiter tells of a case in which, after a countrywide search, the most qualified candidate for a new position was found to be already employed by the client company. "It was months," he said, "before the VP of personnel could hold up his head around the office."

In an effort to prevent such embarrassing incidents, and to make it possible to promote from within in most cases, personnel specialists have devised two tools: appraisals and executive inventories.

Appraisals

Formal appraisals were first applied to rank-and-file employees. Each supervisor was asked to rate each of his subordinates on a simple form on such matters as quality and quantity of work, attitude toward the company and toward fellow employees. This practice, known as "merit-rating," is still widespread. Often supervisors are given special training in using the rating blanks, a step generally necessary because not all supervisors have the same standards; what one considers "good quality" work, another may feel is "only fair"; and the same difficulty may occur with the answers to other questions. It is also necessary to caution supervisors against what is known as "the halo effect"—the tendency to believe that if a man turns in a good (or bad) performance in some areas, he is equally good or bad in all the others. Also, since supervisors are supposed to talk over the ratings with the employees in order to help them improve, the training will probably encompass pointers on conducting the discussions.

Unionized companies sometimes have difficulty in introducing or operating merit-rating plans, for unions tend to feel that both promotions and so-called merit increases within a rate range should depend largely on straight seniority. This is partly because they distrust the fairness of management or supervisory subjective judgments, and partly because more of their members are likely to get raises under the seniority system. But even if merit increases are given automatically because of length of service, many companies believe the merit-rating plans are valuable because the discussions with employees provide an opportunity to counsel them on what is expected and how they can improve. Also, although companies may be compelled to consider seniority in promotions to the first-line supervisory level, they usually have more leeway to take merit into account than they do in the granting of merit raises.

Executive merit rating, commonly called "appraisal," is a later development, which has shown astonishing growth since World War II. Here more variegated systems have been developed since an executive's job is much more complex.

One method—more widely accepted some years ago than it is now—is trait rating. Under this system, the personnel department, with the cooperation, or at least the blessing, of top management, draws up a list of traits that it believes might be valuable to a manager, and his superior is asked to mark him excellent, good, fair, or poor on each one. Generally, job knowledge and job performance have a place on such blanks, but are overshadowed by a longer list of personality qualifications ranging from "accuracy" to "vision," and from "perseverance" to a "sense of humor." Some have even listed such vague terms as "personality" and "acceptability."

In order to make it a little easier for the superior to judge the extent to which a subordinate possesses these traits, companies may include descriptive phrases. For example, a large chemical company offers the following choices for the single trait, cooperation:

1. Concedes nothing. Obstructive, antagonistic.
2. Poor mixer. Tries to run with the ball. Occasionally indulges in obstructive argument.
3. Generally adapts self to persons and situations. Responsive to leadership and reasonably tactful.
4. Willing and eager to please. Works in complete harmony with the group. Adaptable and courteous.
5. Adapts self very well without sacrificing standards. Goes out of his way to promote the common end.

The rater is instructed to check the group of phrases that best describes the man he is rating, to cross out any that do not apply, and underline phrases in other blocks that will help to clarify the appraisal.

The trouble with the trait rating plans is that no one has ever proved that certain traits are essential to the handling of all executive jobs. Some very successful executives have been comparatively tactless, some have lacked a

---

Traits used on appraisal forms of eight companies

Ability to delegate	Habits	Personal appearance
Ability to sell ideas	Health	Personality
Acceptability	Human relations	Physical energy
Accuracy		Planning
Adaptability		Poise
Ambition	Imagination	Product knowledge
Analytical ability	Industriousness	
Attitude	Initiative	
	Integrity	Quality of work
	Intelligence	Quantity of work
Capacity to learn		
Capacity to supervise		
Character	Job knowledge	Reliability
Commands confidence	Job performance	Resourcefulness
and respect	Judgment	Responsibility
Cooperativeness		
Coordination		
Creative ability	Leadership	Self-confidence
	Loyalty	Sense of humor
Decisiveness		
Dependability	Maturity	Tactfulness
		Thoroughness
		Training of personnel
Educational level	Oral expression	
Emotional stability	Organizing ability	
Enthusiasm	Originality	Vision
Foresight	Perseverance	Written expression

---

sense of humor, many are not particularly accurate, and some are not even emotionally stable. If an executive possessed all the traits desirable in a human being (which is what some of the rating blanks appear to call for), he would function superbly. But the fact is that no one does, and it is often more important for a man to possess two or three desirable characteristics to a superlative degree than it is for him to exemplify some of each of the desirable qualities. Finally, many psychologists believe that traits, or at least many of the traits listed on these blanks, are not necessarily constant—that a man may exhibit a trait in one situation and not in another.

Moreover, the trait rating forms ignore the fact that what a company actually wants from an executive is results—in the way of production, sales, sound handling of finance, or whatever his particular function happens to be. Of late, there has been a tendency to recognize this through the development of blanks that require the boss to list the duties of the job in the order of their importance and to comment on the way the incumbent is handling each, giving facts and figures wherever possible. Other forms ask such specific questions as:

Does he meet production or service requirements of the job? Are his assignments accomplished on time? Does he keep within his budget? Has he furthered cost control?

One big advantage of the job-oriented forms is that they make it easier for the boss to discuss the score with the man he has rated—as he is nearly always supposed to do since one of the purposes of the rating is to encourage improvement. Most bosses find it embarrassing to tell a man to his face that he lacks personality or a sense of humor. And the man who is informed that he hasn't enough "vision" or "leadership" is likely to feel pretty baffled about the whole thing. But if he is asked why he hasn't been meeting schedules, he may take a realistic look at his own shortcomings and resolve to improve. Or the boss may find that conditions beyond the man's control, which his superiors have the power to correct, are hampering his performance.

In an effort to get around the difficulty of breaking down executive success into its components, some firms have dispensed with both performance items and traits. Instead they ask general questions that allow the rater to answer in his own words. Popular queries of this type are: What are the man's strongest points? What are his weaknesses? What should be done to help him improve? Questions such as these may be appended to the trait and performance ratings also.

Here again, some troubles develop. Very few department and division heads can write an informative report on a man's performance and character. Further, even apparently simple questions mean different things to different people. For example, American Cyanamid Company discovered that, to raters who had credited subordinates with "ability to go far," distance was entirely relative.

"Take a department head," said L. B. Olsen, a psychologist who worked on the Cyanamid studies. "He may think he's come pretty far, and that any man who will eventually be ready for a job like his should be credited with unlimited capacity for advancement. To another man the same question may mean, 'Will he some day be able to handle the president's job?' "

To bring a variety of viewpoints to bear, some companies using essay-type ratings have the boss bring in other executives on his own level. The group then "talks out" the rating, while one of the number takes notes.

Still another type of rating, at present used by only a few companies, is what is known as the forced-choice method. Where this technique is employed, the rater is confronted with twenty or thirty blocks of statements and indicates the statement in each group that is most applicable to the man he is rating and the one that is least applicable. For example:

Block 1	Block 2
Always does things on time	Is very well suited to his job
Does not get along well with others	Has no trouble making decisions
Keeps his department very neat	Well-liked by those who work for him
Has an excellent personal appearance	Does not readily accept criticism
Needs more training	A good candidate for promotion

It can be seen that all the statements in one block might well apply to a single person; conversely, none of them might apply. Nevertheless, the rater is compelled to check a "most" and a "least" in each block—hence the term "forced choice."

Some of the items that appear uncomplimentary may not count one way or the other. Some that appear complimentary may actually reduce the score since, in view of the choice allowed, checking them amounts to damning the man with faint praise. Hence proponents of this system claim that it has built-in safeguards against partiality. On the other hand, there are some who say that because the boss does not know how his ratings will be scored, he often finds that he has given an impression of his subordinates quite different from what he intended.

Like many other staff-developed techniques, executive appraisals are to some extent a controversial subject. Often they are introduced by a staff department and meet with some resistance from the line, both because the appraisals and the subsequent discussions of them take extra time and because the line executives are reluctant to face the interviews. They don't like to tell a man about his faults, and perhaps have to justify their judgments to him. On the other hand, if a man gets a very good rating, they may be hard put to it to explain why he doesn't deserve an immediate raise or promotion. They are probably aware, also, that the approach of appraisal time occasions nervousness among their subordinates and thus hinders concentration on the work. It has even been said that in attempting to counsel his subordinates, particularly about their personal characteristics as revealed by trait rating forms, the superior is in effect "playing God."[13]

The principal rebuttal to this argument was well expressed by the man in charge of management development for a large company: "Nearly every action affecting people is based in part on judgments about them, conscious or unconscious. In my experience, intuitive, unexpressed judgments are much less likely to be considerate or sound than those which result from examination and discussion."[14]

Management inventories

In general, promotion from within is a wise policy. There is nothing more discouraging to those currently on the job than to see a new man brought in to fill a higher position for which they have the experience and training.

Nearly all companies have such a policy, or at least state that they do; but some follow it more closely than others. Some even appear to hope that eventually they will be able to grow executives under glass, so to speak: hiring crops of college graduates, training them, and promoting them as they become qualified, until eventually it will not be necessary ever to hire from outside except for the beginning jobs.

[13] Douglas McGregor, "An Uneasy Look at Performance Appraisal," *Harvard Business Review*, May–June, 1957, p. 90.
[14] Harold Mayfield, "In Defense of Performance Appraisal," *Harvard Business Review*, March–April, 1960, p. 82.

Probably no company has reached this goal. Most go outside occasionally, as the growth in the number and activities of the executive recruitment firms shows. It is also questionable whether such a closed system would be desirable, even if it were possible, since it might mean an entirely ingrown management.

Another objective in formulating promotion policies is to avoid the development of indispensable men. A company feels uneasy with such a man: first, because he is in a position to demand more in the way of pay and perquisites than it may feel it should grant, and, second, because it will be vulnerable if he should die or quit. Also, many companies point out, indispensability may work to a man's own disadvantage since he cannot be promoted if there is no one who can replace him.

Thus in some organizations the ideal has been to have a backup man or men for each job of any importance, someone ready to step into the superior's shoes if the latter should leave or be transferred or promoted. The tool used in keeping track of the backup men is the management inventory, an example of which is shown in Figure 1. A man's promotability is judged by the facts shown on his appraisals, which may include a rating on promotability and will usually contain data on the further training he needs to become promotable.

TRAINING

Training is, perhaps, the fastest-growing segment of personnel activities. Companies run schools of their own; they arrange for special courses; they pay tuition for school, college, and correspondence courses; often they pay people for the time spent in attending classes. Many personnel departments include training departments; still more have at least one executive, generally known as the training director, who devotes full time to this activity.

The subject matter of the courses and the methods of training naturally vary with the jobs of the students, who may be rank-and-file workers, those being groomed for supervisory jobs, first-line supervisors, young college graduates, or seasoned executives.

The first form of training a new employee encounters is known as orientation training. This is designed to give him a general view of what the company does, how it is organized, what benefits it offers, and what its general rules and regulations are. Most of the information is likely to be embodied in an employee handbook which is distributed to all employees, and in the case of a rank-and-file worker, the orientation may consist only of a brief explanation by a member of the personnel department or the supervisor under whom the employee will work. Orientation training can, however, be more elaborate, particularly in the case of supervisory and management employees. Some companies show movies explaining company activities; others arrange for a lecture or a series of lectures on the company and its practices. In some cases, the new employee spends anywhere from a day to several months in each department to gain first-hand experience in the various types of work and an overall view of how the activities of one department affect those of other departments.

If the new employee is an unskilled or a semiskilled worker—a machine operator, say—he will be given on-the-job training by his foreman or by an experienced operator whom the foreman assigns to help him. This will probably be a simple matter of a few days. The trainer will explain what is to be done, show the new man how to do it, then watch him do it and correct his mistakes.

Apprenticeship training

People are sometimes said to be "serving an apprenticeship" when they are merely receiving hit-or-miss on-the-job training. Actually, apprenticeship training is a definite course, combining selected job experience with classroom training, examinations in each phase of the work, and eventual graduation to the status of journeyman in a skilled trade. It is, in fact, the lineal descendant of the apprenticeship that was practiced under the old guild system in the Middle Ages. Unlike his medieval counterpart, however, the modern apprentice is paid while learning, and his course lasts only three or four years (the length depending on the trade) instead of seven, as in the early days. Also, though both he and the company generally sign articles of indenture— in which the company agrees to provide training in all phases of the work, and he agrees to work diligently—the modern apprentice is, of course, not indentured in the sense that he cannot quit.

"Approved apprenticeship programs" are programs approved by Federal or state apprenticeship agencies, and these must fulfill certain definite conditions. Among other things, they must incorporate a certain number of classroom hours (the number depending on the trade), and—most important of all— approval may require that the program be under the direction of a joint union-management committee.

Classroom training consists of work in such subjects as mathematics, blueprint reading, and trade theory, and may be conducted on the company premises or at a nearby school. While on the job the apprentice works with journeymen and learns while he works. Written examinations are given in each phase of the classroom work, and the apprentice must also pass tests in job skill—showing that he can perform various phases of the job to the satisfaction of the foreman, or perhaps to that of representatives of management and labor.

The apprentice usually starts at a rate about half that of a journeyman and receives wage increases every six months. Then at graduation he is raised to the regular rate for the trade.

Only certain trades are what is known as "apprenticeable," that is, commonly learned through a formal apprenticeship. These are skilled trades with a more or less defined scope of activity: carpenters, electricians, and machinists, for example.

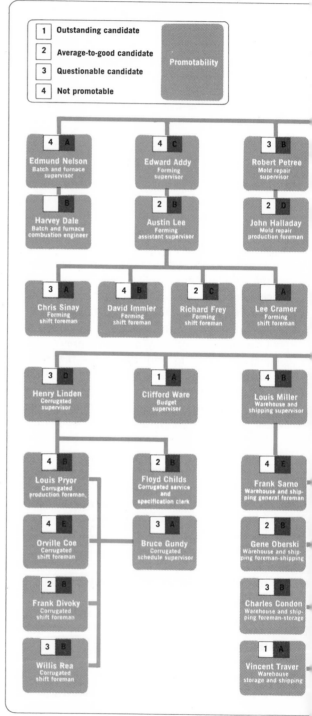

FIGURE 1 Owens-Illinois plant (sample, not an actual plant).

Present performance

Outstanding	A
Good	B
Doubtful	C
Doubtful, because new	D
Not up to standard	E

George Lucas
Plant manager

3 B Fred Orth
Industrial engineer

2 A Eugene Latzko
Machine repair supervisor

2 B Ben Majeska
Selecting supervisor

2 B Walter Sauer
Laboratory supervisor

4 C Bert Lentz
Quality and specifications supervisor

2 A Albert Beebe
Industrial engineer

4 B Kenneth Hines
Machine repair production foreman

2 B Calvin Miles
Selecting assistant supervisor

4 A James Murnen
Quality and specifications draftsman

3 D Virgil Huber
Quality and specifications office manager

3 D Leslie Meek
Industrial engineer

2 B James Todd
Selecting shift foreman

4 A Harry Whipple
Selecting shift foreman

4 B Albert Kozicky
Selecting shift foreman

4 E Stuart Hatch
Selecting shift foreman

4 B Herman Kruse
Selecting assembly and supervision

3 B Loren Prescott
Plant engineer

4 C Leslie Beal
Plant auditor

4 B Arthur Stofer
Purchasing and stores supervisor

1 A Paul Richards
Personnel director

2 A Daniel Wilusz
Service manager

3 B Conrad Ott
Electrical foreman

4 B George Walzak
Payroll supervisor

4 B Elmer Woolf
Stores supervisor

2 B Ted Marino
Director men's activities

2 B Edward Bryant
Schedule supervisor

4 C Philip McCune
General maintenance foreman

3 B George Allen
Chief general accountant

2 B John Stringer
Stock receiving clerk

3 A Alice Connor
Director women's activities

4 B Rex Rejent
Traffic supervisor

2 B Keith Zeditz
Schedule and job order supervisor

4 C Harold Horton
Chief bonus clerk

3 C Gordon Tipton
Newspaper editor

3 E Jack Meinert
Service correspondent

1 B Donald Zulka
Safety director

4 C Stanley Smith
Service correspondent

Automation and the widespread use of electronic controls in industry have created new training needs, for few of the old skilled workers are equipped to keep them in running order or to repair them when they break down. Manufacturers of the equipment, aware that this might well prove an obstacle to sales, conduct schools of their own for customers' repairmen, and a company will often send a man or group of men to take the training, paying both their wages and their living expenses while they are away. There have even been cases in which a company has sent a man abroad to a foreign supplier's plant to learn about new types of machinery. Some companies, however, find the courses offered by the manufacturers insufficient and conduct programs of their own similar to a true apprenticeship in that they include both classroom work and training on the job and continue for as long as three or four years.

Outside training

Many companies encourage all employees down to the rank-and-file levels to improve their skills and general knowledge by taking outside courses. Some will pay half the tuition or all of it if the employee passes. Usually the courses must be in some way related to the job (for example, a machinist might study engineering at night) if the company is to finance it, but some companies interpret this provision loosely and will pay or help to pay for almost any type of serious training that the employee wishes to take.

Supervisory training

Supervisory training is much broader and in general concentrates on human relations, at least at the first step. Most companies feel that the men they promote to first-line supervision are likely to know enough about the actual work not to need further training in it; but they may well need pointers on the best ways of handling their men.

Supervisors are also instructed in company policies, often in company organization and the flow of work, so that they may see where their groups' work fits into the picture. It is quite common also for them to receive training in cost reduction, work scheduling, and similar subjects that will help them plan the work of their groups. Training in the provisions of the union contract is also usual since companies are well aware that the supervisor is continually confronted with demands from the union steward and will not know whether he is supposed to grant them unless he is familiar with the contract. Some companies conduct courses for the foremen every time a new contract is signed.

Training methods are many and varied: Lectures, selected reading courses, demonstrations are all used, but by far the most popular type of training for supervisors is the discussion group, in which the case study type of training is used.

The case study technique has been utilized a great deal for human relations training. Under this method, a case of human relations difficulty, real or imaginary, is presented to the group, and each member suggests a course of action. Then the group members criticize the solutions suggested and together thrash out the best method of handling the matter.

Specific cases are employed also in what is called the psychodrama or role-playing form of training in human relations. In this case, one of the group takes the part of the subordinate and another of his supervisor, and the two act out an interview.

For example, the group may be given the following case: A subordinate has been absent without excuse; he has not called to say he would not be in. Further (and this is a condition that cannot be changed) he will not say why he was absent, even though he is fired for it. Perhaps he was involved in a lawsuit or was taking a relative to an insane asylum—whatever the cause, it is something that he would almost rather die than reveal, and the supervisor will get nowhere pressing him for an answer. Yet he is a good workman and the supervisor does not wish to fire him.

One member of the group takes the part of the supervisor and another member that of the employee, and the dialogue between them is extemporaneous. Then other members of the group criticize the approach of the supervisor and make suggestions for handling the case. A variation of this is to tape-record the conversation and let the man who took the part of the supervisor hear his own performance—some people are stunned when they do.

One of the values of this type of training is that it produces a curious psychological effect. The man who takes the part of the employee actually begins to feel as the employee would feel—frightened of the supervisor and yet entirely committed to his own position. Similarly, the supervisor's indignation and bafflement become very real to him, and he is enabled to practice human relations techniques in a situation very close to a real one. Thus he can learn from his mistakes without suffering difficulties on the job because of them.

Management development

The most varied training techniques are those applied to the development of managers. Interest in the subject has been intense during the past two decades.

This is largely the effect of World War II and the industrial expansion that occurred while the war was in progress and afterwards. Coming as it did immediately after a severe and long-drawn-out depression, expansion found companies generally unprepared to staff the new executive positions that had to be created when new and larger activities were undertaken. During the 1930s managers tended not to move from company to company very much; they stayed where they were because they knew that jobs were hard to get. With little mobility in the executive ranks and contraction rather than expansion the rule in business enterprises, there was little need for "promotable" executives, for there were few opportunities for promotions. And since business failures and contractions had left many people out of work, it was always possible to hire from outside if a company could not fill an executive job from the ranks of its own employees.

All that changed practically overnight, or at least within a year or two. While the economy slept, those in executive positions had been growing older, and no one had been trained to take their places, though many of them were only a few years away from retirement. And there was little possibility of hiring new managers from outside, for the ranks of the unemployed thinned rapidly.

It was then that the idea of management development began to arouse widespread interest. Companies wanted to avoid being caught again so badly without candidates for new jobs or without replacements for key men who died, retired, or left for other jobs. Some large companies had always had a form of management training for young college graduates; others that had

FIGURE 2   Monsanto Chemical Company: Methods of developing key employees (with suggestions by Lyndall F. Urwick).

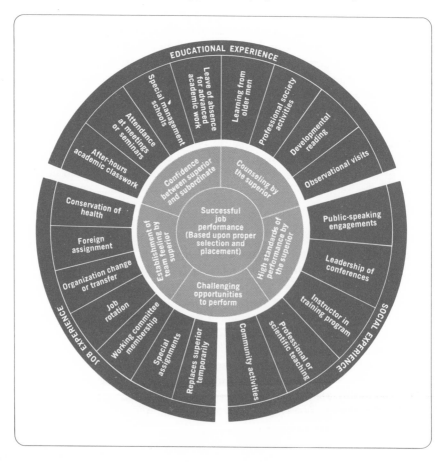

never felt the need installed it. But by far the greatest expansion took place in the area of middle management training, which was largely a new field.

Subject matter, as in the case of the foremen, was sometimes human relations; sometimes phases of the managers' own specialties. Sometimes survey courses were given in other specialties, or in management principles, organization, or other general management subjects.

By far the most popular form of training, as in the case of the foremen, was the discussion group, used especially for human relations training, but other training techniques were also employed, and additional methods as well. Job rotation, having people spend months in each of several departments, has been used for middle management executives as well as for the management trainees, for whom it is almost standard procedure. A term as assistant to a top executive may also be used as a form of training since it will enable a middle management executive who has been handling some specialized function to gain an overall view of the corporation's activities. Or an executive may be assigned to make a special study, partly because the findings are needed and partly as a form of training. Committee assignments may be employed as a means of training also.

Companies also make broad use of outside facilities in training their executives. Men may be detached from their duties and assigned to attend, say, Harvard Graduate School of Business or some similar institution for a year or a semester while drawing their full salaries. Shorter courses and seminars conducted by universities and such organizations as the American Management Association are also used.

In 1955, General Electric Company founded a staff college at Crotonville, New York, and between that time and the end of 1968, several thousand executives from four levels of management attended a nine-week advanced management course. During this time they were completely detached from their jobs and paid their full salaries. The cost of tuition and room and board, amounting to over $2,500, was assessed against the divisional budgets, which ensured that the divisional managers would not send anyone unless they believed he could profit from the training.

The course itself dealt not with such specialties as accounting or production, but with management theory and economic, social, and political issues, and used, according to its director, a "very bookish and abstract approach."[15] Techniques included lectures by outside speakers, who presented widely varying viewpoints, and by executives. There were also reading assignments, question-and-answer sessions, individual student projects, special seminars, and discussion groups.

All this may be attributed to a feeling on the part of top executives that business experience alone does not provide the breadth of viewpoint necessary to manage a large company whose activities affect so many different people and even the economy itself.

[15] *Business Week,* Mar. 4, 1961, p. 51. This program was discontinued for a time, but started again in 1964.

Bell Telephone Company went even further and developed an Institute of Humanistic Studies for Executives, conducted at the University of Pennsylvania. The group of courses took ten months to complete and covered such subjects as the Bhagavad Gita and James Joyce's *Ulysses*. "In the final and most popular course, 'American Civilization,' they [the executives] spent twelve weeks discussing such subjects as the making of the Constitution, the Haymarket Riot and the industrialization of America, *Sister Carrie* and the revolution in American sex mores, *Main Street* and the disillusionment of the 1920s, and *The Lonely Crowd* and the American character structure."[16]

Sensitivity training   A fairly new type of management education, and one that has both ardent supporters and severe detractors, is what is known as "sensitivity training," which is designed to increase the manager's understanding of himself and of his own impact on others.

The training takes the form of a group discussion, and though a leader trained in the technique is present, the group may decide on the subject of discussion or suggest changes in procedure. In the course of the discussion, stress and frustration may be generated, since practically no holds are barred.

For example, one article on the subject[17] describes a session in which a participant called George Franklin becomes disturbed at the apparent lack of purpose in the discussion and announces that he's sick of wasting his time. Then:

> George Franklin became the focus of the discussion. "What do you mean, George, by saying this is nonsense?" "What are you really mad at, George?" George was getting uncomfortable. These were questions difficult for him to answer. Gradually, he began to realize that a large part of the group disagreed with him; then he began to wonder why. He was learning something about people he hadn't known before.

Or, as another advocate of the method put it:

> There is no other educational process that I am aware of in which conflict is generated, respected, and cherished. Conflict, hostility, frustration become motivations for growth as well as food for learning. . . . As these experiences are "worked through" and the learnings internalized, participants soon begin to experience a deeper sense of self-awareness and acceptance. These, in turn, lead to an increased awareness and acceptance of others.[18]

Conversely, there are those who believe that hearing concentrated home truths can have an adverse effect on the manager. For example, George Odiorne of the University of Michigan quotes a participant:

---

[16] E. Digby Baltzell, "Bell Telephone's Experiment in Education," *Harper's*, March, 1955.
[17] Irving R. Weschler, Marvin A. Klemes, and Clovis Shepherd, "A New Focus in Executive Training," *Advanced Management Journal*, May, 1955, pp. 19–22.
[18] Chris Argyris of Yale, "In Defense of Laboratory Education," address given at Cornell University Conference on Industrial Relations, Feb. 28, 1963. "Laboratory education" is another name for sensitivity training.

We sat around the Princeton Inn flagellating one another for days on end. After I graduated from Harvard B School I bought a gray flannel suit and some half glasses and went into the family business. I was doing pretty well; the company was making a profit and growing. Then I went to this thing. Now I have to get it out of my system that I am an incompetent slob who is riding on his ancestor's coattails. A lot of those guys spent the whole time crying about the vice presidents who run the business while they hold inherited stock. A few of them who married the boss's daughter wanted to have a public catharsis over the fact that nobody respected them because they were executives who married their jobs. . . . I've got to keep busy to shake that horrible mess at Princeton and get back to making a buck for the company.[19]

Some differences of opinion   As with all movements that arouse great enthusiasm on the part of some, dissenting voices have been heard on management development. Many people believe that the best management training is on-the-job training in a situation where there is competition for promotion and the necessity of dealing with real problems. They also point out that the man who has the right qualifications in the first place will train himself, take the courses he needs on his own initiative, read widely on the subjects that will help him, and learn from experience.

Some disillusionment has also set in among those who were originally among the strong supporters of the management development programs. At the beginning of 1962, the *Wall Street Journal* reported, university programs were becoming less popular:

A number of companies started taking a hard look at executive development programs during the 1960–61 recession when, searching for ways to cut costs, they sent fewer men to seminars. This reappraisal is continuing despite the general economic recovery.

As an official of one major corporation explains: "The difficulty in evaluating these programs is that you darned well know they can be real eye-openers for the right men. But it's impossible, given the nebulous nature of the thing, to figure the direct return to the company on its investment."[20]

Unless there is a major depression, however, it is unlikely that management development programs will disappear. Companies may become more selective of both the courses and the men they send to them, but the movement itself is likely to grow, even if more slowly than it did earlier. The growing specialization of industry makes it more difficult for middle management executives to gain overall experience than in the past, even if they have the greatest ambition and will to learn. At the same time, if industry continues to expand, it will need more and more executives who know something more than narrow specialties, and the only way it can hope to obtain them is to help managers toward self-development.

[19] At the same meeting at Cornell. In answer to this, Argyris pointed out that the group to which the man belonged had voted to continue the training.
[20] Feb. 21, 1962.

SUMMARY

The staffing function encompasses recruitment, selection, transfers, promotions, and training.

The most difficult phase of staffing may be said to be selection, whether the choice is among candidates from outside the company or among people already employed when a higher job opens up and promotion is in order. Checks on past performance, interviews, and psychological tests are often used in selection; but a large area remains for judgment since none of these will show conclusively that one person is better than another for a given job. Often, however, they help to eliminate many who are entirely unfit.

One method of checking on the performance of those already on the job is the periodic rating by superiors—called "merit rating" in the case of rank-and-file employees and "appraisal" in the case of executives.

Company training programs have become more and more important in recent years, particularly programs for executive training and development, and in many cases the training is designed to broaden viewpoints rather than to teach skills.

Review Questions

1.   What types of psychological tests are available for use in industry?
2.   Do you agree with the criticism of personality tests mentioned in the text?
3.   Do you believe that executive appraisals are a good idea? Would you rather work for a company that had them than for one that did not?
4.   If you were a manager, would you find it difficult to discuss a subordinate's failings with him at regular intervals?
5.   What is a management inventory?
6.   Do you believe that study and discussion of such topics as *Main Street* and the disillusionment of the 1920s, the Haymarket Riot and the industrialization of America are valuable training for executives? Why?
7.   Do you agree with the supporters or the critics of sensitivity training? Why? Would you feel free to tell other participants in such a session exactly what you really thought of them? Would you object to having others tell you unpleasant home truths about yourself? Do you think you would learn something from such sessions?

Case Study One / Who Will Run Hotspur International?*

Hotspur Electric Company is a U.S. manufacturer of major appliances, industrial tools, and motors, with annual sales of $80 million. A company in London

* From *International Management*, June, 1963, pp. 35–38. Written with the advice and help of Paul H. Kiernan, president of an executive search (executive recruiting) firm with offices in New York and London.

has been licensed to produce and sell Hotspur products and, in a joint venture with another company, Hotspur is erecting a factory in São Paulo, Brazil. Now it plans to set up a full-scale international company and is looking for a man to manage it.

The candidates for the job are Charles Brown, 55, manager of Hotspur's main factory; Felix Slimmermeyer, 46, the company's export manager; J. Pennington Smythe, 51, head of the London licensee; and David F. Thornton, Jr., 38, son of the chairman of the board.

David F. Thornton, Sr. (called DFT), and a management consultant, I. M. Wise, interview the four candidates as follows:

WISE: I'll ask each man five far-reaching questions, and you can dig for details whenever you want. Shall we start with number one?

DFT: Fine. That would be Brown. He's an engineer, an inventor, and knows everything there is to know about Hotspur equipment. He's been my right-hand man for over ten years. (*Snaps on intercom.*) Send in Brown.

WISE: (*shuffling his papers, as Brown sits at the end of the table*) Mr. Brown, you and the others have been involved in all Hotspur's plans to extend its overseas operations. Now I'd like your personal views on the move, how well you think it'll succeed.

BROWN: If anything, the move is long overdue. We have a fine line of prodducts, a line that foreigners have shown a great interest in. No company makes as precise and efficient a small motor as we do. Our washers and industrial cleaners stand up better than any on the market. And everywhere you look, the demand is increasing for our type of product. So I see a steadily increasing world market—

DFT: (*tapping on table*) How about the competition? Can we compete with locals and the Japanese?

BROMN: We can because we make a high-quality, fully guaranteed product. We must insist on this quality, and no one will be able to touch us. Of course in many areas we will have to join forces with locals.

WISE: Where should our world headquarters be?

BROWN: Here, right here in Exeter. Why not? Our management policy is set up here, our technical know-how is here. And with jet travel, we're as close to our markets as any city you can name. Also, we know our laws and our economy are stable.

WISE: So you'd headquarter in the United States. Then where would you manufacture, do research, have our principal distribution centers?

BROWN: For the time being, I'd settle for our present factories—here in the United States, in London, and the one being built in Brazil. Our Brazilian plant might one day be able to supply neighboring countries as well. And I see no reason why the British plant, despite current differences with the Common Market, cannot supply much of Europe. At least for the time being. We probably should have a major distribution center on the Continent, maybe one in Mexico, and perhaps one in the Philippines or Australia. As for research, I think we should continue pretty much what we are doing—do our research here. We have the personnel, the laboratories, and can get better value for our research dollar here.

WISE: For executive positions overseas, to what extent should we rely on nationals or Americans?

BROWN: My view is that a qualified man is a qualified man wherever you find him. But for the time being I think we should rely most heavily on seasoned Americans, while at the same time training foreigners and seeing to what extent they can take over. I wouldn't go too far in catering to nationalistic whims or pride.

WISE: Now for the big question, Mr. Brown. We'd like you to look at your background, your talents, and tell us why you should be our man.

BROWN: With all modesty, I would point out that I've spent thirty-five years— most of my adult life—in furthering the interests and improving the products of Hotspur. Dozens of innovations—noncorrosive plastic gears, electronic controls—have been engineered by me. Our products sell because they are good, mechanically good, and they satisfy human needs. At the same time, especially in recent years, I have been involved in many of the company's other problems —its financing, sales, personnel. Also, I have a wide circle of friends among foreign engineers, scientists, and businessmen.

WISE: Thank you very much, Mr. Brown. (*As Brown goes out, Wise rearranges his papers.*) The next, I guess, would be Felix Slimmermeyer.

DFT: Our export manager, and a crackerjack salesman. He used to sell for our biggest competitors. (*Chuckles.*) He was doing so well ten years ago, we decided we needed him more. (*Snaps intercom.*) Slimmermeyer.

SLIMMERMEYER: (*taking seat*) Gentlemen.

WISE: First, give us your views of our plans to expand overseas.

SLIM: I think the potential there is fantastic. In fact, I'd say that in ten years our sales abroad will be far more than our sales in the United States. In fact, we should start to look at the United States as no more than a regional market for Hotspur. We'd have others in Europe, South America, Africa, and so on.

WISE: Where should we have our headquarters?

SLIM: A good question. I've heard rumors we're going to locate in Geneva. That would be a mistake. There've been changes in Swiss tax laws, and restrictions on what foreign personnel you can bring in. We should select some place in central Europe, perhaps Brussels, for a sales center.

DFT: Would you like to live in Brussels?

SLIM: Yes. But there's no place in this world my wife and I wouldn't be happy. We like people—

WISE: Where should we manufacture, do research?

SLIM:The plant in São Paulo, I think, should not have got started right now—though it will eventually pay off long range. The market isn't well enough developed there. But we've got to get a plant going in some free zone, perhaps the Canal Zone or Panama. From there we can serve all South America, North and Central America. But first I'd say we should quickly have a plant on the coast of France or Belgium, and in Italy to serve that part of Europe, North

Africa and the Middle East. We should also get started in the Far East, perhaps with a small plant in Australia.

DFT: What about research?

SLIM: It's a good way to squander money. Let's stick with what we're doing here.

WISE: Who should hold the key executive positions abroad, nationals or Americans?

SLIM: A touchy question. Actually, we have the talent here. They speak our language, know our policy. But we have to get along with people abroad. We have to let them into the act. So I'd start with seasoned Hotspur men, but then I'd make every effort to develop foreigners to fill some of the key jobs—but not policy making.

WISE: Now, take a look at yourself, Slim. Why are you qualified to head the International Company?

SLIM: First, because as export manager and during many trips abroad, I've become very familiar with the marketing problems and potential of the various areas of the world. My job hasn't been a simple marketing one, either. For the past ten years, I've become closely involved with tax, tariff, personnel problems, and I've constantly had to deal with people overseas and at home. The personnel problems are gigantic in a job like this, but I like people and I know how to get them moving.

WISE: That's all for now, Slim.

DFT: (as Slimmermeyer leaves) You might say we absorbed J. Pennington Smythe as head of his own small manufacturing firm. Earlier he had been controller of a big British outfit. (Snapping intercom.) Send in Smythe.

WISE: (as Smythe gets settled) Mr. Smythe, give us your views of Hotspur's short-range and long-range prospects in going international.

SMYTHE: I feel that continued studies of the financial requirements of the move, as well as the personnel needs, will be essential for it to succeed. Our potential in Europe at this stage is probably not too good, unless we can pour large amounts of money into the area. Already ahead of us in this area are some pretty tough competitors. Our best chance here would be some kind of joint relationship with one of these companies. The same for Japan.

DFT: You think we can compete in Japan?

SMYTHE: Only on the basis of the technical excellence of our products, and as a partner with a Japanese company. But overall, I think our move is sound, because there is a great potential for our equipment everywhere and we have enough capital to go after our share of the market, as we have done in England.

WISE: Where should we have our headquarters?

SMYTHE: That depends. If the main consideration was staying close to the parent company, we could effectively stay here right in Exeter. But from a psychological standpoint, it might be wise to avoid both the United States and Europe and set up headquarters in some neutral, reasonably stable point like— oh heavens, I don't know—perhaps Liberia.

DFT: Would your wife live in Liberia?

SMYTHE: Oh yes. She's Italian, you know, and quite world-minded. She'd find it a challenge.

WISE: Where should we produce, market, and do research?

SMYTHE: If there were a joint venture with a European firm, the Continent would be an extremely logical place to do much of our research. Much fine work is being done. But the big problem is that no research is inexpensive, unless it is directed toward the goals that management has in mind. So administering the work, and tying it in with the efforts of the parent company, would be difficult.

About manufacturing, we've already talked a bit about that. Joint ventures would be the only thing for Europe and Japan, and there would—at least eventually—have to be factories in these areas. In regard to other areas, South America, portions of Central America, I think the opportunities for production in one country and shipments to another are somewhat limited. Brazilian production would supply Brazil. Mexican production, if we have it, will supply Mexico. It might be possible to find a Central American location that would serve several countries, but we would have to study this carefully. Actually, our international program will not do away with exports, either. In some areas, there will be advantages in importing some products from the United States, in others, from Europe.

WISE: Smythe, to what extent can we rely on nationals for key executive positions overseas?

SMYTHE: Very largely. We must. In only that way can we work with local governments, trade unions, and understand local customs. An alternative would be to select truly "international men" who have been educated to think in a multination framework.

WISE: Now take a step back, and tell us how you qualify for heading our international operations?

SMYTHE: First, by virtue of being English, I have been exposed all my life to the concept of world business. Second—if you'll forgive me for being frank—I think a non-American would be more acceptable, from a psychological standpoint, in most parts of the world. But most important, I believe that my background and training in the financial area are very significant. Our operations, if we go in for joint ventures more, must be largely governed by financial and statistical considerations and on the operation of investment and return.

DFT: Thank you, Smythe. . . . Now we'll get a look at my son, Davie. Don't pull any punches, because I'm not at all sure he is the man we want. But he's been groomed in the business, as an errand boy, a mechanic, a salesman, now as our industrial relations director. (*into intercom*) Send in my son.

WISE: David, what do you think of Hotspur's plans?

DAVID: As I have indicated in numerous conferences, I think our expansion overseas is solid and inescapable. We have become an international company, and it is up to us to expand in marketing and manufacturing in all regions open to us. That means everywhere. At the same time, I think we have done a poor job in moving fast enough into the expanding European market. But there are still opportunities there, if we find the right partners. We also have wonderful opportunities in Africa, in Latin America, even in Asia. But we must move resolutely, and with a huge investment—even if it means siphoning off all our U.S. profits.

WISE: Where should our world headquarters be?

DAVID: Here is a matter that requires close study. My choice would be Geneva or Zurich, which already are the world headquarters for many firms.

WISE: Where should we have factories?

DAVID: Eventually, in every corner of the world. For the time being, we should manufacture wherever there is a market for our products, and where there appears likely to be a market in the years just ahead. That means in Europe, in Australia, in Israel, in Mexico. The plant in São Paulo had my firm backing, despite the current muddle in United States-Brazil trade, because Brazil's 70 million people need our washers, our refrigerators, our industrial goods—and more Brazilians will be able to buy them in the not-too-distant future. Let us gamble on the world's crying need for more machines and comfort, and in the meantime aggressively sell to that portion of the public that has the means to buy now. Only in that way can we keep one step ahead of the Japanese, the Germans, the fast-moving Italians.

DFT: And where do we do our research?

DAVID: Wherever there are talented men with ideas for new products, improved machines. Of course we can't go to work at setting up laboratories everywhere. But we should start with the knowledge that important technical achievements are taking place everywhere. We should keep in close touch with this work, and wherever the activity—and the market—justifies, we should get active.

WISE: David, to what extent can we rely on nationals for filling our overseas executive posts?

DAVID: Almost completely. If we have a plant in Brazil, we should find a qualified Brazilian to run it for us. Selecting such a man would be one of the most critical jobs for the head of our international company. We must stop thinking of ourselves as an American company. We'll be a world company.

WISE: Now a look inward. How do you qualify for the job of international manager?

DAVID: Because I have a broad knowledge of Hotspur's activities—at home and abroad—and because I think in world terms. I have studied in England, traveled the length of South America, climbed the hills of Jerusalem. I speak Spanish, and can understand German, French, and Italian. At Hotspur, I've played every position, practically. But, most important, I qualify for this job because I have a desire and tenacity to work with, understand, adapt myself to doing business with all people.

WISE: That will be it, David. (As the door swings behind David) Whew! There we have it—four distinct, qualified, and invigorating approaches to the same problem. Now the point, DFT, is that each of these four men has good qualifications for the job, but each has limitations. The big question: How do you weigh general qualifications against a particular limitation? For example, is

Slimmermeyer's rather unsophisticated view of people offset by his marketing know-how and drive? Will Smythe's methodical approach help or deter your program?

DFT: We'll have to balance all these things.

1. Which of the four candidates would you select for the job?
2. What qualifications for the job does each man have? What are his limitations?
3. Why do you think the qualifications of the man you chose outweigh his limitations?

Case Study Two / Selection of Executive for Promotion to Presidency*

Almost every employee, whether a file clerk or an executive, demonstrates assets and liabilities in the performance of his work. Where the assets of an employee clearly outweigh his liabilities, his boss might say that the employee's liabilities are a small price to pay for his assets, and such a person might be considered for promotion. On the other hand, where the assets are clearly outweighed by the liabilities, the boss might say the price paid is excessive, and such a person would not be considered promotable. Before a man is selected for promotion, his best assets are often balanced against his major limitations.

From the following six biographies, you are requested to (1) state in one or two words the chief asset and the chief liability of each man if he were to become company president, and (2) rate the price paid for the asset—that is, balance the limitation against the asset by choosing one of the following:

a. The asset very clearly outweighs the limitations.
b. The asset is a little greater than the limitations.
c. The man's asset is less than the man's limitations.

1. *Phil M., Vice-president, Personnel.* Most agree that Phil is a real personnel expert. He's given us a personnel program that both the social scientists and our cost accountants think is fine. But most also agree he goes overboard in trying to substitute scientific results for human judgment. For example, he refuses to hire any applicant who fails even one of the employment tests—even if he fails by only a single point and favorably impresses all the people who interview him.
2. *Jack M., Comptroller.* Most agree that Jack is extremely bright and competitive. When he worked out our financial reorganization, he got the company one of the most favorable interest rates in the industry. But most

* From Earl Planty. The idea for this exercise came from L. E. Bassler, in a Master's thesis done at the University of Illinois, 1959.

also agree there's doubt about his motives. Several times he didn't hesitate to step on toes to feather his own nest.

3. *Mac C., Vic-president, Sales, Major Appliance Division.* Most agree that Mac brings out the best in his immediate subordinates. An unusually large proportion of them have moved on higher in the organization. But most also agree he leans on their judgment. On several occasions time ran out and a crucial decision wasn't made because his staff couldn't reach agreement.

4. *Carl L., Vice-president, Research and Development.* Most agree that Carl is a real creative thinker. His ideas have given us some outstanding patents. But most also agree that he's stubborn as a mule. He's impossible to talk out of a nonproductive project even after it's bled his budget and most of his own staff think it's pointless.

5. *Ed N., Vice-president, Heavy Equipment Division.* Most agree that Ed's division is usually one big happy family. His turnover, absenteeism, spoilage, and grievance figures are consistently among the lowest in the company. But most also agree he's extravagant with his workers. His division regularly runs up one of the biggest employee relations bills in the company.

6. *Joe L., Vice-president, Engineering.* Most agree that Joe is extremely competent and hardworking. He's given us an advanced technology and low capital investment per unit output. But most also agree that he cannot tolerate subordinates less competent and hardworking than himself. The result is a chronic and serious turnover problem among his immediate staff.

You are a close business friend of the board chairman of Blake, Inc. He lunched with you today to tell you that Blake's president just died of a heart attack and the board is hurriedly trying to replace him from within the top management group.

Advanced age, health, and other considerations have ruled out all but the above six candidates. He asked you to recommend one of the six and to give your reasons. You have the above reports on the six men, gained at lunch to help you, plus the following:

Blake was incorporated forty years ago. Its primary product lines are in the industrial and consumer electronic fields. Its 1968 net sales ($10 million) and earnings were the fourth and third highest in the company's history. The board of directors perceives no urgent problems at the present time. It is Blake tradition to select presidents strictly on the basis of individual merit. Thus, any top management position may be considered a springboard to the presidency.

The characteristics described for each man are, by board consensus, the strongest and weakest points of the man for the presidency. With regard to such things as general intelligence, education, knowledge of the company and the industry, public relations ability, and so on, the men are rated about equally favorably.

Which one of the six men do you choose for president? Why?

The Dynamic Corporation of America is just what its name implies: a progressive and aggressive company in which sales have been increasing every year since it was founded fifteen years ago. Its headquarters are in the Middle West, and it has major manufacturing facilities in the West and in Canada. It has been expanding rapidly abroad as well, in developing countries and in Western Europe.

The company's chief executive is one of the country's most outstanding managers and has contributed greatly to the growth of the company. His chief assistant, who has the title of vice-president, had many years' experience in operations research in the Air Force. In his present post, he serves as a kind of chief of staff, supervising operations research studies, mergers and acquisitions, and long-range planning.

Because the company has plans for further expansion, problems of coordination are expected to increase considerably. Many new younger men are joining the organization; operations are becoming more scattered geographically; and the work is becoming more diverse.

The president needs to reduce his burden of coordination, and he wants to be sure that further growth occurs smoothly. Hence he directs his assistant to hire a specialist in organization planning. Eventually, the choice is narrowed down to three candidates:

Organization Specialist A has had many years' experience in operations research and organization planning in the Air Force. (He is a graduate of the Air Force Academy.) After leaving the service, he became second-in-command of an engineering consulting firm in the East. During the last few years he has been in charge of the successful reorganization of a large corporation. More recently he has been working on product development. He is a good man, although not as articulate as his prospective employers.

Organization Specialist B also served in the Air Force, but only during World War II, and left the service as a junior officer. Then he spent several years with the Marshall Plan in Europe and thereafter worked on the reorganizations of two major corporations, making good contributions under difficult circumstances. During the last two years he has been working as a consultant but is not happy with the variety of assignments and the heavy traveling involved. He is, therefore, looking for a new connection.

Organization Specialist C served in the Air Force during the Korean War in a minor capacity. For the last thirteen years he has been with a large company whose products are somewhat similar to those of the Dynamic Corporation. At first he worked in the employee relations department, then in training activities, and later on mergers. He set up the organization of the international division. Now he is looking for promotion and a larger opportunity, but he is still rather naïve and overcautious.

In making the choice, the Dynamic Corporation must consider that it wants the new man to work no more than two years on the new organization structure and the preparation of the manual. Thereafter he is to succeed the president's chief assistant, who is to go on to more important responsibilities.

1. If you were the assistant, which of these men would you want to hire?
2. State the advantages and disadvantages of hiring each one, and give reasons for your final choice.

Selected Readings

"Use of Tests in Employee Selection," Mason Haire, *Harvard Business Review*, January, 1950, pp. 42–51. A balanced view of the values and limitations of psychological tests.

"Staffing and Developing the Organization," Raymond E. Katzell, and "Measurement in the Selection and Development Process," Albert P. Maslow, *Behavioral Science Research in Industrial Relations*, Industrial Relations Counselors, Inc., New York, 1962, pp. 107–148. Analyses of the staffing problem from the behavioral science viewpoint.

The Brain Watchers, Martin L. Gross, Random House, Inc., New York, 1962. A harshly critical view of personality tests. (Other types of tests are not discussed.)

The Development of Executive Talent: A Handbook of Management Development Techniques and Case Studies, M. Joseph Dooher and Vivienne Marquis (eds.), American Management Association, New York, 1952. A handbook drawn from the experience of many companies, covering viewpoints, principles, and techniques. Authors include personnel managers and others holding important positions in industry.

Manpower Planning for High Talent Personnel, Eric W. Vetter, Bureau of Industrial Relations, Graduate School of Business Administration, The University of Michigan, Ann Arbor, Mich., 1967. Techniques of forecasting manpower needs, developing recruitment policies, selection methods, and training programs, and evaluating and controlling the programs set up. Includes case stories describing practices of leading firms.

The Effectiveness of University Management Development Programs, Kenneth R. Andrews, Division of Research, Graduate School of Business Administration, Harvard University, Boston, 1966. A lengthy study of the effectiveness of university executive training programs.

Executive Obsolescence, Frederick C. Haas, American Management Association, Research Study #90, New York, 1968. An examination of the characteristics and causes of executive obsolescence and the measures which might be taken to prevent and correct it.

18

ADMINISTRATION

OF

COMPENSATION

*The problem of status and payment is made
more complex because it evokes powerful
emotions—emotions about economic security
and about the value attributed to one's own
work as compared with that of others.*
Elliott Jaques: *Measurement of Responsibility*

*Progress mainly depends on the extent to which
the strongest and not necessarily the highest
forces of human nature can be utilised for the
increase of social good.*
Alfred Marshall

18 At a time when many factory workers and office employees were getting $15 to $20 a week or even less, Henry Ford, Sr., the founder of the Ford Motor Company, suddenly announced that his plants would pay a minimum wage of $5 a day. Applicants flocked to his factory gates, not only from nearby communities, but from other parts of the country.

The lure of more money is definitely one of the most potent in attracting recruits, whether they are machine operators or executives, and high-paying industries and companies are apt to draw recruits away from those who pay less. Simply paying more is not the answer to the staffing problem, however, or even to the recruitment aspect of it. When companies begin bidding against each other for applicants on the basis of pay alone, they may find that none of them is better off and all have raised their costs. Something of this sort has occurred in the last fifteen years in college recruiting for technical personnel. Each year the beginning salaries go up, and yet recruiting becomes no easier for anyone.

It is, however, important that a company keep its pay schedule somewhere near what other companies in the industry and the area are paying, and most make an effort to do so. One tool used for this purpose is the salary (or wage) survey, a questionnaire sent to other companies that are likely to be drawing on the same labor market. Generally, this will give job titles, describe the actual responsibilities of each job, and ask what wages and other types of compensation are being paid for similar work. There is also published information on which companies can draw. The Bureau of Labor Statistics of the U.S. Department of Labor has conducted a number of surveys of this nature for various jobs in different sections of the country. Some trade associations and industry groups provide similar services for their members.

JOB EVALUATION

It is not enough, however, for a company to make its pay schedule equal to the average in other companies, or even to that of the very highest paying. This may be important to new applicants, but once people are on the job, other factors assume equal importance: the relation of their pay to that of others in the company, the frequency of increases, and the basis on which increases are given. A man may be getting a good salary, quite adequate for his needs; but if he finds that someone doing less important work is getting more, it naturally rankles. Similarly, it seems only fair that after a man has been on the job for a while and has improved his skills, he should get some recognition in the form of extra pay.

"Fair wages and salaries" are not easy figures to arrive at. Most people would grant that it is only fair that the president of a company should get more than the typist or the man who operates a machine, because it is quite obvious that his job requires more skill and entails greater responsibility. But should the typist who handles difficult statistical copywork get more than the girl at

410

the next desk who types only letters and manuscripts but also takes some dictation and takes care of a few files?

A person's wage or salary cannot be entirely dependent on how good he is at his job; it must be related to the nature of the job itself—its difficulty and the amount of responsibility it entails. To determine what the *jobs* are worth is the function of job evaluation. Differences in individual performance can then be taken care of by providing rate ranges rather than single rates for each job.

There are three principal systems of evaluating jobs: (1) the ranking method, (2) the point system, and (3) the factor-comparison method. In each case, job descriptions—lists of actual duties and responsibilities—are gathered from incumbents and their superiors before the evaluation takes place.

Under the ranking method, duties and other factors affecting the job are examined, and jobs are arranged in order from the highest to the lowest. To facilitate this ranking, key or benchmark jobs may be selected and the others slotted between them. For example, the most highly skilled job held by a nonsupervisory employee in a factory is likely to be that of tool- and diemaker, the lowest that of sweeper. In between are other jobs that are obviously below that of the tool- and diemaker and above that of the sweeper. When two or three of these have been carefully scrutinized and placed in the scale, it is easier to slot the remaining jobs by comparing them with those already ranked.

Under the point system, the various factors the company is supposedly paying for are selected—e.g., skill, physical effort, and responsibility—and the maximum number of points allowable for each is determined. The tool- and diemaker will then receive the maximum number of points for skill, and other jobs proportionately less according to the amount of skill they require. Points are also given for unavoidable hazards on the job, on the theory that an employee should be compensated for running risks and for unpleasant working conditions. The total number of points determines the "labor grade" into which each job falls, and hence the wage rate.

As the name implies, the factor-comparison method also makes use of job factors, but with the difference that each job is ranked by each factor in turn; then the portion of the total salary paid for this factor is determined. This in turn determines the weight to be given to each factor in arriving at a final ranking.

The table on the next page shows the factors used in one company's job evaluation plan and the percentage of total pay that depends on each one.

It is important to keep in mind that job evaluation is used only to determine *relative* pay—which jobs pay more than others and by what percentage. The actual wages or salaries are, in the main, determined by the rates currently in force. Let us say that the highest rate is $5 an hour and the lowest $2 an hour. After the evaluation has been made, the rates for the highest and lowest grades will probably be kept unchanged, and the number of grades, which may range from three to as many as fifty, will determine the increments as one goes up the scale. With a spread of $3 between the highest and the lowest and

Factor	Percentage
Education	15
Job training and experience	15
Job complexity and scope	25
Accountability for errors	10
Contact with others inside the company	5
Contact with others outside the company	10
Functional guidance of the work of others	10
Confidential information	5
Work surroundings	2.5
Physical effort	2.5
	100.0

thirty jobs in between, it would be possible to use increments of 10 cents an hour.

When a job evaluation is first installed, some inequities are usually discovered. Some jobs will be paying too much; others will be paying too little. Companies are reluctant to cut back those who are getting too much for the jobs they are doing since a pay cut would be quite sure to arouse anger. However, when new people are hired for these overpaid jobs, they can be paid no more than the evaluation calls for. On the other hand, those who are getting too little are generally raised. Overall, therefore, installation of a job evaluation system is likely to cost the company money. It is believed, however, that bringing order into the pay structure will bring returns that will offset this disadvantage—lower employee turnover and less discontent.

How scientific is job evaluation? The answer is: Not very. There is an essential illogic in adding together such things as "working conditions" and "skill required," and none of the factors can be evaluated except by judgment, which is likely to be fallible to some extent. However, it may be said that job evaluation is fairer and more nearly scientific than setting pay scales without careful study of the job content. Without it many more inequities are likely to occur in a large company.

This is not to say that, once established, a job evaluation plan will operate without difficulty. On the contrary, there are forces at work that are continually acting to distort the wage structure. General increases arrived at through collective bargaining may not change the ranking of the jobs, but there are other factors to be taken into account.

Most important of these is the relative scarcity of certain types of labor. If a job offered at the scale called for by the job evaluation finds no takers, what is the company to do? If it raises the rate, it must, to be entirely fair, raise the pay of everyone in the same grade and the rates of everyone above them. Often this will be prohibitively expensive.

This dilemma may be illustrated by the situation in the engineering field, though the engineering jobs may not come under an evaluation system. The competitive recruiting in the colleges has driven some companies to raise the pay of beginners by $50 a month or more each year. Thus an engineer who was hired the previous year and has won a raise in the meantime may find himself getting no more than the new recruits.

Another difficulty, found most often in white-collar jobs, stems from tradition. It is generally considered that the company president's secretary should be the highest paid of all secretaries. Yet suppose the work done by the sales manager's secretary is actually more demanding and requires greater skill. Strictly in accordance with job evaluation, the latter should get higher pay.

Again, rank-and-file workers are generally paid time and a half for overtime, while foremen often are not, since they tend to be "exempt" employees (exempt, that is, from the provisions of the Fair Labor Standards Act, which requires time and a half for overtime) and not subject to the provisions of the union contract if there is one. When overtime is heavy, therefore, the foreman may actually be taking home less than the men under him.

Companies deal with these problems as best they may, sometimes with a certain degree of unfairness. When it is difficult to hire certain skills, they may take on new employees at the middle or the top of the rate ranges rather than at the bottom. This can mean that inexperienced employees who have just come on the job are getting as much as or more than those who are doing the same type of work and doing it much better. If the older employees find out what is happening (and they usually do), results can be embarrassing.

For example: A bank advertised for comptometer operators, offering to pay the salary at the top of the rate range, which employees on the job attained only after three years' experience. One of the applicants turned out to be already employed on the job.

"But you work here already," said the personnel manager.

"I did," said the girl. "But I'm resigning as of now, and applying for the job you advertised."

Disconcerted, the personnel manager offered her the higher pay at once. She took it and returned to spread the story in the department. Immediately, seven more experienced operators appeared to claim similar amounts, and there was nothing to do but give them increases too.

Some companies have faced this situation forthrightly and added evaluation points for the scarcity of employees in the category. Similarly some have, in evaluating secretaries' jobs, added points based on the status of their bosses.

One way of ensuring that supervisors' pay will always be higher than that of the people under them is to make the differential large in the first place. Some companies have a rule that a supervisor must get at least 25 per cent more than the highest-paid man in his group. Another method is to pay him straight time for overtime or to allow him time off when he has worked overtime, thus preserving his hourly differential, at least.

If the general level of wages and salaries were constant, most of these difficulties would not arise. But this has not been true for a long time; hence compensation plans need constant policing and overhauling. Large companies may have wage and salary administrators—executives in the personnel department whose work is solely ensuring fairness and consistency in the pay structure.

HIGHER MANAGERS' PAY

If one looks at the figures on higher managers' pay, it seems difficult to explain why they are paid as they are. For example, two vice-presidents in the same company are doing what appear to be equally difficult jobs; yet they may be receiving widely different salaries. Again, the top man in one company may be getting much less than the top man in another company in the same industry, even though he appears (judging by profitability) to be doing a better job. Or a top manager may be paid a very small base salary to which an enormous bonus may be added in some years. (Eugene Grace, for many years the chief executive of Bethlehem Steel, used to get a $12,000-a-year salary to which a bonus of over $1 million might be added.) Sometimes the chief executive is not the highest-paid man in the organization.

Turning from the figures, which present a seemingly irrational situation, to the explanations of economists and writers on the subject, one receives some, though not full, illumination.

For the most part, the classical economists tended to talk about the determination of profits to the owners rather than compensation to management. However, John Stuart Mill, writing about a hundred years ago, did speak of payment for the "great assiduity and often no ordinary skill . . . to exercise control with efficiency if the concern is large and complicated."[1]

The German and French economists took a somewhat more sophisticated view. Thus, J. B. Say, who held that the "profits of industry must include remuneration for those who follow scientific pursuits as well as profits of the master-agent or adventurer in industry,"[2] believed that payments were made partly for the exercise of personal qualities and partly as a reward for "monopoly" because entry into many fields was not easy.

However, it was Alfred Marshall who first stressed that the manager in the modern business contributes "organization":

> The earnings of a successful business, looked at from the point of view of the business man himself, are the aggregate of the earnings, firstly, of his own ability, secondly, of his plant and other material capital, and thirdly, of his good-will, or business organization and connection. But really it is more than the sum of these: for his efficiency depends partly on his being in that particular business; and if he were to sell it at a fair price, and then engage himself in another business, his income would probably be much diminished. The whole value of his business connection to him when working . . . is a notable instance of Conjuncture or Opportunity *value*.[3]

[1] *Principles of Political Economy*, book 2, chap. 15, sec. 1.
[2] *A Treatise on Political Economy*, book 2, chap. 7.
[3] *Principles of Economics*, 8th ed., Macmillan & Co., Ltd., London, 1930, p. 625.

These "conjunctive earnings" Marshall called "composite quasi rent," a temporary advantage caused by a fixity of the supply of managerial ability, which were determined "by bargaining, supplemented by custom and notions of fairness."[4]

Today the economist's most commonly held theoretical explanation is an application of the "marginal approach." That is, a profit-maximizing businessman would be willing to pay an additional manager an amount equal to that by which the firm's income would be increased by hiring him.

But the actual determination of managerial pay in industry tends to proceed along rather different lines.

Effect of company size   First of all, executive compensation tends to vary with the size of the company. Larger companies in an industry tend to pay more to their executives, especially those in the top echelons, than the smaller companies do. This is clearly explicable on the ground that the larger companies have larger sales revenue and therefore greater ability to pay. In addition, large companies tend to have more levels of management; hence there is room for more differentials between top to bottom, making for higher compensation at the top.

Fluctuations   Second, compensation tends to fluctuate much less than sales, and sales to fluctuate much less than profits. The extent to which executives' pay may be independent of sales and profit fluctuations is confirmed by a study made by J. C. Baker[5] in which he analyzed the pay of 1,000 officers and directors in 100 large industrial companies from 1928 to 1932. He found that the total net income of these companies fell by 99 per cent from 1929 to 1932, but officers' salaries dropped by a mere 2.5 per cent. A study by David R. Roberts of executive compensation in more than 900 companies for the years 1945, 1948, 1949, and 1950[6] produced many strikingly similar findings. Again in the 1950-to-1960 period, corporate profits after taxes did not rise, but the compensation of corporate officers increased approximately 75 per cent.[7]

Effect of the industry   Third, industries in which innovation is important and which have comparative freedom of action tend to pay higher compensation to their executives than those that change slowly and are more regulated by government.

For example, the chemical and automotive industries are noted for rapidity of change, especially of product types. They also tend to be relatively free from governmental regulation. Executives in these industries tend to be among the highest paid in American industry. Several of the principal executives of

[4] *Ibid.*, p. 626.
[5] *Executive Salaries and Bonus Plans,* McGraw-Hill Book Company, New York, 1938.
[6] *Fortune,* April, 1955, p. 111.
[7] Ernest Dale, "Executives Who Can't Manage," *Atlantic Monthly,* July, 1962, p. 59.

General Motors each receive total compensation of around a half million dollars, and the top men at Du Pont (chemicals) each get several hundred thousand dollars a year.

On the other hand, companies in industries whose operations change more slowly, such as banks, insurance companies, and public utilities, tend to pay their executives less.

This has been explained on the ground that in the innovating industries, the executive takes a bigger risk. He must innovate, and if his innovations turn out to be unwise, he may find himself out of a job. In the industries in which actions are more or less prescribed, on the other hand, it is more difficult to make a really bad mistake, and such companies tend to pay lower compensation. These include banks, public utilities, and insurance companies, which are all closely regulated by government agencies. Lately, however, compensation seems to be rising in some companies in these fields.

Job changes   A fourth possible generalization about executive compensation is that highly paid management men do not seem to achieve top brackets mainly by changing companies. Roberts found that in a three-year period only between 1 and 2 per cent of some 15,000 executives studied had left their jobs, whereas exits of manufacturing employees averaged from 20 to 35 per cent a year. The large majority of executive separations are due to retirement and death rather than to voluntary separations, and for those who did move, a bigger job, more responsibility, greater opportunity for future growth were considerably more important than increased income. Lack of accord with the company's managerial policies and discharges were almost as important.[8]

Job changes are thus not made for financial reasons alone as a rule, but rather because of the prospect of nonmonetary as well as monetary gains. Monetary gains may be substantial—a 50 per cent increase or more, for example. But the moves are likely to be made to a higher-ranking position, such as from division manager to vice-president, or vice-president to president rather than to jobs similar in function and pay (though this applies less often to staff specialists, who tend to move horizontally).

One reason for the seeming immobility of so many managers may be the accumulation of "experience capital" with one company, such as knowledge of the firm's ways and technology or the good opinions of superiors, which most executives are reluctant to jettison, especially since they do not really know what the difficulties elsewhere might be. And, of course, human inertia also exerts a powerful force against a move; also, various forms of deferred compensation may make it financially costly for an executive to move.

Forms of compensation

Taxes take a rising share of rising income. In the very high income brackets, a relatively small share of any increase is left to the taxpayer. On the other hand,

8 *Business Week,* May 2, 1953, p. 120.

high corporate tax rates reduce the cost of high executive salaries. A $200,000-a-year executive will actually cost the company only around $100,000.

This twofold effect has sparked a search for ways in which high executives can be given raises without being subject to the full impact of higher tax rates. Stock options, pensions, and other forms of deferred compensation are among these.

Under a stock option plan, an executive is given an option to buy stock—issued by the company but not yet sold—at a given price. If the stock goes up, he can buy in at the lower price, hold it for the requisite period, then sell it and pay the lower capital gains tax on the proceeds.

In 1964, there was a temporary shift from stock options to cash bonuses because of two major revisions in the Internal Revenue Code. First, the life of a stock option was shortened from ten to five years, and second, it became necessary for an executive to hold the stock for three years instead of six months in order to pay only the capital gains tax rather than the regular income tax on any profit.

In the meantime, however, most companies modified their stock option plans to conform to the new regulations, and the number of stock option plans now appears to be greater than the number in force at the time of the 1964 IRS ruling. It has been estimated that stock options now account for one-third to one-half of the after-tax pay package.[9]

Again, a company pays no income taxes on the money it puts into a pension plan (provided the plan conforms to certain Treasury regulations), and the executives who later profit by it pay no taxes on the money that is paid in. True, they will pay on the income they receive after retirement, but in the meantime they are profiting by a form of tax-free savings. (This, of course, is also true of rank-and-file employees who are under a company-paid pension plan.)

Then, there are other forms of deferred compensation. For example, a company may undertake to pay an executive well for very occasional services as a consultant after he retires. He will pay income tax on what he receives then, of course, but presumably he will be in a lower bracket at that time and the bite will not be so large. Moreover, as in the case of the pension, he will not have to save so much of his highly taxed salary for his old age as he otherwise might have to; hence he will have more for his living expenses now. This is also true when the company pays for life or health insurance for him.

The deferred cash bonus, to be paid on retirement, is another form of deferred compensation. So is the restricted stock option, whereby the executive buys stock from the company but does not benefit from it until after retirement.

New forms of compensation for executives are constantly being developed. For example, in some cases companies help executives finance the purchase of

9 Wilbur G. Lewellen, "Executives Lose Out, Even with Options," *Harvard Business Review,* January–February, 1968, pp. 128 and 140.

land for speculation. It has also been suggested that companies provide custom-made pay packages, allowing each executive to determine the form in which he will receive his compensation, that is, the percentages to be paid in the form of salary, bonuses, insurance, and so on.

The greater part of executive compensation, however, is usually in the form of salaries and bonuses, and as mentioned earlier, the latter may be larger than the former. These are both, of course, fully taxable as income if they are paid in cash. (Sometimes they take the form of stock options.)

Bonuses are theoretically supposed to supply a form of incentive compensation for managers—the better their performance, the higher their bonuses. Quite often this is the case.[10] It is difficult, however, to devise a plan in which only a man's own efforts will count toward a bonus since the total performance of a company depends on the efforts of so many. Thus a company may set aside a certain percentage of profits, after a given return on capital, for payment of executive bonuses, and the total amount allowed cannot be said to depend on the work of a single man, even the company president, except in special cases. Then the money set aside may be allocated to divisions or departments in accordance with their relative performance, and finally to individuals in accordance with their superiors' judgment of their contributions.

More direct acknowledgment of outstanding individual performance is provided in some companies through the payment of special bonuses for extraordinary achievement: a research breakthrough, for example, that results in a highly profitable new product; outstanding work in reorganizing a plant or a department; settlement of a costly strike on reasonable terms after others have tried and failed; and similar performance beyond what is generally expected.

Theoretically, expense accounts are not compensation at all. The executive who collects money from the company on this score is merely getting back his own money that he has had to spend on company business—for entertaining customers, hotel bills, and plane fares. If a company wants its executives to belong to an expensive country club so that they may entertain customers there, it seems only fair that it should pay the dues. Similarly, it may want to save an executive's valuable time by placing a company car or plane at his disposal.

However, it is undeniable that part of this expense money does constitute a form of extra income in some cases. If an executive can entertain a customer at lunch almost every day and often at dinner too, he is getting a large number of free meals. Similarly, he may attend a business meeting of one kind or another at a resort and in this way get a partial vacation free.

Some companies have been fairly indifferent in this matter, and some executives—and rank-and-file salesmen—have taken advantage of "business expense" provisions which make money received in compensation for business expenses nontaxable. But it is very difficult for a company to draw up rules

---

[10] There have been instances, however, in which top executives have received increased bonuses in years when the company's performance was declining.

ensuring that its executives will be reimbursed for *all* legitimate business expenses and yet prevent *any* freeloading. Nor has the Internal Revenue Service been entirely successful in attempting to differentiate for tax purposes. Almost any type of general rule is likely to be unfair to some.

Company salary structures

In a series of studies conducted over a number of years, the American Management Association has found that there is a fairly constant relationship between the pay of the chief executive and the compensation of the next two highest-paid executives. This seems to prevail generally, regardless of the industry, though of course the actual amounts will differ widely.

The second highest-paid executive, the Association has found, tends to get around 70 per cent as much as the top man, while the third highest-paid man gets about 40 per cent. However, the similarity does not extend to the *positions* held by the second and third highest men. In some companies, the second man is the top financial officer; in others, he is the head of the manufacturing or the marketing function. If the chairman of the board is active in the management of the company, he may be the second highest-paid man. Conversely, if he is actually the chief executive officer, he will be the highest paid and the president the second highest paid.

Some companies have attempted to align executive jobs in accordance with some more or less objective idea of their value to the company, and set ranges for each job; that is, they use a form of job evaluation. The executive's pay *range,* then, will depend on his job, and his actual pay on how well he does it. These plans, however, can seldom be extended very far up in the executive ranks, because the higher a man is in the corporate hierarchy, the more he tends to make his own job.

One interesting idea on the compensation of executives (and others) has been advanced by Elliott Jaques in his book *Measurement of Responsibility.*[11] From a study of the decisions a man is empowered to make, he suggested the criterion should be "the maximum length of time the decisions made by a person on his own initiative committed resources of the Company." Thus top industry researchers like "Boss Kettering" at General Motors or Nobel Prize winner Irving Langmuir at General Electric might not report on their activities for months or years. But rank-and-file research personnel as a rule will have to check fairly constantly with their superiors on the approaches they are using and the results they are achieving. However, Prof. T. T. Paterson of the University of Strathclyde in Scotland has pointed out[12] that the time-span measurement plan would entail formidable administrative problems. For example, a comprehensive study of the time spans in different regions and industries would be needed. Also, since total compensation may include a variety of fringe benefits, accurate calculations would be extremely difficult, if not impossible.

[11] Tavistock Publications, Ltd., London, 1956.
[12] "The Jacques System; Impractical?" *New Society,* Dec. 19, 1963, pp. 9ff.

SUMMARY

While the absolute amount of pay is important in attracting and holding employees and executives, both may be as much concerned about the relation of their compensation to the amounts paid to others in the same company, especially to those at or near their own level. For this reason, companies often go to great lengths to try to ensure an equitable internal pay structure.

The principal way of doing this is to adopt some form of job evaluation, in which an attempt is made to determine the relative value and difficulty of the various jobs.

Job evaluation plans seldom apply to very high executive jobs, however, since the higher a man's position, the more likely he is to make his own job; thus it is difficult to evaluate the job as such, rather than the incumbent.

Higher managers often receive a "pay package" rather than a straight salary. Thus they may be compensated not only by salaries, but by bonuses (which sometimes amount to more than their salaries), stock option plans, and various forms of deferred compensation, in addition to regular pensions.

In general, too, a higher manager's pay depends not only on his position, but on the industry and on company size.

Review Questions

1. What is job evaluation? How does it differ from the merit ratings and executive appraisals described in the last chapter?
2. What is the point system of job evaluation? The factor comparison method? The ranking method? Which do you believe is the fairest method?
3. What are some of the factors that tend to distort a job evaluation?
4. Do you think it is fair for new employees to get the same rate as those who have been on the job a year or two, assuming that skill increases with experience with the company? Suppose, however, that you were the office manager and found yourself unable to get any new stenographers unless you hired them at the top of the rate range. What would you do then?
5. What are stock options? Can you think of any reason why it might be desirable for the stockholders to agree to them?
6. Do stock options cost the stockholders anything?

Case Study / Executive Job Evaluation

You are the president of a comparatively small one-plant company. The executives reporting to you are:

1. *The treasurer and controller,* who is the chief accounting officer and also handles banking relations and relations with stockholders. The company is

closely held, however, and plans no stock issues. Also, it seldom finds it necessary to borrow funds. The treasurer-controller also manages the office, which has twenty employees.

2. *The plant manager.* Production is a fairly routine matter, since the company produces a staple product that has not changed in a number of years. There are about one hundred production employees.

3. *The sales manager,* who supervises a sales force of ten men and is also the company's star salesman. Much of the company's business is due to his contacts.

4. *The personnel manager.* His responsibilities include recruitment, preliminary selection of employees for both plant and office, development of training programs, and initiation and administration of various employee benefit plans, such as the pension system. He supervises a staff of three people. The company has no union.

5. *The research director.* This man has recently been hired with two assistants to work on development of a revolutionary new product that might enable the company to grow into a big one. Its feasibility has not yet been determined, however, although both you and the research director are very sanguine about it. You hired him and his assistants because he came to you with the idea, and you were enough impressed with it to invest some money in the development.

1. These executives are all on the same level on the organization chart since they all report to you. Would you, therefore, pay them all alike? Why or why not?

2. Suppose you determined to have an executive job evaluation plan using a point system. To what factors would you assign points, and how many would you give each man on each factor?

Selected Readings

Top Executive Pay Package, Leonard Randolph Burgess, Graduate School of Business, Columbia University, and The Free Press of Glencoe, New York, 1963. The major trends in the principal types of remuneration and their significance.

Equitable Payment: A General Theory of Work, Differential Payment and Individual Progress, Elliott Jaques, William Heinemann, Ltd., London, 1961. A more complete development of the theory advanced in *The Measurement of Responsibility* mentioned in the text.

"Manpower Management and Employment Relations," Dale Yoder, in W. Grant Ireson and Eugene L. Grant (eds.), *Handbook of Industrial Engineering and Management,* Prentice-Hall, Inc., Englewood Cliffs, N.J., 1955, pp. 241–246. The various systems of job evaluation and their application.

Compensating the Corporate Executive, G. T. Washington and V. H. Rothschild, 2d ed., The Ronald Press Company, New York, 1962. In two volumes: vol. 1

deals with salaries, profit participation, and deferred compensation; vol. 2 deals with stock, pension, and insurance plans.

Executive Compensation in Large Industrial Corporations, Wilbur G. Lewellen, National Bureau of Economic Research, New York, 1968. This study of the compensation of the five highest paid positions in fifty key companies finds that compensation has shifted from direct cash payments toward deferred and contingent rewards. Stock-based pay schemes have provided from one-third to one-half of all the after-tax compensation. In "real" terms, aggregate remuneration has not grown at all over the last twenty-five years.

19

DIRECTION

The boss should neither be a brute
Nor yet a father-substitute,
But should remember if he can
That Employee is also Man.
Kenneth Boulding

19 The directing phase of the management job is what many people think of as management itself: telling people what to do and seeing that they do it. Not only must the manager have plans he wants carried out, not only must he divide the work and hire people who are capable of doing it, he must also compel or induce people to use their capabilities.

Most of the researchers who have attempted to assess the results of different styles of direction have confined their studies to rank-and-file employees and first-line supervisors, in the factory or the office. Both Frederick Taylor and Elton Mayo assumed that the men at higher levels were, in general, so committed to company goals that the only problem was to transmit their viewpoint to those down the line. Later observers are not so convinced of this, but it is more difficult to study managers in the mass since they seldom form as homogeneous a group as, say, all employees under a first-line supervisor or all first-line supervisors in a single plant.

Yet getting middle managers, and sometimes even those near the top, to use their capabilities to the full is still a problem for their superiors. And undoubtedly much may be learned about the proper direction of managers from the many studies conducted among those lower down in the organizational hierarchy. Some of the more important studies, including one dealing with middle managers and specialists, are outlined in this chapter.

Of course, a good part of the power of business managers to get the people under them to obey orders rests on their power to impose sanctions: to reward and punish. They may give or withhold raises and promotions, dismiss the recalcitrant, or, in the case of rank-and-file production employees, lay off a man temporarily without pay. Not all managers have complete (or even much) power to use these sanctions—first-line supervisors seldom do nowadays—but all can make recommendations that will generally carry weight. Also, most managers have the power to bawl out or otherwise reprove their subordinates verbally, and reproof is so distasteful to many people that it amounts to a punishment.

In general, too, people tend to recognize that the manager's position gives him a right to issue orders. It appears only natural to most people that the owner of a business should be allowed to decide how it should be run, and if the owner, or the owners in the case of a publicly held company, delegate the authority to managers, most people are inclined to accept the idea that the managers have a right to give orders. It is also generally recognized that the absence of any direction would lead to chaos in a situation where different types of work must be coordinated.

These factors are usually sufficient to prevent open rebellion in a group of subordinates, but they have never been sufficient to induce people to put forth their best efforts, and the tendency to give only half-hearted service may be so general that the manager may come to accept it as natural. Indeed, he may not know how high the standards actually could be if everyone gave of his best.

EARLY ATTEMPTS AT SOLUTION

The inadequacy of the conventional reward-and-punishment system has always been recognized to some extent, but down through the nineteenth century and well into the twentieth managers tended to regard it as at least good enough. When Frederick Taylor found the men in the shop "soldiering," as he called it, his answer was to increase the possible financial rewards and make them more easily attainable. However, this did not, as we have seen, produce the mental revolution he had hoped would ensue.

But the scientific management movement was concerned with more than pay systems. It also sought to make work easier by providing more orderly surroundings, better lighting, and better ventilation. In part because of this and in part because of the influence of the welfare workers whom industry began to call on for help on personnel problems in the years just before World War I, companies started trying to provide more attractive working conditions.

Up to this time, physical surroundings in most factories were unpleasant, sometimes horribly so. Buildings were drab, workplaces were poorly lighted, washrooms were often dirty and sometimes nonexistent. Employees brought their lunches and—if the factory were in a city—had no place to eat them except at their workplaces.

In the newer factories and offices the situation was better. Not only were lighting and ventilation improved and factory interiors made cleaner and more orderly, but employers began providing better employee facilities. Many of them opened cafeterias in which employees could buy nourishing food at low cost. Some companies even beautified their grounds with flowers and shrubs, provided athletic fields, and organized teams and social clubs for their employees.

Industrial psychology introduced

Just before World War I, managers began to hope that the comparatively new science of psychology would provide more effective means of tapping the latent potential of their employees. "The economic experimental psychology offers no more inspiring idea than this adjustment of work and psyche by which mental dissatisfaction in the work, mental depression and discouragement, may be replaced . . . by overflowing joy and perfect inner harmony," wrote Hugo Münsterberg, who may be called the first of the industrial psychologists.[1] Interest continued high during the 1920s, particularly in psychological tests to ensure better placement of employees and in various welfare measures. Some experimental work, most notably the Hawthorne studies, was done on other factors.

[1] *Psychology and Industrial Efficiency*, Constable & Co., Ltd., London; Houghton Mifflin Company, Boston, 1913, p. 309.

The Depression and World War II

With the advent of the Great Depression of the 1930s, managers had less time to consider the rosy possibilities promised by the new science. Many companies were fighting for bare survival. In addition, the power to discharge acquired new force. Losing a job was a major catastrophe; once out of work, a man was likely to stay unemployed for months or even years, and if he found a new job, it might well be worse than the one he had been dislodged from. A manager who was having trouble with an employee frequently needed to do no more than take him to the window and show him the line of job seekers at the gate to induce at least ostensible compliance.

But if the threat of punishment acquired new force, the promise of reward became more nebulous, for promotions and raises were often impossible as contraction rather than expansion became the general rule. Sometimes raises individuals had won through good work were wiped out by across-the-board wage and salary cuts.

Employees did, perhaps, work harder than before. But a situation in which fear provided the principal motivating force did not give rise to the whole-hearted cooperation that managers had always hoped for. Instead, it produced sit-down strikes in many industries and widespread unionization. Organization of the unions was, of course, made easier by the Wagner Act, which forbade employers to fire employees for union activity. But it would be inaccurate to say that the act was the primary cause of the great wave of unionization that swept the mass-production industries at the time. Rather, both the unionization and the act arose from the same cause, the feeling among many people that their work situations had become intolerable and that there was no hope of anything better unless they rebelled.

After the outbreak of World War II, employment mounted rapidly, and soon the threat of dismissal lost almost all its force. A man who was fired could often go across the street and get another job at higher pay.

Meanwhile, unions had begun to write into their contracts provisions that curtailed the manager's power to impose sanctions. A man who was laid off for a few days without pay or dismissed for disobedience or incompetence might bring a grievance alleging that the penalty was unfair, and an arbitrator might force management to rescind it. Unions sought also, and with a large measure of success, to make both raises and promotions largely dependent on seniority rather than on the superior's judgment of performance.

In the years since World War II, it has seldom been quite so easy to get a new job as it was in wartime, but, except in certain areas, employment has remained reasonably high most of the time and the requirement that employers place weight on seniority in distributing the rewards has become, if anything, stronger and more general. And so has the tendency to resist disciplinary measures through the use of grievance procedures.

LEADERSHIP

One possible approach to the problem of employee motivation is to attempt to provide inspiring leadership. The fact that a leader can have an immense effect on the performance of those under him has always been recognized. In armies, for example, it has been noted for centuries that while some officers receive only grudging obedience, others are able to inspire their men to do the seemingly impossible and to do it willingly. The same phenomenon has been noted in other organizations, including business organizations. It is not surprising, therefore, that business would like to discover some way of selecting better leaders and/or training its managers in effective leadership techniques. But while the power of good leadership to produce extraordinary results is a fact, it is difficult to produce facts about what it actually consists of.

When the man in the street talks of leadership ability, he generally means what has been called "charismatic" leadership, *charisma* being the Greek word for gift. In this view, no matter what group such a natural leader finds himself in, he will be recognized for what he is and others will accept his authority.

Undoubtedly some people do give the impression of being natural leaders of this type. Lytton Strachey wrote of Florence Nightingale:

> As for her voice, it was true of it, even more than of her countenance, that it had that in it "one must fain call master." Those clear tones were in no need of emphasis: "I never heard her raise her voice," said one of her companions. "Only, when she had spoken, it seemed as if nothing could follow but obedience." Once, when she had given some direction, a doctor ventured to remark that the thing could not be done. "But it must be done," said Miss Nightingale. A chance bystander, who heard the words, never forgot through all his life the irresistible authority of them. And they were spoken quietly—very quietly indeed.[2]

Again, a middle management executive writes about his boss, the president of a small company:

> He was in his element as a personal leader of men. I have never known a man who could so easily sway the minds of men, who could turn a meeting from a gathering of gloom to a mass of enthusiasm with only a few phrases of optimism and assurance. The men he gathered around him . . . wanted to capture some of his enthusiasm and conviction— and they did.

We need, however, to inquire further before accepting the view that leadership is a single trait of personality that will make itself felt under all circumstances and with all people at all times. A few examples will cast doubt on this theory.

Hitler, an obscure house painter in his youth, rose to power in Germany

2 "Florence Nightingale," in *Eminent Victorians*, Penguin Books, Inc., Baltimore, in association with Chatto & Windus, Ltd., London, 1948, p. 148 (first published in 1918).

apparently by sheer force of personality, and unquestionably he was able to inspire strong adherence in many people, perhaps in the majority of the German population at one time. Yet as a soldier in World War I, he never rose higher than corporal, even when heavy casualties created many new openings. Surely if his leadership ability had been an inherent part of his personality, he would have been made a sergeant, even if lack of education automatically kept him from a commission.

Moreover, when he staged his first *putsch* for power in the 1920s, the reaction in both Germany and the world at large was laughter. He was considered merely a funny little man with delusions of grandeur.

Or take Winston Churchill, the natural leader to whom Britain turned in World War II and who rose magnificently to the occasion. At the end of the war, his leadership was decisively rejected at the polls despite the great esteem in which he was still held. And before the war, although he had long been prominent in politics, he was never able to gain the leadership of his party or become prime minister.

It is clear that we must look beyond the simple view of leadership expressed by one executive in a round table discussion: "We can recognize a boy who is going to lead at the fifth grade level. Other boys will hang around him and follow him."[3] Almost anyone can remember such a "natural leader" of his childhood or early youth who never rose above mediocrity in later life or even sank below the average.

It may be questioned, for example, whether Florence Nightingale's voice and manner alone would have been sufficient to enforce obedience if it had not been known that she had powerful backing in England and if she had not developed a careful strategy for winning acceptance from those who were at first disposed to regard her as a nuisance. One may wonder also whether the bystander who reported the incident may not have been one who already admired her for her work and her character and had, therefore, attuned his ears to hear a master's voice.

Moreover, one may question whether the company president who turned a meeting from gloom to optimism did not owe something to his official status. It is quite possible that his subordinates felt he knew more about the situation and the possibilities than they did.

And even aside from this, some studies have shown that leadership may depend to some extent on status itself. Some investigations have demonstrated, for example, that leadership in community activities may be a function of social class.[4] It has also been found that those of higher position tend to take the lead in business discussion groups for which no leader has been formally appointed.[5]

Nevertheless, although status or esteem may be reinforcing factors, it is

[3] *What Makes an Executive? Report of a Round Table on Executive Potential and Performance,* Columbia University Press, New York, 1955, p. 65.
[4] Bernard M. Bass, *Leadership, Psychology, and Organizational Behavior,* Harper & Row, Publishers, Incorporated, New York, 1960, p. 273.
[5] *Ibid.,* p. 269.

evident that some people do exercise a kind of charismatic leadership, influence apparently achieved through force of personality alone. And in view of the results an inspiring leader can obtain, it seems important to determine the ingredients of this type of leadership ability.

Trait theory

Originally, researchers in the field attempted to split leadership ability into its components by identifying the traits of character and personality that mark the leader. If it could be shown that all leaders possessed certain traits in common, then it might be concluded that those traits added up to natural leadership ability.

In 1940, Charles Bird examined twenty lists of traits attributed to leaders in various surveys and found that none of the traits appeared on all lists. Leaders were characterized by a wide variety of traits ranging all the way from "neatness" to "nobility."[6]

After reviewing an even larger number of studies, conducted among groups ranging from children to military, business, and professional personnel, William O. Jenkins stated categorically: "No single trait or group of characteristics has been isolated which sets off the leader from the members of his group."[7]

If one considers that a trait is a constant and inherent part of personality, this conclusion is undoubtedly justified. However, if a less rigid view is taken and there is recognition of the fact that the same person may exhibit a given trait in some circumstances and not in others, one may say that there are three traits essential for leadership.

First of all, there is intelligence—not intelligence as an absolute quality but intelligence relative to the intelligence of the followers. More than one study has shown that leaders tend to be more intelligent than their followers, although they might not be considered very intelligent if compared with members of some other group. Moreover, if a person is very much more intelligent than the potential followers, they are unlikely to choose him for their leader.[8] (This is probably because a highly intelligent person is usually uninterested in leading a merely average group or perhaps because people find it difficult to understand the aims or even the language of someone who is very much more intelligent than they are.)

Second, self-confidence, or at least the ability to appear self-confident, appears to be necessary for leadership. But a person who is self-confident in one situation may be anything but assured in an entirely different case. Some businessmen who are very confident in their normal situations have found themselves baffled and frustrated in trying to get their ideas across when they join government. Again, one manager reported that a foreman chosen because he was believed to have natural leadership ability lost all confidence when he

[6] Charles Bird, *Social Psychology*, Appleton-Century-Crofts, Inc., New York, 1940, p. 378.
[7] W. O. Jenkins, "A Review of Leadership Studies with Particular Reference to Military Problems," *Psychological Bulletin*, vol. 44, 1947, pp. 74–75.
[8] Bass, *op. cit.*, p. 177.

was put in charge of activities with which he was unfamiliar: "When someone tries to ask him a question, he hides in the washroom."

The third trait that might be mentioned is initiative, for it goes without saying that the person who does not initiate action or ideas cannot be called a leader. But again the man who exhibits initiative under one set of circumstances may not display it under others. As a simple illustration, the man who is able to suggest entertaining new activities to a social group may not display much initiative in business, and vice versa.

Significantly, these three qualities—although under several different names —appeared on the majority of the lists Bird examined. And this occurred despite the fact that some of the studies were conducted among students, many of whom apparently confused popularity with leadership. (Although a person who is popular with the potential followers may find it easier to assume leadership, not all those who are well liked are leaders, and sometimes leaders are respected but not regarded with any particular warmth.)

Significantly, also, Jenkins found that leaders did have one thing in common, although it could not be called a trait. "The only common factor," he wrote, "appeared to be that leaders in a particular field need and tend to possess superior general or technical competence or knowledge in that area."[9] And superior general or technical knowledge in many fields (although perhaps not in all) generally requires superior intelligence. Again, self-confidence is likely to be a product of competence in the activities in which the group is engaged and so is initiative, for no one is likely to feel self-confident in a situation he does not understand or to exhibit initiative in an unfamiliar field.

Situational theory

More generally accepted today than the trait theory, therefore, is what is known as the "situational theory," which Jenkins stated as follows: "Leadership is specific to the particular situation under investigation."[10]

Thus, leaving aside such factors as status (official position) and esteem because of past achievements or achievements in another field (e.g., generals who become presidents), it is often said that the choice of a leader depends on the problems the group is facing and on the character of the group itself. Leadership in this view falls to the man who is best able to help the group reach its goals.

This theory is well illustrated by some interesting studies conducted during World War II, when men were being trained for the Office of Strategic Services, the cloak-and-dagger group whose members were parachuted behind enemy lines to make contact with resistance forces in enemy-occupied territory. The findings are especially revealing because the groups who chose the leaders knew nothing of their civilian status or their past achievements.

In one case, the group was given the problem of getting over a high wall.

[9] *Op. cit.,* p. 75.
[10] *Ibid.,* p. 75.

(Actually, there were two walls, but the participants could not see the second wall until they got to the top of the first one. A log was available to be used as a bridge.) The report on this states:

> The original leader in this situation was often the man who got to the top of the wall first. If this was his only qualification, he soon lost his authority when others got up beside him, but a man with some aptitude for leadership could gain a decided advantage simply by getting to the top first. The good leader would see that too many men did not crowd the top of the wall while the log was being passed up; he would have the stronger men remain below to pass up the log but yet avoid the predicament of having the last man a heavy, awkward person who could not reach the top without help from below. Similarly, he would direct traffic across the log to the other side, sending a lithe, confident man first to help the more timid and awkward ones, who would come in the middle while he or some other brought up the rear.[11]

In another case the problem was getting a delicate range finder (represented by a log) across a brook that the participants were instructed to consider a raging torrent with steep banks. Here something of the same situation developed:

> Sometimes the group formally elected a leader at the start and retained him to the end despite his demonstrated lack of competence. More often some man would assert himself by proposing a plan of action or by asking each man for his ideas and thus taking charge of the discussion. If he succeeded in gaining the lead in either of these ways, he might continue to guide his teammates from then on, even though his ideas were faulty and his plans poorly conceived. But a man who took the lead at the beginning was not always directing things at the end. . . . Sometimes a man who started by guiding the discussion lost his place when the work began to one who was more adept in manipulating physical objects. On another occasion, a man would lose his leadership when a teammate proposed a new idea that was adopted by the others, who then turned to this second man for direction in its execution. If it worked, the group was apt to regard him as the leader from that point on. Not infrequently, two or more men competed for leadership throughout the task, acknowledgment shifting from one to the other as they varied momentarily in resourcefulness or power. But it was not always the most assertive individual who dominated the enterprise. He might try for leadership and even hold it for a time, but the group might reject him eventually in favor of a quieter member who had made suggestions that had really worked.[12]

Similarly, in discussion groups, it was often the man who could keep the discussion proceeding in an orderly way who took over the leadership, even

---

[11] The OSS Assessment Staff, *Assessment of Men: Selection of Personnel for the Office of Strategic Services*, Holt, Rinehart and Winston, Inc., New York, 1948, pp. 100–101.
[12] *Ibid.*, p. 98.

though another leader might have been elected by formal vote of the group in the beginning.[13]

Voice, appearance, and manner sometimes had a bearing also but mainly on the initial choice of a leader. When leaders of discussion groups were chosen by formal vote at the start, it was found that selection often depended on "some unique characteristic of the individual, such as his greater age or white hair, which made him stand out as a personage."[14]

Another study, by Richard LaPiere, has shown that different types of groups (e.g., reveling, serious) chose different types of leaders.[15] This is not surprising. One would not expect a serious person to be the life of the party in a social group, particularly one that is bent on wild enjoyment.

Closely allied to the situational theory of leadership is the view that the leader may be representative of the group and the best fitted to articulate its desires. W. O. Jenkins observed that his review of the many studies of leadership showed that ". . . leaders tend to exhibit certain characteristics in common with the members of their group. Two of the more obvious of these characteristics are interests and social background."[16]

In some cases the leader may possess the characteristics of the group in exaggerated form. This could account for Hitler's early rise. Hard conditions in Germany had given many Germans a feeling of self-pity and a general sense of having been wronged, and in Hitler this feeling was especially strong. It has been said that tears came into his eyes when he spoke of his early hardships.

Later on, of course, when he had demonstrated his ability to acquire a following, he won backing from industrialists and others who thought he could help them achieve their aim of putting labor and liberal groups in their place. Also, he demonstrated his ability to achieve at least one of the aims of the majority of the population by seizing the Rhineland, an enterprise that succeeded mainly because of weakness and hesitation on the part of the nations that later allied against him.

Similarly, the representation theory may account for the leadership in gangs of juvenile delinquents. Sometimes the leader turns out to be actually psychotic, whereas the followers, although "disturbed," cannot be considered insane.

Leader behavior

Another line of attack has been to examine how successful leaders behave and compare their behavior with that of less successful leaders. Studies at Ohio State University conducted over a period of years resulted in the "Leader

---

[13] *Ibid.*, p. 131.
[14] *Ibid.*, p. 131. The tendency to select an older man may have been due to the fact that many people to some extent associate age with status and dignity. Also, group members may be able to accept direction from an older person without loss of self-esteem because they feel: "Since he's older than I am, he *should* know more."
[15] *Collective Behavior*, McGraw-Hill Book Company, New York, 1930, p. 34.
[16] *Op. cit.*, p. 75.

Behavior Description Questionnaire," a multiple-choice instrument through which people who have an opportunity to examine leader behavior can indicate how frequently a given leader behaves in a given way.[17]

There is, of course, the possibility of a halo effect. That is, observers, particularly when they are the leader's subordinates or superiors, will tend to believe that a man whose behavior is good or bad in one respect is good or bad in all respects. But scores on two factors, called "consideration" and "initiating structure," were found to be independent of the others. The former, of course, refers to consideration for the followers and the latter to logical planning and coordination of the work. Although some evidence has accumulated that supervisors and managers who score high on both factors tend to be good leaders, some studies have led to puzzling results. For example, in one study which covered groups under both production and nonproduction foremen, production foremen who scored high on initiating structure also received high efficiency ratings from their superiors, but in the case of the nonproduction foremen a high score on the same factor was negatively correlated with high efficiency ratings. However, there were less absenteeism and fewer accidents among the subordinates of both types of foremen who scored high on consideration than among the subordinates of those who scored poorly on that factor.

Other interesting work on the type of leadership or supervision that is likely to prove most effective has been done under the auspices of the Institute of Human Relations at the University of Michigan by Rensis Likert, Daniel Katz, and others, who compared the type of supervision employed in high-productivity groups with that used in low-productivity groups. High-productivity supervisors participated less in the actual work than the low-productivity supervisors; they were more "employee-centered" and spent more time talking to employees informally. But, and this seemed to be one of the most important findings, they actually supervised the work less closely than the low-productivity supervisors and left their employees freer to make decisions about methods and procedures. Also they were less closely supervised by their own superiors. Overall, in fact, these studies tended to show that democratic leadership produces better results than autocratic leadership.[18]

THE HUMAN RELATIONS APPROACH

For a number of years, also, there has been renewed interest in the psychology of the employee. From the late 1930s, when the growth of unions in the mass-production industries signaled to managers that something was wrong with their relations with employees, concern with human relations has mounted.

[17] Ralph M. Stogdill and Alvin E. Coons (eds.), *Leader Behavior: Its Description and Measurement,* Monograph R-88, Bureau of Business Research, Ohio State University, 1957.
[18] See, for example, Daniel Katz, Nathan Maccoby, and Nancy C. Morse, *Productivity, Supervision and Morale in an Office Situation,* University of Michigan Institute for Social Research, Ann Arbor, Mich., 1950.

Adjusting the worker

Some of the work done in pursuit of better relations has been concerned with adjustment of the worker to the work. In part, this has taken the form of a straightforward effort to ensure better placement, on the theory that the fewer square pegs set in round holes, the better performance and attitude will be. Another type of program takes in more territory in that it considers adjustment both on and off the job. This is employee counseling, first adopted at Western Electric as a result of some of the findings of the Hawthorne studies.

At Hawthorne, and in most other cases of employee counseling, the counselors have been instructed to use what is called "nondirective interviewing." The interviewer who employs this technique is described as following rather than leading the interviewee. Instead of asking questions, he confines himself to such responses as "I see" or "Tell me more about it," or he simply repeats the gist of what the employee has said—e.g., "You're wondering where to turn" or "You believe your supervisor is unfair." Interviewers are also cautioned to look behind employees' complaints and treat them as symptoms of the "personal situation which gradually is disclosed as the interview progresses."[19]

In some cases, this counseling process may amount almost to a form of instant psychoanalysis, in which the worker solves his own problems through gaining knowledge of himself as he talks. In the best-known account of the Hawthorne studies, Roethlisberger and Dickson tell of a neurotic, probably somewhat psychotic, employee who began the interview by complaining of persecution by his supervisor and ended by saying: *"You know, I think the reason that I can't stand Mr. Jones [the supervisor] is that every time I look at him he reminds me of my stepfather."*[20]

More typical, perhaps, is a hypothetical case cited to explain the technique —the case of an employee who asks for a transfer:

> Throughout the interview, she [the counselor] is constantly looking for "leads" in what Mary says which will indicate the most probable area in which the real trouble lies. It may well be, for example, that her dissatisfaction with her work is an expression of complications arising in her personal life outside the plant. . . . In problems of this kind . . . the counselor's sole object is to lead the employee to a clear understanding of her problems such that she herself comes to realize what action to take and then assumes responsibility for taking it.[21]

In this case, it appeared, Mary's difficulties were not personal. She was a capable, hardworking girl interested in getting ahead, and she had a clear idea of the type of work she wanted to do. The counselor asked her whether she had discussed the situation with her supervisor, and as the interview progressed the girl lost her fear of doing so. Later the supervisor himself approached the

[19] Fritz Roethlisberger and W. J. Dickson, *Management and the Worker*, Harvard University Press, Cambridge, Mass., 1939, p. 280.
[20] *Ibid.*, p. 310.
[21] *Ibid.*, p. 599.

counselor to talk about the situation and confided that he was perplexed about what to do. Then:

> The counselor at this stage may ask the supervisor a number of ques-
> tions, such as: Did Mary tell you why she is dissatisfied with her work?
> Do you see any possibilities for advancement within your own department
> which would obviate the necessity for a transfer? Do you think that Mary
> understands these possibilities? . . . Following this discussion . . . he
> [the supervisor] then calls Mary up to his desk and gives her a more
> adequate understanding of the situation. . . . she goes back to her work
> in better spirits. She is restored to her normal effectiveness and her
> efficiency may rise.[22]

Counseling of this kind, as the Hawthorne researchers saw it, would provide a means of making employees happier in their work. The counselor might also, in some measure, raise questions about the shop situations that were making for maladjustment and provide a continuous feedback to management on the state of employee morale—without, of course, reference to individual names since he must betray no confidences. In other cases, whether counseling has been practiced by counselors hired for the purpose, by members of the personnel department who have other duties, or by supervisors trained in the process, it has been designed merely to "let employees blow off steam."

Counseling is practiced in some companies today, but at Hawthorne it was discontinued twenty years later, in 1956, by management decision. Ten years after that Dickson and Roethlisberger wrote a book[23] in which they attempted to sum up its achievements and its failures and to uncover the reasons why it was less effective than they had thought it would be.

Counseling did alleviate some interpersonal difficulties, the two concluded, but it failed almost completely to get at the real difficulties, which were due not to the faults of individuals but to the way in which work is organized in most large plants. ". . . it seems to us in retrospect," they wrote, "that counseling was all around the edges of a problem that it could never quite get on the table for discussion. . . ."

> Counseling should have remained an innovative role to the very end—a
> constructive force in the direction of a constant self-examination by the
> Company of its task structure, payment systems, incentive systems, cost
> reduction programs, and of its policies. . . . But, as we now know, this
> did not come to pass. . . . And for this counseling shares a joint respon-
> sibility with management.[24]

Employee satisfactions

Counseling was, in any case, only one of the phases of the human relations approach that grew out of the Hawthorne studies, and many companies did not

---

[22] *Ibid.,* pp. 600–601.
[23] *Counseling in an Organization: A Sequel to the Hawthorne Researches,* Division of Research, Graduate School of Business Administration, Harvard University, Boston, 1966.
[24] *Ibid.,* pp. 469–470 and 472.

adopt the practice even though they attempted to make use of the Hawthorne findings.

Greater interest was aroused by the indications that factors other than money had a major effect on productivity. Some even hailed the results as marking "the end of economic man"—the end, that is, of the concept that money is the principal means of inducing higher work output or even very important in comparison with the other satisfactions an employee may derive from his job. This led to the belief that management could obtain good employee relations by providing the nonfinancial satisfactions that employees were seeking in their work. Roethlisberger has described the things employees really want in this way:

> People at work . . . like to feel important and to have their work recognized as important. Although they are interested in the size of their pay envelopes, this is not a matter of first concern. Sometimes they are more interested in having their pay reflect accurately the relative social importance to them of the different jobs they do. Sometimes even still more important than maintenance of socially accepted wage differentials is the way their superiors treat them.
>
> They like to work in an atmosphere of approval. They like to be praised rather than blamed. They do not like to have to admit their mistakes— at least not publicly. They like to know what is expected of them and where they stand in relation to their boss's expectations. They like to have some warning of the changes that may affect them.
>
> They like to feel independent in their relations to their superiors . . . to be able to express their feelings to them without being misunderstood. They like to be consulted about and participate in the actions that will personally affect them. In short, employees, like most people, want to be treated as belonging to and being an integral part of some group.[25]

Surveys of employee opinion have confirmed the fact that the absolute amount of the paycheck may be less important to many people than the relation their pay bears to the pay of others and that employees do value highly the other satisfactions Roethlisberger mentions—e.g., job security, "a feeling of belonging," and being treated like an individual rather than like a cog in a machine.

Various lists have been drawn up of the factors that provide employee satisfactions, and many of the techniques discussed in the last two chapters have been developed in an effort to provide them. Job evaluation plans have been used to ensure that wages and salaries for various levels of work bear a logical relationship to one another, and merit rating plans have been introduced to let employees know what the boss expects from them and how well they are meeting his expectations. Supervisory and management training courses have been instituted to ensure that supervisors "treat employees like individuals" and refrain from reproving them in front of others and that they explain the reasons for changes and orders whenever possible.

[25] "The Human Equation in Employee Productivity," speech before the Personnel Group of the National Retail Dry Goods Association, 1950.

More recently, however, there has been somewhat of a change in viewpoint. Psychologists and sociologists have begun to point out that people exert effort to satisfy their needs, and once a need is satisfied, it no longer provides motivation to further effort.

A. H. Maslow has suggested that there is a hierarchy of human needs and that once a lower need is fairly well satisfied, a man can be motivated only by a desire to satisfy the next higher need. In ascending order, he lists the needs as follows:

1. Physiological needs, of which the most important is the need for food and other things necessary for survival.
2. The need for safety from danger, threat, and deprivation.
3. Social needs for association with one's fellows, for friendship and love.
4. The need for self-esteem, for self-respect, the respect of one's fellows, status.
5. The need for self-fulfillment through development of powers and skills and a chance to use creativity.[26]

It follows from this that only the two top needs are likely to provide perpetual motivation, for they are the only needs that cannot be completely satisfied. Perhaps this is true only of the very top need, for past achievements may satisfy the need for status and self-respect, but a sense of developing powers and skills can come only from continuing effort.

This theory is undoubtedly correct in its broad outlines, but human needs and desires are much more complex than a simple listing would indicate. If a man is starving, he will probably place his need for food above everything else; he may risk his life for something to eat. But some people will practically starve themselves in an effort to satisfy one of the higher needs. Also, people differ in their estimate of how much is "enough." As one example, there are people who are so afraid of poverty that they cannot feel safe from deprivation even when they possess enormous amounts of money.

Yet there is no denying that the greatest motivation is provided by a chance to work toward the fulfillment of the fifth and highest need. People who display the greatest enthusiasm for their work are usually those whose fields permit them to aim toward satisfaction of this need, those who have an opportunity for creativity and for continual development of their skills and powers.

In fact, after conducting studies of a number of different middle managers and specialists in several companies, Prof. Frederick Herzberg of the University of Pittsburgh came to the conclusion that such things as working conditions, pay scales, and supervisory attitudes are merely what he called "hygiene factors." Just as lack of medical hygiene may cause disease but hygienic conditions will not cure it, so, he found, poor pay, unpleasant supervisors, or bad working conditions may cause dissatisfaction but correcting these conditions will not provide positive motivation; it will only permit the true motivators to

---

[26] *Motivation and Personality*, Harper & Row, Publishers, Incorporated, New York, 1954.

operate. Positive motivation, he said, is provided only by a chance for self-actualization—for achievement, in other words—and furthermore, ". . . the accumulation of achievement must lead to a feeling of personal growth . . . accompanied by a sense of increasing responsibility."[27]

Changing managers' attitudes

The human relations movement prompted a great many companies to introduce courses in human relations for both first-line supervisors and higher managers. In general, the aim of these courses was to familiarize managers with the findings of research in the field and to help them apply these findings. This amounted, in many cases, to introducing the managers to new techniques rather than attempting to change the managers themselves.

Now many behavioral scientists have begun to believe that the key to good human relations lies in the managers' attitudes and that these must be changed if the techniques are to work; otherwise, they will be used only sporadically or not at all in the actual job situation. The fact that a man can give the right answers to a questionnaire on human relations does not necessarily mean that he can maintain good human relations in practice.

Douglas McGregor, who served as president of Antioch College and later as professor of management at MIT, believed that much of the failure of the human relations approach as it was actually applied in industry stemmed from the fact that most managers worked on what he called "Theory X" regarding human nature in general and employee nature in particular. In brief, Theory X, as McGregor described it, holds that human beings just naturally dislike work and must be coerced into putting forth adequate effort on the job; further, it holds that most people want security above all and will attempt to avoid responsibility whenever they can.[28]

In contrast, McGregor proposed that managers adopt what he called "Theory Y," which includes the following propositions:

> 1. *The expenditure of physical and mental effort in work is as natural as play or rest.* . . . *Depending upon controllable conditions, work may be a source of satisfaction . . . or a source of punishment.* . . .
> 2. *Man will exercise self-direction and self-control in the service of objectives to which he is committed.*
> 3. *Commitment to objectives is a function of the rewards associated with their achievement.* The most significant of such rewards, e.g., the satisfaction of ego and self-actualization needs, can be the direct products of effort directed toward organizational objectives.
> 4. *The average human being learns, under proper conditions, not only to accept but to seek responsibility.* . . .

[27] See Frederick Herzberg, Bernard Mausner, and Barbara Bloch Snyderman, *The Motivation to Work,* 2d ed., John Wiley & Sons, Inc., New York, 1959. An extract from this book appears in Ernest Dale, *Readings in Management: Landmarks and New Frontiers,* McGraw-Hill Book Company, New York, 1965, pp. 305–309.
[28] Douglas McGregor, *The Human Side of Enterprise,* McGraw-Hill Book Company, New York, 1960, pp. 33–43. Copyright 1960, McGraw-Hill Book Company, Inc. Used with permission of McGraw-Hill Book Company.

5.   *The capacity to exercise a relatively high degree of imagination, ingenuity, and creativity in the solution of organizational problems is widely, not narrowly, distributed in the population.*

6.   *Under the conditions of modern industrial life, the intellectual potentialities of the average human being are only partially utilized.*[29]

Mere intellectual acceptance of a new theory like Theory Y—or any of the other theories regarding human motivation—is seldom sufficient to change a way of looking at things that has become ingrained through a lifetime. Hence there has been a search for new methods of training managers in human relations.

One of these new methods is the sensitivity training described in the chapter on staffing. Another is the use of the managerial grid (Figure 1). The attempt,

[29] *Ibid.,* pp. 47–48.

FIGURE 1   The management grid. (From *Harvard Business Review,* November–December, 1964, p. 136.)

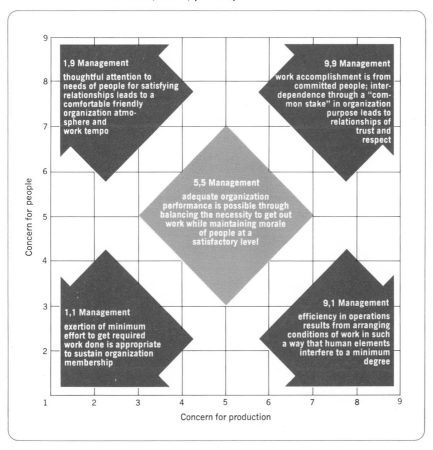

1,9 Management
thoughtful attention to needs of people for satisfying relationships leads to a comfortable friendly organization atmosphere and work tempo

9,9 Management
work accomplishment is from committed people; interdependence through a "common stake" in organization purpose leads to relationships of trust and respect

5,5 Management
adequate organization performance is possible through balancing the necessity to get out work while maintaining morale of people at a satisfactory level

1,1 Management
exertion of minimum effort to get required work done is appropriate to sustain organization membership

9,1 Management
efficiency in operations results from arranging conditions of work in such a way that human elements interfere to a minimum degree

Concern for people

Concern for production

of course, is to induce managers to take a 9,9 position, which emphasizes maximum concern for both production and people. The first step in this type of development is to conduct grid seminars, which are somewhat similar to sensitivity training sessions, except that the meetings are more structured and there is less personal criticism. In a second phase of the program, each work group or department decides on its own ground rules for reaching a 9,9 position and on the relationships that should prevail. Then there are meetings to foster intergroup teamwork, organizational goal setting, and the use of task forces for problem solving. The final phase is to assess the changes and help ensure that there is no slipping back.[30]

These techniques are an attempt to inculcate what Mayo called "knowledge of acquaintance," as contrasted with mere "knowledge about," the first drawn from direct experience and the latter from reflection and abstract thinking.[31]

Beyond this, many behavioral scientists feel that if employees understand objectives and have a chance to express their own opinions—perhaps see those opinions acted on in some cases—they will gain a feeling of participation in the enterprise, and only as they participate can they have an opportunity for self-actualization. Rensis Likert's linking-pin plan of organization is based on this idea.

Likert lists four systems of management, which he calls (1) exploitative authoritative, (2) benevolent authoritative, (3) consultative, and (4) participative-group. The first two terms are self-explanatory, but the difference between the last two may require some clarification. In the consultative type of management, as Likert defines it, superiors place "substantial" confidence in employees, whereas under the participative-group type, there is "complete" confidence in employees and organizational goals are established by group action except in crisis situations.[32]

Another method of fostering participation that is being increasingly urged on management by various writers is what is called "management by objectives." Under this system, the employee and the superior sit down together and agree on the objectives the employee should attain; then, having had a hand in setting the goals, it is argued, the employee naturally feels a greater commitment to reach them.

GROUPS AND GROUP DYNAMICS

The study of small groups and of group dynamics—the ways in which members of a group interact with each other and the effect of the group as a whole on its members—may be considered a phase of the study of human relations, but it is discussed separately here because it has come to constitute a spe-

---

[30] Robert R. Blake, Jane S. Mouton, Louis B. Barnes, and Larry E. Greiner, "Breakthrough in Organization Development," *Harvard Business Review*, November–December, 1964, pp. 133–155.

[31] Elton Mayo, *The Social Problems of an Industrial Civilization*, Division of Research, Graduate School of Business Administration, Harvard University, Boston, 1945, p. 16.

[32] Robert C. Albrook, "Participative Management: Time for a Second Look," *Fortune*, May, 1967, p. 167.

cialized field on its own account. In much of human relations theory, the primary unit is the individual; in the group dynamics branch of the field, the small face-to-face group is the primary unit to be studied.

This, of course, is in line with the theories of Elton Mayo, who held that ". . . in industry and in other human situations the administrator is dealing with well-knit human groups and not with a horde of individuals."[33] But the study of group dynamics began before the Hawthorne findings were widely publicized with attempts to show that a group is something more than the sum of its parts. For example, G. B. Watson concluded from the experimental evidence available in the 1920s and from his own comparison of the intellectual efficiency of a group with the efficiency of the members when they worked by themselves that the product of group thinking is distinctly superior to that of the average person in the group and even to that of the best member—sometimes further above the best than the best is above the average.[34]

In an effort to invoke the extra power provided by interactions within a group, some companies have been using a technique called brainstorming, in which a group gets together to generate new ideas. Each man throws into the discussion any suggestion for solving a given problem that comes into his head, and the others are debarred from pooh-poohing it no matter how foolish it seems. Instead, they throw out new suggestions, perhaps stimulated by those already made. In this way, it is claimed, one mind strikes sparks from another, and eventually valuable new ideas are hammered out.

But if working in groups may stimulate people to develop new ideas and raise their productivity, group solidarity may also influence them to cut down production and to set group standards far below what they might be, as Frederick Taylor found out. Group solidarity may also produce resistance to change or acceptance of it, and the task of the administrator is to use group dynamics in such a way that the solidarity of the group contributes to a favorable attitude toward high standards and acceptance of necessary changes. In this connection, a statement by Dorwin Cartwright (Director, Research Center for Group Dynamics, University of Michigan) of the principles of group dynamics may be helpful:

> 1. If the group is to be used effectively as a medium of change, those people who are to be changed and those who are to exert influence for change must have a strong sense of belonging to the same group.
> 2. The more attractive the group is to its members, the greater is the influence that the group can exert on its members.
> 3. In attempts to change attitudes, values, or behavior, the more relevant they are to the basis of attraction to the group, the greater will be the influence that the group can exert upon them. . . . If a man joins a union mainly to keep his job and to improve his working conditions, he may be largely uninfluenced by the union's attempt to modify his attitudes toward national and international affairs.

[33] *Op. cit.*, p. 111.
[34] "Do Groups Think More Effectively than Individuals?" *The Journal of Abnormal and Social Psychology*, vol. 23, 1928–1929, pp. 328–336.

4. The greater the prestige of a group member in the eyes of the other members, the greater the influence he can exert.

5. Efforts to change individuals or subparts of a group which, if successful, would have the result of making them deviate from the norms of the group will encounter strong resistance.

6. Strong pressure for changes in the group can be established by creating a shared perception by members of the need for change, thus making the source of pressure for change lie within the group.

7. Information relating to the need for change, plans for change, and consequences of change must be shared by all relevant people in the group.

8. Changes in one part of a group produce strain in other related parts which can be reduced only by eliminating the change or by bringing about readjustments in related parts.[35]

Principles 2, 3, and 4 are fairly obvious. Experience with incentive systems under which workers have been reluctant to produce much above the average of their groups has amply demonstrated the truth of principle 5. Principle 8 is exemplified by the reaction reported in many companies when first-line supervisors are given a course in human relations—"They ought to give that course to my boss."

Principles 1, 5, 6, and 7 offer the best clues to action for those in direct charge of small groups. Kurt Lewin, the founder of the group dynamics school, was a strong advocate of democratic supervision, of breaking down the barriers between the leaders and the led (principle 1). One of his most famous experiments was with two comparable groups of ten-year-old children engaged in theatrical mask making. In one group, leadership was authoritative: the children were told what to do, when to do it, and which of them were to work together. In the other group, all "policy" decisions were put up to the group and the children themselves were allowed to choose among various suggested alternatives; also, the children were allowed to pick their own workmates. Lewin reported that hostility was thirty times as frequent in the autocratic group as in the other and aggression was eight times as frequent.[36]

In another well-known experiment by Ronald Lippitt and Ralph K. White, it was found that boys working under democratic leadership were industrious and continued working after the leaders left the room. But those under authoritative leadership were either rebellious or cowed into apathy while the leaders were present and ceased working the moment the leaders left the room.[37]

These studies, of course, involved children and temporary experimental situations; thus it might be questioned whether the findings are applicable to adults in more or less permanent jobs. But some experiments in actual work situations have shown similar results.

[35] Dorwin Cartwright, "Achieving Change in People; Some Applications of Group Dynamics," in Keith Davis and William G. Scott (eds.), *Readings in Human Relations*, McGraw-Hill Book Company, New York, 1959, pp. 219–230. From *Human Relations*, no. 4, copyright 1951, pp. 381–392.

[36] Kurt Lewin, Ronald Lippitt, and Ralph K. White, "Patterns of Aggressive Behavior in Experimentally Created 'Social Climates,'" *The Journal of Social Psychology*, vol. 10, 1939, pp. 271–299.

[37] See W. J. H. Sprott, *Human Groups*, Penguin Books, Inc., Baltimore, 1958, pp. 32–33.

One well-known instance, often cited, is the case of the Harwood Manufacturing Company. There operators just below standard were brought into conferences and given an opportunity to voice complaints about machines, materials, and other factors affecting their output. Then the conference leader would promise specific help on the problems whenever possible: "I'll have the mechanic look at your machine," for example. Finally, he asked: "Now if all these things are taken care of, how many units per hour can you make in the next ten days?" Operators might promise a rise of 20 units per hour, or 30 to 50 per cent, and when they themselves set the goal, they invariably achieved it. When the group made no decision or the decision was forced upon it by the conference leader, there was no increase.

Group dynamics principles 6 and 7 bear a strong resemblance to a concept advanced in the 1920s by Mary Parker Follett, a social worker who became an adviser to businessmen on personnel problems. She called this concept "the law of the situation" and explained it as follows:

> One *person* should not give orders to another *person*, but both should agree to take their orders from the situation. . . . My cook or my stenographer points out the law of the situation, and I, if I recognize it as such, accept it even although it may reverse some "order" I have given. . . . If those in supervisory positions should depersonalize orders, then there would be no overbearing authority on the one hand, nor on the other that dangerous *laissez-aller* which comes from the fear of exercising authority. . . .
>
> I call it depersonalizing because there is not time to go any further into the matter. I think it really is a matter of *repersonalizing*.[38]

Miss Follett, however, thought the application of the law of the situation would lie with the individual subordinate and his superior. Under the group dynamics concept, the group as a whole would be brought to see the need for change ("shared perception") so that the force exerted by the group as a whole would act to foster the change rather than to obstruct it. Thus there would be no need for any of the members to deviate from the group norm and run into conflict with it. Principle 7 simply points out the need to make available to the group the facts that will enable it to discern the law of the situation.

Certainly, when the law of the situation is immediately apparent, managers find little difficulty in motivating people to put forth their best efforts. For example, when a water main breaks and is flooding the plant, repairmen will often take it for granted that they must work through lunch and coffee breaks in order to prevent further heavy damage. But in many instances it is more difficult for employees to discern or to accept the law of the situation because the total situation is so far removed from their own small jobs. For example, a company that controls waste is more likely to prosper, other things being equal, than one that allows it to develop; and if it prospers, it can pay its employees more and provide them with more benefits. But to individual employees or a small group, the amount of time or materials they could save

[38] Henry C. Metcalf and L. Urwick (eds.), *Dynamic Administration: The Collected Papers of Mary Parker Follett,* Harper & Row, Publishers, Incorporated, New York, 1941, pp. 59–60.

by avoiding waste may seem so insignificant as to have no effect whatever on the total situation of the company. Also, they may feel that larger company profits may have little effect on their own compensation. Therefore, exhortations about the importance of controlling waste may have no effect. Thus the problem for the manager is to organize the work in such a way that the law of the situation is the law not of the total company situation but of the work group's own situation.

For example, in a coal mine in England small groups of miners worked together, each man in the group being capable of doing all the jobs, and payment was according to the amount the group produced. Thus each one understood the complete work cycle and could easily discern the law of the situation so far as the immediate work group was concerned. Then it became possible to introduce greater mechanization, and with the change in methods a change in organization was instituted, specialization by shifts and specialization by individual crew members. This should, according to the creed of scientific management, have produced greater efficiency; instead, there was less efficiency as well as a great deal of discontent among the workers. Since efficiency depended on coordination from outside and poor work by one shift could vitiate the efforts of another, the law of the situation was no longer so clear. A man might work very efficiently at his specialized job only to find that production did not increase accordingly because others—with whom he had little contact—were not doing their part.

Does this mean that mechanization should have been abandoned? No, it was found quite possible to utilize the new technology but largely do away with the specialization and give the team as a whole responsibility for assignment of men to shifts and jobs.[39]

WHERE DO WE STAND NOW?

Time after time in the last fifty or sixty years, management has thought itself on the verge of a solution to its human relations problems, only to find the mental revolution that Frederick Taylor promised it receding into the distance again. Some companies have succeeded in developing, perhaps not Münsterberg's "overflowing joy and perfect harmony," but at least above-average productivity and some degree of enthusiasm among both executives and the rank and file. But in many companies the average employee, and sometimes even the average manager or specialist, is likely to be apathetic toward his work and to produce at much less than his full capacity. Hostility is by no means unknown, even in companies that have spent millions on human relations activities. What is wrong? The answer must be a matter of speculation at best.

Improved working conditions

First, take the matter of brighter and more comfortable working conditions. When people are unaccustomed to them, improvements undoubtedly foster

39 E. L. Trist, G. W. Higgin, H. Murray, and A. B. Pollock, *Organizational Choice*, Tavistock Institute, London, 1963.

attitudes that make for efforts to achieve higher productivity, plus a certain amount of gratitude to management, especially if neighboring plants do not provide the same advantages. But once people become used to better surroundings, these results tend to disappear. Gratitude is not a feeling human beings can long sustain. Often they come to regard as a right what they once thought of as a privilege.

No one would claim that pleasant surroundings, good lighting, good cafeterias, and so on, are valueless or unimportant. Poor lighting can make for poor performance since a person who cannot see clearly what he is doing is likely to produce work of poor quality. In addition, eyestrain can cause irritability; so may such things as dirty washrooms, lack of proper places to eat, and crowded conditions.

But after the initial shot-in-the-arm of improvements has worn off, they do not so much exert a positive effect on attitude and productivity as set the stage for good relations and high productivity. As Frederick Herzberg has pointed out, unpleasant working conditions can cause dissatisfaction but pleasant working conditions are not positive motivators.

Better placement

Münsterberg thought that with the development of psychological tests, each person could be placed in the job he was best fitted for. In his opinion, this would in itself produce great interest in the job.

Good placement is, in fact, an important factor in both morale and productivity, but there are two reasons why Münsterberg's theory is inadequate. First, half a century later, psychological tests are not yet infallible, although they may be valuable aids in placement. Second, the perfect job for each person—one that he is capable of doing superlatively well and yet one that offers him a certain amount of challenge—does not necessarily exist in the company in which he happens to be employed.

The human relations approach

Implicit in the human relations approach is the theory that democratic leadership is superior to authoritarian leadership. Still, many have found that their efforts to promote productivity through this means have not met with a great deal of success. Are the findings of the sociologists and psychologists then untrue or incomplete?

One difficulty has been that there has been some misuse of the findings. Some managers have regarded them merely as gimmicks that they can use to manipulate others. They have hoped that provision of nonfinancial incentives in a perfunctory way will make employees less likely to demand pay increases. If they solicit the opinions of their subordinates, it is not because they really want to hear them but because they hope that the subordinates will be more ready to accept decisions already made if they have a chance to let off steam first.

It is this misuse of the findings of the social scientists that has led to a good deal of criticism of the human relations approach. For example, Lewis Corey wrote:

> The anti-democratic "human relations" experts misuse psychological findings. . . . [One researcher] reports that the workers kept telling him and his associates that they joined unions for greater job security and higher pay; but . . . psychologists decided that the workers' real, if unconscious, motive "was a craving to improve the emotional situation surrounding their jobs." So, the practitioners conclude, if you can use psychology to give the workers "emotional release" and "ego involvement," they will forget about their pay.[40]

Perhaps, too, even some sincere managers have been content with a shallow view of the findings of the social scientists. For example, they accept the importance of the nonfinancial incentives (as listed by, say, Roethlisberger) but overlook some important corollaries that a little self-examination would enable them to discover. Thus they appoint a supervisor merely because he has a pleasant personality and disregard the fact that praise from a person who really knows the work and is able to appreciate the exact degree of excellence is far more satisfactory than praise from one who is merely trying to be nice.

Again, some managers have interpreted the human relations approach to mean sugarcoating rules in coy language. This is not likely to make the regulations any more palatable (although courtesy is, of course, always desirable). Consider, for example, this extract from an employee relations handbook in which the "papa knows best" attitude clearly shows:

> A department store may be compared to a ship loaded with a big cargo of merchandise off on a definite voyage. The course is charted, the destination is set, but smooth sailing and a safe arrival at the desired port depend on the knowledge and leadership of the Captain and the cooperation, ability, and loyalty of the crew. The Management of the store is the Captain, and the members of the organization the crew. The destination is the same—success for both![41]

A person who can address employees in that strain simply does not regard them as adults but as children (and very small children, at that) who must be cozened into doing their jobs. This is a very different attitude from the one adopted by the researchers at Hawthorne—or by any good social scientist, for that matter.

In some cases, also, democratic leadership has been interpreted to mean the abdication of leadership. Thus, after a term as a line executive, as president of Antioch College, Douglas McGregor wrote:

[40] "Human Relations Minus Unionism," *Labor and Nation*, Spring, 1950, p. 50, quoted in Loren Baritz, *The Servants of Power*, Wesleyan University Press, Middletown, Conn., 1960, p. 175. As the title implies, the Baritz book advances more or less the same viewpoint, the "servants of power" being the social scientists who work on human relations in industry.
[41] *How To Prepare and Publish an Employee Manual*, 3d ed., American Management Association, New York, 1947, p. 20.

Before coming to Antioch, I had observed and worked with top executives as an adviser in a number of organizations. I thought I knew how they felt about their responsibilities and what led them to behave as they did. I even thought that I could create a role for myself that would enable me to avoid some of the difficulties they encountered.

I was wrong! It took the direct experience of becoming a line executive and meeting personally the problems involved to teach me what no amount of observation of other people could have taught.

I believed, for example, that a leader could operate successfully as a kind of adviser to his organization. I thought I could avoid being a "boss." Unconsciously, I suspect, I hoped to duck the unpleasant necessity of making difficult decisions, of taking responsibility for one course of action among many uncertain alternatives, of making mistakes and taking the consequences. I thought that maybe I could operate so that everyone would like me—that "good human relations" would eliminate all discord and disagreement.

I couldn't have been more wrong. . . . I finally began to realize that a leader cannot avoid the exercise of authority any more than he can avoid responsibility for what happens to his organization. . . . Moreover, since no important decision ever pleases everyone in the organization, he must also absorb the displeasure, and sometimes severe hostility, of those who would have taken a different course.[42]

Another explanation might be that management has been reluctant to try some of the best findings of recent years. For example, Rensis Likert reported a case in which a manager had brought his group from the worst of its kind in the company to the best through the use of democratic leadership combined with high standards of performance. Yet the manager's boss, a vice-president, continued to insist that more pressure was needed. The manager was transferred to another position and again demonstrated the value of his methods, but it made no difference. The original group was broken up into two groups, and the old type of supervision was reinstated. In fact, Dr. Likert has found that where results in experimental groups have been excellent, the practices that produced these results have not often spread to other departments in the same company.[43]

There are several possible explanations for this irrational behavior on the part of higher management. One, suggested by Dr. Likert, is that a manager who is used to operating in a certain way feels that his skills are being made obsolete by new methods. Another and simpler view was advanced by an industry man: Perhaps the vice-president felt that his own position was threatened by his subordinate's success since it might occur to the president that the manager should have the vice-president's job. A third possibility is that the vice-president was so committed to Theory X that he was unable to believe the evidence.

A fourth possibility is that managers are reluctant to relinquish any portion

[42] *Antioch Notes*, vol. 31, no. 9, May 1, 1954.
[43] Address to the Organization Development Council, New York, June 14, 1962.

of their power to command, as they must if they are to allow their subordinates to take a meaningful part in decision making. They may even feel that they know so much more than their subordinates do that consultation is merely a waste of time.

Also, there is growing recognition that although democratic supervision works very well with some people, there are others who do no better under participative management than they do under a more autocratic rule. In one case, Victor H. Vroom studied the effects of more democratic leadership on supervisors in a large trucking company and found that although the supervisors who were independent by nature were more productive when their superiors adopted a more democratic attitude, there was no change in the productivity of the more dependent types.[44]

Still another reason advanced for the frequent failure of the human relations approach to produce revolutionary results is that it has not dealt with a key point: the nature of the work itself.

From the standpoint of the worker, Charles R. Walker and Robert Guest have noted, many production jobs have the following characteristics: "(1) mechanically controlled work pace, (2) repetitiveness, (3) minimum skill, (4) predetermination of tools and techniques, (5) minute subdivision of product, (6) surface mental attention."[45] This is practically a prescription for work likely to induce apathy. The man cannot control his work pace, he can use no judgment, and he is in no way challenged to improve his skill after he has learned the motions necessary.

One difficulty in assessing the effect of monotonous work on morale and productivity is the tendency to believe that the interest the job itself can hold depends entirely on the amount of variety in it. A little-noticed book by a young man who tried a succession of jobs of an unskilled or semiskilled kind makes an important distinction:

> A mistake commonly made by people studying the nature of employment is the assumption that "monotonous" work is not pleasant and "varied" work is. If by monotony is meant the repetition of the same elements in an unchanging sequence, then the most monotonous of all work is acting. Night after night, it might be argued, the worker is required to go through an identical pattern of bodily movements, of words, and of vocal inflections. Nobody, however, will seriously say that acting is monotonous. The question is, why is it not? . . . The unpleasantness of a job has nothing to do with whether it is repetitive or not. It depends solely on how many parts of a man are being used and how well they are being used.[46]

Even the dullest man has a brain, and it is not used at all when his job is merely to turn a few screws. In fact, only an infinitesimal portion of his muscles is utilized. Another paragraph in the same book is also significant:

[44] *Some Personality Determinants of the Effects of Participation*, Prentice-Hall, Inc., Englewood Cliffs, N.J., 1960.
[45] *Man on the Assembly Line*, Harvard University Press, Cambridge, Mass., 1952, p. 19.
[46] Niall Brennan, *The Making of a Moron*, Sheed & Ward, Inc., New York, 1953, pp. 79 and 81.

It is fundamental to the dignity of man that he own his work. . . . By "owning" his work, I mean that he must do it in his own way, in his own time, and subject to his own conditions. That is, he must have a chance of making decisions himself as to the manner of its execution; he shall not be superintended by a stopwatch or time clock but shall exercise his own judgment as to the time it takes . . . and the series of judgments involved in the execution of the work, including the ultimate judgment—that of passing the act of judgment to another—shall be his.[47]

(It might be pointed out that allowing the worker to judge the time his work will take does not mean that he must be allowed to dawdle. Rather, given an overall deadline for completion of a job, he can be allowed to judge how much time to allot to each portion of the task. And making daily and hourly decisions about the conduct of the work gives more opportunity for self-actualization than can be obtained by an occasional chance to express an opinion on changes.)

Argyris has expressed the same view:

The employee must be provided with more "power" over *his own work environment* and therefore he must be given responsibility, authority, and increased control over the decision-making that affects his immediate work environment. He must become self-responsible.

This suggestion is supported by the writer's findings. The degree of self-actualization increases sharply for individuals as their dependence, subordination, and submissiveness are decreased and as their control over their work is increased and as the time perspective is enlarged.[48]

This concept explains a great many things. It explains why workers on a mechanized assembly line sometimes work extra fast for a short period so that they can later slow down and still keep up with the line—in other words, gain a slight measure of control over the pace of their work, which is ordinarily set by the speed of the line. It explains why the high-productivity supervisors in the Survey Research Center studies were those who supervised their subordinates less closely and were themselves supervised less closely by their own superiors. It even throws new light on what the Hawthorne girls called the absence of "slave-driving supervisors"—for in the test room they set their own work pace.

This concept also explains why some profit-sharing plans are extremely successful and others are not. For example, at the Lincoln Electric Company, often cited as a shining example of the value of profit sharing:

Jim Macy . . . manufactures gas tanks. . . . In a 12-by-12-foot area formed by the raw materials he needs, he solders inlets, then arc-welds the sections of the tank, tests it under air pressure, attaches mounting brackets, and thoroughly cleans the finished job before sending it on.

[47] *Ibid.*, p. 175.
[48] *Personality and Organization: The Conflict between System and the Individual*, Harper & Row, Publishers, Incorporated, New York, 1957, p. 181.

. . . Jim also does without inspectors. He is on piecework and guarantees the quality of his product. The company provides the tools and materials and, in effect, buys from him a certain number of pieces of a definite quality at a specified price. He is so independent that he might almost as well be across the street.[49]

Another very successful profit-sharing plan, known as the Scanlon plan,[50] combines profit sharing with opportunity for self-actualization since it allows workers a very large share in planning and policy making through representatives elected to a committee. After the plan was first introduced at the Adamson Company, a manufacturer of steel tanks, a competitor is said to have told the president: "My God, Adamson, you have a tank welded and done in the time it takes us to set it up."

Still another company in which employees not only participate in profits but have a share in overall policy making in planning, designing, establishing new departments, and so on, is the Cyril Bath Company in Solon, Ohio. As Cyril Bath explains it:

A management committee, consisting of five shop men and four men from the office, including me, helps run the business. . . . We don't scold people who make mistakes because we think they feel worse about it than we do anyway. Their personal interests are involved, too. Once, years ago, when there was no money to buy a new crane we needed, a maintenance man was designated to tell the management committee that the boys would forego their next bonus to buy the crane. . . . We paid the bonus and bought the crane because we realized we had assets of good will not shown on the balance sheet. . . .

The workers in the shop not only make the bonuses that are paid and earn the wages they get, but they have pulled the rest out of some pretty deep holes. At times we undertake something in the way of special machinery which proves to be beyond us. In circumstances like this, when the engineers have worn out their pencils and the office brains are all dismayed, time and again, someone from the tool room or the die shop or the assembly floor has pulled us out.[51]

At the time the Scanlon plan was introduced in the Adamson Company, the organization was small enough for employees to recognize the law of the situation and realize how their contributions would affect profitability and their own share in the profits. The same is true of the Cyril Bath Company, which is still a small one. Thus fusion of company goals and personal goals was easier than it would be in large companies that adopted similar measures, for in a large company the extent to which any one person on a lower level can affect profitability is generally infinitesimal. Also, the contributions of individual employees are more clearly visible throughout the organization in a small company, and thus extra contributions bring greater rewards in the form of ego satisfaction.

[49] Blake Clark, "A Factory Full of Partners," *Reader's Digest*, June, 1962, pp. 134–135.
[50] Named after Joseph Scanlon, who was an official of the United Steelworkers when the plan was introduced and later became a member of the faculty at MIT.
[51] "Cooperative Capitalism," address at Columbia University, Feb. 27, 1952.

Another great obstacle to providing proper motivation is that the rewards—both financial and nonfinancial—often depend on factors that have nothing to do with job performance. Lyman W. Porter and Edward E. Lawler III point out:

> The employee's opportunities to gain considerable amounts of intrinsic rewards from performing his job duties in a superior fashion are frequently limited by the mechanical, machine-controlled nature of his work. Furthermore, his chance to assume new, more interesting duties (with higher pay) by working harder on his current job is probably sharply curtailed both in terms of the way in which the organization has arranged the work flow and by union contract that might exist.[52]

The usual financial incentive system, either group or individual, is not the answer, for although such a system may initially increase productivity somewhat, it does not really tap the full potential of those who work under it. Quite aside from any pressures exerted by fellow workers to keep production down to an average level, there are good reasons for this. Financial incentive systems pay for extra productivity when methods, tools, and other job conditions remain constant; a change in methods, whether originated by an employee on the job or by some staff department, generally means that the incentive rates are cut. Thus employee productivity eventually reaches a plateau—and the financial incentives only help to keep it there; they do not motivate anyone to find better ways of doing the job, which is the only way in which an employee can continue to increase his contribution indefinitely.

Now, in some industries, some apathy-producing work may be unavoidable; not only efficiency but company survival may require a fine subdivision of tasks that allows no room for ego satisfaction or self-actualization. But many companies have organized plant and office on the assembly line system because they have been convinced without any real proof that it is the efficient way for everyone. Certainly, many more companies than actually do could broaden the jobs of the rank and file and give them more responsibility than they do at present. Even more certainly, many subordinate managers could be allowed more leeway than they have now.

In addition, automation may offer a new chance for companies that have heretofore had to remove all planning from the jurisdiction of those who do the work. When machines perform all the operations on a given part or assembly and it is passed from one operation to another automatically, the main work for human beings will be making adjustments and keeping the line running. This is skilled work calling for a degree of judgment and planning, and if managers take advantage of the opportunity offered, it may be possible to dispense with a great deal of the old assembly line monotony.

But this will not mean that direction will no longer be a problem for the manager. Not everyone wants to be completely or even largely autonomous, according to some social scientists, for some are happier under authoritative supervision. One psychologist, Clare Graves of Union College in Schenectady,

---

[52] "What Job Attitudes Tell about Motivation," *Harvard Business Review*, January–February, 1968, p. 121.

has even suggested that as many as half the people in northeastern United States and a larger proportion nationwide may fall into this category.[53]

While general observation indicates that these estimates may be too high, it is undeniable that some proportion of the employees in every company will be of this type. Hence direction must be adjusted not only to the department but even to individuals within the department. The manager should also be aware that many of those who appear to have no interest in gaining either ego satisfaction or self-actualization from their jobs may seem incurably apathetic only because they have lost hope of ever having a chance to get either. Such people can often be brought to accept more responsibility and take a greater interest by very gradual steps toward providing them with more stimulating work, along with reassurance that they are doing well when they begin to show the first signs of being able to handle the increased responsibilities and meet higher standards of performance.

SUMMARY

In the directing phase of his job, the manager tells people what to do and sees that they do it. His objective here, of course, is to get everyone to do the best work he is capable of.

This result has never been achieved merely by threats of dismissal; restriction of output was common even before there was widespread unionization. Financial incentives may produce some improvement, but the optimum cannot be achieved by a system of financial rewards alone. The Taylor system never produced the mental revolution that its originator expected it to, nor have similar systems developed later.

Good leadership is undoubtedly a factor, but despite a great number of studies of the subject, there is no sure prescription either for those who are charged with appointing leaders or for those who hope to be good leaders. Some clues that will be of value to both, however, have been developed. Apparently the good leader is one who possesses superior technical ability in the activities in which he is engaged and, because he can trust his own ability and knowledge, is able to exhibit self-confidence and initiative. In addition, he shows consideration for his followers and appreciation of their needs and goals; often he is able to do so because he is like them in some respects, although he is generally more intelligent and better informed about the work than they are. Also, in many cases, he is democratic in his attitude toward them and allows them to contribute to his decisions.

The Hawthorne studies gave rise to great interest in nonfinancial incentives of one kind or another, and it was often postulated that if the work and the environment could satisfy employee needs, there would be greater motivation to produce. More recently, it has been pointed out that once a need is largely satisfied, it can no longer motivate a person further and that there are only

---

[53] Albrook, *op. cit.*, p. 170.

two human needs that can never be completely satisfied—the need for self-esteem and status and the need for self-fulfillment, or self-actualization, through the continuing development of one's powers and skills. Hence it is held that jobs should be so designed, wherever possible, that they afford an opportunity to work toward satisfaction of these two needs.

If employees are to seek these satisfactions, it is sometimes said, their jobs must allow them to "control their own work"—set their own work pace and make decisions about how to do it—that is, jobs should be less finely divided, and the divorce between planning and doing should not be as complete as the members of the scientific management movement thought it should be. In other words, employees at all levels should be given more responsibility, for the capacity to assume responsibility for results and even to innovate creatively is more widely diffused in the population than most managers appear to believe. Some of the companies that seem to be enjoying the best results appear to have organized their work along these lines and in addition have provided liberal financial rewards in the form of profit sharing.

Overall, it appears that providing employees and managers with more opportunity to gain self-actualization from their work—plus a democratic, although not entirely laissez-faire, environment—is likely to produce the best results provided that good performance is recognized by financial rewards greater than the average and by an opportunity to gain greater recognition. However, some social scientists are coming to believe that not everyone is willing to assume responsibility and that autocratic (but considerate) supervision may be best for some people, and this is undoubtedly true. Although the proportion of the general population who fall into this category may not be large, the manager must be able to distinguish between different types of people and suit his type of supervision to his subordinates.

Review Questions

1. What is the directing phase of the management job?
2. Distinguish between the trait theory of leadership and the situational theory. Which do you believe is more likely to be true?
3. What are some of the nonfinancial satisfactions that employees want from their jobs? Do you believe there are others besides those listed in the text?
4. Why have some social scientists begun to believe that providing employee satisfactions does not provide motivation?
5. What is the "law of the situation" and how may it be used in motivation? Can you think of any case in which everyone will clearly see the law of the situation and obey it?
6. In the Institute of Human Relations studies, who supervised more closely, the high-productivity supervisors or the low-productivity supervisors?
7. What does Frederick Herzberg believe are hygiene factors rather than true motivators?

8. What does Chris Argyris believe is of the utmost importance in promoting interest in a job? Do you agree with him?
9. If Argyris is right, did Mayo interpret the Hawthorne results correctly? If not, what did Mayo fail to take into account?
10. Distinguish between Theory X and Theory Y, as set forth by Douglas McGregor. Which theory do you think would work best in most situations?
11. What are some of the reasons why the human relations approach has not always lived up to its promise?

Case Study One / The Stenographic Pool

Harold Bridge is the new office manager of the Hendricks Publishing Company. He has been hired with the understanding that he is to reduce expenses in every way possible.

A number of executives have private secretaries, who often work overtime when there is a press of work, and they are paid time and a half when they do so even though the normal workweek is only thirty-five hours. At other times, the secretaries have very little to do and may even spend their time reading during normal working hours.

There is also a stenographic pool on which a number of other men in the company draw when they have letters to write or other typed material to get out. This pool is always working under high pressure because of the volume of work, but in view of the need for economy Harold does not feel justified in increasing its size.

It occurs to him that the secretaries' idle time could be utilized. Therefore he announces that all secretaries who do not have any work from their bosses should join the pool temporarily to help out with the extra work.

1. Was this a wise move?
2. What do you think happened?

Case Study Two / Work Sampling

You are planning to introduce a new technique called "work sampling." Under this system, an observer makes a random tour through a department and records what each person is doing at the instant he observes him: working, preparing to work, traveling between jobs, standing idle, and so on.

The objective of this procedure is not to check up on individuals, but to determine how management can change conditions in order to make it possible for the employees to work more steadily and so get more done. The findings might, however, reflect on individual supervisors. Since each section is considered separately, a supervisor whose section shows a much larger proportion of nonproductive time than those of his colleagues might be charged with poor planning or poor direction.

What steps would you take before starting to use the technique in order to minimize human relations difficulties?

Selected Readings

Managerial Psychology, Harold J. Leavitt, University of Chicago Press, Chicago, 1964. Contains an up-to-date summary of the latest important findings of behavioral science on different aspects of direction.

Leadership, Psychology and Organization Behavior, Bernard M. Bass, Harper & Row, Publishers, Incorporated, New York, 1960. Findings of a large number of research studies on leadership.

The Social Psychology of Industry, J. A. C. Brown, Penguin Books, Inc., Baltimore, 1954. A review of psychological findings on morale, leadership, and productivity in industry.

Behavioral Science Research in Industrial Relations: Symposium conducted by Industrial Relations Counselors, Inc., New York, 1962. Summaries of basic research in behavioral science by a number of university scientists: Frederick I. Herzberg on the basic needs and satisfactions of the individual, Chris Argyris on the behavior of executives within the organization, Leonard R. Sayles on new concepts in work group theory, and others.

Applying Behavioral Science Research in Industry: Symposium conducted by Industrial Relations Counselors, Inc., New York, 1964. A second symposium in which participants were from industry: Paul Buchanan of Standard Oil of New Jersey; William Mallenkopf of Procter & Gamble; Orlo Crissey of General Motors; Frank Smith of Sears, Roebuck; and Walter McNamara of IBM.

Motivation and Productivity, Saul W. Gellerman, American Management Association, New York, 1963. A history of the study of motivation and of the research over the last thirty years. Deals also with application of the findings.

The Practice of Management, Peter Drucker, Harper & Row, Publishers, Incorporated, New York, 1954, chap. 21. Some criticisms of the human relations approach as it is practiced, and some suggestions regarding the organization of planning and doing.

Management and the Social Sciences, Tom Lupton, Hutchinson & Co. (Publishers), Ltd., London, 1967. Sets forth some of the more important findings of research studies in the social science field and explains their application to the manager's problems and their relevance to organization theory.

Politics and Social Science, W. J. M. MacKenzie, Penguin Books, Inc., Baltimore, 1967 (paperback). Reports on research findings that are applicable to company organizations as well as to politics.

The Bureaucratic Phenomenon, Michel Crozier, The University of Chicago Press, Chicago, 1964. (Originally published in 1963 by Éditions du Seuil, Paris.) An examination of the effect of bureaucratic organization on efficiency and on the employees within the bureaucracy.

Organization and Environment: Managing Differentiation and Integration, Paul R. Lawrence and Jay W. Lorsch, Division of Research, Harvard Graduate School of Business Administration, Cambridge, Mass., 1967. Studies of the ways in which organizations in changing environments differ from those in stable industries.

20

CONTROL

Capitalistic practice turns the unit of money into a tool of rational cost-profit calculations, of which the towering monument is double entry bookkeeping.
Joseph A. Schumpeter: *Capitalism, Socialism and Democracy*

The cornerstone of the modern enterprise—a delicate and shifting balance between decentralization of operations and coordination of control. Donaldson Brown

20

"By their fruits ye shall know them," says the Biblical injunction, and the fruits of the organization's efforts are the final concern of every manager. The sooner he knows the results of the steps he has taken in accordance with his plans, the easier it will be for him to take any corrective action necessary—in other words, the more control he has over his business.

But analytical methods of measurement and quick reporting took many years to evolve. For a long time company books showed only the general results —how much the owner made. At the end of the year, the bookkeeper (later the accountant) would produce an income statement showing expenses, revenues, and the difference between the two (the profit), plus a balance sheet listing assets, liabilities, and the difference (surplus). The owner could then see approximately what had happened, but the figures gave him little or no information on why it had happened or on what he could do to improve matters.

Sales revenues were not broken down by products or territories, which made it difficult, if not impossible, to determine which items or areas were doing better than others.

Secondly, expenses were not analyzed by manageable functions. Thus accounting department expenses might not be separated from manufacturing expenses, and if the owner did not know how much he was spending on a department, he obviously could not determine whether it was too much or too little.

Thirdly, it was impossible to judge trends from year to year, for the records were not comparable. Credit expense might be included in sales expense one year, in financial expense the next; factory administrative expense might be lumped into general company overhead one year and appear as part of plant expense the next. And even where comparable data had existed for a number of years, many bookkeepers did not take the trouble to make a comparison, partly because it did not often occur to them that they should do so and partly because they were afraid of the odium that the presentation of the facts might bring down on them.

Finally, even where comparisons were possible, it was often difficult to judge the merits of one performance as against another because there was no way of telling the reasons for the variations in figures. Thus, the wage bill might be higher one year than it was the year before because of greater output (and the employment of more people), because wage rates had risen, because labor was less efficient, or because of a combination of these factors. Yet the bookkeeper might not trouble himself with any explanation. He usually lacked the opportunity, the knowledge, or the courage to do so. In any case, he was so busy with his regular chores—keeping a record of sales and expenses, being very accurate with his payroll figures, keeping account of the main items of property—that he was unable to put his mind on devising reports that would be really useful to his boss.

Businesses were usually small enough to permit the master's eye to be everywhere, and if the chief executive were alert and intelligent enough, he could make up for his bookkeeper's lack of analytical ability. Even so, he often had difficulty. Thus Thomas Sutherland, one of the managing directors of the Peninsular & Oriental Steam Navigation Company, wrote to his accountant in 1875:

> During my late investigation of the Company's expenditure, I found the utmost difficulty . . . and in no case was it more difficult than in the case of the London Office itself. From the elements of expenditure up to Portage Bills all the charges are so scattered about, that to collect the various threads and knit them together entailed a most unsatisfactory amount of trouble. Constantly, I had to send back Statements to Mr. Miller and others which my own knowledge of the subject enabled me to tell were incomplete, and it occupied many days, if not weeks, to collect all the returns relating to Stations and bring them together in such a way as to give a complete and accurate bird's-eye-view of the cost of these Establishments.[1]

The modern concept of control envisages a system that not only provides a historical record of what has happened to the business as a whole but pinpoints the reasons why it has happened, and provides data that enable the chief executive or the department head to take corrective steps if he finds he is on the wrong track. Also, the system should enable managers to identify trends—in costs, in markets, in all aspects of the business—and so afford a guide for future action.

This is exactly what the alert and astute Mr. Sutherland was after. In the same memorandum he wrote:

> The present system of Bookkeeping in the Accountant's Department is admirably suited for the end it has in view, viz., that of ascertaining once a year or oftener the profits upon the Company's transactions; but it is evident that in a business of this kind much detailed information is necessary regarding the working of the Company, and this information should be obtainable in such a practical form, as to enable the Directors to see readily and clearly the causes at work in favour of or against the success of the Company's operations. . . . I assume that a ship of the *Cathay* class for a voyage to Bombay costs between £5,000 and £6,000; but it is clear that a difference of £500 in the correctness of my assumption and the actual fact is equal to the difference in the profit and loss upon the Company's operations on that line. It is not right that our knowledge upon a point of this kind should be so vague as it is, or that when one begins to think about the matter it should require three weeks to compose a statement which only comes to our hands after the immediate interest in the question of which it treats has expired.[2]

Specifically, he called for a ship's ledger detailed enough to make clear why some ships were losing money and others were making money; another ledger covering "stations" or offices; and a third dealing with the traffic between port and port to enable management "to determine how far it is necessary to provide further for the requirements of some ports, or to abandon trade with others."[3]

As companies began to grow, the difficulties of controlling the operations without the proper type of reports multiplied. Many companies undoubtedly made a good deal less than they could have because the managers had no real knowledge of what was happening and, lacking Sutherland's acumen, did not know what data to demand from their accounting departments. Cases of this type are cited in the writings of Harrington Emerson, and he and other members of the scientific management movement were perhaps responsible in part for the later development of better control systems, or at least for increased attention to the need for them.

To be workable, control reports must produce figures that are truly comparable from one period to another and from one section of the business to another. Second, they must be coordinated so that they not only portray the results in different sections of the business but make plain the reasons why the business is or is not doing as well as could be expected. Finally, they must be presented in such form that the manager can get the "bird's-eye-view" Sutherland demanded, form an estimate of his situation, and lay the groundwork for future action. They must enable him to apply what Frederick Taylor called "management by exception"—that is, they must pinpoint the exceptional situations rather than compel him to devote attention to a mass of routine data that do not signal any need for action. In most cases, data of a recurring nature will be presented, but in some cases they will be the findings of a special analysis made to pinpoint a problem or an individual responsibility.

THE CONTROLLER

It is the job of the controller to develop the type of reports that will be most valuable to management, either at management's request (as in the case of the P. & O.) or on his own initiative. If he can provide the right kind of data in a really usable form, he will be worth many times his salary (and will often get a higher one in consequence). Men and women who can post figures to account books and run up totals on an adding machine are plentiful. The true controllers who can envision the business both as a whole and as the sum of its parts and develop the type of reports that make possible true control are rare and valuable.

The controller might be described as essentially the great "balancer," or at least as the man who provides top management with the information necessary to act in that capacity. The operating man is primarily concerned with pushing out a large volume of production, but if he were allowed to pursue this end without controls, the result might be excessive stocks in the factory

[3] *Ibid.*, p. 1328.

or on the dealers' shelves. He may delight in expensive machinery or beautiful plants, far more elaborate than are necessary or desirable. The sales manager, on the other hand, may be interested in maximizing volume, even at the expense of production schedules (he will want to put favorite customers ahead of schedule). In the interest of larger volume, he may want to increase selling expenses to the point where the added sales no longer pay their way or where price discounts cut seriously into revenue. As Judge Jerome Frank, former head of the SEC, put it:

> Every man is likely to overemphasize and treat as fundamental those aspects of life which are his peculiar daily concern. To most dentists, you and I are, basically, but teeth surrounded by bodies. To most under-takers we are incipient corpses; to most actors, parts of a potential audience; to most policemen, possible criminals; to most taxi drivers, fares. . . . We make life in the image of our own activities.[4]

Now, of course, all department heads are concerned with the financial aspects of their jobs, and they often work hard to reduce their departmental costs. But they may not be sufficiently concerned with costs from the viewpoint of the company as a whole, and it often happens that increased costs in one department will really decrease overall company costs.

In aiding in across-the-board coordination, the controller is "a second wave of attack . . . he supplements but does not supplant."[5] Each manager must use controls of his own. Those who engage in control work are often tempted to remedy what they find amiss, but, as Alvin Brown points out, they should stick to the collection, arrangement, and analyses of the facts: "But, when the facts fail and when judgment must be substituted, this warrant runs out. Judgment belongs to the operating man, and the financial man who assumes to exercise that faculty is speaking out of turn."[6]

SOME TYPES OF REPORTS

A great deal of progress has been made in the twentieth century, and particularly in the last few decades, in development of reports that provide the type of information needed.

For example, Figure 1 shows a system of reporting developed for an oil company which provides the type of information Sutherland called for in fairly concise form, plus graphs that depict trends in the last few years. The hand-written notes are added before the report is presented to management to high-light the important points: the downturn in volume, the lower net per-gallon profit, and so on.

---

[4] In an address to the Controller's Institute, quoted in David R. Anderson and Leo A. Schmidt, *Practical Controllership*, 2d ed., Richard D. Irwin, Inc., Homewood, Ill., 1961, p. 445.
[5] Alvin Brown, *Financial Approach to Industrial Operations*, Society for the Advancement of Management, New York, 1957, pp. 9, 13.
[6] *Ibid.*, p. 13.

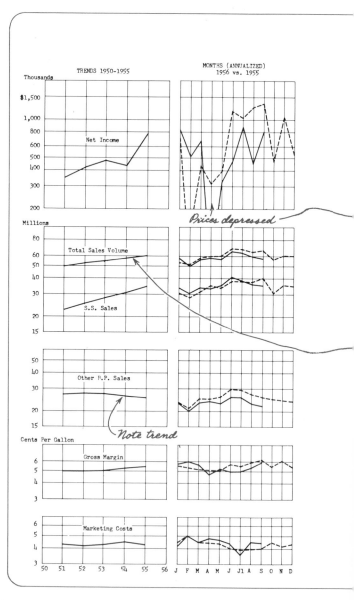

FIGURE 1 Example of a control report for a fictitious unit. (From John G. McLean, "Better Reports for Better Control," *Harvard Business Review*, May–June, 1957, p. 98.)

DIVISION "A"

MARKETING – MANUFACTURING – NATURAL GASOLINE PLANTS

COMBINED NET INCOME BEFORE TAXES: BULK PLANT AND SERVICE STATION BUSINESS

Decline in gross margin due primarily to volume; secondarily to prices

	Net Income Before Taxes ($000)	Return on Net Investment	Sales Volume (000 Gals)	S/S Volume (000 Gals)	Other Bulk Plant Sales (000 Gals)	Gross Margin Per Gal.	Marketing Costs Per Gal.	Net Income Per Gal.
	348		49,451	22,416	27,035	.0497	.0427	.0070
	413		52,715	25,551	27,164	.0494	.0425	.0069
	478		55,833	28,243	27,410	.0507	.0421	.0086
	435		57,896	30,719	27,177	.0522	.0447	.0075
	768	10.8	60,481	34,544	25,937	.0552	.0425	.0127
	69		4,762	2,799	1,963	.0571	.0426	.0145
	42		4,222	2,545	1,677	.0600	.0500	.0100
h	57		4,733	2,769	1,964	.0570	.0451	.0119
	168	8.9	13,717	8,113	5,604	.0580	.0458	.0122
.1	3		4,816	2,810	2,006	.0481	.0474	.0007
	26		4,790	2,856	1,934	.0523	.0469	.0054
	38		5,517	3,339	2,178	.0499	.0431	.0068
	67	4.1	15,123	9,005	6,118	.0501	.0457	.0044
	75		5,383	3,197	2,186	.0500	.0360	.0140
	37		4,973	3,056	1,917	.0525	.0451	.0074
	68		4,785	2,928	1,857	.0585	.0444	.0141
	180	9.4	15,141	9,181	5,960	.0535	.0416	.0119
to Date	415	7.5	43,981	26,299	17,682	.0537	.0443	.0094

Note low return on investment; also down from last year

Net income per gallon lower than .0101 in jobber channel

VARIANCE FROM LAST YEAR

Qtr	60	2.3	218	490	(272)	.0047	.0005	.0042
Qtr	(99)	(5.4)	(632)	117	(749)	(.0032)	.0030	(.0062)
Qtr	(133)	(7.6)	(1,493)	(471)	(1,022)	(.0046)	.0023	(.0069)
Qtr								
to Date	(172)	(3.5)	(1,907)	136	(2,043)	(.0013)	.0021	(.0034)
ange	(29.3)		(4.2)	0.5	(10.4)	(2.4)	5.0	(26.6)

reverses favorable volume [tr]end of last 5 years

Decline in net income per gallon due primarily to rising unit costs

VARIANCE FROM FORECAST

Qtr			(506)					
Qtr			(1,410)					
Qtr			(2,285)					
Qtr								
to Date			(4,201)					
ange			(8.7)					

[th]is is one of few divisions [sh]owing decline in [ne]t income

Continues down trend of last 3 years

Unit costs up because volume well below forecast

ANALYSIS OF CHANGE IN NET INCOME: 9 MONTHS

Causes of Variation	($000)	Per Gal.
Gross Margin Inc. -(Dec.) from change in:		
Volume	(128)	
Price	(23)	
Mdse. Cost	(11)	
Net Change-Gross Margin	(162)	(.0013)
Marketing Costs Inc. -(Dec.) from change in:		
Over. & Oper. Expense	7	.0020
Taxes	-	.0001
Depreciation	19	.0006
Misc. Income	-	(.0001)
T.B.A. Commissions	4	-
Subtotal	30	.0026
Loss (Gain) on Assets	(20)	(.0005)
Net Change-Mktg. Costs	10	.0021
Net Income Inc. -(Dec.)	(172)	(.0034)

MONTHLY AVERAGES

	Number of Service Stations	Total Gasoline Gallons Per S.S.	Total Motor Oil Per S.S.	Ratio of Total Motor Oil to Gasoline
1956	239	11,990	176	1.47
1955	232	12,247	216	1.76
Change	7	(257)	(40)	(0.29)
% Change	3.0	(2.1)	(18.5)	

MONTHLY AVERAGES - BULK PLANT SALES (EXCLUDING SERVICE STATION SALES)

	Number of Bulk Plants	Total Gasoline Per B.P.	Total Other Light Oil Per B.P.	Total Lube Oils Per B.P.
1956	99	17,083	2,017	722
1955	104	18,352	1,906	739
Change	(5)	(1,269)	111	(17)
% Change	(4.8)	(6.9)	5.8	(2.3)

Note declines in gasoline and motor oil sales per service station and in gasoline sales per bulk plant

In this case, management looks first at a quarterly report showing figures for the company as a whole and then turns to reports on the performance of each major division like the one shown. Reasons for any deviation from plans can be traced down through reports for each of six regions and for each of the functional departments within a region.

Top management may then ask subordinate managers for explanations of deviations from plans. Obviously, in the fictitious example shown, income and return on investment fell off because sales volume was well below the forecast, and management can now go straight to the essential point and investigate the reasons for the decline in volume. There has been no general recession since—as one of the handwritten notes shows—this is one of the few divisions in which net profit was lower.

Another type of control report presented quarterly to top management is shown in Figure 2. This is a small company, which not only manufactures its own products but purchases other products for resale. The report is presented, along with other figures, to show how much gross profit the company is earning on purchases from each of its suppliers. In this way, the top managers can tell at a glance which of the purchased products are producing the most worthwhile profit. They may find that certain types of purchased products should be discontinued, or (if freight is eating into profits too sharply) the report might spark a search for nearer suppliers.

Two of the other controls used by the board of directors of this small company are shown in Figures 3 and 4. The cash summary shows the cash position at the beginning of the monthly period and at the end. Note that this is not a statement of assets; not all the money currently in the bank actually belongs to the company. For example, the taxes it has withheld from employees are merely resting temporarily in its bank account. The statement does, however, indicate the flow of cash and show how much is available to meet immediate commitments. Compared with a cash budget, it will show whether or not the cash flow is meeting expectations and if not, where the discrepancies are occurring. These cash summaries are kept in loose-leaf notebook form, making possible comparisons from month to month.

The statement of "current position" (Figure 4) is kept weekly and can easily be put on a daily basis if management so desires. These summaries are also entered in a book so that figures may be kept for later comparison between weeks.

Reports of the type described above are an individual matter which will vary among different industries and among different companies within an industry, and even within the same company from time to time. Probably no company is *completely* satisfied with its reports.

There are, however, a number of control tools that are applicable to any company. Among these are budgets, breakeven analysis, and sales analysis (all of which are also among the tools of planning), ratio analysis, and standard costs. Still others are available for special controls in various departments.

	Six Months Ended June 30, 1968		Nine Months Ended Sept. 30, 1968		Twelve Months Ended Dec. 31, 1968	
Item	Amount	%	Amount	%	Amount	%
SIKA						
Sales						
Less - freight						
Net sales						
Material cost						
Gross profit						
WHITE BORO						
Sales						
Less - freight						
Net sales						
Material cost						
Gross profit						
C-32						
Sales						
Less - freight						
Net sales						
Material cost						
Gross profit						
R-46 AND NORTON MISCELLANEOUS						
Sales						
Less - freight						
Net sales						
Material cost						
Gross profit						
ALUMINA						
Sales						
Less - freight						
Net sales						
Material cost						
Gross profit						
TOTAL						
Sales						
Less - freight						
Net sales						
Material cost						
Gross profit						

STATEMENT OF GROSS PROFIT—PURCHASED GOODS

FIGURE 2 Statement of gross profit—purchased goods.

CASH SUMMARY					
Period from_____, 19____ through_____, 19____					
			Opening bank balance		
RECEIPTS					
Accounts receivable					
Discounts taken					
Group insurance					
Withholding					
Social security					
Interest					
Scrap sales					
S-F sales					
Boro sales					
Super sales					
Cor sales					
Sika sales					
White sales					
Alumina sales					
Dividends					
Notes receivable					
Treasury stock					
Treasury notes					
Surplus					
			TOTAL RECEIPTS		
EXPENDITURES					
Materials					
Boro ore					
Emery ore					
Corundum ore					
Resale					
SiC					
White					
S-F					
Purchased Alumina					
Containers					
Freight					
Compensation					
Payroll					
Salaries					
Bonus					
Commissions					
Pensions					

Page 1

FIGURE 3 Cash summary.

Insurance							
Group							
Life							
Plant protection							
All other							
Taxes							
Federal							
State							
Local							
Withholding							
Social security							
O.A.B.							
Utilities							
Water							
Fuel							
Light and power							
Expense accounts							
Advertising							
Auto							
Laboratory							
Office							
Selling							
Travel							
Donations							
General							
Entertainment							
Factory equipment							
No. 1							
No. 2							
No. 3							
Factory supplies							
Repair supplies							
Dividends							
Preferred							
Common							
Miscellaneous							
Discounts allowed							
Corundum expense							
Interest							
Treasury stock							
Surplus							
Notes payable							
Treasury notes							
Ground maintenance							
			TOTAL EXPENDITURES				
			Closing bank balance				

CURRENT POSITION					
Date	Cash	Accounts receivable	Accounts payable	Net	Notes
Example: 12-1-68	$500,000	$300,000	$200,000	$600,000	Tax payment due 12/15, common dividend 12/20.

FIGURE 4   Current position.

BUDGETS

Comparison of performance against budget is one of the best methods of determining whether or not the company is spending more or less than it had planned to, and of tracing the reasons for overages and underages and making any corrections necessary. Ordinarily, the manager of a department or division is required to explain any overrun (or any overrun that amounts to more than 5 or 10 per cent) to his superior. In some companies explanations of underruns are required also, on the theory that the too economical manager may not be doing all the things he should be doing with the money allotted to him or may have been too greedy in forecasting his requirements.

The value of the budget as a tool of control depends to a large extent on how quickly actual expenditures can be reported to those responsible for them and on the breakdown within the budget. If a manager gets the figures several weeks after the money has been spent, there is little he can do about an overrun. Or if the report of the actual expenses shows merely the amount by which he is over his budget, it provides no clue to the reasons, and he will not know what steps he should take to economize.

The breakdown will be finer, of course, in the case of the lower echelons than at the top. Thus top management may look no further than the overall figure for direct labor or plant overhead unless there is indication that something is wrong. But the plant manager may receive a statement of actual versus budgeted expenses for each department—for light and power, for machinery repairs, for supervision, and for other items.

There is often much that can be done about these costs, even about some that are ordinarily regarded as fixed, or at least semivariable. For example, take light and power. It is possible to waste both by not turning off machines or lights promptly. In addition, one part of a plant's electric bill depends on peak usage, even if only for a short time. By arranging matters so that several machines which draw heavy current are not used simultaneously, a plant manager can often cut this portion of the bill.

Again, in the case of capital budgets, top management is interested mainly in the total cost of a new plant or facility as compared with the predicted cost. The project manager, on the other hand, will be interested in labor and material costs in relation to the percentage of completion week by week as the project progresses. If a plant is being built by a contractor on a lump-sum contract, this is the contractor's headache; the company people need concern themselves only with whether he is following the specifications and proceeding fast enough to get the job done on the promised date. But in many cases, the contracts are let on a different basis. For example, the company may have a time and material contract, under which it agrees to pay the contractor the cost of labor and material, plus percentages for overhead and his profit. Or it may have a cost-plus contract, under which the contractor will get back his costs plus a percentage of them or a fixed sum as profit. In that case, it is the company project manager who must watch the costs, for the contractor has little incentive to keep them down.

It is important, however, that top management have, in all cases, a way of tracing differences between actual and budgeted costs to the man and the factors ultimately responsible. A simplified version of how this may be done is shown in Figure 5.

In this hypothetical case, the company's profit was a half million less than it had budgeted for. Top management asks its division managers, each of whom is responsible for the profit on a group of products, for an explanation. The manager of X division examines the statements for the plants under his jurisdiction and discovers that plant No. 1 accounts for a large part of the variance. Now the plant manager is on the spot; so he looks at the figures by departments and by foremen, and it appears that Foreman Jones is responsible for the largest percentage of the discrepancy. Further, indirect labor and indirect materials used for his section are the main cause of his poor showing.

Now it may be that Foreman Jones should be detached from the payroll as soon as possible, or it may be that he needs help from above. Knowing exactly where the greater part of his overage came from, his superiors are in a position to decide fairly.

Let us say that in this case repair expenses are charged, not to a general maintenance budget, but to the departments and sections in which the work is done, and it is excessive repair expenses that are causing the unduly high indirect labor and material costs. Is Foreman Jones allowing his men to abuse the machines, or abusing them himself by having them overloaded beyond their capacity? Or in his zeal to get out production, is he running them without maintenance until minor difficulties turn into major breakdowns? In that case, he needs at least some reorientation on his responsibilities.

But perhaps he is saddled with a group of machines so old that the breakdowns are inevitable, and his poor showing can be improved only by buying him some new equipment. Or perhaps the machines are poorly designed for the job they are to do, and some engineering help is needed to make the corrections.

On the sales side, variations from budgeted revenue and expenses may be traced down through the regions and districts to individual salesmen, and the showings compared with quotas if the latter have been set realistically on the basis of market research. (Some companies set quotas too high deliberately,

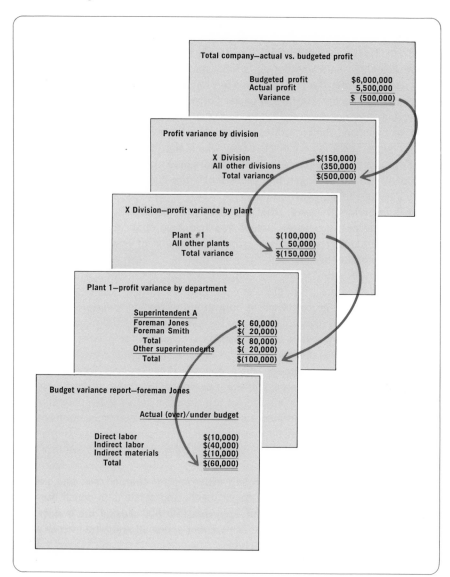

FIGURE 5 A company profit variance from objective can be isolated. (From George E. Altmansberger, "Building an Integrated Reports System," *Reports to Top Management for Effective Planning and Control,* American Management Association, New York, 1953, p. 113.)

in the hope of raising the salesmen's sights. The psychological value of doing so may be questioned since an unattainable goal is likely to produce less incentive than an attainable one. In any case, those who do so should have more realistic figures for control purposes, even if they do not show them to the salesmen.)

Budgets are an excellent tool for both planning and control, but they have their shortcomings.

Thus the budget is usually based on historical trends, and these may not continue. It may also be influenced by what top management would like to happen. Naturally top management is interested in larger dollar and percentage profits, lower costs, and greater market penetration, and may hopefully budget on the basis that these will materialize, even though the chances of their doing so are not very great.

Also, the budget in its final form may be the result, not of examination of the probable facts in the light of pure reason, but of a good deal of negotiation and self-protective maneuvering among the parties involved. There is a strong personal safety factor built into every budget, for each executive is conscious that if he does not "make budget" he will be subject to criticism or even punishment. Hence he is likely to insist on goals that he is sure to reach even though he could do a good deal better. His superiors, on the other hand, may try to pare his budget each year in order to give him a higher goal to shoot at.

Again, if an executive finds that he is likely to exceed his budget and sees no way to meet it legitimately, he may reduce expenditures in a way that will cause trouble later. A plant manager, for example, may neglect to keep his machines in good repair as long as he can continue running them at all, and the results may not show up until some time later—preferably when he has moved on to another job. Some companies are so aware of this possibility that they employ a second control: headquarters inspectors to descend on plants at random intervals and take a good look at the equipment. Or, to take another example, a sales manager may sell in advance, i.e., get orders now that he would ordinarily get only a year later. Then he meets his budget this year, but next year's sales are likely to fall off because his customers have been forward-buying. (This is a typical occurrence among auto dealers, especially if they can take advantage of a manufacturer's sales contest to boost their current record.) Or an executive who is bent on expansion but cannot get top approval for it may start to erect one part of an addition to a plant. Thus he may be able to force top management to accede to his request for the rest of the funds needed.

Finally, there is the psychological reaction of those who have to work within the budget framework. While, on the one hand, people like to know what they are working for and how they will be judged, on the other, many of them are resentful of budget restrictions. This seeming incompatibility between the needs of the enterprise for system and the needs of individuals for elbowroom is as yet a largely unresolved problem. It is part of the larger problem of formal organization.

STANDARD COSTS

Standard costs are developed by working out the cost of the materials and labor that go into each unit of the product and adding a standard overhead rate. Since the amount of overhead actually applicable to each unit of product will vary with the number of units, and since the amount of labor (and the labor rates) may also vary, actual costs will seldom exactly equal standard.

The fact of a variance, which nearly always exists, is not important; what is important is the reason for it. If variances for each element of standard cost are shown, they indicate where corrective steps should be taken.

For example, if a variance in material cost is due to higher prices, there is not much the company can do about it except, perhaps, look for cheaper vendors or substitute materials. But if it is due to the use of more material to produce the same amount of product, it indicates that there may be waste. (Poor adjustment of machines, for example, can cause excessive scrap.) Thus the accounts may show both usage variance and material-price variance.

Similarly, labor variances may be broken down into variances in labor hours (the difference between the amount time studies or past experience shows should be needed and the actual amount) and variances in labor rates. If labor hours are greater than standard, inefficient utilization of labor may be indicated. If changes in labor rates are due to increases in basic rates, that is one thing; if they are due to excessive use of overtime (at time and a half), poor scheduling of the work may be indicated.

Variances in burden or overhead are most likely to occur because of changes in volume. If volume is high, the burden will be "overabsorbed" because it will be spread over more units; if it is low, the burden applicable to each unit of product will be increased. But a variation here could occur also because actual out-of-pocket overhead costs were rising because of more and larger staff departments, more supervision, and so on. These increases might be justified, or they might not. The important point in control is that the managers know *what is actually occurring* and have a chance to weigh the pros and cons in the light of the facts.

Standard costs are not, of course, set once and for all and never changed to take account of changing conditions. But generally they remain unchanged for at least a year.

RATIO ANALYSIS

Ernest R. Breech, for many years chairman of the board of the Ford Motor Company and one of the main architects of its recovery after a long downturn, used to present a copy of James H. Bliss's book on ratio analysis[7] to every young man whom he thought to be of high managerial caliber. He considered ratio analysis one of the most important management tools.

Perhaps the single most important ratio is the relationship of profits after taxes to investment, the percentage return on investment. This ratio should be compared with what is ideally desirable (i.e., the highest figure the company might reasonably expect to make), with past accomplishment, and with the same ratio in other comparable companies. As an absolute minimum this ratio

[7] *Financial and Operating Ratios in Management,* The Ronald Press Company, New York, 1923.

should be at least greater than the interest on good bonds; otherwise there is no return for the greater risk of enterprise.

Other ratios may be used to pinpoint reasons why the return on investment is less than it might be or to gauge the inherent strength of the company. Among the most important, perhaps, are the following:

Net sales to working capital   The adequate utilization of working capital is vital, since it affects the primary measure of results: return on investment. However, a balance must be struck, because too small a ratio of working capital to sales might leave the company unable to take advantage of increased demand. It might have to delay increasing its production for thirty days or so until the revenue from sales came in.

What the ratio should be depends on the product. In general, working capital will be lower in relation to sales volume in cases where the product is perishable and unit costs are low. Thus annual sales of agricultural products like fruit and butter might be twelve times working capital; while in furniture they might be only twice as large—that is, the company might need working capital equal to one-half annual sales. Where the product is perishable, inventory must turn over rapidly, and the same working capital can be used again and again in the course of a year.

Net sales to inventory   Other things being equal, the greater the turnover of inventory, the higher the profit on investment.

Net sales to accounts receivable   This ratio depends on four factors: the value of sales in dollars, the credit terms (number of days in which accounts are payable with or without discount), the percentage of the merchandise sold on credit, and the collection policies of the company. Assuming a relatively constant rate of sales, all on credit, "The net sales during any fiscal period should bear approximately the same relationship to accounts receivable that the length of the fiscal period bears to the length of the credit period."[8] For example, if the credit period is thirty days, the ratio of annual net sales to accounts receivable should be not less than twelve to one since not more than one-twelfth should be outstanding at any one time.

Quick ratio   This is the ratio of quick assets, or assets immediately realizable, to accounts payable. Credit men hold that this should be at least one to one, meaning that the company is able to meet all bills likely to be presented for payment.

Current ratio   This is the ratio of current assets (cash, receivables, working capital) to current liabilities. In contrast to the liabilities (accounts payable) used in the quick ratio, current liabilities will include some debts that have

[8] R. Parker Eastwood, *Sales Control by Quantitative Methods*, Columbia University Press, New York, 1940, p. 51.

already been incurred but are not immediately payable—for example, tax liabilities.

Percentage of accounts payable on which discounts are earned   A good working rule is that the company should be paying its bills at least promptly enough to take advantage of discounts offered for payment within ten or thirty days.

Administrative expense to sales   Administrative expense, since it is to some extent a fixed cost, should be strictly predetermined and limited.

These ratios are easily used as tools of control. As a minimum, a small company might use a set of basic controls as follows:

1	Quick ratio	1 to 1—The company should be able to cover all its immediate obligations at any time.
2	Current ratio	1.5 to 1—Cash plus receivables should be at least 50 per cent greater than current liabilities.
3	Working capital to net sales	Working capital should be at least 15 per cent of annual sales to ensure funds to finance current sales.
4	Accounts payable current: discounted	**Preferably 100 per cent**: should be paid promptly enough to take advantage of discounts.
5	Long-term debt to total capital	Long-term debt should be no more than one-third of total capital, to ensure a good margin of safety.
6	Administrative expense: sales	Administrative expense should be no more than $7\frac{1}{2}$ per cent of total sales.

These ratios can be plotted week by week on a chart in order that management may see at a glance how well it is meeting its objectives. Figures 6 and 7 show examples of such graphs.

Ratios that reveal defects in the financial structure   A basic ratio of this type is the ratio of sales to net worth; another is the ratio of sales to assets. In general, the higher the ratio of sales to net worth, the more effectively the company is using its capital; but this is true only up to a point. Undercapitalization can be a source of weakness as well. For example, Chrysler Corporation achieved a very high ratio over a period of years by doing a tremendously large assembly job in crowded quarters. But when the facilities were no longer competitive costwise, considerable and persistent losses were incurred.

The ratio of sales to fixed assets indicates the balance between sales on the one hand and plant and machinery on the other. It should increase somewhat faster than the ratio of sales to net worth, since depreciation charges will tend to reduce the investment in plant. Again a high ratio indicates a good utilization of capital, but it can be too high if it exists because of a failure to modernize facilities that will show up later in increased costs.

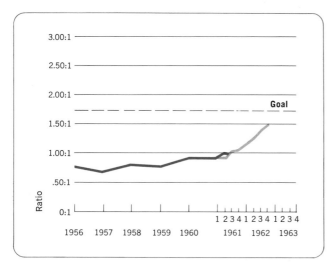

FIGURE 6   Current ratio. (The lighter line is a forecast.)

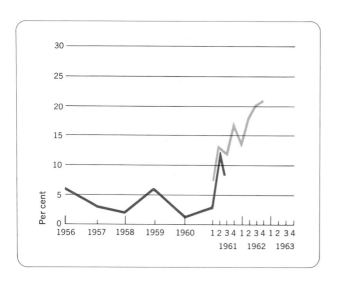

FIGURE 7   Pretax profit as a percentage of net sales. (The lighter line is a forecast.)

SOME OTHER COMPARISONS

Any well-established company, of course, easily meets the financial ratio requirements. Some, therefore, use other measures as well.

An important one is share of the market—the ratio of company sales to total sales in the industry. If a company is a large one engaged in many different industries, it will examine the share of the market of each of its product divisions.

The important point here is not the actual percentage, but the trend. Other things being equal, a company may have a very small percentage of the total market and still be doing very well. But if its market share is steadily decreasing, one of two things is happening: Either competitors are taking business away from it or it is not growing as fast as it should in view of a broadening market.

This may be illustrated by an example. During and shortly after World War II, a brewery in a metropolitan area continued to show rising sales and profits, and its owners—who left everything to a general manager—were highly satisfied with the results. Share of the market was decreasing but this was a factor they never examined. If they had, they would have seen that competitors' sales were rising much faster than theirs and perhaps would have been moved to call the general manager to account. Then sales and profits suddenly dropped, and the owners hired a management consulting firm to find out why.

The actual situation was this: The market was growing with rising incomes, and with war and postwar shortages the producers could not meet the demand; therefore consumers took what they could get. The brewery roof had begun leaking, and the water diluted the beer, but the general manager did not bother to have it repaired. His brewmaster quit after a disagreement and was never replaced. Thus the product had degenerated to the point where customers bought it only when they could not get other brands, and as soon as competitors could supply the market, the buyers flocked to them. The owners' only recourse at this point was to get a new general manager and put in more capital to restore the plant and try to win back their market.

Another measure is the ratio of input to output, which is a measure of the utilization of the company's plant and personnel. An increase in production without a corresponding increase in man-hours worked or new equipment shows rising productivity, and indicates better utilization of men or machines, or both. Some output and input measures used include:

Output	Input
Sales billed	Man-hours worked
Units sold	Payroll dollars
Units produced	Floor space
	First cost of plant and equipment

Labor productivity (output per manhour) is sometimes thought to reflect only how hard the employees are working. If it falls, the layman is likely to conclude that the employees are lying down on the job. Industrial engineers and managers know that the amount of effort employees are putting forth is only one factor in labor productivity. A change of method can bring a bigger rise than any amount of extra effort on the part of employees.

A comparatively new industrial engineering technique called "work sampling" has demonstrated this in many companies. In a work sampling study, random observations are made of groups of workers, and the proportion of time they spend actually working, waiting for materials, looking for tools, conversing, and so on is recorded. Most studies show that although employees do waste some time—a few quite a lot of time—the greater part of the loss occurs because management does not make it possible for them to work a good proportion of the day.

As a guide to investors, *Forbes* magazine publishes four ratios of different kinds which, while not really instruments of immediate control, may give management a chance to see how well it is doing by its stockholders in comparison with its competitors. These ratios shown for a five-year period for individual companies within an industry are:

1.   Net income per share as a percentage of investor's equity per share.
2.   Percentage increase in stockholders' equity per share.
3.   Ratio of earnings paid out in dividends to earnings plowed back into the business.
4.   Increase in per share earnings as a percentage of the plow-back.

Use of the per share figures removes the effect of new stock issues, which might well distort the picture. If total earnings double and the number of shares also doubles, stockholders actually may be no better off—will be no better off, in fact, unless the new shares have been distributed to them in the form of stock dividends.

Figure 8 shows an example of such a report. (Company names are given in the magazine, but are omitted here because the charts were published some time ago and the picture may well be entirely different today.)

Figure 9 shows another method of employing ratio analysis in control, one that can be used only if the requisite figures from comparable companies in the same industry are available. In Great Britain, an organization called the Centre for Interfirm Comparison, Ltd., collects the data and provides the participants with an industry-wide picture in which companies are designated by code letters rather than by name since many would be reluctant to disclose the information to competitors otherwise. Not much work of this type has been done in the United States, however.

ADMINISTRATIVE EXPENSE ANALYSIS

Administrative expenses are somewhat like taxes; they creep up stealthily, and once they have risen it seems hard, almost impossible, to cut them back. And they appear to be an inevitable concomitant of growth.

Thus a young man starts out with a printing shop. He gets the orders, sets the type, and runs the press. If he has some success, he may find that he has no time to keep accounts of expenditures and receipts, which he will need for tax purposes as well as for his own guidance in quoting prices. So he is compelled to take on a secretary-bookkeeper. Immediately, this adds several thousand dollars to his expenses, and, of course, net profits may be cut by the same amount. However, since he can now spend more time selling,

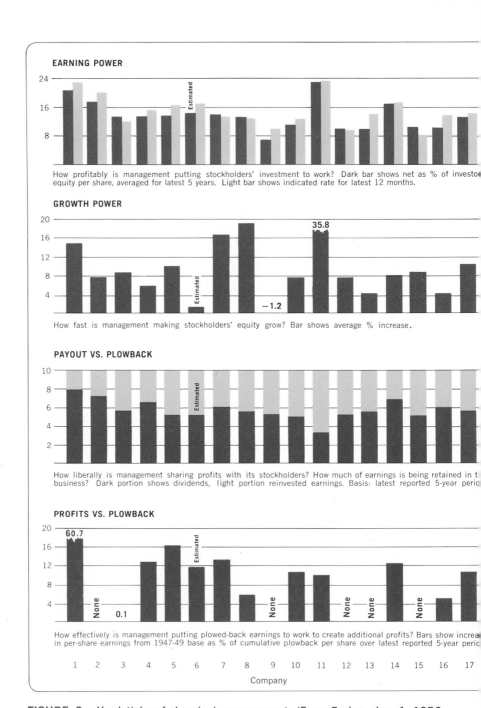

FIGURE 8 Yardsticks of chemical management. (From *Forbes*, Jan. 1, 1956, p. 28.)

increased revenue may more than make up for this, which is, of course, why he incurred the expense.

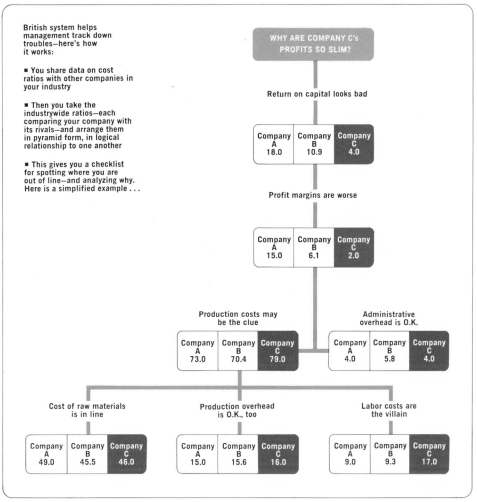

British system helps management track down troubles—here's how it works:

■ You share data on cost ratios with other companies in your industry

■ Then you take the industrywide ratios—each comparing your company with its rivals—and arrange them in pyramid form, in logical relationship to one another

■ This gives you a checklist for spotting where you are out of line—and analyzing why. Here is a simplified example . . .

WHY ARE COMPANY C's PROFITS SO SLIM?

Return on capital looks bad

Company A	Company B	Company C
18.0	10.9	4.0

Profit margins are worse

Company A	Company B	Company C
15.0	6.1	2.0

Production costs may be the clue

Company A	Company B	Company C
73.0	70.4	79.0

Administrative overhead is O.K.

Company A	Company B	Company C
4.0	5.8	4.0

Cost of raw materials is in line

Company A	Company B	Company C
49.0	45.5	46.0

Production overhead is O.K., too

Company A	Company B	Company C
15.0	15.6	16.0

Labor costs are the villain

Company A	Company B	Company C
9.0	9.3	17.0

FIGURE 9   (From *Business Week,* Nov. 24, 1962, p. 128.)

If his business continues to grow, his administrative expense is likely to continue to rise: when he adds several printers, he may need a foreman to supervise them; and if he is successful enough to have a large organization, he will need several foremen, plus perhaps a purchasing department, an accounting department, an estimating department, and other staff groups. His administrative expense will tend to rise, not as a straight line, but as a series of steps as the various functions become too large for him to handle himself (Figure 10).

Administrative expenses cover all human work not directly concerned with making and selling: general management expense (payments to the top officers and their general and personal staffs), special staffs—accounting, personnel,

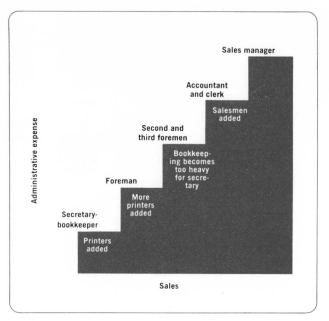

FIGURE 10   Rise in administrative expense in a small printing company.

office, engineering, and production planning and control, time study groups, sales administration—in other words, all wages and salaries for people who handle administration or assist the administrators.

Overall, Seymour Melman[9] has shown that the A/P ratio (administration as a percentage of production personnel) has grown historically in Western countries, especially in the United States and England, and that the percentage is likely to rise further, as Figure 11 shows.

There are many such studies confirming the rise in the A/P ratio. What are the causes of this rise? And the consequences?

The most important reason for the rise in the A/P ratio is the rapidly increasing need for specialization in industry due to the growing complexity of the technical problems. Even in manufacturing, the specialized advisers are increasing faster than those engaged directly in production.

A second though less important reason is the extent to which government and labor unions now impinge on company management. Reports to government (Internal Revenue, the SEC, and many other agencies) mean larger and more specialized accounting departments. The rise of unions has meant that more special study must be devoted to industrial relations, and such concessions as pensions, insurance, and other fringe benefits have also greatly complicated the accounting problem.

[9] *Dynamic Factors in Industrial Productivity,* Basil Blackwell, Oxford, 1956, pp. 131–132.

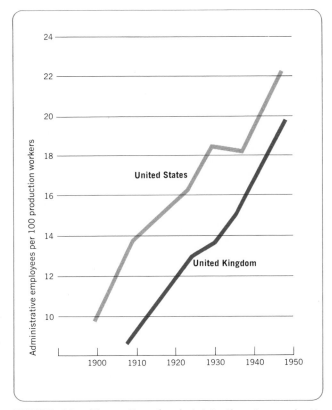

FIGURE 11   The ratio of administration to production personnel in the manufacturing industries of Great Britain and the United States, 1899–1948. (From Seymour Melman, *Dynamic Factors in Industrial Productivity,* Basil Blackwell, Oxford, 1956, p. 131.)

Now, specialized individuals and staffs can often save the company more money than it could make by larger production and sales. A research man may invent an important new product; a methods man may discover a new method that reduces direct labor costs substantially. In addition, staff can anticipate the shape of things to come and help the company develop plans to meet changing circumstances.

But administrative expense may also increase merely because staff tends to beget more staff, according to the well-known Parkinson's Law. In his book by that name,[10] a spoof but one which may have a considerable element of truth, Professor C. Northcote Parkinson illustrated this by pointing out that Britain's shrinking colonial empire was seemingly requiring an ever-rising number of people to administer it. One reason for this, perhaps, is that staff

[10] John Murray (publishers), Ltd., London, 1958.

often seeks new tasks and new responsibilities in order to justify its existence and an increase in size in order to appear more important.

Basically, management employs staff in the hope that it will increase sales or reduce expenses per unit of output, or at least keep them from rising too fast. But this hope may prove a Fata Morgana.

For example, one aircraft company attempted to survive in a declining market through the use of staff. From 1951 to 1956, the company was growing, and staff was increasing in proportion to productive employees. The biggest increases took place in service and field engineering, whose personnel multiplied five times; in quality control, with an increase of 300 per cent; and in manufacturing engineering, with 250 per cent. The total increase in staff as a percentage of direct labor amounted to 13 per cent.

In the next few years, sales fell off. Yet the company kept the staffs at full strength in the hope that they would develop engineering and quality improvements that would enable it to capture a larger share of a declining market. But despite the increase in the A/P ratio (which grew because the productive labor force dropped), the larger sales were not achieved. Company profits were cut substantially.[11]

Another problem raised by the increase in staffs is the possibility that it contributes to inflation. Ruth P. Mack of the National Bureau of Economic Research in the *Review of Economics and Statistics* (1959)[12] examined the trend in costs and prices between 1947 and 1957 and found that the increase in nonproductive labor—in administrative jobs, marketing, advertising, and research—plus heavy outlay for office equipment, had caused a widening gap between selling prices and direct costs (wages and raw materials). If this is true, the increase may have been a major factor in creeping inflation.

There have, however, been cases where sharply rising costs for new staff have materially contributed to profits and ability to compete, even though the gains have taken time to materialize. For example, when Westinghouse decentralized its operations in the period 1936 to 1939, there was an immediate rise in administrative costs since each decentralized division needed a staff of its own, and more staff men were needed at headquarters to coordinate the decentralized operations. For a time, the A/P ratio rose sharply without a corresponding increase in return. But after three years, the increase began to justify itself in increased asset turnover, share of the market, and performance relative to the general state of the economy. Figure 12, which is based on elaborate statistical studies, shows the results graphically. The thick solid line on the chart represents additional administrative expense, the heavy broken line additional profits—that is, the two lines show the rises in administrative expense and profits over what they would have been if the pre-1935 relationship with GE had continued. The lighter lines show the trends in costs (broken line) and profits (solid line) over the same period as two-year moving averages of actual data.

[11] S. B. Alpert and H. Weitz, *Decision-making, Growth and Failure,* The Institute of Management Sciences, Baltimore, Oct. 20, 1960.
[12] *Business Week,* Oct. 10, 1959, p. 176.

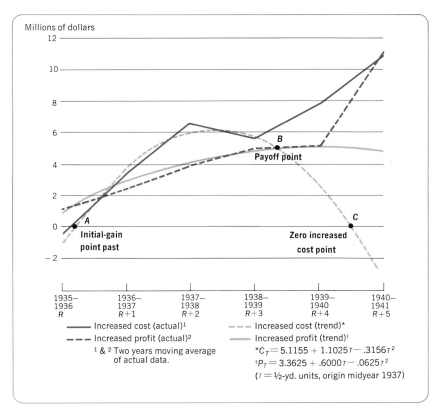

FIGURE 12 "Timing pattern" net gains or losses of the Westinghouse reorganization, 1935–1941.

The area to the right of point A shows what happened after 1936. While relative costs were, for a while, still higher than relative profits, the latter started rising at a much faster rate than the former until, at point B, the new plan began to pay off; and as can be seen from the graph, results were good over the long run.

Since many of the data of this later period were influenced by the impact of the defense program, which drastically changed the product mix of the two companies, the trends of the earlier years were extrapolated to determine what would have happened if normal conditions had prevailed throughout the period.

BREAKEVEN ANALYSIS

A company's breakeven point (see Chapter 16 on planning) does not remain constant. If the fixed costs rise (and there may well be an increase greater than foreseen), the breakeven point will rise, and it will take more sales (in units) to make the same profit. Figure 13 illustrates the effect of a rise in this segment of total costs. A price rise will produce the opposite effect, but a rise in material and/or labor costs per unit of product will mean that the line representing variable costs will rise more steeply than anticipated.

It is important, for this reason, to compare the projections of the breakeven points for various products or divisions with the actual breakeven points during the year. If this is not done, management will lack the really pertinent facts on which to base important decisions.

For example, one large diversified company called in a consultant to determine why one of its divisions had ceased to make money. It hoped he could suggest some way in which it could increase its sales volume. When the consultant drew the breakeven chart, however, he discovered that it looked like the one in Figure 14. It was evident that, under prevailing circumstances, the company could not stop losing money even if it could sell enough to keep the plant operating at capacity. Parallel lines meet only at infinity.

The reason for this was twofold. First, prices had dropped, and the division (which had a great deal of competition) had had to follow industry trends. Second, material prices had risen, and since material cost was 80 per cent of total cost, anything the division did in the way of reducing manufacturing costs would not be of much use. It could not reduce material costs; it had to pay the market price. If it achieved a sizable reduction in all other costs—say, 10 per cent—total costs would be cut only 2 per cent (10 per cent of 20 per cent), and the difference would not be enough to enable it to break even.

The question, therefore, was not: How can the division increase its sales?

FIGURE 13   Breakeven diagrams illustrating effect of fixed costs upon "crossover" point and profits. (From R. Parker Eastwood, *Sales Control by Quantitative Methods*, Columbia University Press, New York, 1940, p. 74.)

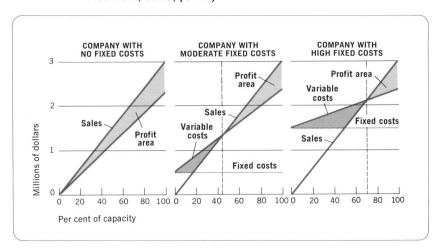

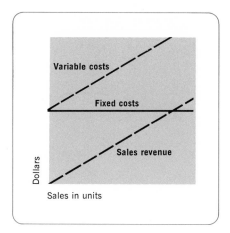

FIGURE 14

but: Should the company eliminate the division entirely, or was the chance that competitors would raise prices (or that raw material prices would drop) good enough to make it worthwhile to ride out a few loss years?

SOME FUTURE POSSIBILITIES

The advent of computers has opened up new possibilities for control since it is now possible to determine what effect a change in one factor will have on all the others.

Figure 15 illustrates this. The key figures here are represented by the dotted line marked "retailers' orders from customers." It is the changes in these figures that set in motion all the other changes, which may be greater or smaller in percentages than the change in sales, and will occur some time afterwards because there is a time lag between the date the orders are placed and the date they are filled.

As retail sales rise to a point 10 per cent above the normal level, retail inventory is depleted, but not by 10 per cent since retailers begin to place larger orders with the distributors. This results, some weeks later, in a 10 per cent drop in distributor inventory and a very large rise in unfilled orders at the factory warehouse since production cannot get going fast enough to replenish the inventory. Similar time lags occur when sales fall 10 per cent below normal. Shortly after they have reached this low point, factory production is cut 52 per cent below normal, though retailers' orders are again on the rise.

In this case, production at capacity (10 per cent above the normal level) can supply customers even for the peak sales periods since sales never rise more than 10 per cent above the normal level. But if management looked at the figures only as of a moment of time, it might well conclude at point A that

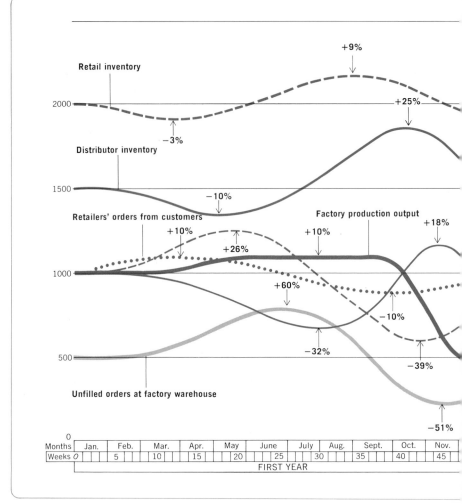

FIGURE 15   Effect of fluctuating retail sales on factory with manufacturing capacity limited to 10 per cent above average sales level.

it needed more capacity since unfilled orders at the factory warehouse are 337 per cent above the normal level.

Jay W. Forrester, professor of industrial management at MIT School of Industrial Management, who developed this analysis,[13] points out that studies of this type might also be used to develop greater stability at the production level.

[13] See *Harvard Business Review*, July–August, 1958, p. 37.

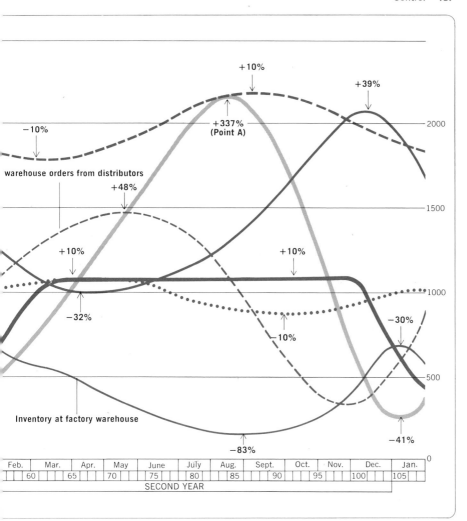

+10%

+39%

−10%

+337%
(Point A)

2000

warehouse orders from distributors

+48%

1500

+10%

+10%

−32%

1000

−10%

−30%

Inventory at factory warehouse

500

−41%

−83%

0

Feb.		Mar.		Apr.		May		June		July		Aug.		Sept.		Oct.		Nov.		Dec.		Jan.
	60		65		70		75		80		85		90		95		100		105	

SECOND YEAR

NONFINANCIAL CONTROLS

Since the major objective of a business is to make a profit, the major controls
used by most businesses are financial measurements of one kind or another.
But there are many areas of business that do not lend themselves to financial
control, and in these areas controls of other types are necessary.

For example, the quality of the product must be controlled. Plans and specifications set up certain standards a product must meet, but there can be no

assurance that it will meet those standards unless there are control measures. A machine set up to produce parts of certain dimensions may get out of adjustment and begin producing either oversize or undersize parts, to mention just one of the things that may happen. It is possible, of course, to have each part inspected and measured, and this is sometimes done. But increasingly, companies are turning to statistical quality control in which only samples of product are inspected. If the size of the sample is calculated correctly, it will be representative of all the parts in a given lot, and it will be possible to accept or reject an entire lot on the basis of the sample.

Then there is production control, which is needed to ensure that production plans are being carried out as expected. The Gantt chart, described in Chapter 6, is one very useful tool for this type of control, for it shows at a glance which parts of a job are behind schedule and enables the manager to take corrective action before delays become serious.

Appraisals of managerial performance may be considered a control technique, especially when the manager and his superior set an objective and then—at the next appraisal—determine how well the objective has been met.

Employee attitude surveys may also be used as a means of control. For example, before-and-after surveys may be used to determine the effect of steps management has taken to improve morale.

In fact, any technique for determining deviation from plans is a control technique.

SUMMARY

Control is the determination of progress toward objectives in accordance with the predetermined plan. Any gap between expectations and performance—on the part of the whole company or any segment of it—is most easily closed if it is detected before it becomes serious. Good control techniques provide information quickly so that action can be taken to correct the discrepancies.

A great deal of control may be exercised through the medium of financial reports, provided they are issued often enough and supply enough information to enable the manager to determine exactly where, and if possible why, deviations from plans are occurring. The information should also be stated in such a way that figures are comparable with the figures for past periods.

Among the tools of financial control are budgets, ratio analysis, standard costs, administrative expense analysis, and breakeven analysis. The use of computers makes possible still more sensitive control techniques.

In addition to the financial controls, many other types are needed to control quality, to ensure that things are being done on time, and to measure the performance of individuals.

It must be remembered that control is not merely seeing that people do what they are supposed to do. Management plans not only to reach certain objectives, but to reach them by certain means. A good control system will indicate not only when there are deviations from the plan but also when external circumstances make it advisable to change the means of gaining the objectives, or even to change the objectives themselves.

Review Questions

1. Define control. Why is it necessary?
2. Why may a budget be considered both a plan and a means of control?
3. What are standard costs? What are some of the ways in which they may be used as a tool of control?
4. What is the quick ratio? Why should it be at least I to I?
5. Why may the ratio of profits after taxes to investment be considered the most important indicator of how the company is doing?
6. Why may a change in the share of the market be more important than an increase or decrease in actual sales?
7. What is administrative expense? Why has it tended to increase in recent years?
8. How is breakeven analysis used as a tool of control?
9. What are some of the controls used in addition to the financial controls?

Case Study One / Solie Bakeries, Inc.*

Several months after the acquisition of bakeries in Maryland had completed the expansion plans of Solie Bakeries, Inc., the president of the company turned over to the controller the task of recommending "a system of controls for branch operations." In making the assignment the president said, "We need better information than we are now receiving to control and also to improve company planning. With so many branches, I find it difficult to keep track of what is really going on." The controller, Mr. James, had only recently been added to the company staff. Before this, he had been a senior accountant in a large public accounting firm.

The original bakery in Newark, New Jersey, conducted a retail door-to-door business selling cakes, pies, bread, and other products to housewives. This company gradually expanded and branches were opened in nearby New Jersey towns. After a number of years of profitable operations in Newark and northern New Jersey, a major expansion program was undertaken. New branches were opened throughout New Jersey, southern New York, and eastern Pennsylvania, and existing bakeries, carrying on the same type of business in Delaware and

* From William H. Newman and James P. Logan, *Business Policies and Management*, 4th ed., South-Western Publishing Co., Cincinnati, 1959. Copyright, Executive Programs, Graduate School of Business, Columbia University, 1954. Reproduced by permission.

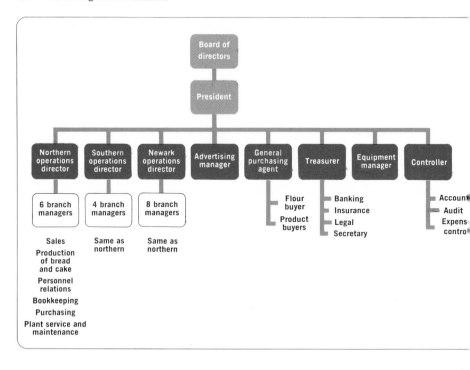

Maryland, were purchased. The purpose of the expansion and mergers was to realize the purported advantages of large-scale operation.

The current organization

Headquarters of the company have remained in Newark, and all senior executives, with the exception of the southern operations director, are located there. The current organization is shown in the chart.

Authority over operations has been decentralized to the branch managers and each branch manager is held responsible for the profit and loss realized in his particular territory. The work assigned to the operations directors is confined to giving advice on current problems to the branch managers and suggesting possible ways of improving operations. These directors have all been successful branch managers in the past. The central functional officers assume authority over their particular fields, and the branch managers are expected to carry out the general directions of these officers. In some cases their authority is exercised concurrently with the branch managers. The duties of the central functional officers are described more fully below.

Although authority over operations is decentralized, the president has established certain policies which are to be followed by the branch managers. The first policy is that of a limited line of products. Each branch is expected to decide upon "specials" for each day of the week and publicize these in advance in order to help reduce the number of items made on any one day. Fancy items which might have only a limited market are discouraged. The branch managers report to the regional operations directors the number of different items baked during a month and are asked for explanations if the number of bread items exceeds 100 or if cake items exceed 150.

Emphasis in production is on volume output at relatively low cost.

Branch operations

Since much of the recent expansion of Solie Bakeries, Inc., was brought about through the purchase of existing bakeries with established lines of products, there are differences in the formulas used in the local plants even for such items as bread and rolls. Pies and other pastry have still more local variation. Suggestions of the regional operations directors tend to bring some uniformity, but local bakers make their own final decisions. This is necessary in order to adapt the formulas to changing local temperature and humidity conditions (which affect fermentation and baking). Quality control is a local responsibility.

Branch managers are in charge of the arrangement of equipment and manufacturing procedures. They receive some help from the operations directors if it is requested. The central equipment manager is in charge of equipment purchases and maintenance routines, but some weight is given to the local managers' opinions when changes are made.

The products to be made on any particular day and the amounts are decided by the branch manager in conjunction with his sales manager. Sales are made direct to consumers from door to door. Each salesman has an assigned route and calls on his customers every day or every other day, depending on the territory. Responsibility for the merchandise rests with the salesmen and they are charged each day for the amount of goods they take out. The men make most sales for cash, but extend weekly credit to some customers. Collection is done by the salesmen. The average number of customers per salesman is 200. Orders for the following day's load are given by the salesman on the basis of orders taken from customers in advance and of average sales expectancy for the particular route. A total is then arrived at for the branch by the sales manager and an order given to the production department for the following day's output. The accuracy of the estimates of the following day's sales determines the losses from sales missed or from stale returns. Bread or cake products not sold on the route are returned by the salesmen. Some items can be redistributed or sold at the branch at a reduced price. Most items, however, are a complete loss because of product perishability. Keeping stale returns low is felt to be a key factor in the success of branch operation. Stale returns and profit together generally make up about 6 per cent of the sales volume.

The rate of turnover of salesmen in some branches is excessively high. These men are paid on commission, and new salesmen realize only about 50 per cent of the earnings of older, established salesmen. The company is currently trying to overcome this difficulty by hiring only married men who can pass certain physical and personality tests. Wages are set by the branch manager as a part of his general responsibility for personnel in his branch.

Minutes of any meetings held at the branches are sent to the operations directors and to the Newark headquarters.

Purchasing

Items purchased by this company fall into three general classes. The first class consists of standard raw materials on which substantial savings can be made through volume purchasing. These are flour, sugar, milk, yeast, lard, and eggs. Flour is the largest single item bought and is purchased from several sources on contracts running about ninety days. It is delivered from the mills to the various branches as needed, in carload lots. The second class consists of raw materials not customarily bought in large quantities, such as nuts, fruits, jams, and jellies. The types and amounts of these ingredients used vary somewhat because of differences in local tastes. The third class consists of items not used directly in the manufacture of bread products. Some of these, such as wrappers, printed boxes, and stationery, have been made standard for the entire company and can be bought in fairly sizable quantities. In addition, delivery equipment and baking machinery must be purchased. The company uses trucks for route deliveries, and purchases these in addition to operating supplies such as tires, oil, and gasoline.

The general purchasing agent for the company supervises buying of all classes of products except equipment and operating supplies. These are purchased by the equipment manager, but he usually confers with the general purchasing agent and the branch manager affected on any major purchase. Authority for emergency purchases with a limit of $100 has been given to the local managers. Some of these managers continue to buy nuts, fruits, jams, and jellies in order to, as they explain, have products adapted to local tastes.

The purchasing department is organized on a product basis. Flour is the largest item of purchase and the general purchasing agent confers weekly with the flour specialist concerning his purchases.

Equipment

Vehicles, machinery, and buildings are under the general responsibility of the equipment manager. He consults with each branch manager on important questions concerning baking equipment. The branch manager is responsible for maintenance work and repairs on trucks. Original purchases of delivery equipment are made by the equipment manager. Mr. Johnson, the equipment manager, spends a large part of his time visiting the branches and talking with the local branch managers and their garage foremen. During these visits he attempts to check on whether or not the maintenance routines which he has specified for trucks and baking equipment are being followed.

Accounting

Monthly profit and loss statements and balance sheets for each branch are filled out by branch bookkeepers according to a system established by the controller. Separate profit and loss statements are made for bread and cake products. In these statements expenses which cannot be directly assigned are charged on the basis of sales volume. Copies of all statements are sent to the regional operations directors and to the Newark office. In addition, weekly sales reports for each branch are distributed to these officers. Monthly reports on advertising expenditures and flour consumption are given to the president.

Bookkeepers at the local branches have all been trained in the Newark office at one time or another. The controller has established all their procedures and does his own hiring and firing. Traveling auditors are also employed to check on the accounting and cash-handling routines at the branches.

Treasurer

Duties of the treasurer are outlined on the organization diagram. He takes care of all banking arrangements and negotiates all insurance contracts. Each branch has a payroll account and a general account at a local bank so that funds can be disbursed for the payroll and regular local expenses. All cash receipts are deposited daily and each month the branch manager is required to send the surplus cash arising from operations to the Newark office. Bills for local purchases have to be approved by the purchasing agent or the equipment manager before they can be paid.

Existing controls

Some of the current controls and control procedures have been illustrated in preceding paragraphs. During his investigation of these procedures, Mr. James (the controller) found that control over inventories varied from branch to branch.

Physical inventories are taken at the end of each month, except in plants which maintain perpetual inventory records. Inventories are valued on the LIFO basis, i.e., last in, first out. Changes in the amounts of finished goods on hand are nominal; so it is simple to compute a ratio of materials expense to sales for each plant. At present, no further detail is reported to the head-quarters office; that is, records do not show expenses by kinds of raw materials.

The practice regarding the withdrawal of materials from inventories varies considerably between plants. At several of the plants, stockmen simply take materials from storerooms upon the oral requests of the bakers. These withdrawals correspond roughly to actual materials usage, but a limited supply of sugar, salt, powdered milk and the like is kept on the mixing floors. In most of these plants at least a few of the items, such as nuts, are kept locked up to prevent "snacking" and pilferage: all other materials are in storerooms open to any of the men handling receipts or withdrawals of materials. A few of the plants have a storekeeper who maintains a perpetual inventory record on all items in stock and must be given a written requisition for any withdrawal.

Quantities to be bought by the purchasing department are estimated on the basis of average requirements in the past adjusted for special promotional efforts. Each branch notifies the purchasing department one month ahead of its "specials" for the coming month.

Recommendations of the controller

The following report was submitted by Mr. James to the president of Solie Bakeries, Inc.:

> The recommendations made in this report are designed to fulfill the objectives of providing more adequate information than is currently available about branch operations and of improving company planning.
>
> (1) *Cash*   In some branches checks are being issued with only one signature. Since correction of this procedure is within the province of the controller's office, instructions have been issued to all branches that signatures of both the bookkeeper and the branch manager will be required. It has also been found that bank accounts are reconciled and verified by the local bookkeeper or one of his subordinates who is also responsible for daily deposits. Since most branches do not have a large enough staff to separate these two tasks, the auditors of the controller's office have been instructed to give special attention to a review of bank reconciliations as part of the internal audit procedure.
>
> (2) *Accounts Receivable*   It is recommended that the amount of accounts uncollected after two weeks be deducted from the salesman's commission.
>
> (3) *Inventories*   It is recommended that each branch adopt a perpetual inventory system. Minimum and maximum stock limits and reorder quantities can be prescribed for each raw material item and a requisition sent to the central purchasing department when materials are needed. A physical inventory should be taken every six months to verify the stock records. This count of inventory should be under the supervision of the branch bookkeeper in order to minimize fraud. In all branches the storekeeper should be made responsible for admission to the storeroom and should designate who is to countersign the stores' requisition. Jams, jellies, nuts, candied fruits, etc., should be kept locked up.
>
> (4) *Fixed Assets*   Control of these assets is currently the responsibility of the equipment manager. The only improvement which appears to be necessary is clarification of the minimum expenditure which must be approved by the board of directors. There is no adequate statement at the moment of the extent of responsibility of the equipment manager for initiating and approving expenditures. It is therefore recommended that the board establish these limits. It is also recommended that a form for requisition of capital expenditures be designed. This will be initiated by the equipment manager and sent to the board of directors for approval. On it can be designated the reasons for the request for expenditure, the amount to be spent, and a description of what is to be purchased.

(5) *Expense Control*   No uniform cost classification or reporting of expenses exists at present. It is therefore recommended that a cost classification and standard costs be worked out for bread production, cake production, branch selling expenses, branch total costs, regional total costs, and for each of the functional fields, advertising, purchasing, equipment, accounting, and finance. Costs should be reported monthly and be given to all officers at Newark as well as to the southern operations director. In the case of production and selling costs the reports should show dollars of expenditure for each cost item expressed in terms of output units, for example, direct labor costs per pound of bread, or heating costs per pound of cake. This information will allow company officers to analyze results three ways: branches can be compared with each other, current and past periods can be compared, and actual results can be compared to standard.

Costs of operating equipment should also be reported in more detail than is done at present. These expenses should be reported in two ways: first, each branch should report costs per mile for gasoline, oil, repairs, etc.; and second, actual expenses charged to each truck and for maintenance of other equipment should be reported.

Since production formulas are not standard for all branches, interbranch comparisons of materials expenses will be difficult. It is recommended that each branch manager write down the formulas actually in use and send copies to the home office. Company auditors can then prepare reports of adherence to these formulas by using information from sales reports and raw material requisitions. Auditors' reports should be sent to the regional operations directors for action. Control over prices of raw materials is made difficult because of random market variations. It is recommended, however, that actual prices by products be reported by the buyers to the general purchasing agent and regional operations directors weekly, and that a monthly summary be sent to the president together with an analysis of trends in materials prices and explanations of significant price changes. It is also recommended that company auditors check the evidence of request for and receipt of bids on purchases of raw materials.

(6) *Sales Information*   Regional operations directors should receive monthly reports of sales by products and by salesmen for all branches. Weekly reports of total sales by product line should also be sent to the operations directors and the president.

It is felt that the system of reports and controls recommended in this report, when added to those currently existing, will provide adequate information for company planning and sound control over operations.

Copies of Mr. James' proposal have been circulated to branch managers and the reaction has been anything but enthusiastic. Several of the managers of branches acquired by merger are already finding it difficult to adjust to "Newark control," and these men are opposed to any further interference with their activities. One of them says, "We should decide whether we are running our bakeries for profits or to pay overhead. I've run this plant for twelve years without so many reports, and nothing has happened to baking bread which makes them necessary now." The operations directors have been noncommittal about the proposal, although one did remark, "Looks like I'll have to hire a new man to tell me what all these figures mean."

1.   Do you think the controls recommended are necessary and desirable? Which ones would you omit, if any? Why?
2.   If you decided to introduce the controls piecemeal, in order to arouse less opposition, which would you introduce first and why?

Case Study Two / Control of Capital Expenditures*

The ABC Metal Manufacturing Company was organized about fifty years ago to take over a foundry in a small town near Toledo. The company prospered and eventually came to include the manufacture of gears, axles, transmissions, metal stampings, and various other automotive parts. It had five plants in the Toledo-Detroit area, each run by a plant manager who had a complete staff, including sales, engineering, personnel, cost, manufacturing, and plant engineering. Heads of these functions at headquarters acted in an advisory capacity to heads of the functions in the plants.

Three of the home office executives exerted greater influence than the others. These were the purchasing agent, the director of personnel, and the plant engineer, who was a really strong man. But he was growing old and no longer enjoyed making frequent visits to the plants as he formerly had. So he had tried to establish a control over capital expenditures that would not handicap operations: Each plant manager was permitted to approve expenditures of $500, but had to obtain home office approval for any project that would cost more than that.

Although there were excellent manufacturing and sales budgets, there were no budgets for plant maintenance, engineering, or research. And the vice-president in charge of plant engineering, while he was quite ready to approve capital expenditures for machinery and equipment, was reluctant to spend anything on building maintenance, expansion, or conveniences for employees.

The plant managers were aware of his peculiarities. Therefore they fell into the habit of approving building projects piecemeal. For instance, a $1,450 job would be completed in segments, each costing only $500. Thus they stayed within the letter of regulations but violated the spirit of their instructions.

In an analysis of plant engineering costs, the chief cost accountant discovered what was happening and called it to the attention of the president, who looked upon it as a clever way of getting needed jobs done. The vice-president

* Reprinted by permission of Northwestern University School of Commerce and William R. Spriegel.

in charge of plant engineering, however, wanted to make an issue of it and even advocated the discharge of one of the best of the plant managers, since he had apparently initiated the practice and had been the most flagrant violator of the spirit of the regulation.

You are a management consultant retained on a regular fee, and the president turns to you for advice.

1.   What would you recommend he do about the plant manager?
2.   What new regulations would you suggest, if any?

Case Study Three / Economy Programs*

The XYZ Warehousing Corporation is a large warehousing organization with storage facilities in a number of large cities. This corporation serves all types of manufacturers, both large and small. However, the bulk of its business comes from the smaller manufacturing enterprises that frequently do not have enough warehouse space to house their inventories—especially during slack sales periods.

   Right after the Korean conflict, direct labor costs commenced to rise and the company sought ways to increase its storage capacity and to decrease its labor costs. The general manager of the concern commenced consulting the managers of his warehousing facilities in the various cities. The following were some of the suggestions which came from these discussions:

Economy no. 1   The manager of the warehouses in city A wrote in to say that with (1) reduction of aisle space to a minimum, and (2) reduction of space assigned to nonstorage activities to a minimum, about 26,622 square feet of storage space—or about 0.5 per cent of the total capacity of the firm—could be reclaimed. He based his total figure on what he felt he could do in his own warehouses, indicating that if he could do this, he saw no reason why the other city managers could not do the same. Assuming that storage space is worth 75 cents a square foot annually, there would be, he argued, a saving of $19,966.50 a year.

Economy no. 2   The manager of another set of warehouses in city B suggested that overtime be held to rock-bottom levels. He indicated that he had been refusing permission to his foremen to use workers overtime at overtime

---

* Adapted by Paul P. Van Riper, Graduate School of Business and Public Administration, Cornell University, from a case used by the Army Controllership Program at Syracuse University.

rates unless they submitted justifications for this twenty-four hours in advance, and that this policy was reducing his overtime costs. He estimated that, if this method were applied throughout the company, a savings of approximately $170,000 could be made during the next twelve months.

During the year 1952 the Syracuse General Depot instituted a "collar the dollar" program. The object of this program was to effect economies through streamlining and improving work methods, consolidating functions, conserving manpower and equipment, salvaging materials, reclaiming storage space, etc. The commanding officer, Colonel George F. B_____, gave this effort his personal attention. By slogans and meetings he endeavored to instill a cost consciousness throughout his entire organization. Leadership in the furtherance of the program was also supplied by the management division of the depot.

The management division prepared an illustrated brochure which described the major accomplishments of the program. This brochure was distributed to key personnel and to the office of the Quartermaster General in Washington, D.C. Two of these economies are described below.

Economy no. 3

A.   The "before" situation

Operating units within the Syracuse General Depot were authorized to submit property issue slips for operating supplies twice monthly on the third and the seventeenth. As a result, the same items were ordered twice a month; work flow was not equalized; and slack time was generated in the depot property branch during interim periods.

B.   The "after" situation

It was determined that space for storage of one month's issues was available within operating units. Local regulations were amended to provide for one issue each month to each activity, with staggered submission dates for property issue slips so that one-third of the depot was supplied each week, leaving the final week of the month free for computation of requirements and issue of due outs.

C.   Results

The number of line items on property issue slips received monthly was reduced by 57 per cent, representing a saving of $30,925 per year. This figure was computed by determining the cost of handling each line item on a requisition. The answer was then multiplied by the reduction in the total number of line items.

Economy no. 4

A.   The "before" situation

In accord with specification JAN, paint was packed for shipment in the engineer supply section by placing each manufacturer's carton into a style 4 reverse wooden box at a cost of $1.90 per carton.

B.   The "after" situation

Authority was granted by the chief of engineers to palletize thirty-six cartons with one style 2 box as a cap. Paint is now shipped strapped to a pallet at a cost of 85 cents per carton, not including the cost of the pallets, which were old ones ready for salvage.

C.   Results

Approximately 3,000 cartons per month have been packed by this method. Savings of $1.05 per carton amounted to an annual saving of about $37,000.

1.   Analyze the four economy actions on proposals described above, and try to decide whether you think these actions are real economies or not.
2.   If you cannot make up your mind about any of them, what additional information would you require in order to make such an analysis?

Selected Readings

Practical Controllership, David R. Anderson and Leo A. Schmidt, Richard D. Irwin, Inc., Homewood, Ill., 1961. The development of the place of control in management, the techniques of control, and the relationship of control to forward planning.

Executive Control—The Catalyst, William Travers Jerome, III, John Wiley & Sons, Inc., New York, 1961. Evaluation of management performance from inside and outside the company, the systems of executive control, the use of the audit. Includes three studies of specific company controls: the return on investment analysis of the Du Pont Company, the "eight key result areas" of the General Electric Company, the control section of Koppers Company.

Higher Management Control, T. G. Rose and D. E. Farr, McGraw-Hill Book Company, New York, 1957. An attempt to arrive at an integrated control structure through special design of the components of control. Covers the fundamentals of control and methods of determining the position of the business in operations and in finance. Concludes with a section on the application of the method and its use by upper management.

Planning and Control Systems: A Framework for Analysis, Robert N. Anthony, Division of Research, Graduate School of Business Administration, Harvard University, Cambridge, Mass., 1965. Presents a system of accounting based on a new classification of accounts.

Controlling Overhead, Harry Tipper, Jr., American Management Association, New York, 1966. Presents a program for overhead control developed through examination of the practices of many companies.

21

INNOVATION

*The central figure on the capitalist stage . . .
is concerned not with the administration of
existing industrial plant and equipment but with
the incessant creation of new plant and
equipment embodying new technologies that
revolutionize existing industrial structures.
Joseph A. Schumpeter: "Capitalism,"
Encyclopedia Britannica*

21

One may think of a manager as purely an administrator, as someone who merely coordinates his work with that of other departments, exercises control to ensure that things proceed according to plan, and sees that his subordinates work to the best of their ability and at the same time keeps them reasonably happy and at peace with each other (and with the organization itself). Or one may consider that "to manage" means, in the words of the late Prof. Joseph A. Schumpeter of Harvard:

> . . . to reform or revolutionize the pattern of production by exploiting an invention or, more generally, an untried technological possibility for producing a new commodity or producing an old one in a new way, by opening up a new source of supply of materials or a new outlet for products, by reorganizing an industry, and so on.
>
> Railroad construction in its earlier stages, electrical power production before the First World War, steam and steel, the motorcar, colonial ventures afford spectacular instances of a large genus which comprises innumerable humbler ones.[1]

The important thing to notice here is that in business an innovation need not necessarily be an invention in the sense of a patentable new product. It may encompass any new procedure that contributes toward corporate objectives. For example, not only the invention of the automobile but the techniques of producing it cheaply enough to place it within the reach of a large number of consumers constituted real innovations. In marketing, a major innovation was the introduction of the supermarket; in finance, the development of installment selling. In personnel administration, there was the discovery of and emphasis on noneconomic aspects of employee-management relations.

Again, there has been a series of far-reaching innovations applicable to the management functions themselves. One example is the use of input-output analysis technique in planning—that is, relating one industry's prospects to those of all others with which it is related—and the development of lead and lag indicators based on the concepts of Wesley C. Mitchell. These techniques were not developed by industry men, but by economists, yet it may be said that the businessmen who recognized their value and hired economists to assist companies in making forecasts were certainly innovators. So were the businessmen who recognized the value of computers and those who have fostered exploration of new ways of using them.

Each of these innovations has been of major significance to our business system, and there are many smaller ones that are being introduced every day. For example, one aerospace company obtained a major government contract partly because of an innovation in production techniques—assembly of a large component in a vertical rather than the conventional horizontal position. To make this possible, it built a tower 105 feet tall, with platforms on which men could work. Then there are such innovations as improved methods of production control, more effective ways of utilizing men and/or machines, new and more efficient layouts for offices or factories, new marketing ideas.

---

[1] *Capitalism, Socialism, and Democracy*, George Allen & Unwin, Ltd., London, 1943, p. 132.

In the late 1940s and the early 1950s, however, both writers on management and managers themselves tended to stress the purely administrative aspects of the managerial job. There was so much pent-up demand at the end of World War II that the main problem was to administer organizations in such a way that lack of coordination, labor strife, or apathy among employees would not get in the way of carrying on business as usual—in much greater volume than in the past.

To be sure, the roadblocks could not always be eliminated without introducing innovations—in personnel policies, in organization, and perhaps even in technology—but many of the problems seemed to arise mainly because of executives' inability to manage their human relations as well as they managed their technical problems. Thus the solutions seemed to lie in getting managers who would fit in with the organization and work harmoniously with others—in other words, managers who would be good business bureaucrats, even if they were nothing else.

Technology made great advances in this period, of course, and companies were not averse to adopting new methods of production or bringing out new products. But there was a tendency to view innovation as the province of some staff group—a research department or methods department—and little appreciation of the fact that the manager himself had opportunities for creativity and needed a temperament that was receptive enough to new ideas to inspire those under him to exercise whatever creativity they might possess.

But like all trends, this one soon gave rise to a countertrend. Opposition came first from writers on management—e.g., William H. Whyte in *The Organization Man*—and later from many managers themselves. Also, as soon as the extra demand generated by wartime shortages abated, it became evident that carrying on business smoothly was not good enough, and the growth companies were those that were not afraid to innovate, not only to change their product lines but to introduce innovations in all parts of management.

Companies began spending more money on research than they ever had before and, in addition, became concerned with a "climate that encourages creativity"—not only in the research and development laboratories but throughout their organizations. In some cases, of course, this concern is purely verbal; managers talk about the need for creativity because it is the fashion to do so, but they continue to prefer harmony to disturbing new ideas and to favor subordinate managers who can produce the former rather than the latter. But the rapid pace of change—in technology, in standards of living, and in competition at home and abroad—has induced genuine interest in creativity and innovation in many companies, even if they are at a loss for ways to ensure that they are getting it.

WHAT IS CREATIVITY?

The first step in innovation, clearly, is the creation of a new idea, often in a flash of inspiration. The story of James Watt and his mother's teakettle is probably apocryphal since steam had been used to provide power even before

Watt was born,[2] but it does illustrate the way in which inspiration may come. Thousands of people could watch steam lift the lid of a kettle before it would occur to someone, seemingly in a flash, that there was a force there that could be put to useful work.

What happens to cause such a flash of insight? No one really knows, even those who have experienced it and produced important creative work.

Arthur Koestler, himself a highly creative writer, has advanced an interesting theory about this, even though—in the nature of things—it is impossible to prove it or disprove it. Koestler holds that the flash of insight takes place when two frames of reference suddenly fuse—"so that a familiar and unnoticed phenomenon . . . is suddenly perceived at an unfamiliar and significant angle. Discovery often means simply the uncovering of something which has always been there but was hidden from the eye by the blinkers of habit."[3]

The realization—by Watt or someone else—that since steam could lift the lid of a teakettle, it could also be a source of power could be regarded as just such a fusion of two frames of reference, the common, taken-for-granted rising of the kettle lid as the water boiled and power for industrial use. Similarly, in the case of Archimedes (which Koestler cites), everyone knew that water in a tub would rise when a body was immersed in it, and probably everyone half consciously realized that the volume of water displaced would be equal to the body's volume. But no one, apparently, had connected this with the possibility of determining the composition of a metal object until the two frames of reference fused in Archimedes' mind.

On the other hand, at least one creative scientist—P. B. Medawar, who won the Nobel Prize for Medicine in 1960—has rejected Koestler's theory. He also rejects a commonly held idea that scientific discoveries arise from a process of induction, that is, from observing phenomena and drawing generalizations from the facts observed. Rather, he believes the process of discovery is "hypothetico-deduction." The scientist creates a hypothesis, "a creative act in the sense that it is the invention of a possible world, or a possible fragment of the world; experiments are then done to find out whether or not that imagined world is, to a good enough approximation, the real one."[4]

According to Medawar, creation of the hypothesis is an "act of imagination" and the mental processes that give rise to it are untraceable, whereas the work that goes into proving or disproving the hypothesis is a rational process, and the two are totally different.[5]

Whatever the sources of sudden inspiration, however, it usually comes only from a great deal of systematic study of a problem and thorough familiarity

[2] In the early eighteenth century, steam engines were used on pumps designed to raise water from mines. See Arthur Pound, *The Turning Wheel*, Doubleday & Company, Inc., Garden City, N.Y., 1934, p. 9.
[3] Arthur Koestler, *The Act of Creation: A Study of the Conscious and Unconscious in Science and Art*, Dell Publishing Co., Inc., New York, 1967 (paperback edition reprinted by permission of The Macmillan Company, New York), p. 108.
[4] Medawar, *The Art of the Soluble*, Methuen & Co., Ltd., London, 1967, p. 89.
[5] "The Reith Lectures Are Discussed" (report of a broadcast), *The Listener* (published by the British Broadcasting Corporation), Jan. 11, 1968, p. 41.

with the field. Occasionally, too much knowledge may inhibit a fresh approach, but this is probably outweighed by the fact that a person unfamiliar with the field may waste time exploring blind alleys that have already been tested. Also, what seems to the novice to be a marvelous new hypothesis may have no relation to the real world at all.

Immersing oneself in a problem and examining all the usual approaches to problems of a similar type is probably a necessary preparation to the creation of an entirely new solution. Then there may be a period of maturation in which the mind brings the idea to fruition, often unconsciously, until the point where it breaks through in a flash of what seems like sudden and inexplicable revelation.

However, for a company that wishes to develop a creative approach to obstacles and opportunities, the problem is not so much to determine the nature of the creative process as to find the answers to two questions: How do we identify creative people? And how do we develop a climate in which creativity can flourish? These questions still receive most attention in relation to research and development departments, although there is a growing interest in answering both on a companywide basis.

STAFFING AND ORGANIZING R & D

There are those who seem to believe that if a company acquires a given number of scientific personnel (all with Ph.D.s), the laws of probability make it practically inevitable that important new discoveries will be made. Perhaps so, but this is an expensive way to attack the problem.

As the editor of *Science* once observed: "When we increase the number of Ph.D.s, do we increase or do we diminish the probability of fostering . . . geniuses? I suspect that in the recent expansion of science quality has been diluted. This impression is based in part on my evaluation of some recent Ph.D. theses. . . . The experimental equipment employed usually is superb; the idea content is often thin."[6] How then, does one identify the creative scientist or engineer?

There is general agreement that high intelligence is a prerequisite, although the most intelligent of a group of candidates is not necessarily the most creative in cases where intelligence is measured by intelligence tests. Also, the creative scientist may not do well on the portions of the tests designed to evaluate verbal skills, although many highly creative scientists have been excellent writers.

There is fairly general agreement, also, that creative people tend to be nonconformists, but, of course, all nonconformists are not creative.

Attempts have been made to develop tests for creativity and also to compare the answers made by creative people to the questions on other tests with those made by people who were considered to be noncreative. Also, some experi-

[6] Philip H. Abelson, "Manpower or Mind Power," *Science,* Jan. 11, 1963, p. 79.

ments have been conducted. For example, in one case in which members of a group were asked to solve a complex problem, it was noted that the more creative tended to ask more questions about the problem itself and the less creative to ask questions that would enable them to synthesize the information they already had.[7]

However, it would seem that creativity cannot be judged on the basis of psychological tests, at least as yet. Rather, it must be judged by past performance, to the extent that evidence is available, and on the basis of interviews by persons who know the field in which the scientist is specializing. A pedestrian Ph.D. thesis based on experiments in which elaborate apparatus was used to test a hypothesis of an unimaginative kind would provide at least negative evidence. And an interview, or perhaps several interviews, might perhaps be the best way of gauging enthusiasm for the field, understanding of it, and ability to consider new approaches. Certainly it would provide negative evidence that would make possible the elimination of those who were definitely noncreative.

Creation of a climate in which creativity can flourish is, perhaps, an important factor in gaining creative scientists and engineers, for those who are creative will be attracted to jobs where the climate is right. But in determining how it will organize research, a company must first determine its research strategy.

Developing a research strategy

As in the case of any other business function, the first step in organizing or reorganizing a research department is to set some sort of boundaries to its explorations, for no one organization can possibly deal with all the possibilities in the scientific world. In other words, a company must develop a research strategy just as it must develop a marketing strategy, a general plan in line with company objectives.

One of the first points to consider is the extent to which the department will engage in basic research and the extent to which it will confine itself to applied research and development.

Basic research is essentially an attempt to advance the frontiers of knowledge, regardless of possible use of the findings. Applied research, on the other hand, is designed to uncover the ways in which theories or facts that have already been discovered can be put to practical use. Thus in his famous experiment with the key and the kite, Benjamin Franklin was conducting basic research; when he applied the theory to the construction of lightning rods, he was engaged in applied research, or perhaps in development, which has been defined as the steps between invention and production: "experimentation,

---

[7] See William H. Reynolds, "Problem-solving and the Creative Process," *MSU* (Michigan State University) *Business Topics*, Autumn, 1967, pp. 7–15, for an account of this and other studies of creativity.

design, development of prototypes, the construction of pilot plants, studies for the use of pilot plant experience in large-scale production."[8]

Basic research may result in major breakthroughs that will make possible important new inventions, but there is no guarantee that this will occur. Further, basic research may take a long time to produce results, and it may be that the results, if there are any, cannot be translated into salable products at any time within the foreseeable future. At any rate, companies seem to be devoting a smaller proportion of their research expenditures to basic research and a larger proportion to applied research and development than they were in the past, for the latter offer a less uncertain way of increasing profitability.

Moreover, the line between basic research and applied research may be somewhat fuzzy. And as Medawar points out, sometimes basic theories are evolved out of what was essentially applied research—for example, he notes, "the growth of a generalized communication theory out of the practical problems of sending messages by telephone."[9]

In planning research strategy, a company must also determine how long it expects to remain in its present fields and what new fields it may want to enter in the future. If the markets for its present products are shrinking, it would not be wise to put much money into attempting to improve the products on a long-term basis.

Still another decision to be made is the extent to which the company will trade investment in R & D for time so that a new product may be brought on the market sooner, before competitors produce something similar. This is often worthwhile. IBM spent $5 billion to speed up the development of the third-generation 360 computer so as to get a jump on competitors, an objective which it achieved.

Finally, it is necessary to decide how receptive the company will be to outside inventions. Some companies make a practice of examining them—and perhaps doing further work on them in their own laboratories—and paying the outside inventor royalties. Others refuse even to glance at inventions sent in from outside because they believe the risk of lawsuits is too great. Work may be going on in their own laboratories on something very similar, perhaps employing the same principles of operation, and if they have looked at the outside contribution, its originator may claim that they have stolen his idea.

Yet there is some evidence that individual inventors have produced more of the important inventions than company laboratories have. One of the main proponents of this thesis was Prof. John Jewkes. In *The Sources of Invention*,[10] he traced the origins of sixty-one important inventions made since 1900 and found that more than half of them were made by independent inventors—for example, air conditioning, the helicopter, the jet engine, the first commercial

[8] Fritz Machlup, *The Production and Distribution of Knowledge in the United States*, Princeton University Press, Princeton, N.J., 1962, p. 150.
[9] *The Art of the Soluble*, pp. 125–126.
[10] John Jewkes, David Sawers, and Richard Stillerman, Macmillan & Co., Ltd., London, and St. Martin's Press, New York, 1958.

plastic (Bakelite), catalytic cracking of petroleum, continuous casting of steel, and quick freezing.

Of course, company research laboratories were far fewer in the years before World War II than they are today. It might be argued, therefore, that a greater proportion of the inventions have been coming from industry in more recent years.

But Prof. Daniel Hamberg traced the origins of twenty-seven important inventions made between 1946 and 1955 and found that almost half originated with independent inventors.[11] And still another study by Prof. Joseph Schmookler showed that as many as 50 to 60 per cent of the inventions of the 1950s were made outside the organized research groups of the corporate industrial laboratories.[12]

Yet important results have come out of company research laboratories—the transistor and laser, to name just two. And although the computer was not a company invention, most of the improvements and many of the new applications have been the product of company development work. Also, many of the great individual inventions were merely advances on other inventions made earlier, and often the big technical advance is the result of many minor improvements rather than one big breakthrough that can be attributed to one person. At least one major study of technological progress shows that in the shipbuilding industry, progress has been due to many small improvements rather than to a revolution or even specific major improvements.[13]

Organizing a company research department

A company research department will be organized under a research director, and finding a good director is, perhaps, the most difficult task of all, for he must be enough of a scientist to win the respect of his researchers, but he must also understand management's aims and be a good administrator as well.

The traditional organization of research departments was to place all physicists in one group, all chemists in another, and so on. This has the superficial advantage of putting together those who have a common tradition and language, who are accustomed to work together, and who know how to get things done in their own field. But this system is giving way to a "constellation" or task-force form of organization, in which engineers and scientists trained in different disciplines work on various aspects of a specific project.

There is, in fact, no reason why both types of organization cannot be used in the same research department. Some types of projects require investigation in only one field; others require the application of scientific knowledge from several fields.

The use of team research in a single field has been criticized on the ground

11 *Essays on the Economics of Research and Development*, Random House, Inc., New York, 1966, p. 27.
12 "Inventors Past and Present," *Review of Economics and Statistics*, August, 1957, pp. 321–33.
13 S. C. Gilfillan, *Inventing the Ship*, Follett Publishing Company, Chicago, 1935.

that it stifles creativity, and it is true that a really creative idea is never developed by a group; if it appears to be a group product, it was always suggested by some one member. However, the use of teams in research does have an important advantage in that it makes it possible to check out a number of approaches to a problem simultaneously. Thus a job that would take an individual inventor years may be completed in months by use of the group approach. Often it is sufficient to have one creative man as group leader and allow him to assign the more routine experimentation—necessary but time-consuming—to his assistants.

Selecting projects

Complete freedom for researchers is, of course, an untenable proposition in a company environment; many might choose to investigate problems that had no relation to company activities, current or possible in the future. Hence, although the researchers themselves may suggest projects, and often do, generally they must be passed upon by the research director and perhaps by a research committee composed of the heads of main departments. Estill Green, formerly director of Bell Telephone Laboratories, one of the most successful company research organizations, and now a director of Xerox Corporation and several other companies, believes that most research workers "need guidance in the choice and pursuit of their tasks, and above all they need to be in the stream of problems."[14]

The last point (immersion in the stream of problems) is particularly important. No one can be creative in a vacuum, by sitting down and waiting for an idea to strike, for then there will be nothing in the environment to stimulate him.

One way of achieving a balance between giving the researcher freedom to pursue any project he believes worthwhile and meeting company need for research findings that it can utilize is to "give the researcher enough rope to hang himself." In this case, there may be a committee composed of executives heading the departments that may be concerned with the outcome—the manufacturing and marketing departments, the financial department, and the long-range planning department. If one member of the group is in favor of the project, the researcher is allowed enough money to "conceptualize" his project, that is, to set up a structure of the principal variables to be explored and their interrelationships. If the researcher cannot conceptualize his idea in this way, his project is discarded without further ado. If he succeeds in doing so, he makes a further presentation to the committee. Usually a number of research projects are presented in conceptualized form and ranked in order of the probability of success and/or the expected payoff. If a project is

14 See Ernest Dale, *Readings in Management: Landmarks and New Frontiers*, McGraw-Hill Book Company, New York, 1965, p. 352. This excerpt was reprinted from *Managing the Search: A Symposium on the Effective Administration of Research Programs*, Graduate School of Business and Public Administration, Cornell University Press, Ithaca, N.Y., 1958, pp. 35–41.

approved, it is turned over to a project director, probably the man who suggested it originally, and he is given the equipment and personnel he needs to achieve his objective.

A "climate conducive to productivity" does not require the complete absence of any regulation whatsoever. Rather, it is a matter of keeping the research organization as simple as possible, with a short chain of command, supervision that is at once approachable and understanding and not too close, and a minimum of red tape. Thus instead of compelling the researcher to fill out forms when he wants a part made for his experiments, some companies allow him or his technician to make it in a small machine shop near the laboratories where an expert machinist is on hand to provide advice and help. Allowing researchers to publish papers regarding their studies, to take part in technical conferences, and perhaps to get their names on the patents even if they assign them to the company are other measures that are often important in attracting and holding good researchers, for scientists are very much concerned with their reputations in their own fields.

INNOVATIONS IN MANAGEMENT

Innovation in management is often a matter of putting together several developments that already exist and using ingenuity or creativity to make the combination work. Walther Rathenau, one of the greatest managers of all times, explained this cogently:

> "Great ideas" . . . lie on the streets. They well up, dozens of them, when we dream, digest, vacation. . . . I imagine how a great industrialist reads in his own biography how the "great idea" of his life is explained, interpreted, and celebrated. But the honest industrialist must laugh at the credulity of the historian. For the great idea when he picked it up was . . . a common possession of all intelligent people; what was missing was the man, the will, the industry, the patience. And if genius was required, it was the genius of the thousand means, of a thousand exits and detours, of persuasiveness and stubbornness.[15]

The thousand exits and detours are not, of course, necessary to bring to fruition the many ideas that, rather than revolutionizing an industry, simply call for a change in procedure, in materials, or in some other phase of business. Many of these simpler ideas can, however, be very important to company success—or at least the sum total of them can have an important impact on the profit and loss statement.

Yet many ideas are lost because they do not get to those who can use them, and thus subordinate managers believe that the company is not interested in their ideas, especially if they work under a man who regards any suggestion of change as a criticism of the way he is doing things at present, and it is almost impossible for a company to avoid having some managers of this type. (Many of them are very good at routine phases of their job.)

[15] *Reflexionen*, S. Hirzel Verlag, Stuttgart, 1908, pp. 87–90.

For rank-and-file workers, there are suggestion systems, of course, and sometimes for first-line supervisors as well. But there is seldom such a system for higher managers; it is usually taken for granted that it is part of their job to make suggestions. But without some way of ensuring that good suggestions are not stymied at some level, many good ideas will never reach anyone who can act on them.

One system of preventing this—which appears to provide maximum inducement to innovation—has been developed by the corporate planning department of Xerox Corporation, one of the fastest growing companies in the country. This system is shown in the diagram in Figure 1. The originator may be anyone in the company, and he may suggest an idea that will be applicable to a division other than his own. If the idea does fit his division, it goes to divisional authority, but the business development and market research departments receive copies. Then divisional management knows that it may be asked what it is doing about a good idea; thus, it will be less inclined to let suggestions get lost in the shuffle or ignore them because they may require changes it does not wish to make.

The programs and procedures suggested may deal with new products or improvements of present products or the development of accessories for them, with developing new or better subsystems, processes, materials, or mechanisms—with practically the whole range of the business.

A system such as this helps to foster a climate of creativity, one that encourages creative managers to stay with the company and managers down the line to retain open minds about new ideas.

SUMMARY

Every true managerial job offers opportunities for innovation. One does not have to be an inventor to innovate profitably.

Today, business and industry are more concerned with innovation than they were a few years ago, and not only in their research departments but in all phases of management, for it is becoming evident that growth is dependent on change and the adoption of new and better ways of doing things.

A new idea often comes in a flash and seems a fortuitous inspiration, and the mental processes that give rise to it sometimes seem untraceable, even to those who have experienced highly creative flashes of inspiration. However, it is evident that the inspiration is most likely to come to those who have immersed themselves in a problem and examined and reexamined all the usual ways of solving it.

A manager cannot consider himself an innovator merely because he throws off an occasional new idea; no matter how good it is, it requires detailed development. And the more far-reaching its possibilities, the more it requires, in Walther Rathenau's phrase, "a thousand means" and "a thousand exits and detours."

Product development, including developments that are actually new inventions, is of great interest to companies today—and they are particularly inter-

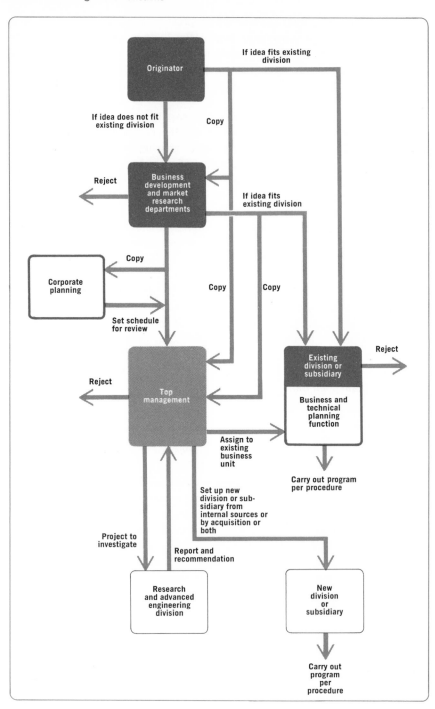

FIGURE 1

ested in getting and holding creative scientists and engineers. Since it is generally recognized that creative people are likely to be somewhat nonconformist, at least to the extent of disliking routines and red tape, and to be interested mainly in following out their own ideas, the problem here is to strike a balance between complete chaos and a too rigid organization of the R & D department.

There are some who claim that truly revolutionary ideas come mainly from individual inventors and that the team approach used in individual laboratories is apt to stifle creativity. However, the team approach has advantages in that it makes it possible to carry on many steps in an investigation simultaneously and so reach results sooner, which is one way of getting a competitive edge.

There is no real reason, however, why an industrial laboratory cannot provide a researcher with as much freedom as he needs to do his work, and certainly some very important innovations have come out of industrial laboratories.

Review Questions

1. Are innovation and invention always synonymous?
2. In which areas of management are innovations possible?
3. What are the advantages of a team approach to invention? Can you think of any possible disadvantages?
4. Why do some companies return proposals by individual inventors without examining them? Do you think this policy is wise? Why or why not?
5. What is the difference between basic research and applied research? Between research and development?
6. Give an example of basic research. Of applied research.
7. Think of some case in which you have evolved an original idea. Does it seem to you that the creation of this idea was the product of the fusion of two different frames of reference?
8. If you were the president of a company in an industry in which new products were constantly introduced, would you think it worthwhile to have your scientists engage in basic research or would you prefer to have them devote their time to applied research and development?

Case Study One / Air Processing, Inc.*

Air Processing, Inc., represents a merger of ten former retail coal and ice companies. Some of the companies were acquired by exchange of stock, whereas others were purchased outright when former owners found competition too severe and were willing, or forced, to sell at quite a low figure. These com-

* From James Healey, Management Services, Columbus, Ohio. Material drawn from the "North Pole Ice and Fuel Company" case in William H. Newman and James P. Logan, *Business Policies and Management*, 4th ed., South-Western Publishing Co., Cincinnati, 1959.

panies are situated in eight cities located within a radius of 100 miles of a central city. In the cities having two companies each, the plants are 6 and 8 miles apart.

Each of these companies had a plant for the manufacture of ice, and all are still in operation. Ice is delivered by truck over rather a wide radius from the plant, the area increasing as competitors have dropped out of the business. Electric refrigerators have virtually eliminated the domestic ice business but there are still a few sales of this kind. There is also a market for crushed ice to be sold to drug stores and restaurants, and there are other miscellaneous users such as hospitals and railroads, some of which buy ice in large cakes.

Coal is purchased from large mining concerns and delivered to the company yards by railroad cars. It is then resold to all types of retail customers who

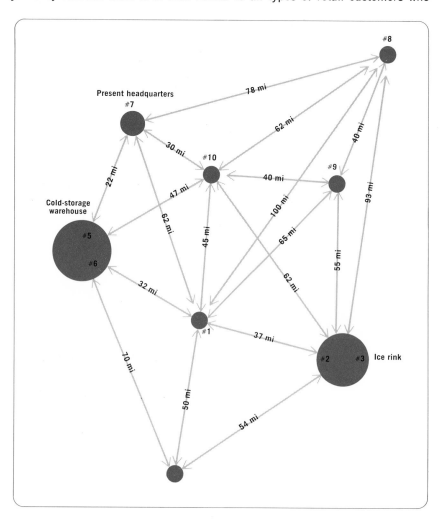

cannot purchase carload lots, delivery being made by truck promptly as orders are received. Coal sales have been adversely affected by fuel oil, but a substantial volume of business is done with domestic, commercial, and industrial users.

All the units which sell coal also retail domestic fuel oil. Company trucks load at a local bulk station of an oil refining concern and make deliveries to residences and various commercial establishments. Typically, the oil is sold on an annual contract under which the company is responsible for seeing that there is an adequate supply of oil in the customers' tanks at all times. Credit is often extended to oil and coal customers.

The headquarters office consisted only of the president, the treasurer, and some office help. In addition, a series of committees was established to deal with such common problems as ice and coal sales, fuel oil sales, heating and air conditioning equipment purchases, ice plant operations, sales promotion, and equipment purchases and maintenance. Appropriate executives from each of the local units were members of these committees, and it was hoped that by pooling their experience the efficiency of each of the units would be improved. Members of the committees were men of long experience and were not inclined to change their methods of operation. The president hoped for voluntary agreement but did not insist on action if the man who knew local conditions did not think it wise. In any event, the operating results have not significantly improved, as was hoped at the time of the merger, and there is now a general agreement among the board of directors that more drastic action must be taken if the company is to be successful in the face of the economic conditions in its industry.

A new president, a former Army officer, has just been appointed and charged with the responsibility of making such changes as are necessary to gain the full benefits of the merger and to put Air Processing, Inc., on a profitable basis. Although he has had no experience in this particular industry, it is expected he will inspire a fresh attack on company problems and will be more aggressive in bringing about changes.

All the local units sell all lines—ice, coal, fuel oil, heating, and air conditioning—and the activities of these are fairly similar. Since each unit has been permitted to continue pretty much along its former pattern, there is no standard form of organization. Ice is sold by the local deliverymen who serve the customers; in addition, most of the companies have one or two men who engage in selling and sales promotion activities. Selling of fuel oil and coal is typically done over the phone and by only occasional personal contact by a sales representative. The deliverymen are not expected to make sales except as their courteous and careful service may affect future orders. Heating and air conditioning equipment is sold principally to contractors, with one salesman in each unit specializing in these units.

A significant feature of developing fuel oil sales is the burner service provided by all the local units. The servicemen make emergency repairs, clean the oil burner, and otherwise maintain the equipment in good working order.

Normally, there is a charge made for this service which just about covers its costs. These services are also provided, at a higher charge, for other heating units and for air conditioning equipment. There is, of course, some risk that the customer will blame the serviceman if his equipment does not work properly, and this may result in the loss of a fuel customer. In general, however, if the service is properly done, it tends to build customer good will.

Each of the units has a coal yard where coal is unloaded from the railroad cars and stored until it is ordered by the customer. Mechanical loaders and specialized dump trucks have done much to reduce the amount of physical labor required in loading and delivering coal.

All the local units have ice plants, which must be operated and maintained at as low cost as possible because of the small demand for ice. In addition, all units have garages and do considerable maintenance work on their equipment.

In each unit there are three or four office personnel. Activities of these people include credit and collections, accounting, cash receipts and disburse-

AIR PROCESSING, INC., SELECTED DATA ON OPERATIONS

Unit number	Trading area Population	Buying unit av. income	Number of employees	Capital investment
1	50,000	$9,500	10	$ 47,000
2 3	500,000	6,200	14	118,000
4	30,000	7,500	9	67,000
5 6	800,000	5,500	20	155,000
7	40,000	8,000	8	61,000
8	40,000	4,200	8	42,000
9	60,000	7,000	9	62,000
10	100,000	6,000	11	83,000

AIR PROCESSING, INC., SALES ($000)

Unit number	Ice	Coal	Fuel oil	H & AC units	Service	Miscellaneous
1	$ 6.6	$ 5.3	$ 30.5	$25.0	$ 5.5	$ 0.7
2	30.0	73.0	110.0	40.5	8.6	15.7
3 4	2.5	0.2	25.0	60.0	4.1	0.4
5 6	40.0	105.0	160.0	72.0	11.4	9.7
7	5.2	7.5	26.0	16.0	4.0	0.2
8	1.3	19.5	9.0	7.2	1.8	—
9	9.8	9.2	32.0	20.1	5.2	0.4
10	11.6	18.8	58.6	32.5	6.5	0.5

ments, local purchasing, insurance, taxes, and the like. Organizational arrangements and procedures for carrying on this work vary considerably between the different units. The total personnel in a unit varies from eight to twenty, depending on sales volume and scope of activities.

The preceding description of activities applies to all the local units. One unit, however, runs a cold storage warehouse. The cold storage plant operates like any other public warehouse: People wishing to store goods pay a fee for the use of the facilities. The plant is located on a railroad siding near a wholesale food market and is used, primarily, for storing a variety of perishable fruits and vegetables. It is also equipped to store a volume of frozen foods.

The only other distinctive activity of any size is an ice skating rink operated by another of the local units. This rink is located on a plot of land adjacent to the ice plant and is open for six months of the year. Admission charges, together with profits from the refreshment concessions, now yield more gross profits than is secured from the sale of ice. Another unit has a separate office 3 miles from its main operations. This office, originally a coal yard, is now maintained solely for sales contacts in the local community.

If you were the new president, what innovations would you introduce in organization, products, or other phases of the business?

Case Study Two / To Innovate or Not to Innovate

In 1950, the president of the Office Equipment Corporation learned of the first successful application of wartime computers to business problems. He was thus confronted with the problem of whether to build computers for an uncertain future or to continue his currently successful line of typewriters, calculating machines, accounting machines, and tabulating equipment.

The company had a large number of satisfied customers, and its rate of return was better than that of comparable companies in the industry. The research department was engaged mainly in improving existing machines so that new models could be introduced every few years. Total sales were on the order of $150 million a year and research expenditures about $3 million. Thus the past record was good, and on the basis of forecasting by extrapolation alone, the future appeared to be assured.

You are the president of the company. You must decide whether to continue the successful strategy of the past or invest large sums of money for research on the high-speed electronic computer.

1. What steps would you take before deciding to pursue the latter course?
2. If you decided to go ahead, what would your goals be for the product itself and for the profit on it?

Selected Readings

The Sources of Invention, John Jewkes, David Sawers, and Richard Stillerman, Macmillan & Co., Ltd., London, and St. Martin's Press, Inc., New York, 1958. An attempt to determine whether individual inventors or organized teams have been mainly responsible for the major inventions of the last fifty years, plus speculations about the future of invention. The last half of the book is devoted to case histories of important inventions.

The Management of Innovation, T. Burns and G. M. Stalker, Tavistock Publications, London, 1961. A discussion of the organization structure of research departments, with consideration of the degree of formal structuring of the activities necessary.

Research, Development and Technological Innovation, James R. Bright, Richard D. Irwin, Inc., Homewood, Ill., 1964. The processes of technological innovation, the discovery and evaluation of new technological concepts, the use of advanced technology (such as automation), and technological planning. Each part of the book is supported by a number of case studies.

Technology and Change, Donald A. Schon, Delacorte Press, New York, 1967. A discussion of the impact of invention and innovation on American social and economic development.

22

REPRESENTATION

*. . . and the moral of that is—"Take care of the sense,
and the sounds will take care of themselves."*
Lewis Carroll: *Alice's Adventures in Wonderland*

*Though we proceed slowly because of our ideologies,
we might not proceed at all without them.*
Joseph Schumpeter: *Science and Technology*

22 Many, if not most, of the constraints imposed on management by the external environment (see Chapter 5) are the product of public opinion. The legal framework reflects public opinion directly, although there is often a time lag between the crystallization of public opinion and the enactment of laws to give it expression.

Again, most unions need public support if they are to enforce their demands (or enforce them without arousing a countervailing public demand for legislation to curb their power), and generally they do not neglect to seek it. Thus if management does not state its position in a way the public can understand, it may find the company's reputation tarnished after a labor dispute has been settled.

Even technology is to some extent influenced by public opinion. For example, the prestige accorded the researcher in a given scientific field by the general public may help to determine how many people will seek training in that field and the amount of money universities find it possible to spend on the training. Although the fact that large numbers of people have been trained in a science does not necessarily ensure that there will be major breakthroughs, it increases the chances that they will occur.

Managers, of course, are part of the general public, and as such they help to form public opinion. And if they are top managers, their opinions often carry more weight than those of other members of the general public. In the first place, they have greater means of communication at their command. They can buy television or advertising space in publications to present their views, and if they are at all well known, they can usually get space in the news columns by giving interviews or making speeches. They may also find it easier to meet and talk with public officials, and the officials may give more weight to what a top manager says than to the opinion of a lone constituent of no particular importance.

Leaving aside all questions of possible campaign contributions, this is probably inevitable, because a top manager of a big corporation has immense prestige; it is only natural that an official should, therefore, regard him as worthy of attention. Also, the manager is often able to point out that his interests and those of many others in the constituency are identical—e.g., "If this legislation goes through, our business will be hurt badly, and that will mean that we'll have to lay off several thousand people." Naturally, no elected official wants to do anything that will cause widespread unemployment and a general recession in his district or state.

But, of course, the manager cannot make his voice heard unless he devotes a considerable amount of time to presenting his views to the general public, to legislators, to government agencies of various kinds, and to others who can help him influence public opinion. For example, if he wants to be sure that his corporation's interests are adequately represented in an industry or trade association, he must be active in that body. And, of course, he must, at least occasionally, talk to important customers and to officials of outside financial groups. Usually, also, he must meet union officials at final bargaining sessions when the actual terms of the contract are agreed upon and at other times as well. Thus there are innumerable occasions when the manager must represent his corporation to persons and groups outside his organization.

Studies of how managers spend their time often show that they may spend as many hours a week with groups and individuals outside their organizations as they do with those inside. For example, a bank president heading an organization of approximately 5,000 employees spent more than 30 hours in a 57¾-hour workweek dealing with outsiders.[1]

External committees	6½ hours
Outside economists	5½ hours
Outside bankers	5 hours
Government officials	4¼ hours
Customers	4 hours
Preparing speeches for delivery to outside groups	2 hours
Social engagements (on business)	2 hours
External phone calls	1 hour

Not all executives devote quite so much time to outside groups, but practically all of them must spend at least some of their time in this way. And this is true not only of top managers but of most middle managers as well. Some companies encourage, almost compel, many of their middle managers to take an active part in community groups.

INCREASE IN NECESSARY CONTACTS

In fact, management must constantly work at making its outside relationships secure if it is to prevent serious problems from arising because of opposition by outside groups. This has always been true, but the number of groups with which management must deal and the frequency of the contacts have both increased.

Companies have always attempted to maintain good relationships with suppliers in order to ensure an uninterrupted source of supply, and in general with banks and other financial institutions, lest funds be withheld in periods of tight money or be forthcoming only in return for a controlling share of the business. Some companies, however, have tried to avoid these relationships by making themselves independent of both suppliers and financiers.

Ernest T. Weir, founder of the National Steel Company, originally owned only tinplate mills and was dependent on U.S. Steel for supplies. This meant that the larger corporation, which was to some extent one of his competitors, had the power to put him out of business any time it wanted to. So he went to Judge Gary, then head of U.S. Steel, and told him, "I must know where I stand." Gary replied that he had planned no hostile action, but added, "As I say, young man, we haven't any such moves in mind now. But who knows about the future?" Since Weir did not choose "to be in business only by the

---

[1] Ernest Dale and Lyndall F. Urwick, *Staff in Organization*, McGraw-Hill Book Company, New York, 1960, p. 37.

sufferance of someone else," he began immediately to plan a more integrated operation in which he would produce his own steel. He also acquired coal and iron ore holdings by purchase and by merger.

Financially, Weir did not feel the same urgency for self-sufficiency, for he was adept at the representation function vis-à-vis the bankers. He obtained a $10,000 loan to finance his first tinplate mill without any collateral, the only stipulation being that his father-in-law, who had no collateral either, cosign the note.

On the other hand, Henry Ford, Sr., founder of the Ford Motor Company, was particularly averse to doing business on the sufferance of financiers and tried to forestall the need for outside financing by the accumulation of reserves.

Most businesses, however, are neither integrated enough to provide all their own raw materials nor able to operate and expand without some recourse to borrowings or the sale of new stock. Hence it is necessary for them to maintain good relations with banks and other financial institutions, and the more friendly the relationships between the financial interests and the top company managers, the smoother the path will be. Even if a company does not plan to borrow any money or float any new stock currently, it must bear in mind that it may wish to do so some time in the future. Thus, someone—and often someone very high up in the company—must represent it to the financial analysts employed by investment counselors, brokers, and others who are in a position to influence the opinion of investors and others on its potential.

The need to deal with labor as an outside group came later, except in a few industries which were unionized very early. For a long time many companies avoided it, in fact, by refusal to recognize unions at all or by the organization of so-called company unions, which were dominated by management. Tactics of this kind are now illegal; moreover, since the unions are stronger, company unions are likely to be of little value to most companies even if they were disposed to ignore the law. The need to bargain regularly—and to discuss matters on which contracts do not present clear-cut directions—has thus imposed additional representation tasks.

The representation function has also become more important because of the growth of enterprises. A corporation employing tens of thousands, and perhaps producing a product or service that is important to a very large number of people, can no longer ignore public opinion, as did many of the managers of the nineteenth or early twentieth centuries. The impact of many corporations on whole sections of the economy, or even on the entire economy, is so great that the decision makers must consider what response their actions are likely to evoke from the general public and from government.

Thus top executives must appear at congressional hearings—lest new laws be passed that will hurt their industries—and endeavor to make their views on the interpretation of existing laws known to opinion makers. And since it is often necessary to work with others in the same industry on these things, outside contact may be required with executives of other companies.

This need for top executives to spend more and more time in representing the company to outside groups is not peculiar to the United States. Professor Sune Carlson, who made a well-known study of how a group of European executives spent their time, found the same development abroad. And his comment regarding the European executives' attitude toward this part of their work is probably equally applicable to American executives:

> Most chief executives were trained for their present jobs at a time when the outside activities of a managing director were less important than today, and they often regard these activities not as a normal part of their job but as an extra burden, which they wishfully think of as being of a temporary nature. Since they hope that life will return to "normal" times soon again, they do not plan their work in such a way as they would if they regarded the present external activities as permanent.[2]

Professor Carlson believes that it would be possible for the chief executives to delegate a good many more of these contacts than they were delegating at the time of the study, and he is probably right. But many of them cannot be delegated, simply because the people to be contacted would regard the failure of the top man to appear as a piece of unwarranted arrogance, and no matter how persuasive the substitute managed to be, he would not get very far in establishing good relations. It would have been unthinkable, for example, for the president of U.S. Steel to have sent a substitute, even a very high-ranking one, to talk with President Kennedy about the rise in steel prices in 1962.

Many department heads cannot delegate a good part of their representation duties for the same reason. A prepared statement presented by an underling is likely to annoy, say, a financial analyst who wants to find out about the company's prospects. He will be satisfied only if he can question a financial executive of high rank or the company president. Also, an important customer who wants special concessions will be less annoyed at a refusal if the reasons for it are carefully explained to him by a top marketing manager rather than transmitted at second hand by a salesman.

PUBLIC RELATIONS AND IDEOLOGY

Up until a short while ago, it was customary in many management circles to consider that management could fulfill its representation function adequately if only it could get enough expert advice. Speakers at management meetings harped constantly on the theme: "Business is doing a good job, but we haven't told the people about it in the right way; we haven't 'sold' our employees or the general public on what we are doing."

Good public relations techniques are, of course, important. There have been cases in which management had more right on its side than did, say, a union or a public agency that was attempting to curb its freedom, yet it lost out because it did not present its case very well. But no amount of pretty language will persuade a group of employees or the general public when the tides of

---

[2] *Executive Behaviour*, C. A. Stromberg Aktiebolag, Stockholm, 1951, pp. 65–66.

public opinion are running strongly against a given action. Hence, *what* management represents may be, in the long run, more important than any public relations techniques it may employ. Management ideology—the way in which managers regard themselves and their function in the economic and social system—must not lag too far behind when public ideology is changing.

It may seem absurd to speak of "management ideology" as though all managers were of one mind, when obviously they differ widely on many important questions. Nevertheless, any set of people somewhat similarly situated tends to develop a common frame of reference that seems to them to embody certain axiomatic beliefs. They may differ from each other in the interpretation of these beliefs and in the emphasis they place on each one, but fundamentally most accept the main points without question:

> The molding of human behavior [by the social environment] is so definite, even in societies like our own, that many alternative ways of doing things remain unconceived or stoutly rejected as "unnatural." (That the study of cultural anthropology has been so illuminating is an index of the feebleness of imaginations cramped by our special cultural traditions.) Explicit discussion on social action springs from the contemplation of alternatives. In the nature of human socialization, the great mass of possible questions for discussion are, as it were, resolved in advance, and the solutions are internalized to become working parts of the personality.[3]

Each of us, of course, lives within several such social environments: nation, church, economic and social brackets, and generation, to name just a few. Occupation also imposes a framework of beliefs, at least on matters that have a direct bearing on the occupational field itself. Thus in recent years elementary and high school teachers have, in general, subscribed to John Dewey's ideas on education, and social workers have adopted a psychoanalytic approach to human problems. While there are always some dissenters from the prevailing view, they are in a minority, the more so in that people tend to choose an occupation whose ideology they can accept. This acceptance is then strengthened by training and by the influence of their superiors.

Statements of management ideology may be found, first, in the writings of original thinkers who developed new ideas and were able to express them in language both understandable and inspirational. These ideas have been disseminated through management organizations, such as the National Association of Manufacturers, the U.S. Chamber of Commerce, the American Management Association, and the Committee for Economic Development. In addition, a series of lectures supported by the McKinsey Foundation for Management Research and sponsored by the Graduate School of Business, Columbia University, has attempted, in the words of the first lecturer, "to coax . . . businessmen out of . . . [their] offices and into the arena of public thought,

---

[3] Francis X. Sutton, Seymour E. Harris, Carl Kaysen, and James Tobin, *The American Business Creed*, Harvard University Press, Cambridge, Mass., 1956, p. 306.

where . . . managerial philosophies can be put to the test of examination by men trained in other disciplines."[4]

No ideology is ever completely static, of course, and although management ideology may have lagged behind some of the changes in public ideology, it is no exception. The first change was centuries in building up; the second has been in progress only for a few decades and to some extent has been grafted onto its predecessor rather than substituted for it.

RISE OF THE PROTESTANT ETHIC

The first big change in managerial ideology occurred gradually between the Middle Ages and the Industrial Revolution. It was clearly identified by Max Weber, the German sociologist whose ideas on bureaucracy were cited in Chapter 10 ("What Is Organization?"), in a series of essays first published in a German periodical and now available in English in his book *The Protestant Ethic and the Spirit of Capitalism.*[5]

Before the Reformation, as Weber saw it, the ideal of the businessman was to conduct his business in a traditional way, do the traditional amount of work, and make the traditional rate of profit. The idea that he should increase his rate of profit by adopting radically new methods or taking more than his regular share of the market by clever competition would have appeared immoral to him.

Not that people in medieval times did not desire to increase their wealth— many of them were unspeakably greedy—but such an attitude was not socially approved, nor was the building of a great business seen as a worthy aim:

> The ideal type of the capitalist entrepreneur . . . gets nothing out of his wealth for himself, except the irrational sense of having done his job well.
>
> But it is just that which seems to the pre-capitalistic man so incomprehensible and mysterious, so unworthy and contemptible. That anyone should be able to make it the sole purpose of his life-work to sink into the grave weighed down with a great material load of money and goods seems to him explicable only as the product of a perverse instinct.[6]
>
> In the most highly capitalistic center of that time, in Florence of the fourteenth and fifteenth centuries, the money and capital market of all the great Powers, this attitude [that the pursuit of money might be a life work] was considered ethically unjustifiable, or at best to be tolerated.[7]

The Protestant Reformation, according to Weber, gave rise to the idea that ambition to make money was not only permissible but laudable. Calvinism with its doctrine of predestination—the theory that some people are born to

---

[4] Ralph J. Cordiner, General Electric Company, *New Frontiers for Professional Managers,* McGraw-Hill Book Company, New York, 1956, pp. vi–vii.
[5] Trans. Talcott Parsons, George Allen & Unwin, Ltd., London, 1930; published in this country by Charles Scribner's Sons, New York.
[6] *Ibid.,* pp. 71–72.
[7] *Ibid.,* pp. 74–75.

be saved and others to be damned—was a powerful influence, he found. Ascetic devotion to business, while it would not, naturally, save a man who had been predestined to hell at birth, would give assurance to the man himself that he must be one of the elect. His success would be a mark of God's favor: "the technical means, not of purchasing salvation, but of getting rid of the fear of damnation."[8]

Most Protestant denominations, to be sure, did not subscribe to the doctrine of predestination, but in one way or another, Weber managed to fit them all into his pattern. For example, he quotes a passage from John Wesley, who, while deploring the bad effects accumulation of wealth often had on people, saw that accumulation as a direct consequence of the industry and frugality advocated by the Methodists, then concluded, "We ought not to prevent people from being diligent and frugal; *we must exhort all Christians to gain all they can, and to save all they can; that is, in effect, to grow rich.*"[9]

Weber's description of the change in business ideology that took place is undoubtedly accurate, but one need not accept his view of its cause. Many other explanations could be suggested. It would be quite possible, for example, to argue that it arose in England—the first country to experience the Industrial Revolution—because of the Black Death. In a society without mass production, a reduction in population can make it possible for everyone to get more, and a reduction in population may have been one reason why England became very prosperous in the fifteenth century. It may have been that the greater opportunities then available aroused ambition in people who had hitherto been content with their traditional lot. The discovery and colonization of the New World had a similar effect. Thus conditions were ripe for the coming of steam and the Industrial Revolution.

The term "Protestant ethic" is, however, a convenient one. It was brought into modern business terminology by William H. Whyte, Jr., in his best-selling book *The Organization Man.*[10] As he used it, and as it will be used here, it has no religious significance. It means merely the spirit of initiative and competition that characterized the entrepreneurs of the eighteenth, nineteenth, and early twentieth centuries and, in fact, characterizes those of today. The German-Jewish immigrant peddler who founded a great department store was exemplifying the Protestant ethic in this sense. So was the Catholic from Ireland who came to this country to better his lot, started as a hod carrier, and became a wealthy contractor. Neither needed to renounce his religious beliefs to adopt such a career.

Basic to the Protestant ethic are the ideas of individualism and free enterprise: that the man of intelligence and industry should be free to start a business and conduct it as he sees fit. The Protestant ethic views the business world in terms laid down by the classical economists (e.g., Adam Smith, Malthus, Ricardo), as one in which many firms in a given industry compete

---

[8] *Ibid.*, p. 115.
[9] *Ibid.*, p. 175. (Weber's italics.)
[10] Whyte, *The Organization Man*, Simon and Schuster, Inc., New York, 1956.

for the customer's dollar and those that are able to provide the best goods at the lowest price are those that survive and prosper.

An economy of this kind was believed to be essentially self-regulating. Unduly high prices or shoddy goods would drive a man out of business very quickly, leaving the field to those who were performing a more socially useful function. If the employees did not like their wages or other conditions of employment, they could always change their jobs or go into business for themselves.

> The captain [of industry] was at once a master builder and an astute financier, but above all a success. He was the active owner of what he had created and then managed. . . . In his role as employer, he provided opportunity for the best of the men he hired to learn from working under him; they might themselves save a portion of their wages, multiply this by a small private speculation, borrow more on their character, and start up on their own. Even as he had done before them, his employees could also become captains of industry.[11]

Business and the public good

Thus, though each man was working for himself alone, it was thought, the sum of men's actions added up to the public good: more and better goods and services at lower prices for everyone; opportunity for everyone; the assurance that no good idea would go begging, since great rewards could be achieved by the man bold enough to take it up. What was good for the individual entrepreneur was good for the country. In the words of Adam Smith, an "invisible hand" regulated the economy.

A business was considered the personal property of the owner-manager, which he could dispose of as he saw fit. His own personal ethics might prevent him from squeezing the last ounce of work out of employees or paying them the very lowest possible wages, but this was a personal matter. The capitalist who acted in this way might be morally condemned in the eyes of the general public and those of his more right-thinking fellows, but no one had the right to forbid him to do so.

In the course of one of his struggles to control a network of railroads, the nineteenth-century capitalist Cornelius Vanderbilt found owners of the New York Central resistant to his demands. In retaliation, he discontinued the connection between his railroad and the Central, and the unfortunate passengers were forced to walk across the frozen Hudson in order to get to New York. His answer to protests was, "Can't I do what I want with my own?"[12]

But systems and ideologies tend to be modified even as they begin to flower. Thus Matthew Josephson writes of the first half of the nineteenth century in the United States:

---

[11] C. Wright Mills, *White Collar*, Oxford University Press, Fair Lawn, N.J., 1951, pp. 5–6.
[12] Matthew Josephson, *The Robber Barons: The Great American Capitalists, 1861–1901*, Harcourt, Brace & World, Inc., New York, 1934, p. 71.

It was not true of course that the early Republic was a millennium of free farmers and artisans; yet in the simplicity of its organization and of its mercantile economy, the nation belonged almost to a pre-capitalist age.[13]

Yet no sooner had large-scale industry and finance got a good start than the investigations and the demands for legislation to dilute the free-wheeling powers of private enterprise began. Vanderbilt's callous action in breaking the railroad connection was investigated by the New York State Legislature (though nothing came of the investigation, and the owners of the Central were forced to accede to his wishes). The Interstate Commerce Act, imposing certain restrictions on the railroads, was passed in 1887, and the first antitrust law was on the books by 1890. Though neither, in practice, imposed much regulation on business at first, they did signify a general public sentiment in favor of at least some minimal restraints.

True, the forces of the marketplace did in many cases operate to compel business to act for the public good. The idea of "one price to everyone" (rather than the price the merchant could bargain out of a customer, perhaps because of his ignorance) helped to make a fortune for Adam Gimbel, founder of Gimbel's department stores,[14] and others in the retail field. It is true also that new inventions that raised the standard of living found ready backers.

In addition, many businessmen were restrained from various kinds of antisocial conduct by their own ethical principles. J. C. Penney, founder of the Penney variety stores, lost his first business, a butcher shop, because he would not bribe his main customer, the chef of a hotel, with an occasional bottle of liquor[15]—a distinctly venial sin, if that, by many people's standards. As another example, Du Pont Company, then a manufacturer of explosives, pioneered in the development of safety measures for the workers quite in the absence of regulations. "What do you do if you see the thermometer [in the mixing vat] going up to an unmanageable level?" Hamilton Barksdale, Du Pont's general manager, once asked a foreman. The latter replied that he would open this and that valve—measures designed to save the plant from destruction. "No" Barksdale told him, "you just run as fast as you can and get behind a barricade. We can rebuild the nitroglycerine plant, but we can't rebuild you."[16]

But the buccaneering types were more flamboyant and hence more visible. Moreover, through mergers and combinations they attempted to reduce the free competition and the control by the forces of the marketplace celebrated by the classical economists. And they often lacked the most elementary sense of public relations; it was not only what they did but the way they did it and

---

[13] Ibid., p. 5. Under mercantile theory, business should be run primarily to strengthen the state—for example, to produce a favorable balance of trade—and the laws governing it should have this end in view.
[14] The first store in Vincennes, Ind., advertised "Fairness and Equality of All Patrons, whether they be Residents of the City, Plainsmen, Traders or Indians." Tom Mahoney, The Great Merchants: The Stories of Twenty Famous Retail Operations and the People Who Made Them Great, Harper & Row, Publishers, Incorporated, New York, 1947, p. 6.
[15] Ibid., pp. 258–259.
[16] Donaldson Brown, Some Reminiscences of an Industrialist, privately printed, 1957, p. 30.

the way they talked that aroused public ire. Charles Yerkes, who controlled the streetcar lines in Chicago until the poor service he provided aroused the citizenry against him, once remarked, "The secret of success in my business is to buy old junk, fix it up a little, and unload it upon other fellows."[17] (This was in the 1890s.)

Thus public sentiment against the "trusts," as large business combinations were called, grew:

> When the U.S. Steel Corp. [which was a combination of several steel companies] was put together in 1901, the impact on public opinion was swift and almost physically tangible. Expressing the prevalent consensus of horror, President Arthur Twining Hadley of Yale remarked that if public sentiment would not regulate such monster businesses, there would be "an emperor in Washington within twenty-five years."[18]

The first dozen years or so of the twentieth century were also the period of the "muckrakers" (as they were called by those who disagreed with them[19]), magazine writers who made a practice of exposing the sins of big business. Some legislation resulted from their efforts (e.g., the Pure Food & Drug Act) and some "trust-busting" was done.

The distrust of big business died down, however. Particularly in the 1920s, business had little reason to complain of hostility from government or the general public. With the Depression of the 1930s, however, public sentiment changed practically overnight, and a number of new laws were passed that affected business directly. This led to renewed emphasis on "free enterprise" in business thinking since business now felt it had to defend many of the freedoms it had taken for granted before.

Business and government today

Few businessmen today believe that the unbridled type of free enterprise that existed for a short time after the Civil War is either feasible or desirable. Most would admit that some types of government regulation are necessary. "Free enterprise" and as little regulation by government as possible are, however, a cardinal article in management ideology, and the belief that the forces of the marketplace will take care of most, if not absolutely all, the regulation needed is still widespread. Managers and their organizations have in the past opposed practically any new legislation of the kind.

Not only is this viewpoint understandable; there is some logic behind it. No one likes to be controlled, even if he has no intention of indulging in any of the practices the controls are designed to curb.[20] Also, the *degree of regu-*

---

[17] Sidney I. Roberts, "Portrait of a Robber Baron: Charles T. Yerkes," *Business History Review*, Harvard Graduate School of Business Administration, Autumn, 1961, p. 344.
[18] John Chamberlain, "A History of American Business," *Fortune*, January, 1962, p. 107.
[19] The term itself was first used by Theodore Roosevelt.
[20] It might be noted in passing that the attitude of organized labor toward any regulation of unions is much the same. Honest labor leaders who would never take a penny from the union cashbox immediately become vocal in opposition when any law is proposed to curb unions in any way, even though it may be aimed at those who are no better than racketeers.

lation is all-important. One can live with a good deal of outside regulation, but after a certain point it becomes intolerable. Free enterprise has been, as the managers claim, an important factor in the growth of industry and mass production, which have brought about enormous rises in the standard of living. If the growth of this country owes a great deal to natural resources, it has been due also to a comparatively open society, without the hereditary aristocracy and a residue of restrictions from precapitalist times that have plagued industry in many other countries.

The quarrel between the managers and those who favor greater government restrictions (unless the latter happen to be socialists, and usually they are not) is over where the dividing line should be drawn. Both favor free enterprise with the minimum restrictions necessary, but they disagree on the interpretation of "necessary."

Thus most managers would agree with "The Law of Free Enterprise" as stated by an assistant attorney general in charge of the Antitrust Division which includes such commandments as "Thou shalt not combine to restrain trade," "Thou shalt not conspire to injure another enterprise," "Thou shalt not commit unfair acts or use unfair methods of competition."[21] But they disagree with any attempt to equate bigness as such with monopoly, and they feel that the administration of antitrust laws has often done just that.

In fact, many managers feel that administration of all legislation that imposes restraints on them has tended to be by those who are actually hostile to private industry and who therefore cannot take a reasonable view of business conduct. Thus *Barron's,* a paper that to some extent represents the views of the financial community, quotes with approval the views of a former staff member of the Securities & Exchange Commission:

> A study [to determine whether SEC regulations have been violated] begins at the desk of an investigator, who is suspicious by nature and starts with the assumption that everyone in the securities business is a crook. The investigator does the spade work, then writes a report, which goes to his supervisor, who pretties up the language and sends it up the ladder, where the process is repeated. The report eventually reaches someone in a position of authority, who reads it and is so impressed with the prose that he runs out and starts proceedings. The sequence has only one flaw—no one ever checks on the validity of the original work.[22]

Business views on labor

Ideologically, management assumes an identity with its employees. Both are necessary to the success of the business, and their interests are largely identical since a company that does not prosper cannot continue to provide employment and higher wages.

---

[21] *Fortune,* January, 1962, p. 95.
[22] Lawrence A. Armour, "Who Watches the Watchdogs?" *Barron's,* Jan. 14, 1963, pp. 12–13.

To the original pure free enterprisers of the nineteenth century, it followed that unionization was a form of disloyalty. This view is held by some even today. For example, a letter in the *Wall Street Journal* in 1963 reads in part, "It has been stated that a strike is a form of war, which it plainly is. It is insurrection within a business structure. Even a small strike is collusion in restraint of trade."[23]

This view is unusual today. Most managers admit that in the "free contracts" between the factory employee and the manager in the nineteenth century, the bargaining was so unequal that some way of redressing the balance was necessary. But they feel that now the pendulum has swung the other way. The unions, they say, have become too powerful and should be curbed by legislation. Thus there is some agitation to make the antitrust laws apply to unions as well as to management, to provide machinery for curbing strikes, and many managements favor "right to work" laws—now in force in some states—that ban the union shop completely.

Probably a good many managers would be glad to see unions disappear altogether; but since they realistically accept the fact that this is not likely to happen in the near future, they merely want to see them weakened as far as possible. Many of them cherish the idea that they, as ethical businessmen, can be trusted to treat their employees well without the compulsion of a union contract. Others simply object to paying out money—which might well go for higher profits—in the form of wage increases.

But the majority of managers who have been accustomed to dealing with unions are undoubtedly sincere when they claim that they have accepted them fully and object only to what they consider excessive demands. If they appear to oppose every new demand with vehemence, it is probably because they realize that a union is by its very nature continually asking for more, and to yield without a struggle would only encourage new demands.

To many of the managers who have grown up in the age of unionization, the necessity to bargain and to observe the terms of the contract is merely one of the conditions of doing business, and they adapt themselves accordingly. On the other hand, in sections of the country that have been largely nonunion, many managers hope to delay unionization as long as possible or prevent it entirely. Managers also have a strong tendency to believe that unions, while necessary or even desirable for production workers, are out of place in the office or among professional workers.

THE NEW IDEOLOGY

The important change in management ideology in recent decades, however, has not been a modification of its attitude toward government and unions but the evolution of an entirely new concept of the manager's role. This has been due to a number of developments, including the divorce of ownership and

[23] Jan. 9, 1963.

control in many large companies, the growth in the size and complexity of the corporations, the belief that management is at least partially a science, and the development of psychology and sociology.

No longer can the manager of a large corporation say with Cornelius Vanderbilt, "Can't I do what I want with my own?" In the first place, it isn't his own; it belongs to the stockholders, and he cannot even claim to be acting under their orders since he has little contact with them.

Further, the great size of the large corporations has led to a tremendous accumulation of power. Five hundred firms, or one-tenth of 1 per cent of the larger U.S. corporations, now account for one-third of all sales, and the sales of the fifty largest are equal to the sales of the remaining 450 in this group.[24] Companies of this size must consider their impact on other groups and on the general public, for power that serves ends contrary to the public good is always in danger of further legal restrictions in a democracy. (The railroads were about the first industry to be strictly regulated, simply because their policies affected so many other industries and so many members of the public.)

Moreover, the manager cannot invoke what has been termed the golden rule of free enterprise—"Where the risk lies, there lies the control"—because he is usually not risking his own capital but that of others. Hence he must justify his power by some other rationale than that available to the entrepreneurial owner-manager.

Social responsibilities

In his new role, therefore, the manager sees himself as an arbiter among the many interests or "publics" affected by the business: the stockholders, the employees, the suppliers, the local community, and the customers. It is his duty to divide the returns from the business equitably by providing a "fair" return to the stockholders, "fair" working conditions and pay for the employees, and "fair" prices to the suppliers and customers and to make the business, in general, an asset to the local community and the nation. This view was expressed as early as the 1920s at least, but it has become much more widespread since World War II.

The manager who views his job in this light attempts to maximize returns to both employees and stockholders—and to the other publics affected by the corporation—as the main purpose of his work. Thus he "tends to stand in contrast to the classical entrepreneur for whom moral responsibilities are treated simply as conditions restricting and defining the range of means he may use in his rational pursuit of profit."[25]

In this view, in other words, the ethical manager is not simply a man whose main aim is to make a profit for the stockholders or himself but who refrains

---

[24] Robert L. Heilbronner, *The Limits of American Capitalism*, Harper Torchbooks, Harper & Row, Publishers, Incorporated, New York, 1967, p. 10.
[25] Sutton *et al., op. cit.,* p. 105.

from unfairness to other groups because of his personal moral standards. Instead, he is *responsible* to these groups as well as to the owners, and he judges his performance by how he fulfills this responsibility as well as by the rate of profit. He sees his authority as stemming, not primarily from the legal rights inherent in ownership, but from his ability to do a good job. His main consideration is to keep the organization stable and growing healthily so that all the groups affected by it may continue to receive increasing returns.

Stated in this absolute way—and many managers do so state it—the concept of social responsibilities leaves the manager of a publicly held corporation open to challenge by the groups whom he is supposed to represent but who have had no part in selecting him.

However, it is doubtful whether many managers actually do believe that they have equal responsibilities to all the publics affected by the conduct of their corporations. Their main objective remains the profitability and stability of their organizations, but they recognize that they cannot ignore the claims of other groups. And many of them, especially in recent years, have given more weight to the claims of these other groups than they ever did in the past.

For instance, it would have been unthinkable to many managers even a few years ago that they had a responsibility to employ members of the "hard-core" unemployed, who may be difficult to train, prone to absenteeism and turnover, and not amenable to discipline. Yet many companies are attempting to do just that today. In part, this is because of their concern for their public "images," and perhaps because of fear of damage to their property in riots, but there also appears to be a genuine feeling on the part of some that they have a duty to help solve the social problem presented by a large group of people who have lost hope of any real participation in the affluent society.

Place of the profit motive

Fortunately, there is much that can be done to square public interests with private interests on the basis of better utilization of investment as measured by its rate of return. Apart from the obvious and great advantages of being legal (when other things may be of doubtful legality) and providing at least a rough way to measure results, this criterion also tends to make coincidental much self-interest in the pursuit of profits and the discharge of social and moral responsibility. That is, reliance on the criterion of profit maximization need not lead to reaction. What is in the interest of the individual executive is often in the interest of the company, particularly if his compensation is arranged accordingly. Also, it is often in the interest of the various publics with which the company deals. This is another way of saying that the service of these interests ensures the best use of the company's resources.

The steadfast pursuit of profit in an institution that contemplates perpetual life exercises a powerful negative sanction, for if the executive fails to take account of factors apparently outside the business, his long-run profits may suffer. If his employment record is unstable, if he treats his employees like numbers, discriminates against them, or assigns them meaningless or deadening work, he is likely to encounter labor trouble. If he treats his suppliers unfairly, he may run short of vital supplies at inconvenient times. If he fails to eliminate unpleasant odors, excessive noise, or industrial eyesores, the community may shun his works, discourage employment there, and ultimately pass ordinances against him. If he raises prices unduly, he may be called before a congressional committee.

It is these potential threats to long-run profits that make the truly responsible executive recognize his proper obligations. Experience has taught industry that compliance is better than compulsion. Thus adherence to the criterion of greater profit need not preclude the fulfillment of social responsibilities.

There have been cases in which companies have found that reducing the "social costs" that their operations imposed on the community have helped them to reduce their own costs, even in the short run. For example, some companies have found that installing equipment to eliminate air or stream pollution has enabled them to salvage valuable material and so more than offset the depreciation on the equipment and the cost of running it.

Some unresolved problems

There are, however, many instances in which a manager must determine how far he is justified in subordinating the interests of his company and his stockholders to the public interest. Some of the unresolved problems in this area include the following:

1. In industries that are "key" in the sense that they act as pacemakers for others and in those that are large, like automobiles and steel, industrial peace is basic. This may lead labor and management to combine at times to raise wages and compensate for the increase in unit labor cost by a price increase. If the product is an important item in the cost of living index, such a price rise may spark other labor demands and contribute to inflationary pressures. This was the issue at the heart of the disagreement between the steel industry and the President of the United States in the spring of 1962. At that time the government held that if industry did not exercise sufficient self-restraint, the government might intervene and restrain it.

   To avoid government intervention of this kind and to maintain as much of a free-working market as possible, many solutions have been suggested. Some lie in elaborate techniques of education, negotiation, mediation, or even arbitration. One practical private solution has been used by the Kaiser Steel Co. and the Steelworkers Union whereby the two parties share gains in productivity, with one-third of the gains going to the workers as a bonus. Another approach has been suggested by the Council of Economic Advisers: The annual increase of productivity in an industry or for industry as a whole might set a ceiling for noninflationary wage increases.

2. To what extent should management hold itself responsible for full employment? If, on the one hand, management is opposed to government measures designed to provide jobs in times of high unemployment (e.g., work
relief), is it not then responsible for providing a reasonably high level of
private employment? On the other hand, it has a responsibility to use the
stockholders' money wisely and not overstaff its plants and offices.

Again, suppose a company that is practically the sole support of a local
community decides to move its plant and office to another section of the
country, for reasons that are quite adequate from a profit-making viewpoint. Is it justified in doing so regardless of the consequences to the
town?

3. If a company includes absolute untruths in its promotion and advertising,
there are legal penalties to take care of the case. But how far is it justified
in stretching the truth in order to put its best foot forward?

4. Theoretically, every company has an obligation to compete just as strongly
as possible so long as the competition is "fair." But, as mentioned earlier,
some companies could, if they went all-out for competition, drive their
major competitors out of business and become virtual monopolies. Where
should management draw the line in this case?

The universal manager

The view that the manager is capable of dealing impartially with all those
affected by the business is based on the premise that he is a professional,
with professional standards. Managers may be, of course, members of one of
the recognized professions. Many of them are engineers or accountants, and
some are lawyers. But the manager's claim to professionalism in current ideology does not rest on this; rather he is supposed to be a professional in management itself.

This has led to the idea that the true manager can manage any type or
phase of business, or, for that matter, any kind of organization—industrial,
government, philanthropic—with equal skill. Curiously, this idea was advanced
centuries ago by Socrates:

Antisthenes . . . though neither skilled in music nor in teaching a chorus,
was able to find out the best masters in these departments . . . if he find
out and select the best men in military affairs, as he has done in the conduct of his choruses, he will probably attain superiority. . . . I say . . .
that over whatever a man may preside, if he knows what he needs, and
is able to provide it, he will be a good president, whether he have the
direction of a chorus, a family, a city, or an army.[26]

[26] Quoted in Albert Lepawsky, *Administration: The Art and Science of Organization and Man-
agement*, Alfred A. Knopf, Inc., New York, 1949, p. 87. Reprinted from Ernest Rhys (ed.),
"Discourse from Xenophon's Memorabilia" (trans. J. S. Watson), in Everyman's Library, J. M.
Dent & Sons, Ltd., Publishers, London, and E. P. Dutton & Co., Inc., New York.

Those who hold this view today argue that the management job is fundamentally the same, no matter what type of organization is being managed: that managing a military campaign is practically identical to managing a business. Essentially proponents of this view are devotees of the school that defines management as the direction of people. They leave unanswered, however, the question of how a manager who is completely unfamiliar with the field knows *what* he wants to direct people to do. If he depends on his staff for this, is he really managing?

The viewpoint that a good manager is essentially an all-purpose manager is, of course, rather flattering to men who hold managerial positions. It enables them to believe that they are "natural leaders" who would come to the top under any circumstances.

For this reason, probably, many managers accept the idea in the abstract. In their management of the day-to-day affairs of their businesses, however, they tend to disregard it. When they come to hire a middle manager, or even an executive vice-president, they are apt to lay down experience in the industry as a fundamental qualification.

And, of course, many successful managers are contemptuous of the whole idea. "I am very tired of these phony manager's managers, who can't produce, can't design, can't sell, and can't even count," one top executive writes.[27]

The social ethic

The view that the manager, whether all-purpose or not, is essentially a coordinator and director of people rather than an innovator is at variance with the Protestant ethic, which was a doctrine of individualism. William H. Whyte, Jr., has termed this phase of management ideology the "social ethic," which he defines as:

> . . . a belief in the group as the source of creativity; a belief in "belongingness" as the ultimate need of the individual; and a belief in the application of science to achieve the belongingness. . . . the gist can be paraphrased thus: Man exists as a unit of society. Of himself, he is isolated, meaningless; only as he collaborates with others does he become worth while. . . . What we think are conflicts are misunderstandings, breakdowns in communication. By applying the methods of science to human relations we can eliminate these obstacles to consensus and create an equilibrium in which society's needs and the needs of the individual are one and the same.[28]

Widespread acceptance of this viewpoint was particularly evident in the 1950s and the early 1960s, when managers were constantly talking of business as a "team effort" and stressing the ability to get along with people and "fit in" with the organization in selecting men for management posts.

[27] In a letter to the author, one of several from managers all over the country expressing somewhat the same idea.
[28] Whyte, *op. cit.*, p. 7.

In good part, this new conception of business was due to the growth in the size and complexity of many companies. When a business becomes very large, increased specialization is necessary, and it is no longer possible for one man to manage every aspect of it personally. He must depend on the help and knowledge of others, and if they do not work well with each other, his difficulties are enormously increased.

To a large extent, however, belief in the social ethic may have been due to the influence of the social scientists, whose views began receiving increased acceptance in industry. Many of them appeared by nature committed to the idea of "togetherness" as an end in itself, as Elton Mayo was.

Of course, many of the managers who talked as though they were committed to the social ethic were, so far as their own careers were concerned, actually devotees of the Protestant ethic. They conformed outwardly to the image of the team worker, but they never lost sight of the fact that it was their showing as individuals that would determine their advancement. Whyte found, however, that the spirit of competition was more common among the older managers than among the younger ones. The younger executives, he said, were ambitious in a "passive" way—expecting to rise almost automatically, not to the top, but to a comfortable plateau where the work would be interesting and well paid but not too strenuous.[29]

However, the social ethic may be somewhat soft-pedaled in management's representation efforts in the future, for the public tends to identify the concept with bureaucracy, and Whyte's book and a number of others that have been widely read have helped to convince many that large companies are bureaucratic.

Now bureaucracy is not wholly bad, although the word itself has unpleasant connotations for most people. Max Weber thought of bureaucracy as the best form of organization since it substituted a rule of law for rule by the whims of the rulers. The British Civil Service is a bureaucracy, but it has long had a reputation for probity and other good qualities, and it ran an empire with considerable skill for a long time.

But a bureaucracy has one major fault: It has difficulty in changing its ways, except very slowly. And because it resists change, it does not attract those who can conceive constructive changes and put them into effect. Some companies are, in fact, already finding it difficult to recruit intelligent young people, in part because they are considered, rightly or wrongly, to be bureaucracies that are more interested in conformity than in originality. The current emphasis on creativity, which was mentioned in the chapter on innovation, is in part an effort to represent business as a more individualistic activity. (Also, quite apart from the representation aspect, companies are becoming more conscious that they must provide an atmosphere that encourages creativity if they are to survive in a world of competition and rapid change.)

---

[29] *Ibid.,* pp. 127–137.

SUMMARY

Managers must spend an increasing proportion of their time representing their companies to outside groups and individuals—government officials, customers, labor unions, suppliers, financial interests, and others—all of whom are likely to have it in their power to hamper company operations in some way.

How much influence management has on these outsiders is in part a matter of good public relations techniques, but *what* the manager chooses to represent may have a greater effect in the long run. Here management ideology is important, for the ideas a manager attempts to promote will depend on his view of his company's function in the economy and the social system.

What has been called the "Protestant ethic" was accepted as axiomatic by most managers from the time of the Industrial Revolution until fairly recently. This doctrine held that a manager should be free to manage his business as he saw fit and that the forces of the marketplace would ensure that resources were used for the benefit of all. It was also a doctrine of individualism, under which managers were supposed to be competitive and to compete for advancement even with others in the same company.

Then this view began to give way to what has been called the "social ethic," in which management was thought of as a group effort and management skill as almost synonymous with skill in getting along with other people.

Concurrent with the rise of the social ethic was the growth of the view that the manager was a professional in management itself and could manage any type of organization and that he was no longer responsible to the stockholders alone but to all groups affected by his organization—employees, customers, the local community, and the general public.

The lines between these varying ideologies have, however, never been very clearly drawn. Thus some managers have been able to accept, ostensibly at least, both the social ethic and the Protestant ethic. Some have bent their principal efforts toward making money for their stockholders (and themselves) and yet have paid substantial attention to the effects of their actions on outside groups. In fact, the two objectives are not necessarily incompatible, for a company that is contemptuous of the welfare of other groups may find itself hampered by strikes, loss of markets, and new government regulations.

There is some evidence that there may be less emphasis on the social ethic in coming years, but the stress on social responsibilities is now greater than ever, and it may grow in the future. For the most part, managers are still opposed to extension of government regulation, but they hope to forestall it by taking action on social matters themselves.

Review Questions

1. Why do executives have to spend more time on the representation function than they formerly did?
2. What is meant by the "Protestant ethic"? The "social ethic"?
3. Do you believe that management should place the interests of its stock-

holders first or that it should consider them only one of the publics to which it is responsible? Why or why not?

4. Do you believe that there is such a thing as a universal manager who can manage any type of organization even if he has had no experience in the field? Why or why not?

5. Do you consider that there is too much government regulation of business today or not enough? If you think there is too much, what laws would you repeal? If you believe there is too little regulation, what new laws would you suggest?

6. The "social ethic" and the social responsibilities of business are not the same thing. How would you distinguish between them?

7. Which do you think has the greatest impact on a company's public image —the skills of its public relations department or its actions? Can you cite an example to support your viewpoint?

Case Study One / The Overoptimistic Supplier

A company asks a group of small suppliers to bid on a contract for supplying a component used in its product. The successful bidder starts the job and then comes to the company and tells it that he has bid too low and is going to lose money on the deal, but that if he can get $50,000 more, he can make a modest profit. The company checks out his figures and finds that he is telling the truth and that even if it pays him the extra money, he will still be doing the job at a price somewhat lower than the next lowest bidder would charge.

Should the company pay him extra or hold him to his contract?

Case Study Two / Moving a Plant

The CDE Company, a producer of furniture, was started in 1890 in a small city in New York State. It is still the biggest employer there. Because the original owners were anxious to avoid unionization, they recruited employees from different countries abroad, believing that a mixture of nationalities would make it difficult for employees to develop solidarity. The growth of the town was, for a long time, a result of the immigration the company had induced.

The company was unionized in the 1930s, however, and signed a contract with the union. Several successive contracts were also agreed to without strikes or serious labor difficulties.

After World War II, a different situation developed: The company announced that the union's demands were so excessive that it would move operations to the South rather than grant them. The union was convinced the company meant what it said and agreed to sign a new contract on the old terms.

At this point, the company announced that it was moving anyway. Its New York State plant was old and inefficient, and it could not hope to survive in competition with newer plants employing cheaper labor in the South.

1.   Do you think the company was justified in moving?
2.   If so, should the matter have been handled differently? How?

Shortly after this, a nearby company, which believed that municipal authorities had treated it unfairly in the matter of taxes, announced that some adjustment in its tax rates must be made or it would move, too. Faced with the loss of two principal employers at the same time, the city government gave in.

3.   Do you believe that the second company was justified in issuing this demand—and threat—at this time?
4.   Why or why not?

Case Study Three / Bob Knowlton*

Bob Knowlton was sitting alone in the conference room in the laboratory. He liked to stay after the others had gone; his appointment as project head was still new enough to give him a deep sense of pleasure. His eyes were on the graphs before him, but in his mind he could hear Dr. Jerrold, the head of the laboratory, saying again, "There's one thing about this place that you can bank on. The sky's the limit for a man who can produce!"

Well, dammit, he said to himself, he had produced. He wasn't kidding anybody. He had come to the Simmons Laboratories two years ago. During a routine testing of some rejected Clanson components he had stumbled on the idea of the photon correlator, and the rest just happened. Jerrold had been enthusiastic; a separate project had been set up for further research and development of the device, and he had gotten the job of running it. The whole sequence of events still seemed a little miraculous to Knowlton.

He was bending over the sheets when he heard someone come in behind him. The man was a stranger—tall, thin, and rather dark. He wore steel-rimmed glasses and had on a very wide leather belt with a large brass buckle.

* Reproduced by permission of Dr. Alex Bavelas.

The stranger smiled and introduced himself. "I'm Simon Fester. Are you Bob Knowlton?" Bob said yes, and they shook hands. Bob waved Fester to a chair. Then he said, "These are the preliminary results of a test we're running. We've got a new gadget by the tail and we're trying to understand it. It's not finished, but I can show you the section we're testing."

He stood up, but Fester was deep in the graphs. After a moment he looked up with an odd grin. "These look like plots of a Jennings surface. I've been playing around with some autocorrelation functions of surfaces—you know that stuff."

Bob, who had no idea what he was referring to, grinned back, nodded, and felt uncomfortable. "Let me show you the monster," he said, and led the way to the workroom.

The next morning Knowlton dropped into Jerrold's office, mentioned that he had talked with Fester, and asked who he was.

"Sit down for a minute," Jerrold said. "I want to talk to you about him. What do you think of him?" Knowlton replied truthfully that he thought Fester was very bright and probably very competent. Jerrold looked pleased.

"We're taking him on," he said. "He's had a good background, and he seems to have ideas about the problems we're tackling here." Knowlton nodded, then instantly wished that Fester would not be placed with him.

"I don't know where he will finally land," Jerrold continued, "but he seems interested in what you're doing. I thought he might spend a little time with you by way of getting started." Knowlton nodded thoughtfully. "If his interest in your work continues, you can add him to your group."

"Well, he seemed to have some good ideas even without knowing exactly what we are doing," Knowlton answered. "I hope he stays; we'd be glad to have him."

Knowlton walked back to the lab with mixed feelings. He told himself that Fester would be good for the group. He was no dunce; he'd produce. Knowlton thought again of Jerrold's promise when he had promoted him—"the man who produces gets ahead in this outfit." The words seemed to him to carry the overtones of a threat now.

The next day Fester didn't appear until midafternoon. He explained that he had had a long lunch with Jerrold, discussing his place in the lab. "Yes," said Knowlton, "I talked with Jerry this morning about it, and we both thought you might work with us for a while."

Fester smiled in a knowing way. "I'd like to," he said.

Knowlton introduced Fester to the other members of the lab. Fester and Line, the mathematician of the group, hit it off well together and spent the rest of the afternoon discussing a method of the analysis of patterns that Line had been worrying over for the last month.

It was 6:30 when Knowlton finally left the lab that night. Shortly after 5, everyone else had left except Fester, and what followed was almost a duel. Knowlton was annoyed that he was being cheated out of his quiet period and finally resentfully determined that Fester should leave first.

Fester was sitting at the conference table reading, and Knowlton was sitting at his desk in the little glass-enclosed cubbyhole that he used during the day when he needed to be undisturbed. Fester had gotten the last year's progress reports out and was studying them carefully. The time dragged. Knowlton doodled on a pad, the tension growing inside him. What the hell did Fester think he was going to find in the reports?

Knowlton finally gave up, and they left the lab together. Fester took several of the reports with him to study in the evening. Knowlton asked him if he thought the reports gave a clear picture of the lab's activities.

"They're excellent," Fester answered with obvious sincerity. "They're not only good reports; what they report is damn good, too!" Knowlton was surprised at the relief he felt and grew almost jovial as he said good night.

Knowlton had been asleep for several hours when he was jerked awake by the telephone. It was Fester. Without any excuses, apparently oblivious of the time, he plunged into an excited recital of how Line's patterning problem could be solved. Completely ignoring the fact that it was two in the morning, he proceeded to explain a new approach to certain of the photon lab problems that he had stumbled on while making analyses of past experiments. Knowlton managed to put some enthusiasm into his own voice and stood there, still half dazed and very uncomfortable, listening to Fester talk endlessly. He not only had discovered a new approach but also had analyzed the inherent weakness of the previous experiment. The following morning Knowlton spent the entire morning with Fester and Line, the mathematician, the usual morning meeting of all the members of the lab having been called off so that they could go over Fester's work.

For the next several days Fester sat in the back office that had been turned over to him and did nothing but read the progress reports of the last six months. Knowlton caught himself feeling apprehensive about the reaction Fester might have to some of this work. He was a little surprised at his own emotions. Although he had put on a convincingly modest face, he had always been proud of the new ground his group had broken in the study of photon measuring devices. Now he wasn't sure, and it seemed to him that Fester might easily show that the line of research they had been following was unsound or even unimaginative.

The next morning the members of the lab, including the girls, sat around the table in the conference room for their regular group meeting. Bob always prided himself on the fact that the work was guided and evaluated by the group as a whole. He was fond of repeating that it was not a waste of time to include secretaries in such meetings because often what started out as a boring attempt to explain fundamentals to them uncovered new ways of regarding these fundamentals that would not have occurred to a lab member.

The group meetings also served Bob in another sense. He admitted to himself that he would have felt far less secure if he had had to direct the work out of his own mind, so to speak. With the group meeting as the principle of leadership, it was always possible to justify the exploration of blind alleys because of the general educational effect on the team. Fester was there, Lucy and Martha were there, and Line was sitting next to Fester, apparently continuing their conversation of the day before. The other members, Bob Davenport, George Thurlow, and Arthur Oliver, were waiting quietly.

Knowlton, for reasons he didn't quite understand, brought up a problem that all of them had previously discussed at length and that they had concluded was impossible to treat experimentally. When Knowlton mentioned it, Davenport remarked that there was hardly any use going over it again, that he was satisfied there was no way of approaching the problem with the equipment and the physical capacities of the lab.

This statement had the effect of a shot of adrenalin on Fester. He said he would like to hear about the problem in detail. Walking to the blackboard, he began setting down the factors as various members of the group discussed the problem and why it had been abandoned. Very early in the discussion it was evident that Fester was going to disagree about the impossibility of attacking it. The group realized this, and their recounting of the reasons why it had been abandoned dwindled away. Then Fester began to speak, and it seemed as if his statement had been prepared the previous night although Knowlton knew this was impossible. He couldn't help being impressed with the organized and logical way in which Fester was presenting ideas that must have occurred to him only a few minutes before.

Fester had some things to say, however, which left Knowlton with a mixture of annoyance, irritation, and a rather smug feeling of superiority in at least one area. Fester thought that the way the problem had been analyzed was really typical of what happens when such thinking is attempted by a group. With an air of sophistication that made it difficult for a listener to dissent, he proceeded to make general comments on the American emphasis on team ideas, satirically describing the ways in which they led to a "high level of mediocrity."

During this time Knowlton observed that Line stared studiously at the floor, and he was very conscious of George Thurlow's and Bob Davenport's glances toward him. Inwardly Knowlton couldn't help feeling that this was one point at least in which Fester was off on the wrong foot. The whole lab, following Jerrold's lead, talked (if it did not always practice) the theory of small research teams as basic organizations for effective research.

Fester insisted that the problem could be approached and that he would like to study it for a while himself. Knowlton ended the morning session by remarking that the meetings would continue. The very fact that a supposedly insoluble problem was now going to get another chance, he said, indicated the value of such meetings. Fester replied that he was not at all averse to meetings for the purpose of informing the group of the progress of its members. He said the point he wanted to make was that creative advances were seldom accomplished in such meetings, that they were achieved by an individual who lived with a problem closely and continuously.

Knowlton said he was very glad that Fester had raised these points and he was sure the group would profit by reexamining the basis on which they had been operating. He agreed that major advances probably came through individual effort, but said that he considered the group meetings useful primarily because of their effect in keeping the group together and in helping the weaker members keep up with the advances of those who worked more easily and quickly.

The meetings went on, and Fester appeared to enjoy them because of the pattern they assumed. It became habitual for him to hold forth, and it was clear that he was without question more brilliant and better prepared on the various subjects being studied than anyone else in the lab.

Knowlton grew increasingly disturbed as he realized that his leadership of the group had been, in fact, taken over. In Knowlton's occasional meetings with Dr. Jerrold, the subject of Fester sometimes came up, and Knowlton commented only on his ability and obvious capacity for work. Somehow Knowlton felt that he could not mention his own discomforts, not only because they revealed a weakness on his part but because it was quite clear that Jerrold himself was considerably impressed with Fester's work and with Fester himself.

Then Knowlton began to feel that the intellectual advantages Fester had brought to the group perhaps did not compensate for the slow loss of the group's cooperative spirit. More and more of the morning meetings were skipped. Fester's opinion of the abilities of the others, with the exception of Line, was obviously low. At times he went to the point of rudeness, refusing to pursue an argument because he claimed that the person who disagreed with him was ignorant of the facts. His impatience with the others also led him to make derogatory remarks about them to Dr. Jerrold.

Knowlton spoke privately with Davenport and Oliver, and it was clear that both of them were uncomfortable with Fester. But Knowlton didn't press the discussion beyond the point where they said that it was sometimes difficult to understand Fester's arguments but embarrassing to ask him to fill in the background. Knowlton did not interview Line in this manner.

About six months after Fester's arrival, a meeting was scheduled in which the sponsors of much of the research were to be told something about its progress. At these meetings it was customary for project heads to make the presentations. Other members of the laboratory groups were invited to other meetings later in the day, but the special meetings usually included only the project heads, the head of the laboratory, and the sponsor.

As the time for the meeting approached, it seemed to Knowlton that he must avoid the presentation at all costs. He felt he could not trust himself to present Fester's ideas in sufficient detail and answer questions about them. On the other hand, he did not see how he could ignore these newer lines of work and present only the things that had been done or started before Fester's arrival. He also felt that it would not be beyond Fester, if he were present at the meeting, to make comments on Knowlton's presentation and reveal its inadequacy. It was also clear that it would not be easy to keep Fester from attending the meeting, in spite of the fact that he was not supposed to go.

Knowlton spoke to Jerrold about the matter. He remarked that Fester would probably like to explain his own contributions but that there was a question of the feelings of the others in the group if Fester alone were invited. Jerrold passed this over lightly by saying that the group would understand Fester's rather different position and that he thought Fester should by all means attend. Knowlton immediately said he thought so too.

Fester's presentation was very successful and he was asked many questions after he had concluded. Later in the evening at a cocktail party for the sponsors and the laboratory force, a little circle of people formed about him, including Jerrold himself. All this disturbed Knowlton, but he joined the circle, praised Fester to Jerrold and to others, and remarked how brilliant some of his work was.

Afterwards, Knowlton began to think of getting a job elsewhere. Within a few weeks he found that a new laboratory was being organized in a nearby city and that he would be able to get a project-head job at slightly more money.

He accepted immediately and notified Jerrold by a letter mailed on Friday night to Jerrold's home. It said that he had found a better position, that there were personal reasons why he didn't want to appear at the lab any more, that he would be glad to come back at a later time to help out if any mix-up regarding past work developed, and that he was sure Fester could supply any leadership the group needed. He hinted that he was leaving because of health problems in his family.

Jerrold was stunned, but he took the letter at its face value. Still, he felt that Knowlton's behavior was quite unaccountable since he had always felt that their relationship had been warm and that Knowlton was happy and productive. He had already decided to place Fester in charge of another project soon to be set up, and had been wondering how to explain this to Knowlton, in view of the obvious contribution Fester was making to his group. He had, as a matter of fact, considered the possibility that Knowlton might add to his staff another person with Fester's type of background and training.

Jerrold made no attempt to meet Knowlton. He felt aggrieved about the whole thing. Fester, too, was surprised, and when Jerrold asked whether he would prefer to stay with the photon group instead of going to the new project, he chose the new project. The photon lab was hard hit. Leadership was given to Line, with the understanding that the assignment would be temporary until someone else could come in and take over.

1.   What management ideology was Knowlton following?
2.   Could he, while still acting on the same ideology, have maintained his position of leadership in his group?
3.   What ideology would you say Jerrold held? What should he have done to prevent what happened?
4.   If you were Jerrold, would you rather have a laboratory project headed by a Knowlton or a Fester? Why?

Selected Readings

The Managerial Revolution, James Burnham, The John Day Company, Inc., New York, 1941. A book that has had a great deal of influence on management ideology. A best seller in its day, it publicized the idea that managers are becoming an elite of professionals.

The Corporation in Modern Society, Edward S. Mason (ed.), Harvard University Press, Cambridge, Mass., 1960. A balanced collection of articles by a number of social scientists on the corporation and the problems it raises.

The Organization Man, William H. Whyte, Jr., Simon and Schuster, Inc., New York, 1956, part I. Whyte's views on the ideology of the organization man are presented in this section in which he contrasts the Protestant ethic and the social ethic.

Issues in Business and Society: Readings and Cases, William T. Greenwood, Houghton Mifflin Company, Boston, 1964. An examination of the relations of business to its many different publics. Subjects covered include the relation of business to the individual; labor-management relations; ethics, religion, and business; management rights and objectives; the social responsibilities of business.

Corporate Social Responsibility, Clarence C. Walton, Wadsworth Publishing Company, Belmont, Calif., 1967. A book that presents the historical development of the idea of social responsibility, reviews the arguments for and against the various concepts of that responsibility, and illustrates the practical applications of the concepts by an analysis of their effect on economic stability and social justice.

The Business Establishment, Earl F. Cheit (ed.), John Wiley & Sons, Inc., New York, 1964. Eight contributions by social scientists on the interrelationship of business and society.

23

THE
THEORY
AND
PRACTICE
OF
DECISION
MAKING

"The cause of lightning," Alice said very decidedly, for she felt quite sure about this, "is the thunder—no, no!" she hastily corrected herself, "I meant the other way."

"It's too late to correct it," said the Red Queen: "When you've once said a thing, that fixes it, and you must take the consequences."
Lewis Carroll: *Through the Looking Glass*

23   As was mentioned earlier, those who define management as decision making are only partly right. Management decisions are always made in the course of one of the true management activities: planning, organizing, staffing, directing, controlling, innovation, and representation. Hence decision making cannot be considered an independent function.

What, then, is decision making? It has been well described as "the focal creative psychic event where knowledge, thought, feeling, and imagination are fused into action."[1] In other words, it is a process that cannot be explained by any formula. The primary characteristic of the process is that it involves uncertainty.

When the objectives are clear and the man in charge knows what will happen if he selects each of the various courses of action open to him, he does not have to make a decision. The circumstances dictate what should be done, and any sane person will do it. But except in purely routine matters, the consequences of management decisions are seldom entirely predictable. The man who decides must weigh the probabilities and balance the risks of each course against the possible gains.

Probabilities can, of course, be determined mathematically, but only in special circumstances. Since a coin will fall either heads or tails, the man who tosses it has one chance in two of getting heads and one chance in four of getting heads twice in succession. Probabilities may also be calculated with fair accuracy when results of a large number of similar cases are known.

But most management decisions of any importance are of the one-of-a-kind variety, if only because some of the variables in the business situation are different from those that affected results of past decisions. Hence the probabilities with which the manager must work are merely estimates, generally based on a largely incomplete set of facts.

THEORIES OF DECISION MAKING

There are many theories designed to show how decisions are, or should be, made in the business world. Both economists and mathematicians have tried their hands at evolving hypotheses, and many writers on the subject have explained decision making in psychological terms.

Traditional economic theory

Economists have long been interested in business decision making because decisions made by companies and investors affect the course of the economy. Thus a general theory setting forth the main basis or bases for business decisions would make it easier to explain how the economy operates and perhaps predict what is likely to happen to it.

Today economists borrow from both mathematics and psychology in

---

[1] G. L. S. Shackle, in C. F. Carter, G. P. Meredith, and G. L. S. Shackle (eds.), *Uncertainty and Business Decisions: A Symposium*, 2d ed., Liverpool University Press, Liverpool, 1957, p. 105

attempting to explain the economy and to make predictions, but traditionally their theory of business decision making was simple: They held that firms always seek to maximize profits and that business decision makers always choose the most profitable course of all those open to them.

The traditional economists also offered a method of determining when a company should stop putting extra resources of one type or another into its operations in the hope of producing extra profit. This was the theory of marginal productivity, which states that as extra inputs of any one type (e.g., labor or equipment) are added, profits increase, but each new increment of profit is smaller than the last one, and at some point the cost of the extra input will exactly equal the extra revenue it will bring in. At that marginal point, the company should stop. To illustrate:

Suppose a company has two salesmen covering New York State, one assigned to New York City and the other to the rest of the state. Because the number of potential customers is very large, the two salesmen do not have time to contact all the prospects, although they do, of course work on the largest ones. If the company splits the state into three territories instead of two and hires a third salesman, both total sales and total profits should increase because the company will be reaching a larger proportion of the market. However, as fourth, fifth, and sixth salesmen (and so on) are added, the customers available to each one become fewer and fewer and the amount each one can sell becomes smaller and smaller, even though total company sales and profits continue to rise. But this process cannot go on indefinitely. At some point, the returns from adding another salesman will exactly equal the cost of having him on the payroll, and at this point the company should stop, for any further additions to the sales force will actually reduce total profits.

Similarly, the marginal point for new machinery designed to save labor would be the point at which the yearly depreciation plus the annual cost of repair and power would exactly equal the annual wages of the labor saved.

Marginal analysis might also be used in pricing. In the case of many products, lower prices mean extra sales, and extra profits will accrue so long as the extra sales are great enough to offset the lower unit profits. Let us say that a company is selling 1,000 units and making a profit of $10 on each one but that if it were to reduce the price by $5 and thereby reduce its unit profit by the same amount, it could sell 3,000 units. This would increase its total profit from $10,000 to $15,000. Up to a point, also, further price cuts might result in greater sales and greater total profits. But as unit profits became smaller and smaller, larger increases in sales would be necessary to ensure that total profit kept growing. Then at some point, further price cuts would not produce enough extra sales to do more than exactly offset what was lost through lower unit profits, and again that would be the marginal point. (This example, of course, disregards the greater absorption of overhead that would occur when sales increased. The absorption of overhead would have to be taken into account in actual business calculations.)

Marginal analysis is useful as a guide to decision making in many cases, but it cannot be used to avoid all risk and so make decisions routine. Other things being equal, it might perhaps do so, but other things are seldom equal. For example, in the case of the salesmen, one would have to assume that the salesmen's compensation, their skill and effort, and the total territory potential would all remain the same. But it is much more likely that the best salesmen would quit if their territories were continually being cut down, to name just one of the uncertainties of the situation. In the case of the new machine, it would be necessary to postulate that labor rates would remain stable and that the company could sell all the output of the machine.

Mathematical decision theory

Mathematical decision theory is concerned with the best way to make decisions under conditions of risk or uncertainty. In this case, conditions of "risk" are those in which the probabilities of various outcomes are known or can be estimated, whereas under "uncertainty," the decision maker is completely ignorant of the odds.

The theory provides a systematic way of laying out the possible outcomes of different decisions when the decision maker faces a complicated problem in which many of the factors that will affect results are completely beyond his control. Factors within his control are called "acts," and those outside his control are called "events."

For example, take the case of the company which makes a profit of $10 on each unit it sells and is able to sell 1,000 units at present prices. The company believes that if it cuts the price, and its unit profit, by $5, it can thereby increase its sales volume, perhaps to 3,000 units, and that it has an excellent chance of doubling sales. The alternatives may be laid out in a payoff table like the following:

Sales volume (units)	Profit at present price	Profit with $5 reduction
1,000	$10,000	$ 5,000
2,000	20,000	10,000
3,000	30,000	15,000

If the company could increase its sales substantially without changing its price, obviously that would be the most profitable course. But it has not yet been able to do so, which is why the reduction is being considered. However, the decision maker believes that there is a 15 per cent chance that sales will increase to 2,000 units anyway and a 5 per cent chance that they will increase to 3,000.

The odds in favor of sales increases are estimated to be much greater if the price cut is adopted. It is thought that there is a 60 per cent chance that volume will double in that case and a 30 per cent chance that it will triple.

This produces the table below. Of course, *unit* profits would increase with greater sales because of greater absorption of overhead, but this factor is ignored in the example, which is merely intended to illustrate the technique.

| | Sales level | | | |
	1,000 units	2,000 units	3,000 units	EMV
Retain price	$10,000	$20,000	$30,000	$12,500*
Reduce price	5,000	10,000	15,000	11,000†

* 10,000 (0.80) + 20,000 (0.15) + 30,000 (0.05) = 12,500
† 5,000 (0.10) + 10,000 (0.60) + 15,000 (0.30) = 11,000

The last column shows the expected monetary value (EMV) of each decision: $12,500 if the price is kept at the present level and $11,000 if it is reduced by $5. This would indicate that the price should be kept where it is.

Of course the $5 cut, which halves the profit margin, is a pretty drastic one. If the cut in unit profits were only 25 per cent and the same odds were used, the EMV would be $16,500; $7,500 (0.10) + $15,000 (0.60) + $22,500 (0.30). If the decision maker were very cautious, he might still keep the price at the current level. But he would have to sell only a few hundred more units to make the $10,000 profit with the reduced profit margin; and, as the odds indicate, there is a very good chance that he can increase his profit substantially by the cut. In this case, the wise decision would seem to be to cut the price.

Or the decision maker might consider cutting the price by only $2, instead of $2.50, which would mean that his unit profit would be cut only by 20 per cent instead of by 25 per cent. In that case, he would have to sell only 250 extra units to maintain his $10,000 profit, an increase that should not be very difficult to achieve. And although the odds that he could double or triple his sales might be somewhat lower than in the case of the larger cut, it would seem that his chances of making more than $10,000 would be very good.

Another mathematical technique that the decision maker may use to improve his grasp of the factors that will affect the outcome of a decision is the decision-tree technique. This has an advantage over the simple payoff table in that it enables the decision maker to see what effect decisions made now will have on the alternatives he will face in the future. This technique is best explained by means of examples.

Let us say that a speculator who has $40,000 to invest is trying to decide which of two blocks of land he should purchase. He is sure that a new high-way will pass one of the blocks and that the route will be announced within six months. If he is fortunate enough to have bought land beside the new highway, he will be able to sell the property at a good profit. Otherwise, he will be able to sell it only for its more normal market price. To be more specific, he must choose one of the three "acts":

1. Buy block A for $25,000 and deposit the remaining $15,000 in a savings bank.

2.   Buy block B for $35,000 and deposit the remaining $5,000 in a savings bank.
3.   Deposit the entire $40,000 in a savings bank.

Once he has chosen one of these acts, the speculator must face the consequences, good or bad, of one of the following "events."

1.   The new highway passes block A.
2.   The new highway passes block B.

The speculator believes that block A can be sold for $40,000 at the end of six months if the highway will go by it, and if it is announced that the highway will take the other route, block A can be sold for $30,000. However, in that case, block B could be sold for $75,000. On the other hand, if the highway goes by block A, block B will bring only $25,000. Money deposited in the savings bank earns interest at the rate of 4 per cent a year; therefore, it will increase by 2 per cent in six months.

Since the speculator has only $40,000, he can purchase only one of the two pieces of land. He would like, of course, to purchase block B for $35,000, then sell it for $75,000 after six months. But since the highway may go the other way, he may be able to get only $25,000 for this property, which means that he will sustain a loss of $10,000. On the other hand, if he buys block A or simply puts the money in the bank, he cannot make such a large profit, but no matter what happens, he will not suffer a loss.

The decision-tree technique enables him to diagram his problem in such a way that its elements become clearer. As he contemplates the alternatives, he is standing at point W in the top diagram in Figure 1 and can choose any one of the three branches of the tree. At the right-hand side of the diagram are figures showing his net worth in each possible case. Thus if he buys block A, he will end with either $45,300 or $55,300, whereas the purchase of block B will leave him with either $30,100 or $80,100.

It is obvious that he will be better off if he purchases block A than he will be if he simply puts the money in the bank, for no matter what happens he will make more by the purchase. Therefore, the act represented by the lowest branch is said to be "dominated" by the act represented by the top branch.

However, the choice between the two top branches of the tree is not obvious. So the speculator resolves his problem in this way:

He envisions himself standing at point X on the diagram six months later, just before the route the highway will take is to be announced. Then he asks himself what he would be willing to sell the property for at that point. This minimum price, or "certainty equivalent," as it is called, will be one that will give him a final net worth between $45,300 and $55,300—obviously he would not accept less than the former amount since he will be sure of it anyway, and he cannot expect that any buyer will be willing to pay more than the $40,000 the property will be worth if the highway passes it. The exact certainty equivalent he chooses will depend on the following:

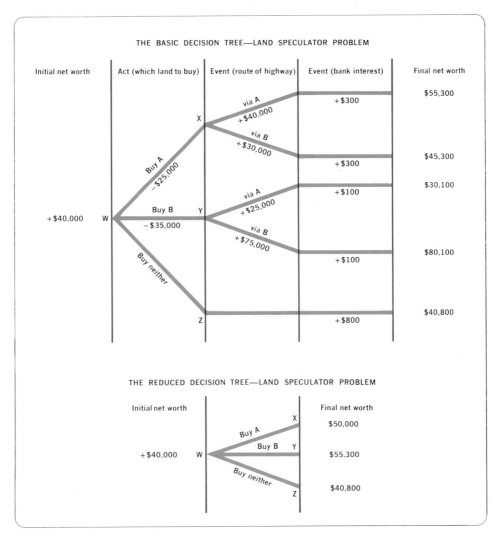

THE BASIC DECISION TREE—LAND SPECULATOR PROBLEM

| Initial net worth | Act (which land to buy) | Event (route of highway) | Event (bank interest) | Final net worth |

via A +$40,000

X

via B +$30,000

Buy A −$25,000

+$300 $55,300

+$300 $45,300

+$40,000   W

Buy B   Y   −$35,000

via A +$25,000

via B +$75,000

+$100 $30,100

+$100 $80,100

Buy neither

Z

+$800 $40,800

THE REDUCED DECISION TREE—LAND SPECULATOR PROBLEM

| Initial net worth | | Final net worth |

X $50,000

Buy A

Buy B   Y

+$40,000   W

$55,300

Buy neither

Z $40,800

FIGURE 1

1. His assessment of the odds that the highway will go by A. (In a case of complete uncertainty, the odds would be 50-50 and, therefore, would not affect the decision.)

2. His current net worth and his need for money at the end of six months. If he will need $51,000 at the time, he would be unwilling to sell for a price that would produce a net worth less than that amount even if he felt that the odds that the highway would go via A were very small. That is, he would not want to give up his chance of getting the $55,300 if he needed $51,000. Similarly, if he needed $48,000, he might be willing to

sell for a smaller amount even though he felt the odds were high that he would have the $55,300, especially since this would eliminate the risk of having only $45,300. The relation the possible profit would bear to his total net worth would influence him also.

Different decision makers would choose different certainty equivalents under these circumstances, but let us say that this speculator selects $50,000.

Then he envisions himself standing at point Y, repeats the process, and chooses a certainty equivalent of $55,300. The certainty equivalent at Z is an actual certainty, $40,800. Then the decision tree could be reduced to the lower diagram shown in Figure 1, and the speculator would buy block B.

In finally choosing to buy block B, the speculator realizes, of course, that he is not going to receive the $55,300 shown in the diagram. He will get either $30,100 or $80,100, but the $55,300 is considered to take the place of the other two for the purpose of making the choice. Another speculator who had access to different information, a different net worth, or a different personality might have assessed this value at $49,000, and in that case he would have chosen to buy block A.

A more complicated case is that of the hypothetical company Emperor Products Corporation. It is normally operating at full capacity, and demand for its product is rising.[2] The sales manager expects a 20 per cent increase in demand, which can be met either by purchasing a new machine or by authorizing overtime. The net cash flow, in the event of the 20 per cent rise in demand, will be $460,000 if the new machine is purchased and $440,000 if the extra production is obtained by the use of overtime. But some in the company say that there is a possibility that sales will not rise; on the contrary, volume *could* drop by 5 per cent, even though the rise is more likely. There is more or less general agreement that there is a 60 per cent probability of a sales rise of 20 per cent and a 40 per cent probability of a 5 per cent drop.

If there were a 5 per cent sales drop, the cash flow would be $340,000 if the company purchased the new equipment and $380,000 if it went the overtime route. The alternatives are then presented in the form of a decision tree. (See Figure 2.)

In order to take account of the probabilities, the decision maker performed the following calculations:

$460,000 × 0.60	$276,000
340,000 × 0.40	136,000
	$412,000
$440,000 × 0.60	$264,000
380,000 × 0.40	152,000
	$416,000

[2] The following, including the illustrations, is drawn from Edward A. McCreary, "How to Grow a Decision Tree," *Think*, March–April, 1967, pp. 13–18, 25. Used by permission of *Think* magazine, published by IBM. Copyright 1967 by International Business Machines Corporation.

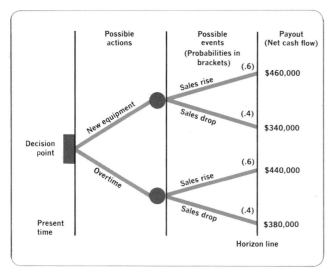

Possible actions

Possible events
(Probabilities in brackets)

Payout
(Net cash flow)

Decision point

New equipment

Sales rise (.6) $460,000

Sales drop (.4) $340,000

Overtime

Sales rise (.6) $440,000

Sales drop (.4) $380,000

Present time

Horizon line

FIGURE 2

This indicated that the company would be well advised to choose the overtime alternative. However, it was not the whole story, because the sales might rise still further in the year following—in fact, the executives agreed, even if the sales dropped 5 per cent in 1967, the odds were 8 in 10 that they would rise 20 per cent in 1968 and 1969 and 2 in 10 that they would increase at least 10 per cent in 1968. Moreover, if sales rose as expected in 1967, the odds were 50-50 that they would increase by either 20 per cent or 10 per cent in 1968.

Thus another decision point would come at the end of 1967, for if a sales rise were expected the next year and the company already had one new machine, it would have to decide whether to buy another new unit or to use its one new machine and authorize overtime. On the other hand, if the company elected to take care of the original 20 per cent rise by using overtime, further rises might compel it to buy two new units or to buy one and continue using overtime.

Figures 3 and 4 show the extension of the decision tree to cover a longer period of time. Figure 3 shows the various possibilities and the subsequent payouts in each case.   In Figure 4, the probabilities are applied to the payouts. Thus on the optimum decision path, the two payout figures in the last column are averaged, because the odds are 50-50, to produce the figure of $994,000. On the branch below this, the $812,000 is made up of 80 per cent of $820,-000 and 20 per cent of $780,000. Also, 60 per cent of $994,000 (596,400) and 40 per cent of $812,000 ($324,800) are added to produce the $921,200. Similar calculations produce the $892,000 figure for the decision to rely on overtime in the first instance. Thus, when the subsequent year's possibilities are taken into account, it appears that the company should purchase the new unit.

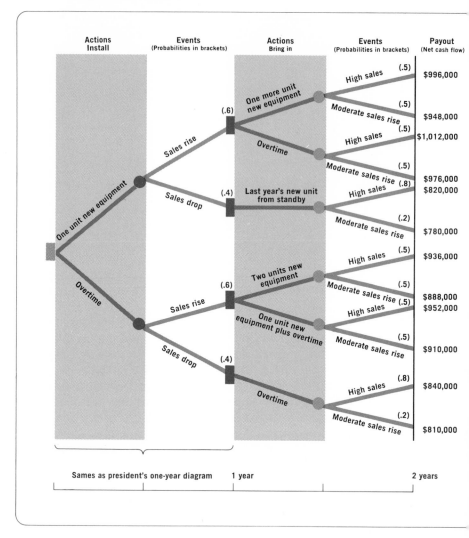

FIGURE 3

Decision theory, it will be noted, does not dictate decisions. Two decision makers who start with the same set of figures may arrive at different answers. Rather its advantage is that it provides an organized way of subdividing a complex problem into small subproblems of manageable size and of taking into account the decision maker's judgment of odds and the extent to which he is willing to take a risk. Its chief contribution may be that it forces the decision maker to take various events (factors over which he has no control) into account, to assess the probabilities that these events will occur, and to determine how much money he is willing to forego to avoid risk in a given

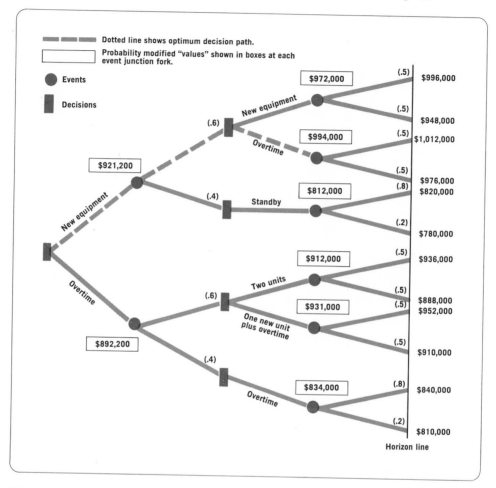

Dotted line shows optimum decision path.

Probability modified "values" shown in boxes at each event junction fork.

● Events

▮ Decisions

FIGURE 4

situation. Extended decision trees can be particularly valuable because a decision made now may limit the alternatives open at some future date, and diagramming the acts enables the decision maker to see this clearly. However, if the tree is extended too far, it will develop so many branches that it will be confusing and the estimates of the probabilities will be less reliable. Some authorities, in fact, believe that a tree should not cover more than a year's time.

A somewhat similar mathematical technique is "venture analysis," which is illustrated in Figure 5. This technique is used by some companies as an aid in deciding how large a new plant should be.

In the case shown in the illustration, the company can expect a 16 per cent return on its investment if demand turns out to be high and it has built a big

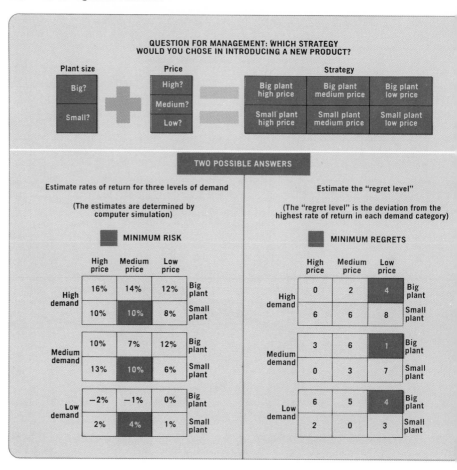

FIGURE 5 Venture analysis. (From *Petroleum Week*, Apr. 7, 1961, p. 34.)

plant and charges a high price. The worst that can happen is that demand will be low after the company has built a big plant and set a high price—if it did not change its price, it could expect to lose 2 per cent. Even with a low price, which might be expected to expand demand somewhat, it would merely break even. But with a small plant and a medium price, it would be assured of making at least a 4 per cent return. Thus if the decision maker were anxious to minimize risk, he might choose to build a small plant and charge a medium price. On the other hand, if he were willing to take a chance in the hope of a big gain, he would select the big plant and a high or medium price.

The figures on the amount of regret management will feel are calculated by subtracting the actual return in each case from the best return the company might have achieved by following a different course. Thus if it builds only a small plant and later finds that the output of a large plant could have been sold at a higher price, the regret level will be 6—the difference between 16 per cent and the actual 10 per cent.

This is a simplified example used merely to illustrate the technique. "Big" and "small" are relative terms, and so are "high," "medium," and "low" when applied to prices. If a company were actually using this technique in decision making, it would probably employ a computer to calculate the percentages for many different plant sizes and many different prices. Also, in a practical business situation, a company that had serious fears that the demand would be low would not build a new plant of any size. If the demand turned out to be low, the best return it could get would be 4 per cent, and it might better put the money in the bank and save itself the trouble.

Estimated probabilities might also be used in the decision on the size of a new plant. A mathematical technique developed by Prof. Robert Schlaifer of Harvard Business School, who has been active in the development of the decision-tree technique, incorporates the guesses of experienced managers and the known statistics, such as the costs of producing in plants of various sizes, and this has actually been tried:

> Paul E. Green of the marketing research group in Du Pont's Fibers Div., actually used management's judgments about the probable sales of the product as part of the data that he fed into a computer. The predictions of experienced sales executives were compiled into a probability curve of potential sales. When these opinions were fed into a computer along with cost data, the computer told Du Pont what size plant to build. The company won't say whether it is following the Bayesian[3] conclusion in this case. But it is certainly encouraging its statisticians to persevere in their work.[4]

Other mathematical decision-making techniques are described in the chapter on operations research. In some cases, these can eliminate the need to make a decision, since they can clearly indicate the most profitable course. However, in many instances they merely provide management with more facts on which to base a decision rather than with the "best decision."

Psychological theories

Theories of decision making based on marginal economics or mathematics all presuppose that the manager is, at least so far as his business decisions are concerned, an "economic man"—that is, he maximizes company profits as far as his ability, the law, and his ethical standards permit.

But some observers do not agree with this premise. Herbert A. Simon, for example, holds that business decision makers do not generally seek the high-

[3] The name comes from an eighteenth-century English clergyman, Thomas Bayes, who developed a mathematical theorem regarding probabilities. In effect, this states that if you discover a given probability that some event will occur and later get additional evidence that points to a different probability, you can estimate the true probability by combining the first probability with the second. Schlaifer's technique combines statistical probabilities derived from large masses of data with probabilities estimated by managers.
[4] "Math + Intuition = Decision," *Business Week*, Mar. 24, 1962, p. 54.

est profit possible. Instead, he believes, they attempt to do what he calls "satisficing." How this differs from profit maximizing he explains in this way:

> While economic man maximizes—selects the best alternative from among all those available to him; his cousin, whom we shall call administrative man, satisfices—looks for a course of action that is satisfactory or "good enough." Examples of satisficing criteria that are familiar to business men, if unfamiliar to most economists, are "share of the market," "adequate profit," "fair price."[5]

According to this theory, only when the attainment falls short of what the manager considers satisficing or adequate does the real search for more profitable courses of action begin. At the same time the level considered satisfactory begins to drop. To illustrate:

If a company has been making, say, 20 per cent on investment for several years, then a satisficing management would probably not attempt to find new ways of increasing the figure until the percentage return fell fairly far. A change of a few percentage points might lead to an attempt to cut costs but not to drastic changes in the company's way of doing business. Only a sizable drop would trigger consideration of entirely new fields, organizational shake-ups, and other far-reaching changes. If these failed to produce results, the level of aspiration would gradually sink until, say, a 10 per cent profit would be considered normal and satisficing.

It is difficult to say, however, whether what looks like satisficing may not, in some cases, actually be long-run profit maximizing. Fear of violating the law, of attracting potential competition, or of losing the good will of the public may keep management from pursuing courses that would seem logical if immediate profit maximizing were the objective. Moreover, most firms do try to increase profits, even when returns are satisfactory, although they cannot, naturally, examine all *possible* courses of action—if they did, they would never get around to acting at all.

Nevertheless, there is some tendency to satisfice in many companies and among some executives at all levels. This is probably due to what the English economist Sir John Hicks called the businessman's "desire for the quiet life"—the desire to keep things as they are if they are reasonably satisfactory, rather than initiate new courses of action that will entail both risk and extra work.

There is also the possibility that a manager may confuse means and ends. In that case, he may concentrate on volume of sales or share of the market rather than on profits. William J. Baumol points out:

> It is not unusual to find a profitable firm in which some segment of its sales can be shown to be highly unprofitable. For example, I have encountered several firms who were losing money on their sales in markets quite distant from the plant where local competition forced the

---

[5] *Administrative Behavior: A Study of Decision-making Processes in Administrative Organization*, 2d ed., The Macmillan Company, New York, 1957, p. xxv.

product price down to a level which did not cover transportation costs. Another case was that of a watch distributor whose sales to small retailers in sparsely settled districts were so few and far between that the salesmen's wages were not made up by the total revenues which they brought in. When such a case is pointed out to management, it is usually quite reluctant to abandon its unprofitable markets. . . . A program which explicitly proposes any cut in sales volume, whatever the profit considerations, is likely to meet a cold reception. In many cases firms do finally perform the radical surgery involved in cutting out an unprofitable line or territory, but this usually occurs after much heart-searching and delay.[6]

As Baumol points out, this may be partly because salaried managers are acting as economic men from their own rather than their companies' viewpoint:

Executive salaries appear to be far more closely correlated with the scale of operations of the firm than with its profitability. And in the modern corporation, which is characterized so often by separation of ownership from management, many executives find it politic to avoid an absolute or relative decline in their operations.[7]

It seems probable, however, that there is true confusion of ends and means. Usually profits grow with sales, and managements are accustomed to thinking of the two as directly related. Hence, to a company that has traditionally increased its profits by increasing its sales, any cutback in sales appears to be a retreat.

On the other hand, tradition can also operate to keep sales down when an increase in volume would produce a higher profit. A company that has prospered by making high-quality products for a small market may be slow to see the possibilities in expansion. An illustration of this is the case of Rolls-Royce. From its founder, I. S. Lloyd points out,[8] later management inherited a set of traditions, "almost instinctive beliefs," which included:

1. There would always be a market for superlative quality in automobile engineering.
2. Rolls-Royce would lose good will by producing in quantity, since quantity and quality were incompatible.
3. Even if this were not so, the customer thought so, and he was always right.
4. Selling a few hundred costly cars had always paid.
5. An inferior component, however cheap, was never justified if something better could be produced, however costly.

Up until 1935, the company had had no difficulty making a profit while acting in accordance with this credo. Whether or not it could have done better

---

[6] *Business Behavior, Value and Growth,* The Macmillan Company, New York, 1959, p. 48.
[7] *Ibid.,* pp. 46–47.
[8] "The Environment of Business Decisions: Some Reflections on the History of Rolls-Royce," *The South African Journal of Economics,* December, 1949, pp. 457–479.

by some revision of its traditions is a matter of speculation, though quite possibly it could have. But in that year, the chassis division began losing money, and the search for ways of correcting the difficulty began:

> Comparisons with the cost breakdown of other vehicles revealed . . . that by far the most important factor was the size of the overhead which had to be spread over 1,000 cars. To achieve the target price of £950 and absorb the overhead meant a reduction in chassis manufacturing costs of about £300. By approximately quadrupling the quantity produced this figure could easily have been reached, but this idea could not be entertained. . . .
>
> The chassis division was obviously living on its name and a complete reorientation of policy was necessary. It was advocated by several people, but until the outbreak of war there was no sign of its evolution.[9]

Lloyd's conclusion was that in most discussions of decision making, "the importance of personality and tradition has been grossly underestimated and, because profit is the most visible index of industrial efficiency, the economist has assumed . . . far more logic and uniformity than is warranted except in the case of the simplest decisions."[10]

Confusion of ends and means may be also the result of the manager's desire for what is known as "psychic income"—that is, nonmonetary personal satisfactions, such as ego aggrandizement. To some men, for example, bigness is attractive for its own sake; others may derive their main psychic income from a large personal staff and an elaborate office; still others, from running a company with a reputation for high quality or scientific advances.

An extreme example of the confusion of ends and means—because, apparently, of an innate desire for show—is the case of General Cardigan as described by Cecil Woodham-Smith in *The Reason Why*, the story of the disastrous charge of the Light Brigade:

> He had visions of a regiment that was nothing less than perfection, of movements executed by men like automatons, more exactly, and above all more swiftly, than ever before. He was in love with speed, the thunder of a charge made him restless with pleasure, and it was observed that the excitement of the horses communicated itself to him, his eye too rolled, his nostrils too dilated. He had plans for new movements, galloping movements, charges from new angles not in the drill book. Mounted on splendid glossy chargers, with brilliant uniforms and dazzling accoutrements, his regiment was to form, reform, wheel, charge, halt, with the precision of a swooping hawk—at break-neck speed.
>
> Though the 15th was a notably efficient regiment, the new commanding officer viewed it with disgust. He demanded more glitter, more dash, and he set to work to drill, polish, pipeclay, reprimand, and discipline the 15th to within an inch of their lives.[11]

As the logical objective of a business is profit making, so the logical objec-

---

[9] *Ibid.*, p. 478.
[10] *Ibid.*, p. 478.
[11] McGraw-Hill Book Company, New York, 1954, p. 34.

tive of a regiment is to win battles. Perhaps speed and precision in cavalry movements were at that time an important factor in victory, but Cardigan carried these means to a ridiculous extent and in pursuit of this subsidiary aim made the real objective less likely of attainment. For example, he made life miserable for the only officers of the regiment who had had experience in actual warfare, those who had served in India. Because of the way in which the British Army was run at that time,[12] these men tended to have smaller private incomes than the others and so were unable to spend money on dashing horses and splendid accoutrements; hence Cardigan would have been glad to drive them out of his command.

A parallel to the Cardigan attitude might be that of some business bureaucrats who visualize a company entirely run by written policies and procedures, with practically every activity prescribed to the last detail.

Some clues to the personality factors that may affect decision making may be drawn from some of the various types described by psychologists. For example, Eduard Spranger has developed the following typology:[13]

1. The economic—interested in what is useful and practical.
2. The aesthetic—his highest values lie in harmony and individuality, pomp and power.
3. The theoretical—chiefly interested in the discovery of truth for its own sake, in diversity and rationality.
4. The social—loves people; other persons are ends; he is kind, sympathetic, and unselfish.
5. The political—interested primarily in power, wants personal power, influence, or renown.
6. The religious—his highest value is the greatest spiritual and absolutely satisfying experience; he is ascetic and looks for experience through self-denial and meditation.

As Spranger stresses, one very seldom encounters a "pure" example of any one of these types; almost all persons are mixtures of all of them in varying degrees. But the components that dominate will have an important effect on a man's decision making. Leaving aside type 6, since a man with a strong orientation of this kind would probably not go into business anyway, one might speculate on the types of decisions each is likely to make.

A man who is primarily interested in what is useful and practical (type 1) would probably be to a large extent interested in profits but would be inclined to the bird-in-hand viewpoint. Thus he might be unwilling to spend money on speculative research. Type 3, the theoretical, on the other hand, might be interested in basic research whether it was ever likely to prove practical or not. Either might, in some circumstances, turn out to be a successful decision maker.

The aesthetic type might be very useful in a company whose place in the

---

[12] An officer might, without being accused of cowardice, get a leave of absence on half pay when his regiment was to be sent on active duty. Those with small or nonexistent private incomes could not, of course, afford to do this.
[13] *Lebensformen* (Types of Men), Max Niemeyer, Halle a/d Saale, Germany, 1922.

sun depends on the quality of its products. But there are times when preoccupation with quality and with harmony in organization is a liability. If a man derives aesthetic satisfaction from pomp, as Lord Cardigan did, he is not likely to make a good chief executive for any organization—except, perhaps, a circus.

The social man, who is kind, sympathetic, and unselfish, will be a popular boss and occasionally a very successful executive who brings out the best in others. But again, his feeling for others may lead him to set standards that are too lax.

Where the political executive can advance his own power, influence, or renown only by advancing his company, he will be an effective decision maker. This is seldom the case, however, unless he is the chief. As a department head, he will be likely to be ruthless in advancing the status of his own department, whether or not the company as a whole will suffer.

For a profit-making organization, perhaps, the most nearly ideal executive would have about equal parts of the economic and theoretical orientations with a strong admixture of the social.

Another typology useful in classifying executives—although again there are very few pure types—is that developed by the psychologist Erich Fromm.[14] Fromm's ideal type is the "productive" man, the man who is chiefly interested in using his capacities to the full and is guided by reason in doing so. Everyone has, to some extent, a productive orientation. But to a greater or lesser extent, everyone is likely to be influenced by one or more of what Fromm describes as nonproductive orientations:

1. *The receptive orientation.* The "person feels the 'source of all good' to be outside, and he believes that the only way to get what he wants—be it something material, be it affection, love, knowledge, pleasure—is to receive it from . . . outside. . . . It is difficult for [such people] to say 'no,' and they are easily caught between conflicting loyalties and promises."

2. *The exploitative orientation.* "The exploitative type does not expect to receive things from others as gifts, but to take them away from others by force or cunning. . . . Such people will tend not to produce ideas but to steal them. . . . It is a striking fact that frequently people with great intelligence proceed in this way, although if they relied on their own gifts they might well be able to have ideas of their own. . . . Because they want to use and exploit people, they 'love' those who, explicitly or implicitly, are promising objects of exploitation, and get 'fed up' with persons whom they have squeezed out."

3. *The hoarding orientation.* "While the receptive and exploitative types are similar inasmuch as both expect to get things from the outside world, the hoarding orientation is essentially different . . . their security is based upon hoarding and saving, while spending is felt to be a threat."

4. *The marketing orientation.* "The character orientation which is rooted in

[14] *Man for Himself,* Holt, Rinehart and Winston, Inc., New York, 1947, pp. 62–117.

the experience of oneself as a commodity and of one's value as exchange value I call the marketing orientation. . . . Others are experienced as commodities like oneself; they . . . do not present *themselves* but their salable part. The difference between people is reduced to a merely quantitative difference of being *more or less* successful, attractive, hence valuable."

As a business executive, the receptive type is not likely to be one who thinks up new ideas, though he may well accept them if they are presented by others in the form of "completed staff work." In fact, he will probably be most pleased with those who do this for him and who not only give him an opportunity to say merely "yes' or "no" but also indicate fairly strongly which he should say. He may be pleasant to deal with, but he is unlikely to make a strong executive.

The exploitative type, on the other hand, though he may borrow all his ideas from others, will be confident, even aggressive, in pressing for new courses of action. He may be the man who prefers to advance by political maneuvering rather than by good work, and if he is clever, he may very well reach a high position. He will value a subordinate who can feed him ideas and allow him to claim credit for them.

The hoarding executive will be a tough man for subordinates to deal with, for he may want to keep all decisions in his own hands, and it will be difficult to justify new expenditures to him. His caution may be valuable under some circumstances, but it may also cause him to miss opportunities. He is likely to seem cold, or at least reserved, to those about him.

The marketing-oriented man is flexible, perhaps too flexible. If the marketing orientation is very strong, he may lack any principles or values of his own and be entirely opportunistic. He is quite willing to become an "organization man" if that is what is required of him.

An interesting psychological theory of what goes on in a decision maker's mind has been developed by an economist, the Professor Shackle whose definition of decision making was quoted on the first page of this chapter.[15] According to this theory, a man confronted with a decision is influenced by what, in his view, are the best possible and the worst possible outcomes of each course of action: "For why dwell upon a moderately good outcome when an excellent one is equally possible? And why stop to consider a moderately bad outcome when a disaster is equally possible?" A second factor is the "degree of surprise" attached to each outcome—that is, how probable the decision maker considers each. The attention directed at each will depend largely on how desirable the best possible outcome is and how probable it is.

This is undoubtedly a fairly good description of what goes on in the decision maker's mind, though some have questioned whether it is not quite possible for a man to contemplate more or less simultaneously the possible results in between the best and the worst as well as the two extremes. Moreover, since

---

[15] Shackle, *op. cit.*, pp. 94–95.

the values assigned to the factors will be subjective, the theory is not of much help in predicting decisions by either individuals or groups.

It is not surprising that the psychology of decision making is difficult to define, for it includes more than can be dealt with by experiment or self-examination. It encompasses the whole philosophical problem of free will versus determinism, a question that has never been answered to everyone's satisfaction.

If one knows a decision maker well, one may sometimes predict his decisions with a fair amount of accuracy, but even then there will be occasional surprises. The cautious man may suddenly take a chance; the very rational man may suddenly act irrationally. The best way to foresee an individual executive's decisions may, perhaps, be to become familiar with the picture of the business (or segment of it) he has in his mind (e.g., Rolls-Royce's high-quality and small-volume idea). But even these pictures are sometimes subject to complete revision under pressure of circumstances.

THE PROCESS OF DECISION MAKING

The decisions to be made in business organizations may be classified as (1) policy decisions, (2) administrative decisions, and (3) executive or ad hoc decisions.

Policy decisions start with the formation of the business. To begin with, there must be an idea or a series of ideas for making a profit—the idea that a new product of a given type will sell or that there is a possible market for an existing product that other companies are not tapping. Someone or some group must decide that a business based on the idea has a good chance of success. Then decisions must be made on company bylaws, on the selection of a board of directors, on the choice of key executives.

Next comes the whole process of building up the business, which involves such major decisions as the following:

The nature of the financial structure (equity or debt capital or both), the amount of working capital needed, accounting policies.

Volume of output, the facilities needed, including the degree of mechanization and automation.

Marketing policies—whether the product will be sold directly to consumers or through distributors, the amount of advertising to be done, prices.

The main outlines of the organization structure.

These policy decisions cannot, of course, be made once and for all. At a later date, the company may find it necessary to change its capital structure, its facilities, its marketing policies, its organization, or any of the other policies listed above.

Below this level there is another series of decisions that must be made, the administrative decisions. These are less important than the policy decisions but still may have a very far-reaching effect. If policy states, for example, that the company will produce a product of a given quality, an administrative decision must be made on the method of quality control that will be utilized. Again, policy decisions will probably be made on the size of the advertising budget, but administrative decisions will be needed for the selection of media and the general copy themes.

Finally, there are the executive decisions, which are made at the point where the work is carried out. Let us say that top management adopts a policy of paying wages equal to the median of the rates paid by comparable companies in the area and that its plan is to have rate ranges, rather than a single rate for each job. Administrative decisions will be required to determine when revisions in the entire rate structure are necessary because of changes in area rates. The executive decision, then, would be whether or not to grant a given employee a merit raise possible within the rate range for his job.

Policy lays down the principles covering the conduct of the business; administrative decisions translate the policies into general courses of action. But since both policies and administrative rulings are intended to be applicable in all cases, they are necessarily stated in somewhat general terms, and no general rule can prescribe the exact course of action in every case that comes up. Hence the need for day-to-day executive decisions. To illustrate:

The distribution of advertising expenditures between broadcasting and print media may be decided in advance, and so may the general themes to be stressed in the advertising copy. But it will not be possible to lay down a general rule to govern acceptance or rejection of each piece of copy. Rejection may be mandatory if a given piece of copy does not stress the required themes, but the mere fact that it does so will not mean that it will accomplish its purpose. An executive decision must be made on each piece of copy submitted.

Thus administrative decisions are made within the framework of policy, executive decisions within the framework of both policy and administrative rulings. But, as shown in Chapter 5, the policy makers, too, must operate within a framework, in their case laid down by state laws of incorporation, the condition of the money markets (which may partially dictate if or how new money is to be raised), and the practices imposed by the union if there is one.

Major policy decisions are often—though not always—put in writing and incorporated in a policy manual or issued in the form of presidential memoranda or letters. Administrative decisions may be available in the form of procedure manuals. Executive decisions are not recorded as such, although, of course, records are kept of most of them in various places. Personnel records will show, for example, when each employee received a raise.

Who makes the decisions?

Classical theory states that decisions should be assigned to the lowest competent level in the organization, which is an excellent rule as far as it goes. The closer a decision maker is to the scene of action, the quicker the decision can be made. And, of course, if too many decisions are passed up the line, higher executives will be overburdened and those in the lower echelons will have little opportunity to use initiative.

The problem is to determine the lowest competent level. Leaving aside the competence of the people who happen to be holding the various jobs (which, of course, will have a bearing), it may be said that the lowest competent level is the lowest level at which the jobholder has both access to all available information pertinent to the decision and the incentive to weigh the factors impartially.

Thus if a man is put in charge of both manufacturing and sales of a given product and is provided with the necessary staff, he may be said to have access to all the information he will need for allocating the funds allotted to him between manufacturing and marketing. And if he is judged, not on the volume of sales or the volume of output, but on the profit his division produces, he has a very strong incentive to allocate the funds in the best possible way. He is not, however, competent to judge how much of the money that the company has available for investment should be spent on his division instead of on other divisions. Only those at central headquarters have access to the knowledge necessary to make this decision. Nor is he likely to be impartial in judging between the needs of his own division and the claims of others. He is competent to make policy only for his own division.

In general, it might be said that only top management, at the company or division level, is competent to make true policy decisions, that administrative decisions can be made by department heads, and that managers, from first-line supervisors up, can make executive decisions.

But the rules regarding the locus of decision making cannot be exact because decisions made in one department or division may force courses of action on others. In actual company situations, also, the line between policy decisions and the other types is not always too clearly drawn. Where top management is anxious to keep close control in its own hands, it may develop "policies" that do much more than lay down a general framework of action and leave little leeway for decision making down the line.

Again, in many instances the locus of decision making may be determined by the extent to which the outcome will affect profits. Perhaps the unwritten theory here is that there is no way to ensure that the incumbent of each position down the line has the judgment to make wise decisions even when he knows all the facts and has the proper incentive. But if a decision will not affect profits very much one way or the other, he cannot do too much harm.

Thus a department head may be authorized to spend up to $500 on capital improvements without asking permission and a plant manager up to $2,000, the amounts increasing as one goes further up the line until the very large appropriations require the approval of the president and the board of directors.

The nature of the industry often has a bearing here. In a company producing one product or products sold in bulk, pricing decisions will generally be reserved for the very top level. In the oil industry, for example, a change of $\frac{1}{2}$ cent a gallon in the price of crude oil can have a tremendous impact on profits. Where there are many different products, mistakes in pricing may tend to cancel each other out and it may be possible to push price decisions further down the line, or at least to allow leeway within certain limits. A department store will probably have a general price policy. Depending on the type of customer it is trying to attract, top management will have decided that it wants a low-priced store, a medium-priced store, or a store that stresses quality at all costs, let prices go where they will. It may even specify a percentage markup over cost for all items. But within these limitations, the department heads determine prices since they select the merchandise and so establish the "costs" to which the markup will apply. They may also decide when it is useless to try to sell items at the regular markup and a reduction or special sale is necessary. Since so many different items are involved, no one mistake in pricing will affect profits too seriously.

Similarly, if a company has a great many products, a decision to change one of them in some way will not be likely to affect overall profits greatly. But in an automobile company, which usually derives most of its profit from the sale of cars, final approval of a new model requires a top management decision.

Rationality and irrationality

Both rational and irrational factors enter into the actual process of decision making, in business and in the rest of life. The extent to which business decisions are rational—that is, made with a view to reaching clearly defined goals and after due consideration of the alternatives and their consequences—depends on the situation and on the personalities of the decision makers. The extent to which even rational business decisions are made with a view to reaching company goals depends on the extent to which the company has been able to make the goals of the decision makers correspond with the organization goals.

In economics, the pattern of rational decision making is often defined as:

1. Making certain assumptions in the interest of simplification so as to make the decision manageable
2. Considering the consequences of various courses of action
3. Relaxing the assumptions

Thus an economist who wanted to determine the possible consequences of a given decision might start by assuming that there were only two firms competing for a market, then go on to consider what would happen if a third, a fourth, and so on, were added (relaxing the assumptions). Similarly, a company might first consider the effect various courses of action would have on its chief competitor, then relax the assumption that only this one competitor need be considered.

Quantifying factors

When mathematical decision theory is used, the factors bearing on a decision are quantified, but the situations in which this theory is useful are those in which the outcomes depend on events over which the decision maker has no control; therefore, the quantities used are merely estimates. There are other cases, however, in which a good many of the quantities used can be exact.

The factors can, perhaps, be most easily quantified in decisions on the purchase of new equipment, not to take care of increased demand but to save on labor costs. If a machine priced at $10,000 will reduce annual costs for the operation by $5,000, it will pay for itself in two years, and other things being equal, it will be a better choice than a machine with a payoff period of four years. Or if the costs of keeping an old machine in repair are higher than the depreciation on a new one, it will be cheaper to make the purchase.

However, there are many refinements that may be introduced into calcula-tions of this nature. For example, it is fairly common for companies to take the time value of money into account in making capital investments of this nature—that is, the return that could be expected if the money were put to other uses. Still other factors, such as improved product quality, are taken into account in what is known as the MAPI formula (MAPI from Machinery and Allied Products Institute, a trade association, which sponsored the formula).

Still, there are certain assumptions implicit in this type of reasoning that should perhaps be relaxed before the final decision is made. It is assumed, for example, that the market for the product will remain constant or grow. But if demand should shrink very far, the labor cost would shrink and the figures embodied in the calculations would change. Another assumption is that the company will not change its product enough to make it possible to eliminate the operation entirely. Still a third assumption is that the best new machine now on the market is the ultimate, at least for several years—that it will not be superseded by something else within a year or two, in which case it might be better to wait.

The decision maker must also weigh the cost of delay and the expense of gathering more information against the risk of proceeding with the facts he already has, which may well be incomplete.

Where possible, hedging is a wise procedure in decisions in which some of the facts are impossible to obtain or cannot be obtained without a large expenditure of time or money. The hedging decision is usually associated with the purchase of raw materials, especially cotton. Textile manufacturers natu-rally want to protect themselves against price fluctuations; they do not want to be holding cotton that loses value while it is in their possession. So they buy and sell cotton simultaneously over a number of months, and if in the end the price of one set of cotton bales has fallen, they may come out even or perhaps ahead because they have sold "futures" at a higher price and can deliver cotton bought at the lower price.

The practice of dollar averaging, sometimes advocated for stock market investment, is a form of hedging also. This practice calls for setting aside a given amount for the purchase of certain stocks each month, regardless of the current state of the market. In this way, an investor buys some shares of a given company at the top of the market, others at the low point, and still others at points in between. In the end, he hopes that what he loses—either in paper value or in actual money when he sells—through buying at the high points will be at least offset by the gains achieved through buying at the low points.

Most economic data are not, in fact, precise in the sense that they can be defined, measured, and accurately verified. At the level of the individual firm, this lack of precision can be illustrated by financial statements, which require an arbitrary cutoff point for determining the actual values of many items—for example, the expiration of fixed assets. A machine or a building may be fully depreciated on the books and have little resale value. Yet it may be serving a useful purpose.

There are also important differences of opinion over the definitions of such accounting concepts as profit and loss. One writer has shown that for

> . . . a group of companies over the eight-year period reviewed, the most restricted application of these [general accounting] principles with rela-tion to profits would have produced an aggregate net profit for all the companies combined of about $125 million, while the most liberal appli-cation would have produced an aggregate net profit of $275 million. It is noteworthy that none of these differences results from the difficulties of the measurement of values (which play such a role in accounting and are a major reason for inaccurate data); they arise exclusively from dif-ferences of opinion as to what constitutes a profit.[16]

Nonquantifiable factors

And, of course, there are some decisions in which the factors cannot be quanti-fied at all. It may not even be possible to judge at some later time whether the choices made were the best possible.

Executive X hired to head the marketing department may increase sales, but would executive Y, who was also a candidate, have done still better? He is now doing somewhat better with another company, but its situation is entirely different—so that proves nothing.

After the introduction of certain personnel policies, employees voted down a union; but would they have done so anyway? And if those policies call for paying higher rates than the union has been able to gain elsewhere, was the move worthwhile? ("Believe me," an executive from a very large company once told a meeting, "you can pay too high a price to keep the union out.")

One cannot evaluate such a decision on the basis of the wage rates alone, for there are many nonquantifiable factors to be considered: If the labor force is not unionized, management generally has greater flexibility in assigning work, in selecting men for layoff, in making promotions to first-line foreman —all of which can be worth money, even though no one can say exactly how much. On the other hand, the company may have simply postponed unioniza-tion and be confronted with labor troubles at a time when competitors whose

[16] Howard C. Greer, "What Are Accepted Principles of Accounting?" *Accounting Review*, March, 1938.

employees have been organized for a long time have arrived at a peaceful *modus vivendi* with the union.

All this leaves a wide area for "judgment" or "hunch," and the two may not differ so widely as is generally supposed.

A hunch may be defined as a sudden feeling that something is going to happen in a certain way—and that, therefore, a certain action is bound to lead to good or bad results. It may be completely irrational, or it may be very nearly a lightning reasoned judgment. Thus the head of a large greeting card company is said to be able to look at cards and tell immediately what will sell. One might say, perhaps, that filed in what, for want of a better term, may be called his "subconscious" is the equivalent of innumerable punched cards that indicate the comparative value of certain colors, shades, themes, and details of design, which are instantaneously checked and weighed against one another to produce an answer in the form of "yes" or "no."

Or a hunch decision may be accurate because the decision maker is actually a sort of one-man cross section of other people's interests and opinions. The news sense a good journalist is said to possess or a good marketing man's hunch of what will sell may be due to this factor.

A hunch decision may, however, be entirely inaccurate. It may be based on wishful thinking or on subconscious associations that have no relevance to the situation.

"Judgment" is difficult to define. The word implies a more reasoned and conscious weighing of the factors, but the reasoning—if a true decision is called for—can never produce a completely airtight conclusion. The case for one course rather than another can never be proved beyond a shadow of a doubt as a theorem in geometry can be.

Possibly, good judgment may be said to be a quality that is inborn but can be greatly improved through long experience. For example, some people have an ability (which is one of the factors sometimes tested on intelligence tests) to judge spatial relationships. This is of great value in driving a car since it enables them to visualize what will happen when they try to pass in a narrow space. But after long driving experience this "feel" for spatial relations, at least in a driving situation, is greatly increased. Further, these people know their own speeds of reaction and how long a car takes to respond when they need to stop or turn suddenly. Similarly, it may be said that some people have naturally good business judgment, but only after they have experienced many different business situations can it reach its full potential.

Most executives themselves do not know how they make decisions. When queried by *Fortune* magazine, company presidents said such things as:

"You don't know how you do it; you just do it."

"It is like asking a pro baseball player to define the swing that has always come natural to him."

"If a vice-president asks me how I was able to choose the right course, I have to say, 'I'm damned if I know.' "[17]

---

[17] John McDonald, "How Businessmen Make Decisions," *Fortune*, August, 1955, p. 85.

The preliminaries to decision making are easier to identify than the process itself. These include economic studies, marketing studies, and cost estimates—not conducted, in the case of top management decisions, by the decision maker himself. In general, too, top management will seek the advice of staff experts and department heads. In some cases, this amounts to allowing the experts to dictate the decision; in others, decisions are a matter of negotiation and compromise.

For example, a study made by this author of the factors that influence the decision to purchase a computer showed that while most companies provided for a check by top management, in some cases it was largely nominal. Top management tended, rather, to ask questions only if the installation did not turn out as promised. This was particularly true in cases where a company was buying its second or third computer.

In studies made at Carnegie-Mellon University, in fact, some evidence has been uncovered that the only real decisions top management is likely to make are the decisions to study various problems:

> By the time a company gets around to a formal study of a problem—whether it's the installation of a stock option plan, retirement benefits, or a computer system—the crucial decision has already unwittingly been made, and it's a pretty good bet the project will go through.[18]

Negotiation as a method of arriving at a decision may seem unlikely in view of the fact that the company president, particularly when he can be assured of the support of the board of directors, in theory has practically unlimited power over the organization, including the power to fire division and department heads. But most company presidents fear the power of passive resistance possessed by subordinates.

By and large, though, company profits and stability are the overriding factor in most business decisions. Most commonly, companies decided to computerize because their studies indicated that the amount they would save in salaries would more than equal the cost of the computer and its upkeep or because their paper work was increasing so fast that they would not be able to get enough people to do it without paying too much. In most large companies, capital appropriations require "justification" in written form, and the justification is practically always almost entirely in quantitative terms.

IMPROVING DECISION MAKING

Perhaps because of the rising interest in psychology among businessmen and the public at large, perhaps because decisions today hinge on many more factors and uncertainties than they did in the past, there has been increasing interest in decision making as a process. Some companies have even gone so

---

[18] "Light on Deciding: Carnegie Studies on Decision Making Come up with New Angles on How and Why Results Are Reached," *Business Week*, Apr. 13, 1957, p. 184.

far as to give their executives courses in it, in the hope that there will be less indecision and more correct decisions down the line.

But both indecision and mistaken decisions are likely to occur less because of lack of knowledge of the process itself than because of unfamiliarity with the subject matter or pressures imposed by superiors.

The man who knows little about a field cannot but feel insecure in taking a position on any aspect of it; therefore, he postpones his decisions as long as he can. Or if he plunges ahead in an effort to appear decisive, he is likely to make a bad mistake.

Company pressures operate in a variety of ways to create indecision. If a man does not know just how far he can take it on himself to make decisions and if at the same time he risks a great deal of blame by overstepping the indefinite bounds, he will make as few clear-cut decisions as possible. This was the situation at Westinghouse before its major reorganization in the 1930s, when subordinate managers had little authority. Their watchword was, "Let East Pittsburgh [headquarters] take care of it." Or if the general attitude at the top is that harmony is to be preserved at all costs, executives down the line will hesitate to make any decisions that will step on other people's toes, however lightly.

How pressure from the top may make for quick but poor decision making is indicated by the following extract from a letter by a middle management executive in a medium-sized company:

> Jack [the company president] left on his vacation the first of the month. Just before he left, he told each department head he wanted a complete budget for 1960 by the 15th, and this was to include an expense budget, a forecast of revenue, and a capital expenditure budget. Our people are keenly aware of Jack's displeasure when his requests are not met. Consequently, there will be a budget ready for him when he gets back. But what a budget! I know right now that many of the critical figures will have been picked right out of the air.

This company's projections, needless to say, have seldom been anywhere near the actual figures. It has, for example, forecast a profit of $1.5 million and found at the end of the year that its net was only $200,000.

Where any of these situations prevail, therefore, improvement in decision making can be fostered by:

1. Giving people more training in areas with which they are too unfamiliar to decide between conflicting views of experts
2. Changing the organization structure and giving people down the line both more authority and more clear-cut authority (Westinghouse solved its problem in this way)
3. Changing the attitude of top management, which is, of course, a feat that can usually be accomplished only by top management itself

Common fallacies

Decision making may also be improved by increased familiarity with the various types of fallacious reasoning that one often encounters in oneself or others. Some of the more important ones may be summarized as follows.

First of all, there is prejudice. It may be argued that "Company X's idea can't be any good because their president is a fuddy-duddy." Or branding a proposal as "theoretical" or "contrary to company policy" may be enough to range some people against it automatically. Similarly, the statement that "everybody is doing it; therefore we ought to" may sound convincing to some. Yet the logical course would be to examine Company X's idea on its own merits (it might be a good one regardless of the personality of the president); to ask whether the "theoretical" proposal would work in practice and if not, why not; to suggest that company policy could be changed if circumstances warrant; and to consider whether what everyone else is doing is necessarily good under the circumstances.

Sometimes a wisecrack will serve to turn attention from the real issues. Politicians, in both government and business, are well aware of this and will often attempt to dispose of an argument they cannot refute logically by a clever remark designed to stigmatize their opponent's point of view as beneath notice.

(On the other hand, of course, there are instances in which wisecracks and slogans are really logical arguments, and couching them in succinct form highlights the illogic of the opponent's position. The medieval reformer who coined the phrase, "When Adam delved and Eve span, who then was the gentleman?" succeeded in this to perfection. Obviously, if one believed the entire human race to be descended from Adam and Eve—and few, if any, would have denied it at the time—one could not simultaneously hold that gentlemen and peasants were two entirely different breeds.)

Analogy is an excellent way of illustrating and driving home a point, but it may also be used as a method of encouraging an unjustified conclusion. Thus a company may be compared to a football team to justify the idea that all criticism must be smothered: "You don't argue with the coach." Yet, while there are points of similarity between a team and a company—both are in a competitive situation—the points of difference are far more important, and the analogy is a false one.

Another device is to select one or a few instances and generalize from them to a whole universe. For example, one might cite the case of a company that had adopted practices unusual in the industry and succeeded thereby. Yet its success might be due almost entirely to the fact that other companies did not follow suit—e.g., with a price cut. When all cut prices, no one has any special advantage.

Still another means of keeping a case from being argued on its own merits is to create a diversion by bringing up points that have nothing to do with the subject at hand. Sometimes this takes the form of a counterattack quite irrelevant to the point at issue. An executive who wishes to squelch another executive's proposal may bring up some mistake the first man made in the past to throw discredit on his new idea.

Even figures can be made to lie. It is possible, for example, to "prove" that product X is more profitable than product Y by including more fixed costs in calculating the short-run cost of Y. In a somewhat similar vein, a justification for a change in components in one large company was based on a comparison of out-of-pocket costs in one case and costs plus a 20 per cent return in the other. The two costs were presented to the top management decision makers as though they were directly comparable.

Why do people use such devices in the attempt to get unsound proposals accepted? Sometimes, of course, they are not very logical thinkers; more often, it is because they have an ax to grind. A department head may be anxious to undertake a project because it will enable his own group to make a better showing at the expense of the company as a whole, or he may be covering up for past mistakes, with the willing assistance of his subordinates. An executive in one of the largest companies in the country explains this in terms of what he calls "circles of mutual support," generally consisting of an executive and his subordinates. What happens then is this:

The top man in the circle commits himself to a goal and to reaching it in a certain manner, and his superiors are told what he plans to do. Those on the lower levels do everything they can to prove that their immediate superior within the circle was right in making the commitment. If he was right, the venture is successful. But if he made a wrong decision on the "how," then the people in the circle still work to prove that the boss was right and to cover up the failure. Thus they may (1) deliberately state new data for top management in such a way that they are bound to be misinterpreted (e.g., by comparing incomparable costs), (2) use ambiguous language in reports, or (3) not transmit the information at all.

This executive cites an instance in which a development department reported "improved component life" in such a way that it appeared to be an advantage when it was, in fact, a negative factor since the components did not last as long as those produced by competitors. In other cases, the department reported improvements from new processes but neglected to mention that they also entailed new disadvantages.

The instances cited above, it should be noted, occurred in a company that is known for good management and highly respected for its research and development work.

How, then, can a decision maker guard against such practices? Perhaps the only way is to ask searching questions about every point mentioned in a report—and about the points that are ignored. Since this requires informing himself about many details—a job he does not have time for—he might possibly use a general staff man to follow up.

In the case of the original justification, the staff man might act as a devil's advocate, bringing out all the reasons why the proposal should not be accepted. In that way, the decision maker can at least be aware of the possible pitfalls as well as of the advantages in any course proposed to him. "A prince," Machiavelli wrote, "should be a great asker of questions." So should a business decision maker, but since he manages a far more complex organization than a sixteenth-century prince did, he may need to have someone suggest the questions to him.

A case example

How both rational and irrational factors may enter into decision making is illustrated by the story of a foreign car manufacturer's experiences in the American market.

The initiative for the move into the American market came from the company's chief export executive, who knew the United States well. Marketing studies—and his own knowledge of the country and of U.S. business conditions—had convinced him that the company could sell a limited but profitable number of cars here provided it could:

1.   Produce a first-class new model car that would emphasize what seemed to be missing in American cars—economy of gas consumption and maneuverability through small size.
2.   Obtain first-class dealers for sales and repairs.
3.   Impress upon the public the idea that the car combined high style and low cost.

His ideas met with considerable opposition both on his own level and at the top. Factory management did not want to produce a separate model for the American market since this would add to its production costs, even though it would also enable it to use excess capacity and so reduce its overhead. It also feared labor troubles if it expanded its work force and then was forced to reduce it again because the American effort was not a success.

Top management studied the experience of its major European competitors in grappling with the American market and found that few of them were successful and many were unsuccessful. It also studied its own showing in competition with American companies abroad, which did not prove much since a low-priced car has greater appeal to the less affluent consumers abroad than to the more prosperous Americans. Then top officials visited the United States to study the matter further and were overwhelmed by the multiplicity of problems and factors involved.

Then J.B., the export manager, played his last card. He threatened to quit, join a competitor, and take it into the U.S. market. The company could not afford to lose him; so top management gave him the go-ahead.

After a few battles with factory management, J.B. got the car he wanted. He personally interviewed dealers and obtained an outstanding group. He directed the efforts of the advertising agency, personally planning the promotion.

His operation was a great success; under his direction, sales doubled every year. In the expectation of continually rising sales, top management began considering a new automated plant.

J.B., however, knew that a large part of the success was the result of his personal management and was doubtful whether he could continue to give all phases of the operation so much personal attention if it became much larger. Hence he initiated a well-planned study of a representative sample of buyers to find out what their incomes and occupations were (an indication of the size of the potential market), why they had bought the car, what they liked about it, what improvements they could suggest, and so on. But before results of the study became known, he died of a heart attack, and his assistant, mainly because he was near at hand and could speak English, was chosen as his successor. This man had few qualifications for directing a marketing operation because his experience had been largely in production.

In the meantime, results of the survey disclosed that at least part of the sales had been due to unsatisfied demand for the products of the company's chief competitor, which was finding it difficult to produce and ship as many cars as the market could absorb. Also, some of the former members of top management had been replaced by men who lacked intensive experience in the automotive industry. They were, it is true, worried about whether the U.S. market would hold out. But, on the other hand, they felt that they had to expand total output in order to operate on a more economic scale and to remain competitive with other European producers, especially in view of the coming European Common Market. For these reasons, they had almost committed themselves to the idea that a new automated factory was necessary. But first they authorized another study by an independent consultant to ascertain the ten-year prospects in the United States.

Each of the different decision makers had a personal interest in the results of the study—and these interests differed somewhat. The chief executive wanted a genuinely independent and professional appraisal of the prospects, but he hoped for a favorable forecast. He had been talking up the American market after J.B.'s death and believed expansion there would help to build his reputation and strengthen his ultimate claim to the presidency. Factory management wanted to expand its own empire but not at the risk of sizable fluctuations. Domestic sales management, on the other hand, wanted the forecast to prove unfavorable; it feared that the interest of top management, and with it much of the money for promotion, might shift to the U.S. market if a large potential were shown.

The new general manager of the U.S. subsidiary had mixed feelings. If a rapidly increasing market were predicted, he would be able to expand his budget and his personal power. If the forecast were unfavorable, he would look good if he did better than expected and would have an excuse if he did not increase sales. His subordinates differed among themselves. Some wanted a prediction of fast expansion; others were conscious of the difficulties it would entail in the way of getting more dealers, supplying spare parts, and so on.

The independent investigator's report began by cautioning, through a *reductio ad absurdum,* against the idea that the future could be directly extrapolated from the past. If the company continued to double sales each year as it had during the last few years, it would capture the entire U.S. car market in a little over six years. Then the report dealt with the total U.S. market for foreign cars at the end of ten years. This was judged on the basis of current surveys and informed opinion, which was surprisingly unanimous. Last, the report discussed the share of the foreign car market the company would have to take to sell the 100,000 cars it was planning to dispose of in the United States.

To reach its goal, even with a much larger share of the market, the company would need a much larger foreign car market in the United States. But if foreign car sales took so large a share of the total market, sales of the Big Three U.S. automobile manufacturers would be reduced significantly and they would probably enter the small-car field.

The more optimistic among the top management men were dissatisfied with these findings, which dashed their hopes of large expansion. So they decided to send "their own man" to check the results. In a short time, though he could not speak English and knew nothing about the United States and its automobile market, the new investigator produced the results his superiors wanted. Sales, he reported, would double and double again; the company could certainly sell 100,000 cars and quite possibly more than that.

All those at the home office who had wished for such a report seized on it with delight. Dissent was smothered by transferring or firing those who disagreed. The new factory was built, money was poured into it, and thousands were added to the payroll. In the United States, hundreds of new dealers were engaged (most of them dealers who also sold other makes and were out to make a quick dollar), inadequate spare parts stores and repair facilities were set up, and an expensive advertising campaign was launched.

For a time, though the company's share of the market did not rise, the total foreign car market did increase, and sales continued to climb. Then the inevitable happened—the Big Three in the United States began producing compact cars to counter foreign competition. Dealers quit, inventories began to pile up, and the factory in Europe was partially shut down and had to lay off workers, who then stormed the offices asking for redress. Finally, the company's car sales dropped to less than 20 per cent of the optimistic forecast. The U.S. manager was sent to Australia, and the company sent men from abroad to take over.

SUMMARY

The simplest theory of business decision making is that the decision makers try to maximize profits and that they consider all courses of action open to them in attempting to do so. This is the theory held by traditional economists, and although it may be partially true—in that business decision makers do generally have the effect on profits in mind—they may not always attempt to maximize them.

Mathematical decision theory is not designed to show how decisions are actually made but rather to help the decision maker who is interested in maximizing profits in a given situation to lay out the alternatives in such a way that he sees the risks and the consequences more clearly.

Psychological theories, on the other hand, are designed to identify what actually goes on in the decision maker's mind when he makes a decision. One of the best known of these theories is Herbert A. Simon's theory that the decision maker attempts to "satisfice" rather than maximize—that is, to find an answer that is good enough—and that the consequences he considers good enough will depend on what has been achieved in the past.

It has also been pointed out that tradition may have a very important influence on decision making, sometimes to the detriment of profits, and that the decision maker's own personality is a very important factor.

Business decisions may be classified in three categories: policy decisions, administrative decisions, and ad hoc, or executive, decisions. Policy decisions set forth goals and general courses of action; administrative decisions determine the means to be used; and executive decisions are those made on a day-to-day basis as particular cases come up. Often the decisions an executive at any given level may make are expressed in monetary terms: he is allowed to spend a stated amount of money without seeking approval from his superiors. Very large expenditures usually require the approval of the board of directors.

In recent years, companies have become very much interested in the whole process of decision making among their executives. Often they have attempted to improve decisions by giving courses in decision making itself. But sometimes executives are indecisive or unable to make good decisions simply because they do not know enough about their own fields. In other cases, companies do not give them enough clear-cut authority, a difficulty that can be corrected by changing the organization structure.

A man may improve his own decision making by guarding against some of the illogical reasons that may be advanced for favoring or disapproving certain courses of action. Where he must depend largely on data supplied to him by others, he should learn enough about the field to ask the right questions or he can employ someone to suggest the right questions to him.

Review Questions

1. Why does a true decision always involve some uncertainty about the outcome?
2. What is marginal theory? Can you suggest a case, other than those mentioned in the text, in which it might be used to advantage?
3. Would you say that a decision to purchase a computer is a policy decision, an administrative decision, or an ad hoc decision?

4. What did Herbert A. Simon mean by "satisficing"? If you were president of a company, would you approve of this type of decision making?
5. In mathematical decision theory, what is meant by an "event"? By an "act"?
6. Do you believe that mathematical decision theory is a good way of arriving at a decision? Why or why not?
7. Do you think that the "types" or "orientations" suggested by Spranger and Fromm are valid ways of classifying people? If not, why not?
8. Give an example of a false analogy, other than the one given in the text.
9. What is meant by "relaxing the assumptions" in decision making? Suppose you were offered two jobs, what assumptions might you make in deciding between them? Then how would you relax the assumptions?

Case Study / A Discussion by the Board of Managers*

Elto, Ltd., in the Netherlands, which manufactures electronic products and sells them at home and abroad, is directing more and more attention to export. Two major customers, one in the Netherlands and the other in France, take 15 per cent and 20 per cent, respectively, of the output.

The company manufactures more than 2,000 different items for stock or to order. Suppliers of raw materials are constantly asking for longer terms of delivery, and at present the stock of most finished products is small. Current orders will take about eight months' production.

The company employs about 3,000 people but has difficulty getting enough skilled labor. Space is not a problem, however, since the factory was considerably enlarged a short time ago.

The top management of the company consists of a president, a sales manager, a production manager, and a controller, who together form a board of managers that meets once a week on Mondays. There is a small research and development department under the production manager, who also does most of the purchasing. The sales manager is in charge of the transportation of the finished product and of the stores.

The president was sales manager before taking over the presidency, and he still takes a special interest in sales (rather too much interest, in the view of the heads of other departments). He has succeeded in considerably improving the spirit prevailing among the managers, which was formerly not good. Among the means he has used to achieve this have been job descriptions for members of management and twenty other principal executives. Introduction of these descriptions has eliminated the confusion about responsibility and authority that was formerly an impediment to cooperation.

Elto, Ltd., is very profitable, but its capitalization leaves much to be desired. It has loans from large shareholders outstanding and bank credit. But the

* By H. Reinoud, director general, Netherlands P.T.T.

bank has already objected to extension of the credit, yielding only reluctantly to Elto's wishes, and has recommended the sale of equities. The large shareholders refuse to consent to this, in part for sentimental reasons.

On Wednesday evening, the sales manager returns from Switzerland with a proposal from one of the company's smaller customers, Makro. Makro is a fairly large wholesaler, but until now it has made most of its purchases in Switzerland rather than from Elto.

Now Makro's Swiss suppliers have formed a cartel, and as a result it must purchase on much less favorable terms than formerly. Moreover, the general manager of Makro knows that some of the companies in the cartel are strongly in favor of eliminating wholesalers altogether. He fears they may squeeze him still further later if he becomes dependent on them.

The manager of Makro has, therefore, proposed that he purchase largely from Elto. He has drafted detailed specifications of the things he will require, including the yearly quantities. In effect, he proposes to take about 25 per cent of Elto's annual output.

However, the Makro manager has some demands. The quality of the items supplied by Elto must be better than heretofore. Its products are often insufficiently finished, they show too much variation, and some items are too easily broken. Further, a fourth part of the order must be delivered as soon as possible, after three months at the latest; after that, a twelfth part of the annual order must be delivered each month. Invoices will be paid four months after they have been received, although Makro will try to reduce the delay over the next few years.

For the time being, the Makro manager is not in favor of a long-term contract, but he is prepared in due course to consider sale of his shares, or some of them, to Elto.

Since he is being pushed by the Swiss suppliers to sign new contracts, the Makro manager wants Elto to decide as soon as possible on his proposals, within three weeks at the latest. He states that he has had some discussions on the subject with other suppliers, including an important Elto competitor, but that he has made his concrete proposals to Elto first.

The sales manager of Elto is very much in favor of accepting the Makro proposal. Makro is a reliable firm with which his company has had long and happy relations. He has told the Makro manager that he will return to his own plant and give him a provisional answer within a week.

Back home, the Elto sales manager is about to inform the president of the proposal when the production manager rings him up about something else; so the sales manager reports on the Makro discussions. The production manager says immediately that it's impossible to accept the contract. There is a shortage of foremen and of all-round skilled employees. Further, his people are becoming very irritated with sales' complaints about quality. Then he's having trouble getting supplies, and just yesterday the controller had serious objections to granting the advances the suppliers were asking. In addition, the president has asked him to pay more attention to research, but he has no time for it. He ends by saying: "We have a good many regular customers on whom we can rely. Let's try to find a way to attend to them properly before we do anything else."

After this not very exhilarating conversation, the sales manager rings up the president. He is still feeling enthusiastic because he knows that the president is very much interested in sales, but he is irritated because of the production manager's remarks. He makes a short report on the proposal and on the production manager's reaction to it. He asks the president: "Hadn't you better come to Switzerland with me next week?"

The president finds it hard not to say "yes" immediately, but the remarks of the production manager, who is doing a good job, worry him a bit. So he compliments the sales manager on the proposal and says he will call a special meeting of the board of managers for the following morning.

The views of the sales manager and the production manager have already been stated.

1. What attitude do you think the other members of the board will take?
2. How should the president finally decide on the proposal?

Selected Readings

Design for Decision, Irwin D. J. Bross, The Macmillan Company, New York, 1953. A discussion of the nature and history of decision making. Explains the concepts of prediction, probability, and values and outlines rules for action. The second half of the book deals with more specialized aspects of decision, such as sequential decisions and decision-making models and systems.

The New Science of Management Decision, Herbert A. Simon, Harper & Row, Publishers, Incorporated, New York, 1960. A comparison of traditional decision-making methods with those possible with computers. The author believes that electronic devices will eventually be able to take over some of the current nonprogrammed (i.e., nonroutine) decisions that now require a human decision maker and that the manager's job will change in consequence.

The Rational Manager: A Systematic Approach to Problem Solving and Decision Making, Charles H. Kepner and Benjamin B. Tregoe, McGraw-Hill Book Company, New York, 1965. A "how-to-do-it" book on the use of available information in decision making. Includes a number of examples showing the application of the techniques described.

"Business Men on Business Decisions," *The Nature of Economic Thought*, G. L. S. Shackle, Cambridge University Press, New York, 1966, pp. 144–159. Results of a survey covering the objectives sought and the criteria used in business decisions.

Decision Making, R. J. Audley, R. B. Braithwaite, Robert Cassen, J. Johnston, Leonard Joy, Anatol Rapoport, Peter Self, and J. W. N. Watkins, The British Broadcasting Corporation, London, 1967. Essays on various facets of decision making by experts in various fields.

4

Management of Foreign Operations

Large companies are increasingly international in scope, and even some comparatively small companies not only sell but produce abroad. And the trends are such that worldwide markets and economic conditions abroad are likely to be of even greater interest to managers in the future. This section is designed to provide the student with some background knowledge of conditions and management problems abroad. First, Chapter 24 deals with the "developed" or industrialized countries of Western Europe, specifically with three of the most important: England, France, and Germany. Then Chapter 25 discusses conditions in the underdeveloped countries. Most of these are struggling for real industrialization and a standard of living comparable to that of Western Europe; hence they may be characterized as "developing." The problems confronting the manager in an industrialized country differ widely from those he faces in an underdeveloped or developing country. In the former, his main problems are likely to be competition and costs. In the latter, he faces additional difficulties: heavy government restrictions, lack of an economic infrastructure (transportation facilities, power supplies, and so on), a shortage of skilled labor, and obstacles imposed by traditions inappropriate in an industrialized economy. Yet the developing countries present a broad new frontier for industry. Many of them have important natural resources and enormous populations that represent potential markets for all types of products. Chapter 26, Managing Abroad, discusses the ways in which companies expand into new countries and the forms of organization they adopt for the management of their international operations, also company practices in the selection of personnel for foreign operations.

24

MANAGEMENT

IN

DEVELOPED

COUNTRIES

*There is not a nation, even among the most
civilized, that has not some fault peculiar
to itself which other nations blame by way of
boast or as a warning.*
Balthasar Gracian: *The Art of Worldly Wisdom*

24 Only comparatively few of the countries of the world can be characterized as "developed"—that is, as possessing any great degree of mass production—and most of these are in Western Europe, where the Industrial Revolution began as early as the eighteenth century.

The extent to which a country can develop by mechanizing its production processes does not depend only on the ability of its citizens to invent or apply machines. The size of the market open to the potential entrepreneur also has a bearing, for a large investment in machines must be spread over a great many units if mechanization is to be profitable. For example, the Ford Motor Company found it unprofitable to produce the Edsel because sales were under 200,000 units.

The United States has been fortunate in this respect because it has a very large domestic market; thus there are few cases in which tariff barriers imposed by other countries will limit its markets to the point where large investments in machinery become unprofitable. (It was the failure of the Edsel in the domestic market that led to its demise.)

Through most of Europe's history, on the other hand, the market was cut up by tariffs and differing types of regulation into a number of comparatively small markets. Thus it was difficult for European companies to obtain the advantages of scale enjoyed by American companies. In 1957, however, an attempt to rectify this situation began with the creation of the European Common Market, made up of France, Germany, Holland, Belgium, Luxembourg, and Italy.

The barriers between countries could not, of course, be reduced all at once, nor did the promoters of the Common Market expect that they would be. Plans were made for gradual reductions, and by the middle of 1967 duties charged by the six ECM countries on goods circulating within the Common Market were down to a fifth of what they had been, and by mid-1968 they were reduced to zero. In the ten-year period between 1957 and 1967, total production in the Common Market rose by more than 50 per cent, as against a 45 per cent increase in the United States and a 30 per cent increase in Great Britain in the same period.

Since the Common Market plans visualized not only the elimination of tariff barriers between Common Market countries but a tariff wall around them, the development has spurred U.S. investment in the six countries in the community. Thus, instead of serving the European market primarily by export of products manufactured in the United States, U.S. companies have opened a great many plants abroad.

This is true to such an extent that some Europeans have become fearful that U.S.-owned companies or their European subsidiaries will come to dominate European industry. A book published in 1967 that expressed this fear was very widely read. The author predicted that "in 15 years the third industrial power of the world after the United States and the Soviet Union may well be not [Western] Europe but American industry in Europe. Already today, in the ninth year of the Common Market, the organization of this European market is essentially American."[1]

But despite the sharp increase in U.S. investment in Western Europe (from $5 billion in 1960 to nearly $20 billion in 1967), that investment amounts to only 5 per cent of total West European investment. Only in certain industries do U.S. companies dominate—for example, they have 80 per cent of the computer market and 50 per cent of the semiconductor market.

To gauge the competitive strength of European companies, it is necessary to know something of the history of development in Western Europe. The three largest countries in Western Europe (largest in terms of population, that is) are Great Britain, France, and Germany. Great Britain, of course, is not included in the Common Market, but probably it will be eventually.

There are important similarities among the Big Three. The populations are about the same size. The people are characterized by industry, intelligence, and a long tradition of religion, culture, and learning. All three countries have important natural resources. Basically all three got a start through the development of coal and iron and steel, though France has been less well endowed in this respect than the other two countries. All have excellent internal (road and rail) and external transportation systems (merchant marine and air service). Their climates are changeable and stimulating for work.

But underlying the similarities are major differences. France has more than twice the area of West Germany or England, which have about the same amount of territory. England relies least on her agriculture and needs a large volume of exports to import her food and raw material requirements. Germany's imports are almost as large as those of Britain, while France is the most nearly self-sufficient. And ways of doing business are different in the three countries.

ENGLAND: A CASE OF ARRESTED DEVELOPMENT

As the first country to experience the Industrial Revolution, England became the workshop of the world in the nineteenth century. Because she could supply manufacturing capacity lacking elsewhere, she was able to support a population far beyond what her arable land could maintain. Other peoples, in effect, paid the British for their skill and the use of their equipment and enabled them to purchase the extra food needed.

By 1850, Britain was far ahead of other European nations in industrial production. She held this superiority for another seventy years until the United States overtook her around 1920. But even earlier, there was a good deal of catching up, not only by the United States but by other European nations, notably Germany.

[1] Jean-Jacques Servan-Schreiber, Éditions du Seuil, Paris, 1967, published in the United States as *The American Challenge*, Atheneum, Publishers, New York, 1968.

There were many reasons why Britain could not maintain her long lead. In some ways, the countries that started later had an advantage: their new plants could incorporate the latest technology. And once they could do their own manufacturing, other countries imported less. Thus the British export income —so important in a country that cannot feed its population from its own agriculture—could not be maintained at the requisite levels. The drain of two world wars also had an important bearing.

Nevertheless, some part of Britain's loss of position must be laid at the door of her managers. They continued to place emphasis on coal and iron and steel, the products that had made them great and wealthy, and were slow to adjust to the up-and-coming industries, such as machinery, artificial silk, chemicals, cars, and electrical goods. Of the last named, for example, Britain's share of world output in 1912 was less than half that of either the United States or Germany, and her automobile production was only 5 per cent that of the United States.[2]

The failure to innovate was in direct contrast to the behavior of British managers during the early days of the Industrial Revolution, when Dr. Johnson described the age as "running mad after innovation; all the business of the world is to be done in a new way."

In the early days, the great staple industries were highly competitive because a large number of small units existed in each. But later on, specialized branches of the basic industries tended to be concentrated in a few hands.

In the beginning, too, companies were founded and managed by those who were "outsiders" as far as the ruling class was concerned. Many of them were Nonconformists in religion; that is, they were not members of the Church of England and for that reason were barred from many posts. But after they acquired large fortunes that rivaled those of the landed aristocrats, they won recognition and began to intermarry with the aristocrats. Then the new industrial aristocrats imitated the customs of the landowners. They adopted their manners (at least in the second and third generations). And among them succession was often by kinship and personal friendship or depended on attendance at a first-class public school[3] or one of the two older universities, Oxford and Cambridge.

> Those with a public school education and business connections had a much better chance of getting to the top . . . while some men have managed to get to the top without special advantages, the odds were heavily against them.[4]

Cartels, associations of companies in the same industry that reduced competition, were quite common, and their restrictive practices made it easy for

---

[2] J. H. Dunning and C. J. Thomas, *British Industry: Change and Development in the Twentieth Century*, Hutchinson & Co. (Publishers), Ltd., London, 1961, p. 16.
[3] In England, a "public school" is actually a private endowed school, equivalent to such schools as Groton and Exeter in this country. There are many such public schools, but only a few really "rate."
[4] Roy Lewis and Rosemary Stewart, *The Boss*, Phoenix House, London, 1958, pp. 95, 99; quoting Dr. G. H. Copeman, *Leaders of British Industry*, Gee & Company, London, 1955.

inefficient firms to stay alive—in the case of family firms, for successors who lacked the ability and interest of their grandfathers and great-grandfathers to continue in control. Many of them did not want to work too long or too hard. They took long weekends, worked short hours, and did not trouble themselves with fresh ideas.

This is not to say that there are no good British managers. The best of them are as good as or better than the best the United States has produced. Many are superbly well informed, far more so than all but a very few American managers. And even as a group the managers display many virtues. They are persistent, and many have a marvelous instinct for successful trading. Another common trait is the ability to compromise when compromise is the better part of valor.

But some of the dynamism that made Britain the world's workshop went out of British management in the twentieth century. Britain could not hope to maintain its dominant position as other countries caught up, but its rate of advance has been much slower than that of France and Germany.

Some of the factors that have tended to discourage initiative have been eliminated in recent years. Laws have been passed against the restrictive practices made possible by monopoly and cartelization. More scholarships have been provided to make it possible for the sons of working-class parents to attend universities and even the top public schools. Thus the hold of "the Establishment," as the ruling groups are called, has been considerably shaken.

Yet results are not at all what might be expected. "What we are up against," says a British publication, "is a peculiar form of English sickness that shows itself in a blank refusal to exploit new developments and which does not appear responsive to the normal financial incentives."[5] The publication goes on to cite a number of inventions that were pioneered in Britain but developed commercially in other countries. Among these were integrated microcircuits for electronic wiring, blind landing for civil aircraft, pivoting-wing aircraft, and computer-controlled machine tools.

FRANCE: THE NEW INDUSTRIAL REVOLUTION

France was one of the pioneers of the Industrial Revolution, but by and large, starting around the middle of the last century, the élan, or drive, seemed to go out of most of French industry. True, it was still expanding and still had outstanding managers in many cases, but its growth was less than that of its principal competitors, especially Britain.

Large sections of the French economy were not industrialized and remained without mass production for a long time. Even in 1955, one-third of the French work force was agricultural, whereas the percentage in Germany was 23, in Holland 20, and in England 5.[6]

[5] The Economist, Mar. 19, 1966, p. 1147.
[6] Robert Marjolin, "Les Chances de la France dans l'Europe de demain," Paris-Presse, July 27, 1955.

Actually, a great part of France's so-called business remained pre-capitalist; that is, the enterprises were no larger than those that existed before the Industrial Revolution. With the obvious exception of "natural" large units in transportation, power, coal, steel, banks, autos, and metallurgy, the typical enterprise was small enough for the owning family to manage and finance it without outside help.

Maximization of profits was not the chief aim, which was, rather, high profit per unit and a small turnover. Emphasis was on quality, good service, and individualism: an enterprise "petit" (small), "boutique" (shoplike), and "parfait" (perfect). The small French enterpriser did not want to work too hard. He wanted to earn enough to live comfortably and avoid risk by saving his money rather than investing it in expansion. Competitors lived and let live; a few big companies coexisted with a lot of small ones. The spirit of the old guild system survived.

In big industry, cartels assured the managers of their markets. Those who tried to break from the system might find themselves unable to raise new capital when they needed it because the financial institutions had no desire to see changes. The few who survived either displayed enough competence to make themselves secure from retaliation or operated in fields in which the "guild" system had no influence.

But after World War II, a "great renewal," in General de Gaulle's phrase, began. Industrial production more than doubled in the 1950s. Exports went up 63 per cent between 1951 and 1960 while those of Britain rose only 18 per cent, an indication that France was able to compete successfully on the international market.

How was France able to effect a sudden transformation of its economy? Marshall Plan aid just after the war helped in the speedy renewal and modernization of capital equipment, and the numerous productivity teams sent out from the United States publicized American methods. Another influence was a sudden spurt in the population, which had remained stationary for decades. This provided a larger demand for goods.

Still another factor, and an important one, was the development of the European Common Market. The knowledge that they would be exposed to strong foreign competition within a given number of years and realization of the great new opportunities gave French managers a strong push.

Impetus was also provided by the government, through "Le Plan" conceived by Jean Monnet, who was also the author of the Common Market idea. This is nothing more than planning on a national scale by coordination of the plans of individual managements. It is designed to prevent uneconomic and unprofitable expansions and ensure that the resources of the country are used in the best possible way.

The government staff for Le Plan consists of a relatively few people: perhaps a hundred engineers, "inspecteurs de finance," agronomists, and others who provide technical help and estimates. Help is provided also by representatives of companies, employers' associations, unions, other government departments, and consumers.

The goal is the maximum economic growth possible with price stability, full employment, and balanced foreign payments. Then assumptions are formulated about the required consumer expenditures, investment, and foreign trade. From these figures an economic table of input-output estimates is drawn up. The table divides the economy into a number of principal sectors and attempts to show what each sector will purchase from every other sector (automobile companies from the steel industry, for example).

Various commissions then work out the details of Le Plan, and the part each major industry will play is decided through discussion and negotiation. With goals agreed upon and markets pinpointed, there is less likelihood that several companies will plan to take over the same markets—in which case, all or most would lose.

No company is compelled to observe the plan, but the government has various practical means of fostering compliance, such as special credit arrangements and tax credits for equipment renewals. Moreover, since the industrialists themselves have a hand in shaping the plans, they are inclined to try to make them work.

GERMANY: THOROUGHNESS AND DILIGENCE

German industry got its real start through the introduction of its own common market in the nineteenth century. In the early part of that period, Germany was not a nation but a collection of small states, each of which tended to put up tariff barriers against the others. It was only as these came down that real industrial development was possible.

It was the great German economist Friedrich List (1789–1846) who pointed out the wastefulness of this situation. The small states, he said, did not provide large enough markets for very large-scale industry; hence a *Zollverein*, or customs union, was necessary. And taking the United States as an example, he advocated not only a wider free trade area, but tariff walls to protect the infant industries inside it. New firms, he said, might find it difficult to compete with established firms in other countries, especially British firms, which had already attained a scale of production that would enable them to drive rivals out of business if they were allowed to compete on equal terms. Since the princes who headed the German states were interested in economic progress, several customs unions were formed, and gradually the separate groups amalgamated.

Visitors were soon impressed with the rapid progress of industrialization. Many capable managers and innovators got their start in the 1830s and 1840s, and some of their descendants are still prominent in German industry today—for example, the Krupps (iron and steel) and the Stinnes (coal). Rail and road transport and banking also developed rapidly. The result was that Germany, which had been overpopulated in relation to the means of production, had a shortage of workers within a few decades and had to draw on outside labor.

Then in 1870 the German states were unified under the leadership of Prussia, and by the turn of the century Germany began to rival England for first place as a producer of iron and steel, had overtaken her in the development of electrical equipment and chemicals, and was also making great strides in overseas trade.

By the outbreak of World War I, Germany was one of the world's leading industrial nations. The general characteristics of German managers at that time may be summed up somewhat as follows:

Strict authoritarianism   The large majority of managers felt strongly that they and they alone should run their enterprises. They might be benevolent dictators who looked after their workers if they were ill and provided retirement income, homes, and recreation. But they were unalterably opposed to labor unions, which they regarded as intruders between themselves and "their own people." And they were often boastful and heavy-handed in exercising their authority.

Diligence   The managers were imbued with the idea of the importance of their task (*Beruf*, or calling). So they worked as hard as possible to prove the seriousness of their intent and to demonstrate that they were doing their duty (*Pflicht getan*) even in the face of great obstacles. Their frugality and their endeavors to save and invest were almost psychotic. In part, this attitude sprang from the old Prussian tradition which held that "one should starve oneself rich."

Thoroughness   Thoroughness was thought to be acquired, first, by training in regular schools and then in the apprentice schools where those who did not go on to higher academic work spent several years learning a trade. Even if a young man finished high school or acquired a university education, he had to learn his business from the ground up in order to become thoroughly familiar with the technology of whatever product he might later manage.

Cartels were prominent in German industry, and they went beyond informal associations. A separate selling company (a syndicate) would be set up to determine the most profitable feasible level of production and allocate shares of the market among the members. If demand fell, the production quotas were reduced to prevent a price decline.

Some of the cartels developed elaborate systems of transfer pricing. There might be an "accounting price" that the syndicate would pay for coal bought from its members and a higher selling price for ordinary consumers. Members profited both because the accounting price was higher than their costs and because they shared in the gains of the syndicate.

The runaway prices after World War I led to the Cartel Decree of 1923, which gave the Reich Minister of Economic Affairs power to bring cartels to account if their actions endangered the public interest. To counter this opposition, the leading cartel managers undertook to explain their actions by what they called "rationalization." They argued that rationing supply to meet demand prevented "destructive pricing practices." In coal mining, for example, it was said that the labor force had been cut by one-third between 1922 and 1926 and the administrative forces by one-fifth, while output rose more than 25 per cent and the wages of those still employed went up substantially.

The law proved ineffective. In 1930, it was felt that the German economy could be improved only by reducing costs and prices and so increasing exports. Consequently the government decreed a 10 per cent decrease in both prices and wages. But because of resistance by the cartels, the price reduction part of this policy never became really effective. Only one cartel was dissolved, and the government never used its power to reduce tariffs in the interest of making the cartels more competitive in the home market.

Then under the Hitler regime, the power of the cartels was increased still further. Only in the post-World War II period was a real effort made to curtail cartelization. Written price-fixing agreements are no longer legal, and contracts providing for the division of markets are not enforceable, although "according to one . . . expert on cartels and trade associations, markets may still be legally divided so long as this is not done by legally enforceable contracts."[7]

If this is true, cartelization may still persist to a considerable extent. In the United States, where such agreements whether written or oral are not only not legally enforceable but illegal to the extent that the parties responsible may go to jail if they are found out, examples of cooperative price fixing by competitors have come to light. Still, there is an immense difference between a legally enforceable contract and a "gentleman's agreement." Parties to the latter are always under the temptation to break away when an opportunity for immediate advantage presents itself.

Germany's remarkable industrial development in the postwar years cannot be entirely attributed to German management. The Allied nations, especially the United States, helped by providing large funds and technical assistance, whereas the intention after World War I had been to keep Germany weak. There was also the Korean War boom, in which Germany shared.

In addition, the German government helped by currency reform in 1948 and an encouraging tax policy. Finally, there was, for the first time, real cooperation with industry on the part of labor unions, which exercised restraint in their demands. Wages rose no more than national productivity or even less, making possible lower costs and more effective competition in international markets. German workers continued to work hard, as they had always done. (The strict apprenticeship training still common has provided a large number of highly skilled young men devoted to the traditions of their crafts.) In return, labor was allowed participation in management in the important coal and steel industries. Under a plan known as "codetermination" the supervisory boards are made up half of members representing labor and half representing man-

[7] David Granick, *The European Executive*, Doubleday & Company, Inc., Garden City, N.Y., 1962, p. 163.

agement or ownership. This in turn has given unions a greater understanding of management problems.

Nevertheless, Germany's showing has been in good part due to an extraordinary display of vigor on the part of management. Not only have some of the older industries, such as coal and steel, recovered from the effects of the war; there are many new enterprisers. The ranks of successful managers have also been swelled by refugees who have transferred their businesses from East Germany.

Efficient nationalized industries exist as well: railways and public utilities, including telephones. Production and sales of the very successful Volkswagen were originally under government auspices, but stock in the company has now been widely distributed.

German managers have learned a great deal from their American counterparts, but they are critical of some modern American practices and attitudes, or what they conceive those attitudes and practices to be. For example, Berthold Beitz, former general manager of Krupp's, once said:

> People say I'm typically American in my methods, but if it's so, it's a very old-fashioned sort of American I am. I'd never get a top job there myself, I'm sure—they're much too particular nowadays. They are more snobbish even than the British—you can't get a really important job in the States unless you've been to one of the best colleges and belong to one or two exclusive clubs. And then all those psychological and intelligence tests—I'm positive I'd never pass.

Many of their pre-1914 characteristics remain unchanged. They work harder than ever, perhaps in order to forget the past. And they have been careful not to go overboard in hiring specialists but have kept close to production and to their customers. They still plan to the last detail and are probably still not as flexible as they might be, or as generous in recognizing the achievements of subordinates. However, they have become much more competitive because the cartels have lost much of their political influence and lower tariffs have compelled them to face competition from abroad.

SOME EUROPEAN COMPARISONS

Certainly, by and large, the French and German managers seem to have avoided so far the relative stagnation of much of British management. The differences in the concepts of the management job and of the qualities needed to fill it might, therefore, be profitably explored.

First, the Continental managers place emphasis on increasing profits rather than on the widespread British and American objective of "satisficing," which includes profitability but places great stress on smoothness and good relations, perhaps even on the quiet life in which disruptive innovations are avoided.

The English organization pattern, especially in many large corporations, has tended to be highly formal. It is accompanied by organization charts, detailed corporate policies, job descriptions, authority limitations, and systematic titling. French and German companies are increasingly adopting this approach also, but the practice of organizational freedom is still quite widespread and is often believed to be more conducive to profit increases than the highly formal organization, for the following reasons:

1. Every incumbent is free to make the most of his job without being hamstrung by excessively close frameworks of organization. It is true that there may be unnecessary duplication, but even duplication is not necessarily frowned upon, for it may provide a check on performance. For example, two tax accountants unknown to each other might be asked to perform the same investigation and come up with recommendations.
2. Job freedom leads to competition and the likely survival of the fittest. Admittedly, the best politician rather than the biggest profit producer might survive, but if the master's eye is constantly on the subordinate's performance, this is not so likely to happen.
3. Job freedom permits flexibility, which is often necessary in exporting and in operation in other countries where everything cannot be spelled out in detail.

Large English companies also tend to be more international than their French or Germany equivalents. For example, their boards of directors may have to include at least two nationalities (e.g., Dutch and English at Unilever and Shell). They are also so large and complex that they cannot always be easily or competently managed by one man; hence the appointment of special committees through which a few men jointly make the principal decisions and the use of "contact" directors who act as intermediaries and negotiators between the board of directors and principal product groups and services.

In the selection of managers, French industry places great emphasis on technical know-how and intellectual attainment; Germany on thorough technical training and the rather mystical idea of the "calling," which Max Weber considered an important part of the Protestant ethic. To the man with such a calling, business is almost a religion.

In Britain, on the other hand, there is not only little emphasis on technical knowledge; possession of it may even be regarded as a disadvantage in the higher posts, where a broader type of education—a liberal arts course, say, at Oxford or Cambridge—has been considered better training for an administrative leader.

If the top man's knowledge is so general, however, he may require more assistants to handle the technical side, and administrative expenses will tend to grow. In addition, it may be more possible for mistakes to occur because he is not too conversant with the details of the business and pays little attention to them.

In examining why Britain lost a £10 million contract for supplying steel plants in Portugal, James R. White found that not only were the prices too high; the British firms were less likely to keep to promised delivery dates than other firms were and did not provide comparable follow-up service. Such omissions as failure to sign the bills of lading, which meant delay at the customs, seemed to be fairly common. So were delays in sending catalogs and price lists, with the result that customers got tired of waiting and placed their orders elsewhere. Not infrequently, delays in shipment were so great that import licenses had expired before the goods arrived.[8]

And if the British discount the value of technical knowledge, they are also inclined to discount the idea of management as a skill and a profession per se. Before World War II, hardly one academic institution was teaching management as such, and the two senior universities, Oxford and Cambridge, have been hostile to admitting the subject to the curriculum.

In fact, the British may have picked their industrial executives as they did their administrators for the colonial service: because they had the "right" background and well-rounded personalities. Thus, recruitment for the service was organized by a man whose own background was "a county family, a house captaincy at Eton, Greats at Oxford, and the cavalry." His preference was to evaluate candidates by the interview alone, and a man might be ruled out entirely on appearance. One, for example, was dismissed from consideration with the notation "pink and unlovely."[9]

A commentator in the liberal *Manchester Guardian Weekly* agrees that there was nothing wrong with these recruitment policies even though Britain eventually lost most of her colonial empire: "It was not their [the recruits'] fault if the governed ceased to accept their right to govern."[10]

But if the colonial service administrators were successful only so long as conditions remained the same, could the selection policy really be said to be successful?

There are many signs that the way in which the German rate of economic advance has outstripped the British is beginning to cause major doubts about traditional ways, in regard to industry at least. For example:

> The English have looked down on education and learning. . . . They claim to have stressed leadership and character. But what, in fact, is meant by leadership? Is it but the capacity to give orders confidently and without reflection? What if the ordered are indifferent and the orders absurd?[11]

Again, the *Economist*[12] cites a survey of the leading chemical companies, which indicates that after the foundations had been laid by businessmen who were also chemists, British industry tended to replace the founders by businessmen with little technical training, while Germany brought in far more qualified chemists. But "more recently, in Britain too, the emphasis has swung; the chemist, flanked by other scientists, has emerged at the top of businesses such as the ICI [Imperial Chemical Industries, one of the world's largest chemical companies]."

[8] "Why Britain Loses Orders for Exports," *The Listener* (publication of the British Broadcasting Company), Mar. 20, 1958, pp. 486–487.
[9] *Manchester Guardian Weekly,* May 10, 1962, p. 10. The "pink" apparently refers to appearance and not to political opinions.
[10] *Ibid.*
[11] Donald MacRae, "Britain's Long Decline," *The Listener,* Nov. 23, 1961, p. 884.
[12] Feb. 18, 1961, p. 688.

In the older industries, however, it may take a long time to change the prevailing pattern.

U.S. VERSUS EUROPEAN INDUSTRY

Although, by and large, some of the European countries have surpassed the United States in rate of growth in the post-World War II period, both per capita income and per capita gross national product in the United States are still larger than in any other country in the world. Also, since the bases on which percentage rate of growth is calculated were smaller in the European countries than in the United States, U.S. rates of growth were probably greater in absolute amounts.

One factor in the difference has been that there are many more large (over $500 million in sales) companies in the United States than in Europe, as the following table[13] shows:

United States	272
Britain	54
Japan	30
Germany	28
France	23
Italy	8

Europeans often tend to conclude that this may have something to do with U.S. industrial superiority since it makes possible not only greater economies of scale but greater subdivision of labor, more automation, and more research; and, in addition, a large company naturally generates more working capital and can often borrow more money, possibly at lower rates, than a smaller organization can. Thus its investment opportunities are greater.

As the Common Market becomes more established, and perhaps takes in other countries, European companies will be able to grow by merger more than they have in the past. Also, widespread use of a turnover tax (a levy on "value added" by a company to the materials it purchases for its products) obviously encourages vertical mergers because the tax can be cut down if a company produces its own raw materials and parts and does not need to purchase them from outside.

The specific advantages of large-scale production may be illustrated by the chemical industry.[14] Chemical executives who examined the differences between American and British chemical processes found that the Americans produced more than twice as much as the British and that two-thirds of the difference was due to differences in the scale of production, for the large scale made possible such things as the use of the latest bulk-handling techniques, automatic bagging, and larger accounting staffs that enabled the U.S.

---

[13] *The Economist,* Jan. 14, 1967.
[14] This case is based on the report of a group of British chemical executives, published under the title *Manpower in the Chemical Industry: A Comparison of British and American Practices,* National Economic Development Office, Her Majesty's Stationery Office, London, 1967.

companies to calculate the costs of various changes in operations more accurately.

Thus what has been called the "technological gap" between U.S. and European industry may be bridged if European industry grows rapidly by merger.

There is also said to be a "management gap," but this may not be so great as is generally supposed. For example, the European chief executive often achieves better coordination than the American chief, who may overdelegate and spend too much time with people and organizations outside his company. Also, the European executive may have greater control over his operations because he tends to know his business thoroughly, although the faster installation of computers in the United States is enabling the U.S. executive to catch up in this respect.

In long-range planning, U.S. management usually does a better job of defining objectives (although it does not always make them as clear as they might be) and a much more systematic job of filling the gap between forecasts and objectives.

Since the European companies tend to be smaller, their organizations tend to be simpler, but leadership is more autocratic than it is in the United States. This has some major disadvantages, of course, but it also provides some advantages: speed in decision making and clear unity of command, for example.

Class barriers between different organization levels are much stronger in Europe than in the United States. Thus younger American executives have much greater upward mobility than their European counterparts, and there is also greater mobility between companies. In addition, American companies put much more effort into the formal training of managers than European companies do. In fact, there is not much recognition in either European companies or European universities of the fact that management is a subject in itself, as distinct from manufacturing and marketing know-how.

Also, the incentives for management are much greater in the United States than in European countries. Managers' compensation, except perhaps in the case of owner-managers of large companies, tends to be much lower in Europe than in the United States, even considering differences in purchasing power. In addition, business management is a much more highly regarded occupation in the United States than it is in Europe.

Because the rewards and opportunities are greater in the United States, the entrepreneurial spirit appears to be more evident than it is abroad, although it may be declining somewhat in the larger bureaucratic organizations. This, together with greater natural resources, a larger market, and a more open society generally, probably accounts for any American superiority that may exist.

SUMMARY

Historically, managers in the developed countries have achieved outstanding success. But success in the past is no guarantee of future progress, or even of staying in the same place, for competition is worldwide and is likely to be increasingly so.

British managers were for many decades the most successful in the world, but later they lost out to the United States and in some respects to Germany. France occupied a leading position in many ways in the early days of the Industrial Revolution, then appeared to lose interest in large-scale industrialization; an important part of its industry remained largely pre-capitalist in nature. Germany, a fairly late starter, managed to catch up with Great Britain in some industries and surpass it in others before World War I. But Germany experienced many difficulties in the period between the two world wars and lost still further ground with a second defeat in World War II.

Since World War II, however, advances in both France and Germany have been remarkable. German managers have achieved results by frugality, emphasis on productivity, and a high rate of investment; in France managers have been helped by government planning. Both countries should be further aided by the Common Market, which gives them a free trade area almost as large as the United States.

Great Britain's problem is essentially that it must export large quantities of manufactured goods if it is to support its large population. It was very successful in doing so during the heyday of British industrial and commercial dominance because other countries were less highly industrialized. Part of Britain's difficulty, however, may be due to British management, which has perhaps clung too long to methods and ideas that made it successful in a different age.

Review Questions

1. What is a cartel?
2. How may the European Common Market be considered an expansion of Friedrich List's idea of *Zollverein?* What were the advantages of the *Zollverein* to Germany?
3. Do you agree with Berthold Beitz's comment on American management? If not, where do you think he is wrong?
4. England, France, and Germany have used somewhat different criteria in selecting managers. Which set of criteria do you think most nearly resembles those used in the United States?
5. What is Le Plan?
6. Does the experience of Great Britain offer any lessons for managers in the United States?
7. In what areas do you think American executives can learn from Europeans, and vice versa?
8. In what ways does the management philosophy in any one of the three European countries discussed differ from the philosophy of American management?
9. If you were a management adviser to the British government, what steps would you advise it to take to improve the performance of British management?

Case Study One / The Pirandello Automobile Company

The Pirandello Automobile Company, located near a city in northern Italy, has a very successful record. Its sales are around $750 million a year, and it has a large percentage of the Italian market. It has an excellent chief executive in his late fifties and competent management in production, finance, and marketing.

The Common Market, however, will deprive the company of tariff protection from the competition of other well-managed companies in France and Germany, and it will have to compete with American companies that have greater resources since some have plants in the Common Market area.

Moreover, the chief executive believes, it will be necessary to introduce radical technical changes and to advertise on a wider scale, not only to take advantage of the broader market, but to enable the company to hold its own. Yet the company does not have enough working capital for these steps.

What course should the chief executive follow?

Case Study Two / The Fawley Refinery

Some years ago the Esso Standard Oil (N.J.) Company considered the alternatives for building a refinery in various parts of Western Europe in order to serve what was then the most rapidly expanding market in the world. Among the principal locations investigated were some in Germany, France, Belgium, Holland, Italy, and Great Britain.

For many economic and noneconomic reasons the British location was preferred. But one major problem remained—namely, the ability of lower management and labor in Britain. From studies and other experiences it was feared that the labor productivity at the British refinery might be considerably below that of some of the other countries. British trade unions have been in the habit of imposing many restrictive work rules, which essentially originated in the Great Depression, such as excessively large work crews, bans on shifting workers from one job to another related to it, premium pay rules, rest pauses on the slightest pretext, strict seniority rules. The company felt that freedom to make work assignments was particularly important because flexible operation was necessary.

The foremen and general foremen sometimes had similarly restrictive rules.

Moreover, some of them were unionized and found it difficult to enforce discipline on subordinates, who might be members of the same union. Many of the foremen were merely reasonably good production workers without experience or even willingness to manage. The whole situation was well summed up by an American management consultant, who said that this was a labor situation of half productivity, half efficiency, half profits, and half pay.

1. If you were this management consultant, how might you try to improve this situation and increase the efficiency of labor so as to persuade Esso to locate in Britain?
2. In framing your recommendations, try to introduce some of the successful American methods of scientific management and human relations.

Selected Readings

The European Executive, David Granick, Doubleday & Company, Inc., Garden City, N.Y., 1962. A first-hand study of the principal characteristics of European executives in major countries.

Management in the Industrial World: An International Analysis, Frederick Harbison and Charles A. Myers, McGraw-Hill Book Company, New York, 1959. A study of management in a number of industrial countries, with emphasis on labor relations.

Why Growth Rates Differ: Postwar Experience in Nine Western Countries, Edward F. Denison, Brookings Institution, Washington, D.C., 1967. Compares productivity increases in Western Europe with those in the United States. Explains that the higher European growth rate is due to a massive switch of resources from agriculture to manufacturing and not to any special management and production techniques.

Promotion and Control of Industry in Postwar France, John Sheahan, Harvard University Press, Cambridge, Mass., 1963. A detailed study of the aluminum, steel, automobile, and cotton textile industries in France. Discusses the impact of government control, pricing, and competition on manufacturing and the market.

APPENDIX

MANAGEMENT IN JAPAN

Perhaps the single most interesting case of industrial development is that of Japan. Japanese gross national product is now the fourth highest in the world, following closely on that of West Germany. If the Japanese economy continues to grow at the amazing speed with which it has been growing (GNP doubled between 1960 and 1967), Japan may become the second most productive country in the world well before the end of the century.

Japan has greatly outdistanced its one-time rivals in Asian development in that its per capita income is eight times that of India or China. Admittedly, Japan is still merely catching up with the developed countries of the world, and her standard of living is still relatively low—per capita income was $750 in 1965, as compared with $3,000 in the United States. But Japan holds the world's record for rate of growth, even though the growth has been somewhat uneven and many smaller companies have fallen by the wayside. Most extraordinary of all has been Japan's ability to increase its exports so as to pay for the increase in imports necessary to keep its industry going. (Japan is the No. 2 customer of the United States.)

The Japanese achievement has been largely due to the mental attitude of the people. When the Portuguese landed on the Island of Tanegashima in 1543, they fired a few volleys into the air. At first the Japanese were deeply disturbed. But then they burst out as one: "We want to learn."

The Japanese desire to learn from other countries was, however, curbed during the next century, and for more than 300 years the country was almost entirely closed to foreign trade—a period which may be said to have ended when Commodore Perry of the U.S. Navy brought a squadron to Japan and demanded that it open its doors.

During the period of seclusion, Japan was ruled by members of the Tokugawa clan. Although the successive emperors were still the official heads of state, the actual power was held by Tokugawa shoguns, whose position was somewhat similar to that of the "mayors of the palace" under the Do-Nothing Kings of France. But changing conditions and the inability of the regime to resist foreign demands weakened it, and when a new emperor, Mutsuhito, came to the throne in 1868, he was able to rule in fact as well as in name. Mutsuhito took the name of Meiji ("enlightened rule") and instituted widespread reforms, decreeing that "wisdom and knowledge shall be sought from all over the world."

Radical changes took place, but the disturbing aspect of change was minimized because the changes were conducted within the framework of tradition, and that framework was strengthened rather than weakened in the process. Ancestor worship, which was part of the Shinto religion, naturally entailed deep respect for elders in the family, and this respect was extended to those in authority (especially the emperor). The head of a business house was regarded much as the head of a family would be, and if his employees owed him respect and obedience, he in turn had obligations to them: to provide stable lifetime employment and stable interpersonal relations. Thus the country maintained the established relationships in the family and in business, which make up so much of the warp and woof of life anywhere.

The custom of never firing a man once he has been hired appears even today to apply to almost all the white-collar workers and to two-thirds of the blue-collar labor force. Common also is the practice of advancement, especially in pay, according to age, length of service, and education. Thus a man in his forties or fifties may get several times the pay of a younger man who is doing the same job. People at all levels are treated with unfailing courtesy, and cooperation is the rule.

In many Japanese companies there is real teamwork. Sometimes it may even be carried too far, as in the "*ringi* system," under which many executives have to be consulted and unanimous agreement must be obtained, at least ostensibly, before action can be taken. In this way, all faces are saved and no one can be criticized if things go wrong.

The consultation may be a time-consuming procedure, but it also helps to ensure that information is circulated, and once decisions are made they are carried out more willingly than they otherwise might be. The traditional rigidity and the paternalistic nature of the enterprises causes headaches where innovations are being considered, of course, and seniority and lifetime jobs may complicate the solution of problems. But just as the ancient abacus produces miracles in the hands of Japanese operators and can sometimes outdo calculating machines, so the amazing teamwork of Japanese managers may enable them to compete successfully with foreign managers using more modern techniques.

Another stabilizing factor has been Buddhism, which in some cases prescribes the correct form for such things as the tea ceremony, miniature gardens, and mental and bodily exercises (the latter may be part of a business training program and of the daily routine of a business executive).

Changes during the Meiji regime

Under Emperor Meiji, who ruled from 1868 to 1912, Japan became a world power in a military sense. It also became an important factor in international trade.

At first, the changes instituted by the Meiji regime were largely improvements in agriculture and in the traditional crafts. Since the population was growing only slowly because of early population control, the growth in agricultural output made it possible to free some of the agricultural labor for industry. For the same reason, it was possible to export agricultural products (also silk) and so gain foreign exchange, which could be used to pay for imports of raw materials and machinery and for technical assistance. By keeping wages from rising as fast as productivity and by generating investment funds through taxation and appeals for frugality, the government was able to start major enterprises in fields still important today, such as railroads, mining, shipbuilding, chemicals, textiles, communications, cement, sugar, and glass.

Later many of these enterprises were sold at low prices to entrepreneurs who had been succesful in private industry. This helped in the creation of the great family companies, known as the *zaibatsu,* which became the foundations of great industrial fortunes.

Young men were sent abroad to learn Western ways, which were then adapted to Japanese needs, and teachers were imported to help spread the knowledge. Leaders in this movement were government officials, university professors, and top executives of the *zaibatsu.*

Taylor's work on scientific management aroused interest in Japan, and his system was introduced in some light industries as early as 1910, although the larger companies preferred to rely on the seniority system and permanent employment to provide motivation. In any case, no mental revolution was needed, for the Japanese worker's sense of duty was such that he considered his interests and those of his management identical anyway.

With low wages and Western (largely American) technology, Japan was able to undersell many American and European companies in their home markets. Thus total production and income had more than doubled by the beginning of World War I in 1914.

Japanese business today

At the end of World War II, Japanese business was disrupted, and the *zaibatsu* were dissolved. Unemployment was widespread, and business was at a standstill. In 1946, gross national product was little more than a third of what it had been in prewar days.

But under a new democratic constitution, the country soon reached and far surpassed its prewar production. In fact, the annual increase in GNP has been greater than that in any Western European country or the United States. New companies were started and became large and powerful, and the *zaibatsu,* although officially split up, still maintained their positions through informal cooperation between the several companies that had once operated as one.

Production   Modern technology, including automation, has been rapidly introduced. Japan is the second largest user of computers in the world, and computers are used in some cases for process control.

Finance   The financing of advanced technology and an increasing scale of production would not have been possible without the help of the banks. Each of the *zaibatsu* had its own bank or was controlled by a bank, and this is still true of some of the larger firms.

There have been several vertical mergers of industrial enterprises controlled by big banks, but the bankers' control is often an obstacle to horizontal mergers since competing companies are likely to be dependent on different banks. Thus there may be many more firms in a given field than there are among the firms' foreign competitors. Until recently (when the number was reduced to six), there were nine major automotive companies in Japan as compared with three (or four) in the United States.

Marketing   A third feature of Japanese industry is the existence of great trading houses, which perform the marketing function for many producers. This type of separation of production and marketing is common in developing countries since it permits sharing of distribution and credit expenses, and it still persists in highly developed Japan.

There are several thousand of these trading houses, but only about ten or a dozen of them are important. These handle three-quarters of Japan's foreign trade and a smaller though sizable portion of the domestic trade. Each of the *zaibatsus* had its own great trading house.

The large trading houses employ very large staffs; some of them have as many as 10,000 people on their payrolls. They perform such services as:

1. Granting of credit, especially by holding inventory in times of sales decline as a cushion for the manufacturers
2. Market research, although in this they may be handicapped by lack of adequate knowledge of foreign conditions and the absence of similar institutions in most other countries
3. Provision of information on imports permitted by foreign countries, customs requirements, and so on
4. Help in drawing up contracts
5. Arranging barter and third-nation trade, as when products are sold to one country for export to another

The great advantage of this separation of basic operating functions is that derived from specialization. The manufacturers can concentrate on production, and the marketers on selling. Also, the trading houses may perform a real lifesaving operation by buying for stock in times when sales are declining.

There are some disadvantages, however. One is that the managers of manufacturing companies may be too oriented to production. Another is that the huge staffs employed by the trading houses make for heavy administrative costs, even in a country where staff salaries are low. Also, they may be slow to act in fast-moving or complicated situations.

Research and development   In the early stages of her industrial development, Japan largely copied foreign processes and products, sometimes without permission. Often, too, the quality was not high, a factor that might be offset in the eyes of purchasers by the much lower prices.

That period ended after the American occupation, and Japanese business began a large-scale purchase of licenses and technical assistance from foreign companies in order to catch up quickly. Japanese managers greatly preferred licensing to joint ventures, and the latter were almost always preferred to the establishment of subsidiaries wholly owned by parent companies in other lands.

During this period, there was widespread application of foreign technology, made easier by the large technical staffs the Japanese companies employed and by the fact that a very large proportion (over 80 per cent) of the Japanese managers was university-trained.

But technology is becoming more complicated, and foreign companies are charging more for licenses. And although the Japanese managers are often willing to pay the higher royalties demanded, they are beginning to look with more favor on joint ventures. In 1967, the government adopted a policy, known as the "liberalization of capital," under which foreign participation is permitted in some industries in which it was forbidden before, and many Japanese managers are hoping to arrange joint ventures of one kind or another under this new rule. They also want to participate in the big international companies as well as share their technology.

But the most important development so far has been the increasing emphasis on research designed to make products more producible and to improve quality, and in quality Japan now scores high in many cases, notably in TV sets, transistor radios, and some electronic components. Now the Japanese are beginning to move into exploratory research, which is similar to basic research, and already some results have been obtained—for example, Sony's invention of the Esaki tunnel diode. In addition, in recent years two Nobel prizes have gone to Japanese.

The role of government managers

The Japanese manager is concerned with the stockholder as only one of his publics. He is equally dedicated to his staff and to his employees, to the firm itself, and to the "company of Japan"—the country regarded as one large firm in which all cooperate.

In serving these publics, the Japanese manager gets intelligent aid from top civil servants, many of whom are brilliant men and some of whom have become top executives in industry. The Japanese system of forecasting the course of the economy and of planning developments is highly sophisticated —and successful.

A considerably larger percentage of GNP is channeled into investment in Japan than in almost any other country, and the guidelines for expansion indicate where growth is possible and where it will result in overexpansion. A "structural change coefficient" is used to determine whether the industrial development is in the right direction—especially whether it is such that it will provide the necessary foreign exchange. Japanese planners have, in fact, done an extraordinary job in shifting Japan's exports from declining to growing fields.

The future

The important problem for management is whether there will be adequate replacements for today's top managers when they move from the scene. Perhaps there will be, for the Japanese are rapidly spreading knowledge of managerial skills and technology.

Toward this end, active participation of younger managers in meetings and deliberations of older managers is often permitted. True, the younger managers defer to their elders in the old tradition, but their participation appears to have gone further than it has anywhere else and to be more successful than it is in other countries. This managerial learning process is likely to continue to be the arch that supports all the rest.

It is also possible that Japanese management may not be able to count indefinitely on devotion to duty on the part of the workers in the lower ranks. Labor-management relations are already becoming a problem in Japan, and the trend is toward greater limitations on managerial action. Also, Marxist elements have a strong influence in the major trade union federation of Japan (Sohyo).

Selected Readings

Japan's Economic Expansion, George C. Allen, Oxford University Press, Fair Lawn, N.J., 1965. A description of the factors that have accelerated industrial development in Japan, including the importation of Western techniques, high investment and savings, quick returns from investment, the revival of the *zaibatsu,* and controls over trade and payments.

The Origins of Entrepreneurship in Meiji Japan, Johannes Hirschmeier, Harvard University Press, Cambridge, Mass., 1965. A helpful examination of the rise of entrepreneurship in Japan during the last century and a half. There is a brief sketch of about fifty of the most successful of the new entrepreneurs.

25

MANAGEMENT

IN

DEVELOPING

COUNTRIES

Slowly comes a hungry people, as a lion creeping nigher,
Glares at one that nods and winks behind a slowly dying fire.
Alfred Tennyson: *Locksley Hall*

25 An underdeveloped country is one that lacks modern industry and modern methods of agriculture. Its inhabitants live mainly by farming small plots, and such industry as exists tends to be labor-intensive, employing few machines and many human hands.

Under such conditions, output per man-hour and per acre of land is low. Total production, even if it were equally distributed, would not suffice to raise the standard of living much above the subsistence level. And often the distribution is enormously unequal: a few rich families have great wealth; the middle class is so small as to be virtually nonexistent; and the great mass of the people live in poverty, sometimes close to starvation.

All countries were once undeveloped, of course, but those of Western Europe were more fortunate than many underdeveloped or developing countries today because their populations were not as yet too large for the land itself to support, as they are in many countries today, and populations grew only slowly. Thus gradual industrialization was quite feasible. Nor were they continually confronted with a contrast between their own sorry lot and that of prosperous industrialized countries, as the developing countries are today.

In some cases, a large proportion of the population lived at a subsistence level, or even suffered from famine when the harvests failed. But they had no reason to suppose that this was not the common and inevitable lot of humanity except for those lucky enough to have been born rich. The United States had an even greater advantage. Not only did it have unlimited land available for the taking; when it became a nation the Industrial Revolution had already started.

In comparatively modern times, two underdeveloped countries, Japan and Russia, have succeeded in pulling themselves up by their bootstraps and joining the ranks of the industrialized nations. Both did it by autocratic means. Some of the developing countries today are attempting the same thing under democratic governments, which makes their task harder in some ways, but may make for better long-run results.[1]

An underdeveloped country can generally get started quickly only by exporting its raw material or hand manufactures and using the proceeds to import capital goods and foreign know-how. This may mean that the government must depress the already low standards of living in order to have more available for export. An autocratic government can do this more easily than a democratic one, which can be thrown out of office if it becomes unpopular.

Today's undeveloped areas include Africa, all Asia with the exception of Japan, Latin America, and parts of Eastern and Southern Europe. Some of the countries within these regions (notably China and parts of Eastern Europe) already lie within the Soviet bloc. The others are the "uncommitted nations," and it is for this reason that their development is considered important to the Western World. It is feared that if their standard of living remains at its

---

[1] Japan's development since World War II, when it has been operating under a democratic government, has been even more remarkable than the progress in the previous development period, which began in 1868 and raised the country to the status of a world power after a long period of isolation.

present level, they may become committed to the Soviet bloc, which is likely to promise much.

There appears to be a broad impression that the non-Soviet world is rigidly divided into "have" and "have-not" nations. On the one side, there are the 400 million people in the United States and Europe who have an annual per capita income of $1,000, or $4,000 for the average family, and on the other hand, approximately two billion people with an average income of $100, or $400 per family. At one end of the scale, there is the United States with over $3,000 per person per annum, and at the other end countries like India and Pakistan, where the annual per capita income is no more than $50 or $60. But there is great diversity within the various countries. For example, there is the prosperous north of Italy and the very poor south. Even in the United States, there are some poverty-stricken areas, as in West Virginia and Kentucky, where the coal mines are exhausted. On the other hand, parts of the state of São Paulo in Brazil are as flourishing as the West Coast of the United States.

To understand the management problem in underdeveloped countries, one must first of all consider their history.

EFFECTS OF COLONIALISM

Many of today's underdeveloped countries have only recently emerged from colonial status. The European colonial powers, mainly England, France, Belgium, the Netherlands, and Portugal, initiated a series of government enterprises: postal service, utilities, railroads, canals, roads, ocean shipping, and a minimum of municipal services. Their nationals also invested money in the colonies and sent in people from home as managers. They traded in local raw materials—rubber in Malaya, cocoa on the West African coast, and jute in India—and occasionally opened manufacturing enterprises. But with labor plentiful and cheap, there was little inducement for them to spend much money for large-scale importation of capital goods.

Colonial powers often introduced a measure of sanitation unknown before, provided some medical care (at least for some of the population), and mitigated famines by improving transportation so that food could be transferred from areas with good harvests to those where crop failures had occurred. To some extent, also, they may have provided better-than-ordinary jobs for some of the population, and in some cases training in management and industrial processes for their native employees. At their best, however, they did little to put the countries they governed on the road to a higher standard of living; at their worst, they exploited their colonies by drawing out raw materials and spending their gains elsewhere.

Independence came earlier to the European colonies in Latin America than to those in Asia and Africa, but it did not produce much improvement. While technically republics, the nations continued under the rule of oligarchies, for the most part descendants of their former conquerors, and of dictators who ruled by force of arms. Recent years, however, have seen the installation of more democratic governments in Latin America. The change came about during the post-World War II period, when the countries of Asia and Africa were gaining independence.

The new rulers of underdeveloped countries faced, and still face, enormous difficulties. They have attained power at a time when a ferment, which has been called "the rising tide of expectations," seems to be general throughout the underdeveloped world. Thus they cannot very well merely allow things to go on as before while they work slowly toward betterment. The high hopes engendered by independence or the elimination of dictators make it likely that they cannot maintain themselves in command unless they show results very shortly.

Aside from their recently acquired freedom and the need for industrialization and improved agricultural methods, however, the underdeveloped countries do not have much in common. India, for example, has had some basic industries for decades, while her neighbor Pakistan has few. In some countries, such as India, the population is already too large for the land to support. In others, such as some in South America, there is still plenty of land in relation to the number of people if it were properly distributed and cultivated, although here, too, the population is rising so rapidly as to constitute a drag on the efforts to raise the standard of living.

Again, a few countries in West Africa or South America have relatively little difficulty in attracting as much foreign capital as they can usefully employ; others have great difficulty in attracting any at all. And the attitudes, the inclination to work and save, and the scales of values of the various peoples vary greatly.

Finally, these underdeveloped countries differ greatly in the rate of development they have achieved in recent years. But even in the more progressive, the primitive flourishes alongside the advanced.

THE ROAD TO GROWTH

Many of the developing countries have borrowed the idea of five-year plans from Russia. Under such a plan, the government sets a goal, such as annual increase in national income, improvements of agricultural yields through various irrigation and fertilizer projects, and expansion of the industries needed to provide the capital goods for further expansion.

Without using the type of force employed in Soviet Russia, which incidentally did not always work out too well, a government has instruments for ensuring that the plans are carried out.

First of all, there are the power of taxation and the possibility of financing new projects through government aid, or of actually carrying them out under government management. Tax inducements can also be offered to private industry which acts to further the plans.

Second, there is government control over imports. A government can refuse to issue import licenses for goods it considers nonessential and so conserve its generally scarce foreign exchange for the goods that will help to fulfill the plans.

Third, it can encourage or discourage the building of plants by foreign companies through laws regarding the repatriation of earnings and capital.

Fourth, it can seek aid from the more industrialized nations, and may play the Western World against the Soviet bloc in this respect.

It is within the framework of such government policy that management of individual enterprises, whether native or foreign-owned, has to operate. Usually there is a national planning commission made up of government officials that develops the plans to reach the desired rate of economic growth.

Goals and needs

In most developing countries, the goal is a modest one, something on the order of an expansion of gross national product at the rate of 3 to 4 per cent per annum overall, and less per capita because of the high rate of population growth in many of the underdeveloped countries.

To achieve this rate of growth, saving is required. In most developing countries approximately a quarter of the national income must be withheld from current consumption, and half of the amount withheld usually must be applied to the provision of public services. The amounts to be spent on these are estimated as follows (as a percentage of national income):

Education	3%
Public health	2%
Economic services (agriculture, geology, communications)	3%
Welfare and administration	4%

The total of 12 per cent is higher than the figure for similar services in developed countries because civil servants are paid more in relation to the general level of wages and salaries. They possess scarce talents and often fill important positions which require them to, say, run large corporations or negotiate barter agreements with foreign countries.

The other 12 to 13 per cent of national income is needed for capital investment, and it tends to go largely into what is known as preinvestment, that is, to provide the services that are necessary if investment in manufacturing is to be feasible: improved transportation facilities; electric power; water for irrigation and industrial and domestic uses; and housing for workers. Not infrequently two-thirds or more of total investment tends to flow into this type of social capital as against one-third for manufacturing.

The financial problem for most underdeveloped countries is, of course, that a 25 per cent rate of saving is just not forthcoming or even likely. Since the incomes of a large proportion of the population are so low, personal consumption is likely to take as much as 85 or 90 per cent of national income. Hence little is left over for investment in either capital goods or education. And those who do have a surplus may send it abroad for safety's sake or use it for conspicuous consumption that stimulates production of luxury goods rather than of necessities. Landowners may use their savings to buy more land rather than to improve the yields from the land they already own. And many poor people keep their savings in the form of silver and gold ornaments, which produce no return.

A basic obstacle to the development of private investment is the lack of effective demand. Prospective managers all over the world have for a long time adopted Andrew Carnegie's attitude: "Give me a market and I'll give you a mill." In the developing countries, there is frequently not enough purchasing power to absorb the output of a plant of economic size.

Second, there is the difficulty of raising capital, unless the prospective manager is very rich himself and can provide it all. There is not likely to be much market for a stock issue in a poor country, and borrowing is often difficult; generally, too, the interest rates are high.

The high interest rates have led to a type of enterprise that is not conducive to economic growth, as a practice on the West Coast of Africa, known as "gold coasting," indicates. A smart local entrepreneur buys standard articles like cigarettes on credit for, say, £105 (about $252) and immediately sells them for £100, or about $240. He can then lend the £100 at 6d a pound for five days (i.e., from one market day to another). In 30 days, when he must repay his debt, he can pay the $252 and have a sizable profit on the transaction.[2]

But difficulty in raising money to build and equip a plant is not the only one faced by the prospective entrepreneur. In overpopulated countries especially, land is often just not available. Government permission may be required to buy it, and this may be withheld either because it is already occupied by people who have no other place to move or because the government itself wants the land for strategic purposes.

Even more important may be the lack of utilities: power, water, good telephone service. Transportation may also present difficulties: railroads may be unable to carry enough of the plant's output to make operation profitable, and roads may be so poor that truck transportation is not feasible.

Still another factor may be the lack of suitable labor. There may be vast numbers of unemployed ready and eager to go to work, but all except a small number may lack the necessary education. Contrast education in a developed country, where *all* children between the ages of 6 and 14 or 15 are in school, with that in an underdeveloped country, where many never go to school at all.

Many of the developing countries are making great efforts to provide more education, but it may be that not all of it is adapted to present needs. Thus the farm boy with a general education may tend to leave his existing employment on the land for the city. His presence, and that of others like him, may mean that an already overcrowded city requires more "social overheads" in the form of municipal services.

What is needed in the country districts is education in better agricultural

---

[2] From P. T. Bauer and B. S. Yamey, *The Economics of Under-developed Countries*, Cambridge University Press, London, 1957, p. 115.

methods. In the cities education might include secondary school education, plus training of the German trade school variety. Underdeveloped countries fall particularly short of technicians and bookkeepers.

In some cases, however, it may be better to bring the plant or factory to the worker in his rural village or small town rather than have him move to the city. In his home habitat, he will find it less difficult to get accustomed to the radically new and unfamiliar working life. He need not make the vast, almost impossible, social adjustment of moving abruptly from his people, his culture, and his ancestors' life.

But the move to the large city is often inevitable because the necessary social overhead is absent in the rural areas. And the transition frequently creates serious maladjustment among the workers and bitterness that may lead to radicalism or at least to deep personal unhappiness. Thus, while industrialization can be achieved more quickly by building plants in or near cities, there are many attendant evils.

Social attitudes

Social attitudes toward the manager's work may also help to discourage private industrialization. There is a widespread belief that the kind of man attracted by managerial work and the way he conducts himself as a manager are considerably affected by what sociologists have called "role expectations." Managers, like others, play a part on the stage of human action, and the attraction of a managerial career is determined partly by prevailing opinion. Such opinion may be broadly classified as *pro* or *contra* management.

Here an important factor is the attitude of opinion leaders. Thus in India some of the religious leaders are opposed to any action leading to the accumulation of wealth, and Gandhi's image of a peasant wearing only a loincloth that he spun and wove himself was a powerful influence against modern technology.

In a society in which political and high government administrative positions are prized—as in France and Russia in the nineteenth century—the most gifted persons may be reluctant to go into business. On the other hand, it is held that in a society that sanctions business and accumulation, business management may well become the ambition of a large number of able men.

However, social attitude is obviously not the only factor in attracting people in underdeveloped countries to a business career or repelling them from it:

1. Quite frequently a business career that results in accumulation may provide a way of buying one's way into the most socially esteemed group. This was often the aim of the early British entrepreneurs; only by accumulating money could they become landowners, and if a man acquired enough he might get a seat in Parliament or a title. If the manager himself could not win acceptance by the aristocracy because of his origin, habits, or language, his children might be able to do so.

2. A career in management may be the only one open to able underprivileged people. In India, the Marawanis, who were not of the dominant Brahman caste, had no chance of gaining respect except by the money route, and some of them have attained eminence in that way. Similarly, immigrants like the Chinese in Southeast Asia and the Lebanese in Africa have found it hard to get recognition except by taking advantage of the open opportunities in business.

3. Money and what it can buy are possible attractions even to those who set the prevailing standards. While a country's leaders who are not in business may scoff at it, they may still want to enjoy its fruits. For example, the civil servants in many developing countries enjoy high status but little wealth, and may inveigh against it. Yet some of them will be tempted by businessmen's offers, or at least by the economic perquisites possible to them, such as luxurious residences and frequent trips to foreign fleshpots.

Thus social attitude toward the manager may prevent or foster management development, but it is not the only influence or even the overwhelming one. In fact, government action can be much more important, because the state can subsidize new enterprises, protect existing enterprises, and adopt a tax policy that will stimulate savings; or it can act to hamper the development of industry.

Government attitudes

In the non-Soviet part of the world, the governments of developing countries include both dictatorships and democracies, and industrial development may be promoted or discouraged by either type.

In some cases, the chief aim of a dictator may be to extract the largest possible amount of money from what may be a stationary or declining economy. This revenue may be used to line the pockets of the regime, to support large military expenditures (so that the dictator may keep his revenue-snatching powers as long as possible), and to maintain a small group of hangers-on and ruling power groups. Even when the economy is expanding, as it may have been under the Trujillo dictatorship in the Dominican Republic, the increase is likely to go merely to swell the dictator's spoils. Thus a large proportion of the people are condemned to a stationary or declining standard of living, and eventually such a government brings about its own overthrow.

On the other hand, some dictatorships may be characterized as benevolent, in that the dictators are genuinely interested in improving the standards of living of the people generally. A government of this type has certain advantages for an underdeveloped country: it can impose its will on those reluctant to go along with the development and make the changes stick, and it can do so with little or no personal corruption. Also, a country under a benevolent dictatorship often finds it easy to attract foreign capital.

But such a military dictatorship has major drawbacks. It is usually ignorant of economics, and particularly of the folkways of economics. Thus the attempt of the Pakistan government to abolish middlemen in agriculture and displace them with civil servants led to a sharp reduction in agricultural trading, both because the new intermediaries lacked competence and because they had little incentive. And even among benevolent dictatorships there tends to be a high degree of centralization, which reduces the volume and diversity of managerial talent. Then, too, dictatorships seldom permit criticism of their actions, which increases the chance of error.

As has been mentioned, one of the fundamental problems of industrialization is the need to extract a large enough surplus from the agricultural population to feed the growing industrial population. Threats, pressure, and force may exert an effect opposite to that desired since the peasants may withhold or reduce their surplus, as has often happened in Russia.

Thus there is much to be said for a democratic endeavor to raise the national income. If rulers who are chosen by and representative of the people get together to discuss alternate goals, the goals and the means of reaching them are likely to achieve wider acceptance. And since a democratic government is always subject to criticism, it can more readily see its mistakes before they become too serious.

Democratic regimes in developing countries have frequently turned toward a democratic socialism, believing in the need for a strong public sector (government ownership and control of strategic investments in power, transport, communication, and heavy industry) and in the need for considerable intervention in the rest of the economy.

This is felt necessary partly because of the absence of capital in the private sector and partly because the leaders were Social Democrats by conviction before they ever held office. The Fabians, the intellectual fathers of the British Labour party in the early twentieth century, believed that once they had the power they could accomplish anything. The socialist leaders of the underdeveloped countries have tended to hold the same view.

But unfortunately, intellectual discussions regarding alternate plans are often so lengthy that the result is agreement on the lowest common denominator, and there is a depressing tendency to regard a plan as something that will automatically reach fulfillment. Thus the democratic regimes are often woefully weak in execution.

THE EMERGENCE OF MANAGERS

There is no doubt that managerial talent exists in every country and that the number of potentially able managers depends largely on the size of the population. The word "potentially" must, however, be stressed; the talent must be found, trained, and given an opportunity before it can function effectively.

The reason for believing in the existence of a potential managerial group in any country is the simple observation that there appears to be little difference in the innate intellectual and business qualities of various peoples. To be sure there are, and will be for a long time, differences in the effectiveness of the managers because of education or the lack of it, environment, traditions, and similar circumstances. And as has been noted, in many societies some of the ablest men may seek careers in fields other than industrial management.

Managers emerge in many different ways. For example, Cyril S. Belshaw has made some fascinating studies of their rise in a part of the world widely accepted as possibly enchanting but impossibly "backward," namely the islands of Melanesia in the Pacific.[3]

Quite often the rise to entrepreneurship was brought about by association with whites. For example, natives recruited as laborers in Queensland returned to their island homes, bringing new values and new ideas. They set up small stores, raised cash crops and cattle herds. Similarly, Melanesians brought up with whites have pioneered various enterprises and taught others to follow suit. In most cases, their early childhood has been traditional, and they have superimposed white values and methods on their original background. Missionaries, health officers, colonial administrators, and occupation forces have also promoted cultural change. And the natives have been quite responsive to changing economic conditions.

Belshaw points out that for management to rise, there must be a market for whatever the people of the country are producing, they must have aid in introducing technology adapted to their needs, and they must accept, to some extent, institutions like the factory or at least intermediary merchants. Under such conditions, it may then be possible for entrepreneurship to develop from existing patterns of society, as follows:

1. The community (which may be quite large in numbers) may develop a commercial activity by itself. For example, in south India one of the Chettiars married a girl from another community against the will of her family. They had to flee and went to Burma, where they set up in the moneylending business, later went into banking and ultimately into industry, and then spread their activities to other countries. The Chettiars now include some of the most important and successful entrepreneurial families in India.

2. The family may begin trading, accumulate some money, and then go into the basic industry of the region—jute in Bengal, textiles in Bombay, for example—first dealing with raw materials, then making a finished product—jute bags or cloth—and finally branch out into other enterprises. The Sarabhai family in Gujarat, India, began making fine textiles in the face of tough British competition after World War I, then went into pharmaceuticals and chemicals, and has now branched out into oil and petrochemicals.

---

[3] "The Cultural Milieu of the Entrepreneur: A Critical Essay," *Explorations in Entrepreneurial History*, vol. 7, no. 3, February, 1955, pp. 146–163; *In Search of Wealth: The Emergence of Business Enterprise in South Eastern Papua*, Memoir of the American Anthropological Association, 1955; *Changing Melanesia: Social Economics of Culture Contact*, Oxford University Press, Fair Lawn, N.J., 1954.

Characteristics of the managers

What kinds of people are most likely to have the characteristics necessary to accomplish saving and expansion? The principal characteristics stressed by writers on the subject are "achievement orientation" and "social deviancy."

David C. McClelland[4] stresses the "achievement motive." Some people, he points out, have an "inner concern" with achievement; they are attracted by problems and get pleasure from solving them. Such persons come from families in which "there has been stress on self-reliance and mastery. They seem to do their best work when it counts for their record and not when other special incentives are introduced, such as pressure from outside, money prizes, or time off from work. They do not necessarily conform to social pressures, like risky operations, prefer experts to friends in their work, and perform better under pressure and long odds."[5]

It is believed that persons with a strong drive to achieve are essential to any development and especially so in underdeveloped countries. Professor McClelland has developed a number of tests. In essence, he has evaluated the achievement motivation reflected in the stories prepared for school use in each country and has found that it showed a high correlation with the national income expected.

This thesis, which has perhaps been stated too briefly here, is an interesting one. But it is rather on the tautological side, for naturally those who are highly achievement motivated are most likely to achieve. Actually, however, lack of achievement may not necessarily be due to failure on Professor McClelland's test, but rather—as he indicates it was in Germany in 1925, for example—to the after-effects of war, famine, and inflation. Still, a method of picking the achieving type in an underdeveloped country might be useful. Essentially McClelland thinks that managerial talent can be increased by such measures as the following:

1. Finding people who like to take moderate risks when their abilities will influence the outcome: people who can carry on energetic and novel instrumental activity, assume responsibility, undertake actions where success or failure can be measured, and anticipate future possibilities.
2. Sending foreign nationals with high achievement motivation to stimulate achievement and set standards for it.
3. Shifting popular values from "traditionally directed" to "other-directed," making people more responsive to needs and challenges. Thus McClelland suggests building factories rather than cottage industries so as to break the traditional pattern, emancipating women as a further break with the past, interesting men in new things (through the widespread introduction

---

[4] *The Achieving Society*, D. Van Nostrand Company, Inc., Princeton, N.J., 1961. (Preliminary study quoted in Benjamin Higgins, *Economic Development*, W. W. Norton & Company, Inc., New York, 1955, pp. 294–301.)
[5] *Ibid.*

of motors, for example), widening horizons by better communication and transportation, and creating "other-directedness" through group plays in schools and similar measures.

In a different viewpoint, the mainspring of economic development is the "social deviant," who is described as a person who goes against the prevailing values and practices. The social deviant is willing to face criticism and even exclusion from the company of those most esteemed in society.

Very clear cases of social deviancy were those who in the Middle Ages loaned out money at interest, often at very high rates. This group was thoroughly disapproved of by the Roman Catholic Church, whose standards of value were then dominant. The government passed laws against moneylenders and prosecuted them at times, and the accepted and dominant society shunned their company. But the moneylenders persisted and helped many people set up businesses. After some centuries, then, some of them became respectable, like the Fuggers of Germany in the sixteenth century. Finally, they managed to get even religious sanction when, in 1545, Calvin, the great Protestant leader of Geneva, wrote his famous letter justifying the charging of interest.[6]

But the question of who the deviants are and how they come to exert themselves still remains. One explanation is that they are "culturally marginal individuals," who are only partly integrated in the culture in which they live.[7] Since they are not fully accepted and do not have to live up wholly to what is expected, they are in a position to make changes that may, in the long run, profoundly alter fundamental values. Levantines (Greeks and Lebanese, and to a lesser extent Syrians and Armenians) and Jews in the West, Chinese in Eastern countries other than their own, and Indians in East Africa have traditionally been such marginal individuals. The Huguenots, French Protestant refugees in the seventeenth century, helped in the development of Britain and Germany. German political refugees in the middle of the nineteenth century and in the 1930s have been instrumental in furthering industrialization in many parts of the world.

Marginal people have helped to bring about contact between an underdeveloped country and international commerce; they have introduced knowhow and special skills, capital, technology, and science; pioneered in the development of commerce and industry and trained native entrepreneurs. Usually they go to parts of the world where their ability is complementary to native skills so that they can live and advance by supplementing local activity rather than competing with it. Characteristically they are willing to accept a low standard of living until they have saved enough to expand their businesses.

A good illustration of the role of marginal men is provided by Professors Bauer and Yamey in their account of the Chinese in Malaya:

[6] For an exposition of the role of the social deviant, see *Change and the Entrepreneur,* Research Center in Entrepreneurial History, Harvard University Press, Cambridge, Mass., 1949, pp. 153–156.
[7] Robert E. Park, *Race and Culture,* The Free Press of Glencoe, New York, 1950, pp. 345–392; and E. V. Stonequist, *The Marginal Man: A Study in Personality and Culture Conflict,* Charles Scribner's Sons, New York, 1937.

It is not unusual to find a Chinese rubber small-holder and his family cultivating a holding of perhaps twenty acres and having interests in half-a-dozen other activities, such as a transport enterprise, a tailor's business, a tapioca plantation, a rubber dealer's business and a garage . . . modern Malaya is very largely a creation of the Chinese. [The local Malayans on the contrary are neither very active nor ambitious, being content to cultivate merely two to three acres of rubber, often with the help of a share-tapper, and for the rest enjoy the leisurely life so pleasant in that part of the world.][8]

But neither social deviance nor the marginal man *by themselves* appear to offer an adequate explanation of the extraordinary transformation of primitive economies into industrial societies. Both existed in Genoa and Florence in the fourteenth and fifteenth centuries without creating a real change, such as occurred in England in the eighteenth century. It is obviously necessary to refine the analysis of conditions under which successful entrepreneurship can flourish.

One such attempt has been made by Professor B. F. Hoselitz in *Sociological Aspects of Economic Growth.*[9] He thinks that the two variables particularly relevant to the problem are (1) the ratio between population and natural resources and (2) the degree of power exercised by central government authority—the smaller the population in relation to the natural resources and the less the exercise of central governmental influence, the more expansionist the economic development. The United States, Canada, and Australia have been the outstanding examples of such an expansionist environment.

Professor Hoselitz considers the Industrial Revolution in England an "in-between" case. The central government did have considerable power and exercised it, partly in the construction of social overhead, partly in the sponsorship of overseas trade. But at the same time there was scope for the social deviant (though not for the "outside" marginal man because the tightly knit social organization was not too friendly to foreigners). There was also an expansion of usable land, partly through the enclosure of the commons and partly through drainage. And there were discoveries of important natural resources, like coal and iron, so that the social deviant with some savings could start his own enterprise with a fair chance of success.

But outside the United States and Western Europe, individual entrepreneurs have rarely, if ever, been successful in taking their countries from the have-not to the have stage. Thus the present leaders of the country, society, race, or tribe may have to initiate the economic development.

From an economic point of view, a basic problem in an entirely under-developed country is the natives' resistance to plans for economic expansion on grounds that appear to be highly irrational. Thus Raymond Firth, the famous anthropologist, tells[10] of the natives of the Trobriand Islands of the

---

[8] *Op. cit.,* pp. 107–108.
[9] The Free Press of Glencoe, New York, 1960, pp. 68–89. See also W. W. Rostow's work, *The Process of Economic Growth,* Cambridge University Press, New York, 1960.
[10] In *Human Types: An Introduction to Social Anthropology,* Thomas Nelson & Sons, Ltd., London, 1956, p. 71.

South Pacific who may go on a fishing expedition instead of diving for pearls, even though they can earn many times as much by the second occupation as by the first. Nearby, in the Solomon Islands, a native would prefer to get three sticks of tobacco for a shilling's worth of his goods rather than two shillings in cash. In New Guinea, the wages for several months' labor might be spent on a gift.

These attitudes, values, and modes of behavior are the result of tradition, training in values, and the collective exercise of a planned system of production and distribution. If the leaders of such a community decide to change some of the objectives and methods of production while preserving the form of organization, then some development may occur.

Professor Firth has illustrated this possibility in his interesting study of the transformation of the Maoris in the period 1840 to 1860.[11] During that time, the Maoris enthusiastically adopted certain Western forms. Within a few years they had built a number of flour mills, greatly expanded the production of wheat, corn, and potatoes, and acquired ships for trading. The total amounted to a considerable increase in wealth. As Firth explains it, this period of rapid economic growth "saw no diametrical alteration in the organization of productive effort or in the system of distribution. Most of the fixed capital was owned communally, by a tribe or a smaller group of relatives, and controlled by the chief of the *hapu* [clan or extended family]. In his hands also lay much of the direction of the work of the community."[12]

The economic growth took place solely because of a change, or rather a reinterpretation, of the objectives of the society. Originally the Maoris competed in canoes, meeting houses, and the amount of traditional food consumed; now they competed in consumption of foreign foods, in coastal vessels, and in flour mills. The extraordinary economic development was brought to an end only when the population was decimated by the Maori Wars of the 1860s.

Government officials as managers

Can modern government officials in developing countries exercise similar influence merely by reinterpreting objectives? The answer almost certainly is no. Usually there are no established systems of production and distribution that could be quickly turned from traditional objectives to modern ones. There is no particular disposition to accept the wishes of officials as binding. And there may be a great diversity of language, custom, and objective among the populations.

On the other hand, modern governments, including those of underdeveloped countries, are able to concentrate enough power in their hands to make themselves a major force for growth. At least the inner core of the permanent civil service often attracts the ablest men because of the great prestige of the top positions, the emoluments, and the job security, and because such positions

[11] *Primitive Economics of the New Zealand Maori*, Routledge & Kegan Paul, Ltd., London, 1929, pp. 456 ff.
[12] *Ibid.*, p. 472.

offer an opportunity to do good for the country and its people. And there is no doubt that important managerial powers have devolved on them and that they enjoy exercising them. Below are some of the ways in which government officials in an underdeveloped country may share in the management of *private* enterprise:

Forecasting   Estimates of the future demand, prices, and investments needed by individual industries may be made by the planning commissions and the various ministers concerned with particular industries.

Planning   Increasingly, four- or five-year plans are worked out in great detail by the planning commissions, and it is very difficult to get permission to set up any enterprise involving an investment of more than $50,000 to $100,000 that is not included in the plan or does not fall within its scope in product mix, location, and so on.

Organization   Any fairly large project may require a license; and to get one, the private businessman may have to spell out in detail the amount to be invested, how it is to be raised, the nature of the product, the volume and method of manufacture, the structure and manning of the organization, the amount and type of labor to be employed, the welfare provisions, the machinery required, the potential markets and methods of selling, the organization of the company and methods of officer remuneration, the start-up date, the foreign exchange required, the location of the land, and how the company proposes to acquire it.

Execution   The government's principal method of participating in execution is through foreign exchange allocation. While this is necessary because foreign exchange tends to be scarce, it can also be used to mete out punishment. Thus a company may find itself unable to import an essential piece of machinery or repair part, ostensibly because time is needed to examine the validity of the claim, but really because the government disapproves of some of the actions of the entrepreneur. The government can also exercise considerable control of execution through its power over the application of local ordinances covering water, power, transportation, fire protection, and so on.

The private sector

People in underdeveloped countries have great patience and sometimes little sense of urgency. The problems are so enormous and so difficult to deal with that solutions will take a long time anyway. And those in a position to act don't like to stick their necks out if they can help it.

If the course of action is indefinite, company organization tends to be so as well. Largely it is based on the objectives and experience of the chief executive. Goals are usually highly personalized; often there is greater emphasis on short-run gains than in more developed countries. If the chief's experience has been in land or mining, he will emphasize production and production processes. If he has a background in trading, he will tend to stress the marketing side.

In either case there is likely to be a lack of balance, which is aggravated by a lack of functionalism. Specialized services like training, personnel work, and even accounting may be part of other jobs. And the tendency toward centralization (largely because there are few to delegate to) may increase the lack of balance. Top management may be overloaded with detail, while at the lower levels there is much redundant staff with ill-defined functions, little responsibility, few incentives, and no hope.

The personal rather than the business aspect is emphasized even more through the prevalence of the family system. The objectives of the family may well take precedence over those of the business. This may produce an emphasis on keeping things as they are, to the detriment of innovation. More often, it may result in a great deal of nepotism and, so far as family members go, an attitude of "from each according to his ability and to each according to his needs," with emphasis on the second part of the admonition rather than on the first. The prevalence of incompetent family members may leave little room near the top for abler nonmembers and even cut down their chances to enter the business at all.

Direction is largely dependent on the availability of management personnel. Finding a capable successor to the founder is often a problem. Sometimes members of the owner's family are sent abroad to study at foreign universities, perhaps also to serve internships in foreign firms. But this form of training is too expensive for many and often frustrating for those who undergo it since they may have to start at low levels of responsibility and pay when they return.

Managers are sometimes hired from the civil service, from the army, or from one of the professions, such as law and accounting. Some management training efforts are being made by governments and universities, but on-the-job training—learning from experience and from superiors—is still the most common type.

In some countries, management societies, both national and local, have been formed to undertake the training of management by the managers themselves, with emphasis on such techniques as industrial engineering, bookkeeping, and accounting because these will have the most immediate value. For foremen, the old United States World War II TWI (Training Within Industry) programs have been helpful in providing information on methods improvement and the handling of personnel. Governments, both native and foreign, are helping by providing instructors.

But while the enthusiasm may be great, the results are not proportionate. There are pioneering managers in almost all the underdeveloped countries, and their problem essentially is the creation of a more mature philosophy of management and techniques particularly suitable to local conditions rather than the blind adoption of either from other countries. They must also overcome the "busyness," selfishness, and tendency to secretiveness on the part of many of the managers.

Foreign managers could, of course, be brought in both to help with on-the-job training and to provide special technical skills until native managers could be trained, and this is done to some extent. But the rigors of living in such a country, the possible lack of tenure, potential discrimination, and the loss of contacts at home all make the jobs hazardous. Perhaps increasing emphasis on an international managerial "civil service" working on a contract basis, such as the United Nations Technical Assistance program now provides on a small scale, might help in part to solve the problem.

Ironically, the weakest aspect of management development in most of these countries is the lack of opportunity for young men who have acquired training on their own, even training abroad. Because they have no experience, they cannot get jobs; and because they cannot get jobs, they cannot acquire experience. It is, therefore, highly desirable that *all* firms hire quotas of young men, even if only to give them experience so that they may utilize their knowledge elsewhere. In the many unfortunate cases of an excess of supply over demand, there might be screening boards composed not only of managers but also of academic personnel and independents.

Even more important, opportunities for advancement should be created. Now the road to the top or the near top is often blocked because of the number of family members who must be taken care of.

Management controls are, paradoxically, both very strong and very weak. Since the conduct of most enterprises is highly personalized, the master's eye attempts to be everywhere, especially in the smaller enterprises. On the other hand, this type of firm has few formal controls except when it is forced to install them by law, action of tax authorities, or the demands of financial institutions. Larger firms utilize more of the formal controls, but the top man is likely to exercise a good deal of personal control and attempt, so far as possible, to be ubiquitous.

Financial controls range from control of the money in the strongbox to highly intricate systems of financial checks and balances. But the more sophisticated forms of control tend to be weak or entirely lacking. Such measures as control of the cost of products and their constituents, marginal and standard costing, budgets, breakeven analysis, and planning of cash flow are little used, and data available may not be comparable. Use of accountancy to aid managerial decisions is rare also. Where books are kept, the practice of keeping several sets for different purposes is not unknown.

In the more advanced countries there is, of course, a larger supply of accounting talent, but this can be secured even in the less advanced countries through the use of outstanding foreign talent. Probably the single most useful control tool in developing countries is the budget because it forces some degree of planning and subsequent check on results. And it is important that data on relevant costs be given to as many executives as possible so that they may develop cost-consciousness.

Manufacturing   The basic problem in setting up and operating manufacturing facilities in developing countries is one of proper *balance* among local labor, raw materials, and local overhead facilities on the one hand, and equipment, technical aid, and raw materials from abroad on the other. Perhaps the best way of bringing about this balance is to adapt equipment to the local repair facilities, operating skills, and scale of production. Larger enterprises, which are able to construct their own labor and power facilities, are often less dependent on local facilities. Another problem of balance is adjustment of scale to growth. The general absence of preinvestment planning is dangerous in developing countries because it may cause a breakdown in coordination of production and consequently disrupt schedules, standardization, and control over the progress of operations.

The supply of raw materials or their quality may be irregular, either because of insufficient output in feeder industries or because of import difficulties. Purchasing departments may be inadequate because they do not know the sources of supply, work on graft, or—in the case of government plants—work under inapplicable regulations identical to those governing administrative agencies. Irregular transportation, or lack of sufficient transportation, may make it difficult to maintain economical production runs unless extra expense is incurred for larger stocks. In the transition stage, therefore, it may be helpful to have both domestic and foreign sources of raw materials if the necessary import licenses can be obtained.

Better quality control is needed if the developing countries are to take full advantage of the export potentials. For example, the beautiful Indian silks could be exported on a much larger scale than at present if the silk threads were of better and more uniform quality.

Irregular quality may also make production more difficult. Use of different types of ores makes for poor yields and irregular slugs. In one country, a great deal of improvement was brought about by proper selection, loading, and consignment at the mines.

Poor quality may result not only from defects in raw materials, but from conditions within the plant itself. Equipment may wear out quickly because of climatic conditions, or it may have been imported second-hand equipment in the first place. The production process itself may be poorly controlled, usually because of human failure. There tends to be a wide difference in the quality of products produced by different workers because of differences in skill, training, attitude, and incentives. Thus there may be a high proportion of rejects. Finally, there may be too much stress on quantity, particularly where plans have to be met or exceeded; and the plant managers may neglect quality as a result.

Apart from the more sophisticated techniques of statistical quality control, much can probably be accomplished by purchase specifications in import licenses.

Maintenance of equipment is not well developed. There is little preventive maintenance (inspection and correction of defects before breakdown) since there is a general tendency to hope that the machines will not break down. The feeling is that when they do, there will be time enough to do something about the trouble. In any case, it might be foolish to anticipate trouble, because little could be done to get parts from abroad because of the strict import licensing, which may prevent ordering or receipt until things come to a standstill. Spare parts should, of course, be provided in adequate quantities at the time the equipment or plant is purchased, but management may hope to avoid the cost of carrying the inventory or lack the necessary working capital. There is also a shortage of trained maintenance mechanics and of outside repair shops.

The latter difficulty could be overcome by setting up central repair shops that would serve several plants and giving them appropriate priorities on imports. The lack of trained maintenance personnel could be overcome by governmental training programs and the use of foreign personnel.

A major aid to many small and struggling enterprises in underdeveloped countries would be the provision of aid through a larger "parent firm" in the form of technical information, joint facilities, or the provision of parts at lower cost through large-scale production, and, finally, through subcontracting work to specialist firms.

Marketing Distribution seems to be the most common activity in many underdeveloped countries. Biggest buyers and sellers in terms of volume are usually the governments, but the stores, open-air stalls, open-window sellers, hawkers, and door-to-door sellers are very numerous.

Most of the latter are conducting pitifully small operations in terms of turnover and income. Traveling from Port-au-Prince in Haiti out into the back country, for example, one encounters thousands of people carrying loads of heavy stuff for dozens of miles to the market in the big town. In this way they are saving the cost of transportation, which may amount to no more than a few pennies.

The real marketing talent (outside the government) tends to be concentrated in the import-export and commission houses. In the seaports, capital cities, and large towns, a few merchants may carry anywhere from a dozen to hundreds of lines. They have the working capital to finance the inventory and the contacts with the intermediaries, and their power may well extend to the larger stores in the small towns and larger villages. And, of course, they have political contacts. It is difficult for a new manufacturer to work outside the "system," and sometimes it is impossible for him to crash into it or to set up his own marketing operations.

Cost of distribution is high because the low per capita income limits demand. This tends to mean low inventory turnover, and there is also considerable risk of default on debts. Hence high profit margins per unit are needed.

It is difficult to distribute mass-produced goods through a marketing mechanism that is incapable of specialization and engages in many stages of the distribution process. Proper coordination of production runs and subsequent sales without inventory loading are difficult if not impossible. To avoid these difficulties, the larger manufacturers tend to establish their own systems of distribution, even though it may involve a herculean effort and tie up a good deal of working capital. At best, perhaps, a compromise can be worked out whereby large orders are obtained directly by the manufacturer while smaller ones go through existing channels of distribution.

But the majority of enterprises are small and tend to be dependent on the merchants, not only for distribution but for working capital to pay for supplies and labor and tide them over difficult periods, even for a part of the fixed investment. This means that the distributor may exercise considerable control over the manufacturer's decisions. In some instances the merchant may market his goods and at the same time import similar products from abroad and sell them in competition. Another device is to stratify markets in order to discriminate effectively among different levels. Sometimes the same product is sold under different labels or at different prices, and prices themselves are frequently not fixed but subject to elaborate bargaining.

Some improvement in marketing efficiency and distribution costs can sometimes be accomplished by joint marketing, perhaps under the sponsorship of the government or through arrangements between noncompeting companies.

Specialist salesmen can, of course, be used for industrial equipment and perhaps for some consumer durables, but it would be difficult and expensive to depend on a sales force for the distribution of many types of consumer goods. In that case, sales promotion and advertising are likely to be helpful in arousing demand for goods people do not know about or are indifferent to because they do not realize their advantages. Conventional promotion methods are, however, not likely to be successful. Where a large proportion of the inhabitants are illiterate, exhibitions and displays are much more effective than the written word. Products must be brought to the people by actual demonstration, with sound trucks to explain their uses.

When the principal exports are agricultural products, minerals, metals, and fuels, not much advertising and promotion are needed, though collective advertising and promotion of such products as tea and fine cotton are being undertaken, and many of the developing countries maintain trade missions abroad.

But the real problem is the export of manufactured goods, which are being produced in quantity and variety in many underdeveloped countries. India, for example, has become quite an exporter of fans, sewing machines, small machinery, finished iron and steel products, and clothing, as well as of the products of her traditional cottage industries. In selling to other underdeveloped countries the big factor is price, while quality and uniformity of quality may be the dominant factor in marketing to more advanced areas. Thus there must be different types of promotion, preferably by specialists in the potential markets.

SUMMARY

Large-scale industrial development, and hence a high standard of living, have characterized very few countries in the past. Now that many former colonies have gained their independence and other comparatively underdeveloped countries have thrown off dictatorships that have hampered their development, widespread efforts are being made to bring the benefits of industrialization to many parts of the world.

Many of the countries that are seeking development have adopted four- or five-year plans, under which agriculture will be made more productive through irrigation and fertilization of the land and capital goods will be imported so that industries may be started or expanded.

There are immense difficulties in the way, however, because the foreign exchange needed to import machinery and know-how can be acquired only by exporting the raw materials and such manufactured goods as are already available and consuming less at home. Since standards of living are already low, this is a difficult problem.

There are many theories about the genesis of industrial development and the type of people who spark it. For example, one is that "achievement-oriented" people are needed and that they might be developed by certain types of education. Another is that "social deviants," or people who are not accepted by the ruling groups in the underdeveloped country, are moved to start new activities in order to improve an otherwise fairly hopeless position. However, it is difficult to fit any one case of development into a general theory.

Considerable progress has been made in some of the countries that are working toward development, but their populations are growing so rapidly that a rise of, say, 3 or 4 per cent in production per year does not produce a comparable rise in the standard of living. Further, the original standard may be so low that even a sizable percentage rise does not mean a great deal.

Review Questions

1. What do the developing countries hope to accomplish by their four- and five-year plans?
2. What are some of the ways in which a government may ensure that such a plan is carried out without using the type of force the Soviet government employed in pursuing industrialization?
3. What are "social overheads"?
4. What are some of the advantages of using democratic methods in development? Some of the disadvantages?
5. What is meant by "the private sector" and "the public sector"?
6. How did Professor McClelland suggest that achievement-oriented people might be developed?
7. Give an example of social deviants who have helped development.

8. What are some of the ways in which the government of a developing country is likely to participate in private industry management?
9. What are some of the problems management is likely to encounter—aside from governmental interference—in an underdeveloped or developing country?

Case Study One / Selling Shoes in India

In the 1930s, Thomas Bata, the chief executive of Bata, the well-known Czechoslovak shoe manufacturer, was traveling through India. He noticed that few people were wearing shoes, and it occurred to him that if only 1 per cent of the large population were to buy his product, it would mean a new market larger than the one he was currently serving in his native land.

The difficulties appeared to be immense, however. The vast majority of India's population could not afford shoes, and in the case of those who could, the climate—always mild and often sweltering—would work against the purchase.

Bata, nevertheless, later decided to sell shoes to the Indians. His first step was to dispatch a group of his executives to India. These men not only had manufacturing and selling experience; they had an inflexible will to succeed. Hitler had begun to occupy their country, and there was no possibility of return.

Suppose you were one of this group of executives. What are some of the steps you would take in order to sell Bata shoes in India?

Case Study Two / Hiring Educated Nationals

An international company is attempting to hire nationals of the countries in which it operates with a view to training them for future positions in management. It has been the company's policy that all new members of the organization start at the bottom and gradually work up to more important work. This policy was adopted because of the intricacies of operation. The company believes that a manager, even after he has reached the point where he delegates very broad powers to others, should have fairly detailed knowledge of what needs to be done.

Many of the candidates come from groups and countries where class distinctions do not normally allow men of high caliber to perform the type of tasks required of trainees and new employees in the company. A number of those hired have left after a very short period of employment.

It is your responsibility to obtain new employees, but you cannot change your company's "start at the bottom" policy. What would you do to attract and hold foreign nationals with university educations or the equivalent?

Case Study Three / The Case of the Miraculous Road Building Corporation

The planning commission of Ruritania recommended a 50 per cent increase in the mileage of roads for the Second Five-year Plan. It is a large country with a short railroad network, which was already badly overtaxed by the First Five-year Plan. There was little scope for inland shipping. Unless at least this minimum extension of the greatly inadequate road system was satisfactorily accomplished, there was no possibility of meeting the country's industrial goals. Only an expanded road system could carry the additional raw materials, machinery, equipment, coal, and food required by the new plan. And it was only an expanded road system that could carry the raw materials and manufactured goods to pay for the increased imports.

The various ministries approved of the road building plans. The parliament ratified it. Ruritania's president was enthusiastic. The consortium of foreign companies that were aiding Ruritania was happy indeed at the proposals. The ministry of construction and road building gave its full support. The finance ministry made all the necessary domestic and foreign funds available. Labor was available. The newspapers and public opinion all gave their wholehearted support.

But at the end of the Second Five-year Plan, there was practically no expansion of the roads, and the existing network had deteriorated.

The government called in the Miraculous Road Building Corporation from the United States. You are in charge of foreign sales and construction. How would you go about carrying out Ruritania's road-building plan?

Selected Readings

Management of Industrial Enterprises in Under-developed Countries, United Nations, New York, 1958. A study by authors from different countries who pool their ideas and experience regarding organization, recruitment, training, labor-management relations, production facilities, marketing, controls, and relations between industry and government.

An International Trade in Managerial Skills, J. S. Fforde, Basil Blackwell, Oxford, 1957. A theoretical and practical essay on the different kinds of ventures in foreign countries—individual ventures, long- and short-term joint ventures, and so on.

The Economics of Under-developed Countries, P. T. Bauer and B. S. Yamey, Cambridge University Press, London, 1957. A handbook that focuses primarily on resource development, but includes several chapters dealing with entrepreneurship and labor problems.

American Business Abroad, Mira Wilkins and Frank E. Hill, Wayne State University Press, Detroit, Mich., 1966. An historical account of Ford Motor Company's operations abroad. Describes a variety of national problems and world changes during sixty years of development.

The Foreign Investment Decision Process, Yair Aharoni, Graduate School of Business Administration, Harvard University, Boston, Mass., 1966. Analyzes some of the ways U.S. firms decide to make direct foreign investments in developing countries. The decision process is related to the policy of the foreign government, and ways are suggested for achieving a harmony of interests.

Economic Growth and Development, Robert E. Baldwin, John Wiley & Sons, Inc., New York, 1966. Considers economic problems of developing countries, discusses the policies at issue, and offers a number of suggestions for coping with the problems.

Overseas Management, T. R. Brannen and F. X. Hodgson, McGraw-Hill Book Company, New York, 1965. Contrasts current technologies with existing ways of life in emerging countries. Discusses training and needs of foreign nationals working for U.S. companies overseas.

26
MANAGING
ABROAD

The business activity of the multinational corporations . . . is almost certain to increase even more rapidly in the future. . . .
Being responsible (or sharing responsibility) for operating industrial undertakings in a number of foreign countries will . . . be as common as it is today for large American manufacturing enterprises to operate in many states of the Union.
David Lilienthal: ''The Multinational Corporation,'' *Management and Corporations 1985*

26 After a rough economic-feasibility survey, starting an enterprise abroad almost always begins with either government negotiations or a search for local partners. Then the question of the appropriate legal instrument (e.g., a separate corporation or a division of the parent company) has to be tackled. Once the operation has begun, the parent company has the difficult choice of (1) controlling foreign operations as closely as domestic operations, (2) giving up almost all pretense of control, or (3) finding some middle way. Perhaps even more important than the degree of control is the question of selection and training of personnel and development of policies regarding their employment.

Development of foreign operations tends to be both attractive and repellent to companies that consider it. On the one hand, it may offer the possibility of greater profits, increased stability, further growth, opportunity for executive talent, and the chance to learn new techniques and acquire new products. On the other hand, the risks may be great. The company may encounter unsuspected pitfalls or, in some countries, face outright expropriation because of a change in government personnel or attitudes.

ADVANTAGES

One attraction, of course, is the possibility of extra opportunities for profit. A study of 100 major U.S. firms, made by McKinsey & Company,[1] showed that over half of them doubled their overseas profits between 1950 and 1960 and that the return on the foreign assets of these companies was higher than the return on their domestic assets. And although rates of return have been somewhat lower in the 1960s, they still appear to be good, especially when receipts from royalties and fees are included.[2]

The same thing is true of many European companies. Some concerns based in smaller countries, such as Holland and Belgium, have traditionally found the bulk of their earnings in foreign countries—for example, Unilever and Philips in Holland and the Société Générale in Belgium. Others have experienced great increases in earnings through investment in underdeveloped countries. Or take the petroleum industry, which is the most international of all. Almost half its earnings come from its foreign operations.

The improvement in stability may be even more marked since one of the problems of many companies in the more mature economies is industry overcapacity. In some industries, the production possible with existing plants and equipment is already greater than can be sold, while a large unmet demand may exist abroad. Thus returns on foreign investments help to keep total earnings stable when domestic sales may be slipping.

By the same token, a company in such an industry can grow through foreign investments when its sales at home cannot be increased because of the existing overcapacity. Under such circumstances, there would be no point in put-

[1] Warren M. Cannon, "The Expansion of American Corporations Abroad," *International Enterprise: A New Dimension of American Business*, McKinsey & Company, Inc., New York, 1962.
[2] Walther Lederer and Frederick Cutler, "International Investments of the United States in 1966," *Survey of Current Business*, September, 1967, pp. 39–52.

ting more money into new domestic capacity, yet there may be surplus funds crying out for investment. American automotive companies, for instance, have gained new markets in this way, and others have been able to show increased earnings in some years largely by improving foreign operations. For Corn Products and IBM, successful foreign operations have supplemented already successful domestic operations and increased the rate of growth.

It is quite possible, of course, for a company to tap foreign markets by export, selling abroad products that it manufactures here. In such a case, it does not even need to have its own foreign sales force; it can sell through agents already living in other countries. It can even have an export company in this country handle all the details, including the appointment of agents, the customs problems, and the currency exchange.

This method of selling abroad is less popular and profitable, relatively speaking, than it used to be, however, even though exports in the 1960s have been high. The rising tide of nationalism in many countries of the world has meant that the importation of finished goods for direct sale may be held to figures far below the market potential or, in the case of some products, forbidden altogether. Governments working for industrialization of their own countries try to conserve their scarce foreign exchange for imports that contribute most importantly to fulfillment of their four- and five-year plans.

The European Common Market also offers a threat to exports from other countries. It means that goods manufactured in the areas outside it will have to compete with those of Continental exporters who enjoy tariff advantages because their plants are located in ECM countries. With a plant or plants located inside the Common Market territory, this disadvantage can be eliminated.

There were tax advantages in some cases also. Many foreign countries have lower corporate income tax rates than the United States, and special tax legislation formerly existed in the United States for the encouragement of foreign trade. It is true that the ultimate effect might be only a postponement of U.S. taxes rather than a remission of them, but in view of the time value of money, this in itself might mean more dollars-and-cents return.

Still other monetary advantages to be derived from setting up plants abroad are the saving in freight rates and the possibility of lower costs through lower wage rates.

For these reasons U.S. export sales have tended to grow more slowly than the sales of U.S. operations abroad.

Finally, operations abroad may add considerably to technical and managerial know-how. Drawing in foreign scientists greatly broadens the possibility of new discoveries, to say nothing of the fact that it may be cheaper to do research abroad. Many American companies have established research centers in Europe for these reasons. Managerially, too, there is much to be learned from other countries, especially from Europe. The British genius for compromise, the French concept of managerial competence superimposed on technical ability, the negotiating and trading methods of the Dutch, the "rationalization" of the Germans—all can make contributions to management know-how.

POSSIBLE DISADVANTAGES

But there are many disadvantages that can negate or offset the advantages.

In the first place, the risk of failure is great. Time may be wasted in looking for opportunities that do not exist. And where the opportunities are good, a company may be too late in attempting to take advantage of them since others may have preempted them earlier. Many petroleum companies were too late in getting into foreign exploration and marketing, for example. Or the opportunities may be there, but the effort and risk necessary to take advantage of them may be out of proportion to the results. Labor rates may be lower than in the United States, but lower productivity may partly offset the differential. There may be many more fringe benefits required by law than the company realized. Government relations may prove to have many hidden (and unpleasant) facets. The native partners whom it may be necessary or advisable to take in may be difficult to work with. Land may not be available, nor a sufficient amount of water or power. For example:

> In many Latin American cities and in the Far East as well, quite often water flows from the mains only at night, the pressure being insufficient during the day. Oftentimes, also, the water is simply cut off on alternate days in sections of the city. . . .
>
> The supply of electric power is frequently inadequate and subject to voltage fluctuations and interruptions of service. In countries like Pakistan and India this can be checked, before the plant is built and without visiting the local utilities company, by noting the daily recurring stoppages of elevator services.[3]

Finally, when all these various difficulties are surmounted, the project itself may be a failure because the expected markets do not materialize, because the raw materials are not available in the quantities and at the prices planned on, because the company cannot get the prices for its products that it thought it could, or for any one of a number of other reasons. The world overseas is strewn with the bodies of white elephants that were once expected to be very profitable. There are abandoned gold and silver mines in Latin America and thousands of abandoned oil wells the world over. The British Labour Government embarked on an ambitious ground-nuts scheme in Africa that proved infeasible; factories have had to be shut down in many parts of the world.

Not all these failures should be criticized in the light of hindsight. Many of them were good, even sound, commercial risks when they were undertaken, but some factor or other did not turn out as expected, or was overlooked, or appeared too late to be considered.

STARTING AN ENTERPRISE ABROAD

Starting an enterprise abroad, even in a country that desperately needs new industry, is often a difficult and frustrating experience today. Certain kinds of foreigners and certain mannerisms are greatly disliked in some foreign coun-

[3] Carl W. Lintner (Parke, Davis & Company), "Handling Construction Problems in Foreign Countries," *Industrial Building*, vol. I, Clapp & Poliak, Inc., New York, 1961, p. 202.

tries, and the subtleties required to overcome these obstacles are not easy to learn. And there may be all kinds of legal restrictions that appear illogical and unjustified.

In an underdeveloped country, a manager must be able to mold all his efforts into the dominating relationships at the time. Unless these are clearly understood, all the techniques, however good, are not likely to be worth much.

In the beginning of the relationship between a more and a less developed country, businessmen from the former frequently had much greater bargaining power than the native officials or managers, for they were backed by the superior political, military, and economic power of their countries. Thus they could enforce contracts and managerial systems, except in cases where the natives could find means to boycott or sabotage agreements.

An outstanding example of such a relationship was that between the British trading companies, which were backed by the power of the British Empire, and many underdeveloped countries. For example, the Royal Nigeria Company was able to obtain grants for the exploitation of northern Nigeria that yielded enormous profits. But after some time this commercial organization endowed with royal sanction was taken over by the Crown itself, and what was then considered a trusteeship was substituted for exploitation.

A British administrator now provided some degree of economic (and personal) protection for the local population and thus cut both the gains and the opportunities of the foreign managers. Minimum prices were set for some of the natives' products, money wages rather than payment in kind were stipulated, and white people were barred from acquiring land. With the growth of a native independence movement, potential local managers received some scope, while local government increasingly shifted its business dealings to local people, at least to native middlemen like traders, brokers, agents, and lawyers, who in turn developed some economic independence, which strengthened their bargaining power.

When independence came, local managers lost the last of their handicaps. Insofar as they had supported the independence movement, their acquaintance with and their financing of the new men of power put them into positions of influence and knowledge. With more to contribute, their bargaining power vis-à-vis foreign managers rose.

Company-governmental negotiations

A company that is interested in establishing itself in a developing country is likely to encounter the government at most steps of the way.

The very possibility of the project depends on the government's plan for production of the product the company is proposing to make. First of all, the company must find out whether there is a gap between the projected output and the amount already licensed. If facilities geared to produce the total volume have already been licensed, it may be difficult to start the enterprise at all, even though the company may be able to produce at less cost than the enterprises already licensed. In some cases, it is true, it may be possible to get the product quota changed, but this is difficult since the economic plans are based on what is feasible in view of the total resources available.

Next, the prospective price of the product has to be ascertained in order to calculate the possible profit and hence the feasibility of the project. The government probably fixes the prices of many so-called essential commodities and may have to be consulted about most others. One of the real snags here is the question whether the price can be maintained over the prospective production period. Many governments reserve the right to change prices if a lower one will give the company what officials consider an "adequate" return. And rate-of-return considerations may lead into the vast morass of what is to be included in capital costs and what in expenses in any one year.

Even when all these intricate data have been collected, it would be foolish to go ahead with a large-scale feasibility study. First, it may well be necessary to obtain a native partner. In certain industries and countries, local partnership is required by government, and in any case it helps to ensure the safety of the investment. In addition, a local partner may be helpful in the attempt to penetrate the maze of government regulations and in getting the project approved or at least sponsored by an important official. Often, too, local partners can help in other ways since they know the local customs, the marketing channels, and many of the other factors that have to be taken into account.

But whether there is a local partner or not, the weary business of getting governmental approval for the license still has to be pursued. To start with, the negotiator must decide whether to begin with the local politicians or with the central government. The former are easier to get to and, once won over, may strengthen the company's bargaining power. The central government, on the other hand, can obviously overrule the local officials, whereas the latter can merely put pressure on the central government. Local officials would naturally like to have the moon for their own areas, but the central government may be unable to deliver simply because it lacks foreign exchange.

Hence success is more likely if the negotiator starts with the central government. But here again, there are difficult alternatives. Logic would appear to favor a first contact with the section of the ministry that deals with the industry contemplated, for starting elsewhere might raise a veritable storm of objections from "channels" to "saving face" from the slighted group. But doing the right thing in this respect may mean abject surrender to some petty bureaucrat more interested in showing his power or in frustrating someone else than in fostering industrial development. The motives of the small bureaucrat may be so complex and shifting as to make him impossible to work with.

Thus to gain some bargaining power in dealing with the petty tyrant, it may be necessary to go higher and present the project in another quarter. But where? Theoretically, one might start with the country's chief executive— president or prime minister—for in theory he can make any decision. But how can the company get at him? And how can it gain his interest and assent when his mind is busy with a thousand and one other problems?

In any case, the head of state will probably fall back on his trusted advisers.

But who are they? If one approaches the minister of finance, he may be interested only in the financial consequences of the project, the minister of power in the consumption of electric power, and so on. The planning commission may be interested, but have no decision-making powers; the minister of industry may see value in the project but be unwilling to offend some of the company's possible native competitors because he may be fighting for his political life.

In any case, the searcher for a license will soon find that a promise by any one minister is meaningless unless it is in writing, and even then it is not to be heavily counted on until it has actually been carried out. And, incidentally, the written promise may be obtained in some cases only by a promise to put the minister or one of his relatives on the board of directors or to give the family business a supply contract or some similar inducement. This is not necessarily true, but it may be.

Another question is whether and when to use diplomatic pressure. On the face of it, this is not desirable; politics and economics may not mix well. But often some matter of trade or aid may be pending, and the implication of a *quid pro quo* can be an important lever.

When the negotiator has threaded his way among these numerous pitfalls, he may have gathered enough information to fill out the necessary license application (perhaps in as many as twenty-four copies). This in itself is a major undertaking because the written word may be more binding than anything that has occurred previously. The negotiator puts down what he thinks the government officials think he should promise, but he must remember all the many viewpoints to be considered. Drawing up a license application that will please all the scrutinizers in the various agencies may be almost as difficult as squaring the circle.

Each ministry may feel obligated to raise questions about the application, and it is the searcher for the license who has to find the answers. Hence it is sometimes vital that the product and application be technically so complex that they cannot be quizzed out of existence. There may be no one to coordinate the inquiring ministries, and our executive in search may have to do the coordination himself. And on the way he may have to make plenty of concessions.

Not infrequently, one particular issue may negate all the work. For instance, it is not unusual for a severe difference of opinion to arise over the issue of a royalty for a patent, process, or product. The government may insist on a rate, say 3 to 5 per cent, that it has been allowing everyone else, feeling that if it were to deviate from past practice it might have to permit reopening of earlier agreements. The company, on the other hand, cannot accept a lower rate than it has been granted in other countries (say 10 per cent) without laying itself open to requests for new contracts elsewhere. Sometimes such an apparently insoluble problem may be resolved by setting the formal royalty at the higher figure but paying only the lower percentage. More often the matter is not resolved at all, and the country may lose the chance for important new production.

Even when the license is granted, many more snags—often unforeseen—may arise. One of the biggest obstacles is likely to be interposed by the finance ministry, which sets the rules for repatriation of dividends and funds designed to amortize the original investment. There are many intricate, hidden, and unforeseen ways in which the investing company may be barred from receiving the money in the form or at the time originally stipulated.

Again, tax rates, import duties, or "reference" prices (stipulated with a view to return on investment) may be changed adversely and suddenly in midstream. Or the foreign exchange necessary to import a basic raw material or spare parts may be withheld—perhaps to put on pressure for more concessions or simply because the necessary exchange is no longer available. Agreements made for years are suddenly revised—"or else."

Yet sometimes the benefits to all parties are resoundingly clear: for example, the use of waste gases produced in a petroleum-rich country for the manufacture of ammonia, the product to be shipped to a nearby developing country for use in the manufacture of low-cost fertilizer, part of which could be exported to provide more foreign exchange. The petroleum country would get payments for gas presently going to waste; the country in which the fertilizer was produced would get it at low cost and without drain on its foreign exchange; and the company financing the project would receive income from both plants.

But before this fortunate result can be reached, many steps have to be undertaken. In the petroleum country, there may be distrust of the power of the foreign manager, which can usually be overcome only by showing that no comparable native operation is able to undertake the project. Many different ministers may have the power of veto, or at least of delay, and satisfying them all will be difficult.

Once all these shoals are successfully avoided, the plant has to be built, and here numerous snags may arise. All the available land may be occupied either by small farmers (whom the ministry of agriculture refuses to dispossess) or by the ministry of defense, which may dislike the native partner. The problems of water and power mentioned earlier will have to be solved, a whole housing colony may have to be built for the workers, and a special railway line constructed to carry the raw materials and finished goods because the company which hoped to use river transportation finds that rapids do not permit sufficiently smooth sailing.

Many of these matters require negotiations with the local officials, and progress may be hampered by local ordinances.

JOINT VENTURES

A joint venture is an association of two or more enterprises formed to accomplish a business objective. Generally those taking part will contribute to the financing of the enterprise and possibly provide managerial talent. Or a joint venture may involve the licensing of one partner by the other to produce a certain product for which the latter holds a patent and the provision of special managerial or technical know-how or the contribution of construction facilities, trademarks, or franchises. Joint ventures are sometimes undertaken in the United States, but they are, perhaps, commoner in other countries.

Financial arrangements

Joint ventures are usually and most frequently characterized by their financial relationship. One common type of relationship is a 50-50 partnership under which each side contributes an equal amount of money to the financing of the enterprise. This has the advantage of giving each party equal rights and duties as well as an equal share of the benefits. But, of course, there is the disadvantage of lack of unity of command; namely, what is to be done in case of disagreement between the two partners? Sometimes nothing short of arbitration will resolve the deadlock.

More frequently the arrangement puts one party or the other in a minority, although joint approval may be required for vital decisions, such as changes in the capital structure, dividend payments, principal appointments, and investment decisions.

Less frequently, there are several partners, and the joint venture becomes a consortium. One of the most famous examples of this is in the oil industry, in which a consortium of several companies operates the Iranian National Oil Company with varying percentages of participation.

Opposition to joint ventures

Many companies are flatly opposed to the whole concept of joint venture. Among these are some of the most prominent United States corporations, such as GM and IBM. Partly, of course, they may speak from bad experience, such as undue interference from partners or too great an insistence on immediate payout as against long-term capital gains. They may also take into consideration the need to concentrate on one product in each country, which may not be the most profitable course from the country's point of view although it is the most profitable for a company with worldwide interests. For example, a particular component may be produced most cheaply in one country, but this may make less of a contribution to the profit in that country than would the assembly of all the components, which is cheaper in another country.

There may be a powerful distrust of the managerial ability and honesty of any potential partner in another country. And this animosity may be particularly directed against any potential governmental participation, especially where the ideology is different. But above all, there is the reluctance to abandon any kind of control over company affairs. This is partly because of the strong desire for omnipotence, partly because of the fear of mistakes that might occur.

Yet the arguments for joint ventures are strong indeed and appear to be gaining. Certainly this is true in the developing countries, as well as in countries like Italy and Japan, and among companies that themselves tend to be short of managerial talent or technical know-how.

Possible advantages

Probably the most important reasons for a joint venture are the real contributions made by the partners to the profitability of the business:

1. *Know-how.* One party is almost sure to have technical know-how: Its executives know the product, the methods of manufacture, and the marketing channels. And it may also have patents without which the product cannot be manufactured. The other party, in this case, may contribute some local know-how, which will be helpful in getting the many permits that must be obtained from the government, in locating land, and in getting local construction help, local production workers, and possibly some managerial and technical talent.
2. *Capital.* One of the partners will usually have adequate capital to finance the whole undertaking or a major part of it. He may even lend the other partner money for participation and be paid back out of the resulting profits.
3. *Protection.* One partner may supply diplomatic protection (as the British did in Kuwait, where they are in petroleum partnership with the local government) or (through its own government) investment guarantees against expropriation or provision for transfer of dividends and amortization of capital.

Dealing with local partners

The search for a good local partner may be as difficult as the search for a marriage partner. On the face of it, the native industrialists with the highest reputations or the largest holdings may seem the most desirable, and are often so in fact. Though they are also the ones most in demand and therefore able to exact the best terms, it may be impossible to operate without them. Also, paying their price may be the cheapest course in the long run.

The second echelon of industrialists, who may be more eager for the deal and seem ready to accept a smaller share of the profits, may prove to be more demanding in fact since they will not have the same feeling of *noblesse oblige*. The foreign negotiator may be forced into semishady commissions at the expense of other shareholders, into putting relatives on the payroll, and making similar concessions.

Below the second level one usually cannot go in an underdeveloped country. Either the partner will be merely a stooge and collector for politicians, or he will be accustomed to such small operations that it will take him years to become acclimated to large ones. He may even be only an amiable farmer who likes to display his water buffaloes, his coconuts, his orchids or—if he is really small peanuts—his single rose bush.

Of course, in the more rapidly developing countries, there is a wider choice of partners, but even there the relationships may be difficult. It may be that differences of opinion can be resolved only by negotiations between principals, and this becomes a time-consuming affair if the company has operations in many countries. And the final agreements on the problems may be informal, unbacked by legal documents. As one partner remarked to his Japanese opposite: "But what do we do when one day I fall out of an airplane, and you fall out of a geisha house?"

The very process of negotiation is strenuous. A prospective native partner may try to tie up the foreign negotiator every available minute so that competitors cannot get to him. And the negotiations may take longer than seems reasonable, especially if procrastination and discussion of matters entirely beside the point are a normal part of local business dealings.

In some cases, there are irreconcilable differences in viewpoint that may make future operations difficult. For example, local partners may want a high unit price and profit for a quick return, while foreign managers may represent large corporations that are interested in long-run profits and so are willing to forego some immediate gain for the sake of overall optimum return over a long period. Or the local partner may have other interests that make it unwise for him to compete too strenuously in the industry.

GROWTH OF OPERATIONS ABROAD

The seeds of growth through foreign operations are generally sown through the export of goods, which may be handled through agents and distributors or through a special sales branch abroad.

The next step is usually taken when strong nationalism and foreign exchange or import restrictions make export of finished goods difficult or impossible. Then a company may pursue one of two roads: It may seek to keep its involvement in foreign countries to a minimum, or it may gradually work its way toward greater involvement in its foreign business.

Noninvolvement may be attained, to some extent, by licensing foreign manufacturers to produce a product protected by trademarks or patents in return for a royalty payment, a specified sum for each unit produced. To achieve the best results in this way, however, a company may have to train the foreign manufacturer's management and engineering staff in production methods and perhaps do some policing to be sure that quality is maintained. Otherwise, it may find its royalties decreasing and its reputation abroad tarnished. If the foreign licensee can issue sublicenses at will, which is sometimes, though rarely, the case, the situation is even more dangerous.

In any case, an increasing number of firms are taking the usually more difficult road of setting up their own facilities abroad. When a country forbids the importation of the finished product or makes it difficult or unprofitable by setting a quota or imposing high tariffs, the company may instead ship the components and start overseas assembly.

Thus the automotive industry started with knocked-down exports. Parts were made in the home country, shipped to the foreign country, and put together in an assembly plant established there. Gradually, some of the parts will be produced in the foreign country, as well as assembled there. Ultimately all the parts may be produced in the foreign country, which may even become an exporter to surrounding countries.

Organization

The simplest form of structure is the branch organization, which is simply an integral part of the parent company—a division or department.

On the other hand, the company may set up a subsidiary, a new corporate entity organized under the laws of the foreign country, and take its profit in the form of dividends. The big advantage here formerly was that as long as it reinvested its profits in expanding and improving the foreign subsidiary it paid no U.S. tax. True, it would probably have to pay foreign income taxes, but these might be set against U.S. taxes on the portion of the profits repatriated, and might be lower than U.S. taxes. Changes in the U.S. tax laws in the 1960s have negated this advantage, however.

Companies do not necessarily confine themselves to any one form of organization for their operations abroad. A concern may have, for example, subsidiaries in some countries and branches in others, and in still others it may license foreign manufacturers. In any case, some provision must be made for coordination of the foreign activities with each other and with the operations of the parent company.

If a company's overseas operations are not complex—say it has only one or two subsidiaries—there may be no special organization required in the home office. In such a case, the parent company president and one or two other executives exercise general supervision over the subsidiaries. Managers abroad contact the various functional departments in the home office—sales, manufacturing, and so on—on special problems that develop. The advantage of this type of organization is that top management has a working knowledge of its operations abroad and can keep close control. If the foreign operations become too large and complex, however, this advantage will probably be lost because the top managers simply will not have enough time to devote to them.

Another possibility is to divide foreign operations on a functional basis. In this instance, subsidiary department heads report directly to the functional officers in the home office—the sales branches abroad to the head of marketing and the plant managers to the manufacturing vice-president, for example. In this way, domestic and foreign operations are closely coordinated with those of the parent company, which may be a decided advantage. On the other hand, there is the danger that there will be a lack of coordination among departments and perhaps a conflict of interest as well. Further, there may be important differences between domestic problems and the problems encountered abroad, and the same executive may not understand both.

When operations abroad reach any size and begin to include several subsidiaries and to reach into a number of different countries, the company will probably organize an international division in the home office to supervise and control them. This will be headed by a general manager (who may have the title of vice-president or president) to whom the general managers of the subsidiaries report. Assisting him will be a staff capable of providing assistance on such matters as finance, sales, manufacturing, economics, and other specialized functions.

Still another possibility is the international corporation or world trade corporation. This is similar to the international division, except that it is a separate corporate entity and is headed by a president and board of directors. Sometimes such a concern is incorporated abroad, perhaps in a European country; sometimes it is incorporated in the United States. The head of the corporation will report directly to the parent company president, and the directors will include members of top management of the parent company as well as the heads of subsidiaries. While he will probably make frequent trips abroad, the president of an international corporation and the members of his staff will generally have their headquarters in or near the home office of the parent company.

Many variations of these forms of organization are possible. For example, the head of the foreign division may have two chief subordinates, one in charge of sales and one in charge of manufacturing. Or there may be general managers for each country or each region in which the company has both sales and manufacturing operations. The head of the international division may have staff men, known as product managers, who provide advice and assistance on the sale of particular product groups. Again, the head of the foreign division may share authority with the parent company controller and the vice-president of manufacturing. Or some one function may be separated from the foreign division and put under the parent company department. For example, Parke, Davis & Company has an overseas operations division, but construction of overseas facilities comes under the domestic engineering department, which includes a special overseas engineering group, several of whom are of foreign ancestry and speak one or more foreign languages.

Control

Some parent companies control their subsidiaries tightly and exercise close supervision over even minor details. Others allow their subsidiaries considerable leeway in operational practices and decisions. Companies may be grouped into three categories in this respect:

1. Subsidiaries are required to keep the home office informed of all operational details and may have to ask home office permission before taking any important action.

2. Subsidiaries are required to submit many reports; however, they have considerable freedom to act without seeking permission in advance.
3. Subsidiaries are permitted almost complete freedom, and only a minimum of information is required by the home office.

The advantages and disadvantages of the three categories of parent company control are as follows:

I. Category 1 (tight control)
   A. Advantages
      1. The parent company is kept closely informed of all matters pertaining to the subsidiary, and the decision making in the home office ensures that subsidiary operations follow home office policy.
      2. Subsidiary managers, conditioned to home office reporting, are more likely to nip problems in the bud and to request help before conditions get out of hand.
      3. Since the brunt of subsidiary operation is borne by the home office, the subsidiary manager does not have to be a man of top management caliber.
      4. Personnel transfers between subsidiaries are more easily effected.
      5. The close touch the parent company has with each subsidiary's operation permits highly integrated, company-wide coordination.
   B. Disadvantages
      1. The subsidiary manager may not have the authority, experience, or initiative to act in emergencies.
      2. Costly time lags may develop in the wait for home office decisions and approvals.
      3. Changes in regional aspects of competition may demand unilateral action. The parent company may insist that rigid standard procedures be used by all subsidiaries without exception.
      4. Highly skilled management men may be deterred from going abroad, or may not stay long once they have arrived, if their chief responsibility is to rubber-stamp and pass along home office directives.
      5. Tight control may be impossibly expensive and its effectiveness illusory.
II. Category 2 (moderate control)
   A. Advantages
      1. The parent company receives most of the essential information relating to the operation of the subsidiaries.
      2. Through data furnished by the many subsidiary reports, the home office can ward off many problems that might otherwise necessitate a policy change.
      3. The performance of different subsidiaries can be readily compared.

4. The close contact between executives in the parent company and those in the subsidiaries makes possible quick communication of new ideas, methods, and other items of interest.

5. Since they must constantly prepare reports and memoranda for the home office, the subsidiary managers are kept abreast of the trends and details of their own operations.

6. The freedom given the executive in charge at the subsidiary to plan and direct operations permits him to use his ingenuity and develops his managerial competence. Further, his morale is likely to be higher if his responsibility is greater.

7. Decisions can be made more quickly and by those closest to the problems.

B. Disadvantages

1. The subsidiary executive may be required to supply so much information to the home office that he will not have sufficient time to function effectively.

2. Good administrators are not necessarily adept paper-work specialists, and vice versa. It may be difficult to fill the top position with a man possessing the desired blend of these sometimes divergent talents.

3. Since the home office receives detailed reports of subsidiary activities but leaves operations to subsidiary management, it may become supercritical of subsidiary results and thereupon set up goals and standards impossible for the manager to meet.

4. Staff specialists may have difficulty in getting their advice accepted.

III. Category 3 (little control)

A. Advantages

1. The subsidiary manager has wide freedom. He can devote full time to his main job as subsidiary manager: realizing profit.

2. Both parent company and subsidiary overhead will be reduced to the extent that decentralized operations eliminate report makers and report checkers. There should be sizable reductions in the personnel required for these activities.

3. Morale at the subsidiary is likely to be quite high since the subsidiary will be functioning primarily on its own. Checks and directives from the home office will be at a minimum.

4. Better decisions may be made by the man on the spot. One company president once cabled the chief of a subsidiary: "You are there; we are here; you make the decisions."

B. Disadvantages

1. The position of the subsidiary manager is a difficult one to fill. He must be exceptionally capable, reliable, and enterprising— a top-caliber executive.

2. Coordinating and integrating overall subsidiary operations become a vexatious problem.

3. The home office may not learn of festering problems until much damage has been done.
4. Intersubsidiary transfers may present headaches since the management practices in the subsidiaries will probably differ widely.

Of the three categories of control, number 2 is likely to be the most effective. Under this system, the home office is adequately provided with information relating to each subsidiary's operation. The subsidiary manager, on the other hand, has sufficient freedom to make decisions in the light of his knowledge of the factors that make his domain uniquely different from that of any of the other company subsidiaries. Category 1 is too inflexible, and category 3 is too deficient in checks and balances.

Areas of parent company control

Whichever form of centralized or decentralized operation a company sets up in its subsidiary operations, there are basic prerogatives that remain with the parent company. Several of these major policy areas are:

1. Control over product or product mix. The parent company determines what products are to be made, discontinued, or replaced, and sets the quality standards.
2. Control over budget and financial matters. This includes the right to specify standard accounting procedures, the financial information to be submitted, and the budget limitations to be observed.
3. Control over the selection, transfer, and promotion of top personnel for foreign operations service (including their remuneration). This control over personnel appointments affords the home office an indirect opportunity to monitor the performance of key personnel at the subsidiaries.
4. Control over major decisions in subsidiary operations: changes in capital stock and in membership of the board of directors. Expansion and retrenchment programs, disposition of profits, and so on are representative of the major points to be decided by the parent company. The home office can view such matters objectively and can relate them to the needs and goals of the company-wide organization.

The formula for an ideal blend of home office control and subsidiary responsibility, however, varies from company to company, it even differs from subsidiary to subsidiary. In the initial stages of subsidiary development, home office control is understandably great. However, as growing-pain problems are resolved and the subsidiary moves forward and makes profits more on its own, something akin to near-independence is usually granted to it. This independence is qualified to the extent that whatever standards are implicit in the company name and reputation must be maintained at the subsidiary.

What criterion is there to determine how successfully a subsidiary operation has been developed? A spokesman for the international division of a leading pharmaceutical company put it this way:

If a country thinks of a company subsidiary as being French, Brazilian or Turkish, then the organization has succeeded. The best arrangement is a group of companies on a string with the home office as a sort of holding company. The home office does little more than set basic policy and procedure and make sure that production standards are maintained.

Selection of personnel

When a company begins operation abroad, it has usually had experience in exporting, and in that case the export manager may become the head of its first subsidiary, particularly if it is a sales subsidiary. If he is also familiar with manufacturing abroad—and some export managers have worked in foreign manufacturing operations—he will be able, with the advice and help of manufacturing specialists from the home office, to get manufacturing operations going also. Otherwise, it may be necessary to hire from the outside.

If a company already has foreign subsidiaries, it may transfer someone from a nearby operation to a new subsidiary—for example, from one Latin American country to another. Or the manager of the foreign division may take on the general management of the subsidiary until he can find or train a man to assume the responsibility.

Companies today do not have as free a hand as they once did in deciding whom to send abroad and for what position. As the tide of nationalist feeling rises, developing countries in particular are not likely to look with favor on a company in which all or even a substantial number of important positions are staffed by people from another country. Thus most companies, even when they are not compelled to do so by law, are attempting to train nationals of the countries in which they operate for increasingly important positions.

It is, of course, necessary that those sent abroad be flexible and not inclined to regard anything different from what they are used to as necessarily inferior. Speaking the language is, of course, a help; so is former residence in the country in which the manager will operate.

But the selection problem is a difficult one. The personnel manager of a company which sends large numbers of American personnel to a very underdeveloped country in which conditions are very different from those in the United States once said: "I've learned one thing—to distrust my own intuition. Every time I meet a man who seems to be just the type we need, one who will be happy abroad and willing to stay long enough to make it worth our while to send him, he always turns out to be the one who gives up after a few months." The same company once hired a psychologist to help with the selection procedure and found that his judgments produced results worse than it had obtained before.

Some companies like to hire single men, particularly for underdeveloped countries, on the theory that they are more adaptable and venturesome and will devote more time to the job. If a man is single, only his own adjustment possibilities have to be considered; if he is married, his wife must be taken into account. While he may like the job, she may be continually pressuring him to apply for a transfer or to quit. If they have children, they will not want to stay long in any country that does not provide what they consider adequate educational facilities. On the other hand, single men may lack stability, be restless, and possibly become involved in indiscretions, whereas married men are likely to be more settled and dependable.

One American oil company with operations in the Middle East made a study of the relative success achieved by the men it sent abroad. It concluded that the best risks were middle-aged men with grown children. The worst were bachelors, young married men with small children, and escapists—that is, those who thought that by going abroad they would escape the problems troubling them at home.

Where surroundings are desertlike, another company has found, people from California or Texas appear to be better bets than those from New England —perhaps because the New Englanders become depressed by the lack of sharp seasonal changes and greenery in summer.

Sometimes the "best" recruit may be described according to his fitness to carry out particular facets of company policy. This consideration may be explored, for example, within the framework of the following questions:

1. Are overseas personnel to be considered company ambassadors, or are they to remain aloof from the cultural environment? Are technical skill and job performance more important than personality, gregariousness, or adaptability?
2. How much autonomy will the subsidiary have? Are decision making and improvisation desired above a more or less rigid following of the blue-prints?
3. What proportion of the personnel will be sent from the parent company and what job categories will they fill? What categories will be filled by nationals? What specific talents will be required to perform the super-visory, technical, and operations work? (In general, companies exerting tight control over subsidiaries prefer to have their citizens in key posi-tions. Companies requiring small control hire nationals for many key positions.)
4. How extensive a training program is necessary for adequate preparation? How much indoctrination will be required (a) at home (b) in the foreign country?
5. What is the nature of the overseas operation? How much of the manu-facturing, sales, marketing, advertising, and other functions will be per-formed at the subsidiary, and what skills are required by both Americans and nationals in performing these functions?

The rationale of a set framework of rules and regulations governing selection of subsidiary personnel has often been overthrown by such contradictory examples as the home office misfit who became a success in the overseas branch and the surprising failure of the home territory star salesman when he went abroad.

Companies that have stressed more or less standard concepts in their selection requirements have not met with as much success in their appointments as those that delve deeper into motivational and sociological aspects.

For example, one company obtained good executives for foreign operations by seeking candidates who displayed:

1. A rational motivation for going abroad
2. Fluency in languages and knowledge of the environment
3. No dominant prejudices regarding races, religions, or cultures
4. No overpowering attachment to Stateside affiliations.

In addition to gauging a candidate on the basis of technical knowledge and general impression, a company may be interested in factors that could play a decisive part in determining whether the man will make a go of it in his work abroad. Among some of these additional considerations are such factors as:

1. *Adjustability.* Will changed food habits, housing, wearing apparel, recreation outlets, work practices, be accepted smoothly?
2. *Resourcefulness.* Is the individual "self-entertaining"? Can he get along with little and make the most of lonely situations?
3. *Marital or emotional ties.* If he is married, does his wife possess the necessary stamina, resourcefulness, and adaptability? If he is unmarried, will the "girl he left behind" impel him to return as soon as possible?

Training   Companies making a substantial investment in the personnel they send abroad take their candidates' training as seriously as their selection. Even wives are given a part in some of the preparation programs.

Many training programs include periodic stays abroad as well as comprehensive training at home. The length of the training period may vary from several months to a couple of years, depending on the responsibility and scope of the final assignment. Companies that provide lengthy and detailed training programs obtain the best results.

In the opinion of many personnel directors for overseas operations, job training should begin as soon as the student decides on a career abroad. The sooner the student has facility in the country's language, the greater his chance for long-run success. The question is often asked: To what extent should the foreign operations man learn the language and be familiar with customs and traditions of the country to which he is going? The optimum is said to be the point where the man's responses to people and situations are almost like those of a native.

In hiring and training, a custom increasingly frowned upon today is taking college graduates, giving them a "quickie" training course, and then sending them off to locations abroad. Regardless of the obvious shortcomings and dangers inherent in this method, it does represent the current major system employed to fill overseas vacancies.

Term of stay   If a man succeeds in an overseas assignment, it is naturally to the interest of the company to keep him there as long as practical. Much, of course, depends on the man and the responsibility of his position. Leave at home is scheduled intermittently when the overseas appointment is considered permanent. Sometimes, as in the assignment of missionaries, a rotation system is practiced: some years in the field, then one year at home. An overseas duty tour ordinarily lasts from three to five years. Whereas a permanent assignment has the advantage of promising good assimilation of the company into the native economy, the rotation assignment has the advantage of periodically refreshing the subsidiary operation in parent company outlook and practices.

It is generally much easier to train the local employees at the subsidiary site than to bring them to the parent company for instruction. Of course, in instances where extraordinary technique is required, or where complete understanding of detailed processes and methods must precede the opening of the subsidiary plant, training at the parent company is necessary.

With the trend toward national pride throughout the world, more and more local employees are assuming key roles in subsidiary supervision. This adds a new requirement for the few Americans who are sent abroad and for the nationals already in supervisory positions: the ability to teach. In time the new appointee may well have to transfer his knowledge and skill to the national.

Operating a subsidiary

The problem of blending the plant into the local community is no less important than the blending of the employee. It is not only incongruous but sometimes ridiculous for a subsidiary to operate as a facsimile of its parent. Successful subsidiary operation, in the opinion of many experienced international companies, is a succession of compromises. Traditions, customs, and local patterns—in work, recreation, meals, and other everyday details—cannot be treated lightly, much less ignored. This is particularly important if the subsidiary depends on the regional market for sales and product distribution.

The matter of compromise is of great importance to successful subsidiary operation. Compromising does not necessarily mean a lowering of standards or the acceptance of a less than good alternative. To be sure, some concessions may be found wanting when compared with domestic practices—but viewed according to the regional outlook, they may be effective, workable answers to problems. Much compromising consists of adapting set ways and textbook precepts to regional requirements. For example, in the United States, personnel administration is often concerned with policies setting uniform standards of behavior. If this system were installed intact in some subsidiaries abroad, it could readily arouse antagonism and resistance. A company that enforces conduct and performance contrary to time-honored traditions and local patterns of behavior will find the going rough indeed.

A company with a trademark item known for its specific ingredients or high-quality workmanship will require that standards be maintained to ensure continued good reputation. The regional programs to maintain these levels may vary from area to area, and holding locals to the standards may be quite a problem. Consider, for example, the variety of attitudes toward work that may be found in different areas:

1. Work is a virtue—the harder one works and the longer, the greater one's prestige.
2. The less work and the less effort one can get away with, the better.
3. Craftsmanship is the hallmark of work success. Time is unimportant. Skill is the important thing.
4. Long rest periods and meal breaks are popular. Employees object to being hurried.

THE MULTINATIONAL COMPANY

Large corporations are becoming increasingly multinational—that is, they produce and sell in all parts of the world and allocate their resources with worldwide production and marketing opportunities in mind.

The basic aim of such a company is to concentrate production where economies of scale will be greatest and to sell its products wherever there is a market that can be profitably supplied. Thus IBM concentrates its European computer plants in France and markets the products in all the Common Market countries. As a matter of fact, the company gave up joint ownership of companies in some countries in order to be free to shift production wherever it would be most worthwhile from a world view.

Again, a textile company may produce fibers in the United States, have the cloth spun and woven in South India, where there are surplus capacity and labor and lower labor costs, then ship it back to the United States for higher-quality dyeing and finally to Hong Kong for finishing. Although the transportation costs may be higher than they would be if all the operations were performed in one country and there will be import duties to pay, overall costs may be lower.

The basic argument for the international company is that production and marketing efficiency can be improved if a firm escapes the narrow confines of economic nationalism, and in this way there is better utilization of resources all over the world. Capital may be raised in one or several countries, raw materials produced in a host of other countries, parts of the product manufactured in still other countries, and the finished products marketed where the demand for them is greatest.

The concept of the international company is quite an old one. Even in the Middle Ages the trading companies organized by monarchs (e.g., the East India Company organized by British monarchs), bankers (the Fuggers in Germany), and merchants (the Hudson's Bay Company) produced and traded in different countries under centralized direction. As transportation and communication improved in the nineteenth century, the concept of the international company grew considerably. Among the main contributors were the Rathenaus (Emil and Walther, father and son), who used the Edison patents to set up general and specialized electrical companies in different parts of the world outside the United States. Walther Rathenau was the coordinating genius, sitting on over a hundred boards of directors in several dozen countries just before World War I, which destroyed the trend toward the internationalization of electrical company management. On a smaller scale, another German industrialist, Danny Heineman, set up the Sofina, which supplied power in different countries.

The movement toward internationalization of large corporations has gained strength in the postwar period, and it would undoubtedly have done so even without the European Common Market, although that may have had an important influence.

The most serious problem that an international company faces is political and economic nationalism and the fear that it may intervene in local affairs or act contrary to the national interest of some of its host countries. For example, it could shift production from one region to another and leave a large number of jobless in the country where plants were originally located. And from the company's own viewpoint, there is always the possibility that its plants may be expropriated when there is a change of government or when war breaks out.

One possible solution to this problem that has been suggested by George Ball, former U.S. Undersecretary of State, and others is the establishment of an international companies' law, perhaps by passage of identical legislation in different countries, with administration by a supranational body. This might impose certain obligations on the international companies (for example, they might be prevented from becoming monopolies), but in return they would receive protection against expropriation and restrictions on the transfer of capital or profits from one country to another. Probably their stock would be held by nationals of many countries, and many different nationalities would be represented on the board of directors.

The International Chamber of Commerce is interested in such a possibility, and so are some governments, but any firm action on it is doubtless some years away. It would be ideal, of course, if, in the words of Shinzo Ohya, president of a large Japanese company (Teijin, Ltd.), there could be "full utilization of the genius of each nation for its own benefit and that of others," but the difficulties are enormous, not only because of nationalistic feelings but because of differing currencies, customs, laws, and other factors.

SUMMARY

It is clear from even this short analysis that managing abroad necessitates consideration of many more factors than must be taken into account in managing at home, and that many of these are more uncertain and more variable. Under these circumstances, it is more difficult than usual to arrive at generalizations to which not too many exceptions can be made. However, a few may be suggested:

1. The trend toward toward operating abroad is rising because of the growth of common market areas, the increase of nationalism within these areas, rising populations and demands, and increasing surplus capacity in a number of domestic industries.
2. The expected return from foreign investments usually has to be greater than the domestic return to compensate for the extra risks.
3. Corporate unity of command is likely to be more diffused because of some share in managerial power by foreign governments and/or local partners.
4. Legal considerations are likely to be dominant in determining the organization structure.
5. Close control of foreign operations from domestic headquarters is likely to be damaging.
6. The selection and training of foreign personnel are best handled in the light of the foreign country's needs rather than through an exact duplication of domestic practices.
7. Foreign personnel, while they may make major contributions, will gradually give way to local talent. The latter is likely to be increasingly represented in the top councils of the large international corporations.
8. The "joint venture," in spite of many well-known drawbacks and some bad experience, is likely to become of increasing importance.

Review Questions

1. What are the advantages of exporting goods to a foreign country as against building a plant and producing them there? What possible disadvantages are there?
2. What are the advantages and disadvantages of centralizing management of foreign subsidiaries or divisions in the home office? Of centralizing management of operations? Of centralizing policy making? Of centralizing control?
3. What kind of training would you advocate for service in the foreign subsidiary of a large company?
4. How would you go about finding outlets for sale of your company's products abroad? How would you go about establishing a plant for production of your company's products in a foreign country?
5. What are some possible advantages and disadvantages of 100 per cent ownership of a foreign subsidiary? Of majority ownership? Of minority ownership?
6. What may be some of the advantages of hiring native personnel for management positions in a foreign subsidiary? Are there any disadvantages?
7. How does a multinational company differ from a national company with operations abroad?
8. What are some of the problems a multinational company may encounter?

━━━━━━━━━━━━━━━━━━━━━━━━━━━━━━━━━━━━━

Case Study / Establishment of Manufacture in Australia*

━━━━━━━━━━━━━━━━━━━━━━━━━━━━━━━━━━━━━

General Motors entered the automobile business in Australia in 1926, establishing assembly plants in the five major cities, Brisbane, Sydney, Melbourne, Adelaide, and Perth. At that time, American car and truck chassis were shipped largely from Canadian operations; English car and truck chassis from Vauxhall Motors in Great Britain were assembled with bodies purchased from Holden's Motor Body Builders, Ltd., in Adelaide. In 1931, General Motors Australia took over Holden's Motor Body Builders, and the name of the company became General Motors–Holden's, Ltd. The common stock was wholly owned by General Motors Corporation.

For several years prior to the outbreak of World War II, pressure had been exerted on the industry by Australian government officials to establish manufacturing facilities in Australia for cars and trucks to be sold in the local market, in New Zealand, and other countries of the Far East. The pressure had its origin in the national desire for greater industrialization of the Australian economy. Preliminary surveys indicated that manufacture in Australia presented many problems and considerable doubt that such manufacture would be economical in comparison to the assembly of parts produced in Canada or the United States on a much larger scale than the volume that the Australian market could provide.

For example, it was possible to import a Chevrolet motor at less than half the cost of producing it in Australia because of the tool and die cost on small-versus large-volume production. It was generally concluded that cars can be assembled in countries entirely devoid of natural resources and primary or secondary industries, even if skilled labor is comparatively scarce, but that far more favorable circumstances than these are essential to manufacture.

The essentials for economical local manufacture were (1) a market large enough to provide economies of mass production, (2) a reasonable number of basic raw materials, especially coal, iron ore, limestone, and other materials needed in the manufacture of steel, (3) primary industries, such as mining, smelting, refining, and lumber, (4) an adequate number of secondary or supporting industries for conversion of raw materials into semifinished and finished products, (5) a sufficient number of specialized industries for the production of items like ball and roller bearings, carburetors, starting motors, brake linings, wheels, and electrical equipment, (6) adequate transportation for raw materials and heavy goods, and (7) experienced personnel and skilled labor.

In Australia the total market for cars and trucks was approximately 100,000 vehicles a year for automobiles largely from American, Canadian, and English sources. At that time automobile and truck sales in the United States were

* Prepared by Harold H. Thurlby.

4 million vehicles. With increasing immigration and the possibilities of export, an expanding market could be anticipated.

Australia has an abundance of good coal, excellent iron ore, limestone, and certain other basic materials needed for automobiles, such as lead, tin, copper, manganese, and other minerals required for steel alloys. Australia has a steel industry, established in 1915, that at the time was operating at a capacity of 2 million ingot tons. The facilities for fabricating sheet steel, however, were very limited. Glass was not being produced but was imported from Belgium and other sources.

Secondary industries were limited. It would be necessary, for example, to set up foundries for gray-iron castings and perhaps malleable iron castings and forgings to obtain the necessary quantity, quality, and variety of supply. Specialized industries were largely lacking in development. Transport was inadequate. Australia has no inland waterways. Rail transportation was handicapped by the fact that, prior to federation, Australian states were autonomous and had installed railways of differing gauges, which necessitated the unloading and reloading of freight and passengers at most state borders. All the major cities depended largely on coastwise shipping, with correspondingly slow traffic and congestion.

During World War II, when Australia was almost cut off from the rest of the world by the Japanese, the Australian government determined, despite these difficulties and as a matter of national security, to have an automotive industry. General Motors and other companies assembling cars in Australia were invited to undertake the manufacture of an automobile there.

In spite of certain reservations about the practicality and timing of the project, General Motors executives felt that the long experience of the corporation in building motor cars both in the United States and abroad, the widespread facilities in Australia, and a policy of helping other nations to help themselves industrially, justified the acceptance of the invitation. In January, 1945, accordingly, the corporation agreed to manufacture an automobile in Australia with the understanding that 10 per cent of the car's list price, and/or 5 per cent by weight, might be represented by imported components and accessories. It was further understood that General Motors was to have the full cooperation of the Commonwealth government and that no special considerations would be given to any competitive company that might also undertake to build a car in Australia.*

When GM decided to build a car in Australia, the first step was to make a complete "on-the-ground" survey to determine the specifications of a car tailored to meet Australian requirements. The survey indicated that the car should be somewhat smaller than the American Chevrolet but larger than the English Vauxhall; that it should have more road clearance than the average car in order to negotiate rough roads in the back country; that it should have better hill-climbing performance in high gear than the lower-horsepower English cars;

---

* No special protection, bounties, or subsidies of any kind were requested. Ownership, in accordance with General Motors policy, was not to be divided with local interests.

that it should be as dustproof as possible for a country of high winds and dust; that it should be extremely economical in fuel consumption since Australia imported all petroleum products and all such products were heavily taxed and severely rationed; and that it had to be light in weight, yet sufficiently rugged to withstand the wear and tear of longer usage than is commonly demanded of American cars.

The specifications were taken to Detroit, along with about thirty technicians from the Australian operations. There specialists in design, engineering, and styling were assigned to design a car. Three prototype cars were built and thoroughly tested at General Motors Proving Ground. When pilot models were rebuilt to satisfaction, seventy-eight technicians went to Australia with them. An 86-mile test course was laid out, including every type of road condition to be expected, and the prototype cars were driven over the course day after day under test-controlled operation. Three more pilot models were built in Australia and subjected to the same rigid tests. From time to time, these cars were "taken down," the parts inspected, and the inevitable specification changes made as dictated by the usage test.

The Holden car,† as produced and introduced in November, 1948, was a single-model five-passenger four-door sedan of 103-inch wheelbase. The road clearance was $8\frac{1}{2}$ inches, or approximately 1 inch greater than in the conventional American car of that date. The engine was a 6-cylinder overhead valve type, similar to Chevrolet, with 3-inch bore and $3\frac{1}{8}$-inch stroke, developing approximately 60 horsepower. Fuel consumption was about 30 miles per gallon at 35 miles per hour. The body had leaf springs in the rear and independent front suspension, like the Buick of 1948. Tires were smaller than on the American cars. The finish, both inside and outside, was plain because Australians preferred utility to chrome and fancy trimmings. The Holden was particularly rugged. It was priced at £675 Australian, or, at the then current rate of exchange, about $2,164.

General Motors—Holden's unit sales were:

	1950	1951
Australian—Holden	20,113	25,177
British—Vauxhall (GM)	16,800	14,915
U.S. and Canadian sources	7,055	5,413

The sales figures for 1951 were not necessarily a true reflection of the demand since dollar restrictions severely curtailed the import of vehicles from American sources and the British source was unable to meet Australian demand.

General Motors—Holden's adopted a policy in 1949, and has since continued it, of developing Australian sources for its components and materials by extending technical assistance and advice to those of its suppliers requiring them. Many suppliers in Australia have expanded plants, added new equipment, and improved manufacturing techniques. The company drew upon other General Motors divisions for advice and services on research and administra-

† Named after a prominent Australian family associated with the automobile industry.

tion. As of December, 1951, the total funds employed by General Motors–Holden's in the manufacture of autombiles in Australia were £22,062,472 Australian, or £2,160 Australian per employee.

Appraise the policy and procedure of General Motors overseas operations in establishing manufacturing operations in Australia.

Selected Readings

Management of International Operations, John Fayerweather, McGraw-Hill Book Company, New York, 1960. Use of the major management techniques in international business. Covers such matters as personnel and labor relations, marketing, finance, organization, operations, and community relations.

The Overseas Americans, Harlan Cleveland, Gerard J. Mangone, and John Clarke Adams, McGraw-Hill Book Company, New York, 1960. Discussion of the qualities that make for effective performance abroad and of the education needed by managers of foreign operations.

International Business: Principles and Problems, Howe Martyn, The Free Press of Glencoe, New York, 1964. The organization, management, and social impact of the multinational business.

Multinational Corporate Planning, George A. Steiner and Warren M. Cannon, The Free Press of Glencoe, New York, 1966. Papers from a conference on problems of multinational corporations. These cover the planning practices of major companies, environment problems, and methods of forecasting results.

International Handbook of Management, Karl E. Ettinger (ed.), McGraw-Hill Book Company, New York, 1965. Articles by sixty-three authors on the major problems of multinational companies in periods of economic and cultural transition. Discussions include comments on the introduction of management techniques in developing countries, training for overseas management, planning, and supervision.

The World-Wide Industrial Enterprise: Its Challenge and Promise, Frederic G. Donner, McGraw-Hill Book Company, New York, 1967. An expansion of three lectures sponsored by the Graduate School of Business, Columbia University (as part of the McKinsey Foundation lecture series). The author, a former chairman of the board of General Motors, discusses the evolution of his company's operations abroad.

5

Current Trends and the Future

Managers have, of course, always used mathematics in attempting to determine the optimum course, in weighing possible gains against possible disadvantages. Since the mid-1950s, however, computers have made possible the use of much more sophisticated techniques of quantifying problems and developing mathematical solutions.

Some of the uses to which computers are put are routine, such as the calculation of payrolls, but in the last few years the applications have greatly broadened. Moreover, it is evident that the number of different types of applications will grow in the future, which means that every manager needs to have some familiarity with what the computer can do and what it cannot do.

The first chapter in this section, Chapter 27, deals with the computer itself, its current possibilities and limitations, and the applications for which it is being used. Chapter 28 discusses another aspect of computerization of importance to management: the effect on employment, on job content (especially the content of management jobs), and on organization structure.

The more sophisticated mathematical techniques are those used in what is known as "management science," or "operations research." These are discussed in Chapter 29 and the appendix that follows it.

But the growing use of computers and mathematical approaches to management problems are only some of the trends that will affect management in the future. Other important changes are considered in the final chapter of the book.

27

HIGH-SPEED

COMPUTERS

A computer is only as good as
the mind of the man who programs it.
Norbert Wiener, quoted in Martin Greenberger (editor):
Management and the Computer of the Future

27 High-speed computers have been described both as "just big adding machines" and as artificial intelligences that are producing a second industrial revolution by increasing man's power to do brain work as much as the introduction of steam (and later electricity) increased his power to do physical work. Neither description is really accurate, although both contain elements of truth.

Computers are of two general types: analog and digital. In analog computers, numbers and letters are translated into electrical quantities: voltages, amperes, and resistances. In digital computers, numbers and letters are translated into electrical impulses. Thus an analog computer measures conditions—flow, stress, and so on—such as might be represented by a graph, and the digital computer counts electrical impulses. The analog computer is employed mainly for scientific work and the control of processes, whereas the digital computer, which handles discrete figures, is the type most widely used in business. There are also "hybrid" computers that have both digital and analog features.

In working with figures, the digital computer performs arithmetical calculations; hence the description of it as a "big adding machine." But it performs these operations at such incredible speeds that it can produce results different not only in degree but in kind from those possible with an ordinary calculator. Computer speeds are now measured in nanoseconds (billionths of a second).

In addition, a computer differs from an adding machine in other important ways. It can compare numbers, determine whether one is larger or smaller than another, then process the data differently in each case. For example, in processing a payroll, it has to multiply hours over forty by time and a half in order to produce the paycheck and hours through forty by the straight-time rate.

Then, although an adding machine may be said to have a memory in that it can retain successive subtotals until the total key is pressed, a computer's memory is not erased when the answer to a problem is found. Moreover, it has what is often called "random access" to that memory, making it somewhat similar to a human memory in that it can bring out and process the things it remembers in any order, regardless of the order in which they were fed in—just as a human being does not have to recall everything that happened during his lifetime up to the time a given event occurred in order to recall that event.[1]

Also, a computer works with various kinds of auxiliary equipment that enable it to perform such feats as reading, writing, and drawing diagrams and pictures. (Some of this equipment is sometimes considered part of the computer itself.) It can even produce an image on sensitized microfilm, which is then developed into a permanent reference record.

---

[1] There is some disagreement over the accuracy of the term "random access," although it is frequently used, for an index must be set up to point to the location of the information being sought. Otherwise, the computer would have to search through an entire storage unit. However, there is apparent random access.

Finally, a computer can process data from remote locations that are connected to it by some type of channel—telephone lines, cables, or microwave links, for example. The data may originate with other computers or with input devices of some kind at the remote locations. This is known as "teleprocessing" or "telecommunications."

CALCULATING MACHINES

Attempts to make machines that will do brain work go back hundreds of years.[2] The French thinker Blaise Pascal invented an adding machine in 1642, and about thirty years later the philosopher Gottfried Leibnitz modified it to make multiplication possible.

Then, in the first half of the nineteenth century, a Cambridge University professor of mathematics, Charles Babbage, conceived and built his "difference machine," which he hoped would make it possible to extend tables of interest or insurance premiums, or tables of tidal ebb and flood, indefinitely and automatically. After the initial figures were fed in, it was only necessary to turn a crank to get out the rest. He also conceived the idea of an "analytical engine" that would be similar to a modern computer in that it would handle a very large number of variables and could be fed by cards with holes punched in them.

Practically all the usual calculating machines contain a counting work, consisting in its original form of horizontal circular disks (Figure 1) on which the figures 0 to 9 appear. Each disk can turn about its vertical axis and is covered by a fixed plate with a hole or "window" in it through which one figure

[2] See the article "Calculating Machines," *Encyclopaedia Britannica*, 13th ed., London and New York, 1926, pp. 972–973.

FIGURE 1

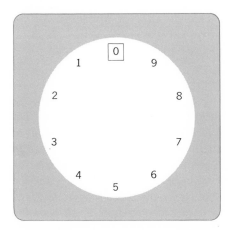

can be seen. If the disk is turned 4 spaces and then 2 spaces, the figure 6, which is the sum of 4 and 2, will appear.

If a series, say six, of such figure disks are placed side by side, their windows lying in a row, then any number of six figures or less can be made to appear—for example, 000373. In order to add 6425 to this number, four of the disks from right to left have to be turned 5, 2, 4, and 6 steps respectively, and the sum 006798 will appear.

But suppose we want to add 6428 to 000373. In that case the first disk must be moved eight spaces beyond the 3, or past the 0 to the 1, and an arrangement for carrying must be introduced. This was achieved in the following way: The axis of a figure disk contains a wheel with teeth including one long tooth, which turns the next wheel as the first disk passes 0. Then if arrangements are added to turn each disk through as many steps as required, we have an addition machine essentially of Pascal's type, though in his machine each disk had to be turned by hand.

Babbage's difference machine was more complicated; as can be seen in Figure 2, it consisted essentially of a series of geared disks. An actual description is impossible without elaborate drawings, but the following may give some idea of the principle on which it operated:

Imagine a number of striking clocks placed in a row, each with only one hand and containing only the striking apparatus. As the hand of the first clock is turned to point to a number on the dial, the clock strikes that number of times. Then suppose the first clock is connected with the second in such a way that *each* of its strokes moves the hand of the second clock one space ahead, but the second cannot strike until the first one stops. Thus, if the hand on the second clock stands at 5, and the first strikes 3, the hand of the second clock will move to 8, and the second clock itself will strike 8 as soon as the first one has stopped striking. This will move the hand of the third clock ahead, and so on.

Using three clocks, one could calculate squares automatically:

	First clock	Second	Third
a.	2	1	0
b.	2	1	1
c.	2	3	4
d.	2	5	9
e.	2	7	16

The first clock is connected to the second and the second to the third, but the hand on the first remains at 2. In the first line (a), the clocks are set at 2, 1, and 0. Then the second clock is struck, which moves the third ahead to 1 (b). Next (c), the first clock is struck, and the second clock moves to 3, the third clock to 4. Striking the first clock again moves the second to 5 and the third to 9 (d); and if the first is struck yet again, the second moves to 7 and the third to 16 (e). The numbers in the third column—1, 4, 9, 16—are the squares of the numbers 1, 2, 3, 4; and the series can be continued indefinitely.

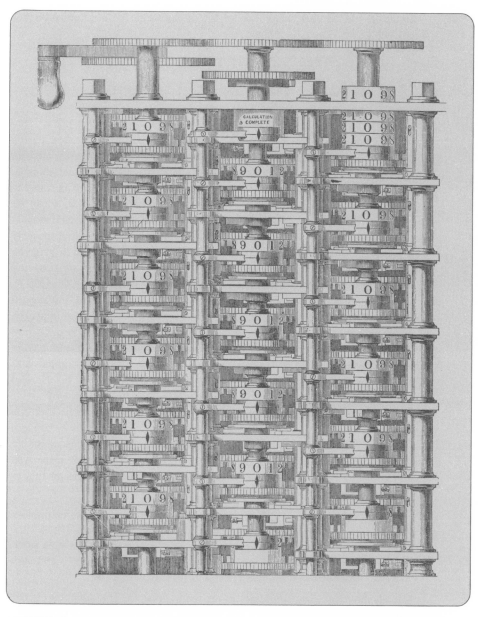

FIGURE 2 "Impression from a woodcut of a small portion of Mr. Babbage's Difference Engine No. 1, the property of Government, at present deposited in the Museum at South Kensington. It was commenced 1823. This portion put together 1833. The construction abandoned 1842. This plate was printed June, 1853. This portion was in the Exhibition 1862." (Facsimile of frontispiece from *Passages from the Life of a Philosopher*, published in 1864.)

Similarly, mechanical calculation of the cubes would be possible with four clocks:

	First clock	Second	Third	Fourth
a.	6	6	1	0
b.	6	6	1	1
c.	6	6	7	8
d.	6	12	19	27
e.	6	18	37	64

In this case, the clocks are set at 6, 6, 1, and 0 to begin with (a), and the third clock is struck first, moving the fourth to 1 (b). Then the second clock is struck, with the result shown in (c). After that the process begins with the first clock, and, as can be seen, the cubes of the numbers 1, 2, 3, 4 can be read in the last column. Again the process might be continued indefinitely. If the first clock, still at 6, were struck again, the second clock would move to 24, the third to 61, the fourth to 125, which is the cube of 5. Driving the whole by turning one handle, as in Babbage's machine, meant a great saving of time and eliminated the possibility of human error.

Babbage finished a part of this "difference machine" in 1834, donating a part of his private fortune to the work and traveling all over Europe in search of parts and tools. He also persuaded the British government to provide him with a subsidy amounting to £17,000. Considering the change in purchasing power, this was equal to at least $1 million today—a rather far-sighted venture for a government of that day, when officials were such strong believers in nonintervention.

Babbage was, however, disappointed in the reception of his machine. It was exhibited in the 1860s at a world exhibition at the Crystal Palace in London; but those in charge had it placed in a dark corner where only six people could see it at a time, and not even clearly at that, while a prominent place was given to various types of new toys. He consigned those responsible for this to oblivion with the words:

> Peace, then, to their memory, aptly enshrined in unknown characters within the penetralia of the temple of oblivion. These celebrities may there at last console themselves in the enjoyment of one enviable privilege denied to them during their earthly career—exemption from the daily consciousness of being "found out."[3]

Actually Babbage's machine was never really finished. The difficulty lay not with his mathematical knowledge but with the hardware available to him. He had only mechanical means, such as gear wheels, ratchets, and levers; and the long train of gears made it hard to get enough power.

Babbage believed that calculating machines would be able to work out

[3] *Passages from the Life of a Philosopher*, Longman, Green, Longman, Roberts & Green, London, 1864, p. 164.

sums of any magnitude and could be so constructed as to be able to perform the most complex mathematical processes and give proofs of mathematical theorems. He also believed that such a machine would be able to play games of skill—chess, for example—and he even proved that a human player would at best gain a draw in playing tic-tac-toe against it. And between tic-tac-toe and chess the difference would be only one of degree.[4] However, the difference in degree is important, for the more complicated the game, the more difficult it is for machines to take account of the entire strategic situation.

OPERATION OF ELECTRONIC COMPUTERS

Although modern desk calculators are, of course, great improvements over those designed by Pascal and Leibnitz, they are not the machines that Babbage envisioned. However, electronic computers can do everything he thought a machine would eventually do (and more) and can do it much faster than he would have believed possible.

It is not feasible to give a detailed description here of how the digital computer works,[5] but essentially it is made up of a multiplicity of circuits each of which may be opened or closed and may in turn open or close other circuits. Thus there is an enormous number of different paths the current may follow.

The input of a computer may be a set of punched cards, a punched tape, a document written with a magnetized pencil, or a printed document. The output may be in the form of other punched cards, tape, disks, strips, printed material (such as a list or a batch of checks), or a picture on a screen. If the output is a picture, it can be modified by a human being using what is called a light pen. Thus when the screen displays a schematic diagram of a given design, the engineer might modify it in some particulars by touching the screen with the pen.

Digital computers are now in their third generation—whenever new computers that embody substantial technological or state-of-the-art improvements are produced, a new generation is said to have been born. The first generation utilized vacuum tubes and had magnetic drums (and sometimes magnetic cores) as memory units. The second employed transistors and used a drum or magnetic cores for the memory unit; but later examples of this generation used disks for memory. The third generation is characterized by a new miniaturized circuitry, so small that as many as 50,000 transistors and diodes would fit in a thimble. The miniaturized circuitry reduces the distance the electrical current travels within the machine and produces greater reliability and lower cost.

---

[4] Hon. Mr. and Mrs. Lionel Tollemade, *Safe Studies*, London, printed for private circulation in 1884.
[5] See William J. Baumol, *Economic Theory and Operations Analysis*, Prentice-Hall, Inc., Englewood Cliffs, N.J., 1961, pp. 422–425, for a simplified description of the workings of a computer.

COMPUTER PROGRAMMING

A computer does not, however, operate without directions from a human being. Its operation is automatic only after a step-by-step set of directions has been worked out and fed into it. Having stored the program, as a set of directions is called, the computer may be instructed to apply it to a new set of data, and then only one instruction—to follow the program—is necessary. Programs are known as "software," in contrast to the hardware, that is, the computer itself and its accessory equipment.

Since a circuit has only two states, open or closed, each step in the program must be expressed in a form that will direct the computer to do one of two things at each step—open or close a circuit. Early programs made use of two symbols, 0 and 1, and the numbers were expressed in binary arithmetic. In decimal arithmetic, moving a figure one place to the left means that it is multiplied by 10; in binary arithmetic, moving a figure one place to the left means that it is multiplied by 2. Thus in binary arithmetic, decimal 1 is written 1 but 2 is written 10, 3 is expressed as 11 (or 2 plus 1 instead of 10 plus 1, as in decimal arithmetic), and 4 (2×2) is 100.

The programming, however, need no longer be in terms of the two symbols 0 and 1. Sometimes an octal system is used—that is, 8 is the base (then 10 equals decimal 8 and 100 equals 64)—or a hexadecimal system, which uses a base of 16 (after 9, the numbers up through 15 are designated by letters). The advantage of these systems over the binary system is that large numbers can be expressed in fewer digits.

There are also computer languages that look more like English. Two of the best known are COBOL (Common Business Oriented Language), which is used for business programs, and FORTRAN (FORmula TRANslation), designed for scientific work.

In every case, each step in the sequence must be thought out by a human being before the program is fed into the machine. A very exact and detailed flow chart of the sequence (Figure 3) must be drawn up before that sequence can be expressed in computer language and fed into the machine. As one computer-language expert explained:

> It's like talking to a moron. You have to tell it every little detail. . . .
> When I was working my way through college, I used to work in a laundry. One of the boys . . . there had very low intelligence. I could say, "Jimmy, go over to that bench and pick up that empty bucket and bring it to me." Jimmy would do it. But if he found that the bucket was full of water instead of empty, he would become very confused. So I would have to tell him to take it to the sink and pour the water out. The trouble was that I had left out a step in his instructions and he didn't have the ability to think what to do. It's the same with machines.
>
> And you have to be careful what you say. . . . You have to be exact. Suppose that you are sitting down in the evening with your wife to have a cup of coffee. . . . You say to your wife, "Please pass the salt." Now your wife knows that you take sugar in your coffee . . . so she passes

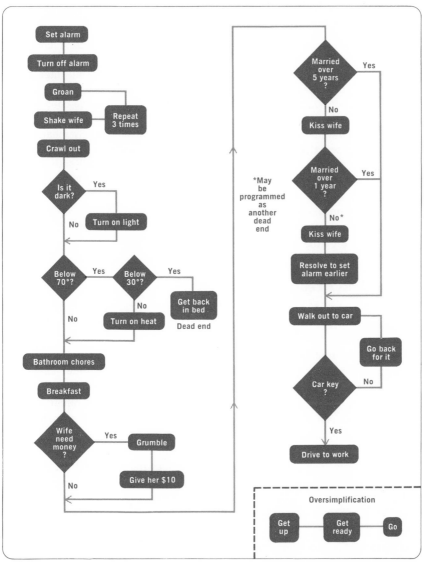

FIGURE 3 Flow diagram of a computer program, "Getting Up in the Morning." This diagram is, of course, intended as a joke, but it is a very good illustration of the way in which directions are given to a computer. Such flow diagrams are used in actual programming to enable the programmer to see whether he has omitted any necessary step. (From William J. Baumol, *Economic Theory and Operations Analysis*, Prentice-Hall, Inc., Englewood Cliffs, N.J., 1961, p. 422.)

you the sugar. But, brother, if you were talking to a machine, you would get salt for your coffee.[6]

A fairly recent development is multiprogramming, in which a computer processes more than one program at a time, or rather it interleaves steps in two or more programs, and the processing is so fast that for all intents and purposes two or more users get results simultaneously. Thus several people in a company or division can use the same computer and yet be conscious of no delay in getting results. This is what is known as "time sharing."

But all programming problems have not been solved, by any means. In a survey of representative companies that were making wide use of third-generation computers,[7] the author found that most of them were well satisfied with the hardware supplied by the manufacturers but were experiencing considerable difficulty with the software that came with it. Some companies, particularly the large ones, develop their own software, but this is often an expensive and time-consuming process and the results may be no better than the programs supplied by the manufacturers.

COMPUTER APPLICATIONS

The possible uses of computers are numerous; they range from the performance of routine clerical operations to development of information needed for top management decisions.

The routine applications are still the most widespread. One has already been mentioned—processing a payroll. In this case, a computer can do in minutes a job that would take several clerks with desk calculators a period of days. Others include such things as handling premiums and commissions in the insurance business, processing stockholder lists and stock transfers and dividend distribution, and various accounting applications.

Then there are frequent applications to production scheduling and control. A computer can "explode" a bill of materials into the number of components needed to fill it, determine the sequence in which they should be processed, and so on.

Inventory control by computer may be used in both manufacturing and retailing. In manufacturing, the source documents used in the control of parts and materials in stock may be requisitions coded in such a way that one of the computer's input devices can read them. In a retail store, each item of merchandise bears a small ticket coded to describe it. When items are sold, the tickets are torn off and sent each day to a central location where the information they carry is either transferred to punched cards or read directly into the computer. The computer subtracts the sales of each item from the quantity on hand the day before. Then every week or every two weeks (this

[6] Robert Sanford, "Some Loose Talk about and with Computers," *Beehive* (United Aircraft Corporation), Fall, 1960, pp. 29–30.
[7] Ernest Dale, *The Impact of Computers on Management,* 1968 (mimeo.). This is a follow-up of the author's earlier study, *The Decision-making Process in the Commercial Use of High-speed Computers,* Graduate School of Business and Public Administration, Cornell University, Ithaca, N.Y., 1964.

could be done daily also), inventory is compared with the planned level and orders are issued.

Then there are the "real-time" applications. (When a computer is said to be operating in real time, it is reporting on what is happening as it is happening, or so soon after the event that the time lag is inconsequential, probably imperceptible to a human being.)

One of the best-known applications of this kind is to airline reservations. An airline that has as many as a thousand or more offices to which passengers come for reservations may tie them all into one central computer. When a prospective passenger states where he wants to go and when, a clerk puts the information into a console on his desk and it is transmitted to a central computer. The computer scans its memory unit to determine whether space is available on the flight the passenger wants to take, and if there is room for him, it sends back a confirming notice. In addition, it records the fact that one more seat on that flight is no longer available. The process is almost instantaneous, even if all the clerks in the system are sending messages at practically the same time.

Computers are also useful in market research and forecasting because they enable the researcher to take account of many more variables. For example, in estimating the demand for cosmetics, only two variables were once used: the number of females over 14 and disposable income. With a computer, forecasts have been based on six variables: one for each of four 10-year age brackets, a fifth for disposable income, and a sixth for the change in disposable income since the previous year. Similarly, manufacturers of TV sets may project the demand for different types of sets.

Computers may also run plants, at least in process industries. Auxiliary equipment can sense such things as temperatures and pressures and feed the information to a computer, which will process it and determine the adjustments to be made. In Great Britain, four computers have been linked together to control a steel mill, the Park Gate Iron and Steel Company in Yorkshire. One handles the accounting, a second controls the production scheduling, a third directs the automatic rolling in the blooming and billet mill, and a fourth, which is fed with a precise description of each customer's order, controls the shearing of the billets.[8]

In an American steel company, the computerization of production planning and control has made possible a reduction in lead time on orders (the time between receipt of an order and delivery). In the past, production-control personnel had to spend five hours each morning trying to find out how much of each order had been produced the day and the night before. Then they analyzed the findings and worked on improving the operations for the rest of the day.

Before computerization, the actual manufacturing operations took only 10 to 15 per cent of the lead time; the rest of it was spent waiting for informa-

[8] "The $5-billion World Market for Computers," *Business Week*, Feb. 19, 1966, p. 118.

tion or for someone to take corrective action. Under the computerized system, the order book and the inventory are examined every 24 hours, and the difference between the order-book quantities and the inventory is the steel-making load in the future. This is picked out and assigned to production according to priority. Then, every 8 hours, the computer prepares the hot-roll—mill line-up.

The company is now operating at a higher level of production, and inventory has been cut 20 per cent or more.

In engineering, also, there are a great many applications, for the rapid processing enables designers to consider many more possible alternatives in cases where a number of variables interact to produce the final result. For example, computers have been found useful in the development of heating and cooling systems for buildings, cases in which the variables include the outside temperatures at various times of the year, the configuration of the building, and the "heat load" from people and machines. Again, in the matter of air pollution control, computer programs have been developed for determining the best results from the simultaneous application of more than one control measure: elimination or partial elimination at the source, treatment, and dispersion through high smokestacks. Obviously, the more pollution eliminated at the source, the less the need for treatment or dispersion, and the more elimination at the source and the more thorough the treatment, the less dispersion is needed. The aim is to discover the combination that will do the job at the lowest cost.

Problems like these can, of course, be worked out with the aid of desk calculators and tables of various kinds or even with a pencil if a person can spend enough time on them. But often each variable can be given so many different values, and the changes would, in turn, affect the values of so many of the other variables, that no one would have the time or the patience to go through the process manually.

For example, suppose a man is trying to draw up a layout of a plant. With only ten departments, there are 3.5 million possibilities. Yet the arrangement of the departments very definitely affects costs—costs of material handling and the cost of the time personnel must spend traveling between departments. Given data on the average number of trips per day, which may be estimated or known from past experience, and on the cost of each trip (the hourly cost for people and transportation equipment), the computer will print out the ten or twenty most economical layouts. In the process, if the program has been planned accordingly, it will automatically discard any layouts that are impractical for various reasons. The programmer may specify, for example, that the shipping and receiving departments must be placed on the perimeter of the building or that certain departments cannot be placed together because vibrations from the machines in one of them would upset delicate precision work in the other.[9]

[9] Drawn from William J. Smith (Computer Equipment Department, General Electric Company), "Use of a Computer in Determining Optimum Plant Layout," *Techniques of Plant Engineering and Maintenance*, vol. XVI, Clapp & Poliak, Inc., New York, 1965, pp. 17–20.

A man with a desk calculator could figure out the costs of each of the 3.5 million possible arrangements, but if he tried to do so, the products and processes would probably have changed so much by the time he finished that the layout he produced would be obsolete. What people do, therefore, when they work out layouts manually is to produce arrangements that are reasonably good and economical but probably not the very best.

Another type of application that some companies are trying is the "data bank." In this case, the computer's memory is filled with all obtainable information on a given subject with a view to enabling it to answer questions which no one has formulated as yet but which may quite possibly come up in the future.

For example, one insurance company has a data bank that includes all the records of the policies it has in force. This makes it possible for general agents to obtain (via telecommunications) immediate up-to-date answers to policyholders' questions. Quite a few other companies have similar systems or are working on them.

The same company has developed an employee data bank that covers all the information about its employees it has been able to obtain: educational background, test scores, work experience, salary changes, findings of appraisals, and many other facts. This is used to obtain regular reports on such things as the average salaries of employees in various categories and the names of employees covered by group insurance. But it can also be utilized to answer questions that may come up in the future—for example, when a given skill is needed, the computer can produce the names of all those who have it, together with information on their other qualifications.

One of the more advanced applications (or "exotic applications," as they are often called) is to the analysis of the risks inherent in different types of capital investment. Others include handling of short-term investment portfolios and integration of cross-functional activities, such as inventory levels, sales, and production.

Another advanced application is what companies are calling the "what if" application. One instance of this is the projection of future profit and loss statements for some years ahead based on present rates of growth and possible management decisions. In other words, the computer is asked: What will happen if we decide to do this instead of that?

And computer applications not only save clerical and executive time, which of course is money-saving as well, they often produce other returns. For example, with a computer a bank found it possible to calculate interest on loans to the half day, which produced a saving of $220,000 a year. In another case, computer calculations are enabling a company to recover excise taxes on parts shipped overseas, and this has produced an annual saving of $400,000.

In addition, many companies are planning new applications. Of the thirty-three companies covered in the author's survey, thirty-two stated that they intended to put their computers to new uses in the future. A great many of these new uses were applications designed to produce better control—e.g., integration of orders and inventory, computerized cash-flow accounting, and the evaluation of the performance of pension fund investments. Others were applications to planning and forecasting and to staffing (personnel data banks and determination of the talent needed in the future). In one case, an application to the organizing function was contemplated: the company proposed to use the computer to determine the clerical expense it would incur with different types of organization.

For some years now, there has been discussion of the possibility of a "total system" under which the computer would forecast sales, schedule production accordingly, determine the budgets and inventories necessary, keep the accounts, and make corrections when new data regarding actual sales and production were fed into it. But no company has yet been able to put such a system into effect.

Even what might be called "subtotal systems," those covering several related areas of the business, are enormously difficult to develop in many cases. For instance, one company has been working for several years on a system that would cover processing of orders, shipping, and billing—which, of course, are closely related to each other. But in this company such a system must be able to handle no fewer than 2 million different freight rates, and each rate may be subject to negotiation between the company and the carrier on such variables as volume, geography, and frequency of shipping. Even the definition of "destination" proved to be rather elusive—it might mean a country, a city, or a single customer.

ARE COMPUTERS BRAINS?

Public imagination has been caught by the performance of large computers, particularly since they can monitor their own operation and correct their own mistakes, make some decisions, and engage in what might be called "learning." Science-fiction writers have foreseen their evolution to the point where they actually develop consciousness and wills of their own.

Monitoring and automatic correction did not, however, originate with computers or in the science of electronics. A purely mechanical example is the governor on a steam engine (Figure 4). The shaft revolves more rapidly as the speed of the engine it governs increases. Eventually centrifugal force causes the balls to fly outward, which closes a valve and reduces the speed of the engine. Automatic correction in an electronic computer—or "feedback," as it is called—is more analogous to the operation of a human mind in that it may involve acting on data that have been "sensed" by one or more auxiliary devices (optical scanners, for example), but it really cannot be called thought.

Machines have been designed also that will imitate some types of human learning in a concrete way. If these proceeded inductively from general principles to specific conclusions, the results would correspond to the reasoning of a very rational human being. But the results are largely arrived at through

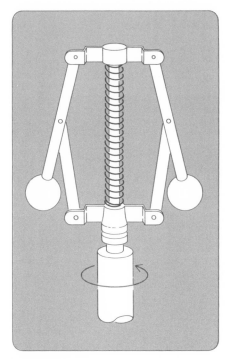

FIGURE 4

a system of trial and error, built into the machine through statistical devices.

A famous illustration of trial-and-error behavior is the cat in the puzzle cage. A cat is put into a cage from which it can escape only by pulling a latch that controls the door. At first, so the theory runs, the cat tries to escape by making a series of movements at random, until by chance it pushes against the latch and opens the door. But each time the experiment is repeated, the cat makes fewer useless movements, and eventually it learns to let itself out at once.

A computer may learn in a similar way—although without the consciousness that the cat undoubtedly possesses. This may be demonstrated by the game of "hexapawn."[10]

In hexapawn, there is a board of only nine squares and each player starts with three pawns (Figure 5). As in chess, a pawn can move one square straight ahead or one square diagonally, but it can capture an opposing piece only when it moves diagonally and can move diagonally only when there is a piece in an immediately adjacent square for it to take. The board is displayed on the computer screen, and the human player who is competing with the

[10] See M. Gardner, "How to Build a Game-learning Machine and Then Teach It to Play and to Win," *Scientific American*, March, 1962, pp. 138–153, and J. L. Hughes and K. J. Engvold, "Hexapawn: A Learning Demonstration," *Datamation*, March, 1968, pp. 67–68, 71–73. (Material published and copyrighted by F. D. Thompson Publications, Inc., Greenwich, Conn. 06830.)

HEXAPAWN

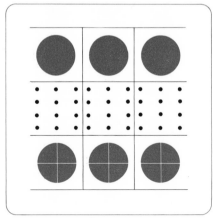

Your move

FIGURE 5

computer makes his moves by touching the screen with a light pen. Because of the simplicity of the game, there are at most only four possible moves for the computer at any stage of the game. A random-number generator selects the computer's move at random from one of the moves possible in the light of the configuration on the board.

The computer learns by losing. Each time it loses a game the move that immediately preceded its loss is wiped from its repertoire; so eventually it can make only winning moves.

In such learning, the initial activity is random but each success increases the chance or probability that the correct answer will recur. Thus such a learning process can be imitated mechanically.

The next step in the imitation of lifelike behavior has been the recognition that the learning process includes more than the gradual reenforcement of responses originally made at random. For example, there are limitations in the range of responses, sudden drops or increases in the degree of error, and sometimes complete changes. But the various changes that occur may have a certain order or predictability. The process may be a stochastic one, in which the probability of one event is a function of the probabilities of other events. For instance, when words are associated in a sentence, each word has a certain probability, which in turn depends on the probabilities of the preceding words. If a sentence begins, "The cat sat on the . . .," the likelihood that the next word will be a noun, such as "mat," is high, whereas the probability that it will be a verb like "go" is almost nil. There have been attempts to build elementary brain activities of this kind into machines, so-called "brain models," which will receive sense data, discriminate, and so on.

But there are great difficulties in doing so. For example, some kinds of behavior involve steps that cannot be specified, or at least cannot be mechanized because of their subjective nature. Also, frequency of occurrence tells us nothing about causes, and the causes of human behavior are complex: goals can suddenly change, for example.

Computers are not really brains. Their work is only as good as the programming, and if essential elements are missing from the program, the computer will not give an accurate response. When UNIVAC, one of the large "mechanical brains," was set to find an ideal couple as a stunt on a television show, the program was unable to pull off the job. The apparently ideally matched couple found themselves in fundamental disagreement as soon as the money provided by the show sponsors for expensive dates ran out. Said the prospective bride:

> After the excitement was over, we didn't go out so often. When we did, it was usually a 50-cent seat in the movies. One night John called and said he was taking me out to dinner. I spent $80 on a new dress and shoes. Then when he came to the house, he had a sack of hamburgers for us to eat at home. . . . I still want to get married, but I'm not trusting any more machines. The old-fashioned methods are best.[11]

What the machine actually did was to sort through thousands of cards and find the man who most nearly corresponded to the girl's definition of the ideal husband and the man's definition of the ideal wife and ensure that they had similar tastes. But the only factors it could consider were those some human being had thought to feed into it. It could not deal with the many thousands of components of varying degrees of importance that go to make up attraction or repulsion between two human beings, simply because no human being could identify them all and program them into the machine. The matter of attitude toward money, which ostensibly proved crucial in this instance, *could* have been programmed if any human being had been able to gauge it accurately in advance.

But there is always the chance that other sources of disagreement would have arisen later, many of them impossible to identify in advance since people themselves often do not know why they like or dislike a fellow human being.

Much of the theory that holds that digital computers can eventually do almost anything a human brain can do may be based on ignorance of human thinking and problem-solving processes. Thus computers can play a limited form of chess by scanning the board and calculating what will happen, up to a point, if a given move is made. To a certain extent, this is what a human being does, but according to Hubert L. Dreyfus of MIT, the human chess player also "zeros in" on a promising situation or a threatening one by a process that cannot yet be duplicated by a computer:

> The player need not be aware of having explicitly considered or explicitly excluded from consideration any of the hundreds of possibilities. . . .
> Still, the specific portion of the board which finally attracts the subject's

---

[11] Joe Hyams, "UNIVAC All Brain, No Heart," *Herald-Tribune*, May 7, 1957.

attention depends on the overall configuration. To understand how this is possible, consider what William James has called the "fringes of consciousness": the ticking of a clock which we notice only if it stops provides a simple example of this sort of marginal awareness. Our vague awareness of the faces in a crowd when we search for a friend is another, more complex and more nearly appropriate case.[12]

And human beings not only utilize "fringe consciousness," they are also able to distinguish the essential from the inessential features of a pattern which may be incomplete, skewed, deformed, or embedded in extraneous matters. In addition, they can take account of the context and "perceive the individual as typical, i.e., situate the individual with respect to a paradigm case."[13]

It is always rash to predict that something will "never" be done, and Dreyfus does not deny that there is a possibility that some day computers designed on entirely new principles may be capable of performance very like that of human beings. However, he makes a very good case for the view that digital computers—however fast and complex they become—will never be able to do so.

Review Questions

1. What is a random-access memory?
2. Why is binary arithmetic sometimes used for computer programs?
3. What is the difference between an analog computer and a digital computer? Which would you say would be more accurate?
4. What types of business transactions are most easily computerized?
5. Every automobile has an analog device (not a computer) that operates in real time. What is it?
6. How does a computer "learn"?

Case Study / Planning the New Plant

Your company is a manufacturer of industrial trucks that has heretofore had only one plant in which it produced all parts and did all the assembly work. But the plant has become very crowded; so management has decided to build a new plant about three miles from the old one for the production of three different subassemblies that go into the product.

The layout of the new plant and its size will, of course, be affected by the

---

[12] *Alchemy and Artificial Intelligence*, The RAND Corporation, Santa Monica, Calif., December, 1965, pp. 21–22.
[13] *Ibid*, pp. 45–56.

number and type of machines needed. Some of the machines used in the manufacture of parts for the three subassemblies can be transferred from the old plant, but others will have to remain there because they are used to make parts that do not go into the three subassemblies as well as some that do. Management is quite willing to purchase some new machines, but, of course, no more than are absolutely needed. It has also specified that there should be no backtracking between plants; parts should not be made in one plant, sent to the other for further processing, then returned to the first plant for assembly.

You are charged with determining what equipment will be needed in the new plant to meet the production goals—the volume of production required has been determined. The company has a computer, and your superior suggests that you use it in your planning. Assuming you know how to program a computer or can get someone to do it for you, what are some of the things you would use it for in this case?

Selected Readings

Cybernetics: The Human Use of Human Beings, 2d ed., Norbert Wiener, The M.I.T. Press, Cambridge, Mass., and John Wiley & Sons, Inc., New York 1961. A clear and farsighted account of the potential of computers by one of the pioneers in the field of artificial intelligence.

Computers and Management: The Leatherbee Lectures, 1967, Hershner Cross, Donald I. Lowry, A. R. Zipf, George Kozmetsky, and Robert N. Anthony, Harvard University Graduate School of Business Administration, Boston, 1967. Lectures by three prominent businessmen whose companies make extensive use of computers, one college dean, and one member of the Department of Defense.

"Artificial Intelligence," Marvin L. Minsky, *Scientific American,* September, 1966, pp. 246–260. A discussion of the extent to which machines can display intelligence—what they have done so far, with some speculations about what they may do in the future.

Management and the Computer of the Future, Martin Greenberger (ed.), The M.I.T. Press, Cambridge, Mass., and John Wiley & Sons, Inc., New York, 1962. A collection of lectures and discussions dealing with scientific and management decision making in relation to computers.

Electronic Computers and Management Control, rev. ed., George Kozmetsky and Paul Kircher, McGraw-Hill Book Company, New York, 1963. The principal management applications of computers.

28

EFFECTS OF

COMPUTERIZATION

ON EMPLOYMENT,

MANAGEMENT JOBS,

AND ORGANIZATION

*The automation and rationalization of decision
making will . . . alter the climate of organizations
in ways important to . . . human concerns. On
balance [the changes] . . . seem to me changes
that will make it easier rather than harder for
the executive's daily work to be a significant
and satisfying part of his life.*
Herbert A. Simon:
The New Science of Management Decision

28 When it became clear that computers would find widespread applications in business, there were some predictions that there would be widespread unemployment among clerical workers because the computers would perform so many of the routine tasks that had formerly required minor decisions or calculations by human beings. The effect on clerical employees, it was sometimes said, would be similar to that experienced by handcraftsmen at the time of the Industrial Revolution; that is, many would be thrown out of work, at least for the short run, and the short run might last several years.

As for the impact on management jobs, three different views were expressed:

1. Some people held that many middle management jobs would disappear because the men at the top would be able to get so much information so quickly that they would be able to make all the day-to-day decisions themselves; also, that such middle management jobs as remained would become so routine that they would scarcely be worthy to be called management jobs.
2. Others believed that middle managers would become more important, though not necessarily more numerous, because computers would provide them with data that would enable them to make more informed decisions.
3. There would not necessarily be any change in the number of middle management jobs or in the decisions made at the middle management level.

If middle management jobs at various levels were to be abolished, it followed that chains of command would be much shorter, with very few levels between top management and the rank and file. Thus, the "flat" organizational chart would become the rule in highly computerized companies.

Finally, there were some predictions that a "computocracy" would become the real power source. That is, that the computer experts would take over much of the top management task, identifying the major problems and determining solutions mathematically with such accuracy that no one could argue with the results of their work.

Now that computers are widely used, to what extent, if any, have the predictions of change come true or appear likely to come true in the near future?

EFFECT ON EMPLOYMENT

Many clerical jobs have been eliminated in highly computerized companies, but this has seldom meant the dismissal of large groups of employees. Most companies have preferred to find other jobs for those whose positions have been abolished and to let natural attrition take care of any excess; that is, as people die, retire, or quit, the companies do not hire others to take their places.

It might appear that this would reduce the total number of clerical jobs available in the economy and so transfer the burden of unemployment to those just entering the labor market, but this does not seem to have happened. There has been no widespread clerical unemployment, for paper work is increasing year by year, and this increase, coupled with business expansion, has been sufficient to take up the slack. In fact, many companies say they had to computerize some of their paper-work operations because they could not get enough people to handle them. One company, for example, used its computer for handling one of its clerical operations even though the unit cost was higher—6 cents per check as against 4 cents per check when low-grade clerical personnel did the work—because it could not find enough clerical workers willing to take the jobs. In other cases, companies say that their computers have simply made it possible for them to offset rising costs of clerical work, that it would be prohibitively expensive for them to hire enough clerical help to take care of all their paper-work operations, which may require processing as many as a million documents in a short period.

In some cases, too, the computer is enabling companies to do things they did not do before because they did not have enough people to do them. For example, take the retail store inventory operations described in the last chapter. It would be quite possible for a store manager to have someone sort sales slips by item, then by size, then by color, and so on, subtract the number of items in each category from the stock on hand at the beginning of the day, and then send a report to the central purchasing department. But in actual fact it was seldom done, and a store might be out of given sizes or colors for some time.

All this is not to say that when more companies computerize their paper work, some serious clerical unemployment may not result, particularly in times of recession. Even small companies that cannot afford to buy or rent the equipment may now use commercial service bureaus which will process batch jobs (such as a payroll) or perhaps provide more or less real-time service through time sharing. Certainly some companies are now employing far fewer clerical workers in some departments than they were formerly. All one can say is that, helped by a general increase in business in the 1960s and by the tendency for paper work to grow faster than other activities, computers have not bred clerical unemployment to date.

For middle managers, so far as numbers of jobs go, much the same is true. Some lower and middle management jobs have been abolished, but, like paper work, middle management work appears to be growing fast enough to offset, or more than offset, this trend.

In some cases, too, computerization has meant an increase in management jobs rather than a decrease even though there were fewer employees to supervise. For example, Hak Chong Lee, Associate Professor of Management at the School of Business, State University of New York at Albany, examined figures on managerial employment before and after computerization in a manufacturing company and a utility and found that the actual numbers of managerial personnel had increased slightly in the departments affected.[1] Another survey

[1] *The Impact of Electronic Data Processing upon the Patterns of Business Organization and Administration*, School of Business, State University of New York, Albany, 1965, pp. 27–31.

of eleven firms in the Minneapolis-St. Louis area[2]—companies that ranged in size from 89 employees to 23,000—found that "there were no cases of middle managers either being eliminated or suffering financial downgrading because of the shift of duties to the computer, although a few were placed at lower levels in the organization."[3]

Still a third survey found that the number of supervisory personnel grew from two to twenty after a general-purpose computer was installed in a manufacturing company and utilized in several departments.[4]

In the author's own most recent survey,[5] which covered thirty-three highly computerized companies in a variety of industries, it was found that some management jobs had been eliminated (mainly lower management rather than middle management jobs) and some jobs had been combined so that only one manager was needed where two or more had been employed earlier. But some new middle management jobs had been created, particularly in inventory management. For example, there is the merchandise information coordinator, an executive with merchandising experience who analyzes the computer records of inventory of staple items (sizes, color, quality, and so on) and brings the needed inventory levels to the attention of vendors and store managers. Another new job that has been created as a result of computerization in some companies is that of the materials manager who provides liaison among purchasing, sales, inventory, and shipping. There is also an increasing number of data input experts and data reporting managers, who are needed as the electronic data-processing (computer) departments grow larger. For example, Figure 1 shows the top organization of an EDP department in a large company, and Figures 2 and 3 show the charts of two of the sections of this department.

The computer's impact on total employment in the thirty-three companies covered in the author's survey may be summarized as follows:

	No. of companies
None (constant employment because of company growth and attrition of personnel)	25
Increase in employment	2
Some decrease in employment	4
Large decrease in employment	2

In almost all cases in which jobs were eliminated, jobholders were reassigned. In some instances they were upgraded, especially into EDP work, for which a surprising number of the displaced personnel were able to qualify with training. In only two cases were actual layoffs necessary.

[2] Roger C. Vergin, "Computer Induced Organization Change," *MSU Business Topics*, Summer, 1967, pp. 62–68.
[3] *Ibid.*, p. 65.
[4] C. Edward Weber, "Change in Managerial Manpower with Mechanization of Data Processing," *The Journal of Business of the University of Chicago*, April, 1959, pp. 151–163.
[5] Ernest Dale, *The Impact of Computers on Management*, 1968 (mimeo.).

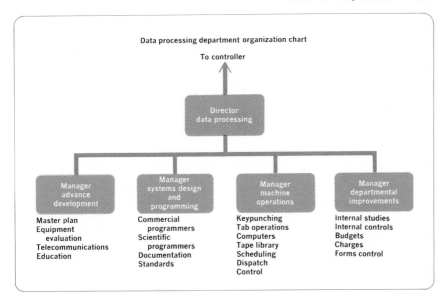

FIGURE 1

EFFECT ON JOB CONTENT

When a company is contemplating purchase or rental of a computer, it generally conducts a feasibility study to determine which of its operations it will be possible to computerize and how procedures must be changed if computerization is to be feasible and profitable. During this period, the work of the lower and middle managers is likely to increase, for people familiar with the operations must take an active part in the study. The managers must also help the programmers understand what is needed and perhaps assist in debugging the system when it is first installed. In addition, they may also have to deal with many human relations problems growing out of the need for transfers and retraining.

But, of course, once the transition period is past, this work will disappear, and so will many of the tasks the middle and lower managers performed before computerization. What, then, will be the nature of their work? Will it be more routine or less routine?

The prediction that middle management jobs would, when not abolished, become more routine does not seem to be borne out by the facts. True, there are at least two studies that have found this prediction justified: one covering a single company[6] and the other covering nineteen companies on the West Coast.[7] But most other surveys have produced diametrically opposite conclusions.

[6] Floyd C. Mann and Lawrence K. Williams, Industrial Relations Research Association, *Proceedings of the Eleventh Annual Meeting*, Madison, Wisc., 1958.
[7] Ida R. Hoos, "When the Computer Takes Over the Office," *Harvard Business Review*, July-August, 1960, pp. 102–112.

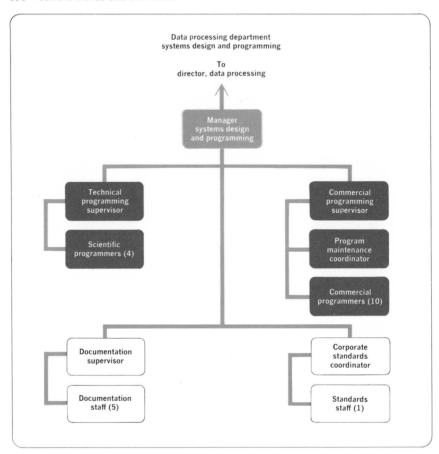

FIGURE 2

One, by Joseph P. Schwitter, which covered thirteen companies in northern Ohio, showed that there were very few changes in lower management jobs and that in general the changes had increased the job content—that is, the managers supervised more people or people with greater knowledge and training, used more mathematical techniques in planning and controlling, had new duties, or needed to use more technical knowledge and judgment. As for middle management jobs, some were not affected at all, and there were nineteen cases in which job content increased, as against only five in which it decreased.[8]

Again, Prof. Roger C. Vergin found that the major effect on middle management jobs in departments most affected by the computer "was not the

[8] "Computer Effect upon Managerial Jobs," *Journal of the Academy of Management*, September, 1965, pp. 233–246.

elimination of some decisions but rather that their task of motivation and coordination was reduced . . . because the number of subordinates in their departments decreased as the clerical work which they had performed was transferred to the computer."[9] Although some of those whose jobs had been transformed in this way felt that they had been downgraded, other surveys have shown that under the same circumstances middle managers generally tend to feel that they require greater skill than ever.

Hak Chong Lee, in a follow-up of his 1965 study, found that the computer tends to upgrade the work of the managers affected by the changes. The parts of the job that are eliminated are the unskilled or clerical components, and the amount of skilled or mental work required increases.[10]

Professor Lee did find that computerization tends to rigidify the work environment by requiring people to finish their tasks within certain specified times. This was true for managers, though to a lesser extent than for clerical employees. Thus, some freedom to set work pace and decide on work methods was lost.

Curiously, in view of the evidence behavioral science has offered that the absence of rigidity of this kind is an important factor in high morale and job satisfaction, the morale of neither the employees nor the managers appeared to have suffered in consequence. The study actually showed that job satisfaction had increased.[11]

But this does not necessarily invalidate the behavioral findings, for there were some offsetting factors, especially for the managers: better knowledge of what they were supposed to do and better understanding of the interrelationship of their jobs with those of others—in other words, better understanding of what Mary Parker Follett called "the law of the situation."

Often, too, managers find that the computer, by taking over the routine parts of their jobs, gives them time to do things they always felt they should be doing but had no time for earlier. Thomas L. Whisler quotes a manager in a computerized distribution system who said that he had, for the first time, an opportunity to get to know his customers and their needs and to give adequate attention to the selection and development of staff.[12]

In cases where managers find themselves in more routine jobs after computerization, it may be because they want it that way—perhaps they were always uncomfortable as decision makers and liked to escape responsibility when they could. At least, one high-level manager complained to the author that the programs became a crutch for many people: After computerization, they stopped using judgment altogether. People felt, he said, "that since our computers are working day and night, even God can sleep peacefully in his Heaven."

[9] Vergin, op. cit., p. 65.
[10] Information Technology and the Work of Managers, Bulletin No. 2, State University of New York at Albany, 1968, pp. 36–37.
[11] Ibid., pp. 37–39.
[12] "The Manager and the Computer," The Journal of Accountancy, January, 1965, p. 29.

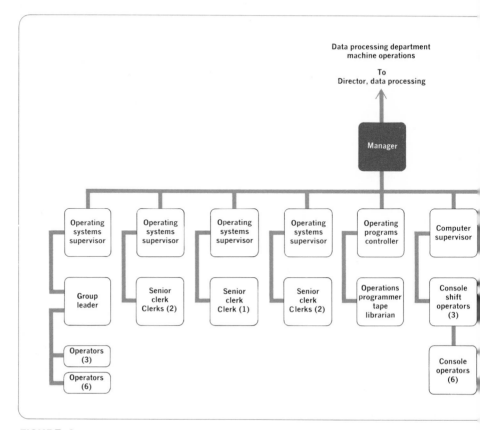

FIGURE 3

EFFECT ON ORGANIZATION STRUCTURE

During the 1960s, there has been some tendency for companies to recentralize, as against a countertrend toward decentralization in the 1950s. But this does not seem entirely, or even largely, due to the advent of computers. Rather it appears that many companies were disappointed in the effects of decentralization for one reason or another—either because they found that it raised costs more than they had expected (because of the need for staff both at headquarters and in the decentralized units) or because they found that it entailed too much loss of control.[13]

In his recent survey of the effects of computerization on management, the author found that although top management could, as predicted by many, get much more information more quickly than in the past, it was still unable to "make all the decisions" by a long shot.

[13] Ernest Dale, *Organization*, American Management Association, New York, 1967, pp. 118–125.

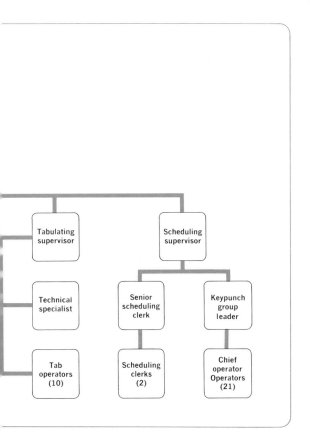

Actually, top executives often do not have enough time to use all the information they already have; often they are overwhelmed by masses of figures and reports. In an increasing number of instances, the problem is to cut down the plethora of information and to ensure that the information top management gets is more relevant to the questions it really must decide. Also, there seems to be some danger in the very speed with which the information is transmitted; this could lead to overemphasis on short-run developments, and decisions that will affect the long run might be made on the basis of facts that are true essentially only for the short run.

In addition, advocates of centralization through computerization have overlooked the role of the general staffs, which are growing in importance as major sources of management information, especially of the type of information that cannot be quantified or anticipated. And in some cases the operating divisions are becoming more independent and are attempting to generate information purely for their own use. This information is not communicated to EDP centers, much less to data banks.

In this survey, companies were asked directly whether the computer had made for more centralization or more decentralization. The replies were as follows:

	No. of companies
No marked effect either way	14
Has caused more centralization	13
Has caused greater decentralization	6

Thus, in almost half the companies questioned (thirty-three in all), there had been no change. It is true that the figures make it appear that centralization was more than twice as frequent as decentralization, but subsequent interviews made it clear that in this context "centralization" generally meant the physical centralization of the computer equipment. For example, inventory data for all locations in several states, a major part of the country, or even the country as a whole might be gathered together for processing at a regional or national computer center.

But even centralization of this kind was not very widespread; when such central systems had been set up, the decisions on changes in inventory levels in response to changing local demands still tended to be made locally or at least to be influenced by the opinion of local managers. On the other hand, the centralized computer department does help to communicate the corporate viewpoint, and increasingly it exercises so-called "functional control" over language, standards, and procedures.

One might almost say there is a trend toward "centralization within decentralization." Information is centralized in regions rather than in divisions or plants, but the local managers retain their traditional decision-making powers except in cases where corporation objectives and/or national trends dictate otherwise.

Also, the movement toward one national center is not nearly so advanced as it is sometimes believed to be. The replies from the twenty-five companies that answered a question on this point were as follows:

	No. of companies
1 national center (including localized data banks)	7
2 centers (East, West)	4
3 centers (East, Midwest, West)	7
4 to 5 centers	1
5 to 10 centers	3
More than 10 centers	3

As for the elimination of levels of management and the consequent enlargement of spans of control, twenty-six companies reported there had been no change in this respect. Seven reported "some impact," which was essentially the elimination of one level in the chain of command. And in these seven cases, the number of levels had ranged from six to twelve—so it cannot be said that the organization charts had become very much flatter.

PLACE OF COMPUTER PERSONNEL

The number of personnel engaged in working with computers, including the number of managers of various phases of the work, has grown enormously in the last few years. In the companies covered by the author's survey, the number of people in the electronic data-processing departments ranged from 230 to more than 2,000, with a median of 500 to 600. The EDP payrolls ranged from $300,000 to more than $15 million, and the median was from $5 million to $6 million. In some instances the EDP payroll was larger than the payroll for all other staffs. Figures 1, 2, and 3 are examples of the type of organization that has grown up since the advent of computers.

But there has been a sizable "communication gap" between top management and the computer experts. A few years ago, there were few top managers who felt that the computer experts could help at all with their important problems. In 1963, one company president told the author: "I am little concerned with computers and know even less about them. I believe they may help to reduce clerical expenses, but they don't help me with the big decisions. Our EDP section made a presentation to our top management committee but made no impression."

This seems to be changing fairly rapidly. As EDP departments have grown in size, they have tended to grow in importance and to become of greater interest to top management. Top managers cannot ignore a department that is costing several million dollars; they naturally become concerned with what they are getting for the money. Also, the demonstrated success of the computer in many applications has aroused top management's interest in it.

Of the thirty-three companies covered in the author's most recent survey,[14] only four said that the gap between top management and the computer experts was widening, whereas twenty-nine reported that it was narrowing. In addition, the EDP experts have made an effort to scale down their claims—which were often excessive earlier—and to improve the intelligibility of their language.

The heads of the EDP function appear to enjoy higher status than they did earlier. Reporting relationships found in the author's 1968 survey were as follows:

	No. of companies
To the president, the chairman of the board, or the executive office	4
To the senior or executive vice-president	4
To the operating vice-president	2
To the vice-president for administration or information	3
To the financial vice-president	5
To the controller, who in some cases had vice-presidential status	9
To the marketing and research vice-president	1
To the assistant controller	1
To the systems manager	1

[14] Dale, *op. cit.*, 1968.

In only one company had there been no improvement in the status of the EDP department since 1964. Six companies reported that the status was "much improved," and twenty-six that it had "improved somewhat."

On the whole, also, the compensation of the EDP groups has risen faster than the compensation of other staff groups. Nine companies stated that compensation was "much improved," twenty-three that it had "improved somewhat," and only one that there had been no improvement.

And not only are EDP men reporting further up in the organization hierarchy, they are in closer contact with top management than they were at the time the author's first survey[15] was conducted. They see the top managers more often, counsel them more, and make presentations to them more frequently.

But the extent to which the gap between the experts and top management is narrowing should not be exaggerated. The gap still exists, and almost everywhere it is still quite wide in that many higher managers have little knowledge of EDP and little contact with EDP personnel.

Top managers still often do not understand the language used by the computer experts, which is full of special terms, and they may not like to ask for definitions for fear of seeming ignorant, especially before a younger man. In addition, experienced top managers are conscious that management is still to a large extent an art rather than a science and that any situation includes many nuances which cannot be quantified or recorded. Thus the answers provided by computers may not be the right ones.

Most companies, in fact, believe that if the computer expert is to be of real value to them, he must know the business as well as the computer techniques, and they find it easier to train someone who knows the business in the techniques rather than attempt to train a man whose whole training has been in computer sciences in the business.

Thus the "computocracy" has not yet materialized, and perhaps it never will. What seems more likely is that general managers will become, if not computer experts, extremely knowledgable about the possibilities and limitations of computers and will be able to judge just how much weight to give to the findings of their experts.

Norbert Wiener once commented on the use of computers by the military: "It is more than likely that the machine may produce a policy which would win a nominal victory on points at the cost of every interest we have at heart, even that of national survival."[16] At present at least, a company that allowed computers to make all the decisions might face equal danger.

SUMMARY

Computers, although they do some types of work very much faster and more accurately than human beings can do it, have not yet caused widespread

---

[15] Ernest Dale, *The Decision-making Process in the Commercial Use of High-speed Computers*, Graduate School of Business and Public Administration, Cornell University, Ithaca, N.Y., 1964.
[16] Quoted in David L. Johnson and Arthur L. Kobler, "The Man-Computer Relationship," *Science*, November, 1962, p. 873.

unemployment even among clerical workers, whose jobs are most likely to be affected. And despite predictions to the contrary, middle management jobs are not disappearing but seem to be becoming more numerous. The main reason is that the amount of work to be done in both categories appears to be increasing more than enough to make up for the elimination of some jobs.

Nor is there much evidence that middle management jobs are becoming more routine, although in some cases the managers have less opportunity to set their own pace and decide on methods. Most middle managers appear to believe that their jobs now require more skill and judgment than before.

The effect on organization has also been slight, although in some cases one level of management has been eliminated.

Computer experts still do not have much influence on top management, but their status within organizations appears to be increasing, and the "communication gap" between the experts and top management is narrowing to some extent.

Review Questions

1. It has been pointed out that management decisions cover five basic areas: (1) defining the problems and arranging them in order of priority; (2) selecting goals; (3) allocating resources; (4) selecting a course of action and implementing it; and (5) appraising results and planning new activities to follow.* Which of these areas do you think the computer could handle? Are there any you think it could not handle? Why?
2. In departments in which much of the work has been computerized, employees and managers may find that the environment has become more rigid in that they have less freedom to set their own pace and decide on their work methods. What factors appear to have offset this lack of freedom and made for higher, rather than lower, job satisfaction?
3. Has computerization resulted in greater centralization of decision making?
4. To what extent is computer work being centralized?
5. What is a feasibility study?

Case Study / A Struggle for Computer Control

In the Hermes Life Insurance Company, the chief executive called for proposals for the computerization of large-scale routine and repetitive applications (such as premium billing, annuity payments, and internal payrolls) and special applications (such as life expectancy studies, market research for new prospects, and the opening of new branch offices). The company had been using conventional punch-card sorting and tabulating equipment.

* Melvin Anshen, "The Manager and the Black Box," *Harvard Business Review*, November-December, 1960, pp. 85–92.

Initially, the following proposals were submitted:

1. The life department (life insurance sales to individuals) wanted to have its own computer but wanted to rent it rather than buy it.
2. The group department (sales of group insurance) wanted to buy a computer.
3. The actuarial department wanted a computer built to its own specifications in order to have one suited to its special needs.
4. The secretary of the company, who was a kind of chief of general staff to the chief executive, argued for farming out the work to the local computer center.

1. You are the company's computer consultant. Set out for the president the pros and cons of each of the proposals.
2. What qualifications would you recommend be set up for those hired to run the computer installation if the company should decide to go ahead with the project?

Selected Readings

Office Automation, George R. Terry, Dow Jones-Irwin, Inc., Homewood, Ill., 1966. Presents current practices in the automation of office work through the use of computers and discusses some of the applications. Chapter 8, "Computers—Managerial Considerations," considers the effect of computers on such phases of managerial work as planning, control, and organizing.

The Shape of Automation for Men and Management, Herbert A. Simon, Harper & Row, Publishers, Incorporated, New York, 1965. The author believes that "the potentialities of a computer for flexible and adaptive cognitive response to a task environment are no narrower and no wider than the potentialities of a human." Includes some speculations on the eventual effects on management jobs and on employment.

Computers and Common Sense: The Myth of Thinking Machines, Mortimer Taube, Columbia University Press, New York, 1961. As the subtitle indicates, the author does not believe that computers are able, or are likely to be able, to replace human decision making.

Computers in Business Management, John Dearden, Dow Jones-Irwin, Inc., Homewood, Ill., 1966. Simplified explanation of computers and programming, plus sections on applications and on the future effect of computers.

29

MANAGEMENT SCIENCE— OPERATIONS RESEARCH*

Operational research has . . . a strictly practical character. Its object is to assist the finding of means to improve the efficiency of operations in progress or planned for the future.

No amount of scientific method can get more out of data than there is in them.

P. M. S. Blackett: "Operational Research," *Studies of War*

29 The scientific management movement was essentially a movement toward the quantification of factors bearing on management decisions. Thus Frederick Taylor wanted to determine by stopwatch measurements the exact time a job should take and use that time in determining pay and production scheduling. Similarly, Harrington Emerson emphasized accurate determination of costs as a basis for management decisions.

Taylor's most ambitious attempt at the quantification of the factors to be considered in decisions was his work on the cutting of metals. Here the decisions to be made were not top or even middle management decisions but those made by mechanics on the shop floor: on the best tools, speeds, and feeds to be used in cutting metals under each of a great many varying conditions.

Through experimentation, Taylor discovered that there were twelve variables to be considered in getting the best results (for example, the quality of the metal to be cut, the diameter of the work, the shape of the cutting edge of the tool, and the chemical composition of the tool steel). Eventually he and his group developed twelve formulas, each representing one of the variables, of which the following is an example:

$$V = \frac{11.9}{F^{0.665} \left(\dfrac{48}{3} D\right)^{0.2373 + 2.4/(18 + 48 D)}}$$

Then the group began trying to develop a sliderule that would enable a mechanic to determine, in a matter of seconds, the correct tools, speeds, and feeds to use in each case. "We went to the great mathematicians, the professors in our universities," Taylor reported later, "and offered them any price to solve that problem for us. Not one of them would touch it; they all said, 'You can solve a problem with four variables if you have your four equations, possibly; beyond that it is an indeterminate problem, and it is all nonsense thinking of getting a mathematical solution for it.' "[1]

Taylor's associates, led by Carl Barth, eventually produced the sliderule he wanted, but it took them eighteen years to do so. Today, high-speed computers and the use of new mathematical techniques would make the problem far easier to solve. In fact, there are cases in which solutions have been found to problems involving thousands of equations.[2]

The more sophisticated mathematical techniques are called management science or operations research (OR for short). Systems analysis utilizes many of the same procedures, but a distinction is often made between this field and OR, as will be explained later.

---

[1] "The Principles of Scientific Management," in *Addresses and Discussions at the Conference on Scientific Management held October 12, 13, 14, 1911*, The Amos Tuck School of Administration and Finance, Dartmouth College, Hanover, N.H., 1912, p. 51.
[2] George B. Dantzig, "Management Science in the World of Today and Tomorrow," *Management Science*, February, 1967, p. C-108.

THE BEGINNING OF OR

OR became recognized as a separate field in World War II. It was introduced in an attempt to determine how Britain, which had excellent fighter planes and pilots but far too few of them, could defend her shores against German bombers and their fighter escorts. Radar had been invented to give warning of attacks, and by plotting the positions of the enemy a ground crew could direct the defenders to positions where they could do the most good.

This required, of course, a determination of such questions as where the enemy aircraft would be after a given length of time, how soon the British planes could get to the point where their pilots could see the enemy, and what strength it would be necessary to pit against any given invading force to ensure probable success in view of the capabilities of both planes and pilots.

The calculations were too complicated for most commanding officers; therefore a small team of about half a dozen scientists was assigned to the Fighter Command. They were highly successful. "It is estimated that radar itself increased the probability of interception by a factor of about 10 but that . . . this small operational research team increased the probability by a further factor of about 2, which together meant that our Air Force was made twenty times more powerful."[3]

Several other applications of the technique were developed during the war —it was applied, for example, to combating U-boats. The depth charges dropped from aircraft on surfacing submarines had had little success. When the OR men analyzed the problem, they found that while the depth charges were set at 35 feet, by the time they went off the submarine had actually reached a depth of between 50 and 150 feet. A setting of the charge at 100 feet was therefore recommended, and a 700 per cent rise in the sinkings followed. Also, knowing the capabilities of the enemy submarines, the OR men were able to determine where and when each one would probably be compelled to surface so that aircraft could be there to bomb it before it could submerge again.

When the United States entered the war, it both borrowed from and added to the knowledge developed by the British teams. Perhaps its most notable achievement in this field was the successful mining of Japanese waters—the development of a pattern of aerial mine laying designed to achieve the maximum results from a limited number of mines.

The similarity of these problems to many encountered in industry is fairly obvious, for many business decisions are essentially a matter of determining how results can be achieved with minimum use of resources.

What, then, is operations research? There are many definitions, but certain key words keep cropping up in most of them. These are "scientific method," "quantitative," "model," "comparison," "optimum," and "decision making." Some of these terms will be discussed in detail later, but at this point they

[3] Sir Charles Goodeve, "Operational Research," *Nature*, Mar. 13, 1948, p. 377.

can be used to construct a definition that will suit the purpose of this text; OR is the application of the scientific method to management problems that can be expressed in quantitative terms. The method used is the construction of mathematical models that permit comparisons of alternative courses of action and determination of the course that will bring optimum results. Its purpose is to aid the executive in decision making.

At this point, the student may well wonder whether OR is anything new. After all, he may ask, hasn't management always attempted to use the scientific method, so far as it was able, even before the scientific management movement developed? Hasn't it always been thinking in quantitative terms? Hasn't it always been constructing models and making comparisons in order to determine the best course of action? And haven't executives normally relied on expert advice?

The answer to all these questions is "yes." How, then, does OR differ from, say, industrial engineering? The difference lies in the fact that OR uses an interdisciplinary approach; that is, it employs teams of experts so that all aspects of a problem may be taken into account.

An industrial engineer may, for example, develop a new shop layout that will make it possible to produce greater output without any increase in either area or personnel. Theoretically, at least, an OR team working in the same plant might include representatives of several physical sciences, mathematics, and engineering, an economist, occasionally a sociologist, and a psychologist. And it would take into account not only the possibility of changing the layout in various ways but the effect of all the other variables in the situation: the future demand, the effect of changes on employees, the possibility of changing the design of the product or the materials used for it, the possibility of changes in the machines, and the various steps in the manufacturing process. All these variables and the relationships between them would be reduced to a mathematical model; then the different possibilities and their effect on profitability would be analyzed through use of a computer.

There is, however, the difficulty that the findings of sociologists, psychologists, and others about the effect on employees of changes of various kinds in layout or production processes are not easily expressed in mathematical terms. Problems arising from them are not, therefore, readily susceptible to OR solutions. OR has proved most successful where all the factors in the problems can be quantified.

Two concepts are important in the OR approach: the concept of a system and the concept of the optimum.

Systems

In OR language, a "system" is a set of interacting variables, but each system is part of a larger system. For example, a single department is a system in which the variables include the procedures, the equipment, the organization structure, and the people. A change in procedures might make it necessary to get new equipment or to change the organization structure in some way, and it might very well affect the attitude of the people in the department or make it necessary for them to learn new skills. Similarly, if some of the people quit and it is, therefore, necessary to hire others with lower skills, a change might be required in procedures, in equipment, or in organization structure. Any change in any one of the variables is likely to affect the others, at least in a minor way.

But a department is part of a larger system—the company as a whole—and any change in it is likely to affect at least some of the variables in other departments. And, of course, the company itself is part of the economic system.

Thus, rather than consider the effect of changes in variables on a single operation—as Frederick Taylor did in his metal-cutting studies—an OR team would consider the effects of any change on manufacturing, marketing, purchasing, and so on.

"Systems analysis" may be considered merely the analysis of a system to identify the controllable and uncontrollable variables and to determine how the system actually operates. In this case, one might say that it is a part of OR.

Sometimes the analysis itself will reveal possible improvements. For example, in one case:

> It was found that many parts that had not been originally scheduled for production were being processed on an emergency basis because lack of them was delaying assembly. . . . The analysis also revealed the cause of the shortages: independent control of withdrawal of parts from stock by both production and replacement-part departments. An organizational change removed this cause of shortage and prepared the way for a comprehensive production and inventory control system.[4]

Such an analysis may eventually produce flow diagrams, but these will take in more territory than the conventional flow chart. The latter, although it is often useful for identifying unnecessary operations and eliminating bottlenecks, usually shows only the flow of physical objects (products in process or papers). The systems analysis diagram, on the other hand, shows the flow of instructions and information as well, and perhaps the points where control is or should be exercised and decisions made.

"Systems analysis" may also be used in a different sense: to designate a technique that is different from OR and one that has a broader scope. The Systems Analysis Office in the Department of Defense considers that OR studies produce exact solutions to well-defined problems and thereby eliminate the need for judgment, whereas systems analysis "presents the decision maker with a range of alternatives representing different mixes of effectiveness and cost. . . . It is part of systems analysis to question the objectives."[5]

[4] Russell L. Ackoff and Maurice W. Sasieni, *Fundamentals of Operations Research,* John Wiley & Sons, Inc., New York, 1968, pp. 28–29.
[5] Alain Enthoven, *Naval Review,* 1965.

Optimum versus suboptimum

In arriving at the solution to a problem, management usually has to consider a number of possible alternatives, none of which is likely to present an ideal solution, i.e., one that provides the greatest possible advantage from every point of view. Each solution has advantages and disadvantages, and each may entail additional problems that will require additional solutions.

An example may be taken from a close baseball game. Let us assume that it is the top of the ninth inning and the team at bat is leading by one run. There are two outs and three men on base, and the pitcher is scheduled to come to bat. But the pitcher is a very poor hitter, and in all probability he will either strike out or ground out. So the situation seemingly calls for a pinch hitter.

This, however, creates a serious problem. If a pinch hitter replaces the pitcher, another pitcher will have to finish the last half of the ninth, and the manager knows that no other pitcher can handle the opposition batters as well; therefore, the probability that the opposition will score will be greatly increased. Yet if the pitcher is not replaced, the team is likely to go into the last half of the ninth with a lead of only one run, which the manager regards as too small for comfort.

The manager is thus torn by two conflicting desires: (1) to prevent the opposition from scoring in the last half of the ninth, (2) to increase his narrow lead by as wide a margin as possible since the opposition still has a chance to add to its score.

Many of the questions a business manager faces are similar. A production manager knows that if one of his machines breaks down, he will not only lose production but have employees standing idle while it is being repaired; and if he has to wait for spare parts, the delay may be a very long one. From the viewpoint of continuous production, therefore, he should keep spares for every part that could possibly break down, perhaps even complete spare machines. But carrying spare parts in inventory costs money; money tied up in inventory is earning no profits. Further, the larger his inventory, the more space he will need to store it, and he may also need more clerks to keep it in order and issue it when it is needed.

Thus complete assurance that production will never be held up and a very small inventory of spare parts are two mutually exclusive suboptimums. The optimum from the production manager's point of view will be the greatest possible production at the lowest possible cost, and to achieve this, he must find a course of action that falls short of each suboptimum to some extent. This illustrates the difference between the "optimum" and the "ideal."

From top management's viewpoint, moreover, the production manager's optimum may be merely a suboptimum. Undoubtedly he can achieve the greatest possible production at the lowest cost if no changes are made in the product. But this will not be top management's optimum if changes will greatly increase sales and overall profits.

In short, the true optimum solution is the one that either maximizes the overall gains or minimizes the overall losses in a given situation. This is the solution an executive tries to arrive at when he weighs possible courses of action. OR is often useful in helping him determine this optimum by reducing the many variables to mathematical terms, which will sometimes represent actual numbers and sometimes mathematical probabilities since often the best that can be ascertained is what is most likely to happen.

One advantage of OR is that it may help to counteract the natural tendency of managers to optimize their own operations at the expense of the company as a whole. In addition, it helps all managers in deciding on what are known as "trade-offs." For example, one might have to decide between a faster machine and one that is more reliable—that is, one can trade off some speed for assurance that the machine will be available when it is needed or trade off some reliability for greater speed. Or one might trade off some measure of reliability and some speed for lower cost. In the absence of rigorous analysis, the manager might be swayed by his own inherent bias—which might be for speed, for reliability, or for low cost. OR makes it possible to determine the optimum combination of the three characteristics.

OR PROBLEMS

The principal types of problems that are susceptible to OR solutions include the following:

1. Allocation
2. Inventory
3. Routing
4. Replacement
5. Queuing
6. Sequencing and coordination
7. Search

Allocation   Allocation problems are problems similar to those for which OR was used during Warld War II. Since resources are never limitless, they must be allocated in such a way as to produce the best possible returns.

One type of allocation problem is the decision on product mix. If a company makes three products and does not have the resources to increase the production of all three—although the demand for each is rising—to which of the products should it allocate the available extra resources (money, equipment, and labor)? One might say offhand that it should increase production of the most profitable product. This is not necessarily the right answer, for the most profitable product may require much more machine and labor time than is needed for the less profitable items; therefore, it may not be possible for the company to produce as much of it as it can of the other two. If there are only two or three products to consider, the answer would be fairly easy to arrive at, but if there are, say, twenty, the problem is a very complex one, involving more variables than can be handled by jotting figures down on a piece of paper.

Or a firm that manufactures several products on which the profit margins are different might have the choice of making them in several different ways. Let us say there are three products—A, B, and C—and three grades of labor —1, 2, and 3. Grade 1 labor has above-average efficiency, grade 2 has average efficiency, and grade 3 is below average. Management will want, of course, to allocate the available labor in such a way as to maximize profits. It might decide, for example, to put out product A entirely with grade 1 labor, product B entirely with grade 2 labor, and product C entirely with grade 3 labor. Or it might decide to use all three grades on each of the products in any one of a number of possible combinations.

Inventory   The inventory problem is, of course, to achieve a balance between the risk of being out of stock and the cost of carrying excess inventory. The inventory may be the inventory of spare parts, of raw materials for production, or of finished goods available for sale.

Ideally, all spare parts or materials and parts for production would come in the plant door exactly when they are needed and products would be finished and ready for shipment just at the time of sale. In the case of parts needed for production, Henry Ford, Sr. actually demanded of a supplier, the Hyatt Roller Bearing Company, that the parts come into his plant no later and no sooner than they were needed. Alfred P. Sloan, then head of Hyatt (and later chief executive of General Motors), used to ride with the engineer of the freight train that carried the bearings in order to ensure that they got there exactly on time. (Ford's purchases accounted for a major part of Hyatt's sales volume.)

However, it is hardly ever possible to arrange matters in that way. Therefore, a company is faced with two questions: How much should we order at one time? And as inventory becomes depleted, at what point should we reorder?

The inventory of finished goods also presents a problem, for inability to meet the demand within a reasonable length of time may mean that sales are lost, and if the inventory is too large, the cost of carrying it may be excessive. This problem is particularly acute for the retailer since he never knows exactly how many of a given item he can sell, and if he does not sell an item, he is out both the cost of the item itself and the cost of carrying it. If the merchandise is perishable, his risk is multiplied.

Routing   The routing problem is illustrated by the following case: Assume that a company has three warehouses—one in Cleveland, one in Boston, and one in Atlanta. It receives orders to ship material as follows:

Amount	Destination
12 truckloads	New York
11 truckloads	Pittsburgh
15 truckloads	Chicago

The dispatcher has plenty of material at each of the warehouses, but the number of trucks available to him is limited:

Number of trucks	Location
6	Cleveland
20	Boston
15	Atlanta

His problem, of course, is to ensure that the goods arrive at their destination in the shortest possible time or at the lowest possible cost.

Replacement   The replacement problem is to determine when equipment should be replaced. The older equipment grows, the more it is likely to lose efficiency, the more repairs it will require, and the less the company can get for it on a trade-in. However, the longer it is kept in service, the less the average annual depreciation cost. (If it were traded in after the first year, the total depreciation—that is, its entire cost less the trade-in allowance—would have to come out of the revenues for that year.)

Queuing   Queuing problems are the problems presented by waiting lines. If mechanics have to wait at tool cribs, for example, they are being paid for time during which they are not productive. Or if customers have to wait too long at, say, a ticket window or a bank teller's window, they may get so annoyed that they take their business somewhere else. Waiting lines at tollbooths on highways may cause unnecessary traffic jams.

But in all these cases, the number of people in line will vary—perhaps there will be none at all at some times and a great many at others—and it is impossible to predict exactly how many there will be at any given time. Also, the time each person spends at the window may vary. Yet providing more facilities—more windows and employees to service them—will cost money. The problem is to find the optimum balance between providing all the facilities necessary to prevent any waiting at all and providing so few that the waits cause losses.

In problems of this nature, of course, the queue need not necessarily be composed of people. It might be made up, for example, of industrial trucks waiting for servicing. Then the longer the waits, the longer the trucks will be out of service. If they have to wait too long for attention, either the company will have to have more trucks than it would otherwise need or it will suffer some delays in production. Yet additional servicing facilities also cost money.

Sequencing and coordination   The problem of waiting times is often not a simple matter of first-come, first-served. There are many cases in which the order in which different jobs are done is important. A common problem of this kind is scheduling in a job shop where each job has a due date and there is a cost attached to lateness. This may be complicated by the fact that the same machines have to be used for several of the jobs and each job requires a different number of machine hours. Also, several of the jobs may utilize many of the same parts, and if identical parts can all be made in one production run, the cost of set-up time will be minimized. But if parts for some of the jobs with later due dates are produced before they are needed, the cost of carrying in-process inventory will be increased.

Sequencing problems are, in effect, problems in coordination. Coordination problems may, however, be described as the problems that arise when a large number of different tasks must be performed in order to complete a single project: a construction project, a product-development project, the manufacture and assembly of large products (e.g., spacecraft).

Search   Search problems are problems of determining how much information to acquire. The wider the search, of course, the greater the cost of acquiring the information. But too little information may mean errors that will cost more than a wider search—errors in observation and errors that occur because the sample is too small.

SOME OR TECHNIQUES

How does an OR man go about solving a problem? The steps in an OR solution are often listed as follows:

1. Formulate the problem.
2. Develop a hypothesis.
3. Derive a solution to the problem.
4. Test the solution.
5. Establish a system of controls over the solution to see that all elements of the plan are working as expected.

This series of steps is, of course, no different from the steps any manager would take in attempting to solve a problem in a rational way. OR differs from ordinary procedure, however, in that the hypothesis is generally expressed as a mathematical model and the solution may be derived by mathematical procedures alone. Also, as in most cases where a scientific method is used, OR uses experimentation, but the experimentation does not require the manipulation of physical objects, only of the terms used in the mathematical model, which may be an equation (or a series of equations) or one or more inequalities. (An inequality may state, for example, that a given quantity must be equal to or less than a certain amount.)

It is also true that in some cases testing the solution may involve actual experimentation: a trial run or the building of a pilot plant, but in many instances only the mathematical work is necessary.

Linear programming

Prominent among the techniques used in operations research is linear programming, which makes it possible to select the optimum when there is a large number of variables, each of which may be given any one of a number of different values. To be susceptible to a solution through linear programming, however, the relationship between the variables must be linear—that is, a change in one variable must produce a proportionate change in another, as in a linear equation in algebra, which is one in which the terms are in the first power only. If we write $Y = 2X$, we have a linear equation because a plot of the possible values of X and Y will be a straight line, as in Figure 1. On the other hand, the introduction of a quantity raised to a higher power produces a curve, as in Figure 2. The relationship between manhours worked and output, for example, is often a linear one up to a point; that is, a 5 per cent increase in manhours will often mean a 5 per cent increase in production.

In addition, a problem may be solved by linear programming only when there are constraints that impose limits on the values that can be given to the variables. Thus it is useful for allocation problems, which arise precisely because the limits of available resources impose constraints on what can be done.

FIGURE 1   Plot of equation $Y = 2X$.

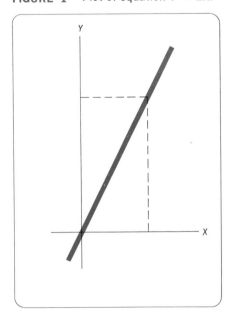

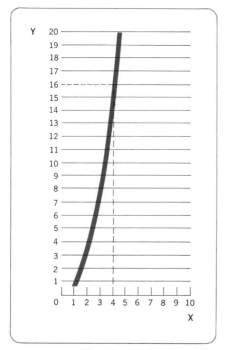

FIGURE 2 Plot of equation $Y = X^2$.

The characteristics of a linear-programming problem are illustrated by the following example:

A company wants to determine how many units of each of two products it should produce. It makes a profit of $1 on each unit of product A and a profit of $1.75 on each unit of product B. The quantities it can produce each day are subject to the following constraints:

1. There are only 24 manhours a day available for work on these products, and it takes 0.4 manhour to produce one unit of product A, 0.8 manhour to produce one unit of product B.
2. Only 200 pounds of material are available for these products, and one unit of product A requires 10 pounds, whereas one unit of product B requires 15 pounds.

In solving this problem, we shall let X stand for the number of units of product A to be produced and Y stand for the number of units of product B. Then the problem becomes one of finding values for X and Y that will maximize P, or profit, in the following equation:

$$P = 1.00X + 1.75Y$$

subject to the following constraints:

$$0.4X + 0.8Y \leqslant 24 \text{ (manhours)}$$
$$10X + 15Y \leqslant 200 \text{ (pounds of material)}$$

There is, of course, also the further constraint that neither X nor Y can be less than zero, for it is obviously impossible to produce less than none of the product.

To facilitate finding the solution, the inequalities are generally restated as equations by adding additional variables for each constraint. In this example, only two are necessary, which we shall express as U and W—U for the unused manhours and W for the unused material. Then the problem is stated as: Maximize:

$$P = 1.00X + 1.75Y$$

Subject to:

$$0.4X + 0.8Y + U = 24$$
$$10X + 15Y + W = 200$$

with X, Y, U, and W all nonnegative.

It will be noted that this problem has the characteristics that are typical of all linear-programming problems:

1. The algebraic statement of the problem is in three parts, as follows:
   a. The objective function, which is the statement of a cost to be minimized or a profit to be maximized.
   b. The operational constraints, which state that the quantity used for each factor of production has to be less than or equal to the available supply. (They might also specify that the quantity of each product has to be at least a certain minimum amount or that the amount of material used has to be at least a certain amount.)
   c. The nonnegativity constraints, which specify that all the unknowns have to be at least equal to zero.
2. All the relationships between the unknowns, in both the objective function and the operational constraints, are linear. That is, all the terms are of the first order; there are no X^2's or Y^3's.

The reader will note that he is asked to solve two equations with four unknowns, something that it is impossible to do algebraically. However, it is possible to solve for any two of the unknowns in terms of the other two, and that is what is done here. Moreover, it can be shown that the optimum value of the objective function (P) will occur when two of the four unknowns are zero.

Therefore, the problem can be solved by letting each successive pair of unknowns be equal to zero and using the resulting values to find the corresponding values of P, discarding all solutions that produce a negative value for any of the variables. Going through this successive solution in this case, the optimum profit is found to be $23.33, which is produced when

$$X = 0 \qquad U = 13.33$$
$$Y = 13.33 \qquad W = 0$$

See the following table for comparison with other solutions:

AVAILABLE PROFITS FOR VARIOUS COMBINATIONS OF ZERO UNKNOWNS

Solution number	X	Y	U	W	Profit
1	0.0	0.0	24.0	200.0	$ 0
2	0.0	30.0	0.0	−250.0	Infeasible
3	0.0	13.33	13.33	0.0	$ 23.33
4	60.0	0.0	0.0	−400.0	Infeasible
5	20.0	0.0	16.0	0.0	$ 20.00
6	−100.0	80.0	0.0	0.0	Infeasible

Now, in practice, it is not necessary to evaluate all the unknowns for each possible combination of zero unknowns. An approach, the "simplex method," has been designed which requires finding the combination of unknowns that will meet all the constraints. Then one proceeds through the following steps iteratively until the optimal solution is found:

1. The available feasible solution is tested for optimality. If it is optimal, the procedure stops; otherwise, it proceeds to step 2.
2. A new feasible solution is produced in which one of the zero unknowns in the former solution is allowed to become as large as possible subject to meeting the conditions of the various constraints. When this is done, one of the former nonzero variables will have become zero. Thus a new solution results in which a former zero variable has become nonzero and a former nonzero variable has become zero. The procedure then returns to step 1 to test this new solution for optimality.

The example illustrates another characteristic of linear programming, namely, that the final values of the unknowns are not necessarily integers. This, of course, could pose problems if X and Y had to be integers, such as the numbers of autos and trucks to be produced. When such integer solutions are definitely required, then another method, called "integer programming," has to be used instead of linear programming.

The example given above is a fairly simple one, in which there are only four unknowns, but the same technique is applicable to much more complex problems that may require the use of a computer. Linear programming may also be done geometrically.

One of the most important uses of linear programming has been in oil refineries to determine the most profitable mix of products. Linear programming has also been used to determine optimal personnel assignments and methods of shipping petroleum (owned versus chartered vessels). It has proved helpful in arriving at make-or-buy decisions, in determining whether to lease or buy computers, in planning crop rotations, and in deciding on purchasing policies.

Routing

Solution of the transportation problem described earlier is also possible through the use of linear programming, though such a problem may be solved through a series of tables. The first of them might be something like this:

Destination	Warehouses (rates per truckload)			Truckloads required
	Cleveland	Boston	Atlanta	
New York	$50	$30	$80	12
Pittsburgh	$40	$45	$75	11
Chicago	$30	$50	$80	15
Truckloads available	6	20	15	41

This table shows that it will cost, for example, $50 to send a truckload from Cleveland to New York and $40 to send one from the same warehouse to Pittsburgh.

Using the table, the dispatcher first develops a feasible solution to the problem, one that will at least get the right number of truckloads to each destination. Starting in the upper left-hand corner, he sends (on paper only) all six of Cleveland's truckloads to New York. Then, since New York actually needs twelve truckloads, he moves over to the next column and sends six more to New York from Boston. This leaves Boston with fourteen trucks, eleven of which he sends to Pittsburgh. Both New York and Pittsburgh are now taken care of, and fifteen truckloads may be sent from Atlanta to Chicago.

This is one possible way of handling the matter, but it is not necessarily the cheapest way, which is the solution the dispatcher is after. To find the cheapest plan, the dispatcher determines the cost of *not using* the routes he has left out—that is, the extra costs he is incurring under his present plan. Various techniques that do not require the use of higher mathematics are available for this.[6]

Nonlinear programming

As noted, the use of linear programming is limited to problems in which the relationships among the unknowns are linear. For example, in a linear-programming problem, the cost of manufacturing 20,000 units of a given product would have to be double the costs of manufacturing 10,000 units. No allow-

[6] See, for example, C. West Churchman, Russell L. Ackoff, and E. Leonard Arnoff, *Introduction to Operations Research*, John Wiley & Sons, Inc., New York, 1957, chap. 11 and appendix 11A.

ance is possible for quantity discounts, which permit the average unit cost to decrease as the number of units increases. Such cost reductions are to be expected in transportation problems, where freight rates per hundred pounds decrease in discrete steps as the size of shipment moves from a less-than-carload lot to the carload and train-load. Marketing problems often entail a declining selling price as the number of units marketed increases. Some of these problems can be solved by another technique, nonlinear programming.

Like linear programming, nonlinear programming is used to find the values of certain variables that will maximize or minimize the value of some objective function subject to certain constraints. However, with nonlinear programming, the relationships among the variables in the objective function and in the constraints need not necessarily be linear. The computations of nonlinear programming are too complex to illustrate in this book; however, notwithstanding this complexity, nonlinear programming is credited with more potential for problem solving than is linear programming. Indeed, the methods of linear programming can be shown to be a special case of those of nonlinear programming.

The order-quantity model

One of the simplest examples of the use of a mathematical model in decision making is in determining the quantity of a given item to be ordered at one time. On the one hand, the larger the quantity ordered each time, the lower the cost of placing orders; on the other hand, the larger the quantity ordered, the greater the cost of holding the inventory. Hence, this is a case in which optimization of the total cost must be sought.

The cost of placing the orders can be represented by the formula

$$\frac{U}{Q} \times CP$$

where U is the number of units needed in a year, Q the quantity ordered, and CP the cost of placing a single order.

If the quantity held in inventory decreases at a regular rate, the average number of units held in the period between orders may be represented by $Q/2$. Then the cost of holding this quantity is multiplied by the cost of holding one unit in inventory.

The formula for the optimum quantity to be purchased at one time works out to

$$Q = \sqrt{\frac{2 \times U \times CP}{CH}}$$

where U is the number of units used in a year, CP is the cost of placing an order, and CH is the cost of holding a unit in inventory.

Where the rate of usage is constant, it is quite easy to determine the minimum amount to be held in inventory—it will simply be the supply needed during the period between the time an order is issued and the time when delivery may be expected, with perhaps a few extra to take account of possible delays in the supplier's plant or in transportation. But in many cases, usage is not constant, and then different techniques must be used. The appendix to this chapter gives two examples of how a retailer might solve the problem of determining how many units to stock when he does not know how many he can sell.

Simulation

Simulation techniques are especially applicable to "what if" problems, cases in which a manager or a technician wants to know: If we do this, what will happen?

Simulation can, of course, be conducted by the manipulation of physical models. For example, one might have a physical model of a machine and actually keep on increasing its speed to determine at what point it would begin to jam, fly apart, or "walk" across the floor. But one may, instead, use a mathematical model in which each of the terms represents one of the variables, and observe the effect on the others when different values are given to one or more of the terms. With the help of a computer, it is possible to examine what will happen in an enormous number of cases—without spending a prohibitive amount of time.

This is very helpful in engineering and design problems, where the medium may be either the mathematical model or a diagram on a screen connected to the computer. In the latter case, the engineer-designer can modify his design by using a light pen. The technique is also applicable to many strictly management problems. As noted in the chapter on computers, some companies are using it to determine what will happen if management makes any one of a number of possible decisions.

It is obviously much cheaper and easier to experiment with a mathematical or diagrammatic simulator than to experiment with real machines (or even physical models of machines). As one Du Pont executive once pointed out, it makes possible penalty-free trial and error:

> If the output of the simulator indicates the pressure vs. time curve going off the top of the chart, you have not broken up any equipment. If you wish to determine the effect of doubling the size of a piece of equipment, you do not have to spend $100,000 to build it; you merely change the term in an equation. . . .[7]

And in simulations of the effect of possible management decisions, the

[7] R. C. Ficke, "Simulation as a Systems Performance Prediction Tool," *Proceedings of the 1964 Systems Engineering Conference*, Clapp & Poliak, Inc., New York, 1964, p. 444.

technique produces even greater savings, for sometimes the use of actual trial and error might be disastrous to the whole company, or almost so.

In some cases, however, the variables that one manipulates are not exact quantities but probabilities. Then what are known as "Monte Carlo techniques" must be used. These make it possible, as William J. Baumol has phrased it, "to stretch as far as possible such few actual data as are available to begin with."[8]

The queuing, or waiting-line, problems are generally solved through the use of these techniques. Since people or objects join the queue at random times and the time required to service them also varies in a random way, a table of random numbers is used to simulate the situation in the system at various times. Thus, if observation has shown that there may be anywhere from one to twenty people in the line at any given moment and that servicing one person may require from one to three minutes, one could simulate the number in the line at various times by picking numbers between 1 and 20 at random, then combine with them random numbers representing the times required for servicing.

If, say, 100 or more possible situations were simulated in this way, the researcher would have a sample that would show how the whole system was actually working. The number of simulations would, of course, have to be large enough to ensure that the sample was representative of the whole, just as a political pollster must ensure that his sample is large enough to be representative of all the voters.

Then the researcher could determine, say, the average waiting time or the longest time it would be necessary for anyone to wait. In the case of machinists waiting at a tool crib, for example, he could use the average time to determine the cost of the time they were losing and compare that cost with the cost of adding an extra clerk. In other cases—for example, people waiting for service at a bank teller's window—the manager might have to use judgment to determine the optimum course, for it would be impossible to say how much the waits were costing, that is, how many people had decided to bank elsewhere after a few experiences of long waits. But the average wait and the longest wait would give him a basis for judging whether the waiting time was likely to be long enough to be intolerable and so produce unfavorable results.

Similar techniques may be used to solve the retailer's inventory problem in cases where the demand is irregular and the retailer runs the risk of either losing sales by being out of stock or losing money through overstocking.

Probabilities may also be used in solving replacement problems in cases where the exact time when failure will occur is not known. An example of this is given in the appendix (light-bulb replacement). (The appendix example of equipment replacement is a simpler one, in that it is presupposed that the

[8] *Economic Theory and Operations Analysis,* Prentice-Hall, Inc., Englewood Cliffs, N.J., 1961, p. 403.

company knows fairly accurately the annual maintenance costs as the equipment grows older.)

Networking

Networking techniques are those used in critical-path scheduling and PERT, techniques described in the chapter on planning. The examples given there were simple ones in which practically all that would be needed to achieve coordination and speeding up of the jobs would be inspection of the networks. However, where the project is one that requires thousands of steps (production of a weapons system, for example), one may have to use higher mathematics and a computer in order to manipulate crew sizes, slack times, and so on, to best advantage.

Decomposition

The technique of decomposition is used when a problem is very complex and it is impossible to start solving it as a whole in the beginning. Therefore, solutions are obtained for parts of it first. This is somewhat different, however, from simply considering each aspect a special problem and perhaps optimizing one aspect at the expense of others rather than optimizing the whole situation. As Russell Ackoff and Maurice W. Sasieni explain it, ". . . we must frequently . . . use the solution obtained from one part as input to a second part, and so on. We may then have to use the output of the last part to reevaluate one or all of the partial solutions previously obtained.[9]

Because the problems for which this technique is used are necessarily the most complex of all, an illustration of the technique cannot be given here. For example, a problem involving 30,000 equations and over a million variables has been optimized by this method.[10]

Game theory

Another technique of operations research, the potential of which has hardly been tapped, is known as "game theory." This provides a basis for determining, under certain specified conditions, the particular strategy that will result in maximum gain or minimum loss no matter what opponents do or do not do. (An opponent would be the enemy general in a military application, a competitor in a business situation.)

The simplest application of the game theory is the two-person, zero-sum game, in which there are only two players and one player can gain only at the expense of the other. These two conditions are generally fulfilled when two

[9] *Op. cit.*, p. 15.
[10] Dantzig, *op. cit.*, p. C-110.

armies are opposing each other. In business they are fulfilled only in special cases: A company has only one competitor, and the size of the market is fixed; thus every gain in sales by one company means an equal loss in sales for the other. In an expanding market, both could gain; in a declining market, one could gain at the expense of the other, but the losses of the weaker company would be greater than the gains of the stronger.

This theory could have the greatest practical usefulness in planning sales promotion strategies. A company that wishes to increase its sales may do so by using one or more of such techniques as the following: (1) a reduction in product price, (2) an increase in the number of salesmen, and (3) a rise in its advertising budget. But since the total market for its products is fixed and it can gain only at the expense of its rival, it must consider what the rival can do to nullify the effect of any of these changes. The competitor might, for example, cut prices too.

The company therefore asks itself questions like these: Assuming we decide to increase our share of the market by cutting prices, what will actually happen if (1) our rival also cuts prices, (2) he increases the number of his salesmen, (3) he raises his advertising budget, or (4) he uses a combination of all three of these tactics? Assuming we decide to try to increase our share of the market by putting on more salesmen, what will actually happen if our rival pursues any of the four courses outlined above?

By evaluating each one of these possible strategies, the company can ascertain the greatest possible damage the rival can inflict. This will reveal either the minimum gain the company is assured of or the maximum loss it can suffer.

Now a rival company or an army will not necessarily adopt the strategy that will inflict the greatest damage on its opponent; there are many cases in which both companies and armies have muffed their chances. But working out the possibilities enables the company to see the worst that can possibly happen and the most it can hope to gain. It may decide to take a chance on the highest possible gain, it may decide to minimize the chance of losses, or it may adopt some course in between.

Of course, the company does not always know exactly what it can hope to gain by cutting its prices, increasing its sales effort, or doing both, but with the aid of a computer, it can simulate various possibilities.

In real life, however, the limitations of the two-person, zero-sum game are not likely to apply. Usually there are more than two competitors, and the demand for most products is not stable. If all competitors cut prices, the market for all may be increased, and possibly all may gain or all may lose. Therefore the losses of one do not necessarily equal the gains of another.

Although some n-person (any number can play) game theories have been worked out, they are not yet developed far enough to be of much use in business. When techniques are refined, however, it may be that theories of this kind will be evolved that will be of practical value to management.

AN EVALUATION OF OR

OR has made invaluable contributions to management and is likely to continue to do so in the future. But if it is to produce the best possible results, it must entail a collaboration between the manager and the OR specialist. The manager knows the many intangible factors that bear on a problem, and he will have to assume the risk if he accepts the OR solution. Thus he must decide when to use OR and when not to use it—and how much of OR to use in solving a given problem.

Even where all the factors in a problem can be accurately quantified, as in many cases where linear-programming techniques are applicable, the manager may have to look upon the solution as only one of the factors he must consider in his decision. Take the simple problem in linear programming explained in this chapter. The OR solution shows that the company will make the largest profit if it devotes all the material available to production of one of the products, which leaves excess manpower available. Presumably, the extra manpower can be used for other tasks; so this does not necessarily constitute a difficulty. If people would have to be laid off, however, the manager would have to take into consideration the effect on labor relations. Also, it might be that some customers would cease to buy the second product from the company if they could not obtain the first one from the same source. There are any number of cases in which the manager might wisely choose to ignore the OR findings. Nevertheless, the OR solutions are valuable because they enable him to see the tangible advantages he is giving up in order to take account of the intangibles.

The simulations of the possible consequences of top management decisions will also be of help, but not in cases where firms are highly sensitive to such factors as governmental fiscal policy, the state of the cold war, foreign trade, trade union pressure, and other variables over which management has no control. They are probably of greatest value in cases where present trends in the industry can be projected with some degree of confidence that they will continue.

If OR is to serve management well, the manager must always remember that it does not relieve him of the responsibility of making decisions himself, except in routine cases. The great danger attached to use of the technique is that managers will do exactly that, for people are apt to accept scientific findings of almost any kind without question. But in dealing with the vast complex of a business situation, the manager is dealing with a problem in which many of the variables are people (managers, employees, customers, those in government agencies, suppliers), and their reactions can never be exactly quantified. Too great a dependence on OR might produce difficulties, just as Frederick Taylor's "scientifically" determined wages did for some firms.

Another difficulty with OR has lain in the difficulty of communication between the OR teams and management. Members of the team usually converse with each other in the language of higher mathematics, which is generally beyond the comprehension of most executives. No matter how brilliant or profound the findings of such a team are, they are absolutely useless unless they can be communicated to those who can act on them.

Then sometimes the difficulty in communication is compounded by a difference in attitude. The OR man may regard his function as that of a pure scientist, one who seeks knowledge for its own sake, and look down on applied science as a somewhat inferior occupation. But OR, whether it is used in business or in some other field, is by its very nature an applied science. If it is not applied to problems in the real world, it is nothing. There is an underlying pure science, mathematics, and advances in mathematics make possible further use of OR. But OR is to mathematics as engineering is to physics; it is the application of the pure science.

THE FUTURE OF OR

Although some of the limitations mentioned are inherent in the OR process itself, others will become less important over time. Management will become better acquainted with the language of the scientists, and the scientists will learn how to translate their language into understandable English—in fact, the communication gap is already narrowing in some companies.

Another factor that will aid the growth of OR is the continued development of the electronic computer. As computers become more sophisticated, many problems now considered insoluble will become susceptible to OR solutions—and in many other cases, management will be able to gauge the exact risks it is taking by following one course of action rather than another.

The use of management science will undoubtedly grow and spread, but it is unlikely that it will ever replace management know-how altogether. Rather, it will provide management with new ways of dealing with many of its present problems in a fairly routinized fashion and give the manager an opportunity to consider many more alternative courses of action than he can at present and to devote more time to the new problems that will undoubtedly arise.

SUMMARY

Operations research, or management science, is the application of the scientific method to management problems that can be expressed in quantitative terms. Generally it requires the use of mathematical models, and solutions are derived by the use of the computer.

Where management must decide between two courses of action (or among several possible courses), there are generally both advantages and disadvantages to each course. The OR techniques enable management to optimize, that is, to select the course in which the advantages outweigh the disadvantages by the greatest possible amount.

Among the problems to which OR techniques are particularly applicable are those in which the aim is to allocate scarce resources in the most profitable way: queuing, or waiting-line, problems, replacement problems, inventory problems, and sequencing and coordination problems.

Review Questions

1.   What is a mathematical model?
2.   What is a system? Would you say that a machine is a system? An iron bar? A person?
3.   What is meant by the optimum?
4.   What OR technique is commonly used for allocation problems?
5.   What is simulation? To what types of problems is it applicable?
6.   What conditions must be fulfilled if linear programming is to be used? Does linear programming make use of the laws of probability?
7.   It is sometimes said that game theory will help companies with their competitive problems. Why is it unlikely to be of great value for this at present?
8.   What are trade-offs?
9.   What is decomposition?

Case Study One / A Sample Problem in Inventory Control

A manufacturer uses 100,000 units of widgets per year. He wishes to determine the quantity Q to order at any one time so that the combined cost of placing orders and holding the goods in inventory is as small as possible. A study reveals that the cost of holding a unit in inventory for a year is $5, and the cost of placing an order is $25. (Widgets cost $50 apiece.)

The $25 figure includes all costs directly associated with placing an order. These could include the wages of purchasing department employees for the time they require to call for tenders and consider them; the cost of the paperwork needed to communicate the order to the supplier; and perhaps any wages required to get the incoming shipment stowed away in the stockroom. The nature and size of these costs will vary from one company to another, but in each case they are the costs that would be saved over the long run if this series of orders were not placed.

The $5 cost of holding one unit in inventory for a year could include such things as interest on the money tied up in the unit, insurance, storage charges, and some allowance for obsolescence, spoilage, perhaps for pilferage, and so on. Often the total of these costs is stated as a percentage of the price of the article, a percentage that varies from about 10 to 40 per cent, depending on the nature of the article. An item subject to spoilage or to obsolescence because of style changes would cost more to hold in inventory than one not so affected. For example, the cost of holding a dollar's worth of standard nails would be lower than the cost of holding a dollar's worth of millinery.

Find the optimum ordering quantity for the widgets and determine how frequently the orders should be placed, assuming 50 weeks of operation per year.

Case Study Two

A company wishes to know how much of each of two products it should manufacture in order to maximize its profits. Product 1 yields a per-unit profit of $7, product 2 a profit of $4. For policy reasons, the company wishes to manufacture at least 3,000 units of product 2. Product 1 requires 3 pounds of material per unit; product 2 requires only 1 pound per unit. There are 30,000 manhours available for manufacturing these two products. Product 1 requires 2 manhours per unit, and product 2 requires 5 manhours per unit.

1. Which of the OR techniques would you use in solving this problem?
2. State the objective function and the constraints in algebraic form.

Case Study Three / Computer-controlled Inventory*

A company uses a computer to control its inventory of maintenance supplies and orders all sizes of each type of item at one time. For example, all sizes and types of brass fittings are ordered quarterly. This company has set minimum and maximum inventories for each item (size and type), as most companies do, but because the computer writes the purchase order automatically, the company also has what it calls a "cycle reorder point," which is between the minimum and the maximum, for each item.

Each quarter, the computer examines the inventory and orders more of every size and type that is below its cycle reorder point—enough more to bring the inventory up to the maximum.

* R. V. Rogers (IBM Corporation, Boulder, Colo.), "Inventory Control for Maintenance Supplies," *Techniques of Plant Engineering and Maintenance*, vol. XIX, Clapp & Poliak, Inc., New York, 1968, pp. 74–76.

However, usage is not at a constant rate, and occasionally special orders must be prepared manually to ensure that the supply will not be exhausted before the computer issues its regular blanket order. If a special order is written, it calls for a quantity only large enough to bring the inventory up to the cycle reorder point, not the maximum.

1. Why doesn't the special order cover a quantity sufficient to bring the inventory up to the maximum? What difficulties would be experienced if it did?
2. How is it possible for a computer to determine how much of each item remains in the inventory when the time comes for reordering?

Selected Readings

Management Control Systems, Robert N. Anthony, John Dearden, and Richard F. Vancil, Richard D. Irwin, Inc., Homewood, Ill., 1965. A detailed study of the relationship of control to management, with emphasis on the systems approach.

Decision and Control: The Meaning of Operational Research and Management Cybernetics, Stafford Beer, John Wiley & Sons, Inc., New York, 1966. A presentation of the concepts of operations research and its possibilities. The book is designed for managers and others who need and want a general understanding of the whole subject.

Fundamentals of Operations Research, Russell L. Ackoff and Maurice W. Sasieni, John Wiley & Sons, Inc., New York, 1968. An introductory textbook which explains many of the mathematical techniques. Methods and techniques are illustrated by real-life cases that show the practical applications of OR.

A Guide to Operational Research, Eric Duckworth, Dover Publications, Inc., New York, 1962. A short, well-written methodological study dealing with the techniques of operations research, its organization, and use.

"Operational Research" in *Studies of War,* P. M. S. Blackett, Oliver & Boyd Ltd., Edinburgh and London, 1962, pp. 161–239. The scope of operations research discussed by one of the originators of the technique.

Linear Programming and the Theory of the Firm, Kenneth E. Boulding and W. Allen Spivey, The Macmillan Company, New York, 1960. Deals with operations research in an understandable and practical way.

Operations Research for Management Decisions, Samuel B. Richmond, The Ronald Press Company, New York, 1968. An introduction to operations research.

APPENDIX

SOME FURTHER APPLICATIONS OF OPERATIONS RESEARCH

As shown in Chapter 29, operations research may be used to assist in problem solving and in decision making at all management levels. Usually this is not done by the application of standard techniques. Rather, each problem is considered in its own right and then an appropriate solution is developed by the use of a judicious mixture of the scientific method, the systems approach, and the basic principles of mathematics and science. However, certain types of problems have been found to occur frequently, and therefore some standard approaches have evolved for their solution. This has been especially the case with problems in inventory management, waiting lines, and equipment replacement. Since one often hears of operations research being used to solve these problems, a few simple examples are presented in this appendix. These are not intended to train the reader in operations research itself, since most real problems are much more complex than these examples. However, it is hoped that they will show the general approaches to problem solving in this area. Some additional readings are listed at the end of the appendix for those who wish to read still more about operations research.

INVENTORY MANAGEMENT

Inventory management is concerned with planning the levels of stock on hand, whether they are stocks of raw materials, work in process, or finished goods. Such stocks are necessary to permit purchasing or manufacturing in efficient quantities and to provide a safety factor for periods of unusually high demand or when new supplies may be unexpectedly cut off. Problems in inventory management generally deal with how many units should be purchased or manufactured at one time and/or with how many units should be carried in stock at all. Examples 1 to 3 are presented to illustrate some of the basic considerations involved in solving such problems.

Example 1

Let us say that 144 units of a certain product are required during the twelve months of a calendar year and that the demand is constant over each working day of this year. The problem is to determine how many of these units should be produced at one time, that is, in one production run. It costs $90 to set up a production run; this figure includes the costs of procuring tools and dies, making patterns, adjusting machines, and so on. The cost is $90 regardless of the number of units produced in the production run. It costs $100 to produce each one of these 144 units, a cost that is also independent of the number produced at one time. It also costs $20 to hold one item in inventory for a year. This cost is 20 per cent of the $100 cost of producing the item and covers insurance and storage charges, interest on the money tied up by the inventory, and allowances for depreciation and spoilage.

Solution to Example 1   The following concepts are used in the solution of this problem:

R = the number of units required for the year
    = 144 units
S = the cost of setting up a production run
    = $90
C = the direct cost of producing one unit
    = $100
I = the percentage of C required to hold one unit in inventory for a year
    = 20 per cent
Q = the number of units to be produced at one time

Since the demand for these units is constant each working day, the production runs can be scheduled in such a way that a new batch of Q items will be placed in inventory just at the time when the last unit of the preceding batch is used. The inventory will have a maximum of Q units and will decrease steadily until it reaches a minimum of zero units. Therefore, the average size of the inventory with be $Q/2$ units, and the annual cost of carrying this inventory will be

$$IC\frac{Q}{2}$$

This annual cost will increase proportionately as Q increases.

There will be R/Q production runs in the year, and therefore the annual costs associated with setting up these runs will be

$$\frac{R}{Q}S$$

These annual costs will decline as Q increases. The annual costs of manufacturing will be RC, regardless of the size of Q.

The total annual costs for production setups and for carrying the units in inventory will be

$$RC+\frac{R}{Q}S+\frac{Q}{2}IC$$

It may be easily proved that the costs are a minimum when

$$Q=\sqrt{\frac{2RS}{IC}}=\sqrt{\frac{2\times144\times90}{0.20\times100}}$$
$$=36\text{ units}$$

(Q is called the "economic order quantity," often abbreviated EOQ; the foregoing formula is often called the EOQ formula.)

In this problem, the minimum total value of these annual costs is

<table>
<tr><td>Direct costs of production:</td><td>$CR =$ $14,400</td></tr>
<tr><td>Costs of setups:</td><td>$\dfrac{R}{Q}S =$ 360</td></tr>
<tr><td>Costs of carrying inventory:</td><td>$\dfrac{Q}{2}IC =$ 360</td></tr>
<tr><td>Minimum total annual costs</td><td>= $15,120</td></tr>
</table>

These costs are based upon 36 units to be produced in each production run—that is, with four such runs in the year—and an average inventory of 18 units.

Example 2

Another basic type of inventory problem considers how many units of some seasonal item should be ordered when only one order is possible and ordering one unit too many or one too few entails costs. Such a problem is often called a "Christmas tree" problem. For example, a merchant wishes to determine how many children's sleds to order. His profit is $3 per sled, and the cost of holding an unsold sled over to the next selling season is $1 The profit of $3, therefore, represents the penalty or "stock-out" cost of having ordered one sled too few; and the $1 is the cost of having one sled too many. The merchant estimates, from past experience, that the number of sleds demanded ("demanded" is not to be confused with "sold") in the forthcoming season will be subject to the following probabilities:

Number of sleds demanded, X	Probability of X*	Probability of X or fewer
10	0.10	0.10
11	0.10	0.20
12	0.20	0.40
13	0.20	0.60
14	0.15	0.75
15	0.15	0.90
16	0.10	1.00
Total	1.00	

* The reader unfamiliar with more technical definitions of probabilities can think of the probability of a demand for, say, fourteen sleds as the fraction of a long number of years in which exactly fourteen sleds would be demanded. That is, one would expect fourteen sleds to be demanded in 15 per cent of such years.

Solution to Example 2　In these circumstances, the merchant might guess that he should stock thirteen sleds; this would take care of his expected demand in 60 per cent of the years. However, he might then wonder if he could expect to secure a larger profit by stocking an additional sled, or fourteen in all. His analysis would be as follows:

Expected gain from fourteenth sled: $3 × 0.40 = $1.20

The per-unit profit of $3 is multiplied by 0.40 since it would be obtained in 40 per cent of the years. That is, the fourteenth sled would be sold whenever the demand was for fourteen, fifteen, or sixteen sleds, and this would occur on average in 40 per cent of the years.

Expected loss from fourteenth sled: $1 × 0.60 = $0.60

The possible unit loss of $1 is multiplied by 0.60, since it would be incurred whenever the fourteenth sled was unsold—that is, whenever the number demanded was thirteen or fewer. This would occur in 60 per cent of the years.

Since the expected gain of $1.20 exceeds the expected loss of $0.60, the merchant would conclude that he would be better off, on the average, by $0.60 per year with the fourteenth sled than without it. He would then decide to stock the fourteenth sled and would repeat the foregoing reasoning for the fifteenth sled:

Expected gain from fifteenth sled: $3 × 0.25 = $0.75
Expected loss from fifteenth sled: $1 × 0.75 = $0.75

Since the merchant would be as well off with this fifteenth sled as without it, he would probably decide to stock it. However, he would not be willing to stock the sixteenth sled since:

Expected gain from sixteenth sled: $3 × 0.10 = $0.30
Expected loss from sixteenth sled: $1 × 0.90 = $0.90

The merchant would, therefore, conclude that he should stock exactly fifteen sleds; this amount would satisfy his demand in 90 per cent of the years, that is, with a probability of 0.90.

The foregoing reasoning can be readily applied to problems having many more possible values of X, the number of items demanded. It forms the basis for the solution to many inventory problems.

Example 3

The Bathurst Better Bagel Bakers produce a certain rare type of bread. Each loaf sells for 30 cents and costs 10 cents to produce. Any loaves left over at the end of a day are sold to a nearby restaurant for 5 cents apiece.

Experience indicates that the demand for this bread varies from six to twelve loaves a day, according to the first table on the next page.

For some reason, the bakery would prefer to limit its production of this bread to nine loaves, as compared with ten at the present time, and wants to determine the change, if any, in its profits that will result.

Number of loaves demanded	Fraction of the days
6	0.10
7	0.10
8	0.15
9	0.25
10	0.20
11	0.15
12	0.05
Total	1.00

Solution to Example 3   To solve this problem, the manager decides to simulate twenty typical days. (Actually twenty days is much too short a period to obtain a good estimate, but it is used in this solution to make demonstration of the technique simpler.)

Table 1 shows the simulated profits for the twenty sample days in each of the two cases: with a stock of nine loaves and with a stock of ten loaves.

The number of loaves demanded each day has no connection with the number of loaves demanded on any other day. Thus the demand is represented by random numbers. In this case, each of 100 random numbers is assigned to a particular demand, in the same proportion as that demand would be expected to occur:

Number of loaves demanded	Fraction of the days	Corresponding set of random numbers
6	0.10	00–09
7	0.10	10–19
8	0.15	20–34
9	0.25	35–59
10	0.20	60–79
11	0.15	80–94
12	0.05	95–99

Now if each of these 100 random numbers were placed in an urn and one drawn out for each day being simulated, a set of such demands would be noted. If this set were large enough, each possible demand would occur the same percentage of the days as that demand could be expected to occur in the real world. It will be noted from Table 1 that on the first day the number 54 was drawn; this was one of the 25 random numbers assigned to the demand for nine loaves, which was expected to occur 25 per cent of the time. Similarly, the random number 19 was drawn for the second day, and this corresponded to a demand for seven loaves. The process was continued for each of the remaining eighteen days.

Another method of obtaining the various demand values is to apportion the circumference of a roulette wheel among the various values in the same pro-

TABLE 1   SIMULATION OF RARE BREAD SALES, BATHURST BETTER BAGEL BAKERS

Day number	Random-number demand value	Number of loaves demanded	If 9 produced		If 10 produced	
			Number sold	Number left over	Number sold	Number left over
1	54	9	9	0	9	1
2	19	7	7	2	7	3
3	79	10	9	0	10	0
4	38	9	9	0	9	1
5	14	7	7	2	7	3
6	95	12	9	0	10	0
7	49	9	9	0	9	1
8	12	7	7	2	7	3
9	39	9	9	0	9	1
10	06	6	6	3	6	4
11	22	8	8	1	8	2
12	31	8	8	1	8	2
13	94	11	9	0	10	0
14	95	12	9	0	10	0
15	16	7	7	2	7	3
16	80	11	9	0	10	0
17	46	9	9	0	9	1
18	21	8	8	1	8	2
19	11	7	7	2	7	3
20	24	8	8	1	8	2
Totals			163	17	168	32

SUMMARIES OF PROFITS

	If 9 produced	If 10 produced
Sales to customers:	163 @ $0.30 = $48.90	168 @ $0.30 = $50.40
Sales to restaurant:	17 @ $0.05 = 0.85	32 @ $0.05 = 1.60
Total	$49.75	$52.00
Production costs:	180 @ $0.10 = $18.00	200 @ $0.10 = $20.00
Profit on item:	$31.75	$32.00
Average daily profits:	$ 1.59	$ 1.60

portion as the demands could be expected to occur in reality. Then a demand value for a particular day could be generated by spinning the wheel. The possible use of this method has caused the term "Monte Carlo simulation" to be applied to problems that include uncertain quantities.

The number of loaves sold to customers equals the number demanded if this latter number is less than the number produced. The number of loaves left over at the end of the day equals zero if the number of loaves sold equals the number produced.

At the end of the 20-day simulated period, the revenues, expenses, and profits can be calculated for each production alternative, and it is seen that profit would be only slightly reduced if the company were to limit its production to nine loaves.

Now the student of mathematics will realize that this particular problem could be solved more efficiently by using basic principles of probability theory to calculate the average daily profits to be expected if nine or ten loaves were produced. If this were done, it would be found that the difference in average daily profits would be larger. (See Table 2.)

This comparison of results by the two methods illustrates the principal disadvantage of Monte Carlo simulation. The results are based on a sample of a finite period of time and are not what could be expected over an indefinitely long period. In this example, the distribution of the demand values, while indicative of a typical sample of 20 days, is not completely representative of the longer term. (See Table 3.)

This disadvantage, however, is offset by the fact that many problems are just too complex to be handled in any other way. It was for these problems

TABLE 2   COMPARISON OF AVERAGE DAILY PROFITS

	With 9 loaves	With 10 loaves
Average number sold to customers	8.35	8.75
Average number sold to restaurant	0.65	1.25
Average daily revenues:		
Customers	$2.5050	$2.6250
Restaurant	.0325	.0625
Total	$2.5375	$2.6875
Less production costs	0.9000	1.0000
Average daily profits	$1.6375	$1.6875

TABLE 3   COMPARISON OF SIMULATED AND EXPECTED NUMBER OF DEMAND VALUES IN 20-DAY SAMPLE

Demand value	Simulated frequency	Expected frequency
6	1	2
7	5	2
8	4	3
9	5	5
10	1	4
11	2	3
12	2	1
Total	20	20
Average	8.7	9.0

that the technique was developed, and as a result, Monte Carlo simulation is one of the more useful OR techniques.

WAITING-LINE SYSTEMS

Almost everyone has had experiences, good and bad, with "waiting-line systems." As a customer, he may have entered the line before a ticket window or before a cash register in a supermarket. He may have complained about the length of this waiting line and perhaps even have become tired of waiting and left the line without being served. With too few facilities, there is this possibility of a loss of customers and of revenue. However, with too many facilities, costs are incurred unnecessarily. As with inventory-control problems, there are cost penalties associated with stocking too many or too few items. In waiting-line problems, these items are servicing facilities—ticket windows, bank tellers, cashiers, repairmen, and so on.

The solutions of waiting-line problems are usually based on the average of and the distribution of the times between the arrivals and the average of and the distribution of the times required to perform the service. They are also based upon the "queue discipline," that is, whether or not all arrivals join the waiting line and also whether or not all customers are served on a "first come, first served" basis. All this information can be used to calculate such properties of the waiting-line system as:

1. The average number of customers in the system at any one time, that is, the average number of customers in the line plus the number being served
2. The average amount of time a customer spends in the system, that is, in waiting in line and being served
3. The average amount of time a customer spends in the line

Properties such as these can be combined with relevant cost considerations to produce measures of effectiveness on which to base the decisions in a given case.

A relatively high level of mathematics is required to determine the foregoing factors in most waiting-line problems. In fact, many such problems are sufficiently involved to preclude any mathematical solution; these have to be studied by simulating the system using the Monte Carlo methods illustrated above. However, there is a type of waiting-line problem which can be analyzed through the use of relatively simple formulas. In this type of problem, the time between successive arrivals is "exponentially distributed" with some specified average, say 5.0 minutes, and the time required to perform the service is exponentially distributed with another specified average, say 2.5 minutes. That these times are "exponentially distributed" is interpreted to mean:

Probability that an arrival occurs later than t_0 hours following its predecessor $= e^{-\lambda t_0}$

Probability that a service requires more than t_0 hours $= e^{-u t_0}$

where λ = the reciprocal of the average time between arrivals
$\quad$ = the average number of arrivals per hour
$\quad u$ = the reciprocal of the average time to perform a service
$\quad$ = the average number of services that could be completed in an hour were the service facility operating continuously throughout that hour

(See Figure A–1 for an example of such an exponential distribution.)

A typical waiting-line problem is presented in Example 4.

Example 4

The time between the arrivals of customers at an information booth is subject to an exponential distribution with $\lambda = 12$ per hour, that is, with the average time between arrivals being $\frac{1}{12}$ hour, or five minutes. The booth is staffed by one employee, and the time required to service a customer is exponentially distributed with an average time of $1/u = 2.5$ minutes, that is, with $u = 24$ per hour. But there are complaints that the waiting times are excessive; therefore, the manager wishes to determine whether or not he should add a second employee.

Solution to Example 4 $\quad$ To determine whether or not a second employee is justified, the management will calculate certain relevant characteristics of the current one-man system. These will then be compared with corresponding

FIGURE A–1 $\quad$ Probability that the time between successive arrivals exceeds t hours $= e^{-\lambda t}$.

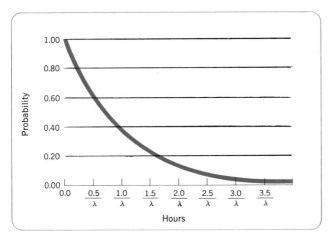

characteristics of the proposed two-man system so as to determine how much improvement a second employee would produce. The relevant characteristics will vary from problem to problem, but for purposes of this example, they are taken to be:

1. P_0 = the probability that there are zero persons in the system when a customer arrives
2. $P(w)$ = the probability that an arriving customer will have to wait for service
3. $E(n)$ = the average number of people in the system, that is, the average number in the queue plus the average number being serviced
4. $E(m)$ = the average number of people in the queue
5. $E(w)$ = the average time a customer spends waiting in the queue

Because the times between arrivals and the times required to perform the service are both exponentially distributed, the foregoing characteristics can be calculated from some relatively simple formulas. This is done as follows, with $\lambda = 12$ customers per hour and $u = 24$ customers per hour.

For the one-employee system

1. P_0 $= 1 - \dfrac{\lambda}{u}$

   $= 1 - \dfrac{12}{24}$

   $= 0.50$
2. $P(w)$ = the probability that there is one or more customers in the system when a customer arrives, that is, 1 minus the probability that there are zero customers

   $= 1 - P_0$

   $= 0.50$
3. $E(n)$ $= \dfrac{\lambda}{u - \lambda} = \dfrac{12}{24 - 12} = 1$ person
4. $E(m) = \dfrac{\lambda^2}{u(u - \lambda)} = \dfrac{12 \times 12}{24(24 - 12)} = 0.5$ person
5. $E(w)$ $= \dfrac{\lambda}{u(u - \lambda)} = \dfrac{12}{24(24 - 12)} = 1/24$ hour

   $= 2.5$ minutes

For the two-employee system

1. P_0 $= \dfrac{1}{1 + \lambda/u + 1/2(\lambda/u)^2[2u/(2u - \lambda)]}$

   $= \dfrac{1}{1 + 1/2 + 1/2(1/2)^2[48/(48 - 12)]}$

   $= 0.60$
2. $P(w)$ = the probability that an arriving customer does not have to wait for service

   = the probability that there are two or more customers already in the system when the new customer arrives, that is, 1 minus the probability that there are zero or one customer

   $= 1 - (P_0 + P_1)$

   $= 1 - (0.60 + 0.30)$

   $= 0.10$

Note: P_1 = the probability that there is one customer in the system

   $= \dfrac{\lambda}{u} P_0$

   $= \dfrac{12}{24} 0.60 = 0.30$

3. $E(n) = \dfrac{\lambda u(\lambda/u)^2}{2(u-\lambda)^2} P_0 + \dfrac{\lambda}{u}$

$= \dfrac{(12)(24)(1/2)^2}{2(12)^2} (0.60) + (1/2)$

$= 0.15 + 0.50 = 0.65$ person

4. $E(m) = E(n) - \dfrac{\lambda}{u}$

$= 0.15$ person

5. $E(w) = \dfrac{u(\lambda/u)^2}{2(u-\lambda)^2} P_0$

$= \dfrac{24(1/2)^2}{2(12)^2} (0.60)$

$= 1/80$ hour

$= 3/4$ minute

The management, on considering these calculations for the one-employee system, might agree that $P(w) = 0.50$ and $E(w) = 2.5$ minutes is excessive. While 50 per cent of the customers, on the average, do not wait at all, many of the remaining 50 per cent must be greatly inconvenienced to produce an average wait of 2.5 minutes. With the addition of the second employee, the probability of a customer having to wait is reduced to 0.10 and the average wait is reduced to 0.75 from 2.5 minutes. The average number of customers in the queue is also reduced. The manager now has to judge whether or not such a marked improvement in the service is worth the cost of the additional employee. This an astute manager will usually be able to do subjectively, perhaps aided by a cost-benefit approach. In this, as in most operations research problems, the techniques do not eliminate the manager or his judgment. However, they do provide facts which can be combined with judgment to produce a better decision than is possible with judgment alone.

Note: The formulas used in this example assume that the waiting-line is in the "steady-state" condition, that is, that the system has been operating long enough for any effects attendant on its starting up to have been removed.

REPLACEMENT PROBLEMS

As the name implies, replacement problems are concerned with determining the age at which certain items should be replaced. These problems are often generalized into two types:

1.   Those dealing with items which fail completely
2.   Those dealing with items whose productivity declines with time.

Example 5, which follows, is typical of the first of these problem types, and Example 6 is typical of the second.

Example 5

The marquee of a theatre has 1,000 light bulbs. Each bulb is replaced individually at a cost of $1 on the day it burns out, and then the entire 1,000 are replaced as a group at a cost of $300 at the end of every k weeks. The probability that a light bulb will fail in the jth week of its life is given by the following table:

Age at failure, j weeks	Probability that a bulb fails in the jth week, p_j
1	0.1
2	0.1
3	0.3
4	0.3
5	0.2
Total	1.0

Example 6

A machine is purchased for $100,000 and may be traded in for an amount R_i following its ith year of service. R_i decreases as i increases. The maintenance costs are M_i during its ith year of service; and M_i increases as i increases. The problem is to determine at what age the machine should be retired so as to minimize the average annual cost per year, given the following values of M_i and R_i:

Number of the year, i	Maintenance cost in year i, M_i	Trade-in value in year i, R_i
1	$ 3,000	$60,000
2	3,500	50,000
3	4,000	40,000
4	4,500	30,000
5	5,000	25,000
6	6,000	20,000
7	7,500	15,000
8	10,000	10,000
9	12,500	8,000
10	15,000	6,000
11	16,500	5,000
12	18,000	5,000

Solution to Example 5 The solution to Example 5 employs the following definitions:

i = the number of a particular week in a k-week schedule; i takes integral values from 1 to k.

j = the age in weeks of a burned-out light bulb; j takes integral values from 1 to $i-1$.

n_i = the average number of light bulbs which burn out and are consequently replaced individually in the ith week.

n_0 = the number of bulbs in the set; in this case, 1,000.

N_{ij} = the average number of light bulbs which were installed in week $i-j$ and which burn out at j weeks of age, that is, in the ith week.

Since the number of bulbs replaced during the ith week includes bulbs of all ages from 1 to $i-1$ weeks,

$$n_i = N_{i1} + \cdots + N_{i,\,i-1}$$

Now, on average, n_{i-j} bulbs were replaced during the week $i-j$, and on average, p_i of these will fail j weeks later, that is, during the ith week. Therefore,

$$N_{ij} = n_{i-j}p_j$$
$$n_i = n_{i-1}p_1 + n_{i-2}p_2 + \cdots + n_1p_{i-1}$$

Therefore, during a k-week cycle, the total number of bulbs to be replaced individually would be

$$n_1 + n_2 + \cdots + n_k$$

Therefore, the total cost of replacing these bulbs at \$1 apiece plus the entire set of \$1,000 at the end of each cycle would be

$$\$(n_1 + n_2 + \cdots + n_k) + \$300$$

Finally, the average cost per week would be

$$\frac{n_1 + n_2 + \cdots + n_k + 300}{k} \quad \text{dollars}$$

Using the supplied data for this problem, n_i are calculated as follows:

$n_0 = 1,000$ bulbs
$n_1 = n_0p_1$
    $= 1,000(0.10) = 100$ bulbs
$n_2 = n_1p_1 + n_0p_2$
    $= 100(0.10) + 1,000(0.10) = 110$ bulbs
$n_3 = n_2p_1 + n_1p_2 + n_0p_3$
    $= 110(0.10) + 100(0.10) + 1,000(0.30) = 321$ bulbs
$n_4 = n_3p_1 + n_2p_2 + n_1p_3 + n_0p_4$
    $= 321(0.10) + 110(0.10) + 100(0.30) + 1,000(0.30)$
    $= 373$ bulbs
$n_5 = n_4p_1 + n_3p_2 + n_2p_3 + n_1p_4 + n_0p_5$
    $= 373(0.10) + 321(0.10) + 110(0.30) + 100(0.30) + 1,000(0.20)$
    $= 332$ bulbs

The average costs per week are calculated as follows for varying values of k.

For $k = 1$ week

Cost of replacing individual bulbs:	
First week, $n_1 = 100$ at \$1	\$ 100
Cost of replacing all bulbs at the end of first week	300
Total cost for one week	\$ 400
Average cost per week	\$ 400

For $k = 2$ weeks

Costs of replacing individual bulbs:	
First week, $n_1 = 100$ at \$1	\$ 100
Second week, $n_2 = 110$ at \$1	110
Cost of replacing all bulbs at the end of second week	300
Total cost for 2 weeks	\$ 510
Average cost per week	\$ 255

For k = 3 weeks

Costs of replacing individual bulbs:

First week, $n_1 = 100$ at $1	$ 100
Second week, $n_2 = 110$ at $1	$ 110
Third week, $n_3 = 321$ at $1	321
Cost of replacing all bulbs at the end of third week	300
Total cost for three weeks	$ 831
Average cost per week	$ 277

For k = 4 weeks

Costs of replacing individual bulbs:

First week, $n_1 = 100$ at $1	$ 100
Second week, $n_2 = 110$ at $1	$ 110
Third week, $n_3 = 321$ at $1	$ 321
Fourth week, $n_4 = 373$ at $1	373
Cost of replacing all bulbs at end of fourth week	300
Total cost for 4 weeks	$1,204
Average cost per week	$ 301

It is left to the reader to verify that the average cost per week for $k = 5$ weeks is $307. Therefore it is concluded with the foregoing costs and probabilities of light-bulb life that the lowest average weekly cost would result with $k = 2$. That is, each bulb would be replaced once it had burned out, and the entire set would be replaced at the end of each two-week period.

Solution to Example 6   The average annual costs for both depreciation and maintenance were calculated for each possible length of life from one to twelve years, and the optimal life of the machine was taken to be the number of years for which the total of these costs is a minimum. The average annual cost for maintenance was the sum of maintenance costs for each year of life divided by the number of years. The average annual cost for depreciation was the purchase price of $100,000 minus the trade-in value for the relevant year divided by the number of years. These costs are displayed in the following table:

	Maintenance			Depreciation			
Year	Annual maint. cost, $	Cumulative maint. cost, $	Average annual cost, $	Trade-in value, $	Total depre-ciation, $	Average annual cost, $	Average of total costs, $
1	3,000	3,000	3,000	60,000	40,000	40,000	43,000
2	3,500	6,500	3,250	50,000	50,000	25,000	28,250
3	4,000	10,500	3,500	40,000	60,000	20,000	23,500
4	4,500	15,000	3,750	30,000	70,000	17,500	21,250
5	5,000	20,000	4,000	25,000	75,000	15,000	19,000
6	6,000	26,000	4,333	20,000	80,000	13,333	17,666
7	7,500	33,500	4,786	15,000	85,000	12,143	16,929
8	10,000	43,500	5,438	10,000	90,000	11,250	16,688
9	12,500	56,000	6,222	8,000	92,000	10,222	16,444
10	15,000	71,000	7,100	6,000	94,000	9,400	16,500
11	16,500	87,500	7,955	5,000	95,000	8,636	16,591
12	18,000	105,500	8,792	5,000	95,000	7,917	16,709

It will be noted that the average annual cost for maintenance increases as the number of years increases; at the same time, the average annual cost for depreciation declines. The annual average of the combined maintenance and depreciation costs is seen to be $43,000 for a life of one year, and then it declines for each additional year of life to a minimum of $16,444 for a life of nine years. Therefore it is concluded that each machine should be traded in for a new one every nine years.

Selected Readings

An Introduction to Quantitative Business Analysis, Ira Horowitz, McGraw-Hill Book Company, New York, 1965.

Quantitative Approaches to Management, R. I. Levin and C. A. Kirkpatrick, McGraw-Hill Book Company, New York, 1965.

Economic Analysis for Business Decisions, Alan S. Manne, McGraw-Hill Book Company, New York, 1961.

Scientific Decision Making in Business, Abe Shuchman, Holt, Rinehart and Winston, Inc., New York, 1963.

Introduction to Operations Research, Frederick S. Hillier and Gerald J. Lieberman, Holden-Day, Inc., San Francisco, 1967.

30

MANAGEMENT

IN

THE

FUTURE

*In a small village, there was an old man
who seemed to know the answer to every
question. A group of young men set out
to confuse him. One of the youths was to
hide a bird behind his back and ask the
old man whether the bird was alive or dead.
If he said it was alive, the youth would kill it;
if he said it was dead, the youth would let
it fly. So they came to the old man and asked:
"What does he have in his hands?"
"A bird," the old man answered. "Is it alive
or dead?" And the old man answered:
"It is in your hands; it is in your hands."*
Indian Folk Tale

30

One way of anticipating the management problems of, say, the year 2000 and immediately after is to extrapolate the trends of a period of comparable length in the immediate past—say, the period from 1933 to 1968–1969. There have been extraordinary advances in the theory and practice of management during this time, as has been shown in the previous chapters. But the advances have been, on the whole, evolutionary rather than revolutionary. There were no major jumps or gaps.

If the future is characterized merely by an extension and intensification of current trends, then the student's task is mainly to analyze these trends and determine their results. This requires the ability to distinguish between temporary phenomena (which may be in evidence for periods as long as ten years) and the more permanent long-term trends.

But many of the readers of this book will become top managers or advisers to top management, and, as such, will have to make up their minds on the question of what is desirable. Then, of course, there is the question of the best way to bring it about. Anyone who attempts long-range planning generally finds that there is a gap between what is desirable, or even necessary, and what is possible without major changes in plans and activities. Then innovation, sometimes comparatively minor, sometimes major, is the only thing that will serve.

But the man who hopes to innovate successfully must remember that every plus has a minus, that any change is likely to entail disadvantages as well as advantages, and that the most he can do is attempt to optimize.

THE EXTERNAL ENVIRONMENT

The tendency of government to expand absolutely as well as in terms of control over the GNP is likely to grow. Increasingly, the capital investment in some possible innovations is so heavy that only government can underwrite it. Space exploration, supersonic air travel, urban renewal, and many aspects of basic research are cases in point. Government is also likely to extend its control over company growth, over the level of employment, and perhaps over prices.

Hence the manager of the future will have to become much more articulate in making the position of his industry clear, both to government agencies and to members of the general public. He will also have to approach questions of government regulation in a more thoughtful way and consider the long-run implications more than managers, as a group, have done in the past, when they often tended to consider only the immediate impact of new government regulations or even to oppose them as a matter of course. Yet some of the regulations that industry spokesmen bitterly contested in the past have, in the long run, proved beneficial to business in general.

Labor unions are not likely to disappear, but they may become less important as the white-collar labor force continues to grow as a percentage of the total labor force. It is possible, of course, that white-collar unionism may develop a real push and begin to take in a greater proportion of the clerical and professional workers. Routinization of white-collar or professional work would tend to foster unionization, and both have been highly routinized in some companies. So would management's neglect or refusal to provide benefits and compensation comparable to those the blue-collar employees win through their unions. However, it is not likely that there will be any real surge in unionization among the white-collar and professional workers unless there is a serious depression that gives rise to salary cuts and great curtailment of opportunity.

Increased government regulation of unions is also quite likely in the future, with perhaps greater government control of the whole process of collective bargaining, for the same reason that government control over industry has increased and is likely to increase in the future—the growing numbers of people who are now affected by what were once thought of as private decisions.

Technology will continue to advance,[1] but managers will still have to cope with technological limitations, although undoubtedly they will be different from the technological limitations of today. Perhaps the principal limitation in this category will be one growing out of the very advances in technology: the cost of having very expensive, highly sophisticated equipment idle even for a short time may be prohibitive, which will mean that managers will have to plan production a long time in advance and will not be as free to make quick adaptations to market demands.

LARGE AND SMALL COMPANIES

Some of the industries that are flourishing today may well be in a serious secular decline by the year 2000. This is not to say that the companies engaged in these industries now will necessarily be out of business or on the way out. It means merely that many will have to change radically if they are to survive. The question, "What business are we really in?" that some companies ask themselves today will become even more pressing as the century draws to its close. In other words, companies will have to define their missions in terms of the needs they are in business to meet rather than in terms of the specific products or services they are supplying, as IBM has defined its mission as supplying information systems rather than office machines and as Ford Motor Company has defined its real product as "transportation" rather than cars and trucks.

Big business will continue to exist and will doubtless become bigger and bigger, at least for a time, but its very size will make for problems of coordination and control that may in the end become unmanageable. Although growth makes for economies of scale, there are offsetting disadvantages that may in the end outweigh the advantages:

[1] See Herman Kahn and Anthony J. Wiener, "A Framework for Speculation," *Daedalus* (Journal of the American Academy of Arts and Sciences), Summer, 1967, pp. 711–716, for a list of a hundred technical innovations likely by the year 2000.

Lack of flexibility   In a small firm, decisions can usually be made more quickly than they can in the large one. There are fewer levels to go through, fewer people to be consulted, less scrutiny of all angles. Alfred P. Sloan, Jr., explained this problem when he was president of General Motors Corporation:

> In practically all our activities we seem to suffer from the inertia result-ing from our great size. It seems to be hard for us to get action when it comes to a matter of putting our ideas across. There are so many people involved. . . . Sometimes I am almost forced to the conclusion that General Motors is so large and its inertia so great that it is impos-sible for us to be leaders.[2]

Of course, as is well known, Sloan and his associates did manage to over-come the then existing difficulties to the extent that the company became a leader in its industry and even in the economy. But it is questionable whether large companies can continue to maintain adequate flexibility with present forms of organization. Certainly a great many large companies are already too inflexible for *optimum* results, although they are able to produce a "satis-ficing" performance, one that is good enough in terms of profitability—at least so long as times are fairly prosperous.

Difficulty of coordination   The problem of keeping all executives in line with company objectives becomes more difficult as the company grows. Consis-tency and pulling together are extraordinarily hard to achieve when there are thousands of people performing tremendously varied activities. It is quite likely that the difficulty increases at a faster rate than the number of em-ployees and executives; i.e., it more than doubles—perhaps triples or quadru-ples—when the number of people is doubled.

Morale   The personal relationships that exist in a small company at least *make it possible* to maintain good morale, although not all small companies do so. For the larger company, the same task is extremely difficult, all but impossible, if by good morale is meant a real interest in the job and in the welfare of the business as a whole rather than apathetic acceptance of orders and the belief that conditions are no worse than they would be elsewhere.

In a study of the relationship between absenteeism, accidents, and the size of pit in the British coal industry, the Acton Society Trust concluded: "Not only was lost time found to increase with size, but it was also established that, when similar geological conditions were being worked, output per man-shift tended to be no larger and was, in fact, often appreciably lower in large pits than in small."[3]

Reinforcement of the idiosyncrasies of the chief executive   In a large com-pany, it is very easy for the chief executive either to assume too much power

---

[2] Speech to the GM Sales Committee, quoted in TNEC Monograph B, *Relative Efficiency of Large, Medium, and Small Business*, Government Printing Office, 1941, pp. 130–131.
[3] The Acton Society Trust, *Size and Morale*, London, 1953, pp. 12–13.

and keep too many decisions in his own hands (with consequent serious delays and mistakes) or to exercise too little power and overlook uncoordinated and/or incorrect decisions lower down. The executive of a small company may also have a predilection either way, but the consequences will not be so serious. If he makes all the major decisions, he can still make them quickly because he is close enough to the scene of action to be aware of all the factors bearing on a given situation. If he lets decision-making powers go to others by default, he will, for the same reason, be immediately aware of the consequences of mistakes and be able to step in to correct them.

Second, the chief executive of a small company is not likely to entertain the delusion of infallibility—he sees the consequences of his own mistakes too quickly. A large corporation, on the other hand, often has a tremendous margin for error, and the chief executive may more easily become isolated from reality by a circle of yes-men.

Again, if the chief executive of a small corporation has a tendency to self-aggrandizement, the limited resources he commands set boundaries to the extent to which he can pursue it. On the other hand, the chief executive of a large corporation may be able to acquire other firms merely for the sake of increasing the size of his company, even though it becomes less rather than more profitable as a result, to spend time on rather useless outside public or government committees, and to make overlavish use of expense accounts.

There are many areas, in fact, in which small companies do better than large ones. For example, there is the production of mobile homes—mass-produced houses that are often 30 or more per cent cheaper than a conventional house and more handsomely furnished because the companies that produce them buy furniture in quantity. No large corporation or investment house —some have tried—has ever succeeded in this industry; yet today it produces one-seventh of all new houses, and its yearly sales are $1 billion. Most of the entrepreneurs who run it are in their twenties and thirties, and their rates of return are much higher than the average in industry as a whole.

In the future, it may well be that the difficulties of managing the giant corporation are going to be such as to encourage the spinning off of activities that make the job of the men at the top unmanageable. Some companies have already begun to divest themselves of enterprises that do not fit in logically (i.e., economically or technically) with their regular operations.

A further development may be a trend away from the integrated company, the company that is as nearly self-sufficient as possible. This may extend not only to the purchase of parts from outside companies—always a feature of the automobile business and others—but to provision of services that most companies have been supplying for themselves. For example, some large companies—especially those in the oil refining industry—often turn over practically all their maintenance work to companies specifically organized to perform that one function.

The same trend could also affect other functions. For example, much of the accounting work could be farmed out to computer centers organized to serve several companies. Outside organizations might also take over much of the research and development work. Both computer centers and research companies exist at the present time, but currently they supply services mainly to small and medium-sized companies that cannot afford to provide their own facilities. It is possible that development of outside services may proceed much further than it has at present and that more companies may divest themselves of functions that are extraneous to their principal activities.

As companies grew, it became increasingly necessary for individuals within them to specialize in the performance of certain functions. The next step may be toward a similar functional specialization on the part of companies.

Any widespread development of this kind is not likely to occur for some time, however, especially since the advent of computers has enabled management to exercise closer control by providing so much more information so much more quickly. But even computers cannot cope with indefinite expansion. The data that a computer supplies depend on the way in which the problem is stated, and deciding what data are actually pertinent to a solution or a prediction may require more physical and psychological proximity to a situation than top management possesses. And each person or group from whom the management scientists gather their data may consciously or unconsciously inject distortion or, by withholding information, invalidate the answers.

In the meantime, despite the great growth of giant corporations, opportunities for small business are likely to increase rather than suffer curtailment. What Kenneth Boulding calls "the principle of interstices" operates to produce chances for new entrepreneurs: "In a pile of large stones, especially if these are fairly regular and round in shape, there will be interstices—holes which can be occupied by stones of smaller sizes, right down to grains of dust."[4]

To set an entire automated plant to work merely to produce a small order would be prohibitively expensive. Yet even a large organization may require small quantities of certain parts or products. Again, automation will produce greater standardization, and because the automated companies have so large an investment in equipment, they will be geared to serve the largest market available—the mass demand from the majority of people. But there are many consumers whose tastes differ from those of the majority, and while their numbers are small in proportion to the numbers in the mass market, they are often large in actual figures. Thus, while it may not be worthwhile for the large corporation to bother with them, the small corporation may enjoy prosperity by catering to their special needs, especially since it possesses greater flexibility and can change its products more easily as those needs change.

Another factor making for greater opportunities for small entrepreneurs is the reluctance of most large corporations to examine the ideas of outside

[4] "The Jungle of Hugeness: The Second Age of Brontosaurus," *The Saturday Review*, Mar. 1, 1958, p. 13.

inventors lest they be accused of patent infringement if they should later invent something similar themselves. Thus an outside inventor must either get financing and form his own company or take his invention to one of the smaller firms. Some new companies and smaller firms have built up good businesses by taking over inventions that the big companies turned down.

EMPLOYMENT

Management's record in handling seasonal employment and in providing other jobs for those displaced by new equipment is likely to improve. Forecasting techniques and faster information through computerization are likely to enable it to improve the already fair record of the past.

In the much more serious cyclical fluctuations caused by large overall reductions in demand, management's power to stem declines in employment is likely to be more limited. In the 1920s, management spokesmen claimed that the economy had reached "new plateaus of prosperity" and that general depressions were things of the past. These claims were shattered by the Great Depression that followed the stock market crash of 1929. And the void that existed has been largely preempted by the Federal government, which controls such major stabilizing factors as unemployment compensation, financial and interest-rate policies, public works, and taxes.

But even here, managers have, on occasion, made important contributions. In the Business Advisory Council, those who exercise important controls on business investment and are able to influence others by example or precept have in their meetings demonstrated an optimism and a determination to avoid a depression that at times has been infectious enough to exert some influence on the course of events. However, the precise degree of this effectiveness is a matter of some doubt—doubtful enough, it would seem, to make it unwise for management to claim too much.

The effect of automation is, of course, already apparent. It makes possible greater output with fewer manhours of labor. But this does not necessarily mean that, as it spreads more widely, there will be permanent large-scale unemployment.

The introduction of mechanization during the Industrial Revolution also made possible greater production with fewer people, and while it caused important and distressing dislocations for some groups and some individuals, the ultimate effect was a wider distribution of goods, higher wages, and shorter hours. Automation is likely to have a somewhat similar effect.

The shorter hours may not take the form of a shorter working day or a four-day week—at least at first. But the trend toward more holidays and longer vacations is already in evidence, and it is obvious that the work is being spread around among more people than it otherwise would be. Eventually, management may wish to trade a four-day week or a six-hour day for the elimination of part of the vacation period, some of the holidays, or the "sabbatical leaves."

In the case of union members, a change to a shorter working week will have to be achieved through negotiation. But it may come about naturally for office employees. The *Wall Street Journal* reported not long ago that in New York City there seemed to be a general trend for the top man to take off early on Friday afternoons in the summer, for the subordinate managers to follow him out the door a little later, and for the secretaries and other clerical workers to escape as soon as they knew all the executives were gone.[5]

Another possible development in employment practices, and one that should make for greater stability of demand, is the gradual disappearance of payment by the hour rather than by the week. This possibility was noted in the first edition of this book, which was published in 1965, when a few companies had already adopted the practice voluntarily. Since then, at least one major union has brought the matter up at the bargaining table, and although the demand for weekly salaries was dropped temporarily, it may be expected that the same demand will be made in the future, perhaps with greater success, and that other unions will take up the idea.

Two developments are likely to foster this change. First, the white-collar working force is increasing faster than the blue-collar force, and there seems to be general agreement that this trend will continue as automation takes over more and more manual tasks. It may, therefore, be easier to have one payroll—a salaried payroll—rather than two, as in most manufacturing companies at present. Second, the advantage of the hourly payments to the employer originally was that he did not pay for time not worked. If an hourly paid employee was absent for any reason whatsoever, he drew no pay. But most hourly paid employees now get sick leave, vacations, holidays with pay—all the benefits that were once the privileges of the salaried. Therefore there is now less value, from the company viewpoint, in having an hourly payment plan for some employees.

What are the possibilities that machines will eventually replace human beings completely and make it possible for people to enjoy all-day leisure with guaranteed annual incomes sufficient not only for minimum comfort and decency but for luxury as well?

"I believe that the entire fabric of our present society will, in one generation, become a superficial fluff of busy-work, keeping us occupied whilst our slaves, the machines, will be doing all the real work for us," George Dantzig has written.[6]

"In one generation," however, seems a little overoptimistic or overpessimistic (depending on whether one regards work as a curse or a blessing). Manufacture and maintenance of the machines themselves will occupy a great many people, to say nothing of the others needed to plan the work of the machines and feed data to them. This prediction may come true eventually, but not by the year 2000 or within the lifetime of anyone now alive.

[5] "Who's in Charge Here? Firms Are Rudderless on Friday Afternoons," July 26, 1968, p.1.
[6] "Management Science in the World of Today and Tomorrow," *Management Science*, February, 1967, p. C-111

If prosperity continues and there are no major wars, undoubtedly there will be many more people engaged mainly in busy-work, or at least in work that might be characterized as desirable but nonessential, just as there are many more today than there were thirty years ago. But it will not be the entire population or even a very sizable segment of it.

THE MANAGEMENT FUNCTIONS

Tomorrow's manager will have to be knowledgable in many more areas than the manager of today has to be. The future manager need not be a mathematician, but he will have to know enough mathematics to understand the premises on which the OR men base their predictions and solutions to problems, and he will have to have enough knowledge of technology in general and of the social sciences in order to evaluate the advice of his experts. He will also have to be aware of general social trends not only in his own country but in many parts of the world, for if his company is at all large, it may be a multinational company or in process of becoming one. At the same time, his primary functions will be the same functions he handles today: planning, organization, staffing, direction, control, innovation, and representation.

Planning   Forecasts should be more accurate than they are today; data on the economy will be available sooner and in greater detail through the use of computers. However, the planning task will be no easier than it is at present, for there may be more uncertainties arising from rapid change. Further, because the computer can simulate so many possibilities so rapidly, management will have many more alternatives to choose among. This may make decisions more difficult, for in dealing with the future, the simulation can show only what will probably happen, not what will happen.

Organization   There is a great need for new types of organization that will make it possible to reduce the coordination problem in the giant company to more manageable size. Divisionalization was an invention in this field that served its purpose well and is still serving it well in some companies, but it is not a complete answer for the future.

The line-staff difficulty, however, may become less important as more companies automate their operations and thus take on more of the character of process industries, in which the division between the two types of functions tends to become blurred. (See pages 213–214.)

Staffing   Undoubtedly, there will be new types of psychological tests, more valid and more reliable than those we have at present, but the staffing problem will be as difficult as it is today, perhaps more difficult, for the number of different skills required will multiply. The main thing that will alleviate the situation will be the possibility of new forms of organization and control that will make it possible to determine more accurately how well people are actually doing on the job.

Direction   Some social scientists are predicting the disappearance of the superior-subordinate relationship—a sort of complete democracy in industry, with management by consensus and everyone deferring to the man with the greatest knowledge and the best ideas, regardless of his official title (if, indeed, people are to have titles at all). Of course, if present trends continue, the entire work force will have more education than the present work force has, but this does not mean that people will be able to coordinate their work without direction from above or that everyone will be able to judge whose ideas are the best. Even in voluntary organizations, such as social clubs, nothing is done without appointing someone to act as chairman and tempo- rary "boss" of those who are working on a project.

However, the working environment will become more democratic in that superiors will have to listen more carefully to the ideas of their subordinates and consider those ideas seriously in making decisions. Superiors will tend also to be less and less authoritarian in their dealings with their subordinates and to regard subordinates as social equals more than they do today.

Control   The greatest advances will probably be made in the field of control —through, as might be expected, the use of computers. A great deal of work, however, remains to be done on identifying the exceptions so that "manage- ment by exception" will become easier and less subject to error.

Innovation   Innovation will continue to be important. Technological innova- tions will come faster and faster, and the task of the manager will be to judge their value to his own company and to make the necessary changes in pro- cedures, organization, and so on, that will enable his company to take the greatest possible advantage of them. Many of the innovations, however, will result in new companies and new industries that will be competitive with some of today's well-established companies.

Representation   The manager's representation task will, as has already been noted, become more important as government control expands and as changes in the social climate occur, probably more rapidly than they have occurred in the past. Managers will also have to decide how far they are justified in assuming social responsibilities when the assumption will be of no direct, and possibly no indirect, benefit to their own companies.

The manager's basic job, in fact, will be very much what it is today. He will still make decisions, although perhaps not the same ones that he makes today. The essential difference will be that he will need greater background knowledge in a wide variety of fields, ranging from sociology and psychology to mathematics, if he is not to allow his decisions to be dictated by "experts."

The manager will also need those intuitive skills that enable him to lead and persuade—in short, to maintain good human relations with his subordinates and associates. According to one prediction, "By 1985 we shall have psychological theories that are as successful as the theories we have in chemistry and biology today. . . . We may expect very rapid advances in the effectiveness and efficiency of our techniques of teaching and our techniques of dealing with human maladjustment."[7] Against this, one may set the prediction by Hugo Münsterberg in 1916, quoted earlier in this book, that "overflowing joy and perfect harmony" would prevail in industrial organizations because psychological tests would make it possible for everyone to be fitted into the right job. Perhaps the prediction will come true eventually, but not by 1985 or even by the year 2000.

SUMMARY

A very marked trend today, and one that is likely to continue for some years, is toward increasingly large companies. The question is, however, whether it can continue indefinitely or whether the losses—through inflexibility, lack of coordination, and poor morale—will begin to outweigh the gains achieved by economies of scale and greater financial resources. One problem for the top managers of the future and their advisers is to determine at what point a company should begin to spin off some of its divisions and activities or, if this is not considered desirable, to devise new forms of organization that will make it possible to manage the bigger giants.

In any case, opportunities for small business will not decrease, but small businesses will have the greatest chance of success when they do not try to compete with big business on its own ground but seek out the interstices and meet consumer needs that are being overlooked. The bigger big business becomes, the more interstices there are likely to be.

Two other trends that are likely to continue are toward automation and computerization. Automation will eventually make possible considerable shortening of working hours; and there are some who predict that computers will eventually be able to solve all management problems, even those in the human relations field, but this is doubtful.

Government regulation of industry is not likely to be greatly modified and may even be intensified, particularly if there should be a major depression. Increased government regulation of labor unions is also quite probable, and the unions are likely to lose strength unless they can organize the white-collar workers, who are becoming more and more numerous while employment in blue-collar jobs is tending to shrink as a percentage of total employment.

Managers of the future will need to be, and will be, better educated than those of today, particularly in mathematics. While some of the decisions they

---

[7] Herbert Simon, "The Corporation: Will It Be Managed by Machines?" in Melvin Anshen and George Leland Bach (eds.), *Management and Corporations 1985*, McGraw-Hill Book Company, New York, 1960, p. 54.

now make may be routinized through the use of computers, human decision making will still be necessary.

Review Questions

1. Why may there be more opportunities for small companies in the future than there are today?
2. Do you think it likely that computers can ever solve all human relations problems? Why or why not?
3. What are some of the advantages of bigness? What are the disadvantages?
4. Do you think it would be a good idea to put present hourly workers on salary?
5. Do you think further government regulation of industry will be necessary in the future? What types of regulation would you like to see instituted? Or do you believe there should be less regulation? If so, what restrictions would you like to see eliminated?
6. Should there be further government regulation of unions? If you think so, what new regulations would you like to see put into effect? Why?
7. What further extension of specialization is possible beyond specialization by individuals? Do you think this would be a good idea? Why?

Case Study One / The Quick Wash Company

The Quick Wash Company, a manufacturer of home washing machines, has been successful and has accumulated a large surplus. However, the number of competing firms—some of which have patented improvements that the company cannot duplicate—is becoming larger and larger. Already it is harder to get business, and there is considerable unused capacity in the industry.

The company therefore decides to reappraise its prospects and, if necessary, to use some of its surplus to purchase other companies making items that might be used to broaden its product line. In the course of the reappraisal, the following questions are asked:

1. What is our real business? What needs are we meeting?
2. Which trends are likely to affect the size of the markets, and what products are likely to be needed to fill the needs of the markets?
3. What products, therefore, should we seek to add to our line?

You are an executive assistant to the president, and he asks you to prepare a report embodying the answers to these questions.

1. How would you answer the first question? Why?
2. What facts would you seek in order to answer the second?

3. What do you think your probable answer to the third question would be?
    (The president expects you to look ahead at least twenty years.)

The Olivetti Typewriter Company, situated in Ivrea in Northern Italy, found
that demand for its products had risen so much that it could not meet it.
There was a shortage of plant capacity and of labor to make certain specialized parts, such as the zipper on the typewriter cover.

The company did not want to add more people in Ivrea because it already
dominated the labor market in the town. It was also concerned with the
increasing centralization of economic regulation in Rome, on the one hand,
and with the increasing radicalism of the workers on the other. Finally, the
president of the company, Adriano Olivetti, was deeply concerned with the
need to offer his employees more than a good pay package and social services.
Dr. Olivetti has asked you to advise him how to deal with this situation.
What is your counsel?

Selected Readings

"Toward the Year 2000: Work in Progress," *Daedalus* (Journal of the Ameri-
    can Academy of Arts and Sciences), Summer, 1967. An analysis of present
    trends and their effect on the future by a number of experts in different
    fields.
Management 2000, The American Foundation for Management Research,
    Inc.,* Hamilton, N.Y., 1968. Addresses given at the dedication of the Foun-
    dation's Manager Learning Center in August, 1967. The speeches covered
    many different aspects of the future of interest to managers.
Management and Corporations 1985, Melvin Anshen and George Leland Bach
    (eds.), McGraw-Hill Book Company, New York, 1960. A symposium held at
    the Graduate School of Industrial Administration, Carnegie Institute of
    Technology. Papers deal with the role of computers, the social character of
    the corporation, the multinational corporation, the future of the underdevel-
    oped countries, and similar subjects.
Management and the Computer of the Future, Martin Greenberger (ed.), The
    M.I.T. Press, Cambridge, Mass., and John Wiley & Sons, Inc., New York,
    1962.

* Founded by the American Management Association.

Glossary of Management Terms

The following glossary contains definitions of many of the management concepts and words used in this book. Basically, the definitions tend to correspond with the meaning of the words as used by managers, which is the sense in which the reader is most likely to encounter them.

There will be differences of opinion, however, even among managers about the meaning of some of the words, and special interpretations of common words are often given by writers on management. These differences are likely to persist as long as there is no widespread attempt at common agreement on basic terms. Hence definitions other than those given here may be in some cases equally good or better. It is believed that as long as a writer or practitioner clearly defines the meaning of the terms he uses, and as long as he uses them consistently, confusion need not result.

Many commonly used management terms are omitted from this glossary, partly because of space shortage and partly because managers use them in the same sense in which they are defined in the dictionary. In addition, a very few extra words not used in the textbook have been included because the reader is likely to come across them in other writings on management.

Accountability   The extent to which a subordinate may be held by his superior to be directly responsible for results, good or bad.

Acquisition   Purchase of one company by another for cash, bonds, or stock in the purchasing company.

Administration   Sometimes used as a synonym for management. In this book the term means directing operations within the framework of policy laid down by higher managers or set by predecessors.

Antitrust laws   Federal laws designed to make possible workable competition and to ensure that the competition is fair.

Appraisal   A formal system of appraising a manager's performance periodically and in writing.

Apprenticeship   A system of training for the skilled trades that encompasses both classroom training and on-the-job training, all conducted in accordance with a formal plan.

Arrow diagramming   See *Critical path scheduling.*

Assistant-to   A staff aide to an executive. The assistant-to is not second in command and has no authority over other immediate subordinates of his chief, although he may *represent* his chief in matters of administrative detail.

Authority, functional   The authority of a central staff group over its counterparts at other locations in cases in which the local manager has line authority over the local staff.

Authority, line   The power to give direct orders to subordinates.

Automation   A system of production in which work in process is transferred from one operation to another without human intervention.

Base pay   Regular salary or wage excluding incentive pay, bonuses, fringe benefits, overtime pay, and all other extra compensation.

Behavioral sciences   Sciences dealing with human behavior, e.g., psychology, sociology, anthropology.

Black box   In concept, an apparatus whose input and output may be observed but whose inner workings are not known. The term is often used, however, in cases where a subsystem (in a computer-controlled system) is purchased from outside rather than designed by the designer of the system. In that case the designer does not care what goes on inside the box (although he probably knows); he is interested only in the output it will produce for a given input.

Bonds   Debt certificates issued by a business, constituting a lien against the physical assets of the enterprise.

Brainstorming   A technique for encouraging innovation by a group. Members suggest any ideas for improvement that come into their heads.

Breakeven point   The volume of sales that will produce enough revenue to cover all costs but no profit.

Burden   See *Overhead.*

Capacity   The total amount it is possible to produce with existing plant and equipment. (Sometimes it is slightly less than the true total. Therefore some companies may, for short periods, produce at more than 100 per cent of capacity.)

Capital   Money invested in a business.

Capital-intensive industry   An industry in which the capital investment per employee is high.

Capital, working   The difference between current assets and current liabilities.

Cartel   An association of companies in the same industry formed to set prices and sometimes to minimize competition by allocation of markets. A cartel may also curtail production in order to prevent price competition.

Cash flow   The amount of cash flowing in and out of a business in a given period.

Centralization   A system of management in which major decisions are made at high levels of management.

Chain of command   The hierarchy of superiors and subordinates.

Charismatic leader   One whose ability to get others to follow him is a natural gift.

COBOL   Common business oriented language. A language for computer programming especially designed for business.

Codetermination   In Germany: the system of having representatives of the union on the board of directors.

Command   Giving of orders.

Common market   An association of a number of countries in an economic unit without tariff or trade restrictions.

Communication   Passing on ideas, information, orders, or instructions in such a way that the recipient understands exactly what is meant.

Communication, two-way   Communication not only from top management down through the chain of command but also the transmission of information, ideas, and feelings in the opposite direction.

Computer, analog   A computer whose function is performed by measurement rather than by counting and in which results are shown by some sort of physical analogy to an actual process—for example, by changes in voltage.

Computer, digital   A computer that functions by counting discrete electronic impulses.

Computer programming   Providing a set of instructions for a computer.

Consortium   A group of companies engaged in a single venture.

Constellation   A team assigned to work together in an effort to solve a problem.

Consultant   Generally, a counselor on business affairs who works with companies in a professional-client relationship rather than as a regular employee, although some consultants work for a single company on a salaried basis.

Control   Ensuring that plans are carried out in line with standards.

Control, span of   The number of subordinates who report directly to a manager.

Coordination   Ensuring that all efforts are bent toward a common objective and that there is no duplication of work that results in wasted effort. Includes resolution of differences of opinion.

Cost, unit   The cost of producing a single unit of product.

Costs, factory   Expenses incurred in the manufacture of a product: labor, material, and plant overhead.

Costs, labor   Wages and fringe benefits.

Costs, standard   Unit costs set in advance of production by determination of the labor and material needed, plus a standard amount of overhead.

Costs, variable   Costs that change with the level of company activity.

Critical path scheduling   A method of scheduling work by means of diagrams that show which jobs must be completed before other jobs can be started. Jobs are indicated by arrows; hence the technique is sometimes called *arrow diagramming.*

Cybernetics   The science of communication and control. The word is derived from the Greek word for steersman (*kubernētēs*), and the study itself is important in the development of management information systems, especially those that utilize computers.

Debenture   A bond issued against the general credit of the company—does not carry a lien against physical assets.

Debt financing   Raising capital by borrowing.

Decentralization   A system of management in which decisions are passed down to lower levels.

Decision making   Choosing among alternatives in cases where there is some uncertainty about the final result of each possible course of action.

Delegation   Passing authority and responsibility to lower levels.

Department   Generally a group of executives and employees engaged in performing a single function or a group of closely related functions. See also *Division.*

Depreciation   Money set aside each year to amortize investment in capital assets whose value declines over time.

Direction   Seeing that subordinates do their work and do it as well as possible. Includes issuing orders, providing instruction, enforcing discipline, and developing *esprit de corps.*

Directors, board of   A group elected by stockholders to provide general guidance for a corporation and to appoint and dismiss the chief executive.

Directors, inside   Directors who are also executives of the company.

Directors, outside   Directors who are not executives of the company.

Diversification   Branching out into new fields.

Division   A segment of a corporation whose head is in charge of all functions necessary to make and market a product, or of all functions in a given geographical area.

Econometrics   A technique of making economic predictions by use of mathematics.

Economic man theory   The theory that money is the principal factor in human motivation.

EDP   Electronic data processing.

Entrepreneur   Originally meant an owner-manager, often the founder of a business, the man who combined land, labor, and capital for productive use. Now sometimes used (e.g., by the economist Joseph A. Schumpeter) for the innovating manager, who may or may not be the owner, or for the manager who makes the crucial decisions in a company (e.g., by Lord Keynes).

Equity   Ownership. Equity financing is financing by the sale of stock.

Exception principle, management by   A method of control under which only exceptional results, good or bad, are flagged for management attention.

Executive office   Term used where a number of executives are shown in the top box on an organization chart. This may indicate a form of group management at the top in some cases; in others, the executive office consists of the chief executive and his principal subordinates and advisers.

Expense, administrative   Outlay for management, clerical, and staff expense.

Expenses   Expenditures that must be covered by current revenues if the company is to make a profit, in contrast to capital investments, only a portion of which (annual depreciation) is chargeable against current revenues in a single year.

Extrapolation   Forecasting by projecting trends to date into the future.

Feasibility study   A study made to determine the way in which procedures would have to be modified if a computer were to be employed and whether or not the use of a computer would be worthwhile.

Feedback   The ability of a machine to sense and correct its own mistakes. May also be used in connection with systems of communication among members of an organization if the results of communications from the top may be easily ascertained by those who issued them.

Float   In critical path scheduling, extra time available for a job because work cannot proceed further until another job that will take longer is completed.

Flow chart   A chart showing the flow of work from one operation to another.

Foreman   Generally the first-line supervisor, one level above the hourly rated employee.

Foreman, functional   A foreman who directs employees in the performance of a single phase of their work (term used by Frederick W. Taylor).

FORTRAN   A language for computer programming designed especially for scientific work. (Word is derived from "formula translation.")

Fringe benefits   Pension plans, insurance plans, vacations, and similar benefits.

Fusion process   The process by which the goals of an individual become identical, to some extent, with those of an organization (term used by E. Wight Bakke).

Games, theory of   Theory used in operations research to develop a technique designed to make possible maximization of gains or minimization of losses regardless of countermoves by competitors.

Gantt chart   A chart on which progress in the various parts of a project (e.g., production of a total amount of product, construction of a building) is plotted against time.

Gross national product (GNP)   The monetary value of the goods and services produced in a country in a year, without subtraction of amounts chargeable to depreciation.

Group dynamics   The interactions among members of a group. Also the study of these interactions with a view to learning how groups can become more effective.

Group executive   A manager who coordinates the work of two or more divisions.

Halo effect   The tendency of managers to assume that a subordinate who is good, bad, or average in one respect is equally good, bad, or average in all others.

Image, company   The general impression the public has of a company.

Incentives, financial   Extra payment for production above a predetermined standard.

Innovation   Development and/or introduction of new ideas, new ways of doing things, or new products.

Integration, backward   Acquisition by a corporation of sources of supplies.

Integration, forward   Acquisition by a corporation of marketing outlets or of manufacturing facilities to reduce the number of intermediaries between the company and the consumer.

Interaction   Reciprocal reactions of people in a group to each other or of variables in a situation or machine.

Interviewing, indirect   Interviewing in which the interviewer does not guide the discussion but says only enough to encourage the person interviewed to express himself freely.

Inventory   Stocks on hand. May be stocks of raw material, of work in process, or of finished goods.

Inventory, management   A listing of the managers within the company and their qualifications, often with notations on when each will be ready for promotion.

Job description   Description of the responsibilities and authority of a position. Generally states also an objective and the relationships to superiors and subordinates. It may cover committee assignments and even standards of performance.

Job element   The smallest discrete motion in a task that can be identified.

Job enlargement   Increasing the responsibilities or variety of a job.

Job evaluation   Systemic determination of the proper relationships among the wages and salaries paid for various jobs within a company.

Joint venture   An enterprise jointly undertaken by two or more companies that are independent of each other.

Justification   Reasons why a project should be undertaken. Generally stated as return to be expected on the investment, although in some cases projects may be justified by pointing out that they are necessary for such things as employee safety, company prestige, or preservation of market share.

Labor-intensive industry   An industry requiring small amounts of capital per employee.

Laboratory education   See *Sensitivity training.*

Law of the situation   The factors in a situation which appear to indicate that a certain course is obviously the sensible one.

Lead and lag method   A method of forecasting based on the idea that certain sets of economic indicators (statistics) have risen or fallen in advance of changes in the economy as a whole, whereas others have changed as the economy moved from prosperity to recession or vice versa, and still others have lagged behind changes in the economy.

Leasing   Renting plant or equipment as opposed to purchasing. A wide variety of leasing arrangements is in use.

Leverage   The ability to operate with a significant ratio of liabilities to gross assets.

Licensing   Granting a license to manufacture a trademarked and/or patented product to another company in return for a royalty on each unit sold.

Line   Concerned with the basic objectives of a company; e.g., in a manufacturing concern, line executives would be concerned with production and sales.

Linear programming   A mathematical technique for determining the optimum in cases where the relationships between the variables are linear.

Make or buy decision   Choice between manufacturing a component of a product in the company's own plants or purchasing it from an outside supplier or suppliers.

Management development Training of managers currently employed to improve their performance in their present jobs and/or to fit them for promotion.

Management, first-line Managers directly over the rank and file.

Management, general Overall management as opposed to management of a specialty.

Management, middle Managers above the first-line supervisors who do not participate in the decisions on overall policy.

Management prerogatives The prerogatives management believes it cannot share with a union if it is to have freedom to manage effectively.

Management science See *Operations research.*

Management, scientific A system of management developed by Frederick W. Taylor and others early in the twentieth century.

Management, top The company policy makers (sometimes just the president).

Manufacturers' agents Independent agents who sell manufacturers' products on a commission basis; they often sell the products of several different manufacturers.

Marginal analysis Analysis to determine the point at which the cost of extra input of one factor (e.g., another employee or another machine) will pay for itself.

Marginal men Groups not fully accepted by the society in which they live.

Marketing All activities connected with sales and distribution.

Marketing research Studies to determine the potential market for a company's products or services and/or how products can be made more salable.

Mercantilism Rules which appear to increase the wealth of a country, largely through governmental action—e.g., imposition of tariffs.

Merger Combination of two companies, generally through an exchange of stock.

Mergers, conglomerate Mergers of companies in entirely different fields.

Mergers, horizontal   Mergers of companies producing the same type of products or services.

Mergers, vertical   Mergers of companies with their suppliers or their marketing outlets.

Merit rating   Formal periodic reporting in writing on how well individual employees are doing their jobs. Similar to *Appraisal* except that appraisal is generally used for rating of managers, merit rating for rating of the rank and file.

Model, mathematical   A description of a system (a machine or a situation) in which the factors are expressed in mathematical terms in such a way that effects of various changes in the real system can be simulated by changing the values given to the mathematical terms.

Monopoly   Control of the sale of a product by one supplier.

Monte Carlo techniques   Techniques used in operations research that make use of the laws of probability.

Motion study   Study of the discrete motions performed in doing a task in order to determine whether it can be performed more efficiently.

Motivation research   A type of marketing research that seeks to determine subconscious reasons why consumers buy given products, or at least the reasons that they are unwilling or unable to express clearly.

Multinational company   A company whose interests cut across national boundaries, one which allocates its resources and its marketing efforts on a worldwide basis. (Also called "transnational company" and "international company.")

Nonlinear programming   An operations research technique that may be used when some of the variables in the mathematical models are raised to a higher power (e.g., X^2).

Numerical control   Direction of machines by magnetic tape or punched cards.

On-line   Term used when computer input or output is directly connected to the computer.

Operations research   Application of quantitative methods to the solution of management problems. It includes a "systems approach" in which a large number rather than a few factors are considered positively by a group of scientists from different fields.

Optimum   The course of action that minimizes overall losses or maximizes overall gains.

Organization   The division of work into managerial positions in the corporate structure and the adaptation of the structure to the people in the organization.

Organization chart   A diagram of positions and their relationship to one another.

Organization, formal   The official relationships of the positions in a corporation, generally shown on an organization chart and embodied in job descriptions.

Organization, informal   The unofficial (interpersonal) relationships in an organization, not shown on the organization chart and even not consistent with it.

Overhead   Costs that do not vary with output over a period of time.

Overshoot method   A technique for forecasting economic activity based on the theory that whenever business activity rises beyond the normal trend level, a reaction is bound to set in.

Partial proprietor   A stockholder (an individual, company, or institution) who holds a considerable proportion of a company's stock but not a controlling (51 per cent or more) amount.

Payout (or payoff) period   The time it takes for an investment (e.g., in a new machine) to pay for itself.

PERT   Program evaluation review technique. A more elaborate version of the critical path technique which takes more factors into account.

Planning   Setting the objectives to be accomplished by a corporation (or a segment of it) over different periods of time and deciding on the major methods of reaching them.

Planning, long-range   Generally, the preparation of plans for five years or more ahead.

Planning, strategic   A complete review of basic company objectives and methods of achieving them, which may result in major changes in either or both.

Planning, tactical   The process of planning short-run changes within the budget.

Policy   A general principle laid down for the guidance of executives in handling their jobs.

Private sector   Industries or activities that are considered the domain of free enterprise.

Procedure   A predetermined series of steps to be taken in doing a task.

Productivity   Output per manhour.

Protestant ethic   Max Weber's term for the view that making money is a worthy occupation and that hard work and individual competitive effort are qualities to be admired for their own sake.

Proxy   A person designated by a stockholder to represent him at the company's annual meeting and vote his shares. Also used for the card that the stockholder uses to appoint his proxy.

Psychic income   Satisfaction, other than monetary, from a job.

Psychodrama   See Role playing.

Public sector   Industries or activities run by the government.

Quality control, statistical   Control of product quality by sampling techniques.

Queuing problem   The problem of determining the facilities to be provided when the need for them varies at random—for example, the optimum number of ticket windows in cases where there may be long queues at some times and no customers at all at other times.

Ratio analysis   A method of judging company performance by examining the relationships between various figures—e.g., the ratio of profits to investment.

Rationalization   Term applied to improvement of industrial efficiency in Germany in the 1920s.

Real-time operation   Term used of a computer that is processing data fast enough for it to be used to control an operation.

Recruitment   Obtaining applicants for a job.

Reliability   The extent to which equipment or systems will operate as necessary to achieve the purpose for which they are intended. Also used to mean the extent to which a psychological test will give consistent results.

Representation   The managerial function of representing the company to outside groups, agencies, or individuals.

Responsibilities   Job duties.

Role playing   Acting out a situation, often used as a technique in human relations training.

Sales analysis   Study of company sales records to determine what customers are buying—what models, what sizes, and so on.

Sales promotion   Development of aids for the salesmen.

Satisficing   Adopting a course that is merely "good enough" from all viewpoints, rather than seeking the best possible course (term used by Herbert A. Simon).

Scalar chain   The chain of command.

Selection   Choosing among the candidates for a job opening.

Seniority   Length of service.

Sensitivity training   A form of training for managers which is designed to make them more sensitive to their effect on others. Conducted by the conference method.

Shop, closed   An arrangement, embodied in a union agreement, under which the employer can hire only people who are already members of the union for jobs within the bargaining unit.

Shop, open   A shop in which it is not necessary for anyone to be a union member in order to get or keep employment.

Shop, union   A union contract arrangement under which the employer may hire people who are not members of the union for jobs in the bargaining unit, but they must all join the union after a certain length of time—for example, after a sixty-day probationary period.

Simulation   Use of a computer to simulate a process. If the mathematical model is correctly developed, changes in the values assigned to variables in the model may show exactly what will happen when changes are made in the variables of the process.

Social deviant   One who is willing to go contrary to the mores of those surrounding him.

Social ethic   Term used by William H. Whyte, Jr., in *The Organization Man* to mean the concept that man is primarily a group member and should subordinate his individuality to the group mores. Used in contradistinction to Weber's *Protestant ethic*, which emphasizes individualism.

Social overheads   Municipal services, such as water supplies and public transportation.

Social responsibilities, management   Management's responsibilities to those other than the owners—e.g., to employees, the local community, or even the national or international economy.

Software   Computer services except hardware and accessories, such as computer programs, training, and other services in a computer installation.

Solid state   The technology concerned with solid materials that can change or mold the character of an electrical value without the use of moving parts or straight magnetic principles. Solid-state parts—e.g., transistors—produce effects through phenomena taking place within or at the junction of solid materials.

Spin-off   A method by which a company may divest itself of one of its divisions. An entirely new corporation is formed and the stock distributed to the shareholders of the first company.

Staff   Experts in techniques who aid the line management to do a better job of reaching corporate objectives.

Staff, general   Staff members who assist an executive with responsibilities he cannot delegate.

Staff, personal   An aide-de-camp or private secretary who helps the manager by making his corporate life easier and more convenient.

Staff, specialized   Executives (and their subordinates) who handle specialized functions that contribute indirectly to the attainment of organization goals. Also those who provide advice on and develop techniques for use in these specialized areas.

Staff work, completed   Staff work whose end product is a single recommendation which a line executive may either approve or disapprove without further investigation.

Staffing   Selecting and hiring managers and employees.

Standard hour   The standard amount of work to be done in an hour.

Standardization   Using one type of component, material, or machine for as many purposes as possible.

Stock, common   Shares in ownership on which the return depends on what the company makes. That return may be nothing or it may be very high.

Stock options   Options granted to executives to purchase stock in the future at a given price approximating the current market price, regardless of its price at the time of purchase. (Sometimes granted to employees as well.)

Stock, preferred   Shares in ownership on which dividends are fixed in advance. Preferred stock dividends must be paid in full before common stockholders receive anything.

Stockholders, institutional   Insurance companies, pension funds, and similar institutions which hold company stock.

Subsidiary   A company controlled wholly or partially by another through ownership of its stock.

Take-home pay   Amount actually included in the paycheck—that is, pay minus deductions for taxes and other purposes, such as contributions to a pension plan.

Tax haven   A country that provides tax advantages for companies incorporated under its laws.

Test, Thematic Apperception   A projective test in which the testee is asked to describe the situations portrayed in a series of rather ambiguous pictures.

Tests, projective   Psychological tests to which the "right" answers are not predetermined and which, therefore, require the testee to project himself.

Therblig   The smallest discrete human motion that can be identified in the performance of a task.

Time study   A method of determining the time necessary to perform a task. Procedure may involve timing the various elements (e.g., very small components of the task such as picking up material, positioning it, or inserting it in the machine) with a stopwatch, totaling the times, and adding "allowances" for such things as fatigue and personal time.

Time value of money   The difference between the value of money on hand today and that of money to be received in the future. The difference is due to the interest or other return that money available now might be producing in the meantime.

Training Within Industry Programs (TWI)   A series of short training programs for first-line supervisors developed during World War II.

Transfer prices   Prices charged by a division when it sells to another division of the same organization.

Trust   A term used in the early twentieth century for combinations of companies that resulted, or were expected to result, in quasi-monopoly. Also used of funds set up for specific purposes and managed by a group of trustees. For example, a company may set up a pension trust to provide money for the payment of pensions.

Turnover, employee   The percentage of the work force who quit, get fired, or are otherwise separated from the payroll in a given period.

Turnover, inventory   The number of times total inventory is used up and replaced in the course of a year.

Unity of command   Only one superior for each person.

Unity of direction   One head and one plan for each segment of the organization.

Validity   The extent to which a psychological test measures what it is designed to measure.

Value analysis   A systematic analysis of each component of a product and of the operations performed on each to determine whether the value contributed by each is great enough to justify the cost.

Vice-president, executive   Generally the second in command to the president.

Wage and salary administration   Maintaining a logical salary and/or wage structure.

Wage and salary survey   A survey of what other companies are paying for various jobs.

Work sampling   A technique to promote efficiency by determining through observation, continuously or at random intervals, exactly how employees are spending their time.

NAME INDEX

SUBJECT INDEX*

*See also Glossary of Management Terms, pp. 755–771.

DATE DUE

GAYLORD			PRINTED IN U.S.A.